2004

Chaucer's *Pardoner's Prologue* and *Tale*

AN ANNOTATED BIBLIOGRAPHY 1900 TO 1995

Marilyn Sutton

The *Pardoner's Tale* is unique among the *Canterbury Tales* in that it showcases a character who also makes several other appearances throughout the *Tales*. One of only three pilgrims to be given a full-length prologue by Chaucer, the Pardoner takes on a dramatic force unequaled among the pilgrims.

A research tool for specialist and graduate student alike, this volume on Chaucer's *Pardoner's Prologue* and *Tale* offers an exhaustive collection of material from the period 1900 to 1995, abstracting and cross-referencing book-length and chapter-length studies, sections of books and chapters, articles, portions of articles, notes, extensive commentary in editions, and representative study guides. There are separate sections for editions and translations; bibliographies, indexes, studies of the manuscript, and textual studies; sources, analogues, and influences for the *Pardoner's Prologue* and *Tale*; the Pardoner portrait in the *General Prologue*; studies of the Pardoner's interruption of the *Wife of Bath*, the *wordes of the Hoost to the Phisicien and the Pardoner*; the *Pardoner's Prologue*; and *The Pardoner's Tale*.

The Chaucer Bibliographies are designed to encompass a complete listing and assessment of scholarship and criticism on the writings of Geoffrey Chaucer, his life, times, and historical context.

MARILYN SUTTON is a professor of English at California State University, Dominguez Hills.

(The Chaucer Bibliographies)

The Chaucer Bibliographies

Chaucer's *Pardoner's Prologue* and *Tale*

AN ANNOTATED BIBLIOGRAPHY

1900 TO 1995

edited by Marilyn Sutton

Published in association with the University of Rochester by

UNIVERSITY OF TORONTO PRESS

Toronto Buffalo London

© University of Toronto Press Incorporated 2000
Toronto Buffalo London
Printed in Canada

ISBN 0-8020-4744-0

Printed on acid-free paper

Canadian Cataloguing in Publication Data

Main entry under title:
Chaucer's Pardoner's prologue and tale : an annotated bibliography
1900–1995

(The Chaucer bibliographies ; 7)
Includes index.
ISBN 0-8020-4744-0

1. Chaucer, Geoffrey, d. 1400. Pardoner's tale. I. Sutton, Marilyn,
1944– . II. Series.
Z8164.C428 2000   016.821'1   C99-9330940-2

University of Toronto Press acknowledges the financial assistance to its
publishing program of the Canada Council for the Arts and the Ontario
Arts Council.

University of Toronto Press acknowledges the financial support for its
publishing activities of the Government of Canada through the Book
Publishing Industry Development Program (BPIDP).

Canadä

For Tom

ಬ Contents

Pardonner's Tale panel from medieval chest, circa 1400. Courtesy of the Museum of London.

ᘒ General Editor's Preface

The Chaucer Bibliographies will encompass, in a series of some eighteen volumes, a complete listing and assessment of scholarship and criticism on the writings of Geoffrey Chaucer (d. 1400), and on his life, times, and historical context. Six volumes — on Chaucer's short poems and *Anelida and Arcite*, on the translations, scientific works, and apocrypha, on the *General Prologue* to the *Canterbury Tales*, on the *Knight's Tale*, on the *Tales* of the Miller, Reeve, and Cook, and on the Wife of Bath's Prologue and Tale — have already appeared. The present volume, on the *Pardoner's Prologue* and *Tale*, extends the coverage of the *Canterbury Tales* by taking up one of the richest and most provocative of Chaucer's portraits. Additional volumes, on the *Tales* of the Physician, Squire, and Franklin, and on those of the Friar, Summoner, Clerk, and Merchant, on the *Tales* of the Monk and Nun's Priest, and, finally, on the *Tales* of the Second Nun, Canon's Yeoman, Manciple, and Parson, with the Retractions, should appear during the coming years. Each volume in the series centers on a particular work, or a connected group of works; most contain material on backgrounds or related writings, and several will be wholly topical in their coverage (taking up music, the visual arts, rhetoric, the life of Chaucer, and other relevant subjects). Although the series perforce places unswerving emphasis on accuracy and comprehensiveness, the distinctive feature of the Chaucer Bibliographies is the fullness and particularity of the annotations provided for each entry. Annotations have averaged one-third to one-half page in the first six volumes; these thick descriptions of intellectual and critical activity (as opposed to simple itemizations or telegraphic summaries) have constituted more than four-fifths of each volume's content.

The individual volumes in the Chaucer Bibliographies series do not therefore constitute a reference work in the ordinary sense of that term. While they attempt to cite every publication on Chaucer worthy of notice from the twentieth century, they go far beyond the usual compilation, bibliographic manual, or guide to research. The bibliographies are not mechanical or machine-produced lists; each volume makes use of the intellectual engagement, learning, and insight of scholars actively at work on Chaucer. The series therefore serves not simply as the collection of all relevant titles on a subject, but as a companion and reliable guide to the reading and study of Chaucer's poetry. In this, the Chaucer Bibliographies represents an innovative and penetrating access to what Chaucer means, and has meant, to his readers. The project offers the full richness and detail of Chaucer's thought and world to a much wider audience than it has, even after one hundred years of energetic scholarship, ever before reached.

Before all else, then, the series provides a means of making practical headway in the study of earlier literature in English and in appreciating its broad cultural contexts. These volumes help make the writing of Chaucer — the earliest figure in the canon of great writers in the English language — more immediate and more directly accessible to all readers. Although readers for six centuries have praised Chaucer as a moving, superb, complex writer, even teachers of his writing sometimes feel at a loss when faced with the linguistic, historical, and critical complexities packed into every line. Consequently, despite his canonical stature, Chaucer has often remained unread, or read only in translation or paraphrase. The goal of this project, at its first level, is to increase the numbers of those who read him with genuine understanding and pleasure by increasing the kinds of things that can be readily known about Chaucer. In offering such broad access to specialized knowledge, the Chaucer Bibliographies is effecting a major change in how Chaucer gets read, at what levels, and by whom.

The Chaucer Bibliographies seeks to intensify the comprehension and enjoyment of beginning readers in university, college, and high school classrooms, presenting themselves as tools to both students and teachers. The series will move undergraduates more quickly from the generalizations and observations of textbooks and instructors to a direct access to the richness and variety of Chaucer's writing, and to its connections with medieval realities and modern understandings. For graduate students, the books will constitute a crucial resource for course work, exam preparation, and research. For non-specialist teachers of Chaucer in survey, masterpiece, and special topic courses, the series provides the means to a broader base of knowledge and to a more intense and shapely preparation than instructors, given the constraints of their work time, were previously able to manage. By clarifying and connecting both recent and long-available materials, and by making them readily accessible, the Chaucer Bibliographies refreshes the teaching and reading of Chaucer, and enables the development of alternative approaches to understanding his writing.

The series holds yet additional resources for specialist readers. The fullness and detail of the annotations in each volume will serve, in the first instance, as a check against duplication and redundancy in academic publication; individual scholars, and editors or readers at presses and journals, will be able to chart the place of new or proposed work quickly. Likewise, Chaucerians engaged with a topic or set of issues will be able to advance or situate their work more readily by reference to the materials in the appropriate volumes within the series. In consolidating the massive work that has been done in the last century or so in medieval studies, and particularly on Chaucer, the bibliographies provide the ground on which new work in Chaucer can build. Their presence in the field will encourage more efficient research on restricted as well as expansive topics, and will likewise facilitate work on the ways in which institutions have fostered and used the reading and study of his writing.

In addition to Chaucerians, the series benefits other specialists in medieval literature in offering ready access to publications on Chaucer that touch on a variety of materials relevant to other fields. Whatever use the materials gathered in these volumes may have for particular queries or problems, they also address interests of a range of scholars whose expertise extends to Chaucer, but whose intellectual concerns have been stymied by the daunting mass of Chaucer scholarship. The Chaucer Bibliographies places interdisciplinary research before scholars in history, art history, and other related areas, and so makes multidisciplinary, collaborative work more possible and even more likely. In short, this massive effort to bring knowledge about Chaucer together strives to open up, rather than to close off, further innovative work on pre-modern culture.

Recent volumes in the series have analyzed, on average, nearly twelve hundred items each; the present volume, in just surpassing that total, reflects the intensity and complexity of the reactions that the Pardoner has provoked over the course of the century. Coverage takes in editions of Chaucer's writing, studies of language, manuscripts, and audiences, his sources and their contexts and intellectual connections, directly relevant background materials (eg, estates satire, medieval science, sermons, the role of the Church and religion in the late Middle Ages), and all publications (in whatever language) bearing directly on Chaucer's poetry. The early volumes have thoroughly fulfilled the promise of the series to sort out and make accessible materials that are confused or obscure, including early philological publications in German and Scandinavian languages, privately printed or scarce volumes, and recent work not only in Britain, North America, and Australia, but more in Europe, Japan, Korea, and elsewhere. But even more strikingly, in bringing together all the materials on specific poems and subjects, these volumes have given new definition to the boundaries of Chaucer studies. Rather than working as a mopping-up operation, telling scholars what they already knew, these volumes attempt to contribute to a new flourishing of Chaucer research and criticism, enabling and even inspiring fresh and solidly grounded interrogations of the poetry. They stand not simply as the summation of a great tradition, but as an impetus for more intense and expanded understandings of Chaucer. The sweeping vision of late medieval writing offered in each volume represents a reconfiguration of knowledge that justifies and fosters informed work by an expanded community of scholars, of whom Chaucerians form merely the core.

In producing volumes that record all relevant titles and that specify — and thereby provide grounds for assessment — the content and interconnections of Chaucerian criticism, the Chaucer Bibliographies defines a new space for itself as a reference tool in its own field, and potentially within affiliated fields as well. The volumes, published and projected, differ markedly in purpose and use from other introductory bibliographies and cumulative listings. Standard bibliographies — unmarked or minimally annotated compilations — furnish helpful listings of publications, but offer limited help to the specialist, and still less orientation or access to the uninitiated. Volumes in the Chaucer Bibliographies project take these publications as a base of information (and make reference to them), but the aim of each volume is to offer in-depth coverage of the work(s) at hand. Contributors initially review annual and collected listings, but acquired learning, developed instincts, and the concentrated reading demanded for the preparation of each volume turn up leads and titles that complete the search. The series through its individual volumes seeks to stand as a definitive companion to the study of Chaucer, a starting point from which future work on the poet will proceed. It addresses itself to an audience beyond the community of professional Chaucerians, inviting non-Chaucerian scholars and non-specialist teachers and students to take part in the continuous process of understanding Chaucer.

The series achieves this inclusiveness through exhaustive itemization, full and strategic commentary, attention to backgrounds and corollary issues, and the demarcation of interrelationships and connected themes; annotations, cross-referencing, generous indices, and the report of significant reviews help insure this high level of comprehensiveness. Its design entails an examination of every relevant published item, in all foreign languages, though contributors rely on their own expertise and discretion in determining the choice and extent of annotations. Information on a 'ghost' or an inaccessible but pointless item may prove as valuable to users of these volumes as careful assessments of central books in the field; it is therefore crucial for contributors not to pass over inadvertently or deliberately omit any 'trivial' writings. The specification of items in these volumes should obviate the need for many vain entanglements in the trammels of scholarship as readers of Chaucer pursue their special interests.

The Chaucer Bibliographies is produced through the work of a diverse and distinguished array of experts. Its format — in which the individual efforts of autonomous scholars take their place within a single project's well articulated, coherent framework — accommodates in a peculiarly appropriate way its broad base and wide appeal. The authors of individual volumes include both distinguished and younger Chaucerians. The comprehensive work for each volume has been carried out over a period of years by an individual scholar or a team in close collaboration, conceiving each volume as a unified intellectual project. Having a collective of more than two dozen Chaucerians actively engaged in the same project has already led to a more thorough cross-checking, a richer array of suggestions and shared information, and a larger number of surprising finds — some obscure, some obvious — than any individual or more limited collaborative effort could have produced.

Since materials for the entire series have been electronically processed and stored, it will be possible for the University of Toronto Press to issue revised editions of volumes, and eventually to produce a general index to all volumes. Plans are underway to generate an updatable CD-ROM version of the Chaucer Bibliographies, which would combine data from multiple volumes and enable a variety of rapid searches through the materials. This electronic version will not replace the issue of individual volumes in hard copy, so that the series will continue to be accessible to a wide range of general users and scholars in a variety of formats.

The work of the Chaucer Bibliographies has been sustained from 1989 to 1995 by a series of grants from the National Endowment for the Humanities (USA), through its Division of Research Programs; without NEH support, it would have been impossible for the collective efforts of the project to continue, or for the work of individual scholars to issue in published form. Library staff at the University of Rochester — in particular, Interlibrary Loan, and the Rossell Hope Robbins Library and its Curator, Dr. Alan Lupack — have provided invaluable and unstinting bibliographic and research aid. Patricia Neill, of the Blake Quarterly (University of Rochester), has furnished crucial editorial and technical expertise in the final stages of preparation. The final and pivotal phases of research and editing were resourcefully and meticulously carried out by Angela Gibson, Karen Sims Parker, and Jennifer Klein at Rochester.

ℬ Preface

The Pardoner's Prologue and Tale

This sixth volume of the Chaucer Bibliographies is devoted to the *Pardoner's Prologue* and *Tale*, texts closely linked to the Pardoner's portrait in the General Prologue, the Interruption of the Wife of Bath, and *The wordes of the Hoost to the Phisicien and the Pardoner*. Since any attempt to identify all discussions of these several texts in a single volume is doomed to inadequacy, this volume concentrates on the Prologue and Tale. Discussions of the Pardoner's portrait are, here, annotated to the degree that they bear on either Prologue or Tale; considerations through 1982 of the pilgrim portrait itself are printed in the third volume of this series, *Chaucer's General Prologue to the "Canterbury Tales"*. Treatments of the Pardoner's Interruption of the Wife of Bath (D 163-187) and the '*wordes of the Hoost*' (C 287-328) are annotated briefly. Consistently an object of fascination, the Pardoner has received attention from virtually every commentator on Chaucer.

Though this volume includes reference to a small number of seminal works appearing at the turn of the century, its aim is to be 'exhaustive' from 1900 through 1995. This volume includes book-length and chapter-length studies, sections of books and chapters, articles, portions of articles, notes, extensive commentary in editions, and representative study guides. Unpublished dissertations are included on a selective basis. Brief annotations are included for a representative selection of reviews treating substantive issues related to the Pardoner's 'texts,' marking critical reception, or supplementing a point; comprehensive lists are available in the *Book Review Index*. A representative sampling of modernizations and translations has also been included although no attempt has been made to represent the numerous adaptations the *Pardoner's Tale* has inspired. Nor has any systematic effort been made to annotate histories of literature, encyclopedias, surveys of medieval culture, anthologies or other general works. Finally, despite repeated attempts, efforts to incorporate criticism published in Japan have met with only partial success.

This volume, as others in the series, builds upon the cumulative bibliographies generated by Hammond (**127**), Griffith (**144**), Crawford (**148**) and Baird (**161**); the selective bibliographies of Baugh (**149**), and Leyerle and Quick (**170**); and annual bibliographies of the Modern Language Association, *Chaucer Review*, and *Studies in the Age of Chaucer*.

The *Pardoner's Tale* is unique among the *Canterbury Tales* in being the central performance of a character who makes a series of appearances in the collection. One of only three pilgrims to be given a full length prologue by Chaucer (the others are the Wife of Bath and the Canon's Yeoman), the Pardoner takes on a dramatic force unequalled among the pilgrims. Yet, despite the clarity of his impact, his several appearances are imbued with a richly evocative ambiguity that draws readers recursively to his 'texts,' puzzling all the while over the complex power of that lure. As a result, criticism of the Pardoner often reveals as much about the psyche of the age, or the commentator as it does about the Pardoner.

Within the frame of the *Canterbury Tales*, the *Pardoner's Prologue* and *Tale* hold a specific identity as one pilgrim presentation within a two-pilgrim Fragment whose place within the order of the other tales has been often debated. Additionally, the *Pardoner's Prologue* and *Tale* invite attention in relation to several other Canterbury texts, most notably the *Wife of Bath's Prologue*, the *Man of Law's Prologue*, and the *Parson's Tale*.

A great satisfaction in working with the Pardoner has been the quality of commentary he inspires. A good many critical works offer rich insights that extend well beyond the Pardoner himself to applications for other pilgrims and insights into Chaucer's artistic practice. Abstracts can never hope to capture the richness of the source; this is particularly the case in richly nuanced longer articles or book length treatments. Commentary on the Pardoner spans the range from specific treatment of a single aspect of the Pardoner's presentation to interrelated treatments of several appearances, and complex studies of the unified 'Pardoner performance.' For all works that treat the *Pardoner's Tale*, the central annotation appears in that section; for works that also present independent commentary on other aspects of the Pardoner's presentations, additional subordinate annotations are included in the respective sections. Works that undertake a single aspect are annotated under the relevant section; those that undertake holistic approaches where separation of elements would seem arbitrary or inaccurate are incorporated within the entry on the *Tale*.

The intent of the entries is to give the reader the information most germane to planning research strategies; the annotations are not intended as substitutes for the whole. Ideally, the number and length of entries for a given work are consistent with impact on the critical tradition; but it is the case that some arguments, in their level of detail or the range of focus, are simply more difficult to summarize than others. Some articles, by their structure, invite a segmentation of annotation that is inappropriate for others. Thus length and number cannot be taken as a sole token of value. Moreover, several issues that weave recurrently through the critical discourse call for a faithfulness to nuance that compels direct citation. These quotations, though necessarily abbreviated, enable the reader to entertain the ideas directly; care has been taken to maintain an authentic context.

The volume is divided into seven sections: 1) Editions and Translations; 2) Bibliographies, Indexes, Studies of the Manuscript and Textual Studies; 3) Sources, Analogues and Influences for the *Pardoner's Prologue and Tale*; 4) The Pardoner portrait in the *General Prologue*; 5) Studies of the Pardoner's Interruption of the Wife of Bath, *The wordes of the Hoost to the Phisicien and the Pardoner* (Physician-Pardoner Link) and Fragment VI; 6) The *Pardoner's Prologue*; and 7) The *Pardoner's Tale* (including the 'epilogue' or solicitation). Full bibliographical references are given with the first reference. Entries are arranged chronologically; the index provides an alphabetized tool directing the reader to the range of annotations on a given topic. Cross-references to works that continue the discussion are included at the end of entries; cross-references within annotations represent works that the author uses significantly.

The first section, Editions, presents a selective list of entries designed to represent as fully as possible the varied aspects of the history of presentation for the *Pardoner's Prologue* and *Tale*. Included are all Middle English editions of critical value as well as those whose supporting material (introductions, notes, glossaries, illustrations or bibliographies) are noteworthy. The list seeks to be comprehensive in its treatment of separate editions of the *Pardoner's Tale* and representative in its inclusion of editions of selected tales that incorporate the *Pardoner's Tale*. Annotations note the basis for the edition (where stated), practices of excerpting (where stated), and supporting material including illustrations. The list of modernizations and translations is more selective, yet aims to demonstrate the distribution of interest in the *Pardoner's Prologue* and *Tale*.

Missing from this volume are summaries of source texts and 'continuations.' Material related to *Roman de la Rose* is incorporated within the volume on Chaucer's *'Romaunt of the Rose'* and *'Boece,' 'Treatise on the Astrolabe,' 'Equatorie of the Planetis,' Lost Works, and Chaucerian Apocrypha* prepared for this series by Russell A. Peck. Criticism deriving from *The Tale of Beryn*, though relevant to understanding the reception of Chaucer's Pardoner, is excluded unless is bears directly on the Pardoner.

Within annotations, textual line references are drawn from *The Riverside Chaucer* (**117**) unless the author being cited has used a different text; any references supplied by the editor (in [ ]) are from **117**. Line numbers without manuscript designation refer to references within the respective section; references to sections of the *Canterbury Tales* beyond the respective section are preceded by Fragment indicators (e.g., line reference to the *General Prologue* in the section devoted to the *General Prologue* appears without a Fragment indicator; line reference to the *General Prologue* within the section devoted to the *Pardoner's Prologue* is preceded by A). Page numbers within annotations are from works cited unless otherwise indicated. Reprints have been recorded when readily available but no attempt has been made to construct a complete publication history of any book.

An effort has been made to preserve the author's spelling and manner of treating terms. In the annotations, I have attempted to follow consistent practices of capitalization and phrasing. One instance, the decision to capitalize 'Old Man,' in cases where the source work does not indicate otherwise, deserves comment. While I recognize that capitalizing the term is tantamount to entering the debate as to whether the Old Man is simply 'an old man' or some symbolic force, it has been necessary to make a choice and, given the attention inspired by his mysterious character, it has been my judgment to treat him in the same manner as characters on the pilgrimage e.g., the Pardoner or the Host. Punctuation of quotations has been adjusted to fit the prose context.

A work of this scope is long in the making and rests on the support of many. I wish to acknowledge A.J. Colaianne, one of the original General Editors, who first invited me to join the Chaucer Bibliographies project. Thomas Hahn, current General Editor, has guided the production of this volume with direction, support and, when needed, provocation. To the editors who precede me in this series I am indebted for the high standard they set. I learned from reviewing an early draft of Kenneth Bleeth's volume on the *Physician's Tale* and benefitted greatly from Monica McAlpine's encouragment and guidance at an early stage of the project. Concurrent with the Chaucer Bibliographies has been the production of the Chaucer Variorum: to Penn Szittya, the editor of the volume on the Pardoner's Prologue and Tale I am deeply greateful for guidance and collegiality; the commentary on early editions is particularly indebted to his fine scholarship.

This project would have been impossible without the dedicated, professional support of several members of the library staff at California State University Dominguez Hills, and particularly that of Faye Phinsee–Clack in Inter-Library Loan and Cecilia Chen in Reference. I wish also to record my gratitude to my colleagues in the English department who urged me to completion, to Professor Burckhard Mohr who translated German sources, and to the student assistants, Paul Sutton and Diane Giarrusso-Barton most notable among them, who assisted in the often tedious tasks inherent in such a project. Angela Gibson of the English Department at the University of Rochester saw the manuscript through its final stages. While the persistent shortcomings in the work are of my own making, the text of the introductory essay has been measurably improved by the comments of Glenn Burger, Linda Geogianna, Richard Osberg, and John Steadman, each of whom read it at an earlier stage. The volume as a whole benefitted greatly from the close reading of Russell Peck of the University of Rochester and an unnamed reader at the University of Toronto Press.

Finally, I wish to recognize the generosity of my children in sharing their time with the Pardoner and their vital energy with me, and the great good spirits of my husband, Tom, whose encouragement offset the myriad setbacks one experiences in tackling such an ambitious project.

ᘒ Abbreviations

LITERARY WORKS CITED

BD	*Book of the Duchess*
ClT	*The Clerk's Tale*
CkT, CkP	*The Cook's Tale, The Cook's Prologue*
CT	*The Canterbury Tales*
CYT	*The Canon's Yeoman's Tale*
Dec	*Decameron* (Boccaccio)
DMC	*De Miseria Humane Conditionis*
Filos	*Il Filostrato* (Boccaccio)
Four P's	*The Playe called the four PP. Pardoner, Palmer, Potycary and Pedlar praise their professions.*
FranT	*The Franklin's Tale*
FrT	*The Friar's Tale*
GP	*The General Prologue*
Interr	*Pardoner's Interruption of the Wife of Bath*
KnT	*The Knight's Tale*
LGW	*The Legend of Good Women*
ManT	*The Manciple's Tale*
Mel	*The Tale of Melibee*
MilT, MilP	*The Miller's Tale, The Miller's Prologue*
MLT	*The Man of Law's Tale*
MkT, MkP	*The Monk's Tale, The Monk's Prologue*
NPT, NPP	*The Nun's Priest's Tale, The Nun's Priest's Prologue*
PardT, PardP	*The Pardoner's Tale, The Pardoner's Prologue*
ParsT, ParsP	*The Parson's Tale, The Parson's Prologue*
PhyT	*The Physician's Tale*

Phy-PardL	*Physician-Pardoner Link*
PP	*Piers Plowman*
PrT	*Prioress' Tale*
Ret	*Chaucer's Retractation*
RR	*The Romance of the Rose*
RvT	*The Reeve's Tale*
ShT	*The Shipman's Tale*
SNT	*The Second Nun's Tale*
SqT	*The Squire's Tale*
SumT	*The Summoner's Tale*
TC	*Troilus and Criseyde*
Tes	*Il Teseida* (Boccaccio)
Thop	*The Tale of Sir Thopas*
WBT, WBP	*The Wife of Bath's Tale, The Wife of Bath's Prologue*

JOURNALS AND REFERENCE WORKS CITED

ABR	*American Benedictine Review*
AI	*American Imago*
AJP	*American Journal of Philology*
ALLCJ	*Association for Literary and Linguistic Computing Journal*
Ang	*Anglia: Zeitschrift für Englische Philologie*
AnglB	*Anglia Beeblatt*
AnM	*Annuale Mediaevale*
Archiv	*Archiv für das Studium der Neueren Sprachen und Literaturen*
AQ	*Arlington Quarterly*
ArQ	*Archiv für Reformationgeschichte*
AWR	*The Anglo-Welsh Review*
BEPIF	*Bulletin des Etudes Portugaises et Bresiliennes*
BHM	*Bulletin of the History of Medicine*
BlakeS	*Blake Studies*
BYUS	*Brigham Young University Studies*
CaFoQ	*California Folklore Quarterly*
C&L	*Christianity and Literature*
CCTEP	*Conference of College Teachers of English of Texas Proceedings*
CE	*College English*

CEA	*CEA-Critic: An Official Journal of the College English Association*
CF	*Classical Folia*
ChauNewsL	*Chaucer Newsletter*
ChauR	*Chaucer Review*
Choice	*Choice*
CL	*Comparative Literature*
CLQ	*Colby Library Quarterly*
Comitatus	*Comitatus: A Journal of Medieval and Renaissance Studies*
CR	*Critical Review* (Canberra, Australia)
CritQ	*Critical Quarterly*
CSR	*Christian Scholar's Review*
CSSH	*Comparative Studies in Society and History*
CW	*Catholic World*
DAI	*Dissertation Abstracts International*
DQR	*Dutch Quarterly Review*
EIC	*Essays in Criticism*
EJ	*English Journal*
ELH	*English Literary History*
ELN	*English Language Notes*
EMS	*English Manuscript Studies 1100-1700*
ES	*English Studies*
ESA	*English Studies in Africa*
Expl	*Explicator*
FCS	*Fifteenth Century Studies*
Greyfriar	*Siena Studies in Literature* (Loudonville, New York)
HLQ	*Huntington Library Quarterly*
JEGP	*Journal of English and Germanic Philology*
JEP	*Journal of Evolutionary Psychology*
JELL	*Journal of English Language and Literature*
JMRS	*Journal of Medieval and Renaissance Studies*
JNT	*Journal of Narrative Technique*
L&T	*Literature and Theology: An International Journal of Theory, Criticism and Culture*
L&P	*Literature and Psychology*
Lang&S	*Language and Style: An International Journal*
LeedsSE	*Leeds Studies in English*
LT	*Levende Talen*

MÆ	*Medium Ævum*
M&H	*Medievalia et Humanistica: Studies in Medieval Renaissance Culture*
MedPers	*Medieval Perspectives*
MichA	*Michigan Academician: Michigan Academy of Science, Arts, and Letters*
MLN	*Modern Language Notes*
MLQ	*Modern Language Quarterly*
MLR	*Modern Language Review*
MP	*Modern Philology*
MQR	*Michigan Quarterly Review*
MS	*Mediaeval Studies*
MSE	*Massachusetts Studies in English*
MusQ	*Musical Quarterly*
N&Q	*Notes and Queries*
Names	*Names: Journal of the American Name Society*
NEJM	*New England Journal of Medicine*
Neophil	*Neophilologus*
NLH	*New Literary History*
NM	*Neuphilologische Mitteilungen*
NYSJM	*New York State Journal of Medicine*
PAPA	*Publications of the Arkansas Philological Association*
PBA	*Proceedings of the British Academy*
PCP	*Pacific Coast Philology*
PLL	*Papers on Language and Literature*
PLPLS-LHS	*Proceedings of the Leeds Philosophical and Literary Society, Literary and Historical Section*
PRev	*Powys Review*
PMASAL	*Papers of the Michigan Academy of Science and Letters*
PMLA	*Publications of the Modern Language Association*
PQ	*Philological Quarterly*
PURBA	*Panjab University Research Bulletin (Arts)*
REL	*Review of English Literature*
RenP	*Renaissance Papers*
RES	*Review of English Studies*
RMR	*Rocky Mountain Review*
RomR	*Romanic Review*
RUO	*Revue de l'Université d'Ottawa*

SAB	*South Atlantic Bulletin: A Quarterly Journal Devoted to Research and Teaching in the Modern Languages and Literature*
SAC	*Studies in the Age of Chaucer*
SCRev	*South Central Review: Journal of the South Central MLA*
SES	*Sophia English Studies*
SFQ	*Southern Folklore Quarterly*
SHUM	*Studies in the Humanities*
SIcon	*Studies in Iconography*
SMC	*Studies in Medieval Culture* (Kalamazoo, Michigan)
SMELL	*Studies in Medieval Language and Literature*
SP	*Studies in Philology*
SSEng	*Sydney Studies in English*
TCEL	*Thought Currents in English Literature*
TSE	*Tulane Studies in English*
TSL	*Tennessee Studies in Literature*
TSLL	*Texas Studies in Literature and Language*
UDR	*University of Dayton Review*
UMSE	*University of Mississippi Studies in English*
UTQ	*University of Toronto Quarterly*
Viator	*Viator: Medieval and Renaissance Studies*
WF	*Western Folklore*
WHR	*Western Humanities Review*
YES	*Yearbook of English Studies*

ॐ Introduction

Composition of the Pardoner's Prologue and Tale

Any question regarding the composition of *PardT* is complicated by the fact that the tale is only one of the Pardoner's several appearances. First introduced as one of a motley assemblage of pilgrims at the end of *GP*, the Pardoner later interrupts the Wife of Bath to compliment her preaching and confuse readers with a reference to his imminent marriage. Following the Physician's *pitous tale*, the Host calls upon the Pardoner for *som myrthe or japes right anon*. This summons places the Pardoner in a game of wits with his pilgrim audience: they, intent on warding off a tale of *ribaudye*; he, pausing with *a draughte of moyste and corny ale* to reflect on a fit rejoinder. Even this fortified pause does not, however, explain the performance in the prologue that follows, and assuredly not the stunning economy of the tale. Were these elements not puzzle enough, at the close of his tale, the Pardoner engages the Host in a test of bravado (arising from 'agonized sincerity,' or is it despair?), only to find his power waning as the Host, coarsely recalling a detail from *GP* portrait, insults the Pardoner into silence. Any comprehensive understanding of *PardP* and *PardT*, then, must address the implicit queries regarding the relationships among the elements within Fragment VI, the sources and 'composition' of *PardP* and *PardT*, the Pardoner's relation to the pilgrims with whom he interacts, and the construction of the pilgrimage frame.

Phy-PardL, *PardP* and *PardT* form a self-contained unit, alternately known as Fragment C (Chaucer Society) or Fragment VI (Ellesmere). Conflicting manuscript evidence and the strong possiblity that, at the time of his death, Chaucer had not determined a final placement for the

Fragment have led to its characterization as the 'Floating Fragment.' Within the Fragment, however, the elements are secure. Interaction between the Host and Pardoner extends the characterization of each and frames the prologue/tale unit between an opening link and closing epilogue. An authoritative review of the manuscript variants and criticism of *Phy-PardL* is provided by Helen Corsa in the Variorum volume of *PhyT* (**562**;cf **58, 532, 534, 538, 542**). Interwoven themes reinforce the unity of the Fragment: ten Brink first raised the connections when he noted that both *PhyT* and *PardT* present physician-swindlers, of the body and soul repectively (**266; 667**; cf **737**); later critics identified a range of thematic interrelationships including the sins of Lechery and Avarice (**685**); the gifts of Nature, Fortune and Grace (**800, 912, 924**); spiritual sickness (**951**); evil (**560; 882**); sudden death (**564**); opposition of virtue/Nature and sin/fortune (**1116**); and the motif of the body (**1103**).

In fact, so great is the evidence for connectedness within the Fragment, and particularly across the elements that feature the Pardoner, that critical discussion frequently scripts the multiple appearances of the Pardoner as scenes in a performance. Inviting as this characterization may be, it privileges dramatic interpretation, a perspective that has shaped critical discussion from Kittredge to Howard (**424**) and dates back at least to Dryden's praise of Chaucer's ability to suit '[t]he Matter and Manner' of the pilgrim tales 'to their different Educations, Humours and Callings, that each would be improper in any other Mouth' (**163**, p 166). Indeed, the Ellesmere manuscript with its placement of pilgrim miniatures at the head of individual tales reveals this interpretive strategy even earlier in the mid-fifteenth century.

Surviving records, with their absence of detail about Chaucer's activity as a poet, offer no guidance for determining conditions of composition. And neither contemporary references internal to *CT* nor manuscript materials provide a basis for more than a web of conjecture on the dating of *PardP* and *PardT*. But, within Fragment VI, the filaments unite with some stability. Scholarly agreement that the source tale originates in folk tradition and that the search for Chaucer's 'lost original' is fruitless has directed attention to Chaucer's reworking of the source elements. Skeat judges *PardT* among the latest written (**7**); Koch narrows the range, placing the composition of the tale around 1389-90 and the prologue between 1389-91. With *PardP*, all traceable source elements predate Chaucer, and Dempster's judgment that 'the character of the Pardoner and the episodes in which he appears are largely the creation of Chaucer' continues to be accepted (**194**, p 409). These facts, together with the stylistic evidence—Furnivall judging *PardP* and *PardT* to belong to 'Chaucer's best time' (**1**, **2**) and Kittredge to the time 'when all his [Chaucer's] powers were at their height' (**668**, p 833)—have generally connected the dating of *PardP* with the line of evidence for *PardT* (**117**, **127**).

More recent scholarship has set the date for *PardP* and *PardT* even later, in the mid 1390's. Brown and Butcher trace the historical context of the politics of religion, specifically policy on papal taxation, to suggest a syncretic process of composition beginning in the late 1370's and extending through the 1390's (**1155**). Lewis associates *PardT* with *MLP* on the basis of the use of Innocent III's *De Miseria Condicionis Humane*, a translation thought to have been made soon after 1390 (**244**). References to Jerome's *Adversus Jovinianum* (**7**, p 279; **117**] relate *PardT* to *WBP* and *MerT*, themselves dated mid-decade but prior to the revised Prologue to *LGW* (c 1395-6). This link provides a basis for dating the Pardoner's interruption of the Wife of Bath. And if, as N. F. Blake speculates, *WBP* and *WBT* were revised, composition may have extended over a prolonged period (**561**). The composition sequence for *PardT* and *ParsT* also bears on understanding the Pardoner's texts—Skeat arguing *ParsT* was written before *PardT* (**7**), Hinckly suggesting *PardT* was originally written for the Parson (**271**; cf **707**, **755**, **756**, **814**) and, more recently, Patterson arguing on the basis of echoes that *ParsT* was written after *PardT* (**949**).

More problematic than the dating of Fragment VI is its placement in the *CT* sequence, a question Corsa describes as holding 'a tantalizing claim on our continued attention' (**116**, p 3). Skeat (**7**) and Pollard (**5**) follow Bradshaw in placing *WBP* (III (D)) after *PardT* (VI (C)), a move which strains verisimilitude by locating the interruption of the Wife after the Pardoner's humiliation into silence. In Ellesmere, Fragment III(D) precedes VI(C). Pratt argues persuasively for the sequence V-VI-VII, an order which all twentieth-century editors adopt (**732**, pp.1141-67; **73**; **81**; **103**; Benson in **117**, p 901).

Early Appreciation of the Pardoner's Prologue and Tale

With no authorial manuscript, the reception of *CT* in Chaucer's lifetime necessarily remains speculative. In one sense, the earliest reception of the Pardoner is inscribed in the text in the reactions of *gentils* and *cherls* as they anticipate his tale. Reception beyond that first audience can be deduced, to a considerable degree, from manuscript evidence: their ownership (**1050**), the order of tales (**730**), their scribal glosses and, in the case of Ellesmere, their illuminations (**284, 435, 902**).

In his examination of the manuscripts as witnesses to Chaucer's work, Penn Szittya finds that 53 of 55 complete or nearly complete manuscripts of *CT* contain *PardT*. (All references to Szittya, unless otherwise indicated, refer to his edition of *PardT* for the Chaucer *Variorum* [forthcoming]). A further indication of early popularity is seen in the fact that 8 manuscripts present *PardT* alone (cf **748**). Only one manuscript of selected tales (a later development perhaps indicating audience preference for tales of piety), includes *PardT* (Ph[1] [now Univ of Texas MS 46]). Paul Strohm traces the development of Chaucer's audience from a close-knit group to a more conservative 'far-flung and disparate secondary audience' (**1002**, p 32). *PardT*, with its frustration of generic expectations and challenges to authority, Strohm argues, finds much greater acceptance with the fourteenth-century audience than it does with the more conservative, expanded audience of the fifteenth century that valued tales reaffirming social hierarchy. Another reflection of the fifteenth-century audience is provided by Lerer's examination of the Helmingham manuscript (Princeton University Library, MS Princeton 100). Noting the manuscript's 'infantile marginalia' together with evidence of wear and repair, Lerer suggests the work served as a utilitarian family manuscript (**1186**, p 93). His examination of the text reveals a work shorn of 'rhetorical sleights, confidential asides, and revealing admissions' (**1186**, p 99), a work of relatively uncomplicated narrative which 'shift[s] our attentions from the problem of authorial self-presentation to more narrowly definable issues in reader response' (**1186**, p 100), in sum, a work appealing to gentry audiences and perhaps child readers (**1109, 1186**). The construction of Chaucer as 'father of English poetry,' Lerer concludes, is the work of later readers.

The finished quality of two early manuscripts—Hengwrt (Hg) and Ellesmere (El)—attests to the great value placed on Chaucer's works within two decades of his death. In his preparation of Hg for the forthcoming Variorum, Szittya emends *PardP* and *PardT* only four times (lines 350, 392, 540, 954). The original scribe corrects it in only 3 lines (lines 329, 420, 911) and later editors agree that its text is very close to Chaucer's own. The substantial representation of glosses in a wide variety of early and reliable manuscripts offers Szittya another approach to early reception, and perhaps even composition history, as he concludes that, though the evidence does not allow us to prove the Hengwrt glosses authorial, 'no other reasonable hypothesis presents itself'(Szittya *Variorum*, forthcoming).

The elaborate and lavishly illuminated Ellesmere similarily evidences high respect and care. In Ellesmere, the Pardoner miniature affords an early fifteenth-century understanding of the Pardoner on the part of an artist or, more probably, a collaborative of scribe, limner, and artist. This visual 'reading' of the Pardoner closely follows the details of the *GP* portrait, though the miniature's placement at the head of the tale seems designed primarily to link tale to teller. There, the beardless Pardoner appears, his *heer as yelow as wex*, hanging *by ounces* and spread on his red-cloaked shoulders. He is capped with a matching red hat, *vernycle* sewn in front, and bearing a colorful *croys of latoun ful of stones*, although his *walet* hangs from his horse's neck rather than resting *in his lappe* and he rides with spurs not mentioned in the text. Renowned for its beauty, the value of the Ellesmere manuscript extends beyond aesthetics to reliability. Significantly, only 25 of the 53 Hg readings Szittya retains for the *Variorum* edition, conflict with El. Judging Ellesemere and Hengwrt 'our best and earliest texts,' Szittya concludes that 'Ellesmere was written by the scribe of Hg, who made only a few more minor errors in El than in Hg, though the ordering of the tales in the two manuscripts is quite different' (Szittya, forthcoming).

In addition to the evidence of manuscript condition and dissemination, two rare glimpses of early reception of *PardT* present themselves in a wooden carving and a continuing text. A carved wooden chest front (c 1400) depicts three scenes in horizontal succession: an apothecary offering what may be a flask of poison to a youth; two youths killing a third; and two youths drinking from a flask while eating (see frontispiece). These carvings provide a rare glimpse into a medieval artist's understanding of *PardT* (**947**, p 172). A second reflection of the unusual impact of *PardT* is found in the Pardoner's appearance in a spurious continuation to the Canterbury pilgrimage, 'The Canterbury Interlude and Merchant's Tale of Beryn' (Northumberland MS 455). This treatment, whose manuscript dates from c 1450-70 (although the texts themselves are earlier—*Beryn* c 1410; *Interlude* c 1420), is the sole reprise for any extant pilgrim, thereby suggesting that 'Chaucer's Pardoner ... seems to have been the one pilgrim who lingered most strongly in the memory of the fifteenth-century audience' (**1167**, p 55).

In addition to scribal notation, the carved chest front and the unique 'continuation,' further indications of reception are found in allusions to the Pardoner among early readers and writers. Heywood's *A Mery Playe betwene the pardoner and the frere the curate and neybour Pratte* (1533) incorporates (Skeat suggests, 'plagiarize[s]') lines from *PardT* (lines 7-48; 49-60); furthermore, the Pardoner in Heywood's *Four P's* resembles Chaucer's Pardoner in tone and attitude (**131**, p 80-1). The Scottish play *Ane Satyre of the Thrie Estaitis*, performed at the Scottish Court in 1540, presents a pardoner with false relics. Chaucer's Pardoner is cited by Roger Ascham against gaming in *Toxophilus* (1544), and passages from *PardT* are incorporated by John Northbrooke into a dialogue on *Dicing between Youth and Age*, where Northbrooke identifies lines 590-602 as Chaucer's own opinion on dicing (**131**, p 115). Passages from *PardT* find their way into *The Institution of a Gentleman* (1555) [lines 603-28; 591-602]. The persuasive force of the Pardoner is recalled in a letter from a parliamentary officer who either identifies the Pardoner's religious affiliation as fraternal or confuses him with Chaucer's Friar: 'Such an Holy Father might have ... converted as many Souls as *Chaucer's* Friar with the Shoulder-bone of the lost Sheep' (1645-6) (**131**, p 224). But it is only towards the close of the eighteenth century that the Pardoner begins to figure as a canonical literary character.

As literary taste moved to endorse Neoclassic principles of regularity, decorum and high seriousness, Chaucer's Gothic style found less favor and the grotesque figure of the Pardoner seemed increasingly alien. Even though Dryden articulates a taste expansive enough to suggest inclusion of the Pardoner, Chaucer, he notes, takes into the compass of *CT* the various:

'Manners and Humours ... of the whole English nation, in his Age. Not a single character had escap'd him. All his Pilgrims are severally distinguish'd from each other; and not only in their Inclinations, but in their very Physiognomies and Persons'(**163**, p 166).

He excludes *PardT* from his modernization of *CT*. The continued absence of the Pardoner is reflected by the playwright Elizabeth Cooper. Seeking, in 1737, a quotation that will do Chaucer, 'the Morning-Star of the English Poetry!' justice, Cooper chooses *PardP* as a relatively obscure text, noting that '[m]ost of his[Chaucer's] principal Tales have been already exhausted by the Moderns...' (**131**, 1:378-9; **163**, p 201-2).

In 1792, whether because *PardT* remained less known than the other tales, or because it was the most likely to find a ready audience, Lipscomb presented a modernization of *PardT* three years before his complete modern edition. But it is not until William Blake's engraving, 'The Canterbury Pilgrims' (1810) that the figure of the Pardoner is etched on the modern consciousness. There the Pardoner appears backside to viewer, posed with pretense as he looks backward over his shoulder to view his antitype, the Host. In the accompanying 'Descriptive Catalogue,' Blake conjures from Chaucer's text a

' ... Pardoner, the Age's Knave, who always commands and domineers over the high and low vulgar. This man is sent in every age for rod and scourge, and for a blight, for a trial of men, to divide the classes of men; he is in the most holy sanctuary, and he is suffered by Providence for wise ends, and has also his great use, and his grand leading destiny.' (cited in **163**, 1:253)

Prior to Blake, the Pardoner was portrayed in a number of individual portraits (Ellesmere, Caxton 1483, Thynne 1522, Stowe 1561, and Urry 1721). Conceptual priority for the decision to set the Pardoner amidst the collective pilgrim company on horseback remains disputed. Thomas Stothard's treatment of the pilgrims on horseback was exhibited first (1807), although Blake claimed that his agent, Robert Cromek, had seen an early sketch of his own and taken the idea to Stothard. Differences can be seen in their collective presentations. Blake aligns the pilgrims in accordance with his symbolic geography (**448**). Stothard portrays the Pardoner, in the words of contemporary William Carey, as 'a sort of jointless, nerveless, compound of youth and imbecility, half-made and loosely-put-together; a limber, herring-backed "Popinjay," fashioned to provide risibility' and offering 'a ludicrous species of effeminacy' (*Critical Description of the Procession of Chaucer's Pilgrims to Canterbury Painted by Thomas Stothard*. London: T. Cadell and W. Davies, 1808, p 63).

The nineteenth century offers plentiful evidence of the Pardoner's impact on readers and artists alike. By the close of the century, *PardT* appears in approximately a dozen modernizations (including some versions for children), and is translated into German, Italian and French. Caroline Spurgeon records that the Victorian poet Leigh Hunt produces a version of *PardT* entitled *Death and the Ruffians* (1855, 1860 [**127**]1845 [**131**]) to which he appends his own poem 'the Tapiser's Tale' (1859) 'attempted in the manner of Chaucer' [**127**, p 228]. Spurgeon next finds the Pardoner mentioned by Charles Dickens who speculates that the memory of Chaucer's Pardoner led the founder of a charitable refuge to exclude a humbug with false relics (letter to Sir James Emerson, 1866) (**285**). A new text of *PardT* appears late in the century with a translation from the Pali 'source,' a Buddha Birth Story, *The Vedabbha Jataka* by H.T. Francis (1884). The increasing influence of the Pardoner through the nineteenth century culminates in the critical commentary of Jusserand (1880) and Kittredge (1893). Indeed, Jusserand writes that Chaucer's Pardoner has become so familiar that an 'unconscious belief creeps into most minds, viz., that half the description does not after all give the idea of anything very extraordinary, and that the other half may be mere fancy' (423). Kittredge, with his treatment of the relation of tale to teller, and Jusserand, with his historical contextualizing of the Pardoner, together set the groundwork for the scholarship of the twentieth century. As G.G. Sedgewick concludes:

'Ever since he [Jusserand] wrote, research and criticism and interpretation have been busy with the *noble ecclesiast*. For the Wife of Bath and the Pardoner exercise a fascination not so much over the unregenerate as over God's elect' (**303**, p 431).

Modern Editions of the Pardoner's Prologue and Tale

This volume reaches back to include the editions of Walter W. Skeat (**3**; **7**) and Alfred W. Pollard (**19**) which establish the scholarly base for Chaucer study in the twentieth century. Skeat publishes *PardT* as part of a school text selection of tales in 1876 before he produces his multi-volume *Complete Works* (the 'Oxford Chaucer,' [**7**]), a contribution that dominates scholarship for forty years. In 1894, Pollard publishes an edition of *CT*, which he follows four years later with the collaborative *Works* (the 'Globe Chaucer,' [**11**]).

Foundational as the editions of Skeat and Pollard are to an understanding of *CT*, the textual history of *PardT* remains unique. Beginning with efforts undertaken on behalf of the original Chaucer Society by Furnivall to print complete transcripts of the six most important manuscripts [1868; 1868a; 1885], and directed by the Society's critical decision to publish specimens of a single tale in an effort to establish a stemma for *CT* as a whole, *PardT* assumes signal importance in the textual history of *CT*. After considering and rejecting *WBP* and *WBT* for the project, Furnivall selects *PardT* because he believes it to be the most varied in its readings (**15**). By 1900 then, the work of Julius Zupitza (**6**), John Koch and F.J. Furnivall, make variants of *PardP* and *PardT* from all known manuscripts (except Cn) available in print (**16**). Building on this groundwork, in 1902, John Koch produces *The Pardoner's Prologue and Tale* as volume 7 of the Englische Textbibliothek series. His work, Szittya notes, stands not only as the first critical edition of *PardP* and *PardT* but as the first critical edition of *any CT* based on a complete collation of all known manuscripts.

The works of Skeat and Pollard continue to set the course for scholarship until they are superseded in 1933 by F.N. Robinson's *The Poetical Works of Chaucer* (**51**). In 1957, the second edition, *The Works of Geoffrey Chaucer*(**71**), with altered readings for both *GP* and *PardT* as well as expanded critical notes, becomes the edition most often cited by scholars as well as that most frequently used by students. More recently, in 1987, the third revised and expanded edition, *The Riverside Chaucer*, edited by Larry D. Benson with the collaboration of thirty-three Chaucerians, has secured the central place of this edition (**117**). Together, these editions emerge as a received norm against which other editors consciously position themselves.

In 1940, Manly and Rickert publish their ground-breaking edition of *CT*—*The Text of the Canterbury Tales, Studied on the Basis of All Known Manuscripts* (**58**)—which presents the second critical version based on all known manuscripts. In the case of the Pardoner, their collations produce a manuscript classification quite different from Koch's and Zupitza's and, consequently, a quite different text. Once Manly and Rickert make manuscript variants more generally available, the debate over base manuscripts is rekindled.

Both Skeat and Pollard follow Ellesmere, setting precedent that is to influence subsequent editors (most notably Robinson) until, in 1958, Donaldson chooses to follow Hengwrt (**73**). Disagreement over manuscript superiority continues, as the annotations in this volume make clear. Both Blake (**108**) and the editors of the *Chaucer Variorum* favor Hg; the working facsimile of Ellesmere (introduced by Hanna [**122**]) and the publication of an elaborate full facsimile by the Huntington Library (**126**) turn attention back to Ellesmere's claims.

The editorial tradition of *PardP* and *PardT* in the twentieth century is noteworthy not only for its priority and prominence, but for its vigor as well. In the ninety-five years reviewed by this bibliography, *PardP* and *PardT* appear in more than 100 editions, apart from anthologies. *PardT* proves a durable favorite of modern editors shaping selected editions. There is no tale with which it has not been matched; in the 30 selections reviewed for this work, it is most frequently included with *GP*, *PrT*, and *NPT*. A review of translations shows that it finds audiences in Danish, German, Spanish, French, Italian, Pali, Russian and most recently Japanese. A frequent base for adaptations (e.g., school plays, a novel, an educational television film), *PardT* appears in the growing number of collections for children. While a comprehensive treatment of adaptations is not included in this volume, a representative selection of adaptations and collections for young children traces the tale's influence (**118, 119**). More notable, however, is the remarkable number of separate editions of *PardT* or the combined *PardT* and *PardP*.

Following Koch's critical edition, *PardP* and *PardT* see separate publication in a number of editions directed to students (**28, 46, 55, 70, 71, 74, 86, 113, 114, 115**); in most of these issues, *PardP* and *PardT* are accompanied by *GP* Pardoner portrait and *Phy-PardL*. Two freestanding translations of *PardT*, one in Danish (**59**), the other a Japanese prose translation (**112**), further indicate the breadth of interest in the work. These editions, addressed to a broadened and often international audience, promise a new generation of diverse critical readers.

Several new visual renderings of the Pardoner also appear in the twentieth-century: Harry Mileham arranges the Pardoner and his fellow pilgrims at an alestake in *Pardoner's Prologue* (1924) (**663a**). A stylized visual representation of the Pardoner is included in the pilgrim collection by Ronald King (**369**) and a film based on woodcuts by Bronislaw Bak (**87**) translates *PardT*, thereby extending the provenance of *PardT* into yet another medium.

Modern Criticism of the Pardoner's Prologue and Tale Sources, Analogues and Influences on the Pardoner's Prologue and Tale

Pardoner's Prologue

The confession of Faus Semblant in the *Roman de la Rose* (11065-11974) has long been recognized as the model for the Pardoner's confession in *PardP* (**186**; **265**; **267**; **573**). Ready comparison of passages can be made by consulting parallels in *Sources and Analogues* (**194**). Beyond specific passages, the more general indebtedness of the Pardoner to Faus Semblant is argued by Lawton (**1048**), Chance (**1101**), Dinshaw (**1117**), and Frese (**1158**); whereas, Calabrese points the debt to Genius (**1170**).

Though French's assertion that *PardP* is original with Chaucer is precisely accurate (**209**), the identification of early analogues and influences continues to intrigue. Jungman suggests that the discussion of an immoral preacher of morality in Augustine's *DDC* provides a significant glose if not a direct source (**245**). The Pardoner's reliance on false relics is early linked to similar practice in *Dec* (Day 6, Nov 10) by Axon (**183**; **694**); though seldom are the similarities developed until the 1980's when Taylor notes a likeness between the Pardoner and Boccaccio's *Ciapelletto* (**1004**). Kirkpatrick points the relationship between the Pardoner and Boccaccio's *Cipolla* (**644**), and Wenzel historically grounds the *topos* of the fraudulent pardoner displaying false relics (**508**). Ganim explores thematic and contextual similarities between Chaucer and Boccaccio, noting the relations of audience to meaning and author to popular culture (**1136**).

Contexts for understanding the Pardoner have also been sought in the medieval dramatic and penitential traditions. Building on discussions of the Pardoner operating within a 'Vice tadition,' Peterson develops the parallels between the Pardoner and Vice in the morality drama (**933**), a relationship Pearsall recognizes while reminding that the Pardoner's special power emanates beyond the confines of any convention (**1050**). Neuss offers a reading of the Pardoner's *moral tale* as a form of moral play (**1145**). Kellogg finds contexts for understanding the Pardoner, his confession, and motivation in Augustinian theology (**590**), as does Miller in the spiritual imagery of eunuchry (**747**).

In two important studies, Patterson demonstrates that the Pardoner is conceived within the multiple contexts of the penitential tradition. In addition to demonstrating similarities to false religious confessions (**932**), Patterson goes on to show how the Pardoner's confession arises from a concept of self-representation grounded in penitential theology (**932**; **1164**).

Study of the Pardoner's *gaude*, wherein he bars those guilty of serious sin from making offerings, suggests the trick was widely known in Chaucer's time. Early analogues have been found in the following works: Der Stricker's *Pfaffe Amîs* (**576**); a 15th century collection of exempla (**192**); Sercambi's 'De Ipocriti et Fraudatores;' a sermon of Odo of Cheriton (d. 1246) (**222**); and John Heywood's *Mery Play betwene the pardoner and the frere* (**193**). Dempster (**194**) prints the selections from *Pfaffe Amîs*, Sercambi, and the 15th century exemplum (*PardP* 377-90) .

The Pardoner's Tale

The relation of the Pardoner's 'Sermon on the Tavern Sins' to the sermon tradition has drawn frequent comment. At the close of the nineteenth century, Lounsbury establishes resemblances between the Pardoner's comments on Gluttony (lines 483-561) and *De Miseria Condicionis Humane* of Lotario dei Segni, later to become Pope Innocent III (**265**). Although additional parallel passages have been noted (**790**; **244**), the issue of direct influence remains unresolved since Lewis also notes similarities with several other works including John of

Wales' *Communiloquium*, Robert Holcot's *Super Liber Sapientiae* and Jerome's *Adversus Jovinianum* (**244**).

The Pardoner's exemplum of the three rioters and the Old Man draws on the widely disseminated folk motif, 'The Treasure Finders Who Murder Each Other'(Aarne-Thompson. *Types of Folktale*, 1961. Type 763; see **219**). By 1881, Richard Morris identifies the earliest known form of the story in the *Vedabbha Jataka*, the fifth century Buddhist 'Book of Birth Stories' in the Pali dialect. That tale, the 48th of 550, introduces the themes of robbers' quarrel, the treasure trove, and covetousness as the root of destruction; conspicuously missing are the Old Man and the ironic coloring of *PardT* (Morris, *Contemporary Review* 39(1881) 728-49). Three years later, two translations of the Pali work appear (Francis and Tawney), one of which is included in the Chaucer Society's *Originals and Analogues* (Clouston 1886). Although this Birth Story is referred to, it is not printed in Dempster's *Sources and Analogues* (1941) and receives slight attention through the period covered by this volume.

In 1941, Tupper summarizes source criticism and prints versions of the Pardoner's story as found in five exempla, three *novelle*— 'Christ and His Disciples,' 'The Hermit, Death, and the Robbers,' and 'The Treasure in the Tiber'as well as two plays—*Rappresentazione di Sant' Antonio* and Hans Sachs' *Der Dot im Stock* (**215**). Of the several forms, Robinson (**51**) judges the tale to resemble most closely 'The Hermit, Death, and the Robbers' (in *Libro di Novelle e di Bel Parlar Gentile*, Florence, 1572, no. 82).

Analogues later than Chaucer likewise abound. Early on, Kittredge notes similarities in plot with Coryat's *Crudities* (**199**), Lowes notes the link between dicing and swearing in four French *balades* (**185**), and Thomas draws a parallel between the Pardoner's description of preaching and Erasmus's *Praise of Folly* (**211**). Later, Wells finds several parallels interpolated by Topsell in *The History of Serpents*, 1608 (**210**).

The dispersion of the folktale motif, with versions in Swahili (**202**) and Arabic (**204**) already identified by the time Tupper wrote, grows increasingly manifest. Analogues have been identified in Spanish (**218, 225**), German (**201, 219**), Arabic (**238**), Portuguese (**240, 249**), and several African languages (**236, 252, 259**); they also include an Irish *scanchai* (**242**), as well as an Islamic tale published in French (**233**).

Modern British and American analogues in the works of writers who may have been directly acquainted with Chaucer include: Kipling, *The Jungle Book* (**261**, **270**); Flannery O'Connor, *Wise Blood* (**234**); Shakespeare, *Romeo and Juliet* (**1019**); Faulkner, 'Lizards in Jamshyd's Courtyard,' (**251**); Jack London, *Just Meat* (**207**, **221**); and David Godfrey, 'River Two Blind Jacks,' (**250**); Bruno Traven, *Der Shatz der Sierra Madre* (1927) later translated as *The Treasure of the Sierra Madre* (1937) and developed as a screenplay (1948; **219**); Conrad, *Victory* (**248**); Wordsworth, 'Resolution and Independence' (**975**); and Sembène Ousmane, *Le Mandat* (**252**); as well as several short stories in contemporary magazines (**221**), and allusions in modern newspapers (**217**). Allusions to the Pardoner himself are seen in Hemingway, *The Sun Also Rises* (**254**) and Sartre, *Saint Genet: Actor and Martyr* (**424**).

Proposing minor sources and particular influences for a tale as rich as *PardT* is a more nebulous operation (though one frequently undertaken). Kittredge notes that legend surrounding the Treasury of St. Mark identifies the corner porphyry figures as four brothers who plot, two against two, and die by poisoning (**199**). Candelaria suggests biographical influence, noting in the *Life-Records* a report of Chaucer having been robbed (three times and one of them near an oak/ *Fowle ok*) as a possible source for the oak tree in *PardT* (**224**). Skeat, Hench, and Robinson all find in the reference to subtly creeping wine (line 565) allusion to contemporary practice (**710**). The Old Man, often judged to be Chaucer's own creation, and assuredly not found in known source texts, nevertheless, recalls analogues traditional and modern (see later discussion). Other borrowings of an incidental character derive from Senecan thought (**205**); Maximian (7; **198**; **212**, **225**); John of Salisbury (**230**); and Chaucer's own tales for the Man of Law and the Parson. Biblical influences reveal themselves in the resonances with Exodus, Ecclesiasticus and Leviticus (**214**, **257**) although, as Pratt suggests, Chaucer may have drawn his knowledge from a preaching compendium rather than from direct sources (**232**). Returning to folktale, Green proposes that the altercation between Host and Pardoner at the close of the *PardT* carries echoes of 'The Friar's Pants,' a medieval folktale turning on cuckoldry, soiled pants, and the worship of relics (**1183**).

Hilary judges the analogues to share enough common elements—

including the search for death, the rioters' attitude toward prototypes of the Old Man, and the association of rats with poison— 'to render it probable that Chaucer knew some related version' of the story (**71**, p 906). The extensive listings in Morris' *Chaucer Source and Analogue Criticism: A Cross-Referenced Guide* provide a valuable point of departure for source study (**253**). Although scholars continue to seek specific sources for the Flanders setting, the theme of the plague, and several characteristics of the Old Man, there remains a scholarly consensus that the achievement of the Pardoner's performance is distinctly Chaucer's.

The Modern Critical Tradition

By the time the century opens, Jusserand and Kittredge have established the Pardoner's performance in the critical consciousness in a way that is to shape subsequent generations of discussion. Jusserand proceeds by examining Papal documents to demonstrate the 'great historical value and the minute accuracy' (436) of Chaucer's Pardoner. But it is Kittredge who moves from vivid characterization to dramatically compelling script. Working from the premise that 'Chaucer always knew what he was about,' Kittredge takes on the charge of dramatic impropriety against the Pardoner's 'harangue.' In the course of his defense, he conjures up an image that is to dominate critical discourse for half a century and hold strong adherents for an additional twenty-five years: he presents a Pardoner sprung from 'a genius eminently dramatic' (**668**, p 829) and fully 'in conformity to nature' (**668**, p 830). The Pardoner is a proud scoundrel, freed from his normal rounds and the 'fear of disagreeable consequences' (**668**, p 830). Having exposed his moral unsoundness, his pride is at stake: '[T]oo clever a knave to wish others to take him for a fool' (**668**, p 831), he enters upon one of his rich store of sermons and soon becomes rapt into his 'conventional earnestness' (**668**, p 831). By the time he arrives at 'the ejaculations on the wickedness of sin and the horrors of homicide, gluttony, lechery, and gambling, which ... form the "application" of the whole discourse,' he is at 'the white heat of zeal' (**668**, p 831). Thus propelled, he moves into his traditional exhortation. With the words of benediction, he encounters his long-dead better nature: 'For once, perhaps, the hideous incongruity between his preaching and the profligate invitation to come up and be pardoned through the efficacy of his trumpery relics has appeared to him' (**668**, p 832). A 'lost soul' with no hope of repentance, he is caught unawares 'in a moment of moral convulsion' (**668**, p 833); to cover the moment, he moves with 'reckless jocularity,' (**668**, p 832) to offer his relics. The Host fails to recognize the Pardoner's jest and replies 'in a strain of coarse raillery' (**668**, p 832) which leaves the Pardoner too angry to speak. Kittredge's scenario of the Pardoner in a 'very paroxysm of agonized sincerity'—a phrase that continues to reverberate—receives wider dissemination when the lectures delivered at Johns Hopkins in 1914, are published as *Chaucer and His Poetry* (**273**, p 217) and become the wellspring of dramatic interpretation. In many respects, the critical history of the Pardoner follows the fortunes of dramatic reading.

When Sedgewick assesses the critical landscape in 'The Progress of Chaucer's Pardoner 1880-1940,' he announces the eradication of three 'critical heresies'— erroneous interpretations of the Flanders locale, the tavern setting, and the sermon genre. Though a strong adherent of dramatic interpretation himself, he argues that each of these distorted readings derives from an undue emphasis on realism (**716**). Manly, who presses realistic readings so far as to hypothesize life models for Chaucer's pilgrims (**286**), suggests in an editorial note (**286**) that locating the exemplum of the drunken rioters in Flanders reflects English national prejudice, a judgment expanded by Norris (**702**); more recently, the theme is taken up by Hilary (**1091**). On the Flanders setting, Sedgewick follows Skeat (**7**) who speculates that the location is derived from a source now lost but available to Chaucer. The critical activity described by Sedgewick as the 'tavern heresy' is introduced and developed by Tupper, challenged by Lowes, then reasserted with modifications by Tupper—the quarrel of the Canterbury critics replacing the 'Quarrels of the Canterbury Pilgrims' (**684**). Simply put, Tupper argues that the Pardoner, himself guilty of the 'sins of the tavern' (and assuredly affected by drink), ironically manifests them while preaching in a tavern (**679, 680**). The insistence on a tavern location, Sedgewick speculates, arises from an over-literal reading of Jusserand's verbal portrait of a typical Pardoner. Later generally discarded, this reading has its adherents; for his part, Robinson supposes both *PardP* and *PardT* to be delivered in a tavern (**51**, p 834; **71**, p 729), a view challenged by Sedgewick (**303**) and Gerould (**316**), and not put forth, in the third edition of Robinson (**117**, p 904). The hypothesis of a tavern location is, in fact, an implication deriving from a larger pattern of interpretation treating the Pardoner's reliance on sermon form.

Both the Pardoner's harangue and his full performance are assessed in relation to the sermon tradition. Numerous critics, taking the sermon as Chaucer's generic model, judge it marred by 'digression' (**676**), lack of coherence (**707**), or the intrusion of irrelevant learning (**666**). Tupper articulates a plan for *CT* wherein each tale represents one of the seven deadly sins; *PardT* embodies Gluttony in its tavern setting and Avarice in the character and exemplum of the Pardoner (**679, 680**). To Lowes' argument that the scheme is unsupportable, Tupper reiterates his belief in Chaucer's 'architectonic use of the Deadly Sins' (**685**), modifying his stand by suggesting the sins form a 'Motif,' with each tale representing a 'Vice.' Still, other comparisons with the sermon form follow (**689**, p 28; **703, 707**). Sedgewick declares the 'Sermon Heresy' dead, suggesting the principle of unity lies in the tale's 'demagogic genius' more potent than logic (**716**, p 440). And he continues to give a reading of the whole 'Pardoner-scheme' reinterpreting the closing as 'a dignified and eloquent farewell' (**716**, p 455).

The complexity of Chaucer's Pardoner-creation insures that several of the issues characterizing the criticism prior to the publication of Robinson's first edition (**51**) elude closure: these include controversies over sources and the continuing identification of analogues; the credibility of the Pardoner (his individual identity, his professional abuses, his psyche and sexuality; the Pardoner's 'tone' in his Interruption of the Wife of Bath; debate as to the placement of Fragment C (**677, 683**); the motivation and degree of control the Pardoner manifests at various points in his performance (**671, 681**); the similarities between his confessional prologue and that of the Wife of Bath; his relationship to his audience; his use of medieval forms (e.g., sermon, allegory) and themes (e.g., seven sins); the power of his exemplum; the interpretation of the events following the exemplum; and, in an article that is to anticipate later interest, study of Chaucer's irony (**701**). Speculation as to the Pardoner's religious affiliation generally settles on his being a friar (**282, 668**), perhaps a Dominican friar (**672**, p 45). Fascination with the character of the Pardoner leads Curry, in a provocative examination of the influence of the Physiognomies on Chaucer, to reveal the Pardoner's 'secret': his identity as a *eunuchus ex nativitate*. Arguing that these characteristics would have been evident to the pilgrim audience, Curry depicts the ostracized Pardoner as feigning sincerity to prepare for a 'master stroke of deception' (**686**, p 603). So provocative is Curry's physiognomical interpretation that it figures in virtually every subsequent treatment of the Pardoner's character.

In the period before and after World War II, defined for Chaucerians by Robinson's first and second editions (1933-57), critics turn from the search for facts—sources, word meanings, physical setting— to the issues of character previously set up by dramatic interpretation (**713, 720, 734, 762**). These include the Pardoner's degree of control during his confession (**736, 740**); his motivation in the benediction and solicitation (**724, 729, 741, 753**); the effectiveness of the exemplum (**718, 720**); and his debt to the sermon tradition (**721, 736, 737, 740, 751**). Lawrence points to the drama implicit in Chaucer's vivid treatment of sin (**726**); Swart sees the sin of *superbia* demonstrated in *PardP* and 'amply documented' in *PardT* (**739**). Renewed speculation as to the Pardoner's religious affiliation leads to his consideration as a canon regular of St. Augustine (**304**) or a questor (**307**).

The methodology of tracing a single integrated scheme, earlier demonstrated by Kittredge and Bronson, is taken up by R.M. Lumiansky and Alfred L. Kellogg in influential treatments (**311, 314**). Lumiansky builds on dramatic interpretation, commenting that, in the case of the Pardoner, the tale proper is more completely subordinated to the total performance than it is with any other pilgrim. He discusses the Pardoner's total 'performance' in eight divisions and describes the Pardoner's effort to replace the imaginary peasant audience of his sermons with the pilgrims themselves, a substitution, he argues, that is completed with the benediction. Kellogg provides a theological reading in which he sees *PardP* and *PardT* as 'an integrated study in Augustinian theology in terms of the secret punishment of evil' (**314**, p 465), with *PardT* mirroring the struggle between the will of God and the Pardoner's own will. But despite the Pardoner's self-damning behavior, he concludes, Chaucer recognizes that the Pardoner manifests the will of God.

Marking significant challenge to dramatic interpretation, several critics undertake symbolic readings of the Pardoner. Charles Owen selects the passage where the revellers find the gold—*No lenger thanne after Deeth they soughte*—as one of five passages where irony is crucial, gold symbolizing death (**742**, p 251). Robert Miller draws from Patristic tradition to read both the Old Man and the Pardoner as manifestations of the *vetus homo*. As the Old Man represents spiritual death, so the Pardoner is a perverse cleric sterile in good works (**747**).

Consideration of the Pardoner's orchestrated performance gives rise, in the 50's, to several examinations of the integration of *PardP* and *PardT* (**725, 729, 733**). These studies join related analyses of order of composition (**713, 715, 744, 761**), plotting of the pilgrim journey (**730**), and relations between the Pardoner and other pilgrims (**734**). Ralph Baldwin suggests a structural pattern that pairs the pilgrim and tale in a 'diptych' with the Parson and his homily; the Pardoner— avaricious, gluttonous, a blasphemer and a simoniac—inevitably moved to contrition by the Parson (**746**).

A new development in the criticism of this time is the examination given to the verbal and rhetorical structure of *CT*: Schlauch conducts a linguistic analysis to identify Chaucer's 'unstilted ease' and verisimilitude (**738**); Schaar treats descriptive technique (**749**); Murata, swearing (**760**); and Kokeritz and Baum study the role of the pun (**743, 751, 756**). One of the most influential studies of style, however, is undertaken by Muscatine who concludes that *PardT*, with its cynicism, preoccupation with death, rhetoric, 'circumstantial realism' and 'vulgarized allegory' both affirms and explores the limits of the medieval moral order (**754**).

Although, in the Sixties, dramatic interpretation leads some to emphasize psychological realism (**778**)— Williams (**804**), Stockton (**772**) and O'Neal (**821**) offering psychoanalytic readings— the period also brings several challenges to this long-dominant interpretive strategy. Arguing that seeking psychological realism in Chaucer is anachronistic, Bronson speculates that, when Chaucer writes the tale (before the epilogue and the headlink), he searches for a means to make those actions consistent, and in so doing, he composed *PardP*. Counterapproaches to these 'dramatic' critics appear, on the one hand, from proponents of 'Robertsonian' or moral reading (**776, 818**) and, on the other, from readers who focus on the nature of the work as fiction. For Robertson, Chaucer's characters' actions accord with their moral natures, setting is iconographic and text exegetical. Payne and Josipovici direct readers to see *CT* as an experiment in the relation of stylistic elaborations to underlying narrative (**781**) or to free the poem from its moral jurisdiction and establish it as a fiction (**796**).

Robert Jordan joins the opponents of psychological reading by urging the replacement of the single focus of dramatic theory with a multiple unity that enables Chaucer to shift attention from nature to supernature (**774**). Seeking to understand why the actions narrated by the Pardoner are so convincing, Harrington moves the focus from realism to narrative pace (**831**). Strang urges readers to interpret allegorically any element that does not make sense literally (**766**). Several critics draw attention to Chaucer's moral purpose in *PardT* (**739, 781, 785, 791**), or his examination of the conflict between moral and immoral (**772, 789, 796**). That Chaucer reaffirms the moral order is evident, Corsa suggests, in the Pardoner's bringing punishment on himself through his blatant hypocrisy (**784**). Ruggiers discusses the Pardoner as manifesting the theory of evil as privation, and *PardP* as Chaucer's subtle comment on evil. Chaucer's theological vision is, he believes, fundamentally comic (**800**).

Nowhere does the focus on Chaucer's fascination with the distinction between the moral and the immoral become sharper than in discussions of the *olde man*, that *restelees kaityf* knocking with his staff on the ground, his *moodres gate*. Despite the range and diversity of proposed readings, and the range of methodologies employed (e.g., folklore studies, iconography, scriptural exegesis, patristics, psychological criticism), the mystery of the Old Man, Chaucer's distinctive synthesis, endures. Though some urge a literal interpretation (**731, 742, 764, 790**); more frequently, the Old Man is read archetypically (**793, 803, 805**) or allegorically— as Death (**273, 314**), Old Age (**711, 733, 844, 936, 1036**), the Messenger of Death (**71**)—or, as indicated earlier, the Pauline *vetus homo* (**323, 757**). On occasion, the Old Man is identified with good (**945**), the inverse of the rioters (**828**), or even Deus (**982**) but, more frequently, his ambiguity is associated with evil—the embodiment of the Pardoner's outcast state (**852**); the Devil (**1022**), Covetousness (**244**), and Avarice (**627**). His presence evokes powerful types including the Wandering Jew (**55, 667, 212, 228**), Odin (**226, 495**), and Wordsworth's Leech Gatherer (**975**); or a state of being such as joylessness (**793**), Despair (**818**), exile (**852**); or the doctrine of the second death (**1176**). Some read him within the frame of convention, e.g., the Old Man's lament (**981**), Noah in the medieval drama (**969**), the 'rash wish' (**910**), or Menippean satire (**982**). The Old Man remains the 'great enigma' of the tale (**851**), with recent criticism only underscoring the power of his unresolved identity (**943**).

Midway through the period framed by the publication of Robinson's second and third editions (1957-87), John Halverson updates Sedgewick's review of criticism. In 'Chaucer's Pardoner and the Progress of Criticism' (1970), Halverson constructs a thoughtful interpretive frame after declaring the issue of the Pardoner's supposed drunkenness closed: the Pardoner is not drunk but 'tongue-loosened' (**851**). Previous critics assume virtually every position on the topic: the Pardoner is drunk (**271, 297, 739, 780, 814**); he isn't drunk (**273, 740**); he isn't necessarily drunk (**769, 786**); or it doesn't matter whether he is drunk (**809**). The apparent superficiality of the question masks, of course, the interpretive issue of control in the Pardoner's confession. Despite Halverson's attempt to close the question, critics through the Nineties feel compelled to assess the Pardoner's degree of inebriation (**1130**) and some, in fact, revive the once discarded consideration of the tavern setting (**1031, 1130**). On a second critical issue, while Halverson concedes that the complexity of the Pardoner's motivation might still be a live topic, he argues that it is inconceivable for the Pardoner, skilled homilist that he is, to be intimidated by the *gentils* (**851**, p 186-7). Halverson reminds readers that they know 'next to nothing' of the 'real' Pardoner (**851**, p 196) and urges them to see the *PardT* as 'a gripping and unexceptionably Christian *memento mori*' (**851**, p 201). He finds recent criticism 'predominantly interpretive and "phenomenological"' (p 193). Thus, Halverson characterizes the criticism of the previous thirty years as manifesting a more holistic or synthetic approach, a more frequent willingness to read the appearances of the Pardoner as a multi-staged sequence, a New Critical propensity to accommodate multiple approaches (e.g., simultaneous naturalistic and theologic readings), and an interest in interpretive approaches be they ironic, spiritual, or psychological.

In addition to sustained interest in topics deriving from dramatic interpetation (Kittredge's seminal work moving into a fifteenth printing), the criticism of the Seventies focuses attention on the thematic relationships within Group C (**864, 924, 941**); symbolic readings of *PardT*; and a closer examination of the Pardoner's two audiences— *lerned* and *lewed* (**848**). Particularly fruitful are the renewed discussions of Chaucer's relation to the sermon tradition (**854, 856, 877, 894, 898, 908, 923, 937, 940, 949**). Though the issue of his religious affiliation receives less attention than in the past (**622, 779**), strong interest in the Pardoner's character continues. As an example, the Pardoner's relation to the figure of Vice in the medieval drama is developed by Kean (**865**), Faulkner (**882**) and Petersen (**933**).

Also during this decade, Muscatine leads readers to see stylistic relationships between the Pardoner and Chaucer. Building on his earlier work, where he characterizes *PardT* as an example of the 'mixed style,' Muscatine notes that the Pardoner is the only pilgrim given powers akin to Chaucer's. These similarities between the poet and pilgrim as both rhetorician and *storyteller* underscore Chaucer's ironic response to the dilemmas of the fourteenth century (**870**). Several critics follow Muscatine's insightful lead in exploring the common ground between Chaucer and the Pardoner (**870, 874, 905, 921**).

In one of several efforts to shift focus from the character of the Pardoner, Barney directs attention to the qualities of his performance (**875**). Several works set studies of Chaucer's art within the context of rhetoric, often giving new emphasis to the quality of *game* (**884, 885, 946, 948**, and **909, 921, 928**). This orientation offers strong direction through the next decade. Howard urges readers to see episodes in *CT* as more thematic than narrative, the overall pattern being one of interlace. In this decade, the discussion of intentionality moves from the Pardoner to Chaucer himself: Quinn arguing for Chaucer's moral seriousness (**916**) while Kean (**865**) and Knight (**884, 885**) hold, as Ruggiers before them, that Chaucer's tone is essentially comic.

In the Eighties, the persistent issue of the Pardoner's sexuality generates considerable interest. The textual basis for the debate over the Pardoner's sexual condition—the Narrator's *I trowe he were a geldyng or a mare* (line 691)—is as enigmatic as it is brief. Both the apparent contradiction with the Pardoner's interruption of the Wife of Bath and the Host's subsequent graphic threat, however, complicate the context. Early in the century, Curry's physiognomic approach (**277**) establishes the groundwork for discussion of the Pardoner's condition as *eunuchus ex nativitate*, a judgment Miller amplifies with patristic sources to depict the Pardoner as *eunuchus non Dei*, a spiritually sterile false cleric (**323**).

In a countermove, several critics undertake moral assessments of the Pardoner by shifting attention to social, psychological, and gendered features of his portrait. McAlpine provides a comprehensive review of critical stances on the Pardoner's sexuality, noting the pervasive influence of the latent homophobic assumptions (**967**). Before McAlpine, Rowland draws from modern medical literature in a dramatic stroke declaring the Pardoner 'a testicular pseudo-hermaphrodite of the feminine type' (**359, 360**). A decade later, Howard urges against reductive readings of the Pardoner; accepting the diagnosis of physical and spiritual eunuchry, he develops an image of the Pardoner as a feminoid or hermaphroditic male, a puzzling grotesque on the margins 'of the ordered world of created goodness' (**424**, p 338-41). Taking up the issue in 1980, McAlpine redirects attention from the term *geldyng* to *mare*, arguing that, while the categories 'effeminate,' 'hermaphrodite,' and 'eunuch,' each account for some of the Pardoner's characteristics, the category 'homosexual' is the only one that accounts for them all. The Pardoner's boast of Avarice, McAlpine continues, should be seen as a screen for his sense of alienation and a plea for acceptance. The Pardoner is a pilgrim and his efforts to relate to Church and community through relics and pardons are indications that he is not a lost soul (**967**, p113; cf **493**; **316, 496, 504, 509**).

More recently, the Pardoner's sexuality has been interpreted metaphorically: Green presents it as a sign of spiritual duplicity (**463**); Knight as a metaphor for the shift from the office of the preacher to private gain (**487**); and Olson finds in the hermaphroditic condition a correlative of the Wycliffite debate over the commingling of spiritual and temporal power. In the early Eighties, the interest in the Pardoner's sexuality led to an MLA forum, 'Thwarted Sexuality in Chaucer's Works,' where, not surprisingly, the tale also figured prominently (**451, 453, 456, 460, 466**).

Common to virtually all treatments of the Pardoner's sexuality in the Eighties (as with interpretations of the meaning of the Old Man) is a recognition of the power invested in intentional ambiguity (cf **457, 462**). This ambiguity leads Carolyn Dinshaw to suggest that the crucial element in understanding the Pardoner is 'the perception that *something* is missing' (**1117**, p 162); from this recognition, she develops a provocative reading of the Pardoner based on the imagery of fragmentation and lack, a 'eunuch hermeneutics.'

Though Di Marco returns to the hunt for sources, suggesting that

Chaucer's inspiration for an 'effeminate, lustful, parasite-prelate' is found in Jerome (**260**), in the Nineties, interest in the Pardoner's sexuality draws largely from feminist and gender studies, gay/lesbian studies, and queer theory, notably their attention to the relationships between representational systems and the body. Several critics draw attention to the Pardoner's body as a site of performance: Steven Kruger sets the Pardoner against a late-medieval construction of male homosexuality to conclude that, if the Pardoner is constructed as 'the medieval equivalent of a gay man,' he is 'a character written out of homophobia' (**1196**, p 120). Moving in a slightly different direction, Glenn Burger, in 'Queer Chaucer,' suggests that the Pardoner's body 'ceaselessly performing gender and sexuality but never getting it "right"' casts light on 'the complexities of a medieval politics of representation' (**1190**, p 163; see also **1169**). Similarily, Rita Copeland claims that, in his body, the Pardoner joins '[t]he social politics of sexuality and the institutional politics of rhetoric' (**1192**, p 149). Dinshaw points out that the queer problematizes sexuality with the Pardoner becoming a kind of 'ideological key to the *Tales*' (**1205**, p 79).

The work of these critics is representative of a larger trend in current criticism which draws on other disciplines (including psychoanalysis, sociology, historiography, ethnography and culture studies) to formulate interdisciplinary approaches. Several treatments of *CT* as a whole emerge as a result of these efforts combined with the waning of dramatic interpretation. The relation of *PardT* to the frame is examined (**979**, **1011**), as are the unities of *theme*—marriage, poets and poetry, inconclusiveness, vow-breaking, fruitfulness (**968**; **1026**, **1069**, **1075**, **1113**)—*imagery* (**983**), *structure* (**962**, **993**; **1049**), and *context* (**1123**). Still others examine Chaucer's stance regarding medieval institutions: Aers (**958**, **1055**), Boitani (**991**), Besserman (**1005**), Cook (**1064**), and Howard (**1092**) argue that Chaucer undertakes a critique of institutions (e.g., pilgrimage, indulgences, relics); although, Storm counters that Chaucer does not repudiate the institutions of his time (**1027**, **1028**).

The impact of contextual influence on Chaucer's art is taken up by several critics: Kirkpatrick arguing against the influence of the *Decameron*(**1016**); Bauschatz considering the influence of scholasticism (**989**); Braswell, the medieval theology of sin (**1006**); Jeffrey and Reiss, scriptural tradition (**1041**) (**1042**); Andreas and

Fleming, ascetic texts (**1034, 1040**) and Calin, the French tradition (**1191**). Emerging from these inquiries comes a fresh examination of the nature of Chaucer's art, including both his humor (**569**) and his moral seriousness (**961, 1030, 1058, 1059, 1070, 1071, 1083, 1093, 1099**). Stevens, in fact, argues that *PardT* represents Chaucer's first poetic statement that art and morals are inextricably linked (**999**).

The artful ambiguity that has long been an acknowledged hallmark of the Pardoner and his tale seems to insure that critical production will not wane; in the last quarter century, interpretive energies push in all directions—psychological, linguistic, deconstructive, feminist, gay, and lesbian studies. Though it may be artificial to fix a center to the activity, three critics articulate approaches (all grounded in psychological readings and two proceeding through deconstruction) that promise to dominate the discourse through century's end. The first of these, Howard, places himself squarely in the line of dramatic interpretation, drawing heavily from psychoanalytic approaches to recreate a mesmerizing figure of the Pardoner, as 'a marginal grotesquerie' (**926**, p 314) who remains 'a mystery, an enigma—sexually anomalous, hermaphroditic, menacing, contradictory' (**926**, p 345). Howard moves on to address the similarities between the Pardoner and Chaucer in gifts of rhetoric, impersonation, and dramatic flair (cf **979, 992, 1036, 1098**). *PardT*, he holds, is a 'grotesquerie' floating at the periphery of the system of interlace that constitutes *CT*.

Leicester takes issue with Howard's characterization of Chaucer's craft as 'unimpersonated artistry' (**964**); Leicester counters with a case for 'impersonated artistry.' Where Howard's construct requires the reader to decide which part of a narrative ought to be assigned to a pilgrim teller, which to the author, Leicester's reading sees the entire narration as the work of a single speaker who directs attention to his various roles. The tales are *texts* rather than performances of pre-existing selves, and these *texts* are to be read with a view to analyzing individual subjects, the *voice* of the texts. Leicester's work focuses the reader on the text itself.

These continuing controversies lead Patterson, in his survey of critical commentary, to conclude that, for the Pardoner and his tale, the basic terms of interpretation remain in dispute. He adds medieval penitential literature to the established contexts of medieval convention and modern psychology. Deeming Chaucer the first post-medieval poet, Patterson demonstrates how Chaucer employs character to develop the relation of self to society: the Pardoner yearns in vain for the liberation of confession and, though he presents glimpses of himself in *PardP*, he remains ignorant of the self-understanding he displaces into fiction in *PardT* (**932**). The Pardoner creates himself *as* language (**949**) and mocks Penance as a means of self-constitution (**1164**).

While it is premature to attempt any retrospective of the twentieth century criticism, an examination of works published 1990-5 acknowledges the debt of Chaucer studies to the prior century, while stimulating interest in the issues of subjectivity (**1142, 1143**) (**1164**), authority (**1132, 1199**), early reception (**1186**), gender (**1193**), and linguistic humor (**1172, 1187**). These, together with the growing influence of other disciplines (e.g., Andreas' use of Bakhtin to articulate the liminal energy in the links) (**568**), new methodologies (e.g. Burger's application of Queer Theory to the Pardoner's performance of masculinity to illuminate the politics of representation) (**1169, 1190**), and the growing international readership promise to both clarify and complicate this most puzzling of pilgrims. In seeking to understand the Pardoner, readers encounter the more general issues of Chaucer's moral intent, his relation to his audience, his attitude towards institutions, and his very nature as an artist. But, the Pardoner's appeal is yet more alluring; for, in the Pardoner, more than any other pilgrim, readers recognize not only aspects of the author but of themselves as well.

ℰ Editions and Translations

A separate edition of *PardP* and *PardT* is being prepared by Penn Szittya, as part of the *Variorum Chaucer*. For consideration of early editors prior to the purview of this listing—Stow, Speght, Urry, Tyrwhitt, and Wright—as well as essays on Thynne, Caxton, Furnivall (**1**), Skeat, (**7**), Manly-Rickert (**58**), and Robinson (**117**), the reader is directed to *Editing Chaucer: The Great Tradition*, ed. Paul G. Ruggiers (Norman, Oklahoma: Pilgrim Books), 1984.

1 *A Six-Text Print of Chaucer's Canterbury Tales in Parallel Columns.* Ed. Frederick J. Furnivall. 8 vols. Chaucer Society, First Series, Numbers 1, 25. London: N. Trübner, 1868. Rpt Berkeley Square House, London: Johnson Reprint Corporation, 1967.
Part I [number 1 rpt] prints specimens of the spurious prologue to *ShT* (pp x-xi) and *GP* portrait (pp 9-21). *Part IV The Tale of Melibeus, The Monk's Tale. The Nun's Priest's Tale. The Doctor's Tale. The Pardoner's Tale. The Wife of Bath's Tale. The Friar's Tale. The Summoner's Tale* [number 25 rpt] prints the text in parallel columns as it appears in the following manuscripts: El, Hg, Cambridge Gg.4.27, Corpus, Petworth, and Landsdowne. In all mss, *PardT* is preceded by *PhyT*; in all but Petworth (where *PardT* is followed by Prologue to *Thop*), *PardT* is followed by *ShT*. In Cambridge and Ellesmere, *PardT* is preceded with portraits of the Pardoner. Furnivall includes the 'Doctor-Pardoner Link' (pp 312-3), the 'Pardoner's Preamble' (pp 314-7), and *PardT* (pp 318-32). Specimens are included of all the variants in 30 manuscripts 'now easily getatable [sic]' (p 333) for the Doctor-Pardoner Link (lines 289-300) and lines 487-8; spurious lines are identified. Reprints of the Ellesmere portraits are bound in the back of the volume.

See **2, 7, 11, 24, 51,71**.

2 *A Temporary Preface to the Chaucer Society's Six-Text Edition of Chaucer's 'Canterbury Tales': Part I, Attempting to Show the True Order of the Tales, and the Days and Stages of the Pilgrimage, etc.* Chaucer Society, Second Series, Number 3. London: N. Trübner, 1868. Furnivall takes up the tale order deciding on: AB¹B²CDEFGHI. This scheme becomes the standard though it is opposed by Bradshaw. See **1**.

- Donald C. Baker, 'Frederick James Furnivall,' in *Editing Chaucer*, (**167**) pp 157-69: 'He followed basically the order suggested to him and worked out by Bradshaw ... Furnivall's own contribution to the order was the shift of Fragment C ... to place no. 4 largely on the strength of the Pardoner's indication that he was hungry ... [this shift] has been quite important and continues to be debated, though it was later abandoned by Skeat himself ... '(p 161).

3 *The Tale of the Man of Lawe, The Pardoneres Tale, The Second Nonnes Tale, The Chanouns Yemannes Tale from the Canterbury Tales.* Ed. Walter W. Skeat. Oxford: Clarendon Press, 1876; rev 2nd ed 1879, rev 1889, 1897, rev 1931, rev 1952, 1962.

This school text follows El 'in general' (p vii) with occasional variations from six others: Hg, Cambridge, Corpus, Petworth, Lansdowne and Harleian. Introductory notes cover 'all that seemed necessary for a right understanding of the text' (p viii). This critical edition includes introductory notes, textual notes at the bottom of the page, critical notes following the text, a glossarial index and an index of proper names. Text includes in Group C: 'The wordes of the Hoost to the Phisicien and the Pardoner' (pp 38-9); 'The Pardoner's Prologue (pp 40-4); and 'The Pardoneres Tale' (pp 44-60). The text is modified: *PardP* omits lines 371, 381, 453; *PardT* omits lines 487, 536, 955 and alters line 549: *A [cursed] thing is wyn and dronkenesse.* Textual notes are included at the bottom of the page. See **7**.

4 *The Harleian MS 7334 of The Canterbury Tales.* Ed. Frederick J. Furnivall. Chaucer Society Publications, First Series, Number 73. London: N. Trübner & Co., 1885.

Prints *GP* portrait (pp 19-21), *Interr* (pp 198-9), *Phy-PardL* (pp 424-5), *PardP* (pp 426-9), and *PardT* (pp 430-44). Contains four spurious lines in *Phy-PardL* (299-300, 305-6); and two in *PardT* (478-9).

5 *Chaucer's Canterbury Tales.* Ed. Alfred W. Pollard. London: Kegan,

Paul & Co., 1886.

An edition of 50 copies on large paper which presents *GP*, and a selection of tales including *PardT* and *PardP*. [Not seen.]

6 *Specimens of All the Accessible Unprinted Manuscripts of the Canterbury Tales: The Doctor-Pardoner Link, and Pardoner's Prologue and Tale*. 4 parts. Ed. Julius Zupitza. With an Introduction by John Koch. Chaucer Society Publications. First Series, Numbers 81, 85, 86, 90. London: Kegan Paul, Trench, Trübner, 1892-7. Rpt *The Doctor-Pardoner Link, and Pardoner's Prologue and Tale*. Ed. Julius Zupitza. New York: Johnson Reprint Corp., 1967.

In an effort preliminary to establishing a stemma for *CT* as a whole, the Chaucer Society printed specimens of a single tale; Furnivall selected *PardT* 'on account of the great number of variations found ... when preparing his Six-Text Print ...' (81:iv). Published in 1892 and 1893, the variants for *Phy-PardL*, *PardP*, and *PardT* are printed as follows: volume 1-3 (edited by Julius Zupitza): Part 1 (number 81), The *Dd.-group*: Dd En¹ Ds Ch En³ Ad¹ Nl; Part 2 (number 85), small groups: Ph¹ Bo² Ha⁵ Ps Se Tc¹ Ra³ Gl Ad² Ht; and Part III (no 86), The *Corpus group*: Cp La Sl² Tc² Ne Ha³ He Ii. For Parts 4-8 see **10**.

7 *The Complete Works of Geoffrey Chaucer*. 6 vols with a supplement, Chaucerian and Other Pieces, vol 7. Ed. W[alter]. W. Skeat. London: Oxford University Press, 1894; Oxford: Clarendon Press, 1894-7. 2nd ed. 1900. Rpt many times thereafter through 1963. Vol IV: *The Canterbury Tales*.

The first complete printed edition of *CT* founded on Ellesmere, collated with the other mss of the *Six-Text* edition (**1, 2**) supplemented by Harley 7334 printed separately by the Chaucer Society: 'Of all the mss, E. is the best in nearly every respect. It not only gives good lines and good sense, but is also (usually) grammatically accurate and thoroughly well spelt' (p xvii). This edition provided for the first time a critical apparatus and set the standard in critical editing. Selected textual notes appear at the foot of the page. Group C comprises *PhyT*; 'Words of the Host to the Phisicien and the Pardoner'(pp 299-300); 'Prologue of the Pardoner's Tale' (pp 301-4); and *PardT* (pp 305-19). Vol V. *Notes to the Canterbury Tales*: Words of the Host, (pp 264-9); *PardP*, (pp 269-275); and *PardT* (pp 275-90). The extensive notes serve as an influential source for students and editors. Vol. VI contains a 310-page, double column glossary with line references. See **3, 8, 9, 11, 27, 29, 36, 41, 42, 45, 51, 66, 84, 96**. For Pardoner, see **267**; for *Phy-PardL*, see

530; for *PardP*, see **570**; for *PardT*, see **669**.

- A. S. G. Edwards, 'Walter W. Skeat,' in *Editing Chaucer* (**167**) pp 171-89: 'He [Skeat] was the first to attempt a comprehensive edition of the works, he provided for the first time an apparatus to illumine them that was reliable and compendious, and he set standards in critical editing which, if they have been subsequently raised, have been raised as a consequence of his work'(p 189).

8 *The Student's Chaucer*. Ed. W[alter] W. Skeat. New York and London: Macmillan: Oxford: Clarendon, 1895.

This work, which presents the 1894 text in a single volume, became the Oxford Standard Authors edition and was reprinted frequently under various imprints through 1967. Includes a brief introduction, an appendix listing doubtful readings and editor's emendations (none for Pardoner), and a 149-page, double-column glossary; no explanatory or textual notes are included. Text includes *GP* portrait (pp 427-8), 'Words of the Host to the Phisicien and Pardoner' (p 555), 'Prologe of the Pardoners Tale' (pp 556-7), *PardT* (pp 558-564) and *Interr* (p 567). This text was also published in three volumes for the World's Classics Series (London: Oxford University Press, 1903-6) and in one volume, with a brief introduction by Louis Untermeyer, for the Modern Library (New York: Random House, 1929). These later printings contain a short glossary. See **7**.

9 *The Works of Geoffrey Chaucer*. [The Kelmscott Chaucer]. Hammersmith, Middlesex: The Kelmscott Press, 1896.

This ornamented edition is printed with 'Chaucer' type in black and red, with 87 woodcut illustrations designed, in at least the initial stages, by Burne-Jones and numerous woodcut borders and initial letters. F.S. Ellis' edition, based on Skeat (**7**) includes additional corrections approved by Skeat [not seen]. For facsimile editions, see **76, 99, 101**.

10 *Specimens of All the Accessible Unprinted Manuscripts of the Canterbury Tales: The Doctor-Pardoner Link, and Pardoner's Prologue and Tale*. Ed. F[rederick] J. Furnivall. With an Introduction by John Koch. Chaucer Society Publications, First Series, Numbers 90-94. London: Kegan, Paul, Trench, Trübner, 1897-8.

Part 4 [1897] no 90 includes 17 mss of the *Pe.-group*: Bw Bo[1] Ds Ha[2] Ld[1] Ld[2] Lc Ln Mm Ph$_2$ Ph3 Ra2 Ry1 Ry2 Sl1 To En[2]; Part 5 consisting of the final array of *PardT* mss and three early editions is published in three sections: the larger part in 1898 and the first and second supplements in 1901 (Number 92).

This work represents the completion of **6** by John Koch and by Furnivall following the death of Julius Zupitza bringing the number of variants printed by the Chaucer Society to 52 of the known 53 mss of *PardP* and *PardT*; for Cn, the exception, see **134**. Includes frontispiece of 'The Yard of the Tabard Inn on the Morning of the 17th of April, 1387' by P.D. Hardy, 1900; the Pardoner wears a hat with vernicle, long hair spread over his shoulders and carries a *croys of latoun* and a *walet*. For Parts 1-3, see **6**.

11 *The Works of Geoffrey Chaucer*. Ed. Alfred W. Pollard, H. Frank Heath, Mark H. Liddell, W.S. McCormick. [The Globe Chaucer]. London and New York: Macmillan 1898/rev 1928. Rpt many times, including Freeport, New York: Books for Libraries Press, 1972.

This critical text of *CT* is based on Ellesmere, conservatively emended by collation with the other mss in the *Six-Text* edition (**1**) and Harley 7334, edited by the Chaucer Society. The double-column text is accompanied by explanatory and textual notes at the foot of the page and a glossary. Text includes *GP* portrait; Tales of the Third Day, Group C comprising 'Wordes to the Phisicien and Pardoner' (lines 287-326), *PhyT* (lines 329-462), 'Preamble of the Pardoners Tale' (pp 145-7), *PardT* (pp 147-54); and the *Interr* (p 156-7). Pollard follows Furnivall in placing *PhyT-PardT* after *FrT*. An earlier separate edition of *CT* had been published by Pollard (London: Macmillan, 1894). See also **19**, **43**.

12 *The Story of the Canterbury Pilgrims. Retold from Chaucer and Others*. Ed. F.J. Harvey Darton. Illustrated by M.L. Kirk. Philadelphia: Lippincott, 1900. Rpt New York: Frederick A. Stokes, 1914.

A free prose translation includes selections from *GP*, *KnT*, *MilT*, *CkT*, *MLT*, *PrT*, *MkT*, *NPT*, *PhyT*, *PardT*, *WBT*, *FrT*, *SumT*, *ClT*, *SqT*, *FranT*, *SNT*, *CYT*, *ManT*, *ParsT*, and 'The Merchant's Second Tale: Beryn' arranged over a five day sequence. Tales of the fourth day include: 'A Gentle Pardoner of Rouncival'(pp 116-9), 'The Pardoner's Tale: The Three Revelers and Death' (pp 120-5), and 'Who'll Buy My Pardons?' (pp 125-6). See **22**.

13 *The Complete Works of Geoffrey Chaucer*. With an Introduction by Thomas R. Lounsbury. 2 vols. New York: Thomas Y. Crowell, 1900.

The source of the text is not indicated. Text includes *GP* portrait (pp

473-4), 'Words of the Host' (p 609), *PardP* (pp 610-1), and *PardT* (pp 612-8). An 82-page double-column glossarial index and an introduction by Lounsbury are included. See **18**.

14 *The Pardoner's Tale. From Chaucer's Canterbury Tales.* Ed. W. Cuthbert Robb. [Standard English Classics]. London: Blackie & Son Ltd., 1900, 1986.

This school edition includes brief introduction, *GP* portrait (pp 18-9), *PardP* (pp 15-19), *PardT* (pp 19-34) and brief explanatory notes; silent deletions occur at lines 534-7 and 950-5.

15 *The Cambridge Ms. Dd.4.24 of Chaucer's Canterbury Tales. Completed by the Egerton Ms. 2726 (the Haistwell Ms.).* Parts I and II. Ed. Frederick J. Furnivall. 2 vols. Chaucer Society Publications, First Series, Numbers 95 and 96. London: Kegan Paul, Trench, Trübner & Co., 1901.

Comments that when Zupitza declined to take *WBP* and *WBT* as the basis for his Specimens (**6**) on the basis of his dislike for the subject, he selected the Pardoner 'which I [Furnivall] then believed to be the Tale most varied in its readings' (p vi). Prints Introduction, *GP* portrait (I: 19-21), *Interr* (I: 171-2), *Phys-PardL* (II:368-9), *PardP* (II: 370-3) and *PardT* (II: 374-88).

16 *The Pardoner's Prologue and Tale.* Ed. John Koch. Englische Textbibliothek.Vol 7. Heidelberg, Carl Winter'sUniversitäts-buchhandlung: Emil Felber, 1902. Adopted by Chaucer Society, Second Series, Numbers 35. 1902. Rpt Oxford: Oxford University Press, 1928.

Koch's text, the first critical edition of *PardT*, appeared originally in 1902 as volume 7 of the Englische Textbibliothek edited by Johannes Hoops, published by Emil Felber, Berlin. Almost immediately, it was adopted by the Chaucer Society. Manly and Rickert took this edition into account in their expanded 1940 volume. The Doctor-Pardoner Link, *PardP* and *PardT* present a genealogy of mss based on a complete collation (with one exception, a never printed manuscript of *PardP* and *PardT* accessible in the Library of the University of Texas). Koch suggests that his classification 'will hold good also for the rest of the C.T., though some mss may have been derived in different portions, from different sources ...'(p xxxv-xxxvi). Koch takes as his aim 'representing the text as if the scribe of the best ms in existence had copied it more carefully and from a better source than evidently was at his disposal' (p xix). Koch concludes that the Ellesmere ms, 'on the

whole the least faulty, must form the basis of a critical text of the C.T.'
(p l[L]xxii). This edition includes introductory material on former editions
of *PardP* and *PardT*, the present edition, the placement and sources of
PardT, and the Pardoner. The edition is supported by extensive notes.
For Pardoner, see **269**; for *PardT,* see **670**. See also **58**.

- Hammond criticizes Koch's effort to construct a genealogical tree
  on the basis of *PardT* (p 112). '[A] "critical" text which assumes
  (1) the correctness of Zupitza's classification of the MSS of the
  Pardoner's Tale, and (2) the applicability of that classification to the
  Prologue, takes positions which are not beyond dispute' (p 169). See
  127.

17 *The Select Chaucer*. Ed. James Logie Robertson. Edinburgh and
   London: William Blackwood, 1902.
   This school edition, which includes an introduction, *GP* and selections
   from *PardT* with sixteen other tales, is based on the El and Harleian
   mss. Notes address chronology, Chaucer's life and times, grammar and
   diction, versification, pronunciation and a 15-page double-column glossary.

18 *The Canterbury Tales by Geoffrey Chaucer*. With an Introduction by
   Thomas R. Lounsbury. New York: Crowell, 1903.
   A school edition with brief notes and glossary and based on **13**; no
   manuscript basis stated.

19 *Chaucer's Canterbury Tales. The Prologue*. Ed. Alfred W. Pollard.
   London and New York: Macmillan, 1903/rev 1905. Rpt London:
   Macmillan, 1932, 1967, and New York: St. Martin's Press, 1967.
   This school edition, reprinted more than twenty-five times, presents *GP*
   with introduction and extensive notes directed to the student interested
   in advanced instruction. Pardoner portrait (pp 24-5) deletes line 691.
   See **11**.

20 *The Canterbury Tales of Geoffrey Chaucer: A Modern Reading
   into Prose of the Prologue and Ten Tales*. Ed. and trans. Percy
   Mackaye. New York: Fox, Duffield & Co., 1904. Reissued as *The
   Canterbury Tales of Geoffrey Chaucer: A Modern Rendering into
   Prose of the Prologue and Nine Tales*. By Percy Mackaye with
   Pictures by Walter Appleton Clark. New York: Avenel Books, 1987.
   A prose rendering of *GP*, *KnT*, *NPT*, *WBP*, *WBT*, *ClT*, *FranT*, *CYT*, *PhyT*,
   Phy-PardL, *PardP*, and *PardT*. Text is based on Skeat (**7**) with the aim
   of erring in the direction of 'literal fidelity' rather than 'literary license'
   (p xxii). Includes a 'stained glass' illustration of 'The Three Rogues

Search in the Woods for Death' (p 80).

21 *The Prioress's Tale and Other Tales by Geoffrey Chaucer Done Into Modern English by Prof. Skeat*. London: Alexander Moring Ltd., 1904.

Skeat presents modernized selections from *PardT* (lines 463-84; 661-894; 488-504) noting that the other matter is interesting but 'altogether irrelevant to the story' (p xv).

22 *Tales of the Canterbury Pilgrims. Retold from Chaucer and Others*. Ed. F.J. Harvey Darton. Introduction by F.J. Furnivall. Illustrations by Hugh Thomson London. 2nd ed. London: Wells Gardner, Darton & Co.; New York: Frederick A. Stokes, 1904 [page references based on this edition].

A free prose translation includes selections from *GP, KnT, MilT, CkT, MLT, PrT, MkT, NPT, PhyT, PardT, WBT, FrT, SumT, ClT, SqT, FranT, SNT, CYT, ManT, ParsT*, and 'The Merchant's Second Tale: Beryn' arranged over a five day sequence. As tales of the fourth day, prints, 'A Gentle Pardoner of Rouncival' (pp 132-7), 'The Pardoner's Tale: The Three Revellers and Death' (pp 138-45), and 'Who'll buy my Pardons?' (pp 146-7). Illustrations include: 'The Pardoner had his cakes and ale' (p 135), 'The three revellers' (p 138), 'They found a great heap of golden florins piled up'(p 143). See **12**.

23 Emerson, Oliver Farrar. *A Middle English Reader*. London and New York: Macmillan, 1905. Rpt 1908-1912 ; rev 1915. Rpt many times through 1950.

Includes *PardT* as an example of the dialect of London from the last decade of the fourteenth century, with text based on El, brief notes and glossary. Omits lines 513-660 and concludes at line 905. See **30**.

24 *Chaucer's Canterbury Tales [Vol 2]: The Tale of Sir Thopas, the Monkes Tale, The Nonne Prestes Tale, The Pardoners Tale, The Squires Tale, The Frankeleyns Tale, The Seconde Nonnes Tale, The Chanons Yomans Tale, The Persones Prologe*. Ed. Alfred W. Pollard. London: Kegan Paul, Trench & Co., 1905. The Dryden Series.

Text is directed to the general reader and based on 'the easiest readings' from the mss of the *Six-Text* edition (**1**) and Harley 7334. *GP* portrait in volume 1 (pp 18-19). Vol 2 includes *Phy-PardL* (lines 290-316 deleted, pp 83); *PardP* (lines 452-3 deleted, pp 84-8) and *PardT* (lines 486-7 deleted, 534-6, 950-5; pp 89-107). Text is supported by brief introduction and glossary in each volume. No notes.

25 *The Works of Geoffrey Chaucer and Others, Being a Reproduction in Facsimile of the First Collected Edition 1532 from the Copy in the British Museum.* Introduction by W[alter] W. Skeat. London: Alexander Moring for the De La More Press and Henry Frowde for the Oxford University Press, 1905.

In an introduction to this facsimile of Thynne's edition, Skeat reviews the history of printed editions of *CT*: Caxton[1] (1477-8), Caxton[2] (1483), Pynson[1] (1493) Wynkyn de Worde (1498), and Pynson[2] (1526). Thynne's edition became the standard for 250 years. Skeat regrets that *CT* are 'the least satisfactory portion' (p xxv) of Thynne's edition, Thynne having drawn from Caxton[1]; Skeat cites Tyrwhitt to the effect that all Thynne's variations from Caxton[2] 'are all, I think, for the worse' (p xxv). Thynne includes the Pardoner portrait in *GP* (pp 18-9), the *Interr* (p 100), 'Wordes of the Hoste' (pp 170-1), *PardP* (pp 171-2), and *PardT* (pp 173-7). Thynne prints the spurious Doctor-Pardoner link. Line numbers (both Chaucer Society and Tyrwhitt) run on the bottom of the page. A woodcut of the Pardoner, one of 13 drawn by Thynne, follows *PardP* (p 172): the Pardoner is shown mounted on a horse with cape and decorated bridle; the Pardoner wears a hat, sword at the left side and beads diagonally across his chest. For later sixteenth- and seventeenth-century versions of Thynne, see **90**.

- James E. Blodgett, 'William Thynne,' in *Editing Chaucer*, pp 35-52: His emendations frequently were based on a limited and flawed understanding of Chaucer's language and a misguided attribution of humanistic practices to Chaucer. Yet modern editors cannot afford to ignore Thynne's edition because Thynne did have access to manuscripts no longer available (52).

26 *Selections from Chaucer.* Ed. Edwin A. Greenlaw. Chicago: Scott, Foresman, 1907.

The text is based on El collated with Hg, Cambridge, Corpus Christi, Petworth, Lansdowne and Harleian; variations from Ellesmere are noted at the foot of the page. Text includes *GP, KnT, MkT* (selections), *NPT, Phy-PardL, PardP* and a condensed version of *PardT* (omits lines 524-660, 946 f). Includes brief textual (by line) notes and 21-page double column glossary.

27 *Chaucer's Canterbury Tales for the Modern Reader.* Ed. Arthur Burrell. Everyman's Library. London: Dent; New York: E.P. Dutton, 1908. Rpt frequently through 1948.

Prints all *CT* with exception of *CkP* and *CkT*. Reference is made to Skeat (**7**) but the basis of the text is not indicated. 'The Pardoneres Tale' (pp 236-52) is one of seven non-modernized tales which are judged 'so plain-spoken, that no amount of editing or alteration will make them suitable for the twentieth century' (pp vii-iii); nevertheless, the text is bowdlerized. The Pardoner is typical of Chaucer's clerics in making us laugh at him. For later Everyman edition, see **72**.

28 *Chaucer: The Pardoner's Tale*. Ed. C.M. Drennan & A.J. Wyatt. London: Tutorial Press, 1910; second edition 1928; rpt with additions and alterations 1958 [page numbers from 1910 edition].
Cites Ellesmere as the best manuscript. Text includes *Pard-PhyL* (pp 43-4), *PardP* and *PardT* (pp 43-62), substantive introduction, explanatory notes and 15-page, double-column glossary. Textual deletions are indicated. The conclusion of *PardT* is 'part of the consummate impudence of the man' (p 26).

29 *The Ellesmere Chaucer, Reproduced in Facsimile*. Preface by Alix Egerton. 2 vols. Manchester: Manchester University Press, 1911. For rpt see **122**.
The third Earl of Ellesmere made this richly decorated Chaucer ms available for reproduction. *Phy-PardL*, *PardP* and *PardT* each begin with a large decorative capital. The first pages of *PardP* and *PardT* are decorated with a demivinet border; the miniature of the Pardoner appears at the opening of *PardT*. This rare facsimile has been reproduced as a working facsimile (**122**). For fuller discussion of the ms, now owned by the Huntington Library, San Marino, California, see **902**. For discussion of the Pardoner's miniature, see **284**, **307**, **335**, **341**, **364**, **375**, **435**, **461**.

30 *Poems of Chaucer: Selections from His Earlier and Later Works*. Ed. Oliver Farrar Emerson. New York: Macmillan, 1911.
CT selections, printed 'as they appear in the best manuscripts' (p vi), include *GP*, *NPT*, *PardT* (pp 132-40; deletions indicated), *MkT* (selections) and *KnT* (selections). Text is supported by introduction, notes, and a 65-page, double-column glossary. See **23**.

31 *Tales from Chaucer*. Ed. Charles Cowden Clarke and Illustrated by Arthur Szyk. London: E.P. Dutton, [1870], 1911. *The Canterbury Tales by Geoffrey Chaucer: Selected Tales Told for Young People*. The Heritage Illustrated Bookshelf. New York: Heritage Press, 1947.
A translation directed to young readers which aims to be '"modernly

antique," prosaically poetic, and comprehensively concise' (Preface). Includes Words of the Host, and *PardT* with full page illustration (pp 125-35).

32 *Chaucer's Canterbury Tales. Selections From The Modern Reader's Chaucer.* Ed. John S.P. Tatlock and Percy MacKaye. Chosen by Carl W. Ziegler. [Macmillan Pocket American and English Classics]. New York: Macmillan, 1912, 1923, 1925.

In this selection drawn from **33**, a modern prose translation of the central portion of *PardT* (pp 82-8) is included with *GP* (pp 17-8; omits reference to *geldyng* or *mare*), *KnT*, *CLT*, and portions of *NPT*, and *WBT*. See **33** complete.

33 *The Complete Poetical Works of Geoffrey Chaucer.* Trans John S.P. Tatlock and Percy MacKaye. The Modern Reader's Chaucer, with 32 illustrations by Warwick Goble. New York: Macmillan, 1912/rev 1938; rpt through 1967. Reissued in paperback without illustrations. Toronto: Collier-Macmillan, 1966. [Not seen.]

This first complete prose translation into Modern English alters words and phrases to avoid 'stumbling blocks' of 'rhyme and excessive rhythm, obscurity, extreme verbosity, and 'excessive coarseness'; variations for the latter are not indicated: asterisks indicate the omission of whole episodes when they are 'incurably gross or voluptuous' (p vii). Includes translation of *Phy-PardL*, *PardP*, and *PardT* (pp 145-56), the *Interr* (p 159), and an illustration, 'The Three Revellers and the Gold' (right facing p 154). See **32**.

34 *Selections from Chaucer, Including His Earlier and His Later Verse and an Example of His Prose.* Ed. Clarence Griffin Child. Boston: D.C. Heath, 1912.

Includes *GP*, *KnT*, *Headlink* to *Thop*, *NPT* and a selection from *PardT* (lines 661-945); the source of the text is not indicated. Blake's 'Canterbury Pilgrims' appears as the frontispiece. Introduction, explanatory notes (pp 178-80) and a 21-page glossary are included. *PardT* presents a story 'of the highest intrinsic merit' possessing 'a special historic insight in that it is of great antiquity' (p 178). Child reads the closing solicitation as 'jesting irony' (p 180).

35 *The College Chaucer.* Ed. Henry Noble MacCracken. New Haven: Yale University Press, 1913; London: Humphrey Milford, 1913; Oxford: Oxford University Press, 1913. Rpt seven times through 1929.

Presents *GP* and parts of 22 tales including the Words of the Host to the Physician and Pardoner (printed as an epilogue to *PhyT*, pp 216-7), *PardP* (pp 218-21) and *PardT* (pp 222-36). The text is based on Ellesmere with the few variants printed at the foot of the page. Includes an extensive glossary (pp 605-713) and appendix with notes on Chaucer's language, life, writings, dates and sources.

36 *The Canterbury Tales of Geoffrey Chaucer. Illustrated after drawings by W. Russell Flint.* 3 vols. A Riccardi Press book published for the Medici Society. London: Philip Lee Warner, 1913. Single volume edition, 1928 [cited here].

The Middle English edition is Skeat's (7). Includes no introduction, notes or glossary. Presents *GP* portrait (pp 20-1); 'The Wordes of the Host to the Phisicien and the Pardoner' (pp 293-4); 'Prologe of the Pardoners Tale' (pp 295-8); *PardT* (pp 299-313); and *Interr* (pp 318-9).

37 Storr, Francis and Hawes Turner. *Canterbury Chimes Or Chaucer Tales Retold for Children.* London: Kegan, Paul, Trench, Trübner & Co.; New York: E.P. Dutton. 2nd ed. 1914.

The introductory material in this second edition of a work originally published in 1878 speaks of the lack of 'supremely good' literature for children, the consequent need for a paraphrase of Chaucer, and mentions some dozen adaptations produced between 1878 and 1914. The Ellesmere miniatures are described as more accurate renderings of the pilgrims than the treatments of Blake and Stothard. The editors suggest that children will not be offended by the 'bad drawing' in these miniatures so much as they will be pleased by the authenticity.

38 *Geoffrey Chaucer's 'Canterbury Tales,' Nach dem Ellesmere Manuscript mit Lesarten, Anmerkungen und einem Glossar.* Ed. John Koch. Heidelberg: Carl Winter, 1915. Englische Textbibliothek 16. Series Editor, Johannes Hoops.

The text, based on Ellesmere, and printed in double columns with notes on the variants at the bottom of the page, includes 'Wordes of the Hoost to the Phisicien and the Pardoner'(p 234), *PardP* (pp 234-7), and *PardT* (pp 237-46). The text is supported by an introduction which treats mss, editions and sources, and 54-page glossary.

39 *Chaucer-Handbuch für Studierende: augsgewählte Texte mit Einleitungen, einem Abriss von Chaucers Versbau und Sprache und einem Wörterverzeichnis.* Ed. Max Kaluza. Leipzig: Bernhard Tauchnitz, 1919/rev 1927.

Presents *GP* portrait (pp 131-2) and *PardT* (pp 170-6; lines 485-660,

895 f deleted). Includes textual notes at the bottom of the page; no explanatory notes; brief glossary.

40 *Los Cuentos de Cantorbery. Versión directa del inglés antiguo con una introducción y notas por Manuel Pérez y del Río-Cosa. Prólogo de Adofo Bonilla y San Martín.* Madrid: Editorial Reus, 1921.

A Spanish translation of *CT*. [Not seen.]

41 *Selections from Chaucer.* Ed. William Allan Neilson and Howard Rollin Patch. New York: Harcourt Brace, 1921.

A selection designed to demonstrate Chaucer's diversity to the general reader and student. The text is based on Skeat (**7**) collated with reprints from the Chaucer Society; variant readings are recorded. Passages 'of least interest' have been omitted; clarity and continuity of plot serve as the priority for what is retained. Text includes 'The wordes of the Host to the Pardoner' (p 361); 'The Prologe of the Pardoners Tale' (pp 361-5); *PardT* (pp 365-77); and *Interr* (p 378). Omits lines 535-36, lines 945 f.

42 *The Canterbury Tales by Geoffrey Chaucer.* Ed. J[ohn]. M[atthews]. Manly. New York: Henry Holt, 1928; London: Harrap, 1928; rpt 1929, 1936.

During the time he was working on **58**, Manly presented this incomplete and bowdlerized edition originally directed to high school and elementary college work: 'Although I believe the text of the Tales here printed to be nearer Chaucer's original than any that has been printed heretofore, it is in no sense an attempt at a critical text' (p vi). Follows Ellesmere order and text 'departing from it only when a study of the other mss seemed clearly to prove that it was in error' (p vii). The introduction (pp 3-147) covers Chaucer's life, times, plan of *CT*, spurious links (including the Pardoner-Shipman Links), language, astrology and brief bibliography. The notes on *PardP* and *PardT* proved influential with later editions. For Pardoner, see **290**; for *PardT*, see **697**.

43 *The Works of Geoffrey Chaucer.* 8 vols. Oxford: Blackwell (printed at the Shakespeare Head Press, Stratford), 1928 (volume 1) and 1929 (vols 2-8). For Pardoner, see vols 1 and 2.

A fine edition; 375 copies printed of which 350 were made available for sale; an additional 11 printed on vellum. Text is based upon Pollard (**11**). *GP* portrait (1: 24-5) is accompanied on the bottom left by a 'freely rendered' Ellesmere miniature. Text includes *Phy-PardL* (2: 115-6) with Pardoner miniature repeated at the bottom left of 2:116, *PardP* (2: 117-

121), and *PardT* (2: 121-37).

44 *Geoffrey Chaucer: The Canterbury Tales*. Ed. Walter W. Skeat. With an Introduction by Louis Untermeyer. New York: Modern Library, 1929. Rpt 1957. A school edition based on Skeat (7). [Not seen.]

45 *The Canterbury Tales by Geoffrey Chaucer*. With Wood Engravings by Eric Gill. 4 vols. Waltham Saint Lawrence, Berkshire, England: Golden Cockerel Press, 1929.

A fine art edition in Middle English and based on Skeat (7); 15 copies on vellum and 485 on paper. The Pardoner *GP* portrait (1:24-6) is bordered by a martyred saint and risen Christ. Volume 3 opens with *PhyT* followed by *Phy-PardL* (3:11-3), *PardP* (3:13-7), and *PardT* (3:17-34). There are no textual headings; wood engravings separate and border tales. No notes.

46 *The Pardoner's Tale. Edited with Introduction and Notes*. Ed. Alfred W. Pollard and M. M. Barber. [Macmillan's English Classics]. London: Macmillan & Co., 1929 rpt many times through 1964.

The text for this frequently reprinted (bowdlerized) school edition is Ellesmere. Text includes 'The Talk on the Road,' *PardP*, *PardT*, and *Interr*. Textual changes number 23; lines 371, 381, 487, and 948-55 are deleted. Supporting materials include an introductory essay (pp vii-xxii), notes (pp 25-48), illustrations of Chaucer's language from *PardT* (pp 49-52) and glossary (pp 53-64).

47 *The Canterbury Tales of Geoffrey Chaucer, together with a version in modern English verse by William Van Wyck, illustrated by Rockwell Kent*. 2 vols. New York: Covici, Friede, 1930. Vol 2.

PardT is included in Tales of the Third Day preceding the tales of Group D. Middle English and modern text are printed in parallel columns (pp 251-61) with a full-page engraving of the Pardoner facing the opening page. *Phy-PardL* and *PardP* are not included. *Interr* follows *WBT* (p 265); *GP* portrait appears in vol. 1 (pp 18-9). This edition was issued as 75 fine copies and 924 numbered copies.

48 *The Canterbury Tales: The Prologue and Four Tales with The Book of the Duchess and Six Lyrics by Geoffrey Chaucer*. Trans. Frank Ernest Hill. Illustrations by Hermann Rosse. London: Longmans, Green and Co., 1930; rpt Longmans Green, 1932; 1931 school edition, rpt 1940, 1960; rpt New York: D. McKay, 1940, 1962.

This poetic translation, one of the first to be widely available, includes *GP*, *KnT*, *PrT*, *NPT*, *PardT*, *BD* (shortened), and six lyrics. For the

Pardoner, includes *GP* portrait (pp 26-8),and *PardT* lines 661-894 (pp 149-56). Black and white illustrations include a pilgrim portrait placed in *GP*, a full page portrayal of the rioters and a headnote portrayal of the Pardoner preaching. Hill acknowledges an earlier translation of *PardT* appearing in *Poems of the English Race*, ed. Raymond MacDonald Alden. New York: Charles Scribner's Sons, 1921, and, in an altered form, in *The Winged Horse Anthology. The Story of Poets and their Poetry*, ed. Joseph Auslander and Frank Ernest Hill. New York: Doubleday, Doran & Co., 1927.

49 *Tales from Chaucer*. Re-told by Eleanor Farjeon. Illustrations by Marjorie Walters. London: Medici Society, 1930. Rpt London: Oxford University Press; Newton, Massachusetts: Branford, 1959.
This prose translation of *CT* includes abbreviated versions of *PardP* (pp 169-70) and *PardT* (pp 171-5). Includes color illustration of the rioters with the gold.

50 *Under the Oak*. A play in Four Scenes, Based on *The Pardoner's Tale* from Chaucer's *Canterbury Tales*. New York: Appleton and Company, 1931.

51 *The Poetical Works of Chaucer*. Ed. F.N. Robinson. London: Oxford University Press, 1933; Cambridge Massachusetts: Houghton Mifflin, 1933. Also published as *The Complete Works of Geoffrey Chaucer*, Student's Cambridge Edition. Boston: Houghton Mifflin, 1933.
2nd ed. with the title *The Works of Geoffrey Chaucer*. Boston: Houghton Mifflin, 1957. Rpt (paperback) London: Oxford University Press, 1974. [The New Cambridge Chaucer].
This influential edition of the Works superseded Skeat's (**7**). The basis of the text for *CT* is Ellesmere collated with the following: 1) the other seven mss printed by the Chaucer Society (Hengwrt, Cambridge Dd.4.24, Cambridge Gg.4.27, Corpus, Petworth, Lansdowne, and Harley 7334); 2) Thynne's edition; and 3) the unpublished Cardigan and Morgan mss Text which includes *GP* portrait (pp 26-7), *Phy-PardL* (pp 178-9), *PardP* (pp 179-81), *PardT* (pp 181-7) and *Interr* (93). Robinson presents the tales in the Ellesmere order, in ten Fragments 1(A)-X. The text is accompanied by a general introduction, headnotes to separate works, explanatory notes at the back of thee text, a glossarial index and bibliographical references (a comprehensive review of scholarship to 1930): all enormously influential. See**71**; for Pardoner, see **295**; for *Interr* and *Phy-PardL*, see **535**; for *PardT*, see **704**. For discussion of

revised edition, see also **117**. See also **65** and **66** for modernizations.

- George Reinecke, 'F.N. Robinson,' in *Editing Chaucer: The Great Tradition*, ed. Paul G. Ruggiers (Norman, Oklahoma: Pilgrim Books, 1984). Pp 231-51. Reinecke reproduces Robinson's five-part 'Tentative Rule' (p 230, 241-2) and applies the first part (modernizations) to *PardT* C 463- 504 (167). 'His [Robinson's] chief preoccupation was the printing of regularly scanned, craftsmanlike, artistically significant lines conforming to his already determined opinions about Chaucer's grammar and meter' (p 250).

52 *The Canterbury Tales*. Ed. Frank E[rnest] Hill. 2 vols. London: Limited Editions Club. 1934. Rev 1 vol. *The Canterbury Tales by Geoffrey Chaucer; Done Into Modern English Verse by Frank Ernest Hill*. With Miniatures by Arthur Szyk. New York: The Heritage Press, 1935/ London: G. Allen & Unwin Ltd., 1936/ rev 1946/ rev Avon, Connecticut: The Heritage Press, 1974. [Page numbers taken from 1935 edition.] 'Words of the Host to the Physician and Pardoner'(p 251-2), *PardP* (pp 252-56), *PardT* (pp 256-68). Full page, color illustration of the Pardoner appears between 264 and 265; two-page color illustration of the pilgrims arriving at the Tabard Inn appears following title page.

53 *The Prologue to the Canterbury Tales, the Prioress's Tale, the Nun's Priest's Tale, the Pardoner's Tale*. Ed. George H. Cowling. New York: Ginn, 1934. Pp ix-xxv rpt in *Rare Early Essays on Geoffrey Chaucer*, ed. Carmen Joseph Dello Buono (Darby, Pennsylvania: Norwood Editions, 1981), 202-19.

The text of this school edition has been normalized to some extent and is supported by an introduction, explanatory notes at the foot of the page and a glossary. For *PardP* see **580**.

54 *Geoffrey Chaucer. Canterbury Tales*. Rendered into Modern English by J.U. Nicolson. With Illustrations by Rockwell Kent and an Introduction by Gordon Hall Gerould. New York: Covici Friede Inc., 1934.

A modernization in rhymed couplets. Includes 'The Words of the Host to the Physician and the Pardoner' (pp 291-2); *PardP* (pp 293-6); *PardT* (pp 297-310); full length portrait (bound between pp 302-3).

55 *Chaucer: The Pardoner's Tale*. Ed. Carleton [Fairchild] Brown. London: The Clarendon Press, 1935, rpt 8 times through 1958, 1979.

This frequently reprinted edition for schools and colleges presents an introductory essay, a brief selected bibliography, notes on the text, notes on Chaucer's English and metre, and a glossary. The text which follows Skeat (7) (with few corrections) includes the Pardoner's portrait (lines 669-714), the *Wordes of the Host to the Physician and the Pardoner* (pp 3-4), *PardP* (pp 5-9) and *PardT* (pp 10-24). An illustration of the opening of *PardP* (Ellesmere ms) is printed facing the *GP* selection(pp 1-2); the Ellesmere pilgrim portrait heads *PardP* (p 5). For Pardoner, see **298**; for *PardP*, see **581**; for *PardT*, see **707**.

- Review by Dorothy Everett, *MÆ* 6(1937), 144-51: Brown 'sets forth a new theory of the evolution' of *PardT* that underscores the differences between the parts of *PardP* and *PardT*.
- Review by H.S.V. Jones, *JEGP* 36(1937), 209-10: Jones questions Brown's conjecture that the Pardoner's sermon was originally intended for the Parson. He argues that context makes it impossible to gloss *cheste* (line 405) as coffin and suggests *pryme* (line 334) means *pryme large* i.e., 9 AM rather than 6 AM.
- Review by Robert K. Root, *Speculum* 11(1936), 523-4: The Introduction of twenty-nine pages contains much sound scholarship and some scholarship which, though erudite, is highly speculative (p 523). Root questions Brown's identification of the Old Man as the Wandering Jew as well as his theory that *PardT* was originally a homily on the sins of the tavern intended as a tale for the Parson. 'I can see no sufficient reason for dismembering what all the manuscripts present as the Pardoner's '''moral tale''' on his unvaried theme of ''avaryce and of swich cursednesse'''(p 524).
- Review by M.B. Rudd, *MLN* 52(1937), 379-81: Brown's theory that the Pardoner's Homily on the Sins was originally intended for the Parson seems 'too clever by half' since Chaucer himself includes the sins of the tavern under Avarice in *ParsT* (p 380).

56 *The Prologue and Four Canterbury Tales [by] Geoffrey Chaucer*. Ed. Gordon Hall Gerould. New York: Ronald Press, 1935.
Referring the reader to Skeat (7) as a basis for his text and Robinson (**51**) for notes, Gerould prints *PardT* with *GP*, *NPT*, *FranT*, *SNT* and eight Middle English lyrics in an edition intended for the general reader. Ends *PardT* at line 945.

57 *The Canterbury Tales by Geoffrey Chaucer*. Ed. Edwin Johnston Howard and Gordon Donley Wilson. Ann Arbor, Michigan: Edwards Brothers [reproduced from typescript], 1937. Rev as *The Canterbury Tales by Geoffrey Chaucer*. Selected and Ed. Edwin Johnston Howard and Gordon Donley Wilson. Oxford, Ohio: Anchor Press, 1942. Rpt New York: Prentice-Hall, 1947.

The source of the text is not indicated. Text includes *GP*, *KnT*, prologues of the Miller, Reeve, Cook, Shipman and Prioress, *PrT*, *Thop*, prologues of *Mel*, Monk and Nun's Priest, *NPT*, *WBP*, *WBT*, prologues of the Friar, Clerk, Merchant, and Franklin, *ClT*, and *FranT*. For the Pardoner, the text includes *GP* portrait (pp 53-4), *Interr* (p 194), *Phy-PardL* (pp 170-1), *PardP* (pp 171-5) and *PardT* (pp 175-89). The text is supported by an introduction, explanatory notes and a 47-page, double-column glossary.

58 *The Text of the Canterbury Tales, Studied on the Basis of All Known Manuscripts*. Ed. John M. Manly and Edith Rickert, with the aid of Mabel Dean, Helen McIntosh and Others. With a Chapter on Illuminations by Margaret Rickert. 8 vols. Chicago: University of Chicago Press; London: Cambridge University Press, 1940.

A study based on the collection at the University of Chicago of photostatic copies of all known mss. This work provides the first critical edition based on all known manuscripts for all tales with the exception of *PardP* and *PardT* which had been provided earlier by Koch (**16**). An introductory essay explains the intention to address the need 'for a text of the Canterbury Tales based throughout upon the evidence afforded by all the extant mss and such early editions as represented mss no longer in existence' (p 1). Provides detailed studies of the physical features, dates, dialects, spellings and provenance of the mss; establishes Hengwrt as 'a ms of the highest importance' (p 276); qualifies authority of Ellesmere. For classification of mss, see volume II *GP* (pp 78-96), 'The Pardoner's Prologue, Tale and Epilogue'(pp 329-39), and 'The Pardoner-Shipman Spurious Links' (p 340). For text and critical notes relevant to the Pardoner, see volume III: *Text and Critical Notes: Part I*: *GP* (text: pp 29-31; notes: p 425) and *Interr* (text: pp 242-3) as well as volume IV: *Text and Critical Notes: Part II*: *Phys-PardL* (text: pp 77-81; notes pp 490-2), *PardP* (text: pp 84-89; notes: 492-3), *PardT* (text: 89-106; notes: 493-5), and spurious Shipman-Pardoner Link (notes: 495-6). The full Corpus of Variants records all readings that differ from the editors' text (Vols V-VIII; volume 7 includes: *Phys-PardL* (pp 33-9), 'The Pardoner's Prologue, Tale, and Epilogue' (pp 40-107). See **51**, **68, 89, 92, 95**. For critical notes on the Pardoner, see **302**; for *Phy-PardL*, see **536**; for *PardP*, see **584**; for *PardT*, see **715**.

- George Kane, 'John M.Manly and Edith Rickert,' *Editing Chaucer* (**167**) pp 207-29. Given the inadvisability of the procedures for classification 'it will be judicious to abstain from using the propositions of this edition as bases for further argument ...' (p 229).

59 *De Tre Drikkebrødre*. Førord af Paul V. Rubow. København: Carit Andersens Forlag, 1946.

An illustrated, Danish prose version of *PardT* designed for young readers.

60 *The Canterbury Tales of Geoffrey Chaucer*. Ed. R.M. Lumiansky. Illustrated by H. Lawrence Hoffman. New York: Simon & Schuster, 1948. Numerous rpts through 1972. Paperback edition, New York: Washington Square Press, 1971.

A modern prose translation following Bradshaw order with a Preface by Mark Van Doren and illustrations by Lawrence Hoffman. Includes *GP*, Words of the Host, *PardP* (with some omissions) and *PardT* as well as a color illustration of the three rioters, 'Then we shall slay this false traitor Death' (p 236).

61 *Canterbury Tales by Geoffrey Chaucer*. Ed. Robert D. French. New York: Appleton-Century-Crofts, 1948. Rpt 1964. Crofts Classics Series. Based on Robinson (**71**), the text includes *GP*, *WBP* and *WBT*, *FrT*, *Phy-PardL* (pp 67-8), *PardP* (pp 68-71), *PardT* (pp 71-84), *PrT*, *Thop*, and *NPT*. The text is accompanied by brief introduction and glossary.

62 *Chaucer's Canterbury Tales (Selected): An Interlinear Translation*. Ed. Vincent F. Hopper. Great Neck, New York: Barron's Educational Series, 1948. Rpt frequently through 1962.

Includes introductory essay, *GP*, most links, twelve tales and *Ret*. For Pardoner, includes *GP* portrait (pp 71-2), *Interr* (pp 211-2), *Phys-PardL* (pp 316-7), *PardP* (pp 317-21), and *PardT* (pp 321-35). The basis of the text is not stated; selections for the Pardoner are not condensed.

63 Colson, J.G. *Search for Death*. A Play for Juniors. Freely adapted from Chaucer's "Pardoner's Tale." London: W.Paxton, 1948. [Not seen.]

64 *Canterbury Tales. A Selective Version by Frederic Whitmore*. New York: Vantage Press, 1949.

This modernization includes *GP*, *KnT*, *NPT*, 'Pardon Vendor's Tale' (p 83), and *FrT*, a selection intended to show Chaucer's mature work. Text is printed without notes, introduction, or glossary.

65 Morrison, Theodore. Ed. and trans., *The Portable Chaucer*. New York:

Viking, 1949; rev 1975. Rpt Harmondsworth: Penguin, 1977 through 1987.

For *CT*, this modernization includes an introductory essay, *GP*, most links, twelve tales, *Ret* and selected bibliography. For Pardoner, the text includes *GP* portrait (pp 71-2), *Phy-PardL* (pp 316-7), *PardP* (pp 317-21), *PardT* (pp 321-35) and *Interr* (pp 211-2). Selections for the Pardoner are not condensed.

66   *The Canterbury Tales*. Trans. Nevill Coghill. London: Penguin, 1951/ rev 1958, 1960, 1977. Rev illustrated selection, woodcuts by Edna Whyte. 2 vols. London: Folio Society, 1956. 2nd ed; 1 vol; 1974. [Page numbers taken from 1960/1977 editions.]

This widely read, verse translation, in rhymed iambic pentameter, adopts the Bradshaw order and is complete except for synopsized versions of *Mel* and *ParsT*. For the Pardoner, the text includes *GP* portrait (pp 37-8/42-3), *Phy-PardL* (pp 257-8/not included in 1977), *PardP* (pp 259-62/ 197-200), *PardT* (pp 262-76/201-14), and *Interr* (pp 279/220-1). Coghill follows Skeat (**7**) and Robinson (**71**). In the illustrated edition, *GP* portrait is accompanied by pictures of clerics, *PardT* by pictures of artifacts, daily life and a stained glass window portraying a peddlar: a commentary with color prints on 'Religion' is also included (pp 168-9). Coghill's translation provides the text for Gila Falkus' sumptuously illustrated *The Canterbury Tales,* Scarborough, Ontario: Prentice-Hall, Canada, Inc. 1986, with Forward by Melvyn Bragg and Introduction John Wain, and picture research by Philippa Lewis. The color illustrations for *PardP* and *PardT* (pp 151-59) include a full page reproduction from the Holkham Bible of the drunken Herod executing John the Baptist; a preacher before a congregation of common folk, BL ms Douce 300 f. 7; the punishment of avaricious in Hell, Bodleian ms Douce 134 f 85; a woodblock from the Master of the Banderloes on lechery; the punishment of lechers, BL ms Douce 134 f 86; a table scene of gluttonous revellers, BL Add. 27695, f. 14; a book of hours illustration showing death on a rampage, London, ca. 1994; and a fine reproduction of a misericord of the three rioters killing each other, from the London museum. See **96**.

67   Davies, W.J., and Myfanwy G. Davies. *The Pardoner's Tale Rendered into Modern English Prose*. London: James Brodie, 1951; Bath: James Brodie, 1976. [Not seen.]

68   *A Chaucer Reader. Selections from The Canterbury Tales*. Ed. Charles W. Dunn. New York: Harcourt, Brace and Company, 1952.

Selections based on Manly-Rickert (**58**) include text of *GP*, *PrT*, *Thop*, *MkT* (selections), *NPT*, *WBP*, *WBT*, *FranT*, *PardP*, *PardT*, and three tales in prose translation: *RvT*, *ClT*, *CYT*. For the Pardoner, the following are included: *GP* portrait (pp 27-8), *Interr* (pp 91-2), *Phy-PardL* translated (pp 152-3), *PardP* (pp 154-7) and *PardT* (pp 158-72). The text is supported by an introduction, glosses in right margin, brief notes preceding each selection, a selected bibliography, and a note on language. For *PardT*, see **734**.

69 *The Canterbury Tales (Selections), Together with Selections from the Shorter Poems by Geoffrey Chaucer*. Ed. Robert Archibald Jelliffe. New York: Scribner's, 1952. The Modern Student's Library.

This text, which aims at a representative selection, includes *GP*, *KnT*, *PrT*, *NPT*, 'The Wordes of the Host to the Pardoner' (lines 318-28), *PardP* (pp 174-7), *PardT* (pp178-92), *Interr* (pp 196-7), *WBT*, *ClT*, *FranT*, and several links. The text is based on Ellesmere with some modifications and is accompanied by a 62-page, double column glossary but no notes. In *PardT*, lines 949-56 are deleted.

70 *Chaucer: the Pardoner's Tale*. Ed. F.W. Robinson. London: James Brodie Ltd., 1953. [Brodie's Notes on Chaucer's The Pardoner's Tale]. Rev London: Pan Books, 1979.

This bowdlerized school text includes *GP* portrait (pp 1-2), *Phy-PardL* (pp 2-3), *PardP* (pp 3-6), and *PardT* (pp 7-19). Text indicates deletions for *PardP* lines 370-3, and *PardT* lines 485-7, 950-5. Supporting materials include introduction, notes, glossary and study questions.

71 *The Works of Geoffrey Chaucer*. Ed. F.N. Robinson. Boston: Houghton-Mifflin, 1957. Rpt in paperback, London: Oxford University Press, 1974.

A revision of **51** with the benefit of the Manly-Rickert edition (**58**); enormously influential. Text includes *GP* portrait (pp 23-4), *Phy-PardL* (pp 148), *PardP* (pp 148-9), *PardT* (pp 150-5) and *Interr* (pp 77-8). Two *PardT* altered readings are recorded for *PardT*; textual notes in the second edition, record two readings altered, in response to Manly-Rickert (**58**) from the 1933 edition of *PardT*. The text is accompanied by a general introduction, headnotes to separate works, explanatory notes (expanded in the second edition) at the back of the text, a glossarial index and bibliographical references (updated from first edition). See **51, 117**. See also **757, 780, 860**.

• Review by R.W. Zandvoort, *ES* 43(1962), 110-115: Zandvoort notes that the 'weak spot' of linguistic apparatus is not remediated in the second edition: notable ommissions from the glossary include: *Desolaat* (598), *Suffisaunt* (932), *thider* (749), *Doom* (637), and *Shapen* (874).

72 *Canterbury Tales*. Ed. A.C. Cawley. Everyman's Library. London: Dent; New York: Dutton, 1958/rev 1975, 1990.

This widely used edition of the complete *CT* is based on Robinson (**71**) and includes *GP* portrait (pp 20-2), *Interr* (pp 162-3), *Phy-PardL* (pp 343-4), *PardP* (pp 344-8), and *PardT* (pp 348-60). The text is supported by an introduction, glosses printed in the right margin, explanatory notes, translations of difficult lines printed at the foot of the page, and a selected bibliography. For *PardT*, see **757**. For the earlier Everyman's Library edition, see **27**.

- Review by R.W. Zandvoort. *ES* 43(1962), 110-115: Zandvoort calls for additional glosses in a second edition, e.g., *in game* (829).

73 *Chaucer's Poetry: An Anthology for the Modern Reader*. Ed. E. Talbot Donaldson. New York: Ronald Press, 1958. 2nd ed. 1975. [Page numbers from 1975 edition.]

Text follows Hg but presents the tales in El order. Second edition includes all *CT* written in verse. Both editions include *GP* portrait (text: pp 28-9; notes pp 1059-61), *Interr* (text: 'An Interlude' pp 196-7), *Phy-PardL* (text: 'The Introduction' pp 405-7), *PardP* (text: pp 407-11; commentary: 1091-3), and *PardT* (text: pp 411-26; commentary: 1093-4); prints lines 919ff separately as subsection 'The Epilogue' (pp 426-7). The spelling system is revised to 'offer the greatest readability that is possible without sacrificing either the phonological values or the general appearance of Middle English orthography' (p iv). Glosses and explanatory notes appear at the foot of the page; a glossary and 62-title bibliography are included; textual notes are not included. Commentary (of about 165 pages) avoids the historical approach: 'the criticism is in general based firmly on the text' (p vii). For Pardoner, see **333**; for *PardP*, see **597**; for *PardT*, see **759**.

- Review by Richard L. Hoffman, 'The Canterbury Tales,' in *Critical Approaches to Six Major English Works*. Ed. Robert M. Lumiansky and Herschel Baker. Philadelphia: University of Pennsylvania Press, 1968; London: Oxford University Press, 1969. Pp 41-80.

74 *The Pardoner's Tale*. Ed. Nevill Coghill and Christopher Tolkien.

[Harrap's English Classics]. London: G.G. Harrap, 1958 rpt many times through 1978.

This text follows Ellesmere with changes (based on another manuscript) noted at the foot of the page; one exception occurs in line 207 where Coghill deletes 'a' on metrical grounds. Includes *GP* portrait (pp 61-2), *Phys-PardL* (pp 63-4), *PardP* (pp 64-9); and *PardT* (pp 69-86). The text is accompanied by textual notes, explanatory notes, and extensive glossary. Detail from Blake's 'The Canterbury Pilgrims' shows the Pardoner with the Summoner, Manciple, Monk, Friar, Tapicer and Prioress.

- Review by R.W. Zandvoort, *ES* 43(1962), 110-5: 'Especially, the writer of the Introduction likes to adapt his style to the raciness of the modern idiom. ... If this is the new 'Oxford accent,' all one can do is pass by and gratefully accept the many virtues of these editions' (p 114). Zandvoort judges 'absurd' the lack of attention to the sound of Chaucer's verse.

75 *The Canterbury Pilgrims and Three Canterbury Tales*. Trans. James J. Donohue. Dubuque, Iowa: The Loras College Press, 1958.
This modernization which includes *GP*, *PardT*, *NPT*, and *SNT* represents a combination of two earlier editions. [Not seen.]

76 *The Works of Geoffrey Chaucer. A Facsimile of the William Morris Kelmscott Chaucer, with the Original 87 Illustrations by Edward Burne-Jones*. Introduction by John T. Winterich. Cleveland and New York: World Publishing Company, 1958.
Introductory notes detail the development of the Kelmscott Chaucer, Morris' extensive role, and the importance of the Kelmscott Press Includes triple-column, eight page glossary; prints *Phy-PardL* (pp 98-9), *PardP* (pp 99-100) and *PardT* with elaborate border on opening page (pp 100-4). See **9, 99, 101**.

77 *Selections from Chaucer: the Prologue, The Nun's Priest's Tale, The Pardoner's Tale, The Squire's Tale*. Ed. Marjorie M. Barber. London: Macmillan, 1961; New York: St. Martin's Press, 1962. The Scholar's Library. General Editor, Guy Boas. [Not seen.]
A school edition based on Pollard (**11**) with introductory notes and glosses on facing pages.

78 *The Canterbury Tales of Geoffrey Chaucer: A Selection*. Ed. Daniel Cook. Garden City, New York: Anchor (Doubleday), 1961.
Includes *GP*, *MlT*, *WBT*, *PardT*, *PrT*, and *NPT*. The text, based on the

Ellesmere and Hengwrt mss, is printed on left-hand pages with annotations on right facing page. An introduction is included.

79 *Geoffrey Chaucer: The Canterbury Tales*. Ed. Mario Praz. 2nd ed. Bari: Adriatica, 1961. Biblioteca italiana di testi inglesi, 1. General Editors, Gabriele Baldini, Agnostino Lombardo, and Giorgio Melchiori.

A school edition with extensive introduction, notes and text based on Robinson (**51**). [Not seen.]

80 *Geoffrey Chaucer. Ausgewählte Cantebury Erzählungen Englisch und Deutsch*. Ed. Martin Lehnert. Halle: VEB Verlag Sprache und Literatur, 1962.

A German translation based on Koch **16** and Hertzberg Von Düring (1886) with English text based on Robinson **71**. Includes *GP* (selections), *MilT, RvT, CkT, WBT, FrT, SumT, PardT* and *ShT* (p xv). The text is supported by notes. [Not seen.]

• Review by Siegfried Wenzel, *JEGP* 62(1963), 680-3: Wenzel questions Lehnert's 'realist' and 'humanist' bias in his choice of selections and questions Lehnert's presumption that tales such as *PardT* are the 'juciest,' best express Chaucer's time and most appeal to our own. He comments on the translation: 'To translate the Pardoner's much debated words, *And Jhesu Crist ... So graunte yow his pardon to receyve* with "Und lasse eure Buße sich genügen" (l 5055) rather misses the meaning' (p 682).

81 *Chaucer's Major Poetry*. Ed. Albert C. Baugh. New York: Appleton-Century Crofts; London: Routledge & Kegan Paul, 1963.

This student text, based apparently on Ellesmere, places extensive annotations at the bottom of the page. Presents the Pardoner portrait (pp 253-4), *Phy-PardL* (pp 489-90), *PardP* (pp 490-2) and *PardT* (pp 493-500). Includes introductory essay, brief bibliography and extensive glossary. Baugh comments that there is no reason to doubt that *PardP* and *PardT* were written about the same time.

82 *Chaucer*. Ed. Louis O. Coxe. New York: Dell, 1963. The Laurel Poetry Series. General Editor, Richard Wilbur.

CT selections include *GP, KnT, MilT, WBP, MerT, FranT, PardP* (pp 200-3), *PardT* (pp 203-16), *NPT*, and *PrT*. The text is based on Skeat (**7**) and Robinson (**71**); very brief introduction, notes and glossary included. For *PardT*, see **780**.

83 *A Taste of Chaucer: Selections from 'The Canterbury Tales'*. Ed. Anne Malcolmson. Illustrations by Enrico Arno. New York: Harcourt,

Brace & World, Inc.; London: Constable Young Books, 1964.
Presents a verse modernization of *PardT* for young readers, 'Three Men in Search of Death.' Illustration shows two rioters drinking in joy over the death of their slain brother.

84 *The Canterbury Tales by Geoffrey Chaucer*. Ed. A. Kent Hieatt and Constance Hieatt. New York: Bantam Books, 1964. Rpt through 1982. [Bantam Dual-Language Series].

A selection based on Skeat (**7**) with facing-page translations, this text includes *GP*, *KnT*, *MilT*, *WBP*, *WBT*, *MerT*, *FranT*, 'Words of the Host to the Pardoner' (lines 318-28: pp 338-9), *PardP* (pp 338-44), *PardT* (pp 344-69), *PrT*, and *NPT*. The text is based on Skeat 'because his spelling is phonetically most consistent' (p vi); some variants are silently supplied from Robinson (**71**) and Donaldson (**73**). An introduction and brief glossary (at the end of the book) is included.

85 Wright, David, ed. *Geoffrey Chaucer: The Canterbury Tales*. London: Barrie and Rockliff, 1964; New York: Random House, 1965.

A prose modernization based on Robinson (**71**) and printed in Chaucer Society order. [Not seen.]

86 *The Pardoner's Prologue and Tale from the Canterbury Tales*. Ed. A.C. Spearing. Cambridge: Cambridge University Press, 1965. Rpt 1979, 1994.

This student text, indebted to Robinson (**71**) and Coghill and Tolkien (**74**), is supported by an introductory essay, explanatory notes and 10-page, double-column glossary. Included are *GP* portrait (pp 92-3), *Phy-PardL* (pp 53-4), *PardP* (pp 55-9), and *PardT* (pp 61-76); frontispiece presents 'The Gambler' from Holbein's *Dance of Death*. For Pardoner, see **366**; for *PardP*, see **603**; for *PardT*, see **801**.

- Review by Helmut Bonheim, *Ang* 85(1967), 212-3: Bonheim praises Spearing's 'reliable text,' 'clear and factual style,' and treatment of the *mors mortis* theme, but cautions against 'the rather unwarranted psychological conclusions' that he draws from the serving boy's remark (212-3).
- Review by P.M. Vermeer, *LT* (April, 1966), 278-81: 'Mr. Spearing is a most discerning critic in his discussion of "Blasphemy in the Tale"... of course the revellers are blasphemers ... but there is blasphemy in a deeper sense as well, for their intention to kill Death may be seen as a "profane parody of God's purpose in the Crucifixion." The Pardoner's way of life is a blasphemous parody

of what it ought to be: he is the embodiment of blasphemy' (279).

87 *The Pardoner's Tale [presented in the Middle English version].* With woodcuts by Bronislaw M. Bak. Chicago: Studio Press, 1966.

This limited edition of 285 copies presents *PardT* in Middle English (edition not specified) together with a series of more than eighty woodcuts originally made for an educational television film. Bronislaw and Hedi Bak note that the woodcuts are intended 'as a translation of Chaucer's tale into visual narrative' (Foreword). *PardT* was chosen 'for its timeless manifestations of human foibles and weaknesses'; of greatest interest was the 'introduction' wherein Chaucer satirized society and the Pardoner (Foreword).

88 King, Ronald. *Geoffrey Chaucer: The Prologue to The Canterbury Tales with original screen images designed by Ronald King.* Editions Alecto, 1966. Rpt Surrey: Circle Press, 1967; 2nd ed. 1978 [Page numbers from 1978.]

An original illustration, a 'mask' of the Pardoner is presented as one of fourteen accompanying a Middle English text (origin not noted though appears to follow Robinson) of *GP.* The illustration is a blending of symbolism and medieval heraldry, inspired in part by the traditions of the African mask. The mask sets out 'to maintain the balance between the real and the transcendent' (p xi). The Pardoner's 'mask' is silver, black, white and purple. A geometric design (suggestive of a game board) of predominantly black, white and silver (with three segments of purple) fills a shape approximately circular; that shape sits at the junction of a cross, two lines black, two lines purple. The circle and cross sit against a silver background.

89 *Selections from the Tales of Canterbury and Short Poems.* Ed. Robert A. Pratt. Boston: Houghton Mifflin, 1966. Riverside Editions. General Editor, Gordon N. Ray.

This Riverside student edition includes 18 tales—*KnT, MilT, RvT, CkT, MLT, ShT, PrT, Thop, NPT, WBT, FrT, SumT, ClT, MerT, SqT, FranT, PardT, ManT*—two links, several prologues and *Ret.* For the Pardoner, text includes *GP* portrait (pp 21-2), *Interr* (pp 194-5), *Phy-PardL* (pp 350-1), *PardP* (pp 351-5), and *PardT* (pp 355-67). Pratt bases the text on Robinson (**71**) admitting readings (silently) from Manly and Rickert (**58**) 'attempting to recreate the text as Chaucer wrote it' (p xxxviii). The text follows the Bradshaw order which Pratt identifies as Chaucer's intention in 1400 (cf **7**). The text is accompanied by an introduction, marginal glosses, and explanatory notes below the text. For complete edition see **100**.

90 *Geoffrey Chaucer: The Works 1532, With Supplementary Material from the Editions of 1542, 1561, 1598 and 1602*. Facsimile edition. Ed. D.S. Brewer. Menston, Yorkshire: Scolar Press, 1969. Rpt (with slight editorial changes) Ilkley, Yorkshire, and London: Scolar Press, 1974, 1976.

This edition offers a conspectus of Chaucer's works as they appeared in the sixteenth and seventeenth centuries. Prints introduction, materials from 1532 edition including *GP* portrait (fol 2), *Interr* (fol xl-xli), *Phy-PardL* (fol lxxv-lxxvi), *PardP* (fol lxxxvi) followed by the Thynne illustration of the Pardoner, and *PardT* (fol lxxvii-lxxix). From the 1561 edition, prints *GP* portrait headed by an illustration. Woodcuts said to be printed from blocks issued by Pynson are interspersed throughout. See **25**.

91 *Chaucer: General Prologue[to] The Canterbury Tales*. Ed. Phyllis Hodgson. London: Athlone Press, 1969.

A school edition based on Ellesmere. Text is supported by introduction and explanatory notes. For Pardoner, see **384**.

92 *The Canterbury Tales: A Selection*. Ed. Donald R. Howard, with the assistance of James Dean. New York: New American Library (Signet Classics), 1969; London: New English Library Limited, 1969. Signet Classic Poetry Series. General Editor, John Hollander.

Includes *GP*, *KnT*, *MilP* and *MilT*, *RvP* and *RvT*, *ShT*, *PrP* and *PrT*, *Thop*, *MkP*, *NPP* and *NPT*, *WBT*, *CLP* and epilogue, *MerP* and *MerT*, *FranP* and *FranT*, *PardP* and *PardT*, *ParP*, and *Ret*. The text is indebted to Manly-Rickert (**58**). Spelling has been normalized and modernized. The text is supported by an introduction, a discussion of pronunciation (with discography), explanatory notes and glosses at the foot of the page, a selected bibliography and a glossary of basic words.

93 *Chaucer: The Prologue and Three Tales*. Ed. with notes and commentary by Francis King and Bruce Steele. Melbourne: F.W. Cheshire Pub. Co., 1969.

Prints *PardP*, *PardT*, *PrT*, and *NPT*. Text is based on Manly-Rickert (**58**) supported by reference to Skeat, Robinson, Baugh, Donaldson and the *Six-Text* (**1**). Inclines to underpunctuation to avoid limiting interpretation. Chaucer is praised for 'fusion of convention and observation' (p 165). Right facing page carries running notes and glosses. Text includes *GP* Pardoner portrait headed by the Ellesmere pilgrim portrait (pp 48-52); 'Prologe of the Pardoners Tale' (pp 62-8); 'Pardoneres Tale' (pp 68-92). See **7, 51, 73, 81**.

94 King, Francis, and Bruce Steele. *Selections from Geoffrey Chaucer's The Canterbury Tales*. Melbourne: F.W. Cheshire, 1969.

Text of *Phy-PardL*, pp 102-3; *PardP*, pp 104-10; *PardT*, pp 110-34; textual notes on *PardT*, pp 314-5; commentary, pp 367-73; 'Concerning Pardoners' (Appendix B) pp 393-5; 'False-Seeming' (Appendix D) pp 395-7. For Pardoner, see **386**; for *PardT*, see **845**.

95 *Geoffrey Chaucer: The Canterbury Tales*. Ed. John Halverson. Indianapolis and New York: Bobbs-Merrill, 1971. The Library of Literature. General Editors, John Henry Raleigh and Ian Watt.

This student edition, based on Robinson (**51, 71**), includes *GP*, 12 tales and associated prologues, 12 tale summaries with excerpts and *Ret*. Included for the Pardoner are *GP* portrait (pp 26-7), *Phys-PardL* ('Wordes of the Host to the Pardoner' pp 334-5), *PardP* (pp 336-40), *PardT* (pp 340-55), and *Interr* (pp 154-5). The text is based on Robinson (**51, 71**), compared line by line with the text and variants of Manly-Rickert (**58**). 'The result is a trifle closer to Ellesmere than either' (p xxi). The text is accompanied by an introduction, brief explanatory notes, selective bibliographic notes, glosses at the foot of the page, and a 44 page, double column glossary.

96 *A Choice of Chaucer's Verse*. Selected with an introduction by Nevill Coghill. London: Faber & Faber, 1972.

Presents text based on Skeat (**7**) with facing modern English paraphrases in verse. Selections include *GP* portrait (pp 158-61), *PardT* lines 333-640 (pp 102-14).

97 *Geoffrey Chaucer: The Canterbury Tales*. [no editor specified]. Introduction note by J.A.W. Bennett. Cambridge: Cornmarket Reprints in association with Magdalene College, 1972.

This facsimile reproduces Pepy's copy of Caxton's second edition (1484) of *CT*. Woodcuts of the pilgrims interspersed through *GP*; the woodcut of the Pardoner appears again at the head of the tale. Text includes 'the Wordes of the Hooste,' *PardP* and *PardT*.

98 *Kenterberiiskie rasskazy*. Trans. I. Kashkin and O. Rumer. Moscow: Khudozh, Biblioteka vsemirnoi literatury. Seriia pervaia, Literatura drevnege vostoka, antichnogo mira, srednikh vekov, vozrozhdeniia, XVII; XVIII vekov. Hudorjestvennaya Litteratura, 1973.

A Russian translation of *CT*. *PardT* includes an egraving showing one reveller dead, a second passed out, flask in hand and a third drinking.

99 *Ornamentation and Illustrations from The Kelmscott Chaucer.* [Printed by William Morris]. Introduction by Fridolf Johnson. New York: Dover, 1973; Toronto: General Publishing Company, 1973; London: Constable, 1973.

Reproduces one hundred pages at seventy per cent size from the Kelmscott Chaucer (**9** and **76**) 'one of the supreme achievements in the history of bookmaking' (p vi). No pages relate to the Pardoner.

100 *The Tales of Canterbury, Complete [by] Geoffrey Chaucer.* Ed. Robert A. Pratt. Boston: Houghton Mifflin, 1974. Rpt New York: Holmes & Meier, 1976.

This expanded version of **89** clarifies that the text is based on Robinson (**71**) with frequent readings admitted from Manly-Rickert (**58**). The aim has been to represent Manly's '"latest common original of all extant manuscripts" (O'), with the correction of all recognizable errors in the transmission to O' of Chaucer's own text (O)' (p 561). Variant readings are listed for *PardP* (4 variants) and *PardT* (14 variants) (p 574). In accordance with Ellesmere tale order, Fragment C follows Fragment F: *PardP* (pp 421-4); *PardT* (pp 424-37). Scenes from *PardT* depicted on a chest front are reprinted from the exhibition catalog for 'Chaucer's London' (p 434). The edition is supported by marginal glosses, introductory essay, and brief glossary. The evolution of Pratt's thinking on the order of *CT* is evident: once having found that the order of no manuscript represented Chaucer's intention at the time of his death, Pratt here notes: 'whatever Chaucer might have planned and done had he lived longer, he seems by 1400 to have conceived and developed a definite arrangement for the groups of tales so far written,' and that is 'the order used for the present text' (p xxxvii).

• Review by Derek Brewer, *YES* 7(1977), 205-8: 'It [The book] has many virtues, but they do not give it preference over works already in the Field' (p 207).

101 *The Kelmscott Chaucer*, a facsimile edition, with *A Companion Volume to the Kelmscott Chaucer* by Duncan Robinson. London: Basilisk Press, 1975.

This facsimile edition reproduces *The Kelmscott Chaucer* with a forward on William Morris, Morris and Chaucer, and the production of the text. F.S. Ellis' edition, based on Skeat (**7**) includes additional corrections approved by Skeat. Text includes 'Wordes of the hoost to the Phisicien and the Pardoner' (pp 98-9); *PardP* (pp 99-100); *PardT* (pp 100-4); *Interr* (p 106). This elaborate edition with ornamented letters and bordered pages includes no introduction, notes or glossary. The companion volume reproduces 85 woodcuts, none related to *PardT*. See **9, 76, 99**.

102 *The Friar's, Summoner's and Pardoner's Tales from The Canterbury Tales*. [London Medieval & Renaissance Series]. Ed. and Introduction by N.R. Havely. London: University of London Press, 1975; New York: Holmes & Meier, 1976 [page numbers from 1976 edition].

Introduction, pp 25-44; text, pp 96-124; commentary, pp 149-161; textual notes, pp 163. The text is based on the Ellesmere ms as printed by the Chaucer Society with reference to other mss printed in their 6-text volume and to the readings and variants in Manly-Rickert (**58**) as well as Skeat (**7**) and Robinson (**71**). Spelling has been normalized and simplified; punctuation is editorial. Introductory materials suggest similarities among Friar, Summoner and Pardoner—e.g., parasites upon the Church, at home in taverns and at the bottom of the moral order among the pilgrims. Specific treatments of the Pardoner (pp 25-8), *PardP* (pp 28-30), *PardT* (pp 30-6) and opinions for discussion (pp 43-44) are included. For Pardoner, see **423**; for *PardP*, see **625**; for *PardT*, see **911**.

• Review by Dorothy Colmer, *YES* 7(1977), 208-9: Havely conforms to editorial policies by which he is 'not uniformly well served' (e.g. providing lexical and explanatory notes on the same page as text). The disadvantage of incomplete glossing is evident (e.g. the dual meaning of *haunt* is obscured). Havely 'carries his learning lightly': a reader of his introductory material 'will proceed to the texts well prepared to enjoy them and to take an informed part in critical discussion' (p 209).

• Review *Choice* 13 (1976), 977-8: Discusses the need for this edition as well as the grouping of the Pardoner, a singularly corrupt character, with the other parasites upon the church. The 'Opinions for discussion' is 'quite useful ... the textual notes and commentary ... are direct and honest' (p 978).

103 *The Complete Poetry and Prose of Geoffrey Chaucer*. Ed. John H. Fisher. New York: Holt, Rinehart, and Winston, 1977/rev 1982; 2nd ed., 1989. Glossary added in 3rd printing (1979); bibliography revised in 7th printing (1982); second edition updates headnotes to 1988 and bibliography to 1987; however, reprints carry unchanged copyright date of 1977.

This edition addressed to the student is based on Ellesmere and follows the Ellesmere order; substantive variants in Hengwrt are listed in textual notes which appear with explanatory notes at the foot of the page. Text includes *GP* portrait (pp 21-2/ 21), *Interr* (p 110/110) and 'Pardoner's Tale' comprising *Phys-PardL* (pp 221-2/ 221-2), *PardP* (pp 222-4/ 222-4), *PardT* (pp 224-31/ 224-31). The Ellesmere miniature of the Pardoner appears at the head of the 'Pardoner's Tale' section. In the second edition, the headnotes are updated to reflect scholarship through 1988 and the bibliography through 1987. Includes a triple column, five-page glossary.

- Review by Ralph Hanna III, *Rev* 1 (1979), 61-71. Hanna praises the comprehensiveness of the volume but notes a confusion of intended audience. The extensive bibliography is directed more to the professional than the undergraduate yet a search for items on *PardT* indicated it was incomplete beyond the *MLA International Bibliography.*

104 *Los Cuentos de Canterbury* / Geoffrey Chaucer. Ed. Pedro Guardia Masso. Barcelona: Bosch, 1978; 2nd ed. Madrid: Cátedra, 1991.

A dual-language translation with Middle English and Spanish on facing pages. Text is supported by introduction, brief notes and bibliography.

105 *The Pardoner's Tale*. Ed. Geoffrey Chaucer. Adapted by Elaine Shelabarger. [Dramascripts]. Basingstoke: Macmillan, 1978.

This script intended for schools, amateur theatrical groups, and youth clubs sets the action in an inn on the Dover Road between London and Canterbury and includes, among its cast, Chaucer.

106 *The Canterbury Tales: Geoffrey Chaucer. A Facsimile and Transcription of the Hengwrt Manuscript, with Variants from the Ellesmere Manuscript*. Ed. Paul G. Ruggiers. Introductions by Donald C. Baker and by A.I. Doyle and M.B. Parkes. Norman, Oklahoma: University of Oklahoma Press, 1979; Folkestone, England: Dawson, 1979. Vol. 1 of *A Variorum Edition of the Works of Geoffrey Chaucer*. General Editors, Paul G. Ruggiers and Donald C. Baker.

This inaugural volume presents the Hengwrt ms, chosen on the basis of age, unedited state, and accuracy, as the foundational text for the *CT* in the new *Variorum Chaucer*. Doyle and Parkes, in an introductory essay, divide the ms into five structural sections, the fourth of which (fols 193-203) contains Group C. For the Pardoner, the edition presents *GP* portrait (volume 10r-1r; pp 34-8); the *Interr* (volume 60r; p 234); *Phy-PardL* 'The myry talkyng of the hoost to the Phisicien and the Pardoner' (volume 195r-v; pp 774-7); *PardP* (volume 195v-197r; pp 777-84); and *PardT* (volume 197v-203v; pp 784-809). Each of *Phy-PardL*, *PardP*, and *PardT* begins with a decorated letter. The variants from Ellesmere appear in the right margin; Lines C 297-8, lacking in Hengwrt, are supplied from Ellesmere. See **108**.

107 *Poetical Works: Geoffrey Chaucer. A Facsimile of Cambridge University ms Gg.4.27.* With Introductions by M.B. Parkes and Richard Beadle. 3 vols. Norman, Oklahoma: Pilgrim Books; Cambridge: D.S. Brewer, 1979.

This ms represents 'the only surviving example of a fifteenth-century attempt to collect Chaucer's major poetical works in one volume' (III: 1). Using Henry Bradshaw's reconstructed foliation, the editors describe the presentation of *GP*: beginning (volume 132) at A, 37; ending (volume 141 \v) at A, 756 (volume I); *WBP* 'beginning abruptly (volume 212) at D, 77' and ending at volume 222 [the *Interr* appears on volume 213] (volume I); *PardP* preceded by missing leaves and beginning (volume 305)[actually marked 304 and recorrected to 303] at C, 387; and *PardT* beginning at volume 305 and continuing through volume 312 (p 3). An illustration of the Pardoner survives at the beginning of *PardT* (volume 306). *PardT* is followed by an inscription 'here foloweth the shipmans tale' and a missing leaf. The editors have supplied *GP* A 757-60, 788-806 from Speght. The nine surviving illustrations are printed in color following the text (volume III). The Pardoner who 'brandishes a "relic"' (p 58) appears robed and hooded, facing right on a horse with decorated bridle and harness (volume 306); Envy, Gluttony and Lechery seated on a goat appear on fols 416, 432, and 433; these representations of the Vices 'are unique in surviving Chaucer manuscripts' (p 59).

108 *The Canterbury Tales by Geoffrey Chaucer. Edited from the Hengwrt Manuscript.* Ed. N.F. Blake. London: Edward Arnold, 1980. York Medieval Texts, Second Series. General Editors, Elizabeth Salter and Derek Pearsall.

Blake presents a conservatively edited text based on Hengwrt (including spelling and tale order) with *Phy-PardT* forming section 9 of the 12 he identifies. Noting that section 10 (*ShT, PrT, Thop, Mel, MkT, NPT*) invariably follows 9, Blake suggests they were separate sections placed in sequence by the compiler of Hengwrt. The 'endlink' of *PardT* serves as a link to *ShT*. The text includes *GP* portrait (pp 59-60), *Interr* (p 183), *Phy-PardL* (*The myry talkyng of the hoost to the phisicien and the pardoner* pp 436-7; lines C 297-8 omitted), *PardP* (pp 438-42), and *PardT* (pp 442-57). A Table of Correspondence relates Blake's sections and lineation to Robinson. Emendations are noted for *PardP* lines 326/7 and *PardT* lines 418, 909. Explanatory notes appear at the foot of the page. An appendix lists all sections found in Ellesmere and lacking in Hengwrt; no instance is listed for the Pardoner. A bibliography and 14-page, double column glossary is included. See **106**; see also **561**.

109 *The Canterbury Tales/Die Canterbury-Erzählungen: Mittelenglisch/ Deutsch.* Trans. and annotated by Heinz Bergner, Waltraud Böttcher, Günter Hagel and Hilmar Sperber. Ed. Heinz Bergner. Stuttgart: Philipp Reclam, 1982.

This dual-language, school edition, based on Robinson (**71**) includes text and commentary for *GP* (pp 44-6), *KnT*, *MilT*, *WBP*, *WBT*, *FranT*, *PardP* (pp 354-61), *PardT* (pp 362-91), *NPT*. Commentary, textual notes and selected bibliographic references for *PardP* and *PardT* appear on pp 532-44. The Middle English text is based on Robinson (**71**). The German prose translation for *PardP* and *PardT* are by W. Bötcher. The Ellesmere miniature of the Pardoner precedes *PardP*.

110 *The Canterbury Tales.* Trans. David Wright. Oxford: Oxford University Press, 1985. Rpt in World Classics Series. Oxford, 1986.[Page numbers refer to 1986 reprint.]

Arguing against the position that Chaucer's language can be read with only a little study, Wright offers his verse translation 'as an introductory prolusion to the real thing' (p xxi). Wright eschews strict adherence to Chaucer's rhyme-schemes yet aims to capture Chaucer's tone by 'contemporary alternatives as half-rhymes, quarter-rhymes, or assonance real or imaginary' (p xx). For the Pardoner, Wright includes *GP* portrait (pp 18-9), *Interr* (pp 223-4), *Phy-PardL* (pp 393-4), *PardP* (pp 394-7), *PardT* (pp 398-410). Translates lines 966-8: 'As for you, Mister Host, come, my dear chap,/ I beg you, shake hands with the pardoner'(p 410). Includes brief introduction, select bibliography and notes.

• Derek Pearsall, *SAC* 9(1987), 199-203: Translation of Chaucer is not only unnecessary but undesirable, since it does, in the end, a disservice to Chaucer's poetry (p 203). This translation is highly accurate but 'every line read in translation seals off Chaucer and his English more finally' (p 200).

111 Geoffrey Chaucer. *Die Canterbury Tales*. Übertragen und herausgegeben von Martin Lehnert. München: Winkler Verlag, 1985.
German text presents *GP* portrait (pp 46-7), *Phy-PardL* (pp 359-60), *PardP* (pp 360-6) and *PardT* (pp 364-77). The Pardoner miniature (Ellesmere) appears between pp 352-3. Includes introductory notes and bibliography.

112 *The Pardoner's Prologue and Tale*, Fragment VI, lines 329-966. Trans. Hisashi Shigeeo. *Meiji Gakuin Review* 384(1985), 1-24.
A Japanese prose translation of *PardP* and *PardT* with general note indicating details of the Pardoner's portrait, the eastern origin of the tale and an Italian analogue (1572). Robinson (**2**) serves as the base text (**71**).

113 *Geoffrey Chaucer: The Pardoner's Tale* [by] Graham Handley; advisory editor Stephen Coote. Harmondsworth, Middlesex: Penguin Passnotes Series, 1986.
Study notes include Middle English text with modern English translation.

114 *Chaucer: The Pardoner's Tale*: (a critical study incorporating Chaucer's text). Ed. C[harles]. W[illiam]. R[euben]. D[utton]. Moseley. [Penguin Masterstudies]. Ed. Stephen Coote and Bryan Loughrey. Harmondsworth, Middlesex: Penguin Books, 1987.
A study guide with text and commentary for *GP* portrait, *Phy-PardL*, *PardP*, and *PardT*. The text is based on Manly-Rickert (**58**) with punctuation added and regularization of spelling; text and notes are printed on facing pages. The text is supported by extensive introductory notes (e.g., the relationship to the audience; Pardoners, Confession and Penance; the closure of *PardP* and *PardT*), a brief glossary, a glossary of rhetorical terms, a brief bibliography and 7 appendices (e.g., relics, the Pardoner's *gaude*, the seven deadly sins).

115 *The Pardoner's Tale by Geoffrey Chaucer*. Ed. Geoffrey Lester. Basingstoke: Macmillan Education, Macmillan Master Guide, 1987.
Notes discuss Chaucer's life and works, medieval background, Chaucer's language, a brief review of critical reception and *GP* portrait, *Interr*, *Phy-PardL*, *PardP*, and *PardT*.

116 *The Physician's Tale*. Ed. Helen Storm Corsa. Norman, Oklahoma:

University of Oklahoma Press, 1987. *A Variorum Edition of the Works of Geoffrey Chaucer*. Vol. 2, Part 17. General Editors, Paul G. Ruggiers, Donald C. Baker, and Daniel J. Ransom.

In addition to the only separate edition of *PhyT*, critical and textual commentary, bibliographical and general indexes, the Variorum presents textual commentary on *Phy-PardL* (pp 45-53) and the order of *CT* (pp 53-61). Critical commentary discusses the relation of *PhyT* to *PardT* (pp 21-4). For *Phy-PardL*, see **562**.

117 *The Riverside Chaucer*. 3rd ed. Ed. F.N. Robinson, General Ed. Larry D. Benson. Boston: Houghton Mifflin, 1987.

This standard complete edition, compiled by 33 Chaucerians and directed to a first reading of Chaucer, updates, expands and revises Robinson (**71**). For the Pardoner, includes *GP* portrait (p 34), *Interr* (p 107), *Phy-PardL* (pp 193-4), *PardP* (pp 194-6), and *PardT* (pp 196-202). The text is supported by a comprehensive (33-page) general introduction, brief introductory notes specific to each section, glosses at the foot of the page, extensive explanatory and selective textual notes, a selective bibliography of primary and secondary sources, a 98-page, double column glossary and an index of proper names. Textual notes cite departures from Robinson (**71**): pp 686, 714; *PardP* and *PardT*, pp 382, 386, 532, 663, 709, 736, 817. Explanatory notes for the Pardoner, *Phy-PardL*, *PardP*, and *PardT* are provided by Christine Ryan Hilary; textual notes are by Ralph Hanna III. For the Pardoner, see **498**; for *PardP* and *PardT*, see **1091**. See **51, 71**.

- Review by Alcuin Blamires, *PRev* 8(1990), 63-4: The subcontracting of editorial tasks results on occasion in inconsistency e.g., when the Host wishes he held the Pardoner's testicles in his hand *In stide of relikes or of senturarie* (line 953), the paginal note offers 'sanctuary, box of relics,' each of which is inappropriate and in fact inconsistent with the end note 'sacred relic.'

118 *Canterbury Tales*. Selected, translated, and adapted by Barbara Cohen. Illustrations by Trina Schart Hyman. New York: Lothrop, Lee and Shepard Books, 1988.

Directed to a young audience, this prose translation includes *NPT*, *WBP*, *WBT*, *FranT*, *PardP* and *PardT* (pp 35-45). Translates the Host's insult as: 'You'd swear your old pants were a saint's relic, though they were stained with your behind' (p 45).

119 *The Canterbury Tales: A Selection*. Retold by Selina Hastings.

Illustrated by Reg Cartwright. New York: Henry Holt, 1988.[Not seen.]

120 *The Canterbury Tales: Nine Tales and the General Prologue*. Ed. V. A. Kolve and Glending Olson. [Norton Critical Edition]. New York: W.W. Norton, 1989.

This critical edition, directed to students encountering Chaucer in Middle English for the first time, employs Skeat (**7**) as copy text and consults the editions of Manly and Rickert (**58**), Robinson (**71**), Baugh (**81**), Donaldson (**73**), Pratt (**89**), Fisher (**103**), and Robinson (**117**) for specific readings. Text includes *GP, KnT, MilT, RvT, WBT, ClT, FranT, PardT, PrT, NPT*, and selected prologues to frame the dramatic context. For the Pardoner, this edition includes *GP* portrait (pp 20-1), *Interr* (pp 109-10), *Phy-PardL* (pp 191-2), *PardP* (pp 192-5), and *PardT* (pp 195-207). Glosses are printed in the right margin, notes at the foot of the page; notes on Chaucer's language and a selected bibliography are included. The text is supported by 1) excerpted sources, analogues, and other medieval writings chosen to encourage students to think in historically relevant ways as well as 2) 10 historically influential critical essays. Background selections for the Pardoner include excerpts from the *RR*, 'The Hermit, Death, and the Robbers' (translated by Kolve from Borghini), and Exemplum 103 from *Liber de Apibus* (also found in **55**). For critical essays relevant to the Pardoner, see **318, 320, 403, 681, 776, 857**.

121 *Geoffrey Chaucer: Die Canterbury-Erzählungen: Mittelenglisch und Deutsch*. Trans. Fritz Kemmler. Ed Jörg O. Fichte. Goldmann Klassiker mit Erläuterungen. Munich: Goldmann Verlag. 1989. 3 vols.

A facing-page original German prose translation of *CT*; the Middle English text is **117** and the translation based on **71**. Volume 2 presents *Phy-PardL* (757-61), *PardP* (761-9), and *PardT* (769-97). German apparatus includes notes, introductions to each tale, guide to pronunciation, history of critical reception, and brief bibliography. The first German and English text of the complete *CT*.

122 *The Ellesmere Manuscript of Chaucer's 'Canterbury Tales': A Working Facsimile*. Introd. Ralph Hanna III. Rochester: Boydell & Brewer, 1989.

A working copy of the text of the Ellesmere Chaucer printed as a line facsimile from the 1911 facsimile; the position of the text on the page follows that of the facsimile; text reproduced at 75 per cent of the size of the facsimile. Hanna's introduction notes the liberties Greggs took in printing the 1911 facsimile, all of which necessarily pertain to this working facsimile. Hanna suggests the wider distribution afforded by this working facsimile will stimulate attention to the degree of editing the Ellesmere received, the status of its individual readings, and the nature of early book trade and scribal habit. See also **29, 58, 902**.

123 *The Canterbury Tales by Geoffrey Chaucer: The General Prologue and Twelve Major Tales in Modern Spelling*. Ed. Michael Murphy. Lanham, Maryland: University Press of America, 1991.

Proceeding from the judgment that some Chaucerians, in their insistance on Middle English, 'act as if the works of the poet should be carefully kept away from the general reader and general student'(p xiv), Murphy presents a 'modspell' edition (with only spelling changed) based on Hengwrt for 'readers who do not want the vagaries of archaic Middle English spelling, nor yet a flat translation' (p xv). Includes Pardoner portrait (pp 23-6), *Phy-PardL* (pp 306-7), *PardP* (pp 307-11) and *PardT* (pp 311-23). The text is supported by a brief general introduction, brief introductory notes on the Pardoner's performance, marginal glosses, textual notes at the foot of the page, brief notes ('Endpapers') on selected topics or terms (e.g., *gentil*, 'Pardoner'), and a brief glossary.

124 Dor, Juliette. *Chaucer: Les contes de Cantorbéry*. Paris: Bibliothèque Médiéval, 1991.

Introduction, bibliography and French translations of *WBP*, *WBT*, *CLT*, *MerT*, *FranT*, *PhyT*, *PardT*, *ShT*, *PrT*, *NPT*, *SNT*, *CYT*, and *ManT*.

125 *The Canterbury Tales by Geoffrey Chaucer*. Trans. Ronald L. Ecker and Eugene J. Crook. Palatka, Florida: Hodge & Braddock, 1993.

A complete modern translation in rhymed verse undertaken over a twenty year period and based on **71** with reference to **81, 89, 103**, and **117**. Includes Pardoner portrait (pp 18-9), *Phy-PardL* (pp 335-6), *PardP* (pp 336-9) and *PardT* (pp 339-52); line numbers for reference and a brief glossary of terms and names are also included.

126 *The New Ellesmere Chaucer Facsimile (of Huntington Library ms EL26 C9)*. Ed. Daniel Woodward and Martin Stevens. Tokyo and San Marino, California: Yushodo and Huntington Library Press, 1995.

A full color facsimile with 240 leaves in the size of the original ms. Contains 23 portraits at the heads of respective tales. Ornate capitals and border designs. Supersedes **29, 122**.

Bibliographies, Indexes, and Textual Studies

127 Hammond, Eleanor P. *Chaucer: A Bibliographical Manual.* Boston: Macmillan, 1908. Rpt New York: P. Smith, 1933.

The first comprehensive, systematic collection of bibliographic materials for modern Chaucer study. Hammond lists editions, modernizations and translations, discussions of sources, analogues, and dates together with a brief bibliography on the Pardoner and pardoners (pp 295-6); comments on links and fragments (pp 150-60); and presents Furnivall's view that the Pardoner tells his tale on the third day. The 'strongly autobiographical character' (p 256) of the framework of *PardT* supports the judgment that it is a work of Chaucer's maturity. Three different positions occupied by Fragment C are outlined (pp 293-4). For *Phy-PardL*, see **532**; for *PardT*, see **674**.

128 Koch, John. 'Die Chaucerforschung seit 1900.' *GRM* 1(1909), 490-507.

A survey of early twentieth-century research particularly useful for European materials; for *PardT* notes Koch's edition (**16**), and H.S. Canby's evidence of Italian sources (**200**).

129 Skeat, W[alter].W. *Early English Proverbs. Chiefly of the Thirteenth and Fourteenth Centuries with Illustrative Quotations.* Oxford: Clarendon Press, 1910.

In this book of proverbs extant before 1400, Skeat notes analogues for *PardT* lines 558 *For Dronkenesse* etc. and 781 *And lightly as it comth, so wol we spende.*

130 Corson, Hiram. *Index of Proper Names and Subjects to Chaucer's Canterbury Tales together with Comparisons and Similes,*

Metaphors and Proverbs, Maxims, etc, in the Same. With an
Introduction by W. W. Skeat. London: Kegan Paul, Trench Trübner &
Co. and Henry Fowde, 1911. Chaucer Society Publications, First Series,
72. Rpt New York: Johnson Reprint [1967].

The index is referenced to the *Six-text* edition (1) and offers a conversion
chart. Part One includes proper names and subjects (including Biblical
allusions). Part Two lists comparisons and similes; metaphors; proverbs,
maxims and sententious expressions; and prayers, entreaties and
imprecations. References are listed for the Pardoner, the Pardoner's
preamble and *PardT*.

131 Spurgeon, Caroline F. E. *Five Hundred Years of Chaucer Criticism
and Allusion, 1357-1900.* 7 Parts. London: Kegan Paul, Trench,
Trübner & Co. and Oxford University Press, 1914-1924. Chaucer
Society Publications, Second Series 48(1914), 49-50(1918), 52(1921),
53(1922), 54(1922), 55(1924), and 56(1924). Rpt Cambridge: Cambridge
University Press, 1925 (as 3 volumes); rev Russell & Russell, 1960.

Modernizations listed include: Lipscomb, 1972(1:403); and Hunt, 'Death
and the Ruffians,' 1845(2:260), 1855(3:22-3). Direct influence on
Heywood, *Four P's* is cited (1:80-1). *PardT* lines 615-7 are cited by
Roger Ascham against swearing (1544, 1:85-6); lines 608-28 in *The
Institution of a Gentleman* (1555, 1:94); and lines 603-28 by John
Northbrooke on age (1577, 1:115). See **143**. For Pardoner, see **285**.

132 Wells, John Edwin. *A Manual of the Writings in Middle English,
1050-1400.* New Haven, Connecticut: Connecticut Academy of Arts
and Sciences, 1916. Rpt 1917, 1923, 1926.

Wells records 'generally accepted views' (p vii) and provides
bibliographic notes on *GP*, *PardP* and *PardT* through 1915; nine
supplements (1919-52) take the coverage through 1945. The complete
revision of Wells' *Manual* (Ed. J. Burke Severs and Albert E. Hartung)
does not include a bibliography in view of the availablility of other
resources. Fragment C is 'the most difficult Fragment to place' as it
lacks a genuine headlink, indication of time or place and connection to
the following material (p 713). *Phy-PardL*, given 'the rather
inappropriate title' (p 715) of the Words of the Host, serves as both an
endlink to *PhyT* and a headlink to *PardT*. *GP* portrait of the Pardoner is
the next to longest in order to begin the exhibition of character that will
continue through *PardP* and *PardT*. *PardP* 'is in Chaucer's best
humorous style' (p 715) exposing the Pardoner's hypocrisy, laying bare

his methods, illuminating his theme and imposing on his audience. *PardT* is 'one of Chaucer's most extraordinary achievements, a narrative of notable power for any period' (p 716). The story is of Eastern origin; though widely treated, no specific source has been identified. Its effect derives from: its suggestiveness, the plague setting, its detail, close realness, dramatic quality, its telling in the form of discourse, the awfulness of the rioters and pathetic yet ominous figure of the Old Man, the rapidity of action, and the inevitability of the outcome. The final solicitation provides relief to the tale of the revelers though the Pardoner is operating 'in all gravity' (p 717).

133 *The Year's Work in English Studies.* London: Oxford University Press and Humphrey Milford. 1921—.
An annual collection of bibliographic essays which from 1921 to 1934 (vol 15) includes entries on Chaucer in the general 'Middle English' chapter, and following 1935 (vol 16) presents a separate 'Chaucer' chapter.

134 Marburg, Clara. 'Notes on the Cardigan Chaucer Manuscript.' *PMLA* 41(1926), 229-51.
Marburg describes the Cardigan manuscript, discusses its relation to other manuscripts of *CT*, and presents a transcription of the *Phy-PardL*, *PardP* and *PardT* (pp 236-51) to enable comparison with the Chaucer Society's *Parallel Text-Specimens* (**1**). Marburg concludes that the Cardigan manuscript belongs to the Dd-subdivision of the A-group, and is most nearly related to Hodson 39 with which it shares a common ancestor influenced by the B-group of manuscripts.

135 Tatlock, John S.P., and Arthur G. Kennedy. *A Concordance to the Complete Works of Geoffrey Chaucer and to the Romaunt of the Rose.* Washington, DC: Carnegie Institution, 1927. Rpt Gloucester, Massachusetts; Peter Smith, 1963.
Based on Pollard (**11**), this concordance includes items relevant to the Pardoner portrait and all aspects of the Pardoner's performance. See **179**.

136 McCormick, Sir William. *The Manuscripts of Chaucer's Canterbury Tales: A Critical Description of Their Contents.* With the assistance of Janet E. Heseltine. Oxford: Clarendon Press, 1933. See **534**.

137 Whiting, Bartlett Jere. *Chaucer's Use of Proverbs.* Harvard Studies in Comparative Literature, 11. Cambridge, Massachusetts: Harvard University Press, 1934.

Chaucer uses more proverbial material than any 'other poet of repute' (p 3). When the Pardoner interrupts the Wife of Bath, she employs a proverb to advise him to wait (D 180 ff). The Pardoner's desire for drink before he begins his tale (line 321 ff) may refer to the proverb: 'A story needs a drink.' In *PardP*, Whiting identifies three proverbial phrases (two of which are comparisons) and one sententious remark; in *PardT*, he notes one proverb (line 781), three proverbial phrases, one of which is a comparison, and four sententious remarks (line 558 ff, 591, 825 and 958 ff). See **129**.

138 Martin, Willard E., Jr. *A Chaucer Bibliography 1925-1933*. Durham, North Carolina: Duke University Press, 1935.

This selective bibliography lists reviews, translations into foreign languages, imitations, children's versions as well as scholarly books and articles.

139 'Chaucer Research, Report No. 1-54.' MLA Committee on Chaucer Research and Bibliography. 1937-66.

Prior to 1966, this report was circulated periodically in mimeographed form. Since the compilation for 1966 ('Report No. 27'), the bibliography, edited by Thomas A. Kirby, has been published annually in *ChauR*, vols 1- present with the following exceptions: volumes 5 and 13 include no annual report; volumes 9 and 15 include two annual reports each. Includes listings of current research, completed research, published works and other notices.

140 Bowden, Muriel. *A Commentary on the General Prologue to the Canterbury Tales*. New York: Macmillan, 1948. Several times rpt (4th printing 1954). 2nd ed. New York: Macmillan, 1967; London: Souvenir Press, 1973, rpt 1981. Portions rpt in *Critics on Chaucer*, ed. Sheila Sullivan. London: Allen and Unwin, 1970; Coral Gables, Florida: University of Miami Press, 1970. Pp 97-104.

A detailed study with a historical orientation (cf **690**), this work also provides a summary of scholarship. For Pardoner, see **307**.

141 Rickert, Edith, compiler. *Chaucer's World*. Ed. Clair C. Olson and Martin M. Crow. Illustrations selected by Margaret Rickert. London: Geoffrey Cumberledge for Oxford University Press, 1948; New York: Columbia University Press, 1948.

Contemporary sources are compiled with illustrations to document fourteenth-century life. Of relevance to the Pardoner and his performance are sections on pilgrimage (pp 259-69), church and churchmen (pp 369-87), prayers for the soul (pp 419-23), the burial of the dead (p 395), description of relics (pp 389-90), confession (p 391), penance (p 392), and 'Attempts to restrain the evil practices of pardoners, 1348, 1368, 1374' (pp 379-80).

142 Baugh, Albert C. 'Fifty Years of Chaucer Scholarship.' *Speculum* 26(1951), 659-72.

From 1900 through 1950, the latter a date by which Baugh considers Chaucer studies to have reached scholarly maturity, he provides an overview of scholarly concerns including textual questions, editions, discussion of sources and analogues, and selective treatment of secondary works.

143 Alderson, William L. 'A Check-list of Supplements to Spurgeon's Chaucer Allusions.' *PQ* 32(1953), 418-27.

Alderson corrects several items cited by Spurgeon (**131**)and adds a check-list of 78 entries. See also **264**.

144 Griffith, Dudley David. *Bibliography of Chaucer 1908-1953*. Seattle: University of Washington Press, 1955.

Planned as a supplement to Hammond (**127**), this listing includes theses, reviews, recordings, modernizations, translations, and children's adaptations. The book incorporates Griffith's earlier work, *A Bibliography of Chaucer, 1908-1924*, University of Washington Publications in Language and Literature, 4(1926). See also **148**.

145 Magoun, Francis P., Jr. *A Chaucer Gazeteer*. Stockholm: Almqvist and Wiksell, 1961: Chicago: University of Chicago Press, 1961.

The book is a conflation of three articles by Magoun: 'Chaucer's Ancient and Biblical World,' *MS* 15(1953), 107-36; 'Chaucer's Great Britain,' *MS* 16(1954), 131-56; and 'Chaucer's Mediaeval World Outside of Great Britain,' *MS* 17(1955), 117-42. For Pardoner, see **345**; for *PardT*, see **768**; see also **156**.

146 Elliott, Ralph W. V. *The Nun's Priest's Tale and The Pardoner's Tale*. [Notes on English Literature]. New York: Barnes & Noble, [not indicated-1965]; London: Basil Blackwell & Mott, 1965.

Notes suggest *PardT* told in a tavern ends with a comic tone. Study questions and notes on Chaucer's language are included.

147 Crow, Martin M., and Clair Olson. *Chaucer Life-Records*. Oxford: Clarendon Press, 1966.

A source book of life-records. Of possible relevance to *PardP* and *PardT* are: records related to Chaucer's being robbed by highwaymen,

1390 (pp 477-489); and an entry from Thomas Gascoigne's *Dictionarium Theologicum* relating to Chaucer's reported repentance at the time of his death (p 547). See **206, 224**.

148 Crawford, William R. *Bibliography of Chaucer 1954-63*. Seattle: University of Washington Press, 1967.

Planned as a supplement to Griffith (**144**); includes reprints of items originally published prior to 1954 and an introductory essay on new directions in Chaucer criticism. Lists items for Pardoner (pp 62-3) and for *Phy-PardL*, *PardP*, and *PardT* (pp 76-8). See also **161**.

149 Baugh, Albert C. *Chaucer*. New York: Appleton-Century-Crofts, 1968. 2nd ed. Arlington Heights, Illinois: HHM Publishing Corp., 1977. Goldentree Bibliographies in Language and Literature. General Editor, O. B. Hardison, Jr.

This selective bibliography lists 16 items on the Pardoner; 57 items on *Phy-PardL*, *PardP*, and *PardT*.

150 Hoffman, Richard L. 'The Canterbury Tales.' In *Critical Approaches to Six Major English Works*. Ed. Robert M. Lumiansky and Herschel Baker. Philadelphia: University of Pennsylvania Press, 1968; London: Oxford University Press, 1968. Pp 41-80.

Hoffman offers a selective overview of Chaucer scholarship from 1940, treating editions (**58, 71, 73**), sources and analogues (**194**), and critical directions with particular emphasis on thematic treatments of *CT*, particularly variations of the theme of love. Hoffman notes that *radix malorum est cupiditas* is the theme of many tales in addition to *PardT*, and *radix bonorum est Caritas* runs through *CT* as a whole.

151 Burrow, J.A., ed. *Geoffrey Chaucer: A Critical Anthology*. Harmondsworth, England, and Baltimore, Maryland: Penguin, 1969. Penguin Critical Anthologies. General Editor, Christopher Ricks.

Brief reference is made to the Pardoner and *PardT* by: John Lydgate (pp 42-4); William Blake (pp 77-83); G. L. Kittredge (pp 119-24); J. M. Manly (pp 126-30); Rosemary Woolf (pp 206-14); and R. E. Kaske (pp 233-9). More extended reference is made in the selection from Nevill Coghill, 'from *The Poet Chaucer*' (pp 156-9)(see **309**): 'the basilisk Pardoner' was more fearful and consequently more hateful than either the Friar or the Summoner (p 157). In *PardT*, Chaucer shows himself 'the first and subtlest ironist' (p 157). Harry Bailey, the Pardoner's nemesis 'voiced the feelings of all England towards Pardoners in his annihilating retort' (p 158-9).

152 'Chaucer Research in Progress.' *NM* 70(1969)—.
An annual compilation lists research projects underway.

153 Myers, A. R. *English Historical Documents*, 1327-1485. Volume 4. General Editor, David C. Douglas. London: Eyre & Spottiswoode, 1969. Presents a wide variety of fundamental sources of English history including entries on: the Flanders campaign of 1339 (pp 65-6); the Black Death, 1348-9 (pp 89-91); an indulgence for refugees from Constantinople, 1454 (pp 715-6); Archbishop Sudbury raising the wages of priests, 1378 (pp 728-9); a bull of Pope Urban VI (p 786); extensive selections on Wyclif and Lollardy (pp 837-77); entries on pilgrim conditions and violence; a selection on the popularity and variety of sermons (pp 821-5); and a selection from the Tale of Beryn (pp 1214-6).

154 Ross, Thomas W. *Chaucer's Bawdy*. New York: Dutton, 1972; Toronto: Clarke, Irwin & Co, 1972.
For Pardoner, see **399**; for *Phy-PardL*, see **548**; for *PardP*, see **617**; for *PardT*, see **872**.

155 Benson, L. D. 'A Reader's Guide to Writings on Chaucer' and 'Chaucer: A Select Bibliography.' In *Geoffrey Chaucer*. Ed. Derek Brewer. Cambridge: D. S. Brewer, 1974. Republished as *Writers and Their Background: Geoffrey Chaucer*. London: Bell, 1974; Athens, Ohio: Ohio University Press, 1975, 1990. Pp 321-51; selective bibliography 352-72.
Benson provides a general overview of critical issues (including the Canon, texts, language, learning and sources), commentary on interpretive criticism and a selective bibliography. Kellogg (**728**) is cited as an example of interpretion from a medieval standpoint. See **892**.

156 Dillon, Bert. *A Chaucer Dictionary: Proper Names and Allusions Excluding Place Names*. Boston: G. K. Hall, 1974; London: George Prior, 1974.
Seeks to provide a guide to names, allusions and borrowings accessible to Chaucer's contemporaries; includes thirty references to *PardT*. Entries are arranged alphabetically with variant spellings, identification, references to other literary works and scholarly studies and a list of occurrences in Chaucer's works. A cross-reference list of titles and a 20-page bibliography is included. See **145, 768**.

157 Scott, A[rthur]. F[inley]. *Who's Who in Chaucer*. London: Elm Tree (Hamilton), 1974.

Fourteen names are glossed for *PardT*: *Adam* (line 505), *Attilla* (line 579), *Avycen* (line 889), *Deeth* (line 675), *Demetrius* (line 621), *Eleyne* (line 951), *Jeremye* (line 635), *Lamuel* (line 584), *Looth* (line 485), *Mathew* (line 634), *Old Man* (line 713), *Ryotoures Thre* (line 661), *Senek* (line 492), *Stilboun* (line 603). See **130** and **156**.

158 Thorpe, James. *A Noble Heritage: The Ellesmere Manuscript of Chaucer's Canterbury Tales*. 2nd ed. published as *Chaucer's Canterbury Tales: The Ellesmere Manuscript*. San Marino, California: The Huntington Library, 1974, 2nd ed. 1978.

In a richly illustrated pamphlet, Thorpe describes the Ellesmere ms produced about 1410 in a commercial scriptorium, held in the Bridgewater Library assembled by Thomas Egerton, and sold in 1917 to H. E. Huntington for one million dollars. Now held at the Huntington Library. Includes color illustration of the beginnning of *PardT* with accompanying pilgrim miniature (p 7) and a black and white reproduction of Blake's *Canterbury Pilgrims* (1810) (pp 8-9). For Pardoner, see **411**; for *PardT*, see **902**.

159 'An Annotated Chaucer Bibliography, 1975—.' *SAC*, 1(1979-present).

The *SAC* bibliographies are designed as a continuation of Hammond (**127**), Griffith (**144**), Crawford (**148**), Baird (**161**), and Fisher (**103**) with short annotations. Entries specific to the Pardoner are included under 'The Pardoner and His Tale' and treatments of the Pardoner in other works are cross-referenced.

160 Courtney, Eleanor Lewer. *Geoffrey Chaucer's 'Canterbury Tales': An Annotated International Bibliography, 1964-1971*. University of Arizona Dissertations, 1975. Director: Christopher F. Carroll. See also *DAI* 37(1976), 327-A.

Following a survey of trends in *CT* criticism, Courtney provides an annotated bibliography of editions, books, articles, dissertations, reprints and reviews. [Not seen.]

161 Baird, Lorrayne Y. *A Bibliography of Chaucer, 1964-1973*. Boston: G. K. Hall, 1977. Reference Guides in Literature. General Editor, Everett Emerson.

Baird continues Crawford's *Bibliography of Chaucer 1954-63* (**148**) and adds festschriften and collections; foreign translations; literary and aesthetic backgrounds; music backgrounds; recordings, films and filmstrips; and musical settings and adaptations. See **173**.

162 Miller, Robert P., ed. *Chaucer: Sources and Backgrounds*. New York: Oxford University Press, 1977.
This useful reference for teaching presents excerpts from the tradition of literary authority within which Chaucer wrote. Brief excerpts include: Augustine, from *On Christian Doctrine* (pp 53-7); Hugh of St. Victor, 'On Clerics'(p 214); Jeun de Meun, 'Fals-Semblant Describes the Friar's Life'(pp 251-4); *ParsT*, 'The Five Fingers of Lechery'(pp360-2); Innocent III, from 'On the Misery of the Human Condition'(pp 484-90); and a pardoner's license (pp 229-30).

163 Brewer, D. S., ed. *Chaucer: The Critical Heritage*. Volume 1, 1385-1837; Volume 2, 1837-1933. London: Routledge and Kegan Paul, 1978.
Includes selections from Deschamps (1385) to Rosemund Tuve (1933). Brewer includes the following extracts with reference to *PardT*: Elizabeth Cooper, 'Soaring in High Life, Pleasant in Low, 1737' (pp 198-203); William Blake, 'Names Alter, Things Never, 1809' (pp 247-8); Frederick James Furnivall, 'Work at Chaucer, 1873' (pp 167-77); John Dryden, 'God's Plenty 1700' (pp 160-172); John William Mackail, 'Daylight and Romance, 1909' (pp 285-99); and John Matthews Manly, 'From Art to Nature, 1926' (pp 384-402).

164 Davis, Norman, Douglas Gray, Patricia Ingham, and Anne Wallace-Hadrill, comp. *A Chaucer Glossary*. Oxford: Clarendon Press, 1979.
Text is based on Skeat (7), the Tatlock-Kennedy *Concordance* (135), and glossaries through to Pratt (100). Presents words used in ways unfamiliar in modern English; the sense is given in order of frequency. A brief list of proper names is also provided. See 181.

165 Gibaldi, Joseph, ed. *Approaches to Teaching Chaucer's Canterbury Tales*. Consultant Editor, Florence H. Ridley. [Approaches to Teaching Masterpieces of World Literature]. New York: Modern Language Association, 1980.
The section on 'Materials'(pp 3-32) identifies texts of selected *CT* that include *PardT*, tapes, records, films, background studies on topics relevant to *PardT*. In Part II, 'Approaches' (pp 35-148), Donald Howard cites *PardT* as one of a number of 'peculiarly Chaucerian moments' where 'Chaucer teaches us how it is possible to take life and the world and one's self very seriously while at the same time seeing the transiency of life, the triviality of the world, and the ballooning potential for roosterhood in almost any self'(p 62). Mary J. Carruthers comments on teaching *PardP* and *PardT* 'wholly within the context of an

Augustinian analysis of the psychology of sin and redemption, the habits of medieval pardoners, and the universal games of confidence-men ...'(p 78). Robert M. Jordan notes that *PardT* demonstrates the closest that Chaucer comes to 'dramatizing' a teller through a tale (p 86). Julia Bolton Holloway notes the relevance of literary texts such as *RR* and *Roman de Renart* to an understanding of the Pardoner. The List of Works Cited includes books, recordings, films and filmstrips (pp 153-67).

166 Ramsey, Roy Vance. 'The Hengwrt and Ellesmere Manuscripts of the *Canterbury Tales*: Different Scribes.' *SB* 35(1982), 133-54.
Argues that Hengwrt and Ellesmere were copied by different scribes with different habits of registering accidentals, proofing finished copy and registering substantive readings. Tables of graphic and graphemic contrasts in Hengwrt and Ellesmere include data on *PardT*. The differences in scribal habits extended to 'substantives and resulted in significant differences in the textual quality of each manuscript' (p 144).

167 Ruggiers, Paul. *Editing Chaucer: The Great Tradition*. Norman, Oklahoma: Pilgrim Books, 1984.
This volume provides an overview of the evolution of the editions of Chaucer including essays on the major early editions as well as post 1900 editions. Included are: 'Walter W. Skeat' by A. S. G. Edwards (pp 171-89); 'John M. Manly and Edith Rickert' by George Kane (pp 207-29); and 'F.N. Robinson' by George Reinecke (pp 231-51). See 7, **51, 58**.

168 Blake, N. F. *The Textual Tradition of the Canterbury Tales*. London: Edward Arnold, 1985.
Through a description of the earliest manuscripts, Blake pursues the evolution of *CT* from Hengwrt, through Corpus, Ha 7334 and Lansdowne, to the a-group manuscripts Dd4.24, Gg4.27, and Ellesmere. Hengwrt, the earliest extant ms, best grounds an understanding of the textual tradition. *PhyT* and *PardT* are joined by a link varied in some mss. In Corpus, the first in which changes are made, an extra couplet included at C 297-8 moralizes that beauty is the cause of Virginia's death. Some of the other changes may have been made to nullify the criticism of lawyers. The scribe of Dd4.24 did not introduce any of the changes found in Corpus, though he did introduce a change which makes the activities of the Pardoner 'progress in a logical way' (p 131). The changes made to *PardP* in various mss are spurious and seldom included

in modern editions.

69 Morris, Lynn King. *Chaucer Source and Analogue Criticism: A Cross-Referenced Guide.* New York and London: Garland, 1985.
Morris provides a guide to the literature on sources and analogues (through 1981) indexed by Chaucerian title, author, origin and title of the source or analogue. See **253**.

70 Leyerle, John, and Anne Quick. *Chaucer: A Bibliographical Introduction.* [Toronto Medieval Bibliographies]. Toronto: University of Toronto Press, 1986.
A selective bibliography designed to facilitate interdisciplinary study. Presents sections on 'Materials for the Study of Chaucer's Works' (including sources and influences), 'Chaucer's Works,' and 'Backgrounds' (including preaching, the Bible and the liturgy). Includes 23 brief annotations for items treating *PardP* and *PardT* (CT 291-307 with cross references).

71 Allen, Mark, and John H. Fisher. *The Essential Chaucer: An Annotated Bibliography of Major Modern Studies.* Boston: G. K.Hall, 1987.
Designed as a research tool for students and a convenient reference for scholars, this work covering 1900-84 (with emphasis on the preceding quarter century) provides annotations for 22 entries relating to the Pardoner and *PardT* as well as brief sections on *GP*, evolution and order. Items 570-591 (pp 148-52) relate to Pardoner and *PardT*; sixteen cross-references identify items related to style and rhetoric, sources and analogues, and relations to other tales.

72 De Weever, Jacqueline. *Chaucer Name Dictionary: A Guide to Astrological, Biblical, Historical, Literary, and Mythological Names in the Works of Geoffrey Chaucer.* New York: Garland Publishing, Inc., 1987.
For names of persons, gods and goddesses, De Weever provides: biographical, historical or mythological information; identification of Chaucer's use; etymological information; and bibliographic references for sources used in the entry. Names considered include: *Ronyan* (p 290/lines 310, 320); *Looth* (p 201/ lines 485-7); *Herodes* (p 162/ lines 488-90); *Adam* (p 7/ lines 505-11); *Baptist John* (p 53/ lines 488-91); *Paul* (pp 252-3/ lines 517-23); *Sampsoun* (pp 293-4/ lines 554-5, 572); *Atilla* (p 46/ lines 579-82); *John* (p 181/ line 752); *Marie* (p 214/ line 685); 'Samuel/ Lamuel' (pp 294, 193/ lines 583-6); *Demetrius* (p 108/ lines 603-28); *Mathew* (p 218/ lines 633-4); *Jeremye* (p 178/ line 635);

Avycen, Qanum (pp 50-1/ lines 889-92); *Eleyne* (p 122/ lines 951-5).

173 Baird-Lange, Lorrayne and Hildegard Schnuttgen, comp. *A Bibliography of Chaucer 1974-1985*. Hamden, Connecticut: Archon, 1988.

Generally follows the plan of **161** with the addition of categories for: Fascimiles, Medieval Women's Studies, and Pedagogy.

Includes items on the Pardoner (1266-70) and *PardT* (1691-1757) with additional cross references in each category.

174 Besserman, Lawrence. *Chaucer and the Bible: A Critical Review of Research, Indexes, and Bibliography*. Garland Reference Library of the Humanities. Vol. 839. New York and London: 1988.

Index 1 lists 46 Biblical allusions for *PardT* (pp 126-33) and 11 for *PardP* (pp 124-6); entries are accompanied by references to relevant primary or secondary supporting texts whose full listings appear in a bibliography. Index 2 lists biblical references in a reverse index. An introductory essay suggests that by creating biblical adepts such as the Pardoner, Chaucer 'problematized' the orthodox claims of the Parson (p 7). The Pardoner like False-Seeming in *RR* turns the Bible into a deadly weapon.

175 Smith, J. J. 'Spelling and Tradition in Fifteenth-Century Copies of Gower's *Confessio Amantis*.' *The English of Chaucer and His Contemporaries*. Essays by M. L. Samuels and J. J. Smith. Ed. J. J. Smith. Aberdeen: Aberdeen University Press, 1988. Pp 96-113.

In a study that seeks to determine the extent and implications of Gowerian forms persisting into the fifteenth and early sixteenth centuries, Smith concludes that the Gower mss were produced within a strong orthographic tradition. In a comparative study with items in *PardP* and *PardT*, he notes no Chaucer manuscript carries *sih* ('saw') or *end(e)* (present participle) and *gh-* type spellings for 'own' appeared in only four texts. Syncopated verbs such as *comþ* ('comes'), despite the fact they were a variable in Chaucer's own language, survive relatively infrequently.

176 Hanna, Ralph III. 'The Hengwrt Manuscript and the Canon of *The Canterbury Tales*.' *EMS* 1(1989), 64-84.

Hanna discusses 'soft' and 'hard' Hengwrtism to conclude that the existence of anomalies between textual quality and tale order argue for the concept of split authority. The quality of Hengwrt is attested by its avoidance of passages such as C 297-8 which is based on scribal reading, yet often included by modern editors (p 76). '[N]one of the tale orders we have received necessarily reflects Chaucer's plan (if indeed he had one) but rather the difficulties of manuscript supervisors trying to make a text left manifestly incomplete at its author's death look like a continuous whole' (p 79).

77 Moorman, Charles. 'One Hundred Years of Editing the *Canterbury Tales.' ChauR* 24(1989), 99-114.

Noting two editorial traditions, the 'conjectural' and the 'conservative,' Moorman notes that eclecticism dominates the last one hundred years of Chaucer textual scholarship. Using a list of *GP* emendations, he suggests that Skeat is a 'conjecturalist *manqué*' (p 103); Skeat's emends Ellesmere in *GP* lines 680, 685, 714 without notation. Robinson, similarly, departed from Ellesmere (*GP* line 686); Pratt, despite his acknowledgement to Ellesmere, makes such heavy use of Manly-Rickert that he moves toward making Hengwrt his base text (*GP* emendation line 686). Closes by urging that we accept the manuscripts we have to be studied, analyzed and grouped where possible rather than 'fancifully improved' (p 112). See **7, 51, 71,** and **89.**

78 Ramsey, Roy Vance. 'F. N. Robinson's Editing of the *Canterbury Tales.' SB* 42(1989), 134-52.

Argues against reliance on Robinson's text (including **117**) on the grounds that: Robinson relied on early editions, working deductively and accepting untenable assumptions, rather than basing his text on manuscript evidence; and relied on his own 'very neat and rigid ideas about Chaucer's meter and grammar' (p 151), smoothing the text inappropriately.

79 Oizumi, Akio, and Kunihiro Miki, eds. *A Complete Concordance to the Works of Geoffrey Chaucer.* Programmed by Kumihiro Mike. 10 vols. Reihe C: Englishe Autoren. Hildesheim, etc.: Olms-Weidmann, 1991-4.

Provides an index of every occurrence of every word in Chaucer, ranking word frequency list, list of hyphenated compounds, and indication of frequency that individual words appear in rhyming position. See **135.**

80 Oizumi, Akio. 'Towards a Rhyme Concordance to Chaucer's Poetical Works.' In *Chaucer to Shakespeare: Essays in Honour of Shinsuke Ando.* Ed. Toshiyuki Takamiya and Richard Beadle. Bury St. Edmunds, Suffolk: D. S. Brewer, 1992. Pp 67-74. Describes the preparation of a sequel to **179.** [Not seen.]

181 Benson, Larry D. *A Glossarial Concordance to the Riverside Chaucer*. 2 vols. New York and London: Garland, 1993.

A comprehensive glossary organized according to headwords of the Middle English Dictionary with lemmas having reference to OED. Volume 2 presents a ranked list of high frequency words including the following: *sinne* (445), *deth* (309), *slen* (307), *dien* (310), *ded* (194). See **164**.

182 Ramsey, Roy Vance. *The Manly-Rickert Text of the "Canterbury Tales."* Lewiston, New York: Edwin Mellen, 1994.

Defends the Manly-Rickert text of *CT* suggesting that it be used in conjunction with Hengwrt, the best-text manuscript to provide an edition that sits between the *Variorum* and student texts. Ramsey critiques the editorial process of Manly and Rickert, examines the context of late medieval manuscript and book production, and evaluates Hengwrt.

Sources, Analogues, and Influences

Pardoner's Prologue

83 Axon, William E.A. 'Italian Influence on Chaucer.' In *Chaucer Memorial Lectures*. Ed. Percy W. Ames. London: Asher and Company, 1900. Pp 83-110.

The passage in *PardP* on false relics is paralleled in Boccaccio (Day 6, Nov 10) though the satire is so obvious it may be based more generally. The plot of *PardT* is almost identical with that of *Cento Novelle Antiche* (Nov 83). *PardT* is most likely based on a recension still undiscovered.

84 Schofield, William Henry. *English Literature From the Norman Conquest to Chaucer*. New York: Haskell House Publishers, 1906. 1914, 1921, 1968.

Chaucer seems to have derived some material for the Pardoner from Bromyard's *Super Libros Sapientiae*, a book of commentaries. Having the Pardoner citing *ensamples*, Chaucer illustrated the technique of 'the common sermoniser'(p 342) who justified his habit by the *lewed* people's love of stories.

86 Fansler, Dean S. *Chaucer and the Roman de la Rose*. Columbia University Studies in English and Comparative Literature, 7. New York: [1914]. Rpt Gloucester, Massachusetts: Peter Smith, 1965.

Fansler evaluates the validity of recorded parallels between Chaucer and *RR*, records new parallels, and attempts to determine Chaucer's attitude to the work. Fansler notes for the first time that the Pardoner's character owes more to *RR* than does the Friar. *PardP* bears many resemblances to Faux-Semblant's self-revelation (e.g., the form of the confession, preaching against avarice, love of food and wine, and reluctance to work with one's hands [line 444]). Unlike Faux-Semblant, the Pardoner is willing to deal with poor people (*GP* 701-4). The Pardoner is so associated with the Friar in Chaucer's mind that he divides a couplet from Faux-Semblant between them (A 256; C 403). Faux-Semblant antagonizes less than the Pardoner because he is less detailed, less human. 'The Pardoner is without doubt one of the most despicable wretches in literature' (p 163). Fansler notes that the proverb attributed by Tyrwhitt to *RR* (lines 407-8) shows indication of coming from the English translation. Mention of *veyne glorie* (line 411), *ipocrisye* (line 410), and *avarice* indicate Chaucer's contact with Reason's sermon on evil priests (*RR* 5792-5839).

187 Cummings, Hubertis M. *The Indebtedness of Chaucer's Works to the Italian Works of Boccaccio*. The Collegiate Press. Menasha, Wisconsin: George Banta Publishing Co., 1916.

Cummings decides it highly improbable that Chaucer used any other Italian works of Boccaccio than *Filos* and *Tes*. Most likely, Chaucer did not know *Dec*; his debt to Boccaccio is that of a borrower who drew specific elements and fitted them to his own design.

188 Sedgwick, W.B. 'Chaucer's "Pardoner's Prologue."' *MLR* 19(1924), 336-7.

Though the reader is surprised that the unscrupulous Pardoner places a restriction on the efficacy of his relics, the restriction is actually cunning: the Pardoner speculates 'that none would voluntarily confess, before the whole parish, to living in deadly sin, by holding back from making an offering'(p 336). Sedgwick is the first to note a similar trick, found in the thirteenth-century German poem of *Pfaffe Ameis*. A slight resemblance is found in the *Dec*. See **192**.

192 Weatherly, Edward H. 'A Note on Chaucer's Pardoner's Prologue.' *MLN* 50(1935), 310-1.

Chaucer's source for the Pardoner's 'blackmail' (lines 377-90) is probably a fourteenth-century exemplum. W.B. Sedgwick noted a thirteenth-century German parallel, *Pfaffe Amies*, where the trick is attributed to a priest. Harleian ms 3938 (ff 124b-125), a fifteenth-century Latin collection presents a closer analogue in attributing the trick not to a priest but to a pardoner from Ferrara, paralleling growing distrust in pardoners. See **188**.

193 Whiting, B.J. 'More on Chaucer's Pardoner's Prologue (VI [C], 377-390).' *MLN* 51(1936), 322-7.

The Pardoner's trick (lines 377-90) is found, in addition to the identified analogues (**188**), twice in a single tale of Giovanni Sercambi—*De Ipocriti et Fraudatores*. The tradition used by Sercambi is followed by Heinrich Bebel (1508), Henri Estienne (Apologie pour Herodote), and, in a slight altered form, by John Heywood in his *Pardoner and Friars* (1533).

194 Dempster, Germaine. 'The Pardoner's Prologue.' In *Sources and Analogues of Chaucer's Canterbury Tales*. Ed. W.F. Bryan and Germaine Dempster. London: Routledge & Kegan Paul; Chicago: University of Chicago Press, 1941. Rpt Atlantic Highlands, New Jersey: Humanities Press, 1958. Pp 409-14.

Although undoubtedly 'the character of the Pardoner and the episodes in which he appears are largely the creation of Chaucer' (p 409), much of *PardP*, particularly the confession of hypocrisy and self-interest, is paralleled by and may have been inspired by Faux-Semblant in the *RR*. Early analogues to the Pardoner's gaude (C 377-90) find analogues in Der Stricker's *Pfaffe Amîs*, Sercambi's novella 51, *De ypocriti et fraudatores*, and a fifteenth-century exemplum from Harleian ms 3938, fols 124b-25 (see pp 437ff). See also **188**, **192**, **193**, **304**.

196 Braddy, Haldeen. 'The French Influence on Chaucer.' In *Companion to Chaucer Studies*. Ed. Beryl Rowland. New York: Oxford University Press, 1968; 1979. Pp 123-38.

Of the eighteen tales relying on writers from across the Channel, *PardT* is one of ten revealing slight dependence. The public confession in *PardP* may have been inspired by the self-interested speeches of Faux-Semblant in *RR* (cf **71**)'which source less probably explains the "*coillons*" reference' in line 925 f (p 134).

Pardoner's Tale

197 Sutta-Pitaka and Khuddaka-Nikaya. *The Vedabbha Jataka Translated From the Pali and Compared With 'The Pardoner's Tale.'* With Introduction and Notes by H.T. Francis. Cambridge: J. Palmer, 1884. Francis presents a Buddhist birth story earlier identified by Morris (1881), as an Indian original. The Buddhist story includes a robbers' quarrel over a treasure trove. 'This covetousness verily is the root of destruction' is said either by the robber left to guard the treasure or the author (p 10).

198 Kittredge, George Lyman. 'Chaucer and Maximianus.' *AJP* 9(1888), 84-5.

The striking similarity of *PardT* lines 728-38 and the first elegy of Maximianus (1:221-36), including the details of the Old Man knocking the ground with his staff and appealing to Mother Earth, suggests Chaucer had likely read Maximianus and imitated him consciously or unconsciously. See **200, 212**.

199 Kittredge, George Lyman. 'Coryat and The Pardoner's Tale.' *MLN* 15(1900), 193-4.

Kittredge locates a legend similar to the plot of *PardT* in Coryat's *Crudities* (1611) and notes that a 1645 diary identifies the legend with the porphyry figures at the corner of the Treasury of St. Mark in Venice. In this analogue, four brothers who plot two against two to secure riches die by poisoning.

200 Canby, Henry Seidel. 'Some Comments on the Sources of Chaucer's "Pardoner's Tale".' *MP* 2(1904-5), 477-87.

Two essentials, the virtuous man who warns, and the group of characters who carry through the poisoning, remain surprisingly constant in the core plot that is behind the *PardT*. Though Canby notes many eastern versions, he traces only 'heirs in the European line' (p 478): two versions of a Persian story from a twelfth century poem of Feridu-'d-Din 'Attar'; the Arabic analogues; *Cento Novelle Antiche* (Gualteruzzi); *Cento novelle antiche* (Borghini); and material worked into the latter portion of an Italian miracle play *Rappresentazione di Sant' Antonio*.

Chaucer inserted an introduction (lines 463-82) and a didactic digression before meeting with the Old Man (possibly influenced by the legend of the Wandering Jew but based on the account of the hermit in the Italian precedents) (cf **12**). Though the immediate source of the story of the three rioters who meet death is not identified, it is probable that an Italian story was Chaucer's immediate source. Next to Chaucer's version, Kipling's telling of the story is the best. See **261**.

201 Hart, Walter Morris. '"The Pardoner's Tale" and "Der Dot im Stock".' *MP* 9(1911-12), 17-22.

Resemblances between the work of Chaucer and Hans Sachs have been noted: Sachs drew from sermon-books and German translations of fabliaux. Sach's *Der Dot im Stock*, 1555, is more closely related to *PardT* than either is to the version in *Cento Novelle Antiche*. Sachs and Chaucer may have used a common source, though the story has not been found in any medieval sermon book. The similarities include: the character of an old hermit protesting mistreatment by the youth; gold treasure in a hollow tree; a trio of profane murderers who vow brotherhood and use chance to select one to go to town; the order of the narrative; the explicit moral; and reference to the murderers' sufferings. See **200**.

201a Lowes, John Livingston. 'Illustrations of Chaucer. Drawn Chiefly from Deschamps.' *RomR* 2(1911), 113-28.

A presentation of passages from four *balades* by Mahieu, Arnaud de Corbie, Deschamps, and an anonymous contemporary illustrates that the link between dicing and swearing in *PardT* (lines 651-3, line 656) was customary in its time.

202 Werner, A. 'Chaucer's "Pardoner's Tale": African Analogue.' *N&Q* 4(1911), 82-3.

A Swahili version of the source story of *PardT* is printed in *Kibaraka* [2nd ed. Zanzibar: UMP, 1896. Pp 89] under the title 'The Heaps of Gold.' In substance, this tale is identical to the Persian Version; Persian settlements on the Swahili coast have resulted in Persian traditions being incorporated with Swahili folk-lore. The Swahili version omits the first and second murders recorded in Persian. The immediate source of the Swahili version is unknown. See **133, 233**.

203 Crane, T.F. 'New Analogues of Old Tales.' *MP* 10(1912-3), 301-16.

Crane was the first to draw attention to two exempla in the Klapper collection (numbers 97, 98) and three in British Library mss (Add ms 11872, number 12; Add ms 27336, number 184; ms Harley 3938, number 26). See also **215**.

204 Andrae, August. 'Zu Longfellow's und Chaucer's Tales.' *AnglB* 27(1916), 84-7.

Andrae identifies as a possible analogue of *PardT* a tale told by Weber of three Arabs who feud over treasure and die by poisoning ('Greed,' 1834). He lists variants of the disputed treasure (p 10) and death-by-poisoning (p 5) themes and notes eight relevant märchen.

205 Ayres, Harry Morgan. 'Chaucer and Seneca.' *RomR* 10(1919), 1-15.

In the Middle Ages, reference to Seneca conferred dignity. In addition to other works (*Mel, ParsT, MLT, TC*), the Pardoner's discourse is 'shot through with Senecan thought, assimilated and adapted to the medieval context'(p 6). Parallel passages are given for lines 513-6, and lines 534-48. Chaucer's first hand acquaintance with Senecan thought seems limited to the Epistles.

206 Kuhl, Ernest P. 'Chaucer and The "Fowle Ok".' *MLN* 36(1921), 157-9. Rpt in Ernest P. Kuhl. *Studies in Chaucer and Shakespeare.* Ed. Elizabeth K. Belting. Beloit, Wisconsin: Belting Publications, 1971, pp 50-3.

Previous critics had read the record variously as indicating one, two (**7**), or possibly three (**673**) robberies. The establishment of three robberies testifies to a considerable amount of travelling in the course of Chaucer's duties at the time of composition of the *CT.* See **147, 224.**

207 Wells, Whitney. 'A New Analogue to the *Pardoner's Tale.*' *MLN* 40(1925), 58-9.

Jack London's *Just Meat* offers an 'interesting pejoration of the ancient Oriental theme' (p 58) that is the core of *PardT.* This tale of a diamond merchant concealing a hoard of diamonds from his partner presents resemblances in motive, number of characters, and deaths by violence and poison. Missing are the warning character and deliberate intention in the death of the first character. Since *Just Meat* was published after London's visit to the Orient, it is possible he encountered some form of the legend to which he added such details as the death agonies of the poisoned men.

208 Cowling, George H. *Chaucer.* London: Methuen, 1927.

PardT, Chaucer's 'most dramatic story,' belongs simultaneously 'to no age and to every age' (p 166). Based on an Eastern story, it finds analogues in the tale of the hermit who found treasure (*Cento Novelle Antiche*) and the satire of a begging friar (*Dec*). It is 'a little masterpiece in the grim and gruesome' (p 167).

209 French, Robert Dudley. *A Chaucer Handbook.* New York: F.S. Crofts & Co., 1927/rev 1947. Pp 192-338.

Noting the capacity for variety in the structure of *CT,* French judges futile attempts to determine intended arrangement or unifying motif. Separate essays on the tale discuss sources and analogues, elements of originality, and indications of date of composition. The Pardoner may have been added late with the Reeve, Miller, Manciple, and Summoner to furnish dramatic incident . *PardP* is original with Chaucer though contemporary sources document similar abuses. *PardT,* originally of

Hindoo origin worked its way westward, the closest parallel being an Italian verse in *Cento Novelle Antiche*. No known version incorporates the background of the plague or the figure of the Old Man. Some of the moral reflections of the sermon are taken from *De Contemptu Mundi*; others, echoed in the *ParsT*, are likely drawn from a common Latin treatise. For *PardT*, see **695**.

210   Wells, Whitney. 'An Unnoted Analogue to the *Pardoner's Tale.*' *MP* 25(1927), 163-4.

In his treatise, 'Of Dragons' in *The History of Serpents* (London 1608, pp 153 ff), Topsell interpolates into his translation of Gesner's *Historia animalium* an analogue of *PardT*. Referring to a printed version but relying on oral tradition—Topsell's tale of an old fisherman and two servants who witness an omen, the meteor, *Draco volans*, then draw up a chair of beaten gold in their nets. After murdering the old fisherman, the servants who seek to escape with the chair by sailing to France are themselves slain in an altercation with a man-of-war. The analogue contains resemblances in motive, number of characters, deliberate plotting, inclusion of warring elements, and 'Canby's *x* factor,' (p 164)— insistence on the warning character— in the form of the *Draco volans*. It differs in the honesty of the Old Man, lack of poison, and the external force responsible for the servant's death. See **200**.

10a   Langhans, Victor. 'Chaucer's Angebliche Übersetzung des Traktates *De Contemptu Mundi* von Innocenz III.' *Ang* 52(1928), 325-49.

Langhans treats *PardT* lines 483f, 498f, 505f, 513f, 516f, 521f, 527f, 529f, 534f, 538f, 547f, and 549f. In the course of arguing that in *LGW* lines 412f(ms Gg 4.27)—the alleged translation of *DMC*—are a later interpolation and should be deleted from the Chaucer canon, Langhans notes that in the case of *PardT*, the manuscripts (especially Ellesmere and Hengwrt) give the Latin text of the original in the margin. Langhans, therefore, concludes that Chaucer did not translate *DMC* as a whole even though he used particular portions of it.

211   Thomas, Russell. 'Ecclesiastical Satire in Chaucer and Erasmus.' *MLN* 45(1930), 394-5.

There is an interesting parallel to the Pardoner's description of preaching (lines 329-31, 392-9, 412-9) in Erasmus's *Praise of Folly*. Probably both were describing familiar contemporary characters or drawing upon a common literary source.

212   Bushnell, Nelson Sherwin. 'The Wandering Jew and *The Pardoner's*

Tale.' *SP* 28(1931),450-60.

210a   Though the 'immortal wanderer' first appeared in Buddhist legend (p 452), by the thirteenth century, through accretion (Pindola, St. John, Malchus, Sameri), a single figure known as the Wandering Jew had evolved. The most important characteristics of the Old Man can be found in this figure—his temperament, immortality, rejuvenation, wanderings, and submission to divine command. Two details—including the knocking on the earth—are found in Maximian. Meek and conscious of divine command, the Old Man serves as a foil to the three rioters and accomplishes his work, as 'three erring mortals have been set on the path to ruin' (p 460). See **198, 200, 667, 672.**

212a   Bolduan, Nils W. 'Chaucer and Matters Medical,' *NEJM* 208 (1933), 1365-8.
        Chaucer is 'well fitted to give an account of fourteenth century Medical Art' (p 1366): the reference to Avicenna (lines 889-90) suggests that the Canon was known to intelligent laity; pestilence (lines 675-9) 'probably refers to the Black Death' (1367).

212b   Coffman, George R. 'Old Age from Horace to Chaucer. Some Literary Affinities and Adventures of an Idea.' *Speculum* 9(1934), 249-77.
        The Horatian idea of old age can be traced through Maximian (elegies), Innocent III (*De Contemptu Mundi*), and Vincent of Beauvais (*Doctrinale*). The Reeve's prologue is the final essence of Chaucer's careful reflection and reading on old age. In the *PardT*, the Old Man's speech is adapted from the first elegy of Maximian (cf **198**). Though Chaucer seems to have employed only parts of the elegy, the evidence suggests knowledge of the entirety. *PardT* demonstrates Chaucer's knowledge of *De Contemptu Mundi*, a familiarity established elsewhere as well (*LGW, MLT*). Whether or not Chaucer read Horace, he is the first to give a full artistic integration of the Horatian idea of old age.

213   Bonaschi, Alberto C. *Italian Currents and Curiosities in the English Literature from Chaucer to Shakespeare*. New York: Italian Chamber of Commerce, 1937.
        Text in English and Italian. The 'entire organism' of *CT* is Italian, 'decidedly taken' from *Dec* (p 8). *PardT* is based on Oriental material which had already been published in Italy in *Cento Novelle Antiche* and the *Novelle* by Morlini. Beyond content, Italian precedents provided Chaucer the 'secret of harmonious composition' (p 10).

214   Immaculate, Sister Mary. '"Sixty" as a Conventional Number and

Other Chauceriana.' *MLQ* 2(1941), 59-66.

Section III comments on the reference to *the first table/ Of heigh Goddes heestes honurable* (lines 639-40). Robinson takes the reference to mean the first five commandments but the medieval tradition (Bede, Aelfric, Dan Jon Gaytryge's sermon) considered Exod. XX, 3 the first commandment, Exod. XX, 2 being introductory. Chaucer would have been familiar with the division of three and seven.

214a Johnson, Dudley R. 'Chaucer and the Bible.' Yale University Dissertation, 1941. See also *DAI* 31(1941), 3506A.

Though Chaucer's knowledge of the Bible came to him largely from secondary sources, he used it wisely. For the quotations in *PardT*, Chaucer may have consulted an exemplum book such as the *Summa Praedicantium* of John Bromyard.

215 Tupper, Frederick. 'The Pardoner's Tale.' In *Sources and Analogues of Chaucer's Canterbury Tales*. Ed. W.F. Bryan and Germaine Dempster. London: Routledge & Kegan Paul, 1941; rpt 1958. Pp 415-38.

There are no direct sources but numerous analogues for *PardT*; Tupper excludes Oriental analogues on the basis that all features found there are also found in Western versions. Tupper quotes from the *novella*,— 'Christ and His Disciples,' 'The Hermit, Death, and The Robbers,' 'The Treasure in the Tiber,'—and *exempla*, notably *De tribus sociis*. He provides portions of two plays—the fifteenth-century *Rappresentazione di Sant'Antonio* and the sixteenth-century *Der Dot im Stock* to demonstrate that some details absent in the *novella* and *exempla* are not necessarily original with Chaucer. Subsidiary material is included to provide parallels to the Old Man and the tavern. See also **198, 200, 203, 212, 607, 679, 680, 701, 707.**

216 Krishnamurti, S. 'A Note on "The Pardoner's Tale", Lines 237-9.' *MLR* 39(1944), 398.

Lines 237-9 refer to the manner in which vine-shoots of Spanish vineyards become intermixed with those of French vineyards nearby rather than the deliberate adulteration by vintners (**710**). This interpretation is evident not only from the use of *growing* and *crepeth*, but from the use of *wyn* and *wynes* wherein Chaucer resorts to a pun (wine/vine).

217 Whiting, B.J. 'Some Chaucer Allusions, 1923-1942,' *N&Q* 187(1944), 288-91.

Suggesting that Chaucer allusions in the work of non-academics offer a hint of the effectiveness of Chaucer education, Whiting notes allusions to lines 333-4 in *The Boston Herald* (1 April 1939), p 9 and possibly line 862 in *The New York Post* (12 July 1941), p 12. See also **131**.

218 Braddy, Haldeen. 'Chaucer's Wandering Hermit and Cabeza de Vaca's Report of Bad Thing.' *CaFoQ* 4(1945), 82-3.

As a New World analogue for the Old Man, Braddy suggests the old wanderer, called Bad Thing by the natives of the American Southwest and reported by Cabeza de Vaca. Bad Thing, who was of small stature and indistinct facial features pointed to a rent in the earth as his home.

219 Kirby, Thomas A. '*The Pardoner's Tale* and *The Treasure of the Sierra Madre*.' *MLN* 66(1951), 269-70.

PardT is a late specimen of an ancient and widely spread folktale identified byAntti Aarne in *The Types of Folktale: A Classification and Bibliography*, 1910. Trans Stith-Thompson, 1928; rpt New York: Burt Franklin, 1971. Number 763 appears under the heading *The Treasure Finders Who Murder One Another*. A close modern analogue is found in Bruno Traven's *The Treasure of The Sierra Madre*, published first in German as *Der Schatz der Sierra Madre* (1927) and later in English (1934), and presented as a film (1948).

220 McPeek, James A.S. 'Chaucer and the Goliards.' *Speculum* 26(1951), 332-6.

Description of the abbot in *Magister Golias de quodam abbate*, a prose satire widely circulated in the thirteenth and fourteenth century, furnishes an analogue in substance and form to passages in *PardT* including references to gluttony (i.e., womb/belly as God, spicing of dishes, attempts to turn substance into accidents).

221 Woolf, Henry Bosley. '"The Pardoner's Tale": Another Analogue.' *MLN* 66(1951), 267-9.

Originating in the Orient, the narrative of the treasure that brings death was known on the Continent during the fourteenth, fifteenth and sixteenth centuries in Italian, French, Portuguese and German versions, in Latin even earlier and, in our day, in stories by Rudyard Kipling and Jack London. 'Winter Fishing,' by Robert M. Coates published in *The New Yorker* March 6, 1943, pp 21-5, offers another analogue. 'Winter Fishing' differs from *PardT* in narrative technique, absence of suspense, and the use of two rather than three comrades. It resembles *PardT* in its differentiation of characters and theme; the florins are replaced by life insurance policies, the dagger and wine by ice-axe and shotgun.

222 Friend, Albert C. 'Analogues in Cheriton to the Pardoner and His Sermon.' *JEGP* 53(1954), 383-8.

The sermons and Fables of Master Odo of Cheriton (died 1245-6) contain parallels to material used by Chaucer in *PardT*. Parallels include a reference to the *develes temple* (line 470), gambling, and oaths. In a sermon on the Epistles, Cheriton gives the earliest known version of the story of a preacher who claims to have relics of such power that only women free from adultery may make an offering (cf *PardT* lines 378-84; cf *Der Pfaffe Amîs*; the *Novelle* of Sercambi). In a sermon on the Gospels, Cheriton describes a preacher who passes off animal bones as holy relics (cf Pardoner lines 350-71).

223 Bloomfield, Morton W. 'The Pardons of Pamplona and The Pardoner of Rounceval: *Piers Plowman* B XVII 252 (C XX 218).' *PQ* 35(1956), 60-8.

Bloomfield examines the suggestion that the term Pamplona in *Piers Plowman* line 252 of Passus XVII of the B Text (*'and purchace al the pardoun of Pampiloun and Rome'*), contains an allusion to the Hospital of St. Mary Rounceval, Charing Cross (**314**). The Bishop of Pamplona issued indulgences for the use of the hospital of St. Mary's Rounceval. This hospital figured in a scandal concerning pardons and alms-collecting in 1382 and was notorious as a distributor of pardons as early as 1378. A 1366 entry in the *Chronicon Johannis de Reading* indicates that 'the brethern' of the hospital 'were involved in a charge of forging a bull of excessive indulgence'(p 68). In addition to his pardons from Rome, Chaucer's Pardoner 'probably also had a few from Pamplona in his bag to continue to give offence to good Englishmen and to anyone indeed who had the good of religion at heart'(p 67).

224 Candelaria, Frederick H. 'Chaucer's "Fowle Ok" and *The Pardoner's Tale.*' *MLN* 71(1956), 321-2.

In specifying an oak tree in the *PardT*, Chaucer distinguishes the tale from its analogues. Awe and reverence were accorded the tree from primitive times, an association that underscores the mythical quality of the 'old man' associated with the tree. Literary precedent for specifying the oak may derive from 'Burying Death', a ceremony in which an effigy of Death is buried under an oak (p 321). A more personal precedent may arise from a robbery Chaucer reportedly suffered at the *fowle Ok* in Kent (*Life-Records of Chaucer*) (p 321). Assuming the relevance of this personal incident, the *PardT* can be dated after September 1390 (p 322), a date consistent with the references to *De Contemptu Mundi*. See **147, 206**.

225 Steadman, John M. '"My Modres Gate" and "El Palo del Viejo".' *N&Q* 203(1958), 323.

In the allusion to 'the ground, which is my modres gate,' (line 729), Chaucer was not indebted to *Of Thre Messagers of Death* (**711**). He has fused the staff mentioned in Maximianus (**198, 731**) with the 'palo del viejo' of Spanish proverb, 'El palo del viejo, pestillo de la puerta de muerte' ... 'An old man's staff is the rapper of death's door' (p 323). This passage in *PardT* represents its only known English occurrence.

226 Barakat, Robert A. 'Odin: Old Man of *The Pardoner's Tale*.' *SFQ* 28(1964), 210-5.

PardT, itself based on folklore, employs numerous folk-motifs, including the symbolic personification of Death in the figure of the Old Man. Sir James Frazer cites a Silesian Spring ceremony where Death is buried under an oak. Odin (Woden) appears to be the prototype of the Old Man: both are weary wanderers, bearing staffs and longing for death. Further, Odin's mother is identified in one myth as Jorth, 'our mother Earth,' thereby establishing a significant parallel with *Leeve mooder, leet me in* (line 731).

227 Lewis, Robert E. 'Chaucer and Pope Innocent III's *De Miseria Humane Conditionis*.' University of Pennsylvania Dissertation, 1964. Director: Robert A. Pratt. See also *DAI*, 25(1964), 7246-7.

Seeking to establish a text of *DMC* as close as possible to the one Chaucer would have used, Lewis compares Chaucer's original with relevant passages in *MLT* with *PardT* and glosses from *MLT*. He then classifies and discusses relevant manuscripts to single out a base text. See **244**.

228 Anderson, George K. *The Legend of the Wandering Jew*. Providence: Brown University Press, 1965, 1970.

In an extensive treatment of the legend of the Wandering Jew, Anderson notes that 'the magnificent passage' (lines 720-38) in *PardT*, 'if valid,' marks a departure from the existing tradition in introducing the lament of the Old Man seeking someone with whom to exchange his fate (p 31). In this detail, as well as in the 'romantic attachments' of character (e.g., the frail aged form, piercing look, and pale withered countenance), Chaucer transmutes the existing legend to complete a prophetic portrait of the Wandering Jew of four or five hundred years later. Echoes of Chaucer's portrait in *PardT* are found in nineteenth century German writers Christian Friedrich Daniel Schubart (p 172), A.W. Schegel (p 191), and Nikolaus Lenau (p 220).

229 Barakat, Robert A. 'Chaucer's *Old Man* in the Americas.' *WF* 24(1965), 33-4.

Two analogues establish the Old Man as a symbol of death in the Americas. Both Cosa Mala in the American Southwest (**218**) and Juan No in Guatamala wear a white cloak, carry a staff, and represent Death.

230 Fleming, John V. 'Chaucer's Clerk and John of Salisbury.' *ELN* 2(1965), 5-6.

The possibility that Chaucer consciously echoed the *Policraticus* of John of Salisbury in his description of the Clerk (*GP* line 308) gains support from the fact that he drew freely on it in *PardT*.

231 Grennen, Joseph E. '"Sampsoun" in The Canterbury Tales: Chaucer Adapting a Source.' *NM* 67(1966), 117-22.

Chapter 89 of the book written by Geoffroy de la Tour-Landry for the edification of his daughters presents a description of a wine-bibber which is closely analogous to the 'tavern haunting tosspot' in *PardT* (p 117). Though the Pardoner attributes the sentiment of lines 549-61 to *Sampsoun* and la Tour-Landry attributes it to Solomon, it is likely that Chaucer drew on La Tour-Landry because the chapter is devoted to a story of Samson with a side reference to a monk sinning through gluttony. *Sampsoun* neither fits the demands of onomatopoeia (Skeat's explanation, **7**), nor the Pardoner's case; if Chaucer was using Samson as a symbol of temperance, the drunk's repetition would be facetious humor. The Monk shows Chaucer adapting the same source to a different occasion (B^2 3141-43); there, the theme is the necessity of keeping 'conseil' (p 121).

232 Pratt, Robert A. 'Chaucer and the Hand that Fed Him.' *Speculum* 41(1966), 619-42.

Chaucer may have been less familiar than previously thought with Seneca, John of Salisbury and the Vulgate Bible. He drew 'raw materials for some of his brilliant passages of characterization, drama, and satire' (p 619) from a preaching compendium. Comparison of passages from John of Wales' *Communiloquium sive summa collationum* show resemblances with the opening description of the rioters (lines 467-9), comments on *glotonye*, particularly *dronkenesse*, and the preaching against *hasardrye* (lines 591-602). *PardT* satirizes the idea of the compendium as the Pardoner boasts that he *saffrons* his *predicaciouns*. Recognizing the familiarity of Chaucer's audience with sermons based on popular preaching manuals provides a context to Chaucer's use of such material. See also **260**.

233 Hamer, Douglas. '"The Pardoner's Tale": A West-African Analogue.' *N&Q* 214(1969), 335-6.

An analogue of *PardT*, probably of Islamic origin and recorded as a version of the Peul, is published in a French translation by Count Aime Olivier de Sandeval in *De l'Atlantique au Niger par le Foutal-Djallon, Carnets de Voyage* (Paris, 1882,1893). Rpt R. Basset, *Contes Populaires d'Afrique* (Paris, 1903). The terminal moralizing, an expanded element, is Moslem. The Old Man differs from the Old Man in *PardT*. See **202, 236**.

234 Gafford, Charlotte K. 'Chaucer's Pardoner and Haze Motes of Georgia.' *Essays in Honor of Richebourg Gaillard McWilliams*. Ed. Howard Creed. Birmingham-Southern College Bulletin 63:2(1970), 9-12.

The Pardoner, like Haze Motes the tragic hero of Flannery O'Connor's *Wise Blood* (1952), is often reviled as 'socially tacky' and 'intellectually underprivileged' (p 9). Both false prophets and spiritual wanderers, they come to a point of redemption. The Old Man 'perhaps the Pardoner's alter-ego' (p 11) is a tragic symbol of the unredeemed. The Pardoner precedes his tale with a public confession, then as Chaucer 'siezes the moment of intensest self-revelation'(**681**), articulates 'a major Mystery' (p 11) with the closing benediction (lines 916-8). For Pardoner, see **389**.

235 Bryant, James C. '*The Pardoner and the Friar* as Reformation Polemic.' *RenP* 71(1971), 17-24.

Pardoner in Heywood's *The Pardoner and the Friar* is reminiscent of Chaucer's Pardoner in showing false relics and rascality.

236 Walker, Warren S. 'Chaucer's "Pardoner's Tale": More African Analogues.' *N&Q* 217(1972), 444-5.

Walker cites three African analogues to *PardT*: a Nupe variant from Western Sudan and a Fulbe or Fulah version from the Upper Niger both included in Antii Aarne and Stith Thompson, *The Types of the Folktale* (Helsinki, 1961); and a Yoruba version cited by Barbara K. and Warren S. Walker, *Nigerian Folk Tales* (New Brunswick, 1961).

See also **202**, **233**.

237 Halaby, Raouf J. 'Arabic Influences on Chaucer: Speculative Essays on a Study of a Literary Relationship.' *DAI* 34(1974), 5911-2A. East Texas State University Dissertation, 1973. Director: Lawrence F. McNamee.

Halaby supports his contention that a literary relationship existed between British and Arabic cultures and that Chaucer borrowed ideas from the Arabs by citing analogues to *PardT* in Ibn al-Maqaffa's 'The Exemplum of the Shrew and the Ignoramus,' 'The Exemplum of the Discoverer of the Treasure' and two other Arabian tales [not seen].

238 Manzalaoui, Mahmoud. 'Chaucer and Science.' In *Geoffrey Chaucer*, Ed. Derek Brewer. Cambridge: D.S. Brewer, 1974. Republished as *Writers and Their Background: Geoffrey Chaucer*. London: Bell, 1974; Athens, Ohio: Ohio University Press, 1975; 1990. Pp 224-61.

The youngest rioter consults an apothecary for rat-poison (lines 852-67) and 'Ibn Sina's *Kitàb al-Qànùn* is cited (lines 889-94) for case-histories which might equal in horror the death of the men on whom the poison was actually used' (p 251).

239 Ginsberg, Warren. '"*Le Grant Translateur*": Chaucer and his Sources.' *DAI* 36(1975), 2843-4A.

Lacking a primary source for the Pardoner's confession, the treatment of avarice in preaching manuals suggests a method of inquiry. Study of *PardT* and rhyme-royal tales demonstrates Chaucer's combination of observation from life with that from literature. [Not seen.]

240 Dias-Ferreira, Julia. 'Another Portuguese Analogue of Chaucer's *Pardoner's Tale*.' *ChauR* 11(1977), 258-60.

The Portuguese analogue collected by W.A. Clouston differs slightly from *PardT* in aim. An additional and closer analogue was recorded in Alentejo, included in the work of J. Leite Vasconcellos, and first published in 1963. This folktale which includes several elements of one of the closest analogues, Christ and His Disciples, and maintains a warning of death merits inclusion in an updated volume of sources and analogues.

241 McGrady, Donald. 'Chaucer and the *Decameron* Reconsidered.' *ChauR* 12(1977), 1-26.

Urging a reconsideration of the viewpoint that Chaucer had no acquaintance with *Dec*, Chaucer notes traces of 'about a dozen *Decameron* stories' in addition to the apology to the reader and details of the cornice (p 15).

242 McKenna, Conan. 'The Irish Analogues to Chaucer's *Pardoner's Tale.' Béaloideas* 45-47(1977-9), 63-77.

McKenna presents three hitherto ignored Irish analogues of *PardT* to suggest the possibility of crossfertilization between folklore and medieval literature. These variants suggest wide distribution of a preceding oral variant which might have been known to Chaucer. *PardT* incorporates elements of oral form (e.g., rapidity of narration, lack of proper names). The technique of *PardT* resembles the Irish '*scanchai*' more than the exemplum.

243 Fox, Alistair. 'Thomas More's *Dialogue* and the *Book of the Tales of Caunterbury*: "Good Mother Wit" and Creative Imitation.' In *Familiar Colloquy: Essays Presented to Arthur Edward Barker*. Ed. Patricia Bruckmann. Ontario: Oberon Press, 1978.

More's understanding of the 'necessary instrumentality of reason' (p 15) in *Dialogue* (1529) leads him to defend the liberal arts in general and poetry in particular. Among the allusions to *CT* are references to *ClT, SqT, ShT, RvT,* and *PardP*. He explicitly refers to *PardP* (C 350-1): For *what reuerent honor is ther daili done vnder the name and oppinion of a saintes relike, to some olde rotten bone that was happely some time as Chaucer saith a bone of some holy Jewes shepe* (139, F-G; cited p 19-20). More's use of ironic overtones and the absence of echo in the standard compilation of proverbs suggest he worked from direct knowledge of Chaucer's text.

244 Lewis, Robert E. ed. *Lotario Dei Segni (Pope Innocent III). De Miseria Condicionis Humane*. The Chaucer Library. Athens: University of Georgia, 1978.

Unlike the Man of Law's Prologue and *MLT*, the main occasion of indebtedness to *DMC* where he translates fairly literally and follows Lotario's order, in *PardT*, Chaucer introduces material from four consecutive chapters (Book II, chapters 17-20), paraphrasing, condensing and altering the order to suit his artistic purposes (p 8). A listing of all possible parallels (pp 8-11) shows many of the ideas medieval commonplaces. While it is impossible to determine that these passages (lines 467-9, 481-2, 483-4, 485-7, 505-7, 488-91, 513-6, 521-3, 517-20, 534-6, 537-46, 547-8, 549-50, 551-2, 560-1, 583-7) did not arise from others sources (e.g., St. Jerome's *Epistola Adversus Jovinianum* or the Vulgate), it is 'striking' (p 11) that the ideas can be found in four consecutive chapters and could all have been written on a one page or one two-page opening. Possible further indebtedness (though the evidence for verbal parallel is not persuasive), may be found in the description of the Old Man (cf. **790**) as well as the allusions to covetousness and the 'three temptations' (p 12). The evidence *PardT* yields for identifying Chaucer's text remains somewhat ambiguous because the translation is not literal. See **227**.

245 Jungman, Robert E. 'The Pardoner's "Confession" and St. Augustine's *De Doctrina Christiana*.' *ChauNewsl* 1(1979), 16-7.

The discrepancy between the highly moral and effectively presented *PardT* and the Pardoner's character, replete with moral flaws, is a striking incongruity. The hypocritical preacher is a late medieval commonplace. F.N. Robinson has noted the parallel to Faux Semblant (**71**). Jungman notes a discussion of an immoral man preaching morality in Augustine's *De Doctrina Christiana* (Book IV, xxvii, 59) which provides, if not an outright source, at least a significant *glose* of the Pardoner's *confession*.

246 Blake, N.F., ed. *The Canterbury Tales*. 1980. See **108**.

Of the many analogues to *PardT*, none is likely Chaucer's source. Much of the moralizing is drawn from Innocent III *De Contemptu Mundi* and from *ParsT* or its source. With the exception of the narrative opening, *PardT* is arranged as 'a typical medieval sermon' (p 442).

247 Diekstra, Frans. 'Chaucer's Way with His Sources: Accident into Substance and Substance into Accident.' *ES* 62(1981a), 215-36.

In *PardT*, the traditional folktale of the hermit and Death is embellished with a frame, digressive ornament imitating pulpit rhetoric, expansions to the themes of death and cupidity, and the conceit of dealing death to Death. Chaucer's use of different contexts encourages different interpretations of otherwise similar rhetorical elements.

248 Purdy, Dwight H. 'Paul and The Pardoner in Conrad's *Victory*.' *TSLL* 23(1981), 197-213.

Conrad's allusion to Paul and the Pardoner in *Victory* indicates the title is 'savage parody' (p 207). Echoes of *PardT* include the characters of Mr. Jones and his two henchmen as shadows of the rioters, their being duped by a tale of hidden treasure, and the double cross leading to death. The resemblances between Mr. Jones and the Pardoner, including sexual anomaly mirroring spiritual malaise, suggest that Conrad knew Chaucer's version of the tale. The Pardoner is a more profound creation: in *CT* forgiveness is possible; Conrad's world is spiritually sterile.

Allusions to Paul provide another link. The rioters unwittingly allude to 1 Cor. with *Deeth shal be deed, if that they may hym hente!* (line 710). Paul's text, the core of *Victory*, functions as mocking echo. In the note to the first edition suggesting a positive connotation to the title, Conrad resembles the Pardoner feigning confessional openness to deceive. See **983**.

249 Williams, Frederick G. 'Chaucer's "The Pardoner's Tale" and "The Tale of the Four Thieves" From Portugal's *Orto do Esposo* Compared.' *BEPIF* 44-5(1983-85), 93-109.

The manuscript of *Orto do Esposo*, unpublished until the twentieth century, is credited to Fr. Hermenegildo de Tancos, a Portuguese contemporary of Chaucer, and contains an exemplum similar to *PardT*. Two references in *PardT* to the wine of Spain reflect Chaucer's familiarity with the peninsula. The literary interest of the Portuguese royal house together with the interaction between England and Portugal make the existence of *PardT* in Portugal 'highly probable' (p 101). Set in Rome, *Orto do Esposo*, is a tale of four thieves who, finding treasure in a tomb, send one of their number to town for food while they await nightfall. Greed leads the three to plan the death of the fourth; he, likewise, plans the poisoning of the three. Similarities between the Italian novelle 82 in Borghini's *Libre di novelle e di bel parlar gentile* and *PardT* suggest that either the novelle is Chaucer's source or each derives from a common source. The source of *Orto do Esposo*, a unique Portuguese variant remains unknown.

250 York, Lorraine M. '"River Two Blind Jacks": Dave Godfrey's Chaucerian Allegory.' *SCL* 9(1984), 206-13.

Dave Godfrey employs the structural elements, methods of narration, and motifs of *PardT* in 'River Two Blind Jacks' [originally published *Tamarack Review* 19 (1961)], an allegory of the contemporary Canadian political scene. Like *PardT*, Godfrey's story is framed by a description of the storytelling process and tells of a deadly feud; unlike *PardT*, Godfrey's narrator is a positive touchstone in relation to his tale as he represents cultural multiplicity in an allegory of national confusion. Names are allegorical: the narrator's grandfather has sought Henri la Mort (death), and loggers Reginald Cocteau (knife/curse) and Albert Godspeed (cooperation) compete. Both works employ motifs of drink, gambling, cursing, unwitting discovery of death, gold placed in specific relation to a tree, the earth as a pit, and man reduced to an animal state.

PardT ends with order superimposed on tension; Godfrey's political allegory ends with social tension unresolved. The Pardoner tells his story to extort money from a *lewed* audience; Godfrey reshapes his story to give sight to 'a culturally blind people'(p 213).

251 Braswell, Mary Flowers. '"Pardners Alike": William Faulkner's Use of The Pardoner's Tale?' *ELN* 23(1985), 66-70.

[Listed as 'Madness, Mayhem, and the Search for Gold: William Faulkner's Use of the Pardoner's Tale' on journal cover and some bibliographies.]

The similarities in theme and plot between William Faulkner's 'Lizards in Jamshyd's Courtyard' (1932) and *PardT* are enough to suggest that Faulkner 'adjusted his myth of Yoknapatawpha County to accommodate the old tale' (p 70). The treasure seekers in both are aided by a guide notable for his age, madness, sermonizing, and freedom from materialism. Additionally, both tales are framed with a sinister, greedy character: the Pardoner and Flem Snopes. In accordance with the conventions of the Middle Ages, the Pardoner is punished by the 'humiliating diatribe' of the Host (p 69); whereas, Flem Snopes devastates his victims and proceeds victorious. When Faulkner adapted this story in *The Hamlet*, he moved away from *PardT* reducing some of the mystique of character and the irony deriving from the theme of partnership.

252 Harrow, Kenneth. 'The Money Order: False Treasure of True Benefice.' In *Interdisciplinary Dimensions of African Literature.* Anyidoho, Kofi; Abioseh M. Porter; Daniel Racine; Janice Spleth. Washington: Three Continents Press, 1985. Pp 75-87.

A comparative analysis of the structure of *Le Mandat*, one of the most successful novels of Sembène Ousmane shows how he hopes 'to lead his audience to a greater degree of social consciousness, thus joining his efforts to those classical models of reform in the past' (p 75). *Le Mandat* has the form of a folk tale in which the arrival of unexpected wealth creates problems. Chaucer's *PardT* is, perhaps, the best example of this kind of parable. The greed of the three 'layabouts'(p 75) is the cause of their demise, the gold merely acting as a catalyst. In the irony of rushing towards that which destroys them we may see a similarity to Medea, where the beauty of the princess attracts the deadly adornment sent by Medea. In Chaucer's tale the moral is religious rather than social. The tale is like a fable taking place in mythic time and space. In

Sembene's *Le Mandat*, the money order is a false treasure bringing misery and setting in motion a series of steps that reveals the flaws of the Dieng family.

253 Morris, Lynn King. *Chaucer Source and Analogue Criticism: A Cross-Referenced Guide*. 1985. See **169**.

In an identification of sources and analogues through 1981, Morris notes 22 entries for *PardP*. Includes 22 entries for *PardP* (pp 155-6) and 151 entries for *PardT* (pp 156-9).

254 Rudat, Wolfgang E.H. 'Jake Barnes, Chaucer's Pardoner, and the Restaurant Scene in Ernest Hemingway's *The Sun Also Rises*.' *Cithara* 26(1987), 48-55.

If the restaurant and taxi ride scene towards the end of *The Sun Also Rises* are informed by allusion to *PardT*, Hemingway is voicing hope rather than disillusionment. The Pardoner and Jake, both sexually disabled, substitute a sense of power and appetite for food and drink for sexual satisfaction. The Host psychologically castrates the Pardoner as Brett does Jake with the masculine aggressiveness of her language. The Pardoner's silent shock is matched by Jake's pointedly feminine rejoinder, 'Yes ... Isn't it pretty to think so?' (p 49). The Host reacts vehemently to the Pardoner's solicitation because he recognizes the causal relation between the Pardoner's sexual anomaly and his selling false relics. Recognizing that the Host has 'psyched him out', the Pardoner 'grasps the truth about himself' (p 51). Once the Host sees the Pardoner's self-recognition, he moves to a conciliatory tone. The Knight, recognizing the psychological situation of the Pardoner and Host, calls for 'a redemptive kiss, a kiss which confirms the Pardoner's part in the Father's creation and the Son's redemption' (p 51). The allusive operation of *PardT*, if indeed it operates as speculated, imbues the last two pages of *The Sun Also Rises* with 'a heroic stature' (p 53).

255 Boitani, Piero. 'The Old Man and the Earth: Alterity and Otherness of a Medieval Story,' In *The Tragic and the Sublime in Medieval Literature*. Cambridge: Cambridge University Press, 1989. Pp 1-19.

In an examination of the mental and representational differences between modern and medieval attitudes towards death, Boitani contrasts the Old Man in *PardT* with Santiago in Hemingway's *The Old Man and The Sea*. The episode of the Old Man is a parable within a parable. The Old Man is 'culturally stratified,' (p 10) half Biblical and half Christian. '[A]n image powefully created through concretions,' the Old

Man 'represents the borderland, the *limen* or threshold where division is oneness, and his uncanniness is therefore supremely, "sublimely" tragic'(p 19). See also **86, 731, 747, 991, 1024**.

- Review by Ronald B. Herzman *SAC* 13(1991), 165-8: The more rigorous analyses of medieval poems are generally more illuminating than the discussions of modern examples. 'I found his discussion of Apoc 9:6 as a source for the Old Man to be genuinely illuminating; the extended reference to Hemingway's Old Man from *The Old Man and the Sea* I did not' (p 167).

256 Wenzel, Siegfried. 'Chaucer's Pardoner and His Relics.' *SAC* 1989. Countering the view that the combination of a pardoner with the display of false relics had few parallels beyond *CT* (**314, 403**), Wenzel presents two hitherto unnoticed pieces of evidence. *Fasciculus morum*, a Latin handbook for preachers written in the early fourteenth century by an anonymous Franciscan, combines the figure of a pardoner with the display of false relics in a simile. A thirteenth-century collection of exempla made by a Dominican friar in Cambridge links a pardoner with the display of relics (not false) in a story dating to Jordan of Saxony (d 1237). Taken together with Canon number 62 of the Fourth Lateran Council which juxtaposed legislation concerning relics and pardoners (it was divided when it entered the Decretals of Pope Gregory IX in 1234), and the evidence of a Middle English sermon noted by Owst (**577**, pp 109-10) and a Wycliffite tract, these instances leave no doubt that 'in Chaucer's time, fraudulent pardoners who displayed fake relics were a well-established *topos* and evidently a historical reality'(p 41). For *Interr*, see **526**.

257 Purdon, L.O. 'The Pardoner's Old Man and Leviticus 19.32,' *ELN* 28(1990), 1-5.
Ecclesiasticus 8:7 (rather than 8:6 as identified by **51** and **117**) and Leviticus 19:32 are the source of lines 742-7. By intentionally omitting the penultimate clause, 'and fear the Lord thy God'(Lev. 19:32), the Old Man reveals the degree to which the Pardoner is aware of 'the doctrine of the second death' (p 3). The Old Man is damned and thus constrained from knowing God; 'like "dives" in hell, [he] is ... forever dying "in death"' (p 4).

258 Boocker, David. 'Heywood's Indulgent Pardoner.' *ELN* 29(1991), 21-30.
Heywood's understanding of Chaucer's satire is shown in his use of

the Pardoner of *CT* in both *The Pardoner and the Friar* and *The Four P's* to critique the preacher of indulgences and the corrupt system that supported him.

259 Hamel, Mary, and Charles Merrill. 'The Analogues of the *Pardoner's Tale* and a New African Version.' *ChauR* 26(1991), 175-83.
A previously unrecorded analogue of *PardT* from the Basakata people of Zaire is assessed against a five-type classification scheme. Within that context, the *masapo*, fable, is a unique example of Type 3 analogues in that it presents three companions and identifies treasure as the cause of death; the creation of the treasure by a controlling figure resembles Type 2 analogues. Similarities to *PardT* include the quest originating from the characters' own volition and the temptations of money, sex and power. '[N]o one would suppose that the *masapo* was ... influenced by Chaucer's tale'(p 181).

260 DiMarco, Vincent. 'Chaucer and the Hand that Led Him.'*LeedsSE*, 23 (1992), 105-26.
Di Marco builds on Pratt (**232**) who demonstrated Chaucer's reliance on the *Communiloquium* to argue that, in the case of the homiletic material at the beginning of *PardT* and in the development of the character of the Pardoner, the *Communiloquium* led Chaucer to the primary source in Jerome's Letter 22 to Eustochium. Details that Chaucer could have found in Jerome's letter include: the quotation *vinum, in quo est luxuria* (Eph 5.18); the image of fires of lust (line 482); references to gluttony. Additionally, the character of the Pardoner might have been shaped by an effeminate heterosexual 'parasite-prelate' and a pattern of seduction also included in the Letter 22 (p 118). See **232**.

261 Thum, D. Maureen. 'Frame and Fictive Voice in Chaucer's "The Pardoner's Tale" and Kipling's "The King's Ankus".' *PQ* 71(1992), 261-79.
Chaucer and Kipling offer parallels in their use of the 'treasure finders' motif: both conflate the motif with other motifs to form a new configuration; embed the narrative in a series of frames; and modify it by the commentary of multiple fictive voices. With Chaucer, the motif becomes a vehicle for social, cultural, historical and religious commentary. An examination of Chaucer's technique reveals his narratorial strategies. The Old Man links the tale of the revelers and treasure finders. The Pardoner is shown to be symptomatic of the commodification of spirituality in the late medieval Church.

262   Sheneman, Paul. 'The Tongue as a Sword:Psalms 56 and 63 and the Pardoner.' *ChauR* 27(1993), 396-400.
Sheneman builds on Besserman's recognition of Psalm 139:4 as a source for *PardP* (412-6) and *GP* (A 712-3) (**174**) but differs by suggesting that the tongue (A 712) is figured as a sword rather than a serpent. Evidence is cited from scripture (Psalm 56 and 63), commentaries and proverbs of the period to support a reading of the Pardoner extorting money by slander.

263   Bennett, Helen T. 'Pope Gregory's *Liber Regulae Pastoralis* and Chaucer's *Canterbury Tales.*' *MedPers* 9(1994), 24-40.
Gregory the Great's *Liber Regulae Pastoralis* influenced medieval handbooks of penance. Both the Pardoner's negative qualities as a preacher and his identity as a sinner are exemplified in the *Liber Regulae Pastoralis*; he perverts the rhetorical ideals of the preacher by leading souls astray and, through his avarice, marks himself as a sinner. In the chapter on the type of man unsuited to rule Gregory includes the Pardoner's text: *Radix omnium malorum est cupiditas* (44:1.110).

264   Johnson, James D. 'Identifying Chaucer Allusions 1981-90: An Annotated Bibliography.' *ChauR* 29(1994), 194-203.
Surveying the years 1981-90, Johnson identifies verbal associations between Thomas More's *Book of the Tales of Caunterbury: 'Good Mother Wit' and Creative Imitation* and *PardP* (**243**) and the influence of *PardT* in the quest for Death in *Romeo and Juliet* (**1019**).

264a   Ruud, Jay. 'The *Pardoner's Tale* and the Parody of the Resurrection.' Proceedings of the Third Dakotas Conference on Earlier British Literature (1995) pp 35-44.
The meaning of the Old Man is understood when he is read in the context of action. The rioters' encounter with the Old Man can be seen as a parody of the Resurrection revolving around the question, ''Whom do you seek?'' Similarities are found in a man asking not to be touched, the direction of the seekers to a particular place, and the consequent running of the seekers. Contrasts are found in that Christ rendered death powerless while the rioters seek vainly to kill death; Mary points to the empty tomb as an emblem of eternal life whereas the Old Man points to gold that leads to death. The Old Man can be seen as a parody of Christ the garderner, the risen Christ; the oak tree can be read as a phallic contrast of the yonic empty tomb. The Pardoner's world lacks the regenerative power of grace: *PardT* reflects the avoidance of the

female (contrary to Dinshaw [1117]); through parody Chaucer asserts that the female is necessary for life and rebirth.

The Pardoner Portrait in the *General Prologue*

65 Lounsbury, Thomas R. *Studies in Chaucer: His Life and Writings*, 3 vols. New York: Harper; London: James R. Osgood, McIlvaine, 1891, 1892. Rpt New York: Russell & Russell, 1962.

Despite Chaucer's agreement with Wyclif on some positions, it would be 'a strained inference' (2.467) to judge him a Wycliffite. Chaucer, in commenting on the frauds of pardoners, used only commonplaces. It is wrong to cast Chaucer as a reformer: he is 'first and foremost a man of letters' (2.469). 'There is nothing that escapes his view, but there is likewise nothing that heats his temper' (p 469). Chaucer had a 'sort of liking' for his religious rascals (2.470); the Pardoner he notes, was *in church a noble ecclesiast* (line 708). For *PardP*, see **571**; for *PardT*, see **666**.

66 Ten Brink, Bernhard. *History of English Literature*. Volume 2. Trans. Horace M. Kennedy and William Clarke Robinson. 3 vols. New York: Henry Holt and Co., 1893; London: G. Bell and Sons, 1893-96.

The Pardoner, 'an unmannerly clown' (p 144), appears appropriately in the company of the unclean Summoner. The Pardoner had the greatest attraction after the Wife of Bath for Chaucer's satiric muse. The Physician, a doctor of the body, serves as a foil to the Pardoner, a 'spiritual doctor of miracles' (p 169). For *PardT*, see **667**.

67 Skeat, W[alter]. W. 'The Pardoner.' *The Complete Works*, 1894. Volume 5: 54-7. See **7**.

Skeat refers the reader 'as to the character of the pardoner' to *PardP* 329-462; *Piers Plowman*; David Lindsay's *Satire of the Three Estaits*; Heywood's *Interlude of the 'Four P's,'* 'which includes a shameless plagiarism from Chaucer's Pardoner's Prologue' (p 54); and Jusserand's works which show that 'Chaucer has not in the least exaggerated' (p 55). *Rouncival* refers to the hospital of the Blessed Mary of Rouncyvalle at Charing, a cell to the Priory of Roncevaux in Navarre. In line 672 *to me* rhymes with *Rome*, an indication that *Rome* is dissyllabic and that the final *e* in such words is pronounced. In line 673 *bar to hym a stif burdoun* means 'sang the bass.' The legend of the vernicle was invented to explain the name; Bernice/Veronica was wrongly explained as the meaning *vera icon*. Line 699 refers to a cross set full of 'probably counterfeit' stones (p 56). Silent on line 691. See **73, 762**. For *Phy-PardL*, see **530**; for *PardP*, see **572**; for *PardT*, see **669**.

268 [Beeching, Henry Charles.] 'The Poetry of Chaucer.' In *Conferences on Books and Men*. London: Smith, Elder & Co., 1900. Pp 269-99. Rpt in *Rare Early Essays on Geoffrey Chaucer*. Ed. Carmen Joseph Dello Buono. Darby, Pennsylvania: Norwood Editions, 1981. Pp 155-85.

Chaucer reserves his 'sarcasm' chiefly for the clerical pilgrims (pp 178-9), and 'shows himself a sympathiser with Wyclif' in attacking friars and pardoners (p 178).

269 Koch, John. *The Pardoner's Prologue and Tale*. 1902. See **16**.

The Pardoner is not exaggerated. The signatures on his documents need not be forgeries. Discrepancies in the description of relics in *GP* and *PardP* suggest *PardP* was written later. Koch sees the Pardoner as a figure drawn from life wherein Chaucer ridiculed abuses rather than institutions of the the Church. For *PardT*, see **670**.

270 Root, Robert K[ilburn]. *The Poetry of Chaucer: A Guide to its Study and Appreciation*. Boston and New York: Houghton Mifflin, 1906/rev 1922; rpt 1934. Rpt Gloucester, Massachusetts: Peter Smith, 1950, 1957.

The Pardoner is not self-deceived; 'his hypocrisy is a part of his profession merely, and he is now on vacation' (p 223). For *PardT*, see **671**.

271 Hinckley, Henry Barrett. 'The Prolog.' *Notes on Chaucer: A Commentary on the Prolog and Six Canterbury Tales*. Northhampton, Massachusetts: Nonotuck Press, 1907. Rpt New York: Haskell House, 1964. Pp 1-49.

For the Pardoner's portrait (pp 44-6) Hinckley includes notes on: *Rouncivalle* (suggesting it was one of the British cells of the Priory of Rouncevaux); the Pardoner (a Dominican friar whose crown should be saved); and *from Berwyck to Ware* as an expression for 'in all of Great Britain.' 'Chaucer's pardoner is perfectly true to the facts of history' (p 44). For *Phy-PardL, PardP,* and *PardT,* see **672.**

272 Coulton, G.G. *Chaucer and His England.* London: Methuen, 1908, rpt in several editions through 1968 and with a new bibliography by T.W. Craik in 1963.

The Pardoner and Summoner, 'parasites that crawled on the skirts of the Church and plied under her broad mantle their dubious trade in sacred things' (p 148), lack even the Friar's redeeming features.

273 Kittredge, George Lyman. 'Chaucer's Discussion of Marriage.' *MP* 9(1911-2), 435-67. Rpt in *Chaucer and His Poetry.* Cambridge, Massachusetts: Harvard University Press, 1915. Rpt many times including anniversary edition with Introduction by B.J. Whiting, 1970. Portions rpt in *Discussions of the Canterbury Tales,* ed. Charles A. Owen, Jr. Boston: Heath, 1961; rpt in *Chaucer Criticism: The Canterbury Tales.* Ed. Richard J. Schoeck and Jerome Taylor. Notre Dame and London: University of Notre Dame Press, 1960 through 1978. Pp 130-59; Rpt in *Chaucer: Modern Essays in Criticism.* Ed. Edward Wagenknecht. New York: Oxford University, 1959. Pp 188-215.

In the essay that introduces the critical construct of the 'Marriage Group'(p 467) in *CT,* Kittredge notes that the pilgrims are *dramatis personae* in a 'Human Comedy' (p 435), their stories speeches that illustrate their character and opinions or relationships with other pilgrims. The *gentils* heading off the Pardoner's attempt to tell a ribald tale exemplifies the way in which a tale can be dramatically motivated. The Pardoner, himself a judge of good preaching, manifests the lively interest the pilgrims take in whatever the Wife says.

274 Legouis, Emile. *Geoffrey Chaucer.* Trans L. Lailavoix. New York: Dutton, 1913. Rpt New York: Russell and Russell, 1961. Originally published in French: *Geoffroy Chaucer.* Paris: Bloud, 1910.

Even when Chaucer moralizes, he 'builds up his picture with so many concrete and precise details that he still retains his customary air of a chronicler' (p 156). His delicate shadings e.g., from the 'brutal revelations made by the Pardoner' to the 'imperceptible irony' accompanying the Parson's virtues elude one-sidedness (p 156). For *PardT,* see **696.**

275 Galloway, James. *The Hospital and Chapel of Saint Mary Roncevall; Elenor of Castile, Queen of England and the monuments erected*

in her memory. London: John Bale, Sons & Danielsson, 1914. Galloway aims to fill a historical gap since no collection of records for this medical institution was conducted before 1907. Sections are included on Roncesvalles, the convents of Saint Mary Roncesvalles in Navarre and Saint Mary Roncevall Charing, and a calendar of the Hospital of St. Mary Roncevall, Charing Cross (1229-1552). Illustrations include: landscape showing St. Mary Rouncevall (previous to 1544), Charing and the seal of Saint Mary Roncevall.

276 Young, Karl. 'Chaucer and the Liturgy.' *MLN* 30(1915), 97-9.
The word *storie* (line 709), usually interpreted as *exemplum*, is like the words *lessoun* (i.e., *lectio*) and *offertorie* (ie, *offertorium*) in that it is a liturgical reference (i.e., *historia*). In the liturgical sense, most of the meanings for *historia* imply a series of narratives. The appropriate gloss for the line is: 'He well knew how to read either a single lesson or the whole string of lessons' (p 99). Perhaps the line suggests humor; certainly it indicates Chaucer's acquaintance with liturgiology.

277 Curry, Walter Clyde. 'The Secret of Chaucer's Pardoner.' *JEGP* 18(1919), 593-606. Rpt in *Chaucer and the Mediaeval Sciences.* New York and London: Oxford University Press, 1926; rpt 1942; 2nd ed. (with bibliography), New York: Barnes & Noble, 1960. Pp 54-70 [page numbers 1919; 1960].
The apparent inconsistencies in Chaucer's portrayal of the Pardoner arise from the Pardoner's appearance and the medieval audience's understanding of it. The critics (**273, 573, 679, 680**), have given too little attention to the Pardoner's appearance and the medieval audience's understanding of it. Chaucer's 'selection of both form and feature' (p 594; 56) is influenced by the physiognomies which relate appearance to character (p 595; 57). Polemon and the physiognomists who follow him associate his high thin voice and glaring eyes with shameless impudence, gluttony, and reveling (p 596; 58). Chaucer's Pardoner 'carries upon his body and has stamped upon his mind and character, the marks of what is well known to the medieval physiognomists as a *eunuchus ex nativitate*'(p 597; 59): wide-open glittering eyes, a long neck, a high-pitched voice and a beardless chin.The mind which accompanies his physical misfortune is full of depravity. So close are the parallels between Polemon's description of Favorinus and Chaucer's Pardoner that Chaucer may have known the account or an anonymous version of it. Chaucer is the first to combine 'a complete, psychological study of the

medieval *eunuchus ex nativitate* and a mordant satire on the abuses practiced in the church of his day'(p 601; 64). For *PardT*, see **686**.

278 Westlake, H.F. *The Parish Gilds of Mediaeval England.* London: Society for Promoting Christian Knowledge, 1919.

Traces the contribution of the parochial gilds to the social life of England between the tenth and sixteenth centuries. Chapter IX treats 'A Gild Hospital: Our Lady of Roncesvalles' which came into existence in 1385 and received legal standing ninety years later (pp 92-103). The hospital over which the gild came to preside was founded in the early part of the reign of Henry III as a cell of the mother-house at Roncesvalles in Navarre, a site known for its charity to pilgrims. The gild inherited a pardon connected with feasts of the Blessed Virgin, two or three hundred notices of which were printed and posted or distributed and sold (p 100).

279 Jusserand, J.J. *English Wayfaring Life in the Middle Ages.* Trans. Lucy Toulmin Smith. 2nd ed. London: T. Fisher Unwin, 1920. Rpt 1921, 1925 (3rd ed.), 1929, 1931(London: Ernest Benn), 1950 (4th ed, Benn).

A study of roamers is undertaken in three parts: English Roads, Lay Wayfarers, and Religious Wayfarers. Religious Wayfarers (in chapter 2) treats the role and conduct of pardoners, their reputation, and their relationship to their audience. As the concept of 'indulgence' shifted down from the idea of commutation to a system based on the theory of the treasury, pardoners, or quaestors, were authorized to distribute pardons and receive offerings. The evidence of papal decrees, registers, penitentials and contemporary accounts indicates that the work was lucrative and their conduct often unscrupulous. Despite exposure by critics, the environment of vain belief yielded a ready audience until they were entirely suppresed by the Council of Trent.

280 Brégy, Katherine. 'The Inclusiveness of Chaucer.' *Catholic World* 115(1922), 304-13.

Chaucer's tolerance stops at the cynicism of the Pardoner. [Not seen.]

281 Emerson, Oliver Farrar. 'Some Notes on Chaucer and Some Conjectures.' *PQ* 2(1923), 81-96. Rpt in *Chaucer Essays and Studies: A Selection From the Writings of Oliver Farrar Emerson, 1860-1927.* Cleveland, Ohio: Western Reserve University Press, 1929, and rpt Freeport, New York: Books for Libraries Press, 1970.

Emerson excludes the Pardoner from consideration as one of the Prioress's *preestes thre* noting that he does not belong to 'a typical

Church group' but has returned from Rome to play upon the fears of the pilgrims 'in a manner thoroughly disapproved of by Chaucer' (p 92).

282 Kennard, Joseph Spencer. *The Friar in Fiction, Sincerity in Art and Other Essays*. New York: Brentano's, 1923.

In a treatment of Friars in English fiction, Kennard interprets the Pardoner as a friar and judges Chaucer's treatment of the Friar and Pardoner among the most important before Shakespeare.

283 Thurston, Herbert. 'The Medieval Pardoner.' *Month* 142(1923), 522-32.

Pardoners were not a professional class drawing support from the institution of the Church. For almost three centuries before Luther, strong ecclesiastical censure was directed against the *quaestuarii*. Even the ignorant were not duped: 'An impudent and amusing rogue, like Chaucer's Pardoner, will often coax a coin from the pockets of those who do not in reality take him at all seriously' (p 532).

284 Piper, Edwin Ford. 'The Miniatures of the Ellesmere Chaucer.' *PQ* 3 (1924), 241-56.

The Ellesmere portraits are the work of 'a realist' (p 255); they represent an interpretation based on careful study of the text of *CT*. Piper notes the Pardoner's loose red gown without girdle, blue hose, soft black shoe, and peaked red cap; the 'professional and characteristic tokens'(p 248) of the vernicle, the *male*, and the latten cross set with showy stones; his weak and retreating chin, yellow tresses spread over his shoulders and his pop eyes staring from a beardless countenance. 'His trappings show individuality. The spur-shank is jointed at the heel; the bridle is a simple headstall with a very long checkbar; the saddle is double-rigged without breaststrap or crupper. Apparently black sweat-leathers run down to the stirrup ...The horse's gait is nondescript, its disposition long-suffering ...' (p 248-9).

285 Spurgeon, Caroline F.E. *Five Hundred Years of Chaucer Criticism and Allusion 1357-1900*. Cambridge: Cambridge University Press, 1925. 3 volumes and a Supplement. Rpt New York: Russell and Russell, 1960.

Spurgeon cites a reference from a letter, author unknown, printed in 1687 that confuses the Pardoner with the Friar: Cleveland is described as such a good preacher that he might have 'converted as many Souls as *Chaucer's* Friar with the Shoulder-bone of the lost Sheep' (1645-6,

1. 224) (See **131**). Dickens suggests in a letter to Sir James Emerson Tennent (1866) that Chaucer meant the Pardoner to be 'a humbug' (3: 82) and that Watts may have had Chaucer in mind when he excluded such a man from his hospital at Rochester.

286 Manly, John Matthews. 'The Canterbury Pilgrims, II: The Summoner, The Friar, and The Pardoner.' *Some New Light on Chaucer*. New York: Henry Holt, 1926; rpt 1951. Rpt Gloucester, Massachusetts: Peter Smith, 1959. Pp 102-30.

Since Chaucer was writing for contemporaries thoroughly familiar with abuses in the sale of pardons, and since he often writes ironically, it is quite possible that the Pardoner's pardons were 'as spurious as were his relics'(p 128). Abuses at the house of Rouncivale during the 1380's and 1390's were widely known. Though the fact that the Pardoner preached leads to speculation that he was in holy orders, several other factors suggest that, if in holy orders at all, he 'was certainly in very minor ones'(p 129). 'On the whole, ... the Pardoner, with his long flaxen hair, his new Italian fashions, and his glaring eyes must have been nearly as familiar to Chaucer's readers as was Rouncival itself, which they passed daily as they journeyed between London and Westminster'(p 130). For *PardT*, see **690, 691**.

287 Quiller-Couch, Sir Arthur T. *The Age of Chaucer*. London: J.M. Dent and Sons, 1926; rpt 1931.

This general work celebrates the humanism and distinctive English quality of Chaucer's work through commentary and selections from contemporary records. Quiller-Couch suggests that the modern reader finds greatest difficulty with Chaucer's clerical pilgrims. In the case of the Pardoner, attitudes to the Papacy are relevant. Both because it made a claim to be above the English law and because it extracted revenue, the Papacy was regarded with mistrust. The Pardoner would have typified the 'unbridled greed of lesser officials' (p 123).

288 Tupper, Frederick. *Types of Society in Medieval Literature*. New York: Holt, 1926. Rpt New York: Biblo and Tannen, 1968.

Tupper draws from previous articles (e.g. **678, 679, 680, 684, 685**) to illustrate Chaucer's ironical association of sins and social types. 'Men lived and loved ... and even sinned in accord with codes and catalogues as rigid as they often were wrong' (p 62). *GP* provides '*individualized conventions* of each class of society'(p 16). To the modern, Chaucer is a portrait painter; to the medieval, he is a 'dextrous expositor or generalizer' (p 17). Despite occasional shifts in order, the sequence of the Seven Deadly Sins established by St. Gregory (seventh century) endured: Pride, Envy, Wrath, Sloth, Avarice, Gluttony and Lust. The Seven Deadly Sins were preached four times a year and proved provocative of great literature (Chaucer, Boccaccio, Dante, Gower, Langland and the *Ancrene Riwle*). The Canterbury pilgrims afford several instances of the ironical association of sins and social types as they move simultaneously toward the cathedral and the Parson's sermon. With the Pardoner, 'that precious rascal'(p 94), the clash between percept and practice is clear. For *PardT*, see **693**.

289 Moore, Samuel. 'Chaucer's Pardoner of Rouncival.' *MP* 25(1927-8), 59-66.

From entries in the *Calendar of the Patent Rolls* (1346, 1351, 1397) and the *Papal Registers* (1355, 1357, 1368) which record indulgences granted for the benefit of London hospitals in the fourteenth century, 'it seems clear that a hospital would have been recognized by a contemporary reader of Chaucer's desciption as an entirely appropriate institution for the Pardoner to be connected with' (p 64). The appropriateness of Rouncival may be found in a patent of July 18, 1382 appointing Nicholas Slake, master of the hospital of St. Mary, Rouncesvalles (the mother-house connected to Rouncival in some form until 1432) to arrest 'all persons whom he shall prove to have collected alms in the realm as proctors of the hospital and converted the same to their own use' (p 65). 'It seems highly probable that a contemporary reader would have interpreted Chaucer's reference to Rouncival in this context ... And I find it very difficult to believe that this interpretation would not have been foreseen by Chaucer himself' (p 66). See also **515**.

290 Manly, John Matthews. *The Canterbury Tales*. 1928. See **42**.

In his notes on the Pardoner's portrait (pp 530, 535-7), Manly discounts the notion that the Pardoner is a late addition to *GP*, discusses indulgences, and judges that the Pardoner could have been either a layman or in minor orders. For *PardT*, see **697**; see also **515**.

291 Dieckmann, Emma Pope M. 'The Meaning of Burdoun in Chaucer.' *MP* 26(1929), 279-82.

The usual gloss of *burdoun* or *burdon* (lines 673, 4165), a word which enters English literature with Chaucer, is 'burden of a song' (p 279). The musical terms fa-burden (Eng) and *faux-bourdon* (Fr), describing a style of part-singing which developed during Chaucer's time, suggest not only a definite kind of singing, but also a humming, droning sound. In line 673, the word refers to the 'monotonous and repetitious ground melody' (p 281) of the Summoner's voice.

292 Chesterton, G.K. *Chaucer*. New York: Farrar & Rinehart, 1932. Rpt 1934; new ed. 1948; second ed. 1959; paperbound 1962.

The contempt that 'normal Catholics' felt for the Papacy's efforts to solicit money 'is written in red-hot letters in Chaucer's account of the Pardoner'(p 43). Chaucer was exactly what the venal Pardoner was not—a gentle Pardoner (p 283). In his treatment of the Pardoner, Chaucer shows his ability to make distinctions, to observe from several angles, 'to realize that even an evil has a right to its own place in the hierarchy of evils; to realize ... there are even things more unpardonable than the Pardoner' (p 283). Chaucer's frame renders him more orthodox and more fundamental than Langland.

293 Bolduan, Nils W. 'Chaucer and Matters Medical.' *NEJM* 208(1933), 1365-68.

Chaucer exhibits the fundamental trait of the scientist—accurate observation—in lines 688-91 'almost a classic description of the eunuch' (p 1368).

294 Mohl, Ruth. *The Three Estates in Medieval and Renaissance Literature*. New York: Columbia University Press, 1933; rpt New York: Frederick Ungar, 1962.

Strictly speaking, *GP* is not a piece of estates literature. Chaucer was 'more interested in character than denunciation' (p 102).

295 Robinson, F.N. *The Works of Geoffrey Chaucer*. 1933/1957. Notes drawn from expanded second edition. See **51**, **71**.

After describing the role of pardoners, Robinson suggests Chaucer's Pardoner was at least in minor orders, that he manifested fraudulent behavior, and that his pardons were likely regarded as spurious. Fals-Semblant in *RR* 'doubtless furnished Chaucer with suggestions for the Pardoner's confession' (p 667). For *Phy-PardL*, see **535**; for *PardT*, see **704**.

296 Lowes, John Livingston. *Geoffrey Chaucer: Lectures Delivered in 1932 on the William J. Cooper Foundation in Swarthmore College*. Oxford: Clarendon Press, 1934. Rpt 1944, 1946, 1949, 1961, 1964. American edition, with the title *Geoffrey Chaucer [and the Development of His Genius]*, Boston: Houghton Mifflin, 1934.

Rpt Bloomington, Indiana: Indiana University Press, 1958.
Chapter 6 'The Human Comedy' deems Chaucer's art 'original'and
'startlingly new'(p 164). In his use of 'Dialogue and action, gesture,
costume and scenery, as in real life,' Chaucer 'conceived and exhibited
the Human Comedy' in ways that anticipate Balzac (p 164). For *PardT*,
see **705**.

297 Sedgwick, Henry Dwight. *Dan Chaucer: An Introduction to the Poet,
His Poetry and His Times*. New York: Bobbs-Merrill, 1934.
The Pardoner is 'the Age's Knave' sent for a rod and scourge 'to
divide the classes of men' (p 269). Just back from the Papal Curia, the
Pardoner rides with the Summoner. For *PardP* and *PardT*, see **706**.

298 Brown, Carleton, ed. *Chaucer: The Pardoner's Tale*, 1935. See
55.
The Pardoner, the most contemptible pilgrim, receives unusually extended
treatment, fully half of the lines devoted to personal description. The
agreement between Chaucer's description and the general reputation
of fourteenth-century pardoners cautions against specific identification
(cs **286**). The Pardoner's directions for relics reflect the influence of
medieval folklore. For *PardP*, see **581**; for *PardT*, see **707**.

299 Piper, Edwin Ford. *Canterbury Pilgrims*. Iowa City, Iowa: Clio Press,
1935.
Two poems on the Pardoner are included in this set of poems inspired
by *CT*: one treating his character ('He runs, the spring of action is not
fame,/ But itch for triumph and smart-alec scoff,/ Inordinate desire of
showing-off') (p 45); the other deriving from *PardT*, its sources, themes
and ironic technique (p 46).

300 Patch, Howard Rollin. *On Rereading Chaucer*. Cambridge,
Massachusetts: Harvard University Press, 1939; 4th printing 1967.
CT reflects a 'hearty belief in human nature'(p 253); in the case of the
Pardoner, the exception tests the rule. The Pardoner's is 'a despised
condition'(p 164), his high-pitched voice revealing 'what was the matter
with him' (p 164), his vanities repulsive. His accompaniment of the
Summoner in song is 'the most violent satire in all of Chaucer's poetry'(p
164). Details such as the Pardoner's 'hopeless solitude' and 'succession
of amours' (p 168) reflect 'a perilous, unlovely existence' (p 168). The
Clerk is most like Chaucer but the Clerk 'would have had no patience
for the Pardoner' (p 169). Chaucer loves all his characters except the
Pardoner, 'and even there he concedes as much as he can bear to' (p

256).
301 Loomis, Roger S. 'Was Chaucer a Laodicean?' *Essays and Studies in Honor of Carleton Brown.* [no editor]. New York: New York University Press, 1940. Pp 129-48. Rpt in *Chaucer Criticism: The Canterbury Tales.* Ed. Richard Schoeck and Jerome Taylor. Notre Dame: Notre Dame University Press, 1960, pp 291-310 [cited here]. Chaucer observed 'a politic discretion in his utterances' (p 308) but was not a Laodicean. In *GP*, the scales are weighted in favor of Wyclif and against the class who opposed him. The Pardoner is one of several rascals, one of three who are morally repulsive and one of two who are also physically repulsive. Wycliffite literature assailed the veneration of relics. Far from 'invariably good-humored'(cited p305) or detached, Chaucer, in such passages as the Host's response to the Pardoner, expresses contempt and loathing of the Pardoner. For *PardT*, see **714**.
302 Manly, John Matthews, and Edith Rickert. *The Text of the Canterbury Tales*, 1940. See **58**.
Volume 3 presents text of the Pardoner portrait (pp 29-31) with critical notes; the reading of *murierly* (line 714) is peculiar but attested by manuscript authority. Volume 5 reports manuscript variants (pp 62-6).
303 Sedgewick G.G. 'The Progress of Chaucer's Pardoner 1880-1940.' *MLQ* 1(1940), 431-58. Rpt in *Chaucer Criticism: The Canterbury Tales.* Ed. Richard J. Schoeck and Jerome Taylor. Notre Dame and London: University of Notre Dame Press, 1960 through 1978. Pp 190-220; Rpt in *Chaucer: Modern Essays in Criticism.* Ed. Edward Wagenknecht. New York: Oxford University Press, 1959. Pp 126-58. Sedgewick cautions against Curry's assumption that physiognomical theory would have been widely known (see **277**), remarking, 'I very much doubt that any of the pilgrims (except Chaucer and the Physician) were familiar, or needed to be, with the Physiognomies'(p 435). The combination of pardoner and *eunuchus* in one person is unusual: 'There are good reasons for thinking that, ... Chaucer put traits of some well-known individual or individuals into the Pardoner's complex' (p 436). In his performance, the Pardoner develops every theme announced in *GP*: irreverence, lust, exhibitionism, physical impotency, avarice, skill as a charlatan, and, by association with the Summoner, drinking. For *PardP*, see **585**; for *PardT*, see **716**.
304 Hamilton, Marie P. 'The Credentials of Chaucer's Pardoner.' *JEGP* 40(1941), 48-72.

Most scholarly attention having focused on the Pardoner as exemplar of the abuses of his calling as questor, his clerical status remains unresolved. Some have judged him to be in minor orders (**286, 295, 298**); some presume him a Dominican friar (**271**), others consider him an illiterate layman (**279**). The Pardoner must have been an Augustinian canon. External evidence (including records showing Austin canons rivaling mendicant friars as purveyors of indulgences) together with the internal evidence (the inclusion of the nickname 'John' in some manuscipts, references to the expectation of manual labor, poverty and chastity, as well as reference to the Pardoner's 'prowess' in church delivering the *lessoun* and *storie*) suggest the Pardoner is either a friar or an Austin canon. He represents the hospital of St. Mary Rouncival, a cell of the Augustinian priory of Roncesvalles in Navarre. The connection of the Pardoner with Rouncival explains, in part, the reaction of the gentle folk: the Augustinian hospital of Rouncivale was a 'degenerate foreign priory, bone of contention between alien schismatics and kings' minions'(p 72). The association with Rouncival also heightens the satire; possibly the Pardoner and Summoner are in the same territory. The Pardoner's long hair and lack of tonsure reveal his worldliness and defiance; the references to marriage, his bravado. The ultimate irony lies in the authenticity of the Pardoner's papal licenses and the orthodoxy of his relics (p 71). The importation of papal bulls in England was repeatedly forbidden: '[e]specially in Court circles with which Chaucer was allied, the papal bulls of the Pardoner would have been no recommendation' (p 71).

305 Sleeth, Charles R. 'The Friendship of Chaucer's Summoner and Pardoner.' *MLN* 56(1941), 138.
Chaucer never draws a damaging conclusion that he can trust an intelligent contemporary reader to draw. The pairing of the Summoner and Pardoner takes on significance when seen in the light of a part of the register of John de Grandisson, Bishop of Exeter from 1327-69. The document reveals 'it was sometimes through connivance with the archdeacon's officials'(p 138) that a false pardoner duped the people.

306 Chute, Marchette. *Geoffrey Chaucer of England*. New York: Dutton, 1946; London: Hale, 1951. Rpt London: Souvenir Press, 1977.
Chaucer was incapable of thinking of humans as a class or group; he thought of them as individuals e.g., he thought of 'a pardoner with a love song running through his head and a glassful of *pigges bones* that

he passed off as holy relics'(p 200). Characters that Chaucer had time to develop, like the Pardoner, take on a reality unsurpassed in any writer other than Shakespeare. Chaucer had no moral purpose in introducing the Pardoner; thus, he was 'running directly counter to the whole spirit of his age'(p 257). 'He described the Pardoner merely because the man was like that, which was a Renaissance point of view ...' (p 257). For *PardT*, see **720**.

07 Bowden, Muriel. *A Commentary on the General Prologue to the Canterbury Tales*. 1948. See **140**.

Chaucer's Pardoner is the only fourteenth-century fully developed portrait of an individual *quaestor*; though he may have borrowed from Boccaccio, it is more likely Chaucer painted from life. He stresses the personal nature of the Pardoner's specific relationship with the Summoner. The doubt cast on the Pardoner's virility may be more scornful jest than literal description. Pardoners were generally engaged in the sale of indulgences, the sale of relics, and in preaching (though no pardoner's sermon has been preserved). Though Chaucer expresses disapproval of the sins of pardoners, unlike Wyclif, he is silent about the theory that gave rise to their office. Whether or not the Pardoner comes from St. Mary Roncevall, it is fitting he claims to do so, for his claim removes 'all necessity for polite discretion'(p 286). Flagrant scandals, particularly those arising from the sale of pardons, brought government action against the Order in the latter part of the fourteenth century. In 1387, there was a particularly open scandal regarding the unauthorized sale of pardons by representatives of this convent. 'The Pardoner may properly be shown to be the scoundrel he is: a lying, avaricious, and shameless cheat, hawking his pigs' bones as relics, preaching eloquent sermons only to deceive, and openly singing love-ditties in his girlish voice to a diseased and wicked summoner' (p 286).

08 Brett-James, Norman G. *Introducing Chaucer*. London: George G. Harrap & Co., 1949.

The Pardoner, 'a thorough-going cheat' (p 65), is one of twelve pilgrims attached to religion. The Pardoner, Friar, Monk and Summoner are presented as seemingly typical churchmen. Chaucer has a poor opinion of relics and reproves the Pardoner for his behavior.

09 Coghill, Nevill. *The Poet Chaucer*. London: Oxford University Press, 1949. The Home University Library of Modern Knowledge, 185. General Editors, Gilbert Murray et al. Rpt 1950, 1955, 1960 (with corrections),

1961, 1964. 2nd ed., London and New York: Oxford University Press, 1967. Oxford paperbacks University Series. General Editors, Michael Abercrombie and A.D. Woozley. Parts rpt in *Chaucer and His Contemporaries*. Ed. Helaine Newstead. New York: Fawcett, 1968. Pp 164-73.

Referring to the Pardoner, Friar and Summoner as 'that religious basilisk and those rival caterpillars' (p 159), Coghill notes Chaucer's 'full comedy of hatred' (p 159) is reserved for the Pardoner. In all that he says of the Pardoner, Chaucer shows himself 'the first and subtlest ironist in English' (p 160). Ironically, the Pardoner's statements are true while he supposes them a mockery; his text is as much a figure of his own doom as of the rioters. The Host voiced 'the feelings of all England towards Pardoners in his annihilating retort'(p 162). See **151**.

310 Hulbert, J.R. 'Chaucer's Pilgrims.' *PMLA* 64(1949), 823-8. Rpt in *Chaucer: Modern Essays in Criticism*. Ed. Edward C. Wagenknecht. New York: Oxford University Press, 1959. Pp 23-9.

Chaucer may have given the specific detail of the Pardoner's 'unhappy physical constitution' (p 26) to fix a type portrait as disgusting but we cannot be sure that he was not expecting contemporary readers to recognize a specific individual. The Pardoner's sketch joins sharp satire to individual traits. See **286**.

311 Lumiansky, Robert M. 'A Conjecture Concerning Chaucer's Pardoner.' *TSE* 1(1949), 1-29. Rpt with minor modifications in Lumiansky, R.M. 'The Pardoner.' *Of Sondry Folk: the Dramatic Principle in the Canterbury Tales*. Austin: Texas University Press, 1955. Rpt through 1980. Pp 201-21. [Page numbers from 1949; 1980.]

The Pardoner alone among the pilgrims lacks an obvious reason for making the pilgrimage. Barred, as a eunuch from birth, from normal satisfactions, the Pardoner (like Shakepeare's Edmund in *King Lear*) 'finds his compensation in matching wits with normal folk and coming off best in the encounter' (p 3; 203). Even in the context of abuses, the Pardoner's behavior must have shocked the pilgrims. His joining the Summoner in song together with his fashions can be seen as 'his effort to test the reactions' of the pilgrims (p 5; 205). For *Interr*, see **519**; for *Phy-PardL* see **539**; for *PardP*, see **588**; for *PardT*, see **724**.

312 Lawrence, William Witherle. *Chaucer and the Canterbury Tales*. New York: Columbia University Press, 1950. Rpt 1969.

In *GP* Chaucer does not follow the pattern of estates; his aim is 'an effect of unstudied realism' (p 57). Despite their realism, Chaucer's portraits are not based on actual people (cs **286**). 'Was Chaucer the kind of man to draw malicious portraits under a thin disguise?' (p 50). For *PardT*, see **726**.

313 Hendrickson, D.W. 'The Pardoner's Hair—Abundant or Sparse?' *MLN* 66(1951), 328-9.

Although some Chaucer editors have referred to the Pardoner's hair as abundant, the text indicates that it is sparse. The words *by ounces* (line 677), and *colpons* (line 679), imply that he is spreading it as far as possible; the phrase *his lokkes that he hadde* (line 677) suggests that he had few. Sparseness of hair is consistent with the physiognomists' interpretation of cunning and deceit.

314 Kellogg, Alfred, and Louis A. Haselmayer. 'Chaucer's Satire of the Pardoner.' *PMLA* 66(1951), 251-77. Rpt with slight revisions in Alfred L. Kellog, *Chaucer, Langland, Arthur*. New Brunswick, New Jersey: Rutgers University Press, 1972, pp 212-44. [Page references from 1951.]

The Pardoner is an artistic creation and 'generic figure' (p 272). Chaucer's satire is 'upon those who make the Pardoner possible' (p 276). Detailed historical information and documentation are provided to show Chaucer's Pardoner is representative in attitudes, practices and credentials. The pardoner, or 'questor', had power neither to forgive sin nor to sell indulgences. He could be authorized to enter diocesan churches by the bishop but was forbidden to do more than read his letters and collect contributions. Particular characteristics include his affiliation with Roncesvalles (which provides a particular name for a generic corruption), his false relics ('an abuse so rare that no contemporary manual even discusses it' (p 275), and his 'ironical juxtaposition' (p 274) with the Summoner. '[N]o force contributed more powerfully to [the conclusion that the Church was suspect] than did the existence of the pardoner' (p 276).

315 Malone, Kemp. *Chapters on Chaucer*. Baltimore, Maryland: Johns Hopkins University Press, 1951. Rpt Westport, Connecticut: Greenwood Press, 1979. Portions rpt in *Discussions of the Canterbury Tales*, ed. Charles A. Owen, Jr. Boston: Heath, 1961. Pp 28-32.

GP is composed of two parts: the first comprised of five groups; the second of a single group which includes the Summoner and Pardoner. Though the Pardoner is a misfit, he is a success in his profession; he meets the standard of conduct as Chaucer found it. The Pardoner's profession is 'most contemptible' (p 177); for him and the Friar there is 'no excuse, no saving grace' (p 185). For *PardT*, see **729**. See also **307, 320**.

316 Gerould, Gordon Hall. 'The Vicious Pardoner' and 'The Limitations of Chaucer.' *Chaucerian Essays*. Princeton, New Jersey: Princeton University Press, 1952. Pp 55-71; 94-102.

Chaucer inconsistently portrays the Pardoner as both riding and at an inn. The reference to the Summoner's 'edible buckler' (line 667) prepares for the Pardoner's pause in lines C 321-2. Chaucer was not specific about the Pardoner's sexual abnormality; critical commentary has explored the implications of *geldyng* but not *mare* (p 59). For *PardT*, see **736**. See **450**.

317 Preston, Raymond. *Chaucer*. London and New York: Sheed and Ward, 1952. Rpt New York: Greenwood Press, 1969.

The Pardoner, a *castrato* riding towards Canterbury, is 'the most vigorous son of False-Seeming' (p 229). Dante would probably have placed him in the eighth circle of hell. Chaucer resists Boccaccio's farcical treatment of Fra Cipolla. The fiend in *FrT* resembles the Pardoner.

318 Donaldson, E. Talbot. 'Chaucer the Pilgrim.' *PMLA* 69(1954), 928-36. Rpt in *Chaucer Criticism: The Canterbury Tales*. Ed. Richard J. Schoeck and Jerome Taylor. Notre Dame and London: University of Notre Dame Press, 1960 through 1978, pp 1-13. Rpt in *Discussions of the Canterbury Tales*. Ed. Charles A. Owen, Jr. Boston: D.C. Heath, 1961, pp 18-24 [page numbers from this edition]. Rpt in *Speaking of Chaucer*, ed. Donaldson. London: Athlone Press; New York: Norton, 1970, pp 1-12; and in *Chaucer, The Canterbury Tales: A Casebook*. Ed. J.J. Anderson. London: Macmillan, 1974, pp 93-104.

In an influential essay, Donaldson separates Chaucer's roles as civil servant, pilgrim and poet. Chaucer the poet can speak as moralist defining what ought to be while Chaucer the pilgrim affirms what is; the result is a comic attitude marked by ironical double vision. Chaucer the pilgrim is not constrained in identifying rascality when it appears in a member of the lower classes; fortunately, for his reputation as a judge of character, Chaucer the pilgrim sees through the Pardoner everywhere except in Church where he remains *a noble ecclesiaste* (line 708). Through the *persona* of Chaucer the pilgrim, the poet presents 'a vision of the social world imposed on one of the moral world' (p 23). His is a moral realism more significant than literary realism.

319 Duncan, Edgar Hill. 'Narrator's Points of View in the Portrait-Sketches, Prologue to the *Canterbury Tales*.' In *Essays in Honor of Walter Clyde Curry*. [No editor]. Vanderbilt Studies in the Humanities, 2. Nashville: Vanderbilt University Press, 1954, pp 77-101.

Examines the device of the narrator with free-ranging points of view. Chaucer's originality lay in imposing the convention on 'the chaotic elements of actuality' (p 101). The portraits of the Pardoner, Monk and Franklin are distinctive in that Chaucer sketches them from a wholly limited view, allowing reported conversation to take the place of omniscience. The Pardoner portrait falls into two parts: the first 25 lines from the narrator's point of view; the second 21 lines wherein the narrator reports the Pardoner's boastful talk, a technique which prepares for the subsequent confession.

320 Hoffman, Arthur W. 'Chaucer's Prologue to Pilgrimage: The Two Voices.' *ELH* 21(1954), 1-16. Rpt in *Chaucer: Modern Essays in Criticism*, ed. Edward C. Wagenknecht. London: Oxford University Press, 1959, pp 30-45 [this edition cited]; In *Discussions of the 'Canterbury Tales*,' ed. and introd. Charles A. Owen, Jr. Boston: D.C. Heath, 1961, pp 9-17; In *Chaucer: The Canterbury Tales—A Casebook*, ed. J.J. Anderson. London: Macmillan, 1974, pp 105-20; and in *The Canterbury Tales: Nine Tales and the General Prologue*. Ed. V. A. Kolve and Glending Olson. New York: W.W. Norton, 1989.

The 'double view of pilgrimage' represented by nature and supernature appears in the portraits as 'a range of motivation' (p 33) extending from Knight and Parson on one end to Summoner and Pardoner on the other. The exterior unity achieved by realistic device and broadly symbolic framework of pilgrimage is made stronger by pairings and by the variations on the theme of earthly and celestial love. With the Summoner and the Pardoner, the theme of love appears in 'a sinister and terrible distortion' (p 41). Their song, *Com hider, love, to me!* is both 'a promiscuous and perverted invitation' and, 'a superb dramatic irony' (p 41) acknowledging their need for the love of God. The Pardoner, 'the ostensible instrument of divine mercy and love' (p 42), abrogates powers theologically reserved to God in offering pretended absolution *a culpa* as well as *a poena*. Compared to the Summoner, however, the Pardoner is an attractive figure. Paradoxically, the pair are emissaries of justice and love: their 'radical physical distinctness ... is at this level the definition of the two aspects of supernature'(p 42); divine love is powerful over these debased instruments. Unwittingly and impotently, both Pardoner and Summoner in their appeal for natural love pray for celestial love (p 42). Both the Physician, concerned with natural healing, and the Pardoner, agent of supernatural healing, 'appear under the rubric of "Physician, heal thyself"' (p 44). The Physician is alienated from God; the Pardoner naturally impotent. The Summoner and Pardoner, with their 'appalling personal deficiency' may suggest by contrast 'the summoning and pardoning' ideally associated with Chaucer's pilgrims (p 45).

321   Swart, J. 'The Construction of Chaucer's *General Prologue.' Neophil* 38(1954), 127-36.

In seven groups of pilgrims, Chaucer has systematically 'put the world before us' (p 135). The Reeve, Miller, Summoner, Pardoner, Manciple, and Chaucer himself appear 'as a kind of echo to the guildsmen' (p 129). '[T]hey are all members of a great and irreligious fraternity that includes all those who prey upon their fellow-men' (p 129). The crimes of the Miller, Manciple, Reeve, Summoner and Pardoner 'may be considered successively worse because of the greater importance of the position of trust that each occupies' (p 129-30).

322   Baldwin, Ralph. *The Unity of the Canterbury Tales. Anglistica 5.* Copenhagen: Rosenkilde and Bagger, 1955. General Editors, Torsten Dahl, Kemp Malone, and Geoffrey Tillotson. Excerpts rpt in *Chaucer Criticism: The Canterbury Tales.* Ed. Richard Schoeck and Jerome Taylor. Notre Dame and London: University of Notre Dame Press, 1960; 10th printing 1978, pp 14-51. Pp 54-7 rpt in *Discussions of the 'Canterbury Tales.'* Ed. and introd. Charles A. Owen, Jr. Boston: D.C. Heath, 1961, pp 25-7.

In his discussion of various medieval methods of characterization and the tradition of the estates, Baldwin gives examples from the Pardoner's portrait. A table analyzing *GP* descriptions shows the following entries for the Pardoner: 7 related to *condicioun*, 11 to *whiche*, 4 to *degree*, and 7 to *array.* 'Chaucer's innovation in the *descriptio* was the inorganic, disordered, and inconsequent piling-up of details' (p 48). He employs the *radix* trait to give a quick glimpse of the interior man in line 691. The artistic diffidence suggested by *I trowe* intimates 'the whole nature of the Pardoner and his desperate attempts at social justification'(p 51). Characterization of the Pardoner is continued in the teller-tale relationship. Particularly with the *cherles*, similes are used eg, the

Pardoner's hair was *as yelow as wex* and hung *as dooth a strike of flex* (lines 675-6). Chaucer transfixes 'travel' details to static *'effictiones'* (p 57) so as to broaden and enliven the Pardoner (line 683). These details of travel become metaphors for the pilgrimage itself. For *PardP*, see **593**; for *PardT*, see **746**.

323 Miller, Robert P. 'Chaucer's Pardoner, the Scriptural Eunuch, and the *Pardoner's Tale.*' *Speculum* 30(1955), 180-99. Rpt in *Chaucer Criticism: The Canterbury Tales*. Ed. Richard J. Schoeck and Jerome Taylor. Notre Dame and London: University of Notre Dame Press, 1960; 10th printing 1978. Pp 221-44. Rpt in *Twentieth Century Interpretations of the Pardoner's Tale: A Collection of Critical Essays*. Ed. Dewey R. Faulkner. Englewood Cliffs: Prentice-Hall, 1973. Pp 43-69.

The Pardoner is a false ecclesiatic and presumptuous hypocrite. Augustinian theology provides more than a general climate of ideas for understanding the Pardoner; the Scriptural imagery represents the Pardoner's character and the *moralite* of his sermon. The medieval author built 'the surface or *cortex* of his work in such a way as to indicate some particular *nucleus*, or inner meaning' (p 181). The detail of eunuchry in the *cortex* of the Pardoner's portrait is clarified by Scriptural references to eunuchs (Deut 23:1; Isaiah 56:3-5; Matthew 19:12) and medieval commentaries. The secret eunuchry (**277**) of the Pardoner exposes his spiritual nature. Both Old and New Testament offer precedent for three varieties of eunuchry: eunuchry by birth, by voluntary chastity (*novus homo*), and by the wilful act of cutting oneself off from good works. The Pardoner is best understood as the third, a *eunuchus non Dei*, a sinner who lives the life of the spiritually sterile *vetus homo*. The impenitent Pardoner contrasts with the Parson, who resembles the good eunuch. Though the Pardoner should work to increase virtue, his increase is wholly material. For *PardT*, see **747**. See also **857**.

324 Schaar, Claes. *The Golden Mirror: Studies in Chaucer's Descriptive Technique and Its Literary Background*. Lund: C.W.K. Gleerup, 1955. Skrifter Utgivna av Kungl. Humanistika Vetenskapssamfundet i Lund, 54. Rpt with index, 1967.

Schaar distinguishes nine types of descriptions of character in 'The Portraits'(pp 167-252); the portrait of the Pardoner is marked by 'objective description' (lines 669-90) and 'description of profession' (lines 692-714). Chaucer tends to describe characters associated with nobility, clergy or learning in a more abstract manner; the stress on concrete description in the Pardoner is compatible with the poet's hint at the Pardoner's 'layman character' (p 212). *GP* portraits do not seem modelled on specific originals (p 490). For *PardT*, see **749**.

325 Baum, Paull F. 'Chaucer's Puns.' *PMLA* 71(1956), 225-46.
Noting the meaning of the Summoner singing a strong bass to the Pardoner's treble, Baum goes on to comment on possible associations of *burdoun* (line 673) with *burd*: young woman, *bourd*: jest, and *burdon*: ninny. Added to the Pardoner's being *a geldyng or a mare* (line 691), these possibilities bear out the suggestion that the Summoner and Pardoner were homosexuals and 'point to the obscene pun' (p 232). For *PardP* see **594**; for *PardT* see **751**.

326 Bloomfield, Morton W. 'The Pardons of Pamplona and The Pardoner of Rounceval: *Piers Plowman* B XVII 252 (C XX 218).' *PQ* 35(1956), 60-8.
Bloomfield examines the suggestion that the term Pamplona in *Piers Plowman* line 252 of Passus XVII of the B Text (*and purchace al the pardoun of Pampiloun and Rome*), contains an allusion to the Hospital of St. Mary Rounceval, Charing Cross (**314**). The Bishop of Pamplona issued indulgences for the use of the hospital of St. Mary's Rounceval. This hospital figured in a scandal concerning pardons and alms-collecting in 1382 and was notorious as a distributor of pardons as early as 1378. A 1366 entry in the *Chronica Johannis de Reading* indicates that 'the brethren' of the hospital 'were involved in a charge of forging a bull of excessive indulgence'(p 68). In addition to his pardons from Rome, Chaucer's Pardoner 'probably also had a few from Pamplona in his bag to continue to give offence to Englishmen and to anyone indeed who had the good of religion at heart'(p 67).

327 Coghill, Nevill. *Geoffrey Chaucer*. London: Longmans, Green for the British Council and the National Book League, 1956. Writers and Their Work, 79. Rpt with revised bibliography, 1959, 1962, 1965. Rpt in *British Writers and Their Work* 1. Lincoln, Nebraska: University of Nebraska Press, 1963. Pp 1-68.
Chaucer drew on medical lore as a modern novelist might draw on Freud in his characterization of the Pardoner as a eunuch from birth. For *PardT*, see **752**.

328 Blake, William. 'A Descriptive Catalogue. Number III.' *The*

Complete Writings of William Blake. Ed. Geoffrey Keynes. London: Oxford University Press, 1957; with additions 1966. Pp 566-75.

The descriptive catalogue for the 1809 exhibition of William Blake's water color illustration of the Canterbury pilgrims originates a characterization of the Pardoner oft to be echoed in criticism: 'the Age's Knave, who always commands and domineers over the high and low vulgar. This man is sent in every age for a rod and scourge, and for a blight, for a trial of men, to divide the classes of men; he is in the most holy sanctuary, and he is suffered by Providence for wise ends, and has also his great use, and his grand leading destiny'(p 570). See **163**.

329 Duino, Russell. 'The Tortured Pardoner.' *EJ* 46 (1957), 320-5, 365.

Chaucer may have characterized the Pardoner with sexual abnormality so as to include among his 'gallery of types of human nature ... a man who had found Hell'(p 325). A misfit, the Pardoner employed his superior intelligence to mock others and, in entering the Church, mocked ideals and beliefs. For the Pardoner, as for Lucifer, there is no turning back. For *PardT*, see **753**.

330 Baum, Paull F. 'Chaucer's Puns: A Supplementary List.' *PMLA* 73 (1958), 167-70.

Adds items to **325, 594, 751**. Baum notes Lilian Horstein's suggestion that *Rouncivale* (line 670) conveys a pun (mannish woman/rouncy) that may be accepted by those who believe the Pardoner a homosexual.

331 Christie, Sister Mary Joannes. *The Provenance of Chaucer's Self Portraits: the Pardoner and the Wife of Bath.* Fordham University Dissertation, 1958. Director: Grover J. Cronin.

Discrepancies between details in the Pardoner's portrait and information provided elsewhere may result from the incompleteness of *CT* or audience expectations directed to multiple levels of meaning. Cicero's *De Inventione* supplies the frame for the description of the Pardoner. Among the details recommended by Cicero and included in *GP* portrait are details revealing inner and outer nature, position in society, and manner of life. Five of Cicero's eleven qualities are developed in *GP*, the remaining in *PardP* and *PardT*.

332 Coghill, Nevill and Christopher Tolkien, eds. *Chaucer: The Pardoner's Tale.* 1958. See **74**.

No real rogue appears in Chaucer's writing before *GP* where, towards the end, he presents 'a sudden *crescendo* of crooks'; the Summoner and Pardoner are the worst, 'monsters' both (p 14). Chaucer's deceptive simplicity masks his congruence with the principles of Cicero (*De Inventione*), Matthieu de Vendome and Geoffrey of Vinsauf. Details convey psychological meaning (e.g., sparse hair: effeminacy; hare-eyes:shameless effrontery, libertinism; and goat-voice:lack of manhood). The Pardoner is a gelding. Of possible significance are the details of Rouncivalle (whose alms collectors were known for abuses) and accompaniment of the Summoner (who had jurisdiction over the Pardoner). For *PardP*, see **596**; for *PardT*, see **758**.

333 Donaldson, E. Talbot, ed. *Chaucer's Poetry*. 1958/rev 1975. See **73**. [Page numbers from 1975.]

Like the Summoner, the Pardoner is 'another corrupter of the ecclesiastical system' (p 1059). The commentary covers the workings of indulgences, and the role of and guidelines for pardoners. By the end of the fourteenth century, the term pardoner was synonymous with rogue. It is unclear whether Chaucer's Pardoner represents the hospital of Roncesvalles or is a complete fraud. The depth of his depravity is symbolized by his eunuchry; his desire to conceal this fact 'becomes the means by which the seemingly triumphant evil of one who has set his heart against man and God is rendered impotent' (p 1061). For *PardP*, see **597**; for *PardT*, see **759**.

334 Owen, Charles A., Jr. 'The Development of the *Canterbury Tales*.' *JEGP* 57(1958), 449-76.

Probably Chaucer began *GP* towards 1387 but 'reworked and added to the *Prologue* as his conception of the *Canterbury Tales* evolved' (p 454). Chaucer expanded his plan to four tales per pilgrim with a revision to Fragment A (mostly likely in 1399, 1400). For *Interr*, see **521**; for *PardT*, see **761**.

335 Dent, Anthony. 'Chaucer and the Horse.'*PLPLS-LHS* 9(1959-62), 1-12.

Explains the vocabulary related to horses and provides notes on the horse ridden by the Pardoner in the Ellesmere illustration.

336 Ethel, Garland. 'Chaucer's Worste Shrewe: The Pardoner.' *MLQ* 20(1959), 211-27.

Wrath not covetousness is the Pardoner's prime motivation. The Pardoner's sexuality is the likeliest determiner of his character; his choice was to accept the 'dispensation of Providence' or succumb to 'immortal hate' (p 227) revenging himself on men whose normality he envied. His effort necessitated 'the whole armor of sin.' Chaucer presents him as 'the wretchedest and vilest of the ecclesiatical sinners'(p 227). It is appropriate to use the standards outlined in *Pars T* to assess the morality of the pilgrims; Chaucer's audience would have recognized such Church teaching from various sources. The Pardoner is the worst of the worst: though impenitent corrupt priests, the Monk and Friar do not express 'contemptuous unconcern for consequent spiritual disaster to others' (p 219). The Pardoner evidences all seven sins, Pride appearing in his acts of civil and ecclesiastical inobedience. Lechery is not dependent on capacity as the Parson made clear in discussing senile lust.

337 Woolf, Rosemary. 'Chaucer as Satirist in the General Prologue to *The Canterbury Tales.*' *CritQ* 1(1959), 150-57. Rpt in *Art and Doctrine: Essays on Medieval Literature.* Ed. Heather O'Donoghue. London: Hambledon Press, 1986, pp 77-84.

Woolf explores Chaucer's methods of satire and the degree to which he was influenced by classical satirists. Chaucer's use of the 'I-character' is new in the way it 'pre-supposes' the poet (p 78), the discrepancy between the naive pilgrim and the witty poet providing much of the meaning. Chaucer achieves a two-fold irony: with the naive pilgrim reporting, the impression is created that most of the information derives from the character's own conversation and his response seems a repetition of what he has been told. The acute satire of Chaucer the poet is seen in choice of detail and in the denunciation of evil in the description of the Pardoner. Chaucer 'extends Horation ridicule to the kind of objects satirised in the Juvenalian tradition, and modifies it by the tone of pretended naivete ... almost certainly learnt ... from Ovid' (p 83). Behind the mask of Chaucer the pilgrim is glimpsed the 'truly personal tone of the satirist, which is quite un-medieval' (p 84).

338 Biggins, D. 'Chaucer's General Prologue, A 696-698.' *N&Q* 205 (1960), 93-5.

The *gobet of the seyl* most often interpreted as referring to Matthew 14:29, more often refers to the incident of Jesus 'claiming' Peter as a disciple. *[H]ente* may be a submerged pun: Christ caught Peter as Peter caught fish. Audaciously, the Pardoner asserts the piece of sail derives from the boat Peter had *before* he became a disciple. Heywood's Pardoner continues the satire in claiming he has a box of bees that stung Eve.

339 Birney, Earle. 'Chaucer's "Gentil" Manciple and His "Gentil" Tale.'

NM 61(1960), 257-67.

Chaucer uses the term *A gentil Maunciple* in the way he uses *a gentil Pardoner*; the 'gentility' reflects 'the self-appointed elevation above the workaday world of the successful rascal' (p 261).

340 Bronson, Bertrand H. *In Search of Chaucer*. Toronto: University of Toronto Press, 1960; London: Oxford University Press, 1960. Rpt University of Toronto Press, 1963, 1967.

Though a spirit of good-nature prevails, *CT* as drama proceeds between strangers motivated by antagonisms. So great is the individualization of the pilgrims that one suspects Chaucer knew models. Though the Pardoner travels with the Summoner, he is fundamentally alone. The most outspoken confessions come from such companionless pilgrims. The Pardoner is in professional rivalry with the Friar and Summoner for the Wife of Bath's purse. Possibly, once Chaucer composed *PardT*, in order to demonstrate the hypocrisy detailed in *GP*, he added the solicitation. For *PardT*, see **764**.

341 Dent, Anthony. 'Pictures from Chaucer.' *History Today* 10(August) 1960, 542-53.

The Ellesmere miniatures are contrasted with Pynson's woodcuts (1491 edition) to reflect 'a social and technical revolution' (p 543) in riding and changes in English life between the reigns of Henry IV and Henry VII. The miniature shows the Pardoner's wallet round the horse's neck; a pull on the strap could bring it *in his lappe*. The woodcut shows a more worldly Pardoner carrying a sword and, in place of the wallet, a pedlar's pack carried on the crupper. Dent suggests printers thought kindly of pardoners, the distributors of printed indulgences.

342 Elliott, R.W.V. *Chaucer's Prologue to the Canterbury Tales*. Notes on English Literature Series. Oxford: Blackwell, 1960; New York: Barnes & Noble, 1963.

Even Chaucer is unable to say anything favorable of the last two 'religious' pilgrims; the Pardoner's office lent itself to wholesale abuse. The Pardoner's portrait depends on similes suggesting smoothness and persuasiveness. Chaucer's use of *gentil* (lines 647, 669) conveys contempt.

343 Miller, B.D.H. 'Chaucer's General Prologue, A 673: Further Evidence.' *N&Q* 205(1960), 404-6.

Following on the suggestions of D. Biggins (**338**) and Paull F. Baum (**325**) that *burdoun*, literally 'staff,' carries the figurative sense of 'phallus,' Miller demonstrates that this figurative sense is 'regularly attached' (p 404) to Middle French *bourdon* from which Middle English *burdoun* is derived. *Bourdon*: 'staff' is first recorded in this sense on the allegorical plane in Jean de Meun's continuation of *RR*. Eustache Deschamps' use of the term in a *Ballade* (MCCXXV) and *Le grand Parangon des nouvelles Nouvelles* [sic] indicate that the sense of *bourdon* as 'phallus' was widely current in French.

344 Schoeck, Richard J. and Jerome Taylor, eds. *Chaucer Criticism: The Canterbury Tales* vol 1. Notre Dame: University of Notre Dame, 1960. Includes: E. Talbot Donaldson. 'Chaucer the Pilgrim.' 1-13 (**318**); George Lyman Kittredge. 'Chaucer's Discussion of Marriage.' 130-159 (**273**); G.G. Sedgewick. 'The Progress of Chaucer's Pardoner, 1880-1940.' 190-220 (**716**); Robert P. Miller, 'Chaucer's Pardoner, the Scriptural Eunuch, and the *Pardoner's Tale*.' 221-44 (**747**); John Matthews Manly. 'Chaucer and the Rhetoricians.' 268-90 (**690**).

345 Magoun, Francis P., Jr. *A Chaucer Gazeteer*. Chicago: University of Chicago Press, 1961. See **145**

An alphabetical listing and discussion of all geographical names and names of either geographical origin or geographical connnections, this work conflates, with minor additions, Magoun's articles in *MS* 15(1953); 16(1954); and 17(1955). Note entries for *Rouncivale* (which implies Westminster), *Rome, Berwyk*, and *Ware*. For *PardT*, see **768**.

346 Owen, Charles A. Jr., 'The Twenty-Nine Pilgrims and the Three Priests.' *MLN* 76(1961), 392-7.

The Pardoner is one of a group of pilgrims whose portraits were added after Chaucer's original plan for *GP*. The addition of these portraits demonstrate Chaucer's decision to employ the interaction of tale and teller as an organizing priniciple and his growing interest in the 'lower orders' (p 397).

347 Schaar, Claes. 'A Postscript to Chaucer Studies.' *ES* 42(1961), 153-6. Schaar defends his earlier analysis (**324**) arguing that Chaucer's portraiture of common people is colored by traditional upper class attitudes and that Chaucer is generally regarded as more modern than he was.

348 Schaut, Quentin L, O.S.B. 'Chaucer's Pardoner and Indulgences,' *Greyfriar* (1961), 25-39.

Schaut reviews the historical development of indulgences and their association with pilgrimages, pardoners, hospitals and accusations of abuse. Improbable as Chaucer's Pardoner may seem, 'after examining the contemporary official documents we feel that nothing has been overdrawn' (p 36). Whereas there may be doubt as to his authorization, the authenticity of his documents, and his status (cleric or lay), there is no doubt as to how he carried out his office or the loathing he inspires. Chaucer's Pardoner is not to be assumed typical; he is 'supreme in his kind' fusing 'all the worst characteristics of the class'(p 39).

349   Brooks, Harold F[letcher]. *Chaucer's Pilgrims: The Artistic Order of the Portraits in the Prologue*. London: Methuen; New York: Barnes & Noble, 1962; rpt 1968.

Moving from group to group of pilgrims in *GP*, one moves down either the social or the moral scale. The Pardoner is the 'nadir of the moral scale' and 'zenith of the satiric' (p 56). His impudence and exhibitionism are overcompensations for his unnatural deficiency. The Pardoner, with his sale of indulgences, is a minister of 'a corrupt institution which imperils men's souls' (p 54). The fusion of tale, prologue and situation results in a uniformity of dramatization.

350   Jordan, Robert M. 'Chaucer's Sense of Illusion: Roadside Drama Reconsidered.' *ELH* 29(1962), 19-33.

The fact that the Pardoner is 'characterized' by his statements adds support to the 'dramatic' interpretation of *CT*, a conception based on the framework suggested in *GP* and the interplay among pilgrims in the links (cf. **307, 681, 690, 691**). The conception of 'roadside drama' has encouraged psychological and historical speculation and deterred understanding of Chaucer's sense of illusion. For *PardT*, see **774**.

351   Reidy, John. 'Grouping of Pilgrims in the General Prologue to *The Canterbury Tales*.' *PMASAL* 47(1962), 595-603.

The Pardoner appears with the Reeve, Miller, Summoner, and Manciple, in a 'rogue's gallery' (p 602) united by swindling. The placement of this sixth group, following the Parson and Plowman whose portraits complete the three estates and 'might have been an effective ending' (p 602), is 'a means of controlling the audience's attitude toward it' (p 603). Chaucer's use of the abrupt break before introducing this group, his ironic tone increasingly violent, and his greater use of physiognomical detail underscore the characterization of these pilgrims as parasites on society.

352   Robertson, D.W., Jr. *A Preface to Chaucer: Studies in Medieval Perspectives*. Princeton: Princeton University Press, 1962.

The details of *GP* portraits are arranged as details in Romanesque and Gothic art with a view to developing the idea rather than 'surface reality' (p 248). For *PardT*, see **776**.

353 Nevo, Ruth. 'Chaucer: Motive and Mask in The "General Prologue".' *MLR* 58(1963), 1-9. Excerpts (pp 2-3; 6-9) rpt in *Critics on Chaucer:Readings in Literary Criticism.* Ed. Sheila Sullivan. Coral Gables: University of Miami Press, 1970. Pp 105-10. Rpt in *Geoffrey Chaucer's The General Prologue to the Canterbury Tales.* Ed. Harold Bloom. New York: Chelsea House Publishers, 1988. Pp 9-20.

Economic motivation is both a principle of selection and criterion of moral judgement in *GP* portraits. *GP* presents 'a clear, socio-economic ranking based upon an analysis of the origins of income' (p 6): the feudal aristocracy are followed in turn by members of the propertied religious orders, those of peasant origin, and finally, parasites like the Pardoner who derive their income from graft. The last group 'argue most cogently for Chaucer's economic insight' (p 5). The intensity of irony in the portraits varies with the degree of discrepancy between profession and action. It is 'irony doubly ironic' that Chaucer, the master of ceremonies, appears as an innocent 'in the masquerade' (p 9). Only with the Pardoner does the 'innocent' narrator drop his politeness. 'For the Pardoner stands at the outer pale of Chaucer's tolerance for humanity. He is a concentrate of the maximum rapacity and the maximum hypocrisy' (p 9). *PardT*, with its text, *radix malorum est cupiditas*, is the most powerful of 'moralities'(p 9).

354 Bowden, Muriel. 'The Influence of Chaucer's Religious and PhilosophicWorld.' *A Reader's Guide to Geoffrey Chaucer.* New York: Farrar, Strauss and Giroux, 1964; rpt 1966. Pp 46-93.

At the bottom of the hierarchy of religious pilgrims stand the Pardoner and Summoner 'that pair of arch-rascals ... presumably on ecclesiastical business'(p 47). In addition to distributing pardons, the fourteenth-century pardoner sold relics and preached. The allusion to *Rouncivale* (line 670) may mean the Pardoner is of dubious morals rather than actually from St. Mary Roncevalle which was known for its wealthy prior, a pardoner, and for a scandal in 1387 concerning the sale of pardons. Chaucer portrayed the life of his time: 'No one can believe that Chaucer did not actually know—if only by observation—such a pardoner ... '(p 75). The portrait stresses vices and repellent physical characteristics; the few details of clothing, however, are selected to reinforce the total effect. For *PardT*, see **782**.

355 Howard, Edwin. *Geoffrey Chaucer.* New York: Twayne, 1964.
The Pardoner's portrait is highly individualized. Critics have emphasized the term *geldyng* and overlooked the implications of the term *mare*. For *Interr*, see also **522**; for *PardT*, see **786**. See also **967**.

356 Huppé, Bernard F. *A Reading of the 'Canterbury Tales.'* Albany: State University of New York, 1964.
The Pardoner is 'the central figure in the triptych of ecclesiastical corruption' (p 218); he not only outdoes the Friar and Summoner in evil, he joyfully calls attention to his own sinfulness. The Pardoner's models are Satan and Judas; he is the chief adversary of the Parson. In *GP*, though the portraits appear dramatic, the method is rhetorical. Chaucer foreshadows dramatic possibilities through pairings and contrasts (e.g., Pardoner and Summoner, Pardoner and *gentils*). Apart from 'gossiping curiosity'(p 24) revealed in comments on the Pardoner's appearance, the narrator, who is a friendly reporter but splendidly obtuse, does not otherwise comment on the Pardoner's evil. 'If anything, his tone is one of worldly approval for a successful operator' (p 24). The Pardoner, as one of the last group of pilgrims, may have been added as Chaucer's recognition of the dramatic possibilities of a human comedy evolved. For *PardP*, see **607**; for *PardT*, see **818**.

357 MacLaine, Allan H. 'The Pardoner.' *The Student's Comprehensive Guide To The Canterbury Tales.* Woodbury, New York: Barron's Educational Series, 1964.
The Pardoner's portrait is discussed pp 38-40. For *Phy-PardL*, see **546**; for *PardP*, see **600**; for *PardT*, see **787**.

358 Mitchell, Charles. 'The Worthiness of Chaucer's Knight.' *MLQ* 25(1964), 66-75.
Taking the Pardoner as a touchstone of evil, the Parson of good, Mitchell positions the Knight midway between them.

359 Rowland, Beryl. 'Animal Imagery and the Pardoner's Abnormality.' *Neophil* 48(1964), 56-60.
Rather than describe the Pardoner with scientific or hermeneutical texts in mind (contra **277**, **323**), Chaucer was more likely reflecting traits of some well known person and 'describing an abnormality of which he was actually aware' (p 57). Chaucer may have employed popular animal lore to convey his diagnosis. Sensing that the Pardoner could not function as a man, Chaucer referred to him as a gelding. The references

to hare and goat suggest bi-sexuality. Consistent with the Pardoner's wenching, hare, goat and mare imply lasciviousness. The Pardoner's peculiarities are 'characteristic of the testicular pseudo-hermaphrodite of the feminine type' (p 58). Sexually abnormal, the Pardoner 'shows the typical desire of the deviate to conform to the sex in which he is reared, although physically he may be unable to do so' (p 58). The Pardoner 'stands revealed as an unhappy, frustrated creature, haunted by his own sexual inadequacy, conscious of his separation from normal life' (p 59). Through the Old Man knocking with his staff at his mother's gate, 'he seems to convey the anguished realization of his male impotency'(p 59).

360   Rowland, Beryl. 'Chaucer's Swallow and Dove "Sittynge on a Berne" ("*MilT*", I, 3258, "*Pard Prol*," VI, 397).' *N&Q* 209(1964), 48-9. See **601**.

361   Cameron, Kenneth Walter. *The Pardoner and His Pardons: Indulgences Circulating in England on the Eve of the Reformation With a Historical Introduction*. Hartford: Transcendental Books, 1965. Cameron discusses printed indulgences circulating in England, identification and location of these indulgences, and evidence of the influence on literature of printed indulgences and provides copies of indulgences, an index of names, places and subjects, a copy of the Ellesmere miniature of the Pardoner, and a bibliographical note on Cameron's works. Cameron finds the portrait of the Pardoner in *GP* and his own account in *PardP* 'realistic entertainment' (p 3). Note 15 draws attention to Canon 62 of the Lateran Council which addresses 'the widespread custom of deceiving pilgrims with "faked" relics' (p 10).

362   Courtney, Neil. 'Chaucer's Poetic Vision.' *CR* 8(1965), 129-40. Chaucer's pilgrims impress by their 'wholeness as individuals' (p 134). Hoffman overstates the superiority of the '"ideal" portraits' (p 134); the essentially religious nature of man is best realized in characters most individualized. The view of the Pardoner is informed by a moral sense though obviates moral judgment. The portrait of the Pardoner is marked by vivid physical detail denoting privation and self-ignorance together with 'ironic affirmation'(p 137) of his social and professional virtues. Master of the arts of his profession, the Pardoner is ignorant of its true nature; yet, in this figure, Chaucer's religious sense 'has come most alive to affirm him as an individual' (p 139).

363 Kiehl, James M. 'Dryden's Zimri and Chaucer's Pardoner: A Comparative Study of Verse Portraiture.' *Thoth* 6(1965), 3-12.

Comparison of Chaucer's portrait of the Pardoner, 'a typical portrait' (p 3), with Dryden's portrait of Zimri reveals substantial differences of method and demonstrates the 'excellencies' of Dryden's portrait (p 3). Chaucer follows more closely the 'Theophrastian model'(p 3) and delineates a type by an amusing example. Dryden, who aims at ridicule, begins with a specific individual and reduces him to a mere type. Chaucer makes more use of images, is more casual in tone and verse form, and, though he too 'disvalues' his subject, he engages in 'an almost fond portrayal'(p 11). The Pardoner's portrait employs specific allusions to establish a context while preserving anonymity; the portrait is 'a provocative accumulation of imagery'(p 6); and incongruous diction e.g., *noble ecclesiaste* subverts the apparent rhetoric of praise. The 'attitude' of Chaucer's portrait is one which 'embraces the whole world, even the "worst" of it'(p 12).

364 Loomis, Roger Sherman. 'The Canterbury Pilgrims.' *A Mirror of Chaucer's World.* Princeton: Princeton University Press, 1965.

That the Pardoner (fig 100) struck the Ellesmere artist's imagination is evident from the details in conformity with the text. The wallet has been slung around the horse's neck to avoid cramping the Pardoner's style. A marginal sketch of a priest holding up a pardon with a seal attached (fig 118) is taken from ms Bodleian Library, Douce 104, fol. 44v. *Piers Plowman.* For *Phy-PardL*, see **547**; for *PardT*, see **798**. See also **299**.

365 Ruggiers, Paul G. *The Art of the Canterbury Tales.* Madison and Milwaukee, Wisconsin: University of Wisconsin Press, 1965. Paperback ed, 1967. Pp 121-30.

In *GP* and links we see the pilgrim in terms of dominant passion and implication with the community. Chaucer's characters combine inward and outward, moral and intellectual. For *PardT*, see **800**.

366 Spearing, A.C. *The Pardoner's Prologue and Tale.* 1965. See **86**.

The Pardoner and Summoner make 'a horrifying pair, whose loathsome outward appearance fully expresses their inner corruption' (p 5). The Pardoner, a lay professional, usurps the role of priest adding that of medicine man. Historical records suggest the Pardoner is an astonishingly accurate picture of the fourteenth-century *quaestor*. The Pardoner is a parody not only of fashion but manhood, his interruption of the Wife of Bath 'an ineffective blind' (p 15). For *PardP*, see **603**; for *PardT*, see **801**.

367 Williams, Arnold. 'Some Documents on English Pardoners, 1350-1400.' In *Medieval Studies in Honor of Urban Tigner Holmes, Jr.* Ed. John Mahoney and John Esten Keller. University of North Carolina Studies in the Romance Languages and Literatures, 56. Chapel Hill, North Carolina: University of North Carolina Press, 1965. Pp 197-207. The Pardoner has received attention due 'the most thorough and shameless scoundrel'(p 197) on the pilgrimage. Williams provides documents from episcopal registers to supplement Jusserand (**279**). The documents cover conflicts between friars and *questors* or pardoners, instructions to diocesan priests not to help *questors*, prohibitions against receiving false *questors*, and against confessing to false friars and *questors*, and a pardoner's license for Roncesvalles (see line 670). The attitude Chaucer implies was shared by some members of the hierarchy though the actual number of complaints in the episcopal registers is rather small and all come from two of the seventeen dioceses in England. The picture Chaucer gives of the friar 'is certainly biased'; that of the Pardoner may also be (p 205). Williams' documents distinguish between friars and pardoners but associate them in knavery. Chaucer apparently lumped them together in the cancelled lines of *GP* (252a-b). 'What more natural then than Chaucer's transference' to the Pardoner of St. Jerome's metaphor adduced by Maidstone in defense of mendicant friars? St. Jerome, in his preface to the Book of Job, argues that he ought to devote himself to the imperishable food of eternal life rather than earn bread by weaving baskets or plaiting screens of palm leaves. For *PardP*, see **604**.

368 Winny, James. *The General Prologue to the Canturbury Tales*. Cambridge: Cambridge University Press, 1965. The Pardoner's 'fraudulent vitality' (p 38) demands exposure. His 'gaily animated manliness, added to his sexual impotence' (p 39) arouses Chaucer's scorn. The Pardoner's lack of creative virtue is reflected in his relics. Through his false promises 'he subverts the process of natural life'(p 40). The presence of Pardoner, Reeve and Summoner introduce 'parasitic forms of life' into the company of healthy pilgrims (p 41). For *PardT*, see **805**.

369 King, Ronald. *Geoffrey Chaucer: The Prologue to The Canterbury*

Tales with original screen images designed by Ronald King. Editions Alecto, 1966. Rpt Surrey: Circle Press, 1967; 2nd ed. 1978 [page numbers from 1978].

An original illustration, a 'mask' of the Pardoner is presented as one of fourteen accompanying a Middle English text (origin not noted) of *GP*. The illustration is a blending of symbolism and medieval heraldry, inspired in part by the traditions of African mask. The mask sets out 'to maintain the balance between the real and the transcendent' (p xi). The Pardoner's 'mask' is silver, black, white and purple. A geometric design (suggestive of a game board) of predominantly black, white and silver (with three segments of purple) fills a shape approximately circular; that shape sits at the junction of a cross, two lines black, two purple. The circle and cross sit against a silver background.

370 Rowland, Beryl. 'The Horse and Rider Figure in Chaucer's Works.' *UTQ* 35(1966), 246-59.

Rowland traces the impact of the Christian Church on the symbol of the horse (traditionally understood as an emblem of generative power) whereby the the horse comes to be equated with the body or with Woman and the rider with the soul or Man. In view of the Pardoner's ambivalent sexuality, his offer of insurance against a fall from a horse is particularly ironic.

371 Mitchell, Charles. 'The Moral Superiority of Chaucer's Pardoner.' *CE* 27(1966), 437-44.

The problem of salvation as it involves the distinction between true and false pardon is prominent in *GP*. The Pardoner offers officialized indulgences meant to free the sinner from the burden of penance. The Pardoner chooses his theme to help loosen the purse strings of the avaricious, and so that by preaching against his own evil, he can rise above his own false pardon while others sink deeper into sin. For *PardT*, see **811**.

372 Schweitzer, Edward C., Jr. 'Chaucer's Pardoner and The Hare.' *ELN* 4(1966-67), 247-50.

Because hares were thought to be hermaphroditic or to change their sex, the association of the Pardoner's eyes with those of the hare (line 684) 'anticipates in its implications of sexual abnormality the line, *I trowe he were a geldyng or a mare* (line 691; p 249). The medieval notion of the hare's sexual peculiarities was commonplace. The *Eunuchus* of Terence, a medieval school text presented the sexuality of the hare as 'ambiguous and perverted'(p 247). The encyclopedists, Vincent of Beauvais, Alexander Neckham, and Bartholomeus Anglicus, agree the sex of the hare is ambiguous. In Christian symbolism, the hare could be interpreted both *in malo* and *in bono*. The Pardoner is the prohibited *lepus* of the Pentateuch. Hugh of St. Cher delineates correspondences between the physical characteristics of the hare and the spiritual characteristics of good prelates: the hare, at once male and female, corresponds to the prelate, 'both father and mother to those in his care,' but the Pardoner is 'the inversion of this norm'(p 249). Chaucer may have built on Biblical commentary treating the hare as a figure of the Jews. Like the Jews, the Pardoner rejects Christ. Eyes *glarynge* like a hare (line 684) may refer to 'eyes of a soul spiritually asleep' (p 250).

373 Stewart, Donald C. 'Chaucer's Perplexing Pardoner.' *CEA* 29 (1966), 4-6.

The Pardoner becomes unduly complex when scholars interpret him in the context of 'single integrated schemes' (p 1). Kittredge opened a Pandora's box (**668**); others including Lumiansky (**311**), Kellogg and Haselmayer (**314**), and Bronson (**340**) followed. The Pardoner acts predictably with the exception of the benediction. Speculation on the Pardoner's motives for joining the pilgrimage is vain. The Pardoner's confession is the result of his drunkenness and may also be a convention whereby Chaucer satirizes pardoners (cf **298**). The benediction and solicitation were, like the tale itself, originally intended for the Parson (cf **271**). The tone of the solicitation is jocular; the Pardoner expects the Host to accept his jest. For *PardT*, see **814**.

374 Tuve, Rosemond. *Allegorical Imagery: Some Mediaeval Books and Their Posterity*. 1966. Pp 176-7. Pp 139-58 rpt as 'Memory and Form'. Geoffrey Chaucer's *The General Prologue to the Canterbury Tales*. Ed. and introd. Harold Bloom. New York: Chelsea House Publishers, 1988. Pp 37-50. Pp 78-116 rpt as 'The Idea of *The Canterbury Tales*.' *Modern Critical Views*. Ed. and introd. Harold Bloom. New York: Chelsea House Publishers, 1985, pp 79-104.

In *GP* the ideal portraits end with a general statement; portraits like the Pardoner's end with a particular detail of 'piquant phrase'(p 103) e.g., the Pardoner sings merrily and loud. The concluding detail encapsulates the pilgrim, suggesting 'an inner reality,' a reality of 'character, frame of mind, place in society,' a reality that will dictate 'choice and treatment of tales' (p 103). For *PardP*, see **605**; for *PardT*, see **815**.

375 Hussey, Maurice [compiler]. *Chaucer's World:A Pictorial Companion*. Cambridge: Cambridge University Press, 1967.
The artist of the Ellesmere manuscript has interpreted the Pardoner correctly (p 138). The Pardoner's self-description as a preacher (lines 395-7) is audacious. *PardT* gains significance from the placement of the Pardoner and Summoner at the end of *GP* where thoughts ought to be of 'Judgement, Heaven and Hell' (p 139). Holbein's sequence of the *Dance of Death* (1538) is most appropriate to illustrate *PardT*. Death comes from the coins; the Old Man is 'only a man with an urge to submit himself to the medieval "death-wish"' (p 139).

376 Adams, George R. 'Sex and Clergy in Chaucer's "General Prologue," *L&P* 18(1968), 215-22.
Chaucer arranges the portraits in *GP* in a meaningful sequence; he describes the clerics such that their personalities are partially or wholly defined by 'what and how they love' (p 215). The Pardoner 'is the picture of the passive homosexual' (p 219). He is described largely by oral motifs and placed at the end of the series. Other structural patterns can be found in the treatment of love (a perversion of appetite in the Pardoner), the use of eyes as a motif (hare-like in the Pardoner), and the Seven Deadly Sins (avarice).

377 Braddy, Haldeen. 'Chaucer's Bilingual Idiom.' *SFQ* 32(1968), 1-6.
Among examples of Chaucer's folksy style, Braddy notes erotic terms and double-entendres. He rejects, however, any implication in lines 672-3 of a homosexual relationship between the Summoner and the Pardoner: *stif burdon* refers to the song.

378 Delasanta, Rodney. 'The Horsemen of the "Canterbury Tales".'*ChauR* 3(1968), 29-36.
'Almost without exception Chaucer introduces or confirms an oblique moral judgment of [the pilgrims] by reference to their riding habits' (p 30). The Pardoner, who rides *al of the newe jet* (line 682) is part of the group (Monk, Merchant, Summoner, Reeve and Wife of Bath) who either rides proudly or has horses of *greet estaat*. This group is contrasted with those who ride poor or un-caparisoned horses as well as those who 'seem compromised by their *inefficiency* as horsemen' (p 31). See 352, 370.

379 Griffith, Richard R. 'The Pardoner.' *A Critical Study Guide to Chaucer's The Canterbury Tales*. Totowa, New Jersey: Littlefield, Adams, 1968. Pp 61-5.

Description of the Pardoner is accompanied by notes on corruption in the sale of pardons, interpetation of *a geldyng or a mare*, the use of detail in the portrait and the sale of relics. The Pardoner's position at the end of the pilgrims reflects his status, morally and socially. The 'preceding four rascals' betray in the main their earthly duties; the Pardoner overtly betrays his spiritual duties. The protest of *gentils* is a direct affront to the Pardoner. He finds himself, like several others, in the position of not being able to tell the tale he had planned but his desire to win carries him forward. For *PardP*, see **610**; for *PardT*, see **830**.

380 Kirby, Thomas A. 'The General Prologue.' In *Companion to Chaucer Studies*. Ed. Beryl Rowland. Toronto, New York, London: Oxford University Press, 1968. Pp 208-28. Rpt 1971. 2nd ed. 1979. [Page numbers from 1968.]

GP portraits fall into two parts; the second (lines 545-714) about one third the length of the first. Chaucer's special interest in religious figures is suggested by his according half his space to them and according the Pardoner the final position. Chaucer follows the order described by rhetoricians of his day, modifying it consciously for particular effect. Chaucer employs several devices in his description of the Pardoner: the use of 'conglomerate detail,' exaggeration, focus on the single quality of hypocrisy, and the 'sudden thrust' in line 691 (p 218). See **837**.

381 Rowland, Beryl 'Chaucer's Imagery.' In *Companion to Chaucer Studies*. Ed. Beryl Rowland. Toronto, New York, and London: Oxford University Press, 1968. Pp 103-22.

Imagery derives its vitality from analogy, 'unifying disparate areas of knowledge in a startling way'(p 103). Chaucer's figures are more 'emotional or intellectual accessories'(p 118) than visual representations. The description of the Pardoner as *a geldyng or a mare* (line 691) denotes his sexual deviancy: the reader deduces that the Pardoner is a hermaphrodite (p 118).

382 Wagenknecht, Edward. *The Personality of Chaucer*. Norman, Oklahoma: University of Oklahoma Press, 1968.

Chaucer creates the Pardoner, one of the greatest literary characters before Shakespeare, 'as a dramatist would have' (p 5). By attaching the Pardoner to Rouncival, an establishment 'in bad odor' (p 59), Chaucer presents a topical reference though his emphasis was on the universal.

383 Braddy, Haldeen. 'Chaucer - Realism or Obscenity?' *AQ* 2(1969), 121-38.

Fundamentally realistic, Chaucer is 'the best example among English authors of liberal-mindedness' (p 138). The Pardoner, like the Summoner, is a 'birdwatcher' (p 126). Though his description 'betokens both emasculation and feminization' (p 126), his goat-like voice associates him with the virility of a male; 'the convivial Pardoner was, not a part-time "homo," but a veteran bird catcher' (p 127). Chaucer 'steered away from homosexuality ... he manifested little, or no, interest in any aspect of aberrant sex, in what one might call sick love' (p 133).

384 Hodgson, Phyllis, ed. *Chaucer: General Prologue [to] The Canterbury Tales*. 1969. See **91**.

Explanatory notes discuss the Pardoner as a stock figure (pp 16-22). At the time of *CT*, analyses of social organization multiplied: themes of the Three Estates, Feudal Aristocracy, and the Clergy and Commons were popular; the main target, the Church, was assailed continuously. Crafty pardoners were criticized in Church statements (1348, 1368, 1374, 1390) and John Heywood's *The Four P's*. Langland, Wyclif and Gower, who also castigated false pardoners, affirmed the ideal. Chaucer veils his comment in irony or ambiguity though his sympathy should not be taken for approval. Notes on moral personifications (pp 22-6) comment on indebtedness to *RR* and the literature of the Seven Deadly Sins: the Pardoner is one of nine pilgrims afflicted with Avarice, the besetting sin; the nature and activities of False Seeming are transferred to the Pardoner in *PardP*. Adroitness at cheating employers binds the Pardoner to the group of lower-class rogues; by faking forgiveness, the Pardoner cheats God Himself. Each pilgrim is defined to some extent by the presence of others; the Pardoner and Squire form a striking contrast 'both claiming attention by their hair style, their song and their pursuit of the latest fashion in dress' (p 36).

385 Hoy, Michael. 'The Pardoner's Tale' and 'Conclusion.' Ed. Michael Hoy and Michael Stevens. London: Norton Bailey, 1969. Pp 103-31; 163-6.

Characters like the Pardoner and Summoner must have represented the corruption that lay close to the heart of the medieval Church. But Chaucer's satire differs from Langland's in that it is tempered with fine humor (p 165). For *PardT*, see **844**.

386 King, Francis, and Bruce Steele. *Selections from Geoffrey Chaucer's The Canterbury Tales.* 1969. See **94**.

Text of Pardoner portrait, Ellesmere miniature and notes, pp 48-52; commentary, pp 358-9. The Pardoner seems beyond pardon since he willingly subjects himself to blasphemy; by comparison, the Summoner seems 'quite human' (p 358). Despite his claims of Avarice, the Pardoner's main aim is 'verbal and practical blasphemy' (p 358). The *vernycle* produces the visual image of Christ, the ideal of mercy and perfected human nature; the Pardoner's grotesque appearance and behavior contrasts sharply. His moral corruption is paralleled by physical and emotional corruption. His 'high-spirited enthusiasm' is a final touch 'which makes him on the one hand a curiously unpleasant version of the Squire and on the other an excellent performer in church' (p 359). For edition, see **93**; for *PardT*, see See **845**.

387 Kiralis, Karl. 'William Blake as an Intellectual and Spiritual Guide to Chaucer's *Canterbury Pilgrims.*' *BlakeS* 1(1969), 139-90.

Blake's critical insights depend on understanding his pictorial guideposts; e.g., the placement of the group of pilgrims, specific arrangement of smaller groups, roles of background and foreground and the use of detail. The pairing of Pardoner and Parson contrasts 'the thieving prostitute of the Christian religion with the perfect and selfless practitioner of Christianity' (p 144). The Pardoner functions as a 'useful blight' (p 144); the manner of response to him separates those who merely wish salvation from those who realize salvation is not simple. The Pardoner's horse acts tightly checked; by contrast, the Squire's horse appears loosely checked much like his lovemaking. The framing of the Prioress between the Pardoner (corrupt church) and Knight (highest representative of the aristocracy) suggests her vacillation between the two sets of values.

388 Currie, Felicity. 'Chaucer's Pardoner Again.' *LeedsSE* 4(1970), 11-22.

Chaucer's Pardoner convinces fellow-pilgrims and critics alike that he is wicked. By placing the Pardoner with the Summoner, 'Chaucer has carefully suggested the general attitude of the pilgrims to the Pardoner' (pp 11-2). For *PardP*, see **612**; for *PardT*, see **848**.

389 Gafford, Charlotte K. 'Chaucer's Pardoner and Haze Motes of Georgia.' *Essays in Honor of Richebourg Gaillard McWilliams.* Ed. Howard Creed. Birmingham-Southern College Bulletin 63, 2(1970).

Birmingham, Alabama: Birmingham-Southern College, 1970. Pp 9-12. Noting criticism of the Pardoner as rogue and homosexual liar, Gafford asks: '[C]ould not Chaucer's Pardoner be considered as a heightened example of the human contradiction that, even though people often do not behave in both of two ways or do both of two things, they must have been originally designed and humanly prepared to have done either? Are only scoundrels, abandoned rascals, and eunuchs to see themselves reflected in the Pardoner' (p 10)?

390 Halverson, John. 'Chaucer's Pardoner and the Progress of Criticism.' *ChauR* 4(1970), 184-202.
Halverson reviews critical opinion (1940-69) noting considerable agreement as well as convergence of interest: the criticism is predominantly interpretive and phenomenological with interest in Freud, spiritual dimension and ironic modes. The Pardoner's portrait, in contrast to that of the Friar, lacks explicitness. Chaucer maintains 'a comparative distance' confining himself to description of physical appearance and professional success (p 196). The Pardoner's sexuality remains his secret. The Pardoner engages in a 'put-on', presenting a sordid image of himself as revenge against the gentlefolk. For *PardT*, see **851**.

391 Hanson, Thomas Bradley. *Stylized Man: The Poetic Use of Physiognomy in Chaucer's Canterbury Tales.* University of Wisconsin Dissertation, 1970. Director: Chauncey Wood and Robert K. Presson.
The Pardoner is discussed together with the group of pilgrims introduced at the end of *GP* and the Host. Chaucer uses as much physiognomic detail for these as he does for all the other pilgrims combined. Hanson takes issue with Curry's interpretation of the Pardoner and contrasts him with the Miller. He suggests that, in the quarrel with the Host, the Pardoner is both exposed and saved from condemnation.

392 Lenaghan, R.T. 'Chaucer's *General Prologue* as History and Literature.' *CSSH* 12(1970), 73-82.
The basic fact of life in the society of *GP* is economic struggle: the pilgrims are their work. Occupational labels in *GP* provide social and economic indicators (p 79) that define the narrator's positions and values. The Pardoner, who manifests 'materialistic drive'(p 78) in selling fake relics, papal pardons, and the service of remitting sins, is grouped with pilgrims such as the Shipman, Miller and Manciple. The stress on 'hustle and competition' (p 79) creates a society different from the

'complementary self-subordination' (p 79) implied by the pattern of the three estates.

393 Spencer, William. 'Are Chaucer's Pilgrims Keyed to the Zodiac?' *ChauR* 4(1970), 147-70.

Chaucer turned to the medieval science of astrology for the 'hidden ground plan' (p 149) of *GP*. The Pardoner is associated with Sagittarius and Jupiter, the former reflected in horse imagery; like the Shipman, he is a 'bad Jupiter character' (p 168). The pilgrims can be matched to lore of pre-Chaucerian astrological authorities: the Pardoner manifests cynicism, credulity and the habit of bringing good into disrepute (Albohazen Haly); is diabolical (Bonatti); lacks virility (Firmicus).

394 Woo, Constance, and William Matthews. 'The Spiritual Purpose of the *Canterbury Tales.*' *Comitatus* 1(1970), 85-109.

The pilgrims acknowledge the spiritual purpose of the pilgrimage in the benedictions at the close of their tales; the Pardoner, 'most paradoxically, is most pious of all, for he calls the whole company to confession' (p 86). Spiritual themes (e.g., body versus soul, ideal versus real) are implicit in the portraits. In the Pardoner's portrait, 'sin is undeniable and horrifying' (p 89), the gap between ideal and real taking the form of lies and deceit. The Pardoner, like the Prioress, Monk and Friar, is characterized by either the absence or perversion of religious detail. The Parson is the perfect Christian counterposed to the Pardoner in economic status, intent, preaching style, and initial reaction from the pilgrims. The *povre person* (line 702) may refer to the Parson (see line 478). For *PardT*, see **853**.

395 Karlen, Arno. 'The Homosexual Heresy.' *ChauR* 6(1971), 44-63.

The Middle Ages was 'no exception to the Western tradition of linking political, religious and sexual deviance' (p 44).

396 Rowland, Beryl. *Blind Beasts: Chaucer's Animal World*. Ohio: Kent State University Press, 1971.

Besides the physical resemblances implied (comparison to the dove inflating and deflating its neck and crop; to the tremulous voice which seems soft but is far-reaching), the Pardoner's self-description as a dove may include an ironic reference to the dove as a symbol of Christ. The comparisons to hare and goat are 'striking and specific' (p 99): Chaucer suggests the Pardoner's eyes are 'bulging, watchful, unnatural'; the Pardoner's voice is 'not that of a normal man'(p 100). Both hare and goat may suggest hermaphroditism (p 100). The image of the hare is simple yet paradoxical: '[t]he Pardoner stands revealed as an unhappy, frustrated creature, haunted by his own sexual inadequacy, conscious of his separation from normal life' (p 102). Through the 'artistic triumph' of this image, Chaucer 'reveals human nature'(p 102) but conceals his own view. For *PardP*, see **614**; for *PardT*, see **860**.

397   Higdon, David Leon. 'Diverse Melodies in Chaucer's "General Prologue".' *Criticism* 14(1972), 97-108.

GP is bounded '[p]hysically, spiritually and spatially' (p 97) by Knight and Pardoner; temporally and metaphorically, it is bounded by songs. Attitudes toward and use of music indicate the moral standing of the pilgrims; the Pardoner, together with the Miller, Summoner, Manciple and Reeve, is associated with loudness, harshness and discord. The Pardoner's voice is compared to a goat (line **688**), his chanting an *offertorie* is surrounded by 'blatant sexual, physical, and monetary negatives' (p 105) and his loudness (line 714) 'emphasizes that he sings only to gain money for himself'(p 106).

398   Kean, P[atricia]. M. *Chaucer and the Making of English Poetry*, vol 2. *The Art of Narrative*. London: Routledge & Kegan Paul, 1972.

The Pardoner exemplifies Chaucerian comedy in that he is a typical character who,because of vice and physical abnormality, stands apart from the norm.   Overemphasis on the Pardoner's lack of normal masculinity and its social consequences risks anachronistic interpretation; the Pardoner is to be understood in the context of medieval ideas regarding *eunuchus ex nativitate*. The norm is conveyed through characters and reference to the observer whose view the reader is made to share.

399   Ross, Thomas W. *Chaucer's Bawdy*. 1972. See **154**.

See entries for *burdoun* (A 673); *geldyng* (691); *hair* (675); *jape* (705); and *Rouncivale* (670). For *Phy-PardL*, see **548**; for *PardP*, see **617**; for *PardT*, see **872**.

400   Condren, Edward I. 'The Pardoner's Bid For Existence.' *Viator* 4 (1973), 177-205.

Though by Chaucer's time pardoners had earned a notorious reputation, the admission of fraud and the hints of sexual abnormality distinguish Chaucer's Pardoner as an individual. Like Faux-Semblant in fraudulence, the Pardoner is essentially different. Critical discussion has typically followed either the psychological approach (**273, 311, 340**) which fails to account for inconsistencies in the Pardoner's behavior, or the exegetical (**323, 352, 356, 866**) which overlooks motive. Generally speaking, the psychological critics rely on the Pardoner's self-description (predominantly in *PardP*), and the exegetical critics on his indirect revelation (predominantly in *PardT*). For *PardP* and *PardT*, see **876**.

401 Eliason, Norman E. 'Personal Names in the *Canterbury Tales.'Names* 21(1973), 137-52.

See entry under **880**.

402 Faulkner, Dewey R. "Introduction". In *Twentieth Century Interpretations of the Pardoner's Tale: A Collection of Critical Essays*. Ed. Dewey R. Faulkner. Englewood Cliffs, New Jersey: Prentice-Hall Inc., 1973.

The Pardoner is a *quaestor* based at the Hospital and chapel of Saint Mary Roncevall at Charing, a convent notorious for abuses in alms-collecting. *Rouncivale* was 'doubtless a fountainhead' (p 2) for the sale of pardons authorized by Pope Boniface IX for his Jubilee Year in 1390. In their own time, pardoners were regarded as having the power to damn souls. The Pardoner's position in *GP* opposes him to the virtuous Knight, animal images suggest a subhuman quality, and he admits duplicitous practices. The Pardoner's sexual privation is a physical symbol which prepares for the spiritual ones. For *PardT*, see **882**.

403 Mann, Jill. 'The Pardoner.' *Chaucer and Medieval Estates Satire: The Literature of Social Classes and the 'General Prologue' to the 'Canterbury Tales'*. Cambridge: Cambridge University Press, 1973; rpt 1987. Pp 145-52.

Chaucer drew his characters from contemporary social life (cf **302**), mediated by the 'social stereotypes' (pp 7-10) found in and perpetuated by estates satire. The 'estate' of the Pardoner figures in satiric literature only in a minor way. The Pardoner is one of four pilgrims who has been interpreted in the light of medieval scientific lore. The introduction of the Pardoner reveals both Pardoner and Summoner to be homosexual, a characterization carried forth, in the case of the Pardoner, in details of effeminacy. In linking the Pardoner's appearance to effeminacy, 'scientific and satiric traditions go hand in hand' (p 148). The homosexual was 'not a new figure in medieval satire'(p 146). Homosexuality, which had appeared as a metaphoric representation of institutional corruption, in the case of the Pardoner has become real and the attribute of an individual. The Pardoner's 'sexual make-up' (p 147) is more important in the portrait at the immediate than the symbolic level. Chaucer's inclusion of a pardoner seems to 'correspond to a stimulus from Langland' (p 149). Chaucer's Pardoner deceives both priest and people. The narrator briefly abandons the Pardoner's viewpoint to 'speak with the Parson's vocabulary of the *feyned flatery and japes* (p 149). The relics, likewise, are introduced in plain terms (lines 694-700). Chaucer is 'far removed' (p 152) from contemporary satires of what relics are meant to be: he targets the contrast between 'the holy awe felt for the supposed relics, and the tawdry nature of their reality' (p 152). 'Amusement, not disgust, is predominant in the final picture of the Pardoner'(p 152).

404 Mehl, Dieter. *Geoffrey Chaucer: Eine Einführung in seine erzählenden Dichtungen.* Berlin: Erich Schmidt, 1973. Trans. (revised and expanded) as *Geoffrey Chaucer: An Introduction to His Narrative Poetry.* Cambridge: Cambridge University Press, 1986 [cited here].

In *GP*, the typical and the individual complement each other: the Pardoner, an 'estate-representative'(p 146), is individuated through his performance of confession, tale and solicitation. The extensive self-portrait of the Pardoner, like that of the Wife of Bath, is largely independent of the frame story and provides a particularly lively link between the pilgrimage and the tales. For *PardP*, see **619**; for *PardT*, see **886**.

405 Mitchell, Jerome and William Provost, ed. 'Chaucer's Parodies of Love.' In *Chaucer: The Love Poet.* Athens, Georgia: University of Georgia Press, 1973. Pp 27-44.

Robert E. Kaske, in the panel discussion session (pp 91-106), builds on earlier treatment of the influence of Canticles on Chaucer to suggest that the Pardoner's song echoes '*Veni, veni, amica mea.*' If so, Chaucer would have placed echoes of Canticles in the mouths of three futile lovers—the Pardoner, Absalom and January thereby showing it an effective vehicle for ironic judgment.

406 Rowland, Beryl. *Animals with Human Faces: A Guide to Animal Symbolism.* Knoxville: University of Tennessee Press, 1973.

Treats the symbolic meaning of hare, goat and horse. For *PardP*, see **620**; for *PardT*, see **887**.

407 Ferrie, Antoine. *Religion et Gens d'Église chez G. Chaucer.* University of Toulouse Dissertation. 1974. Director: V. Dupont. [Not seen.]

A comprehensive overview of the pilgrims with discussion of the Pardoner, Prioress, Second Nun, Nun's Priest, Monk, Friar, Summoner and Parson.

108 Kernan, Anne. 'The Archwife and The Eunuch.' *ELH* 41(1974), 1-25.

The Pardoner and the Wife of Bath are 'kindred spirits'(331): both are concerned with fashion, particularly headgear; both use the Offertory for self advancement; and both are extensively travelled. For *Interr,* see **524**; for *PardT*, see **894**.

109 Manning, Stephen. 'Chaucer's Pardoner: Sex and Non-sex.' *SAB* 39(1974), 17-26.

When the Host invites the Pardoner to tell a tale, the Pardoner replies that first *I wol bothe drynke, and eten of a cake* (line 322 corrected). In *GP*, Chaucer the pilgrim introduces the Pardoner singing with the Summoner *Com hider,love, to me!* (line 672 corrected). 'Thus Chaucer introduces a pattern of imagery which Freudian critics call *oral*, which basically involves taking in or spitting out of the mouth, and biting' (p 17). Figuratively they incorporate into it 'such matters as the acquisition of knowledge or of wealth, cursing, nagging, vows, "biting" sarcasm, and so forth' (p 17). A strong aggressive element underlies this pattern. Figuratively, the Pardoner 'takes in' gullible people with *feyned flaterye and japes* (line 705 corrected). The Pardoner 'substitutes oral aggression for phallic aggression' (p 21). Interestingly, Chaucer compares the Pardoner to three animals normally associated with lechery—the hare (line 684), goat (line 688), and the horse (lines 689-91). '[T]he Pardoner's being a gelding or mare is analogous to oral castration is analogous to spiritual death and these analogies reinforce ... each other' (p 25).

110 Parr, Roger P. 'Chaucer's Art of Portraiture.' *SMC* 4(1974), 428-36.

GP portraits reveal Chaucer's originality. Unlike contemporary practice, in Chaucer's portraits, *notatio*, the description of moral qualities, predominates over *effictio* and *descriptio*, physical description. *GP* portraits entice the audience, and by differentiating the pilgrim with a minimum of detail, distinguish the individual from the group.

111 Thorpe, James. *A Noble Heritage: The Ellesmere Manuscript of Chaucer's Canterbury Tales.* 1974. See **158**.

The Pardoner is a perversion of his own tale: muddled by drink, guilty of avarice, conscious of the fakery of his relics and lacking in masculinity. The Pardoner, portrayed with a long red cloak and red hat adorned with the talisman of a veronica, is an official of the Church as are one third of the pilgrims. For *PardT*, see **902**.

412 Deligiorgis, Stavros. 'Poetics of Anagogy for Chaucer: *The Canterbury Tales.*' In *Geoffrey Chaucer: A Collection of Original Articles.* Ed. George D. Economou. New York: McGraw-Hill, 1975. Pp 129-41.

The reader must become a pilgrim. *PardT* 'is dialectical—however cynical—to the end'(p 133). The Host's 'explosion' (p 133) is less a punishment than 'the victory of dialectics suggesting the checking game between statement and life'(p 133). Since forgiveness is a dialectic, the Host and Pardoner are reconciled. By acknowledging deceit, the Pardoner earns the grace of the Host. 'The two are one theme; *the* theme, and what makes as much "literature" of readers or listeners as they, in their passivity, make of it' (p 133).

413 Donaldson, E. Talbot. 'Chaucer's Three "P's": Pandarus, Pardoner, and Poet.' *MQR* 14(1975), 282-301.

The Pardoner, Pandarus and the poet, all artists, try to redefine reality and end by celebrating the failure of love. Despite prostituting his art, the Pardoner's art remains valid; he is less successful in recreating himself as a vicious man. The Pardoner is the literal symbol of the man who can neither love nor be loved: 'Cut off from human affection, he uses his art to acquire money, which is something humanity respects' (p 293). The Pardoner and Pandarus represent 'deep impulses' that Chaucer may have recognized in himself (p 297). 'The only profound optimism such as Chaucer's is one that results from a pessimism so profound that one has no choice, short of death, but to accept it and go on from there' (p 297). For *PardT*, see **905**.

414 Eckhardt, Caroline D. 'The Number of Chaucer's Pilgrims: A Review and Reappraisal.' *YES* 5(1975), 1-18. Rpt in *Essays in the Numerical Criticism of Medieval Literature.* Ed. Caroline D. Eckhardt. Lewisburg, Pennsylvania: Bucknell University Press; London Associated University Presses, 1980. Pp 156-84.

Eckhardt reviews previous discussion of the number of pilgrims offering three classifications for explanations of the discrepancy between *nyne and twenty* pilgrims (line 24) and the thirty identified pilgrims. She concludes that the deliberate miscounting of the pilgrims indicates Chaucer's ironic attitude to the Narrator who characteristically puts forth hasty verdicts that invite correction by the reader.

415 Engelhardt, George J. 'The Ecclesiastical Pilgrims of the *Canterbury*

Tales: A Study in Ethology.' *MS* 37(1975), 287-315.
In the ethology of *GP*, the Pardoner represents '[t]he reprobate sense in its ultimate ignominy' (p 307). Consummating idolatry with sodomy, he has converted Christ's pardon into a commodity. His 'desiccated manhood'(p 307) symbolizes simony; his effeminacy portends tribulation of the second advent. For *PardT*, see **907**.

416 Green, Eugene. 'The Voices of the Pilgrims in the *General Prologue to the Canterbury Tales*.' *Style* 9(1975), 55-81.
Stylistic analysis demonstrates that the illusion of recollected conviviality in *GP* derives from Chaucer's creative use of convention. The voices of narrator and pilgrim blend in 'counterpoint' (p 57) to exemplify the influence of the natural and eternal (cf **320**). The Pardoner's portrait is marked by hyperbole (*noble ecclesiaste*), use of place name (*Rouncivale*), allusion to *RR* (the song of love in Dame Gladnesse's portrait transformed in line 672), and the tone of hypocrisy in the description of the Pardoner as 'a mock sermonist'(lines 709-14) (p 75).

417 McVeigh, Terence A. 'Chaucer's Portraits of The Pardoner and Summoner and Wyclif's Tractatus De Simonia.' *CF* 29(1975), 54-8.
In his portraits of the Pardoner and the Summoner, Chaucer employs images of leprosy and homosexuality to symbolize the spiritual degeneration of simony. In so doing, Chaucer borrows from medieval tradition, as reflected by Wyclif's *Tractatus De Simonia*, where simony is depicted as spiritual sodomy and the allegorical equivalent of leprosy. The ecclesiastical tradition represented by Wyclif provides a more immediate source than either the Augustinian tradition (**314**) or the medieval exegetical tradition. See also **323**.

418 Quinn, Esther C. 'Religion in Chaucer's Canterbury Tales: A Study in Language and Structure.' In *Geoffrey Chaucer: A Collection of Original Articles*. [Contemporary Studies in Literature]. Ed. George D. Economou. New York: McGraw-Hill, 1975. Pp 55-73.
In *GP*, three fraudulent aspects of the Pardoner's activities are singled out: his sale of relics, his sale of pardons and his preaching. The 'depraved' Pardoner employs his verbal skill to appropriate the functions of the priest in performing the liturgy and absolving sinners from Penance. It is part of Chaucer's irony that, though the Pardoner is a minor functionary, the name 'pardoner' suggests mighty powers. For *PardT*, see **916**.

419 Taitt, Peter S. *Incubus and Ideal: Ecclesiastical Figures in Chaucer* *and Langland.* Salzburg: Institut für Englische Sprache und Literatur, Universität Salzburg, 1975.

The Pardoner commits one of the less common offenses ascribed to pardoners: the showing of false relics. The description of the Pardoner incorporates four references to lechery (*stif burdoun*, hare-like eyes, goat-like voice, and line 691). Together with irony these references create a 'portrait of a thoroughgoing and unashamed scoundrel' (p 43). For *PardT*, see **918**.

420 Wetherbee, Winthrop. 'Some Intellectual Themes in Chaucer's Poetry.' In *Geoffrey Chaucer: A Collection of Original Articles.* Ed. George D. Economou. New York: McGraw-Hill, 1975. Pp 75-91.
Chaucer, 'probably the most learned of medieval English poets' (p 75), was fundamentally conservative in his attitude toward authority in church and state. The portrait of the Pardoner, like that of the Friar, shows that Chaucer shares Langland's sense of 'pervasive demoralization' (p 87) in the church and Wyclif's criticism of the abuse of authority. Chaucer emphasizes obstacles to vision and knowledge in the situations of his characters and dramatizes 'their inherent capacities for love and spirituality' (p 89). Knowledge of the Pardoner's congenital sexual deficiency engenders greater sympathy for him than the Friar. In the Pardoner's 'fascination with hazard and blasphemy, his nervous eloquence and vivid evocation of the *timor mortis*'(p 89), we see 'the perversion of what is basically a deeply religious nature' (p 89). For *PardT*, see **920**.

421 David, Alfred. *The Strumpet Muse: Art and Morals in Chaucer's Poetry.* Bloomington, Indiana: Indiana University Press, 1976.
Chaucer progressively experienced tension between his obligations as a medieval author and his own artistic vision, his 'strumpet Muse'(p 7). The Pardoner is one of several pilgrims who embody ironic images of the poet. The Pardoner and 'his stock' appear at the end of the pilgrims as they express in its 'most outrageous form the discrepancy between ideal and reality'(p 72): [t]hey symbolize respectively the sickness and impotence that have infected the medieval Church and, indeed, the whole society' (p 71).

422 See **427** below.

423 Havely, N[icholas]. R., ed. *The Friar's, Summoner's and Pardoner's Tales from The Canterbury Tales.* 1976. See **102**.
The Pardoner and Summoner are appropriately last in *GP*, the worst of

the tricksters and 'among the most sinister-looking'(p 25). Though as grotesque as the Summoner, the Pardoner, who was probably a member of the clergy (p 25), is both higher in the Church hierarchy and more sophisticated in extortion. Like the Friar and the Summoner, the Pardoner represents active corruption in the Church and the poisoning of the relationship between Church and laity. Approximating 'the art of an illusionist' (p 28) with his hypocrisy, the Pardoner can play clergyman or clown as is seen in the link to *PhysT*. For *PardP* see **625**; for *PardT* see **911**.

424 Howard, Donald. *The Idea of the Canterbury Tales*. Berkeley, University of California Press, 1976; paperback edition 1978. [Page numbers from 1978]; 'Memory and Form' pp 139-58 revised from '*The Canterbury Tales*: Memory and Form.' *ELH* 38(1971), 319-28; rpt in *Geoffrey Chaucer's 'The General Prologue to the Canterbury Tales.'* Ed. Harold Bloom. New York: Chelsea House Publishers, 1988. Pp 37-50; Pp 78-116 rpt as 'The Idea of *The Canterbury Tales*.' In *Geoffrey Chaucer*. Ed. and introd. Harold Bloom. [Modern Critical Views]. New York: Chelsea House Publishers, 1985. Pp 79-104.
The inclusion of the 'startling figure of the Pardoner' (p 97), a corruption of the institution of indulgence, in *GP* is partial evidence that the ideal of pilgrimage was discredited by Chaucer's time. *GP* presents the Pardoner in the third of three increasingly ironic mnemonic groups, each introduced by an idealized figure (Parson, Plowman: Miller, Manciple, Reeve, Summoner, Pardoner, Host). This group is lower in status, more given to swindling and fonder of fabliaux than the other entrepreneurs. The Pardoner's portrait concludes with a 'piquant phrase' (p 115): the concluding detail encapsulates the pilgrim, suggesting 'an inner reality,' that will dictate 'choice and treatment of tales' (p 115). The Pardoner functions as 'a marginal grotesquerie' in the *CT*; he belongs to the '*banished world* of the Middle Ages' (p 341). 'He is meant to haunt us,' to be central to the idea of *CT* (p 342). Hence, we must eschew diagnoses that discount his seriousness e.g., that he is drunk, an obvious eunuch, or the 'modern stereotype of a homosexual' (p 345). He is 'feminoid in a starkly physical way' (e.g., voice, hair, beard) (p 344). He remains 'a mystery, an enigma—sexually anomalous, hermaphroditic, menacing, contradictory' (p 345). We know him to be a *eunuchus ex nativitate*, symbolic in the exegetical tradition of the deprival of grace. The use of traditional lecherous animals makes him seem obscene. If

he is a *eunuchus ex nativitate*, doesn't this suggest 'we are all born in sin? Doesn't it demand that we become involved in his deformity, see ourselves in it' (p 372)? The Pardoner's behavior is a defense against society's uncharitable reaction to him. The Pardoner's asexuality throws into relief a stratum of *CT* that treats domestic life and sexuality: like Jean-Paul Sartre's *Saint Genet: Actor and Martyr*, he puts all about him in perspective. The Pardoner is like 'a grotesque mirror-image' of both the institution at the heart of *CT* and of Chaucer, himself (p 376). Chaucer and the Pardoner possess gifts of rhetoric, impersonation and dramatic flair; both role-play themselves in ironical spirit. The figure of the Pardoner unmasks Chaucer the artist. Chaucer states his intent as the reverse of the Pardoner's in *Ret*. For *Phy-PardL*, see **555**; for *PardP*, see **629**; for *PardT*, see **926**.

- Review by Lee Patterson *UTQ* 48(1979), 263-282: Howard's reliance on the relation of tale to teller is at odds with his concern for metastructure; it allows 'a splendid psychological reading' which distracts from larger narrative significance (p 273).

425 Moore, Bruce. '"I Wol No Lenger Pleye with Thee": Chaucer's Rejection of the Pardoner.' *Parergon* 14 (1976), 52-62.
The Pardoner portrait is the 'most tonally uneasy' (p 53). The most varied and professional performer, he is a curious mix of power and sterility. He attempts to present himself as sexually potent while at the same time flaunting his abnormality. For *PardT*, see **930**.

426 Peterson, Joyce. 'With Feigned Flattery: The Pardoner as Vice.' *ChauR* 10(1976), 326-36.
The *feyned flaterye* attributed to the Pardoner (line 705) can really only represent Chaucer the Pilgrim's experience during the pilgrimage since nothing in the Pardoner's 'catalogue of tricks' (lines 335-90) suggests flattery. For *PardP*, see **631**; for *PardT*, see **933**.

427 Schmidt, A.V.C. 'The General Prologue to The Canterbury Tales and The Canon Yeoman's Prologue and Tale.' New York: Holmes and Meier, 1976.
Notes on the Pardoner suggest he is a parody 'of the elegant Squire in his negligent dandyism' (p 150).

428 Zacher, Christian K. *Curiosity and Pilgrimage: The Literature of Discovery in Fourteenth-Century England.* Baltimore: Johns Hopkins University Press, 1976.
Chaucer's pilgrims and tales reflect the 'culturally energizing tension'

between the vice of curiosity (*curiositas*) and the pious practice of pilgrimage (p 90). The pilgrimage frame enabled Chaucer to 'mirror his conservative attitude toward both the remembered ideals of pilgrimage and its contemporary decline' (p 90) as a curiosity-ridden institution. The tensions between the unity required by the pact and the contest reflect a larger pattern of oppositions, stressing the basic instability of this social group and of life in late fourteenth-century England. The disruptive Pardoner challenges whatever stability the Knight represents. The Pardoner is one of a group of 'extraterritorial vagrants, morally *exorbitans*, emblems of curiosity'(p 94). Most of the pilgrims are seen and see themselves in a mutual iconic struggle that 'pits the selfless against the assertive' (p 95). As a pair, the Summoner and Pardoner are contrasted with the Parson and Plowman. Freer from supervision than the Friar and Summoner, he is bolder and more corrupting. The Pardoner, who has joined the pilgrimage to sell relics and indulgences, is the 'most ruinous to the Church and its members' (p 94). With his deceptive tale-telling, he does in miniature what *CT* does as a whole. The inherent disorderliness of the pilgrimage almost makes the Host's pact seem necessary. For *PardT*, see **938**.

429 Cespedes, Frank V. 'Chaucer's Pardoner and Preaching.' *ELH* 44 (1977), 1-18.

An important foundation of the opposition of the Pardoner's and Parson's portraits in *GP* is the *res et verba* distinction drawn by Paul in his epistle to Timothy. The opposition is extended with the Pardoner's over-expressiveness, his artificial pains *to wel affile his tonge* (line 712), and the Parson's refusal to tell a fable. For *Interr*, see **527**; for *PardP*, see **632**; for *PardT*, see **940**.

430 Evans, Gillian. *Chaucer*. [Authors in Their Age]. Glasgow and London: Blackie, 1977.

'If the Summoner stands for hell, the Pardoner stands for death' (p 74). A 'lost soul'(cf **273**), Chaucer's Pardoner is a caricature of the worst members of his profession. Chaucer's irony turns to bitter sarcasm when he describes the Pardoner. *PardT* is heavily ironic, its goal being to encourage hearers to abandon the vices the Pardoner exemplifies.

431 Gardner, John. 'Fragment VI and VII: The Theme of Pride and The Uses of Unreliable Art.' *The Poetry of Chaucer*. Carbondale: Southern Illinois University Press, 1977. Pp 293-315 mostly.

The Pardoner unites a role generally acknowledged to be perverse with 'a crippled physical and spiritual nature' (p 232). The Pardoner is 'instantly identifiable as a eunuch or a homosexual [line 691]. Whichever he really is, he plays, and brazenly, the role of homosexual'(p 301). To infer moralizing on Chaucer's part in this detail is to misunderstand Chaucer (contra **323, 336**). The Pardoner's problem is more a social than a spiritual one. For *Phy-PardL*, see **556**; for *PardT*, see **941**.

432 Knight, Stephen. 'Politics and Chaucer's Poetry.' *The Radical Reader*. Ed. Stephen Knight and Michael Wilding. Sydney: Wild & Woolley, 1977. Pp 169-92.

Chaucer employs Gothic structural style which he associates with the serious mode and which corresponds with medieval epistemology. The structure 'recapitulates a Christian, idealist, non-material view of knowledge'(p 179). The techniques of characterization support the structural pattern in that ideal types are presented ideally and characters like the Pardoner are presented with 'sense-available detail'(p 180). Though the weight of Church authority is against the Pardoner, he seems partially redeemed by vitality and self-knowledge. Critics have not sufficiently recognized that Chaucer's mastery reaches from style through characterization and structure to create themes (p 182). In a world where feudal economic patterns are giving way to capitalistic patterns, 'worldly, comic individuals'(p 184), like the Pardoner, are also petty capitalists.

433 Owen, Charles A., Jr. *Pilgrimage and Storytelling in the Canterbury Tales: The Dialectic of 'Ernest' and 'Game'*. Norman, Oklahoma: University of Oklahoma Press, 1977.

Ch 2: The portraits of the five churls, Monk and Friar, were added c 1396, creating a 'lighter, more gamey and more gamesome' (p 46) tone, while presenting a society threatened by church corruption. With these additions, the society was less firmly established than in the earlier form and 'the indeterminacies of game superseded the certainties of pilgrimage'(p 47). Ch 3: The friendship of the Summoner and the Pardoner is the only one described. 'Like many of his kind, [the Pardoner] only half-wills the concealment of his peculiarities' (p 82). The Pardoner makes no effort to appear clerical. He stresses the relics over the pardons since they are not depleted through use. The Pardoner is a 'shrewder villain' (p 83) than the Summoner. His satisfaction in his appearance and his pride in his ill-earned income keep him in the world of comedy. The Pardoner's portrait is closely linked to his performance, his sample sermon justifying the term *noble eccleasiaste*. The closing position of the Pardoner's portrait emphasizes the forces of corruption in society and the ignorance on which they prey. For *Interr*, see **528**; for *Phy-PardL*, see **557**; for *PardP*, see **633**; for *PardT*, see **943**.

434 Pison, Thomas. 'Liminality in *The Canterbury Tales.*' *Genre* 10(1977), 157-71.

The *CT* can be analyzed as a *rite de passage*: separated from structural positions in medieval society by the liminal space of the pilgrimage, co-workers, such as the Pardoner and Summoner, are released to critique each other. The liminality of *CT* moves the ground for evaluation from profession to person. Social status is redefined by the interplay between *gentilesse* and churlishness. Chaucer's use of the term *gentil*, which more often applies to values than station, is used ironically in line 669.

435 Stemmler, Theo. Ed. *The Ellesmere Miniatures of The Canterbury Pilgrims*. Mannheim: University of Mannheim, 1977.

Stemmler reproduces the Ellesmere miniatures together with *GP* text that supplied many of the details. Besides being the only complete set of illuminations, the Ellesmere miniatures are notable for their artistic quality and early date. The miniaturist follows Chaucer's description of the Pardoner in every detail. Together with the Cook and Summonner, 'this pale eunuch is an impressive study of human repulsiveness' (p xx).

436 Stevenson, Warren. 'Interpreting Blake's Canterbury Pilgrims.' *CLQ* 13(1977), 115-26.

Blake's archetypal method is not constrained in *The Canterbury Pilgrims*, the quasi-realism of his commentary notwithstanding. The full figure of the Pardoner is turned toward the leering Summoner. The Pardoner's jewel encrusted cross together with the large red crosses on his back and wallet 'emphasize both his office and his flagitious hypocrisy' (p 122). The Pardoner's horse struggles to get the bit between his teeth; the Pardoner is the sole pilgrim to have relinquished his grip on the reins. The Pardoner's 'swastika-like contortion' contrasts with the Host's cruciform position (p 122). The Pardoner's 'demonic duplicity' finds it analogue in 'Chaucer's "angelic" duplicity' (p 125).

437 Allen, Orphia Jane. 'Blake's Archetypal Criticism: *The Canterbury Pilgrims.*' *Genre* 11(1978), 173-89.

The Pardoner is the epitome of 'Urizenic perversion' (p 179), a perverted leader standing in contrast to the creative leadership of the Parson and the poet. Both Blake and Chaucer are masters of irony; the Pardoner is Chaucer's ironic masterpiece. The structure of Blake's *The Canterbury Pilgrims* is dominated by two iconographical motifs—the cross and the net—both Blakean symbols of repression. The cross is found in the Pardoner's 'Swastika-like contortion' (p 188); the Pardoner's clothing has a 'filmy, net-like appearance.'

438 Hughes, Geoffrey. 'Gold and Iron: Semantic Change and Social Change in Chaucer's Prologue,' *Standpunte* 137.31 no 5. 1978. Rpt in *Geoffrey Chaucer's 'The General Prologue to the Canterbury Tales.'* Ed. Harold Bloom. New York: Chelsea House Publishers, 1988. Pp 73-84.
Semantic content is an indispensably revealing factor of *CT*. The nuances of words conveying acquisition form an important semantic thread. Words such as *winne*, and *bisynesse* which with the Pardoner connote his 'cynical profit-motivation' (p 83) connote religious dedication with the Clerk and Parson.

439 Jennings, Margaret. 'Chaucer's Beards.' *Archiv* 215(1978), 362-8. [Not seen.]

440 Keiser, George R. 'In Defense of the Bradshaw Shift.' *ChR* 12(1978), 191-201.
MlT endlink 'calls attention to Harry Bailley's sensitivity to criticism of swearing and the related tavern vices and, thus, makes us more aware of the effect that the Pardoner's Tale must have had on Harry. With that awareness, we can understand more readily the anxieties that cause Harry's rude explosion when the Pardoner makes his implications explicit in C 941-45' (p 199).

441 Martin, Loy D. 'History and Form in the General Prologue to the Canterbury Tales.' *ELH* 45(1978), 1-17. Rpt in *Geoffrey Chaucer's The General Prologue to the Canterbury Tales.* Ed. Harold Bloom. New York: Chelsea House Publishers, 1988. Pp 51-65.
Chaucer adapted the rhetorical catalogue to define 'an extraordinary mode of human experience or knowledge' (p 10). His ambivalence toward social transformation reflected itself in a dialectic between linear time and timelessness. *GP* portraits employ the form of the Chaucerian catalogue noting moral as well as physical attributes such as location, class, social type, profession and the way the pilgrim relates to money. The Pardoner is satirized for his economic opportunism. The detail Chaucer devotes to the normal life of each pilgrim emphasizes the degree of departure represented by the pilgrimage. The understanding

of the Pardoner is affected by perspective. The Pardoner's speaking ability being the means of his profit, *PardT* demonstrates his tools. Since the Pardoner denounces himself for avarice in *PardP*, *PardT* condemns the teller. The Pardoner and most of the pilgrims share a spirit of penance and confession engendered by the pilgrimage. Harry Bailly mistakenly reads the Pardoner's invitation as sincere.

442 Morgan, Gerald. 'The Design of the *General Prologue* to the *Canterbury Tales*.' *ES* 59(1978), 481-98.

The sequence of *GP* portraits, following the late fourteenth-century ranks of English society, closes appropriately with the morally vicious Pardoner. By placing the Summoner and the Pardoner at the end, Chaucer 'reminds us of the final Christian truths of judgment and of grace' (p 498).

443 Coletti, Theresa. 'The Pardoner's Vernicle and the Image of Man in the *Pardoner's Tale*.' *ChauNewsL* 1:1(1979), 10-2.

The vernicle, an iconic tag, serves 'as a vehicle for condemning the Pardoner' yet suggests 'an ambivalent hint of hope for him' (p 11). *PardT* weaves the themes implied by the vernicle—the juxtaposition of the Old Man and the New Man, the image of man, man's relationship to God, and the nature of flesh and spirit—while undermining the positive associations implicit in the vernicle. By punctuating his treatment of the tavern sins with references to Christ's sacrificial death, the Pardoner at once 'defiles and dismembers the body of Christ just as he corrupts his own' (p 11) and also holds out hope for man. The vernicle, like the Knight's call for reconciliation, suggests that the Pardoner 'still has a place in the Christian community' (p 12). For *PardT*, see **952**.

444 Fleming, John V. 'Chaucer's Ascetical Images.' *C&L* 28(1979), 19-26.

Chaucer enriches his portraits with a 'privileged exegetical vocabulary'(p 24) of images consciously drawn from the literature of medieval asceticism. With the image of the purse or 'wallet' (line 686), Chaucer yokes sterility and fecundity, underscoring the victory of flesh over spirit as the Pardoner, a gelding, amasses silver. Though the phallic possibilities of the medieval purse were evident in medieval art, Chaucer probably departed from the literary portrait of the Lover in *RR*. The 'purse question' (p 24) dominated thirteenth- and fourteenth-century discussions of ascetic perfection, discussions largely centering around debates concerning the mendicant orders. The literature of asceticism stressed 'the primacy of the visual imagination'(p 25). Images which nourished the ascetic imagination for a thousand years, stimulating a desire for 'a new nature, a new creation' came to inform 'the most powerful description of the imperfect creation' which Chaucer saw about him (p 25).

445 Miskimin, Alice. 'The Illustrated Eighteenth-Century Chaucer.' *MP* 77 (1979), 26-55.

Vertue's neo-Gothic portraits in the 1721 Urry edition sum up an iconographical tradition as they focus on the pilgrims 'as an array of moral, social, and psychological types' (p 32). In turning to illustrate tales rather than tellers, later eighteenth-century artists reflect a shift of interest toward Chaucerian narrative. For *PardT*, see **955**.

446 Rowland, Beryl. 'Chaucer's Idea of the Pardoner.' *ChauR* 14(1979-80), 140-54.

Rowland takes up the question: 'why should a diabolically clever, self-confessed charlatan try to persuade his listeners to behave in the same way as his customary dupes?'(p 140). Chaucer presents 'a disastrous physical ambivalence as both counterpart and cause' (p 150) of the Pardoner's behavior. Curry (**277**) and Howard (**926**) related the Pardoner's moral condition to his biology. Previously, Rowland (**601**) suggested the Pardoner was 'a testicular pseudo-hermaphrodite of the feminine type'(p 143). This paper adduces evidence from ancient and medieval authors to demonstrate 'the values attached to the hermaphrodite were ambivalent. The hermaphrodite could be the image of perfection; it could also be an image of frustration or incontinence. Philosophically, it meant an ideal unity; physically, it was an evil and a misfortune' (p 148). Chaucer draws upon the medieval understanding that 'the hermaphrodite's dual nature represented a duplicity, a doubleness of character' (p 149).

447 Weissman, Hope Phyllis. 'The Pardoner's Vernicle, the Wife's Coverchiefs, and Saint Paul.' *ChauNewsL* 1:2(1979), 10-12.

As Coletti has noted (**952**), the Pardoner's *vernicle* (line 685) is both a badge of professional accreditation and an allusion to, and parody of, the doctrine of man as *imago Dei* (cf **443**). Beyond that, the vernicle, indeed the Pardoner's entire headgear, serves as an iconographic device symbolically linking the Pardoner and the Wife of Bath. Each wears headgear that is an imitation and a travesty of the Pauline paradigm (1 Cor 11:3-10); the headgear suggests the 'feminization of the Pardoner and the masculinization of the Wife' (p 11). The travesty of the Pardoner may go further, his long hair serving as a symbol of *ignominia*. 'By acting out the negative consequences of sex-role reification, the mock knight and the drag queen also are issuing an implicit invitation' (p 12) to transcend sex differences *in Domino* (Gal 3:28). See **952**.

448 Bowden, Betsy. 'The Artistic and Interpretive Context of Blake's "Canterbury Pilgrims".' *Blake: an Illistrated Quarterly* (1980), 164-90.

The details of Blake's Pardoner can be explained by a combination of Chaucer's text, Urry's illustration (1721), and Blake's own imagination. Blake's Pardoner is like the Ellesmere Pardoner and unlike the renderings of Thynne (1532), Stowe (1561), and Urry (1721) in that he carries the *croys of latoun* (line 699), a symbol of repression in Blake's rendering. The Pardoner is positioned in Blake's *Chaucer's Canterbury Pilgrims* (1810) in several dynamic binary relationships. The Pardoner and Parson, placed in polar opposition and bisected by the cruciform Host, represent Evil and Good: the Pardoner/Summoner placed in relation to the Prioress/Second Nun suggest a relationship between 'evil elements of organized religion' (p 182) and the questionable 'innocence of vanity' (p 182); the Pardoner/Summoner combined with the Monk/Friar underscore a statement about avaricious clergymen. In the painting, Blake links Pardoner and Prioress by contrasting hands; in the *Descriptive Catalogue* (1809), he links Pardoner, Prioress and Wife of Bath in 'an unresolved syntactic ambivalence' (p 181) with word echoes (blight:rank; rank: blight).

449 Donaldson, E. Talbot. 'Chaucer in the Twentieth Century: Presidential Address to the New Chaucer Society, 1979.' *SAC* 2(1980), 7-13.

Chaucer's 'imitation of down-to-earth honesty' together with his 'occasional shows of endearing incompetence' have led critics to imagine he has said something other than what he has said (p 9). Conflicting evidence exists on the issue of the Pardoner's sexuality: *stif burdoun* has been interpreted as a pun reflecting homosexuality; *geldyng* and *mare* bring their own suggestions and, if Curry is correct, the Pardoner is sexless (**277**). Chaucer captures the paradoxical nature of human beings; in fact, 'there is good evidence that the Pardoner is and is not homosexual' (p 9).

450 McAlpine, Monica E. 'The Pardoner's Homosexuality and How It Matters.' *PMLA* 95(1980), 8-22. Rpt in *Geoffrey Chaucer's 'The*

Pardoner's Tale.' Modern Critical Interpretations. Ed. and introd Harold Bloom. New York: Chelsea House Publishers, 1988. Pp 103-24.

Previous commentary on the narrator's remark, *I trowe he were a geldyng or a mare* (line 691) has focused on the implications of *geldyng* (usually taken as eunuch). Evidence from other medieval texts suggests that *mare* should be translated 'homosexual.' The portrait of the Pardoner is a pastiche of allusions to effeminacy, hermaphroditism, and eunuchry. These categories can account for some of the Pardoner's characteristics: only homosexuality can account for all of them. The narrator finds the Pardoner's professional expertise as important as his sexual identity. Uncertain himself, the narrator presents the Pardoner more as a puzzle to be solved than a pilgrim to be judged (p 14). His song (line 672) suggests a desire for acceptance. Readers are forced to seek 'a nonreductive appreciation of his sexuality and its spiritual implications' (p 18). 'Chaucer may be seen as using his art, and especially its indirection and allusiveness, to challenge the sexual phobias of his readers' (p 18). Avarice is a screen sin: the Pardoner is obsessively interested in states of sin and in the body as source, instrument, and victim of sin (p 15). The *vernicle* (line 685) 'asserts the dignity of the Pardoner, whatever his sexual status, as part of Christ' and 'asserts the necessity of each reader's responding to the Pardoner in the context of Christian love'(p 19). For *PardP*, see **638**; for *PardT*, see **967**.

451 Ridley, Florence H. 'Chaucerian Criticism: The Significance of Varying Perspectives,' *NM* 81(1980) 131-41.

Commenting on the 1976 MLA session 'Thwarted Sexuality in the Works of Chaucer' as 'imaginative constructs derived from Chaucer's poetry' (p 141), Ridley concisely surveys critical appraisals of the Pardoner, a pilgrim who consistently inspires little sympathy.

452 Donaldson, E. Talbot. 'Adventures in the Adversative Conjunction in the General Prologue to the *Canterbury Tales*, or, What's before the *But*?' In *So meny people, longages, and tonges: Philological Essays in Scots and Mediaeval English Presented to Angus McIntosh.* Ed. Michael Benskin and M.L. Samuels. Edinburgh: Benskin and Samuels, 1981. Pp 355-66.

The Narrator uses *but* in both a logical and illogical way though the latter is indicated twice as frequently as the former. The Pardoner's portrait contains seven adversative *buts*; that is, they 'introduce a statement of the nature of an exception, objection, limitation, or contrast to what has gone before' (OED cited p 357). The Pardoner evokes a series of *buts* (lines 676, 679, 680, 692, 707, 710) from the Narrator that seem to trace a trajectory from 'ill-ease' to gradual acceptance (p 355). 'The but discriminates between the fine trappings of the Pardoner's performance as noble ecclesiast and his genuine role as recipient of what the Offertory might produce' (p 358).

453 Donaldson, E. Talbot. Part III of 'Thwarted Sexuality in Chaucer's Works.' *Florilegium* 3(1981), 256-8.
Donaldson finds examples of thwarted sexuality in Chaucer's works infrequent. He differs with Howard (**424**) and Ridley (**459**) in making a distinction between love and sexuality. The Pardoner is not sexually thwarted but 'sexually wholly deprived'(p 258). Love 'cannot apparently exist' (p 258) in the Pardoner; asexuality is the symbol not the cause of his lovelessness. Unable to love, the Pardoner, like Pandarus and Chaucer, produces 'art of a high order, which is a surrogate, perhaps, for love'(p 258). See **456, 459, 460**.

454 Duder, Clyburn. *'Thematic Relationships Between Hagiographical References and "The Canterbury Tales."* DAI 41(1981). University of North Dakota Dissertation,1980.
The aim of this dissertation is to demonstrate a relationship between the life and symbolic representation of a saint and the corresponding reference and allusion in *CT.* The appendix lists all saints in *CT* (including Paul, Ronyan, and Veronica) and a separate chapter is provided on the Pardoner.

455 Friedman, John Block. 'Another Look at Chaucer and The Physiognomists.' *SP* 78(1981), 138-52.
Reading humoural type from physical signs (cf **277**) is particularly well suited to characters like the Pardoner who are fully developed at the outset and unlikely to be altered by their pilgrimage.

456 Howard, Donald R. Part I of 'Thwarted Sexuality in Chaucer's Works.' *Florilegium* 3(1981), 243-9.
No matter how we diagnose the Pardoner's physical disorder, 'sex is thwarted by his body, by nature—that greatest of ironists'(p 243). The Pardoner shares thwarted gender identity with the Wife of Bath and the Prioress. The medieval lesson about sexuality was a lesson of *contemptus mundi,* that it was the nature of sexuality to be thwarted. See **452, 453, 459, 460**.

457 Lawton, D[avid] A. 'The Pardoner's Tale: Morality and its Context.'

In *Studies in Chaucer*. Ed. G.A. Wilkes and A.P. Riemer. Sydney: University of Sydney, 1981. Pp 38-63. Rpt as 'The Pardoner: Morality and its Context.' In *Chaucer's Narrators*. Cambridge: D.S. Brewer, 1985; Wolfeboro, New Hampshire: Boydell and Brewer, 1986. Pp 17-35. [Page numbers from 1981.]

GP presents a portrait 'of memorable abnormality and extreme villainy'(p 38). The juxtaposition of tale and teller have typically led critics to rationalize the Pardoner in psychological or spiritual terms or to rationalize his tale as a moral commentary on his person (p 38). The portrait is 'comically overdrawn' (p 51) as is clear from his relics. The critical investigations of the Pardoner's sexuality overlook the fact that to the pilgrims the Pardoner remained sexually anomalous. The Pardoner is immediately identified as a phony and is clearly unpleasant. A grotesque, he mirrors and challenges the grotesque in ourselves and our world (p 53). For *PardT*, see **979**.

458 Morgan, G[erald]. 'Rhetorical Perspectives in the *General Prologue* to the *Canterbury Tales*.' *ES* 62(1981), 411-22.

This article builds on **442**. The purpose of schematic representation of types is found in Chaucer's rhetorical tradition. *GP* exhibits the range of human nature in a comic rather than satiric way. Ironic detachment is less pervasive in *GP* than Donaldson (**333**) believes (p 416). The demonstrative portraits serve as an epideictic device intended to elicit specific emotional responses. Physical description implies moral judgment. In the Pardoner's lack of vitality and unfashionable appearance there is a deformation of the ideal of courtly youth (p 417).

459 Ridley, Florence. Part IV of 'Thwarted Sexuality in Chaucer's Works.' *Florilegium* 3(1981), 258-63.

Ridley provides a summation to the thematic panel **452, 453, 456, 460, 466**. Thwarted sexuality 'is a timeless aspect of the human condition' (p 261). Because Chaucer has refused to give explicit explanations of his characters' behavior, we supply them. The Pardoner has been described as sexually thwarted and therefore: a necrophiliac, an hermaphrodite, a gelding *and* a mare, a revolting abomination, or a tragic victim of hypocrites. Most of these constructs depend on 'selective reading' and 'fertile imagination' (p 262). The degree to which such readings are responses to, rather than interpretations of, the text should be recognized.

460 Rowland, Beryl. Part II of 'Thwarted Sexuality in Chaucer's Works.'

Florilegium 3(1981), 250-6.

Rowland had described the Pardoner as a hermaphrodite (**359, 360**). Here she suggests 'that a contemporary audience might have found the diagnosis less exceptional than modern critics, and that Chaucer used the hermaphroditic condition as a complex central figure, reflecting it in imagery in both Prologue and Tale, in order to make a specific indictment' (p 254). The hermaphroditic diagnosis is congruent with the Pardoner's relationship with the Summoner, his shoulder-length hair, his concern with fashion, his hairless face, and his amorous aspirations. He demonstrates the desire of the sex in which he was raised; his cry *Sampsoun, Sampsoun* epitomizes sexual frustration as does the Wife of Bath's *Allas! allas! that evere love was synne!* The Pardoner bodies forth the lesson that 'human nature remains self-deceiving and incomplete' (p 256). See **452, 453, 456, 459,** and **466.**

461 Stevens, Martin. 'The Ellesmere Miniatures as Illustrations of Chaucer's *Canterbury Tales.*' *SIcon* 7-8(1981-82), 113-34.

The illustrations of the Ellesmere manuscript are ahead of their time in portraying a surprisingly close reading of the text. The Pardoner's portrait is partly descriptive and largely narrative. The physical picture of the Pardoner is conveyed by selected details e.g., his effeminate hair and 'provocatively commercial' collection of 'junk items' (p 118). Figure 4 of the Ellesmere miniatures is unmistakable in its rendering of Chaucer's description (e.g., *colpons* of hair, clean shaven, wearing a vernicle, eyes *glarynge*, carrying cross, wallet and collection of pardons). In their placement at the head of their respective tales, the illuminations help bridge *GP* portrait with the tale itself.

462 Benson, C. David. 'Chaucer's Pardoner: His Sexuality and Modern Critics.' *Mediaevalia* 8(1982), 337-49.

Benson opposes psychological readings of the Pardoner (contra **273, 365, 424**), to argue that the 'excessive modern preoccupation' with his sexuality 'distorts Chaucer's method of characterization by demanding certainty where none exists' (p 338). Critical interpretation of *I trowe he were a geldyng or a mare* (line 691) often fails to consider the qualifier *I trowe*, the doubt created by animal metaphors, and the fact that two possibilities, by their nature, 'mock any attempt at precise identification'(p 339). Curry inaugurated the sexual interpretation of the Pardoner (**686**), but his evidence for eunuchry is not as conclusive as generally thought; further, the allusion to hare and goat more likely suggests unspecified lust. The homosexual thesis (316) is likewise insufficiently grounded, often resulting from the critic becoming Chaucer's collaborator. Misguided efforts to describe the 'real' Pardoner trivialize Chaucer's accomplishment: 'the vague and contradictory hints of sexual peculiarity ... prepare us for the more serious ecclesiastical corruptions to follow'(p 346).

463   Green, Richard Firth. 'The Sexual Normality of Chaucer's Pardoner.' *Mediaevalia* 8(1982), 351-8.

Green casts his argument as an appendix to **1058**; he argues the text offers no hint of a homosexual relationship between Pardoner and Summoner nor of sexual incapacity in the Pardoner. The Pardoner's effeminacy is appropriate because he is a parody of the Christian virtue of mercy, a feminine virtue; in addition, the doubleness of his physical nature may reflect his spiritual duplicity. Further, in the context of the Middle Ages, his effeminacy could be taken as an emblem of his carnality (p 357).

464   Higgs, Elton D. 'The Old Order and the "Newe World" in the General Prologue to the *Canterbury Tales.*' *HLQ* 45(1982), 155-73.

GP portraits reveal tensions between the Old Order (e.g. feudalism, rural economy, unchallenged Church) of the fourteenth century and 'the forces of plague, urbanization, and entrepreneurship which were pushing toward fragmentation of the society and a greater degree of individualism' (p 155). The Pardoner contrasts with the Knight, Clerk, and Parson, and serves as 'a negative summation of the theme of disorder ...' (p 169). He represents unprincipled manipulation of people counterpoised against the ideal of old rural service (e.g. Parson and Plowman). The representatives of disorder are given progressively more attention in each of the three sections. The Pardoner is one of five pilgrims who violate *commune profit*. With the Manciple, Reeve and Summoner, he is associated with towns, a mobile population and the flow of money. His eunuchry and related behavior suggest he has so much self-loathing he finds it impossible to participate as part of an ordered society.

465   Leicester, H. Marshall. '"Synne Horrible": The Pardoner's Exegesis of His Tale, and Chaucer's.' In *Acts of Interpretation: The Text in its Contexts, 700-1600: Essays on Medieval and Renaissance Literature in Honor of E. Talbot Donaldson.* Ed. Mary J. Carruthers and Elizabeth D. Kirk. Norman, Oklahoma: Pilgrim Books, 1982. Pp

25-50.

There is something 'conspicuous and aggressive about the Pardoner's failure to conceal his various evils'(p 29). From the obvious fakery of his bulls and relics to his physical peculiarities, the Pardoner's manner invites an interpretation later confirmed by his tale.

466 Sylvia, Daniel; Donald R. Howard; E. Talbot Donaldson; Florence Ridley; Beryl Rowland. 'Thwarted Sexuality in Chaucer's Works.' *Florilegium* 3(1982), 239-67.

Daniel Sylvia introduces (pp 239-42) papers originally presented at a special MLA session on thwarted sexuality 'and one of its subspecies, thwarted love' (p 240). Donald Howard discusses the term 'sexuality' and examines Chaucer's presentation of the Pardoner as thwarted in his sexuality (Part I pp 243-9, **456**). Beryl Rowland similarly examines the Wife of Bath and the Pardoner (Part II pp 250-6, **460**). E. Talbot Donaldson differs from Howard and Rowland in his distinction between love and sexuality (Part III pp 256-8, **452** and **453**). He proposes that the Pardoner is self-thwarted, and, that like Pandarus and Chaucer, the Pardoner prefers art to experience, possibly as a consequence of thwarted sexuality. Florence Ridley distinguishing between 'traditional' criticism and 'psychoanalytic creative commentary,'(p 242) suggests that all criticism is self-reflexive (Part IV pp 258-63, **459**). Noting that Chaucer has deliberately left the matter of thwarted sexuality open, she demonstrates the dramatic creativity of critics enticed to interpret the Pardoner.

467 Wurtele, Douglas. 'Some Uses of Physiognomical Lore in Chaucer's *Canterbury Tales.*' *ChauR* 17(1982), 130-41.

The physiognomical lore in *GP* is not random and folklorish, but based on authority of several treatises widely known in Chaucer's time: they represent 'a mode of popular wisdom' (p 133). Though Curry has read the physiognomical details as simple characterization (**277**); they are better understood as a technique of Chaucer the ironist. They are inserted into the portraits by the narrator, 'a fellow evidently versed in the wisdom to be acquired from studying those physical details upon which the physiognomists base their predictions about human behavior' (p 134). The voice of *GP* is that of a pilgrim observer engaged in a display of physiognomical wisdom to meet the Host's demand for 'best sentence.' When viewed in relation to the physical lore in the *Secreta*, the details of hair, eye and voice convey damaging implications (e.g.

timidity, arrogance, *folye*, and *womanhede*). The pervasive motif is betrayal. Readily accessible to the pilgrims (including the Pardoner), the implications of physiognomical lore are held up to the scrutiny of Chaucer the poet who might be more skeptical of physiognomists' theories than the pilgrims.

468 Burnley, David. *A Guide to Chaucer's Language*. Norman: University of Oklahoma Press, 1983. See **161**.

In a treatment of interpretive implications of grammar and syntax, Burnley notes that line 693 presents simple negation characteristic of an informal style. For *PardT*, see **1007**.

469 Cooper, Helen. *The Structure of the Canterbury Tales*. London: Duckworth, 1983.

Even when a narrator is as fallible as the Pardoner, the story remains untouched; rhetorically, a tale against avarice is suited to a pardoner. 'The tales of evil are the clearest example of false felicity carried over from their tellers' (p 217). The Pardoner's vision is of a godless world: he may boast of paradox in telling a moral tale 'but the fit between teller and tale is all too close' (p 217). The one homosexual relationship hinted at in *CT* can be viewed within the larger theme of friendship between men. For *PardP*, see **642**; for *PardT*, see **1008**.

470 Eberle, Patricia J. 'Commercial Language and the Commercial Outlook in the *General Prologue*.' *ChauR* 18(1983), 161-74. Rpt in *Geoffrey Chaucer's The General Prologue to the Canterbury Tales*. Ed. Harold Bloom. New York: Chelsea House Publishers, 1988. Pp 113-23.

References to money in *GP* have been interpreted as within the tradition of venality satire and prelude to the Pardoner's sermon and tale (cf **353**); yet *GP* lacks the explicit condemnations of venality typical of the convention.

471 Ginsberg, Warren. 'The Cast of Character: Chaucer and the Conventions of Originality.' In *The Cast of Character: The Representation of Personality in Ancient and Medieval Literature*. Toronto: University of Toronto Press, 1983. Pp 134-65.

Chaucer's characters manifest a 'submerged conventionality' (p 141): irony often results from the juxtaposition of conventional expectations and behavior in *CT*. The Pardoner derives power from 'his conscious denial of the processes of literary typology' (p 142). By introducing images with spiritual connotations (e.g., the dove, the Old Man) yet allowing only literal meaning, the Pardoner reveals his lack of faith.

472 Knight, Stephen. 'Chaucer's Pardoner in Performance.' *SSEng* 9 (1983-4), 21-36.

The Pardoner is a type arising from the tradition of a speaker simultaneously confessing and performing villainy (cf *Faux Semblant*). Such contradiction is particularly disruptive in the medieval context where the individual is seen as a fragment of a social whole, and fulfilling a role is understood as a social duty rather than falseness to individuality. The Pardoner, 'a deeply shocking figure' is 'a truly dialectical figure in that the contemporary vigour of one system—external values—is the cause of its overthrow'(p 32). The Pardoner is 'a self-conscious, anti-communal, individualist revolutionary' (p 32). The late fourteenth century shows an increasing awareness that the public 'semblance' may be 'false' (p 34). Chaucer's imagination derives power from the rapidly developing social and cultural individualism. The Pardoner's obsession with cash receives context from the transition from the 'use value' system of the manorial economy to a cash economy. For *PardT*, see **1017**.

473 Owen, Charles A., Jr. 'Development of the Art of Portraiture in Chaucer's *General Prologue*.' *LeedsSE* 14(1983), 116-33.

The Pardoner's portrait, as one of the later and possibly 'added' portraits, exemplifies Chaucer's developing technique. Building toward an identity rather than asserting it (p 117), Chaucer challenges the traditional sequence of *effictio* preceding *notatio*. The Pardoner's portrait employs negative superlatives to establish distinction. The marked use of simile (6 in 46 lines) is characteristic of the portraits of four of the five churls as well as all three of the possibly inserted portraits. Other features that suggest Chaucer's 'widening range of artistic possibilities'(p 125), his 'creative collaboration' (p 127) with his audience and his changing evaluation of the world he lived in (p 128) include: 'the moral comedy of praise for scoundrels' (p 126), groupings which offset the Parson-Plowman pair with the Summoner-Pardoner pair, and the misapplied value statement *noble ecclesiaste*. By the time of the Pardoner's portrait, the portraits have become 'improvisations where the freedom of pilgrims and author invites and challenges the participation of the reader'(p 130).

474 Rhodes, James F. 'The Pardoner's *Vernycle* and His *Vera Icon*.' *MLS* 13(1983), 34-40.

A fuller knowledge of the tradition of the Veronica illuminates the nature of the Pardoner. The association of the Veronica story with the Crucifixion did not occur until the fourteenth century. Though 'the *vernycle* seems to have been something like a standard part of the "uniform" of Pardoners' (pp 37-8), Chaucer may suggest deeper significance. The *vernycle* represents many of the things the Pardoner outwardly covets (e.g., youth, power of miracles, redemptive grace) and inwardly may represent a receptivity. Pilgrim badge and sacred face, the *vernycle* may associate the Pardoner with Christ's ministry: 'bearing that image of Christ who has not yet fulfilled his earthly mission, may make the Pardoner ... a questor for the true image too' (p 38).

475 Shoaf, R[ichard] A. *Dante, Chaucer and the Currency of the Word: Money, Images and Reference in Late Medieval Poetry.* Norman, Oklahoma: Pilgrim Books Inc., 1983. Chap 13: 'The Pardoner and the Word of Death,' pp 211-27 rpt in *Geoffrey Chaucer's 'The Pardoner's Tale.'* [Modern Critical Interpretations]. Ed. and introd. Harold Bloom. New York: Chelsea House Publishers, 1988, pp 139-58.

The Pardoner 'is the most skillful, theatrical, and elusive' (p 211) of Chaucer's posers. Whatever the specifics, the Pardoner's identity remains a question to others 'and therefore almost certainly a question to himself' (p 213). The pattern of his obsession is clear: 'ravaged personality, mutilated; a brilliant mind, unbalanced; abnormal sensitivity; a probable desire to be saved, ... a profession which involves merchandising out of the store of Redemption and the treasury of Christ' (p 215). The Pardoner 'counterpoises' (p 214) the Knight's position within *GP*, his virtues and his lack of passion. For *PardP* and *PardT*, see **1026.**

476 Smith, Sarah Stanbury. '"Game in Myn Hood": The Traditions of A Comic Proverb.' *SIcon* 9(1983), 1-12.

The hood that can both conceal the face and reveal public identity is an apt symbol for conveying the disparity between reality and appearances. Noting that the origin for the connection between 'hood' and violations of public identity may derive from a Latin pun (*cucullus*:cowl; *cuculus*:cuckold), Smith identifies comic nuances in Chaucer, other medieval writers and manuscript illuminators. The dual association of the hood with hypocrisy and adultery is relevant to the Pardoner; in packing away his hood, the Pardoner shows his wish to replace his conventional identity with a particular one: 'bare head and glaring eyes advertising his own flesh, and his cap with its Veronica advertising his relics for sale'(p 2). The stashing of the hood may also be a sign of his own celebration of his overt hypocrisy. 'As the arch-hypocrite turned confessor, he flaunts his profession and shows us his tricks, while he removes the single article of clothing that might signify pretense'(p 3).

477 Traversi, Derek. *The Canterbury Tales: A Reading.* Newark, Deleware: University of Delaware Press, 1983.
Chapter 2. The Pardoner is the most disquieting and sinister of the pilgrims though comedy of an un-moralizing nature is the essence of the portrait. He exploits God's mercy as his companion, the Summoner, exploits God's justice. The opposite of the Parson, the Pardoner divorces ostensible function from visible reality (p 28). Humor arises from the juxtaposition of his incompatible features and the list of objects that characterize his trade. For *PardP*, see **645**; for *PardT*, see **1030**.

478 Ames, Ruth M. *God's Plenty: Chaucer's Christian Humanism.* Chicago: Loyola University Press, 1984.
The Pardoner, together with the Summoner, is one of the two most shameful characters in *CT*: 'opposite sides of a counterfeit coin' (p 57). Falsely pardoning the guilty, the Pardoner is the antithesis of Christ. Whatever Christian value might originally have been connected with the Pardoner's profession, Chaucer finds none viable. Chaucer does not use the reference to pardons from Rome as an opportunity to register Wycliffite sentiments against the Pope. For *PardT*, see **1033**.

479 Kane, George. *Chaucer.* [Past Masters Series]. Oxford: Oxford University Press, 1984.
Chaucer's pilgrims are dramatizations of estates satire which specified typical shortcomings. Writing in a 'closed system' where religion prescribed answers to fundamental questions, Chaucer, nevertheless, explored existing value conflicts shaped by the sexual and acquisitive urge. The Pardoner, the 'consummate conman' (p 109) and the Summoner represent the worst dishonesty in preying on human weakness and the fear of damnation. They produce a grotesque comedy. Successes in their own way, we see how their success renders them deficient in integrity.

480 Bloom, Harold. Introduction. *Geoffrey Chaucer.* Modern Critical Views. Ed. and introd. Harold Bloom. New York: Cheslea House Publishers, 1985. Pp 1-6.
Chaucer is, like Shakespeare, Cervantes and Tolstoi, one of those great

writers who defeats almost all criticism. The Pardoner, like the Wife of Bath, calls into question virtually every mode of criticism. In their vitality, they are representations of 'what a human being *might* be' (p 2). 'The Pardoner *is* the interior and even Iago, even Goneril and Regan, Cornwall and Edmund, do not give us a fiercer sense of intolerable resonance on the way down and out'(p 4). No codes of criticism will explain 'the Pardoner's more-than-Dostoevskian intermixture of supernatural faith and preternatural chicanery?' (p 4). The critic must 'become a vitalizing interpreter in the service of an art whose burden is only to carry more life forward into a time without boundaries' (p 6).

481   Lindahl, Carl. 'The Festive Form of the *Canterbury Tales*.' *ELH* 52 (1985), 531-74. Rpt in *Earnest Games: Folkloric Patterns in the Canterbury Tales*. Bloomington: Indiana University Press, 1987. Pp 44-61.

The performancs in CT contain an 'elaborate hierarchical structure' (p 550) drawn from medieval festival. Festival art must appeal broadly; a challenge such as that of the *gentils* to the classes such as the Pardoner, Reeve, Miller and Summoner were the principal performers and beneficiaries in these festivals. See **500**.

482   Orton, P.R. 'Chaucer's General Prologue, A 673 *Burdoun* and Some Sixteenth-Century Puns.' *ELN* 23 (1985), 3-4.

Although the musical sense of *burdoun*, 'ground melody' is explicit in context, the meaning 'phallus' is implied (p 3) (**325, 338, 343**). In Middle English, *burdoun* became confused with the native *burden, burthen*, 'load'. Shakespeare puns on *burden* as both 'load' and 'ground melody' in *Two Gentlemen of Verona* (I.ii.85); Sir Thomas Wyatt plays on the possibilities of *burden* as 'load' and 'phallus' in *Ye Old Mule* (p 4).

483   Pearsall, Derek. *The Canterbury Tales*. London: George Allen & Unwin, 1985.

Pearsall reviews critical approaches to *GP* with particular attention to the discussion of *persona*. In *GP*, all characters are described in terms of profession (cf **403**) and are recipients of approbation, often superlative, in terms of their performance (line 708) though not their morality. '... Chaucer has taken over the kind of detail customarily employed to satirise the representatives of the estates ... and has removed the elements of explicit moral condemnation' (p 67). The viciousness of the Pardoner 'is described in the same phlegmatic manner' as his repulsiveness 'to suggest that both have the objective status of observed attributes' (p 70). The Pardoner and the Wife of Bath are the 'supreme examples' of 'Chaucer's interest in the portrayal of character "in performance"' (p 91). The *GP* portrait is 'entirely and in detail consistent' with the Pardoner's self-portrayal in *PardP* (p 91). For *PardT*, see **1050**.

484 Brosnahan, Leger. '"And Don Thyn Hood" And Other Hoods in Chaucer.' *ChauR* 21(1986), 45-52.

One of twenty-two times Chaucer uses *hood* or *howve* to mean common cloth hood occurs in the description of the Pardoner (lines 680-1). The fact that the Canon wears a one-piece coat and hood and the Pardoner a detachable hood may provide slight evidence of the clerical status of the Canon and the lay status of the Pardoner.

485 Drucker, Trudy. 'Some Medical Allusions in The Canterbury Tales.' *NYSJM* 68(1986), 444-7.

Medical symptoms predominate so with the Pardoner and the Summoner that one could suppose the piglrimage is undertaken in gratitude. Drucker cites a description from an endocrinologist to support her interpretation that the Pardoner is 'beyond question' (p 444) a eunuch.

486 Ellis, Roger. *Patterns of Religious Narrative in the Canterbury Tales.* London: Croom Helm; Totowa, New Jersey; Barnes & Noble, 1986.

GP authorizes a reading of *CT* as a continuous sequence, functioning on both the literal and symbolic levels. The idea of storytelling enunciated in the frame provides the key to the primary significance of each tale. The tale, however, cannot be read simply as a reflex of the respective pilgrim in *GP*; there is a gap between what *GP*, a 'cast list,' and the framing narrative tells us about pilgrims. The presentation of the Pardoner in *GP* is closely related to *PardP* but has few clear links to *PardT*. For *PardP*, see **650**; for *PardT*, see **1067**.

487 Knight, Stephen. *Geoffrey Chaucer.* Oxford: Basil Blackwell, 1986.

The individuation like the mobility of the Pardoner is indicative of changing experience in the fourteenth century. The Pardoner is based on Faux Semblant, best translated as 'Bogus Exterior' or 'Misleading Appearance' (p 126). His 'unnatural sexuality'(p 81) is a metaphor for the way in which his skills are shifted from the proper role of preacher to his private gain: in its sterility, his homosexuality becomes a code for containment. As a 'role-abusing servitor'(p 73), the Pardoner like the other churls is indicative that the authority of traditional role-models was decreasing. For *PardT*, see **1070, 1071**.

488 Needham, Paul. *The Printer and the Pardoner: An Unrecorded Indulgence Printed by William Caxton for the Hospital of St. Mary Rounceval, Charing Cross.* Washington, D.C.: Library of Congress, 1986.

A project of the Center for the Book, this volume reprints an unrecorded Caxton indulgence as it was discovered in strips of the binding of the Rosenwald Sammelband. Also included are brief essays on William Caxton, early indulgence printing and its survival, indulgence printing in England, the hospital of St. Mary Rounceval, and indulgences issued by St. Mary Rounceval.

489 Nolan, Barbara. "'A Poet Ther Was'": Chaucer's Voices in the General Prologue to *The Canterbury Tales.' PMLA* 101(1986), 154-69. Rpt in *Geoffrey Chaucer's The General Prologue to the Canterbury Tales.* Ed. Harold Bloom. New York: Chelsea House Publishers, 1988. Pp 125-147.

'[T]hree voices and three attitudes toward poetic authority vie for control in the *Prologue*—the "clerk's," the pilgrim's and the Host's' (p 158). The Pardoner follows the Host in purely secular play. Unlike the voice of the 'clerk,' concerned with causality, hierarchy and order, that of Host and Pardoner offer 'the disorders, sexual exploits, and trivialities of quotidian life' (p 166). The pilgrim Chaucer's voice is 'as richly various and morally dense and stubbornly inconclusive as its total subject'(p 166).

490 Olson, Paul A. *The 'Canterbury Tales' and the Good Society.* Princeton: Princeton University Press, 1986.

Olson reads Chaucer's language from within the linguistic and semiotic system of the fourteenth-century intellectual milieu. In *GP*, Chaucer moves from court to city to country (where the Pardoner operates) and from top to bottom in the moral order to show disintegrative forces at work. 'The presentation of the Pardoner and the Summoner as grotesque parodies of the Church arises out of late fourteenth-century English theological disputes over the hierarchy'(p 185). The homosexuality of the Pardoner and Summoner reflects 'Wycliffite episcopal debate over the "hermaphroditic" commingling of temporal and spiritual power in the exercise of the apostolic office of the keys' (p 39). In the portraits of the Summoner (representing the excommunication curse) and the Pardoner (representing the indulgence), Chaucer exposes 'the Epicurean root of Wyclif's problem with the keys' (p 183). The Pardoner sells true pardons (cf **304, 314**). For *PardT*, see **1077**.

491 Richardson, Janette. 'Intention and the Pardoner.' In *Chaucer and the Craft of Fiction*. Ed. Leigh A. Arrathoon. Rochester, Michigan: Solaris Press, 1986. Pp 85-95.

The Pardoner is a public speaker whose very mode of existence depends on his ability to persuade unsophisticated audiences to buy his pardons. His exclamatory style is undercut by his goat-like voice and his attempts to hide his homosexuality provoke a rude response from the Host. For *PardT*, see **1079**.

492 Benson, Larry. *The Riverside Chaucer*. 1987. See **117**.

For Pardoner, see **498**; for *PardP*, see **655**; for *PardT*, see **1091**.

493 Bowden, Betsy. *Chaucer Aloud: The Varieties of Textual Interpretation*. Philadelphia: University of Pennsylvania Press, 1987.

Bowden explores 'divergent yet valid responses' (p 3) to the Pardoner in pre-Victorian readers' responses 'after and before the eighteenth century'(pp 77-93); in the eighteenth century (pp 94-113), as well as in performance analysis of taped readings of crucial passages (accompanying tape). Blake's 'misunderstood moral stance' (p 81) replaced the previously established interpretation of the Pardoner as a comic figure with that of a wicked figure. The Pardoner in the *Prologue* to the *Tale of Beryn* 'is clearly a buffoon' (p 89); the Pardoners in Heywood's *A mery Play betwene the Pardoner and the frere, the curate and neybour Pratt* (1533) and *Four P's* (1544) offer 'a comic satire on Roman Catholic abuses'(p 92). The eighteenth century presents a range of interpretations, the most influential being that of Pope/ Betterton. Demonstrating that '[t]extual interpretations do vary extensively within the identical sociohistorical context' (p 109), Bowden cites the evidence of modernization (William Lipscomb), translation (French, 'probably the Abbé Prévost' p 100), and Elizabeth Cooper, a critical reader uninvolved 'with running battles of the scholarly establishment'(p 109). Various twentieth-century views are inferred from taped readings (pp 114-131). For *PardP*, see **652**; for *PardT*, see **1087**.

• Review by Richard Osberg, *SAC* 11(1989), 186-8: Another set of chapters, based on reception aesthetics and Caroline Spurgeon's magisterial *Five Hundred Years of Chaucer Criticism and Allusion*, studies the responses of pre-Victorian readers, whose frequently execrable modernization (e.g., Lipscomb's) or additions (e.g., *The*

Tale of Beryn) or paintings (e.g., Stothard's) are read as diachronic evidence of variety, despite the philological ineptness and historical misinformation of their authors. Bowden relegates a third source of evidence, varying interpretations in contemporary criticism, to bibliographical notes.

494 Dent, Judith Anne. 'Sickness and the "Siker Way"; Themes of Illness and Health in Chaucer.' *DAI* 48(1987). Washington University Dissertation.

Chaucer's deep interest in medicine is reflected in the portrait of the Pardoner, Summoner and Cook; there, the misapplication of medical thought and practice leads to a result at once comic and pathetic.

495 Fritz, Donald W. 'Reflections in a Golden Florin: Chaucer's Narcissistic Pardoner.' *ChauR* 21(1987), 338-59.

The Pardoner's portrait suggests 'a smoothness and freshness of prepubertal adolescence'(p 339). From the 'jarring juxtaposition' of the effeminate Pardoner and the burly Host in *GP*, their collision is inevitable. The Host embodies the *senex* archetype; he is a figure of authority with whom the Pardoner, *puer*, must collide or unite. The Pardoner resembles the Host in that both are 'mother-bound'(p 352), a condition that may make them psychologically suspicious of each other from the outset. For *PardP*, see **653**; for *PardT*, see **1088**.

496 Gillam, Doreen, 'Chaucer's Canterbury Mare.' *NM* 88(1987), 192-99.

Gillam seeks to establish a lexical context for Chaucer's use of *mare* (line 691) to describe the Pardoner who is 'almost certainly a eunuch and very probably a homosexual too'(p 192). Chaucer uses a pilgrim's mount to describe character by extension; with the Pardoner, he applies to the man himself terms that may derive from the sale of horseflesh. Such terms place the Pardoner in the commercial sphere where he operates. Mares were not highly regarded (of the pilgrims, only the Plowman and the Cook ride mares). 'In a sense the Pardoner *is* the Summoner's mount, the pair of them constituting a travesty of the traditionally (and often sexually) symbolic horse and rider figure'(p 193). If there is a *double-entendre* (mare: female horse; mare: spectre/hag), it contributes to the sense of menace in the Pardoner's portrait. The pejorative use of *mare* for a woman extends back to Chaucer's time. Generally associated with lechery, and in women specifically with shameless sexuality, it is not improbable that the term was extended to

mean 'an effeminate homosexual.' A faintly discernible common
European tradition, evidenced in twelfth-century France (cf **403**, p146)
and vigorous in thirteenth-centry Scandinavia links 'effeminate
homosexuality' with 'female horses'(p 199). See also **450**.

497 Grennen, Joseph E. 'The Pardoner, The Host and The Depth of
Chaucerian Insult.' *ELN* 25(1987), 18-24.

The Pardoner's *vernycle* (line 685) is recalled in the Host's retort (lines
946-50) which imagines an imprint of the Pardoner's *fundement*
(buttocks, anus) on his breeches—'quite clearly a sacrilegious version
of the image of Christ's face imprinted in blood on Veronica's veil' (p
21). For *PardT*, see **1089**.

498 Hilary, Christine Ryan. [notes] *The Riverside Chaucer*. Ed. Larry
D. Benson. See **117**.

Ryan outlines the system of indulgences and surveys critical discussion
of the Pardoner's abuses, his clerical status, and sexuality. For *PardP*,
see **655**; for *PardT*, see **1091**.

499 Howard, Donald R. *Chaucer: His Life, His Works, His World*. New
York: E.P. Dutton, 1987. [Page numbers from this edition]. Published
simultaneously in the United Kingdom under the title *Chaucer and the
Medieval World*. London: Weidenfield and Nicholson, 1987.

The Pardoner, Chaucer's 'most vivid and frightening' (p 16) pilgrim
operates as an illusionist through glibness. Though Chaucer does not
create an individual psychology, he employs temperament, personal
reaction formations and individual quirks to account for character. The
Pardoner's physical repugnance finds a counterpart in his depravity. In
view of the medieval tradition of a male-female Christ, the Pardoner's
androgynous quality suggests an Antichrist figure: 'the Pardoner is an
archetypal figure, one of those figures we encounter in dreams, a
grotesque man-woman whose evil reveals to us, like a mirror, the evil in
ourselves and warns us of its punishment' (p 490). For *PardT*, see
1092.

500 Lindahl, Carl. *Earnest Games: Folkloric Patterns in the Canterbury
Tales*. Bloomington: Indiana University Press, 1987.

Lindahl builds on his earlier discussion of festival form (**481**). Discussing
CT as an 'act of community self-definition' (p 19), Lindahl ranks the
pilgrims as they would have been in a fourteenth-century household.
Though a Pardoner should rank with the Host, Gildsman, Shipman, Nun's
Priest and Chaucer the Pilgrim as the 'upper middle class' (p 23),

accorded the privilege of dining with the Squire, Chaucer's Pardoner is so abhorrent he may have been denied the honor. The Pardoner is one of thirteen pilgrims who were regular travellers, a group that includes Chaucer's finest narrators. For *PardT*, see **1094**.

501 Stone, Brian. *Chaucer*. Harmondsworth: Penguin Critical Studies, 1987; rpt 1989.

The Pardoner is one of the 'depraved' pilgrims, (the other groups being the 'good' and the 'worldly-striving') (p 32). A 'perverted lecher and corrupt minor church official' (p 78), the Pardoner astonishes with 'brilliant energy' (p 32). For *PardT*, see **1097**.

502 Bloom, Harold. "Introduction." *Geoffrey Chaucer's 'The General Prologue to the Canterbury Tales.'* Ed. and introd. Harold Bloom. New York: Chelsea House Publishers, 1988.

This collection which reprints 10 essays includes the following with reference to the Pardoner: 'Commercial Language and the Commercial Outlook in the General Prologue,' pp 113-23 (**470**); 'Memory and Form,' pp 37-50 (**424**); 'Gold and Iron: Semantic Change and Social Change in Chaucer's Prologue,' pp 73-84 (**439**); 'Medieval Estates Satire and the General Prologue,' pp 21-36 (**403**); 'Chaucer: Motive and Mask in the General Prologue,' pp 9-20 (**353**); 'History and Form in the General Prologue to the *Canterbury Tales*,' pp 51-65 (**441**); '"A Poet Ther Was": Chaucer's Voices in the General Prologue to *The Canterbury Tales*,' pp 125-47 (**489**). In a brief introductory essay, Bloom notes the Pardoner is such a distinctive artistic achievement as to call into question virtually every mode of criticism. In his ability to engender himself through reflection on his own acts, the Pardoner presages the complexity of Shakespearean characters.

503 Dinshaw, Carolyn. 'Eunuch Hermeneutics.' *ELH* 55(1988), 27-51. Revised version rpt as 'Eunuch Hermeneutics.' In *Chaucer's Sexual Poetics*. Madison: University of Wisconsin Press, 1989. Pp 156-84.

The Pardoner surrounds himself with substitute objects (e.g., relics, sealed documents) to compensate for his lacking parts. Knowing their falsity, he persists in the belief they can make him whole: the eunuch's hermeneutics proceeds by 'double affirmations ... the incompatible affirmations of knowledge and belief' (p 28). The Pardoner 'both exposes and is caught in language's double truth' (p 39). The Pardoner is a fetishist. See also **506**. For *Interr*, see **529**; for *Phy-PardL*, see **565**; for *PardT*, see **1103** and **1117**.

504 Emmerson, Richard Kenneth, and Ronald B. Herzman. '*The Canterbury Tales* in Eschatological Perspective.' In *The Use and Abuse of Eschatology in the Middle Ages*. Ed. Werner Verbeke, Daniel Verhelst, and Andries Welkenhuysen. Mediaevalia Lovaniensia 1:15. Leuven: Leuven University Press, 1988. Pp 404-24.

Chaucer provides 'an apocalyptic urgency' (p 424) by charging the Pardoner's portrait with allusions to Simon Magnus and Antichrist. Since medieval exegetes labelled simony 'spiritual sodomy' (p 423), the Pardoner's spiritual associations parallel his implied homosexual relationship with the Summoner (lines 669-73). For *PardT*, see **1104**.

505 Andrew, Malcolm. 'Context and Judgement in the *General Prologue*.' *ChauR* 23(1989), 316-37.

Andrew surveys critical approaches to *GP* (**273, 403, 434, 441**) to argue against imposing contexts on *GP* as a basis for judgment. Chaucer creates a fiction of travel which decontextualizes the pilgrims. Statements on the Pardoner's sexuality 'generate an unspecific response to the symbolic and evocative potential of these allusions' (p 325). Place names, such as *Rouncivale* are designed to 'release a set of traditional associations and prejudices' (p 330).

506 Dinshaw, Carolyn. *Chaucer's Sexual Poetics*. Madison: University of Wisconsin Press, 1989.

Dinshaw draws from Lacan to expand her treatment of the Pardoner in **503**. She finds that the Pardoner problematizes many of the terms she has employed to describe the patriarchal hermeneutic e.g., 'the passage of a woman between men and her stripping, reclothing, marriage, and domestication' (p 156). The Pardoner does not allow himself to be stripped, revealed or known; rather, he creates a screen in part through his consciously chosen dress, his stated theme and what appears to be playing 'at homosexual display' (p 157). In hermeneutic terms, 'the Pardoner's clothed body suggests that the existence of the letter of the text does not at all ensure the existence of a spirit, a truth beneath it' (p 157); in fact, the Pardoner leaves open the possibility that there is nothing underneath his representations. He is defined in terms of absence within a context of masculinity, identity and power. His sense of his own lack represents his view of language and reveals 'a hermeneutics of the partial, or, for short, eunuch hermeneutics' (p 158-9). Surrounding himself with objects (e.g., relics, documents, words), he holds on to the belief that they make him whole but 'the eunuch's hermeneutics proceeds by double affirmations, double truths, the incompatible positions of recognition and disavowel, knowledge and belief' (p 159). For *PardT*, see **1117**.

507 Vance, Eugene. 'Chaucer's Pardoner: Relics, Discourse, and Frames of Propriety.' *NLH* 20(1989), 723-45.

The Pardoner attempts to establish his credibility with sealed texts and *vernicle*. The profusion of sealed texts is intended in part to keep his unwhole body in one piece; however, his body functions as 'an exterior sign of his inability to retain the spiritual character of ordination' (p 736). The Pardoner may be a sodomist; if so, that signifies his character as a simoniac (p 736). The Pardoner has supplied himself with a variety of sacks that collect the treasures of 'the horizontal economy of this world' while subverting the 'vertical economy of salvation' (p 737). See **504**.

508 Wenzel, Siegfried. 'Chaucer's Pardoner and His Relics.' *SAC* 11 (1989), 37-41.

Countering the view that the combination of a pardoner with the display of false relics had few parallels beyond *CT*, (cf **314**, **403**), Wenzel presents two hitherto unnoticed pieces of evidence. *Fasciculus morum*, a Latin handbook for preachers written in the early fourteenth century by an anonymous Franciscan, combines the figure of a pardoner with the display of false relics in a simile. A thirteenth-century collection of *exempla* made by a Dominican friar in Cambridge links a pardoner with the display of relics (not false) in a story dating to Jordan of Saxony (d. 1237). Taken together with Canon no. 62 of the Fourth Lateran Council which juxtaposed legislation concerning relics and pardoners (it was divided when it entered the Decretals of Pope Gregory IX in 1234), and the evidence of a Middle English sermon (noted by Owst in **577**, 109-110) and a Wycliffite tract, these instances leave no doubt that 'in Chaucer's time, fraudulent pardoners who displayed fake relics were a well-established topos and evidently a historical reality'(p 41).

509 Wetherbee, Winthrop, *Geoffrey Chaucer: The Canterbury Tales.* [Landmarks of Literature]. Cambridge: Cambridge University Press, 1989.

The Pardoner's response to isolation is defiant exhibitionism. Aside from the homosexual overtones of his friendship with the Summoner, they are emblematic of the deeper need of those chronically isolated by their profession or personal traits beyond their control. Taken together, the Summoner and Pardoner show professional greed, exploitation of the authority of the Church and personal corruption; 'they bring Chaucer's anatomy of a society in flux to an appropriately ominous conclusion' (p 36). The comments about the Pardoner's sexual deficiency are as close as the narrator comes to joking about something a pilgrim cannot help; they indicate the world of *CT* is a cruel one that already stigmatizes aberrant behavior. For *PardT*, see **1126**.

510 Frese, Dolores Warwick. *An 'Ars Legendi' for Chaucer's 'Canterbury Tales': Reconstructive Readings*. Gainsville: University of Florida Press, 1991.

No other pilgrim is so prejudiced prior to the telling of his tale as the Pardoner is by his portrait. The opening of the portrait announces a continuity with the Summoner, a coupling that is repeated sufficiently to signal deviance. The Pardoner's terminal position in the pilgrimage, the coupling of money and male sexuality, the Pardoner's gelded state and the insinuations of 'sexual usury' all encourage retrospective re-readings. For *PardT*, see **1158**.

511 Kearney, Milo. *The Role of Swine Symbolism in Medieval Culture*. Lewiston: Edwin Mellen Press, 1991.

Kearney traces the pig as a symbol as it appeared through the fifteenth-century in the history, art, music, myth and literature of northern Europe. This symbol is related to man's search for truth about himself and his relationship to the universe. The Pardoner's *pigges bones* (A 700) may draw additional meaning from the use of swine as images of sin.

512 Patterson, Lee. *Chaucer and the Subject of History*. Madison: University of Wisconsin Press, 1991.

Working from the concept that Chaucerian character is 'an open site for negotiating the problematic relationship between outer and inner,' (p 16) Patterson discusses the Pardoner as both 'real' (in that he possesses inwardness) and fabricated from the materials of literary convention and medieval religious culture. The Pardoner both 'asserts and subverts the idea of a unitary selfhood' (p 423). His subjectivity constructed in alignment with the medieval understanding of sin as privation, his performance is best understood in terms of medieval confessional habits. The Pardoner's discourse is offered as 'an act of penance that seeks to atone for the transgression that has resulted in his "castration," whether it be real or only presumed' (p 372). For *PardP* and *PardT*, see **1164**.

513 Calabrese, Michael A. '"Make a Mark That Shows": Orphean Song, Orphean Sexuality, and the Exile of Chaucer's Pardoner.' *Viator* 24 (1993), 269- 86.
Genius's discourse on Orpheus and homosexual 'writing' in *RR* provides a vocabulary for discussion of the Pardoner's sexuality. The speech in which the relations among Orpheus, sodomy, Nature and death are developed is at the core of the Pardoner. The Pardoner's implied sexual behavior is 'a metaphor for, and a reflection of, his social, professional, and spiritual life ...'(p 270). The Pardoner, like Orpheus, is an eloquent artist, a preacher and a manipulator of audience; unlike Orpheus, he cannot realize his claim to control destiny. Linking themes of procreation and writing, Genius develops views on language, law, homosexuality, and art—all issues in *PardT*. 'Ovid, Orpheus, Chaucer, and the Pardoner are all artists, are all, in some sense, servants of love, and are all vulnerable to exile and death as they explore various and profoundly different ways to "write themselves" in books of immortality' (p 286). See also **958, 967, 1117, 1142, 1143**.

514 Kim, Jaewhan. 'Geoffrey Chaucer and the Medieval Science: Centered Upon Canterbury Tales.'*JELL* 39 (1993), 249-61. [In Korean with English abstract].
Chaucer often employs scientific materials, drawn from principles familiar in his day, in metaphors. His knowledge of physiognomy provides techniques in character portrayal.

515 Maxfield, Donald K. 'St. Mary Rouncivale, Charing Cross: The Hospital of Chaucer's Pardoner.' *ChauR* 28(1993), 148-63.
Maxfield adduces historical evidence to trace broad outlines for understanding medieval hospitals and their pardoners, the clerical class to which pardoners belonged, and the history of St. Mary Rouncivale, Charing Cross. After noting the multiple missions of medieval hospitals as health-care giving, soul-curing and benefice-providing institutions (p 149), he establishes the role of pardoners (*quaestorii* or *quaestores*) as raising funds through alms and rewarding repentant alms-givers with indulgences. Maxfield cites extensive records to document: the establishment of St. Mary Rouncivale and its relationship to Roncesvalles; the condemnation of false pardoners; and the criticism of false indulgences. He comments that, even if Chaucer's Pardoner was legitimate, 'most—if not all—of his indulgences were false' (p 157). Maxfield concludes that Chaucer may have selected *Rouncivale*

for his Pardoner because of his own familiarity with both Roncesvalles and Charing Cross and, more importantly, for ironic effect: '... what possibly could be more ironic than to make one of these historically pilgrim-oriented hospitals the apparent sponsor of his evil character?'(p 158). Any ironic effect would be intensified by giving the Pardoner characteristics and vices particularly abhorrent to the Augustinian tradition e.g., long hair, gluttony, concupiscence, cupidity, and avoidance of hard labor (p 158). See also **275, 286, 289, 314, 326.**

516 Bloom, Harold. 'Chaucer: The Wife of Bath, the Pardoner, and Shakespearean Character.' In *The Western Canon: The Books and School of the Ages*. Ed. Harold Bloom. New York: Harcourt Brace and Company, 1994. Pp 105-26.
In this commentary on 'canonical' works marked by 'their sublimity and their representative nature' (p 2), Bloom considers Chaucer to follow only Shakespeare as the foremost writer in English. The Pardoner he judges to be 'the most crucial' (p 119) Chaucerian character for Shakespeare. Like the Wife of Bath, the Pardoner is inward and individual; unlike her, he is 'ancestor of all Western literary characters condemned to nihilism' (p 119). Inspired by False Seeming, the Pardoner is closer to Iago: 'No one could love the Pardoner, or Iago; but no one resists their negative exuberance' (p 119).

516a Patton, Celeste A. 'Chaucer's Poetics of the Female Body.'Pennsylvania State University Dissertation, 1995. Director: Robert R. Edwards. See also *DAI* 56, 0545.
Chaucer uses the female body to signify a range of characters from ideal types to vile grotesques. He rarely employs the female body for the comic grotesque and reserves the feminized male grotesque for his more serious rhetorical creations such as the Pardoner.

16b Gross, Gregory 'Trade Secrets: Chaucer, the Pardoner, the Critics.' *MLS* 25(1995), pp 1-36.
Gross sets out to historicize the Pardoner and discover the common ground between twentieth century constructions of gay identity and Chaucer's presentation of the Pardoner. A review of criticism on the Pardoner's sexuality from Kittredge **(668)** through Dinshaw **(506)** reveals an essentialist strain which reads the Pardoner as a homosexual. The rhetoric of secrecy, which in the nineteenth century was a vehicle for expressing anxiety about public morality, becomes, in the twentieth century, a vehicle for anxiety about sexuality **(277, 303, 323, 450,**

462, 506). Essentialist readings mistakenly proceed from the anachronistic premise that the body is 'encoded by sexuality' (p 15). When critical attention is refocused from identity to behavior, connections can be found among the Pardoner's sexual habits, and the nature of his trade and his use of rhetoric; these connections are elucidated by the medieval literary tradition that conflated sodomy and idolatry and read sodomy as an analogue of 'unproductive' language (p 2). The Pardoner's characterization as a *ful vicious man* may refer to his 'misuse of rhetoric for socially unproductive ends' (p 29) as well as to his physical nature.

❧ The Pardoner's Interruption of The Wife of Bath

517 Patch, Howard Rollin. *On Rereading Chaucer.* 1939.
The 'hardened bluff' involved in the Pardoner's interruption of the Wife of Bath is 'piercingly sad' (p 164). Unlike the Wife, the Pardoner has no friendships, 'only the dark satisfaction of his pride' (p 166). For Pardoner, see **300**; for *PardP*, see **582**; for *PardT*, see **712**.

518 Moore, Arthur K. 'Alysoun's Other Tonne.' *MLN* 59(1944), 481-3.
The Pardoner's interruption (D 168) incites the Wife of Bath to take up the convention *qui capit uxorem.* Chaucer is probably the first to cast a woman in this role; unlike earlier Latin and French treatments of the convention, Chaucer 'camouflages a threadbare pattern with a merry account of a wife's adventures with five husbands' (p 483).

519 Lumiansky, R.M. 'A Conjecture Concerning Chaucer's Pardoner.' 1949. Rpt with minor modifications in 'The Pardoner.' *Of Sondry Folk: The Dramatic Principle in the Canterbury Tales.* R.M. Lumiansky. Austin: University of Texas Press, 1955, rpt through 1980. [Page numbers from 1949; 1980.]
Lumiansky is convinced *PardT* follows *WBT* (contra **686**). In the Wife of Bath, the Pardoner recognizes a kindred spirit: she, diverging from established behavior in marriage; he, in confession and pardon. The Pardoner interprets the pilgrims' lack of remonstrance to the Wife of Bath's heresy as an 'affectation of worldliness in regard to accepted moral laws' (p 8; 207); he concludes their worldliness is deep enough 'to bear the revelation of his own [scurrilous] gross tricks' (p 10; 209). It may be at this point that the Pardoner decides the Host, 'already

bested by various Pilgrims' (p 8; 207) and the pilgrim characterized by the highest degree of 'affected sophistication' (p 7; 206), is his most likely victim. If the Pardoner is a member of a mendicant order, his mention of a plan to wed is simply another example of disregard for rules. For Pardoner, see **311**; for *Phy-PardL*, see **539**; for *PardP*, see **588**; for *PardT*, see **724**.

520 Moore, Arthur K. 'The Pardoner's Interruption of The *Wife of Bath's Prologue.' MLQ* 10(1949), 49-57.

The Pardoner's interruption of *WBP* does not break the continuity; rather, it motivates with 'good-natured badinage'(p 50) the second and longer part of the general discussion of marriage. *WBP* fuses two related subjects: marriage and celibacy (through line 162), and *tribulacion in mariage* (line 193 to end). The Pardoner is answered by the Wife's accounts of marriage; the religious are 'twitted' (p 49) by her burlesque of an antifeminist satire, a feat that becomes a 'spectacular attack on ecclesiastical authority' (p 56).

521 Owen, Charles A., Jr. 'The Development of the *Canterbury Tales.' JEGP* 57(1958), 449-76.

The interruption (lines 161-92) was probably added at the time of composition of *PardP* and *PardT* though it may have been part of Chaucer's original plan to prepare for the Pardoner's confession. The first 162 lines of *WBP* were originally intended to follow *MLT* and introduce *ShT*. For *GP*, see **334**; for *PardT*, see **761**.

522 Howard, Edwin. *Geoffrey Chaucer.* 1964.

It is noteworthy that when the Pardoner interrupts the Wife of Bath to say he is contemplating marriage that she makes no derogatory remarks about his manhood. For Pardoner, see **355** for *PardT*, see **786**.

523 Jordan, Robert M. *Chaucer and the Shape of Creation: The Aesthetic Possibilities of Inorganic Structure.* Cambridge, Massachusetts: Harvard University Press, 1967.

The Pardoner's response to the Wife of Bath is oblique and 'remarkably self-effacing' (p 219). His courteous language underscores the Wife's shrewishness. His interruption is to be interpreted in the context of *PardP* and *PardT*: 'Chaucer was no doubt quite aware of the intricate play of ironies he was here setting in motion' (p 220). The Pardoner embodies the anti-feminist view. For *PardT*, see **819**.

524 Kernan, Anne. 'The Archwife and The Eunuch.' 1974. See **408**.

The Pardoner's interruption of *WBP* serves not only as a marker of a logical division but a 'more significant dramatic center than has yet been recognized'(p 1). Apparent opposites, the Pardoner and the Wife of Bath are 'exemplars of *cupiditas* and of distorted and barren sexuality'(p 25). The impotent Pardoner is intrigued by the Wife's depiction of husbands enslaved by their wives' sexual demands. The Pardoner's interruption of the Wife of Bath 'epitomizes in dramatic form the fundamental accord of *amor prauus* between them' (p 25). For Pardoner, see **408**; for *PardT*, see **894**.

525 Gallick, Susan. 'A Look at Chaucer and His Preachers.' *Speculum* 50 (1975), 456-76.
The Pardoner sees *WBP* as an antifeminist exhortation against marrying and submitting the male body to insatiable female drives. Seeing no discrepancy between the Wife's character and her preaching, he fails to see beneath the pulpit rhetoric that described women from the male point of view (p 463). For *Phy-PardL*, see **550**; for *PardP*, see **624**; for *PardT*, see **908**.

526 Wenzel, Siegfried. 'Chaucer and the Language of Contemporary Preaching.' *SP* 73(1976), 138-61.
By characterizing lay people as pseudo-preachers, as in the Pardoner's compliment to the Wife of Bath (D 165), Chaucer makes them the butt of his irony. For *PardT*, see **937**.

527 Cespedes, Frank V. 'Chaucer's Pardoner and Preaching.'1977. See **429**.
Familiarity with Paul's epistle to Timothy lends significance to the Pardoner's ironic interruption of the Wife of Bath: the epistle not only provides the Pardoner's 'theme,' it contains material concerning preaching and a digression on widows. The Pardoner's announcement of a pending marriage parodies the Wife's announcement that she hopes to marry again. Pitting one *noble prechour* against another, the Pardoner's interruption underscores the gap in the Wife's character between her words (claiming sensuality) and deeds. For *PardP*, see **632**; for *PardT*, see **940**.

528 Owen, Charles A. Jr. *Pilgrimage and Storytelling in the Canterbury Tales: The Dialectic of 'Ernest' and 'Game.'* 1977. See **433**.
The Pardoner and the Friar who both interrupt the Wife share in the hypocritical misuse of the powers of absolution. The fact that the Pardoner interrupts when the Wife is discussing the debt of husbands indicates a position near Fragment D for Fragment C, the only part of

CT without indication of time or place. Recognizing pretense, the Wife contemptuously reduces the Pardoner from mockery to acquiescence. For *Phy-PardL*, see **557**; for *PardP*, see **633** for *PardT*, see **943**.

529 Dinshaw, Carolyn. 'Eunuch Hermeneutics.' 1988. See **503**. Pilgrims in *CT* are never brought together only coincidentally: similarities between the Wife of Bath and the Pardoner are apparent even in their clothes-consciousness. The eunuch Pardoner embodies a truth about language that explains why the Wife's fantasy of a perfect marriage (analogous to the perfect glossing of a text) remains an unfulfilled dream (p 27). The Wife presents herself as the image of a text: the 'heterosexual hermeneutic' likens a text to woman's body, 'to be stripped and penetrated by male interpreters'(p 28). The Pardoner enunciates the hermeneutics of the partial, eunuch hermeneutics; that is, the 'only possible strategy of using language in a postlapsarian world'(p 28). The Pardoner not only obsessively desires wholeness himself, he knows the pilgrims desire it as well. His claim that he was about to wed a wife plays on the pilgrims' desire to believe in the integrity of the body, 'the integrity of *his* body, and of their own pilgrim body' (p 42). For *Phy-PardL*, see **565**; for *PardT*, see **1103**.

Physician-Pardoner Link; Spurious Doctor-Pardoner Link

530 Skeat. W[alter] W., ed. *The Complete Works of Geoffrey Chaucer.* 1894. See **7**.
Skeat includes variants identified by Furnivall lines 289-92 and 297-300. *Ronyan* and *rinian* are likely corruptions of *Ronan*, a saint about whom little is known. *Ale-stake* refers to a bar projecting horizontally from an inn and bearing a sign around which a garland was frequently suspended. The effort of the decent folk to suppress the Pardoner's *mirth* or *japes* indicates the popular estimate of his character. For Pardoner, see **267**; for *PardP*, see **572**; for *PardT*, see **669**.

531 *The Works of Geoffrey Chaucer.* [The Globe Chaucer]. Ed. Alfred W. Pollard, H. Frank Heath, Mark H. Liddell, W.S. McCormick. 1898. Pollard comments that lines 291-2 in Cp and Ha4 are 'more vigorous' than their Hengwrt or Ellesmere counterparts (p 145). For edition, see **11**.

532 Hammond, Eleanor P. *Chaucer: A Bibliographic Manual.* 1933. See **127**.

CT was first circulated in separable booklets giving rise to confusion about order; e.g. in some manuscripts, *NPT* appears 'incongruously after the Pardoner, its headlink carrying the Monk-interruption as usual' (p 243). The inclusion of the spurious Pardoner-Shipman link in nearly all mss of the group which connects *MLT* and *SqT* demonstrates how scribes altered links to fit conditions that arose from displacement (pp 243, 283-4). See also **674**.

533 Tatlock, John S.P. '*Bretherhed* in Chaucer's *Prolog.*' *MLN* 31(1916), 139-42.

Note 1 on *GP* line 509 comments that *seynt(e)* is generally monosyllabic in Chaucer. With *seynte Marie*, the word seems disyllabic though in *God blesse hem, and oure lady Seinte Marie!* (*Phy-PardL* line 308) the line might be 9-syllables (p 139).

534 McCormick, Sir William. *The Manuscripts of Chaucer's Canterbury Tales: A Critical Description of Their Contents.* With the assistance of Janet E. Heseltine. Oxford: Clarendon, 1933.

In a collation of 57 complete or practically complete mss, the 'standard' *Phy-PardL* (p xx) and the 'added' Pardoner-Shipman link (p xxvi) are reviewed. *Phy-PardL* lines 287-328 is found between *PhyT* and *PardT* in all but 11 mss (in 3 mss the leaves containing it are missing; in 3 mss all Group C is missing and in 5 mss, Group C is split and the link was originally missing). *PhyT* is followed by *ShT* in 4 mss, and by *FranT* in 1 mss (in Trinity Oxford, To, the first two lines of the link are written then stroked and marked *vacat* between *PrT* and *PardT*). The Pardoner-Shipman, an 'added' link of 12 lines, occurs in 19 mss: invariably, the link precedes *ShT* and refers to the Pardoner in the second line. The link follows *PardT* in 14 mss, *Gamelyn* in 4 mss and *ClT* in 1 mss. In Fitzwilliam, F1, *PardT* is broken off at line 962 where two lines are added and the link follows. Egerton 2863, En2, lacks a leaf; after the first 6 lines, the link is missing.

535 Robinson, F.N. *The Works of Geoffrey Chaucer.* 1933/1957. Notes drawn from expanded second edition. See **51**.

Robinson combines the two forms of *Phy-PardL* (cf **58**). Robinson notes Brussendorff's suggestion that lines 297-8 may have been cancelled by Chaucer. For Pardoner, see **295**; for *PardT*, see **704**.

536 *The Text of the Canterbury Tales, Studied on the Basis of All Known Manuscripts.* Ed. John M. Manly and Edith Rickert. 1940. See **58**.

Most modern editors have been reluctant to adopt one version of *Phy-*

PardL over the other; Manly and Rickert note, as a result, these editors have 'erred in making a composite text, taking such lines as they could use from both versions' (2.325). Though there is reason to believe Chaucer wrote all the lines, an editor is not justified in combining them. The link was composed by Chaucer in parts at two different times; the later version appearing in Hengwrt and Ellesmere. See also **116**.

537   Shelly, Percy Van Dyke. *The Living Chaucer*. Philadelphia: University of Pennsylvania Press, 1940; reissued 1968.

The portrait of the Pardoner is a 'miracle[s] of telling details' (p 198) built of facts 'that come straight out of life and not from the poet's invention or reading' (p 198). The links are, in some ways, the most interesting parts of *CT*; the Pardoner is one of three characters best served by the links. The Pardoner's interruption of the Wife of Bath separates the two main topics of her discourse. Nothing could reveal the Pardoner's cynicism as effectively as his attempted solicitation. Chaucer includes scenes of incomparable vividness for their own sake e.g., the visit to the apothecary's shop.

538   Dempster, Germaine. 'A Chapter of the Manuscript History of the *Canterbury Tales*: The Ancestor of Group *d*, the Origin of its Texts, Tale-Order, and Spurious Links.' *PMLA* 63(1948), 456-84.

Assessing the materials available to the *d* editor and the amalgamation of that material, Dempster notes the presence of the spurious Pardoner-Shipman Link and the revised and expanded form of the *Phy-PardL* differentiating the lost ancestor of ms group d (d) from the lost ancestor of ms group c (c).

539   Lumiansky, R. M. 'A Conjecture Concerning Chaucer's Pardoner.' 1949. See **311**.

Just before calling upon the Pardoner, the Host demonstrates several of his affectations: his use of medical terminology, a forced connection between his pity and his need for a merry tale, his French *beel amy*. The Pardoner is ready when his turn comes. He bargains for a halt to assemble the pilgrims so as to make his appeal most effective. He recognizes 'the wisdom of supporting his appeal by emphasis upon the true value of his wares' (p 29). Already considering the Host a potential victim, the Pardoner echoes *Seint Ronyon* as a test. For *Interr*, see **519**; for *PardP*, see **588**; for *PardT*, see **724**.

540   Sledd, James. '*Canterbury Tales*, C 310, 320: "*By Seint Ronyan*".'

MS 13(1951), 226-33.
St Ronyan has puzzled modern scholars as well as medieval scribes. The identification of Ronyan with Ninian is correct; the cult of St. Ninian affords at least a minimal explanation of the Host's oath. The confusion of Ronyan-Ninian, originally suggested by Hinckley (**672**) has been accepted by Robinson (**71**), and Brown (**55**). Brown quotes the anonymous fifteenth-century translation of Higden's *Polychronicon: Seynte Ninian otherwise callede of commune peple Seynt Ronyon* (p 227). Understanding of the Host's and Pardoner's oath is built on the notes of Skeat (**7**), Manly (**58**), Tupper (**685**), Robinson (**71**), and Brown (**55**). The cult of St. Ninian, a great saint in Scotland, was known in England. Both Host and Pardoner might be familiar with Ninian; the Host would more likely know him by a vulgar form. The root irony of the oath lies in St. Ninian's fast; Ninian took the poorest food through Lent and abstained completely from Holy Thursday till after Easter Mass. The Pardoner invited disaster in mocking the Host's pronunciation, and announced ribaudry by incongruously invoking Ninian in a tavern near Easter time. See also **545**.

541 Gerould, Gordon Hall. 'Chaucer's Calendar of Saints.' *Chaucerian Essays*. Princeton: Princeton University Press, 1952. Pp 3-32.
Chaucer's 42 references to saints outside of *ParsT* are for the most part casual. The Pardoner's mocking echo of the Host (*Ronyon* line 320) is given 18 different forms by copyists. Gerould surveys critical treatment (**530, 535**) and notes modern editors have varied the final syllable to rhyme first with *man* then *anon*. Rejecting Tupper's suggestion of *runnion* (with its potential scabrous meanings [**685**]) on the grounds that scribes failed to notice such meanings, Gerould concludes: 'It is evident that we shall never know what saint Chaucer meant Harry Bailly to have had in mind when he swore by St. Ronyan' (p 11).

542 Dempster, Germaine. 'A Period in the Development of the *Canterbury Tales* Marriage Group and of Blocks B² and C.' *PMLA* 68(1953), 1142-59.
One of three links employing pieces previously composed for *CT*, *Phy-PardL* opens with a previous endlink to the story of Virginian. These links, together with the *Shipman-Prioress Link*, are the sole source for some characteristics of the Host—'overawed husband,' distorting

medical terms, annoyance at classical allusions, strange Latin and strange oaths (p 1153). *Phy-PardL* is notable for the Pardoner's blundering attempt to use learned words and his use of oaths betraying a combination of ignorance and self assurance. The links were probably written near the middle of the Canterbury period at a time when Chaucer conceived of the Host as a witty character and realized that previously written tales could serve in the Marriage Group. The arranging of the Marriage Group led to the arranging and linking operation in Blocks B^2 and C. *PardP* and *PardT* were written before the links and not linked to any other piece.

543 Kökeritz, Helge. 'Rhetorical Word-Play in Chaucer.' *PMLA* 69(1954), 937-52.

Discusses *in terme/ to erme* (lines 310-1) as an example of 'traductio,' and *Seint Ronyon* (lines 310, 320) as 'significatio.' See **592, 743**.

544 Severs, J. Burke. 'Author's Revision in Block C of the *Canterbury Tales*,' *Speculum* 29(1954), 512-30.

Chaucer did revise *Phy-PardL* rewriting 4 of its 38 lines, striking out 4 and substituting new lines for them, and adding a new couplet—'all praiseworthy improvements in coherence, forcefulness, and subtle enrichment of character portrayal' (p 530). Counters Manly-Rickert (**58**) in arguing lines 299-328 were composed as a unit and probably authorial in origin; consequently, no 12-line epilogue exists independent of the full link. Study of Chaucer's alterations here results in 'a new sense of his consummate artistry'(p 530). For *PardT*, see **744**. See also **562**.

545 Hamp, Eric P. 'St. Ninian/Ronyan Again.' *Celtica* 3(1956), 290-4.

Hamp traces the changes from *n* to *r* in Middle Irish phonology: (1) Old Irish had two phonemes /N/ (emphatic) and /n/ (nonemphatic); (2) /n/ a short continuant with alveolar contact was close in articulation to /r'/ a single flap alveolar; (3) by 1300 the allophone /n/ had become [r'] so English speakers rendered it with their [r] phoneme; (4) by 1500 [r'] had become /r/ with nasalization of the following vowel. See **540**; see also **554**.

546 Maclaine, Allan H. 'Introduction to the Pardoner's Tale.' *The Student's Comprehensive Guide To The Canterbury Tales*. 1964. See **357**.

Phy-PardL discussed pp 196-7. For *PardP*, see **60**; for *PardT*, see **787**.

547 Loomis, Roger Sherman. 'The Pardoner's Headlink and Tale.' *A Mirror of Chaucer's World*. 1965. See **364**.

Fig 167, 'Drinking at an Ale-Stake,' (lines 320-2) depicts a hermit drinking in front of a tavern, from which an ale-stake projects. Fig 172 'An Apothecary's Shop'(line 314) illustrates *triacha*, Chaucer's *triacle* and shows a customer, an apothecary and his apprentice. For *PardT*, see **798**.

548 Ross, Thomas W. *Chaucer's Bawdy*. New York: Dutton, 1972. See **154**.

See entries for *amy* (line 318), *jape* (line 319), *jurdones* (line 305), *ribaudye*(line 324), *ronyon* (lines 309-10, 320), and *urynals* (line 305). For Pardoner, see **399**; for *PardP* see **617**; for *PardT*, see **872**.

549 *The Tales of Canterbury*. Complete. Ed. Robert A. Pratt. 1974. See **100**.

Pratt states simply: 'Chaucer wrote a 12-line "endlink"' (p 420). See **562**.

550 Gallick, Susan. 'A Look at Chaucer and His Preachers.' 1975. See **525**.

In several *CT*, prologues, and links, Chaucer demonstrates the pilgrim audience's awareness of sermon conventions. The Pardoner attempts to satisfy the conflicting demands of Host (line 319) and pilgrims (lines 324-6) and ends by antagonizing both. For *PardP*, see **624**; for *PardT*, see **908**.

551 Joseph, Gerhard. 'The Gifts Of Nature, Fortune, and Grace in The *Physician's, Pardoner's* and *Parson's Tales*.' *ChauR* 9(1975), 237-45 The Host clearly addresses the Physician (lines 292-300) but his reference to the *yiftes of Fortune and of Nature* acts as a thematic hinge, 'Janus-like,' bridging the 'apparently disparate sections of Group C' (p 237). Few readers have tried to link thematically *PhyT* and *PardT*. The suitability of the tale to the Physician remains debatable; by contrast, the integration of the *PardP* and *PardT* is 'well nigh perfect' (p 242). The power of that connection has overshadowed the more tenuous integration of the Physician's and Pardoner's performance. For *PardT*, see **912**.

552 Haines, R. Michael. 'Fortune, Nature, and Grace in Fragment C.' *ChauR* 10(1976), 220-35.

What the Host says of the gifts of Fortune and Nature (lines 292-300) is relatively orthodox in the light of what the Parson says (lines 450-7). He omits, however, any mention of Grace. Chaucer revised the link with the *ParsT* in mind and possibly to make the theme of Fortune-

Nature-Grace more explicit in Fragment C. For *PardT*, see **924**.

553 Harrington, Norman T. 'Experience, Art, and The Framing of The *Canterbury Tales.*' *ChauR* 10(1976), 187-200.

The role of the frame is normative, offering a gauge for testing the validity of truths conveyed by literature. The framing material of *CT* 'represents the last and most complex literary structure' (p 190) in which Chaucer explores the ways art (the world of the tales) and experience (the world of the links) amend each other. The links juxtapose the reality of 'unfolding and intensely felt experience' (p 191) and the reality of the literary artifacts. The Pardoner offers a particularly rich example of the interplay between two tales and a confessional link. The interplay of link and tale engages the reader in a complicated series of perspectives in which art and experience qualify one another to dramatize Chaucer's preoccupations with the complexity of ordinary human experience. 'In no other poem in the language is quite so much demanded of a reader' (p 199). For *PardP*, see **628**; for *PardT*, see **925**.

554 Haskell, Ann S. 'The Pardoner's St. Ronyan.' *Essays on Chaucer's Saints*. Studies in English Literature, 107. The Hague-Paris: Mouton & Co., 1976. Pp 17-25.

A knowledge of the 'lore' surrounding a saint offers a key to Chaucer. Though scholarly inquiry has favored links to St. Ronyan (C 310, 320) as St. Ninian or 'runian', the Breton St. Ronan accords with two premises: that Chaucer made use of the opportunities for satire he himself created, and that names that vary least from preferred manuscript tradition should be given first consideration. The suitability of St. Ronan to the Pardoner is found in treatment of women, personality, and the suggestion of deviation. St. Ronan's symbols are likewise appropriate—holly (bisexuality), spider web and wolf (avarice)—as is his attribute of a bell. The extended celebration of his feast occurred both in 1377, a year Chaucer visited France, and 1395 a possible year of composition for *PardT*.

555 Howard, Donald. *The Idea of the Canterbury Tales.* 1976, 1978 [page numbers from 1978]. 'The "Floating" Fragment' pp 333-9 rpt in *Geoffrey Chaucer's The Pardoner's Tale*. [Modern Critical Interpretations]. Ed. Harold Bloom. New York: Chelsea House Publishers, 1988. Pp 43-7.

The Pardoner is introduced last, the Parson is the last to tell his tale:

final placement being rhetorically emphatic, the juxtaposition forces a comparison. The Pardoner's sermon, designed to sell false pardons, is a thriller on divine retribution: the Parson's treatise, intended to show the Way, is a manual for individual conduct. As the Pardoner is a pariah among pilgrims, so his performance floats 'on the periphery of the interlaced structure'(p 338). If *PhyT* and *PardT* come in sequence it is because of contrasts; *PardT* offering a mysterious, grim and natural punishment for evil, *PhyT* a simplistic, cold moralism. *ParsT* is appropriately placed at the end of *CT*. *PardT*, an anti-sermon, coupled with *PhyT*, belongs in no ordered structure. For Pardoner, see **424**; for *PardP*, see **629**; for *PardT*, see **926**.

556 Gardner, John. 'Fragment VI and VII: The Theme of Pride and The Uses of Unreliable Art.' 1977. See **431**.

Considering the Physician a sanctimonious fool, the Pardoner enjoys the irony and obscenity of the Host's characterization, *lyk a prelat, by Seint Ronyan* [line 310]. The Pardoner's echo *It shal be doon ... by Seint Ronyon!* [line 320] may indicate the Pardoner's offense at being asked for mere *japes* while the Physician has been praised. Both are dissemblers. Perhaps it is when the company peremptorily protests *ribaudye* that the Pardoner begins to plan his revenge (pp 299-300). The Pardoner replies to the Host's use of *Thou beel amy* [line 318] merrily and with obscene puns on drinking and eating of a *cake* (*cah-keh, caw-keh*, 'cock') (p 302). For *PardT*, see **941**.

557 Owen, Charles A. Jr. *Pilgrimage and Storytelling in the Canterbury Tales: The Dialectic of 'Ernest' and 'Game.'* 1977. See **433**.

With *beel amy*, the Host's instinct for *sooth pley, quaad pley* lights on the Pardoner foreshadowing the later insult to virility, recalling the *GP* portrait, and provoking the Pardoner's performance. For *Interr*, see **528**; for *PardP*, see **633**; for *PardT*, see **943**.

558 Blake, N.F., ed. *The Canterbury Tales.* 1980. See **108**. Omits lines 297-8 from Ellesmere. For *PardP*, see **637**.

559 Donaldson, E. Talbot. 'Gallic Flies in Chaucer's English Word Web.' In *New Perspectives in Chaucer Criticism*. Ed. Donald M. Rose. Norman, Oklahoma: Pilgrim Books, 1981. Pp 193-202.

In an examination of the effect of French constructions, Donaldson notes the mild *double entendre* in *cors* (line 304) which appears before the Host moves to the masculinity of the Physician and the contrast of the Pardoner.

560 Brown, Emerson Jr., 'What is Chaucer Doing With the Physician and His Tale?' *PQ* 60(1981) 129-49.

PhyT is connected to *PardT* by a link indisputably genuine. Group C is intended to follow Group F: *FranT* and *ParsT* present a logically sequential treatment of the problem of evil. The Franklin introduces the problem of causality but glosses over it; the Physician takes up the same theme but offers irrelevant or conflicting causes; the Pardoner operates in a world permeated by evil, understands his own evil, yet is unable to do anything about it. Together, the three tales approach the symbolic center of *CT*, a work about a world in need of Canterbury.

561 Blake, N. F. *The Textual Tradition of the Canterbury Tales*. London: Edward Arnold, 1985. See **108**.

Through a description of the earliest manuscripts, Blake pursues the evolution of *CT* from Hengwrt, through Corpus, Ha 7334 and Lansdowne, to the a-group manuscripts Dd 4.24, Gg 4.27, and Ellesmere. Hengwrt, the earliest extant manuscript best grounds an understanding of the textual tradition. *PhyT* and *PardT* are joined by a link varied in some mss. In Corpus, the first in which changes are made, an extra couplet included at lines 297-8 moralizes that beauty is the cause of Virginia's death. Some of the other changes may have been made to nullify the criticism of lawyers. The scribe of Dd 4.24 did not introduce any of the changes found in Corpus, though he did introduce a change which makes the activities of the Pardoner 'progress in a logical way' (p 131). The changes made to *PardP* in various mss are spurious and seldom included in modern editions.

562 Chaucer, Geoffrey. *The Physician's Tale*. In *Variorum Edition of Works of Geoffrey Chaucer* vol. 2. *Canterbury Tales*. Ed. Helen Storm Corsa. 1987. Pp 45-53. See **116**.

PhyT and *PardT* 'are welded together by a link that is Chaucerian, and in the late-Chaucerian style' (p 53). Corsa notes that, though ten manuscripts lack *Phy-PardL*, its necessity was established by Koch who indicated that the first verse of *PardP* (line 329) would be unintelligible without it. Manuscripts including the link offer two distinct versions (pp 46-7), differing most markedly in the first twelve lines. The history of debate on two remaining issues is briefly traced: line 299 *a* and lines 297-8. Following a brief review of the history of the printed editions, Corsa charts variants (pp 50-53). A table of correspondences for *Phy-PardL* is offered (p 62). While the link is genuine and establishes the sequence of *PhyT* and *PardT*, the pair of tales 'floats' within the larger sequence of *CT*. Corsa reviews the debate on placement (**1, 2; 7**). Scholars divide between those who attempt a placement and those who declare the placement cannot be determined. Corsa reviews the approaches of Tatlock (**33**); Manly-Rickert (**58**); and Doyle (**107**). In similar fashion, she reviews the range of positions taken on the question of whether early editors followed thematic or motif relationships. See also **6, 16, 531, 536, 544, 683, 968**.

563   De Weever, Jacqueline. 1987. See **172**.

Gives detail for *Ronyan* (p 290/lines 310, 320).

564   Lee, Brian. 'The Position and Purpose of the *Physician's Tale.' ChauR* 22(1987), 141-60.

Fragment C represents a conscious pairing of two tales of sudden death following *FranT* where sudden death is narrowly averted. Both *PhyT* and *PardT* 'induce a painful catharsis' (p 149): the former, the Host tries to pass over; the latter, provokes a scatological rejection. Virginia's virtue in *PhyT* is the opposite of the rioters' condition and, unlike the rioters, she attends to her moral guides. The Physician's *Forsaketh synne er synne yow forsake* (line 286) cues *PardT*.

565   Dinshaw, Carolyn. 'Eunuch Hermeneutics.' 1988. See **503**.

The sequence of *PhyT-PardT* is not coincidental. The Physician is the pilgrim most concerned with the body. The Pardoner follows as if to explain the world of *PhyT* as a castrated world, cut off from natural justice (p 30). For *Interr*, see **529**; for *PardT,* see **1103**.

566   Bitterling, Klaus. 'Goon A-Blakeberyed.' *NM* 94 (1993), 279-86.

Bitterling draws on two exegetical traditions—the interpretation of the Biblical words for 'blackberry' or 'bramble' as 'vice' or 'sin' and the interpretation of the picking of berries in the wood as a spiritually dangerous activity—to support the interpretation of *goon a-blackberyed* as 'to go to perdition, to be damned to all eternity.' For *PardP*, see **662**; see also **589**.

567   Rudat, Wolgang E. H. 'Revealing the Church's *Pryvetee*: The Pardoner and Various Otherworldly Loins.' *Earnest Exuberance in Chaucer's Poetics: Textual Games in the "Canterbury Tales".* New York, Lewiston, 1993. Pp 121-158.

Rudat provides a phallic reading of the Pardoner's interruption of the Wife of Bath: *Up stirte the Pardoner, and that anon.* See also **1187**.

568   Andreas, James R. '"Wordes Betwene": The Rhetoric of the

Canterbury Links.' *ChauR* 29 (1994), 45-64.
Tracing the literary theory of Mikhail Bakhtin to medieval source texts in Geoffrey of Vinsauf and others, Andreas assesses the role of the links and interruptions. The Pardoner's interruption of the Wife of Bath, the words between the pilgrims and the Host, and the interaction of Host and pilgrims following *PardT*, and consistent with Bakhtin's view that laughter dissipates aggression and liberates, all provide occasions for discourse in dialogue with previous and subsequent discourse. The links 'are perhaps Chaucer's unique and most characteristic contribution to medieval and world literature' (p 60): they provide liminal moments, provoke interaction, offer 'mediation between characters, author, and audience' (p 60), and 'represent the preeminently dialogical, existential moment when the individual articulates his or her choices and is judged communally for those choices' (p 61).

569 Crafton, John Michael. '"Paradoxicum Semiotica": Signs, Comedy, and Mystery in Fragment VI of the "Canterbury Tales".' In *Chaucer's Humor: Critical Essays*. Ed. Jean E. Jost. New York and London: Garland, 1994. Pp 163-86.
Examining Chaucer's comedy as a function of the paradox of language, Crafton notes that, in *PhyT* and *PardT*, Chaucer presents and undermines caricatures of the Realist and Nominalist positions. Much of the comedy of *PardT* derives from the discrepancy between language and truth: as the Pardoner preaches agaist the sins he exhibits, the disjunction between signifier and signified is manifest; the Pardoner literalizes his metaphor; and undermines the success of his theory with his performance. Rather than a stance of skepticism, Chaucer's word play should be seen as 'necessary play,' a play that 'interrupts the systems of human construction and allows the divine comedy to exist ...' (p 183).

569a Bowers, John M. 'Chaste Marriage: Fashion and Texts at the Court of Richard II.' *PCP* 30(1995), 15-26.
The Pardoner reveals Chaucer's 'most savage' satire of 'Ricardian sexual fashion' (p 21). In the Pardoner's vaunting comment about his plans to wed, he announces his intent to follow the example of the king by entering a chaste marriage, a practice of 'sexual hypocrisy posing as virtuous Christian abstinence' (p 23).

❧ Pardoner's Prologue

570 Skeat, Walter W. *The Tale of the Man of Lawe, The Pardoneres Tale, The Second Nonnes Tale, The Chanouns Yemannes Tale from The Canterbury Tales.* 1877.
Introductory notes discuss relics and comment on Heywood's 'close plagiarism' (p xxvi) of a Pardoner in *The Four P's*. *PardP* suggests that Chaucer knew Boccaccio's Friar Cipolla Day 6 Tale 10. For *PardT*, see **664**.

571 Lounsbury, Thomas R. *Studies in Chaucer: His Life and Writings.* 1892. See **265**.
Comparison lines for *RR* and *PardP* are provided: 2009 *RR*/420 *PardP*; 6837/117. For *PardT*, see **666**.

572 Skeat, W[alter] W. 'The Pardoneres Prologue.' *The Complete Works of Geoffrey Chaucer.* Vol 5. 1894. Pp 269-75. See **7**.
Skeat notes that the novel by Morlinus cited as a source of *PardT* (III: 442) contains the expression *radice malorum cupiditate affecti*; he points to contemporary examples of pardoners carrying relics including a 'shameless plagiarism' (p 54) in Heywood's 'Interlude of the *Four P's*,' a humorous description in Sir David Lyndesay's 'Satire of the Three Estates,' and the portrayal of Frate Cipolla in *Dec* (Day 6). Given prevailing attitudes toward Jews, line 351 is remarkable for *hooly Jew*; Skeat speculates that the Pardoner may have wished to indicate the sheep once belonged to Jacob. The significance of the Pardoner's earnings of 100 marks a year (line 390) is clear when contrasted with Chaucer's pension of 20 marks granted in 1367 and increased till it became £61 13s. 4d. in the last year of his life. In line 406 *blakeberied* is a variation of *gon a blake-berying*. Skeat follows Tyrwhitt in pointing

a parallel between lines 407-8 and *RR* lines 5763-4. Line 445 seems to imply some of the apostles made baskets: Paul provided an example of working with his hands; in imitation of him, St. Arsenius made baskets. For Pardoner, see **267**; for *Phy-PardL*, see **530**; for *PardT*, see **669**.

573 Tupper, Frederick. 'The Quarrels of the Canterbury Pilgrims.' *JEGP* 14(1915), 256-70.

The 'literary *motif* of clash between present and practice'(p 257) evident in the Pardoner is found also in False-Seeming of *RR* who preached abstinence and poverty while indulging his appetites and pursuing coin.

574 Hemingway, Samuel B. 'The Two St. Pauls.' *MLN* 32(1917), 57-8.

The fact that Langland (PP B xv, 235 f) and Chaucer (line 443 f) both ascribe the trade of basket-making to St. Paul the apostle, whereas tradition indicates his trade was tent-making, may result from confusion with St. Paul the Hermit whose 'tunic' in medieval art is a mat of palm leaves (*Sacred and Legendary Art* 6th ed., p 748).

575 Hinckley, Henry Barrett. 'Chauceriana.' *MP* 16(1918-9), 39-48.

Line 406 *a blakeberyed*: The relation between the verbal in *ed* and the Anglo-Saxon verbal in *ao* was noted (**7**) but the intermediate *eth* form is rare. Passages from 'Sir Ferumbras' are cited to show the rarity of the *eth* form. C 953 *seintuarie* is used collectively for 'sacred things'(p 43).

576 Sedgwick, W.B. 'Chaucer's Pardoner's Prologue.' *MLR* 19(1924), 336-7.

The restriction the Pardoner places on his relics (lines 377-87) is actually cunning: the Pardoner speculates that none would 'virtually confess, before the whole parish, to living in deadly sin, by holding back from making an offering'(p 336). Sedgwick is the first to note a similar trick, found in the thirteenth-century German poem of *Pfaffe Ameis* [sic]. A slight resemblance is found in the *Dec*.

577 Owst, G.R. *Preaching in Medieval England: an Introduction to Sermon Manuscripts of the Period, c. 1350-1450.* Cambridge: Cambridge University Press, 1926.

Chapter 3 'Wandering Stars' examines pardoners ('quaestors'), their credentials, their role with Indulgences, and the conflicts posed by their delivery of sermons. Chaucer's picture in *PardP* 'is to be verified fully by the official declarations of the Church' (p 99). Owst suggests that the silence in sermons regarding their abuses may be an indication of the 'general disdain' for them (p 109).

578 Rutter, G[eorge] M. 'An Holy Jewes Shepe.' *MLN* 43(1928), 536. Skeat's (**572**) suggestion that the sheep's shoulder bone (lines 350-1) was Jacob's does not explain why it was 'owned by a holy Jew'(p 536). Rutter speculates that the *hooly Jew* might be Gideon whose fleece drew water from heaven (Judg. VI).

579 Thomas, Russell. 'Ecclesiastical Satire in Chaucer and Erasmus.' *MLN* 45(1930), 394-5.
There is an interesting parallel to the Pardoner's description of preaching (lines 329-31, 392-9, 412-9) in Erasmus's *Praise of Folly*. Probably both were describing familiar contemporary characters or drawing upon a common literary source.

580 Cowling, George H. 'England in Chaucer's Day,' *Chaucer: The Prologue and Three Tales*. Ed. George H. Cowling. London: Ginn and Company, Ltd., 1934, pp ix-xxv. Rpt in *Rare Early Essays on Geoffrey Chaucer*, ed. Carmen Joseph Dello Buono (Darby, Pennsylvania: Norwood Editions, 1981), 203-19.
'Chaucer accepted the faith and rites of the Church, and appears to have studied to some extent the philosophy and theology of the schools; but like the rest of his fellow-men he accepted the popular belief in the miraculous workings of devil and saint' (pp 215-6). Such beliefs account for why Chaucer wrote *PardP*. See **53**.

581 Brown, Carleton. *Chaucer: The Pardoner's Tale*. 1935. See **55**.
The 'flippancy' and 'cynicism' of *PardP* is at odds with the seriousness of *PardT*. *PardP* is not a sermon but an illustration of pulpit methods. *PardP* and *PardT* are delivered in a tavern (cf **680**) while the Pardoner continues to drink. For Pardoner, see **298**; for *PardT*, see **707**.

582 Patch, Howard Rollin. *On Rereading Chaucer*. 1939. See **300**.
The Pardoner's 'long discourse' is all defense (p 164). Against the backdrop of spring, suggesting an emotional turbulence, the Pardoner 'is moved to lay bare his inmost hypocrisies and yet falls into others as he does so' (p 154). The Pardoner's description of himself preaching is grotesque. Chaucer's 'most unsparing couplet in all his works' is: *Thus spitte I out my venym under hewe/ Of hoolynesse, to semen hooly and trewe* (lines 421-22; p 166). For *Interr*, see **517**; for *PardT*, see **712**.

583 Henkin, Leo J. 'Jacob and the Hooly Jew.' *MLN* 55(1940), 254-9.

Though Skeat's suggestion (**572**) that Jacob might be the *hooly Jew*, to whose sheep's shoulder bone the Pardoner ascribed magical powers (lines 350-71), has been generally followed (cf **269**; **271**; **286**; **295**) there is little basis for it. Likewise, the alternate identification of Gideon. Jacob's wizardry, while involving sheep, was accomplished by wooden rods. In drawing a parallel between Jacob's effects and the Pardoner's claim, Skeat ignored many points of variance. The attempt to ascribe the sheep's shoulder bone to a particular individual is gratuitous: despite two opportunities, Chaucer avoided identification. *ParsT* unequivocally damns false *enchantours* who use such bones. It would be incongruous to identify the holy Jew given the exposure of the practices as pagan. The Pardoner's attribution of the relic to a *hooly Jew* would increase its potency in the eyes of a superstitious audience.

584   Manly, John Matthews and Edith Rickert. *The Text of the Canterbury Tales*. 1940. See **58**.

Provides notes for lines 331, 333-4, 334, 346, 350, 356, 366, 392 and 461. For Pardoner, see **302**; for *PardT*, see **715**; for *Phy-PardL*, see **536**.

585   Sedgewick, G. G. 'The Progress of Chaucer's Pardoner, 1880-1940.' 1940. See **303**.

The *gentils'* protest is dramatically useful, warding off fabliau and prompting doctrine. Following the example of the Wife of Bath, the Pardoner provides an exhibition and commentary on his technique. *PardP* is artfully constructed to simulate improvisation. With *A moral tale yet I yow telle kan* (line 460), the Pardoner can address his double audience (past and present) as one. For *PardT*, see **716**.

586   Henkin, Leo J. 'The Pardoner's Sheep-bone and Lapidary Lore.' *BHM* 10(1941), 504-12.

The relic-like virtues the Pardoner attributes to the *sholder-boon/ whiche that was of an hooly Jewes sheep* (lines 350-1) are not found in hagiography. The virtues and ritual use of the relic have significant parallels in folk medicine (**581**). A 'more conclusive correspondence' (p 512) is shown with the occult properties of precious stones of lapidary lore. Though no one stone or lapidary has been identified in all details with the powers of the sheepbone, practically every detail featured in the Pardoner's recipe has its duplicate in the prescriptive powers of precious stones, and there is hardly a stone which is not credited with one or more of the virtues claimed for the shoulder bone relic (p 505).

587 Speirs, John. 'Chaucer: The Canterbury Tales.' *Scrutiny* 12(1943-4), 35-57.

PardP is 'a poor thing' in comparison to *WBP* for all the life has gone into *PardT* (p 35). In *PardT*, 'the sermon grows out of the tale and is embedded in it' (p 36). The digression is an exhibition of the Pardoner's skill as spellbinder and a representation of his persona. The Old Man has the force of Elde; ultimately, the recognition that Death is not a person comes with the force of shock.

588 Lumiansky, R.M. 'A Conjecture Concerning Chaucer's Pardoner.' 1949. See **311**.

The Pardoner delivers his prologue and tale to a group which has halted. In *PardP*, as in *PardT*, the Pardoner flatters the pilgrims by inviting them to join in laughing at the gullibility of his normal peasant audiences and suggests the value of his wares with four defenses: a flattering appeal to the pilgrims' worldliness based on his monetary success; a claim for the efficacy of his absolution despite his fraudulent methods; an insistence he is no worse than others; and a claim that a *ful vicious man* can tell a moral tale. For *Interr*, see **519**; for *Phy-PardL*, see **539**; for *PardT*, see **724**.

589 Cross, James E. 'On The Meaning Of "A-blakeberyed".' *RES* 2 (1951), 372-4.

Analysis of extant dialect words for 'blackberry'(*mooch* and *mitch*) indicate a connection between 'blackberrying' and 'playing truant.' The translation of line 406 as: 'I care not when they are buried, though their souls play truant,' supports the theory that the Pardoner regarded himself as an official of the Church.

590 Kellogg, Alfred L. 'An Augustinian Interpretation of Chaucer's Pardoner.' *Speculum* 26(1951), 465-81. Rpt in Alfred L. Kellogg, *Chaucer, Langland, Arthur: Essays in Middle English Literature*. New Brunswick, New Jersey: Rutgers University Press, 1972. Pp 245-68.

PardP presents a 'concentrated study of the evil, destructive side of the Pardoner'(p 470): the 'genesis of evil within his soul, his revelling in the physical sins, his delight in overturning the good he sees about him'(p 472). Chaucer gives us 'the key' to the Pardoner's personality in the speech wherein the Pardoner 'climaxes his cynical disclosures' (lines 439-63) (p 470). The Pardoner pronounces the aversion of his will from God together with the proud refusal of the will to serve God. 'A more completely satisfactory fulfillment of the Augustinian definition of pride would be difficult to find'(p 471). Despite his efforts to hide the judgment of God, *PardP* manifests the Pardoner's attempt to pervert the good. The Pardoner's sins are simultaneously the typical sins of all pardoners—*avaricia, gula, luxuria*—and the final three sins in the progress of the seven deadly sins. The sins of the sermon are related through the seven deadly sins to the theme of avarice (contra **581**). The Pardoner's attempts to pervert order (lines 398-9) are typical of the defiant apostate. Irony is appropriate to his mind inverted by sin. For Pardoner, see **314**; for *PardT*, see **728**.

591 Gross, Seymour L. 'Conscious Verbal Repetition in The Pardoner's "Prologue".' *N&Q* 198(1953), 413-4.

The Pardoner's confession, revenge for the insult of the *gentils* (line 324), is intended to caste a 'disturbing shadow of hypocrisy' (p 413) over *PardT*. Conscious verbal repetition of the Pardoner's intent (*wynne, avarice, coveitise*) results in a revolting self-characterization. For *PardT*, see **741**.

592 Kökeritz, Helge. 'Rhetorical Word-Play in Chaucer.' 1954. See **543**.

Discusses *beryed/ a-blakeberyed* (lines 405-6), 'no doubt a pun' (p 949), as an example of *traductio*. See also **594**.

593 Baldwin, Ralph. *The Unity of the Canterbury Tales.* 1955. See **322**.

PardP serves as a link between two structures: the tales told by the pilgrims (part of the inner structure) and the frame of the tales created for the reader (Pp 54-7). For *PardT*, see **746**.

594 Baum, Paull F. 'Chaucer's Puns.' 1956. See **325**.

Baum concurs with Kökeritz (**743**) that *beryed/ a-blakeberyed* (lines 405-6) is a pun. For Pardoner, see **330**; for *PardT*, see **751**.

595 Friend, Albert C. 'The Dangerous Theme of the Pardoner.' *MLQ* 18(1957), 305-8

The Pardoner shows 'that Chaucer could give a biting, but humorous, criticism of a difficult issue' (p 308); Chaucer's satire of the Pardoner, in the form of a sermon rooted in 1 Tim 6:10, attacked churchmen who preached for money. In 1395, Robert Lychlade, a secular clerk who preached on the same subject was censured, an indication of the tension of the times when even the suggestion that members of the clergy were greedy or in need of reform could be taken as heresy (p 307).

596 Coghill, Nevill, and Christopher Tolkien. *Chaucer: The Pardoner's Tale.* 1958. See **332**.

PardP, like *PardT*, is to be imagined spoken 'outside the Alestake or

Inn where he [the Pardoner] stops to wet his whistle' (p 23); beginning 'pint-pot in hand' (p 23), the Pardoner does not stop for breath until he solicits the pilgrims. The Pardoner's self-disclosure does not strain realism if the reader takes account of Chaucer's conventions; Chaucer presents the Pardoner, off-duty, boasting to his friends and prepares the reader for the Pardoner's actions at the close of his sermon. For Pardoner, see **74**; for *PardT*, see **758**.

597 Donaldson, E. Talbot. *Chaucer's Poetry: An Anthology for the Modern Reader*. 1958. See **73**.

The situation of False-Seeming in *RR* provided Chaucer with 'the essential framework' for the Pardoner, 'the most repellently sterile of Chaucer's characters'(p 1091). By converting grace into cash, the Pardoner perverts salvation to accomplish his own damnation. With 'rankest hypocrisy' the Pardoner presents himself as 'an accomplished wencher' (p 1092); apparently, his reference to Saint Runion is sexual. For Pardoner, see **333**; for *PardT*, see **759**.

598 Bronson, Bertrand H. *In Search of Chaucer*. 1960. See **340**.

The self-disclosure of the Pardoner is insidiously provocative. The theories of Kittredge (**681**) and Gerould (**736**), though persuasively argued and dramatically appealing, rest on an assumed intention of psychological realism—a technical achievement probably unknown before the eighteenth century. The answer to the puzzle of the Pardoner may lie in the conditions of composition. Perhaps to create a pause, to develop the character of the Pardoner more fully, or to lengthen the block of narrative to the customary reading time of one hour to one hour and a quarter, the confession was written as a prologue. For *PardT*, see **764**.

599 Pratt, Robert A. 'Chaucer's Pardoner's Prologue, 444-7.' *Expl* 21 (1962), 14.

The Pardoner is like the Wife of Bath in his abhorrence of asceticism. His reference to making baskets likely derives from Jerome's letter *Ad Rusticum Monachum* (CXXV, 11).

600 Maclaine, Allan H. 'The Pardoner's Prologue.' *The Student's Comprehensive Guide To The Canterbury Tales*. 1964. See **357**.

PardP (pp 197-201) is divided into four narrative units. For *Phy-PardL*, see **546**; for *PardT,* see **787**.

601 Rowland, Beryl. 'Chaucer's Swallow and Dove "Sittynge on a Berne" ("*MilT*," I, 3258, "*Pard P*," VI, 397).' *N&Q* 11(1964), 48-9.

GP description of the Pardoner's voice (lines 688 and 714) corresponds to the voice of a dove. The same proverbial expression (*MilT* I 3258; *PardP* VI 397) is used for Alison's voice and the Pardoner's gestures, the comparison in the former being to the swallow, in the latter to the dove (lines 395-7). If based on the *Bestiary* where the dove is compared to the good preacher, the reference is heavily ironical. The *GP* portrait and later depiction of the Pardoner use complementary traits to 'throw graphic light on human behaviour'(p 49).

602 Thomas, R. George. 'Two Points of View: The Pardoner's Prologue and Tale.' *AWR* 14(1964), 13-7.

See entry under **785**.

603 Spearing, A.C., ed. *The Pardoner's Prologue and Tale.* 1965. See **86**.

PardP is told in a tavern though it is not clear at what point the journey resumes. Through the combination of a surface accuracy of detail with the underlying convention of the confession, *PardP* achieves a powerful economy of self-exposure. The Pardoner, a 'strange fusion of fascination and horror,' (p 23) blatantly re-enacts his wickedness, projecting his own will and absorbing that of his audience. While perverting the preacher's art, the Pardoner achieves an effect more powerful than the true preacher (e.g., the Parson). For Pardoner, see **366**; for *PardT*, see **801**.

604 Williams, Arnold. 'Some Documents on English Pardoners, 1350-1400.' 1965. See **367**.

Williams presents a selection from '*Protectorium Pauperis*: A Defense of the Begging Friars by Richard of Maidstone, O. Carm. (d 1396)' to suggest why the Pardoner will not make baskets (line 445). Williams' documents distinguish between friars and pardoners but associate them in knavery. Chaucer apparently lumped them together in the cancelled lines of *GP* (252a-b). 'What more natural then than Chaucer's transference' to the Pardoner of St. Jerome's metaphor adduced by Maidstone in defense of mendicant friars (p 207)? St. Jerome, in his preface to the Book of Job, argues that he ought devote himself to the imperishable food of eternal life rather than earn bread by weaving baskets or plaiting screens of palm leaves. The Pardoner's boast that he can *assoille* (line 387, 913) is paralleled by complaints that *questors* absolve the ignorant from perjuries, murders, and other sins. The implication of fraud in the Pardoner's confession receives confirmation

from the letters of Grandisson and Brantigham in the episcopal records.
605 Tuve, Rosemond. 'Allegorical Imagery: Some Mediaeval Books and Their Posterity.' 1966. Excerpt (Pp 176-7) rpt as 'from Allegorical Imagery.' In *Twentieth Century Interpretations of the Pardoner's Tale: A Collection of Critical Essays*. Ed. Dewey R. Faulkner. Englewood Cliffs: Prentice-Hall, 1973. Pp 117-8. [Page references from this edition.]
Tuve suggests a relation between the self-revelations of Chaucer's Pardoner and Avarice in Guillaume de Deguileville's, *Pèlerinage de la vie humaine*. Psychological interpretations (cf **681**) have found the 'blatant and exultant tone' (p 118) of the Pardoner's self-revelation embarrassing, but the tone is explained if the Pardoner is seen as the very essence of Covetousness. The Pardoner shares 'an unmistakable ecstatic timbre' (p 118) with all the characters who present an evil in Guillaume. For Pardoner, see **374**; for *PardT*, see **815**.
606 Boyd, Beverly. *Chaucer and the Liturgy*. Philadelphia: Dorrance and Co., 1967.
Chaucer's references to the Mass touch on liturgical detail but do not describe it. The Offertory is the aspect of the Mass most frequently singled out (e.g., *GP* 709-14). The sermon was preached after the Gospel, after the Creed or after the Offertory: *PardP* 400-02 places the Offertory after the sermon. Though most of Chaucer's references to Penance are in *ParsT*, he comments by implication through the Pardoner's hypocritical behavior.
607 Huppé, Bernard F. 'The Pardoner.' *A Reading of the 'Canterbury Tales'*. 1967. See **356**.
CT must be read with the expectation that the sense is designed to embody 'an underlying meaning in accord with Christian truth' (p 9). (cf **776**) The Pardoner suffers despair, the occasion for which is his physical affliction. The Pardoner's resentment results in cupidity becoming both his motivation and his theme. He painstakingly secures his credentials, reads his audience, and plots his strategy. The Pardoner is 'a serpent prepared to sting, silently, swiftly, with his tongue' (p 211). Through the blasphemous image of the dove, the Pardoner likens himself to 'the great Dove, who brooded over the waters, and gave the apostles the gift of tongues' (p 213). The Pardoner's pride in idleness is related to his Despair, a branch of Sloth. In his declaration for drink and a wench in every town he may both pretend to himself and recognize

his pretense. For *PardT*, see **818**.

608 Myers, Doris E. 'The *Artes Praedicandi* and Chaucer's Canterbury Preachers.' *DAI* 28(1967), 2215-6. University of Nebraska Dissertation, 1967. Director: Paul A. Olson.

The comic deviations of perverse preachers like the Pardoner, the friar in *SumT* and the Wife of Bath can be normed against the standard of the worthy Parson and his conventional sermon. The Pardoner's self-revelation is patterned after the treatment of the preacher's character in the *ars praedicandi*. The medical imagery in *Phy-PardL,* together with the structural and stylistic levels of the Pardoner's sermon, displays his avarice.

609 Curtis, Penelope. 'The Pardoner's "Jape".' *CR* 11(1968), 15-31. Rpt in *Geoffrey Chaucer's 'The Pardoner's Tale.'* [Modern Critical Interpretations]. Ed. Harold Bloom. New York: Chelsea House Publishers, 1988. Pp 23-42.

Between the beginning of *GP* which not only presents the pilgrimage as ended but renders its end (p 15) and the Parson's sermon which points a way out of the poem, the 'meaning of the journey is tested by the pressures under which the company is placed' (p 15). The prologues and links are highly selective (indicative of changing perceptions) and dramatically shaped: *PardP* and *Phy-PardL* most tests 'the depth of purpose' (p 15). The 'almost hypnotically fluid power' of the Pardoner's discourse masks the careful progression in his *pleye* (p 15). As the Pardoner attempts to bring the company under his influence, he tries to 'dissolve their *milieu,* to suspend time, and to remake the identity of his hearers' (p 16) as *lewed peple* who will become his fools. The Physician-Pardoner Fragment achieves a 'unity of depth' (p 17). The Pardoner is set apart; he works in paradox and antithesis, mingling 'address and struggle' (p 19) throughout *PardP*. He imitates himself showing an ability to 'produce his "lost" self like a dazzlingly sarcastic credential' (p 19). In the Pardoner, we have '"confession" for its own perverse sake' (p 21). As he discriminates between his audiences, *lewed* and *gentil,* we focus on his inner state. For *PardT*, see **827**.

610 Griffith, Richard R. *A Critical Study Guide to Chaucer's Canterbury Tales.* 1968. See **379**.

The Pardoner preaches against Gluttony as well as Avarice in part because it is on physical pleasures that his audience is most likely to have spent the money he wished to divert. Underlying the portrayal of the Pardoner are the closely related questions of the efficacy of the 'bad priest' and the tolerance of evil by an omnipotent God. Though the Pardoner tries to make himself appear guilty of Lechery, he almost neglects to preach against it. The Pardoner's life itself is a blasphemy. For *PardT*, see **830**.

611 Ramsey, Vance. 'Modes of Irony in the Canterbury Tales.' In *Companion to Chaucer Studies*. Ed. Beryl Rowland. Toronto, New York, and London: Oxford University Press, 1968; rev ed with index 1979. Pp 291-312.

The Pardoner exemplifies *irony of manner*; though his confession is made with conscious irony, the Pardoner is largely unaware of serving as a 'living example ... and warning ... of the final truth of his sermon' (p 299). Meaning, in Chaucer, is established by the whole, rather than the part, irony being both characteristic of the age and integral to Chaucer's art.

612 Currie, Felicity. 'Chaucer's Pardoner Again.' 1970. See **388**.

The Pardoner works toward the identification of his 'two audiences' through the Prologue and Tale. *PardP* and *PardT* are unified by the similarity of the *lewed peple* and the rioters. For *PardT*, see **848**.

613 McCracken, Samuel. 'Confessional Prologue and the Topography of the Canon's Yeoman.' *MP* 68(1971), 289-91.

PardT is one of four tales (including *WBT*, *MerT*, and *CYT*) prefaced by a confession that is differentiated from other prologues (e.g., *MLT*, *SNT*, and *FrT*). With *PardT*, the structural pattern consists of a link with the previous tale (287-328), a confessional prologue (329-462), and the tale (463-96).

614 Rowland, Beryl. *Blind Beasts: Chaucer's Animal World*. 1971. See **396**.

The Pardoner displays characteristics 'of the testicular pseudohermaphrodite of the feminine type' (p 100): this interpretation is consistent with the Host's address as *thou beel amy* (line 318), the Pardoner's silence (lines 952-7), the pun on *burdoun*, and the relationship to the Summoner. The sheepbone employs 'a confusion of ideas associated with Holy Men, wells, saints' bones, lucky sheep bones and charms' (p 151). For *PardT*, see **860**.

615 Khinoy, Stephan A. 'Inside Chaucer's Pardoner?' *ChauR* 6(1972), 255-67.

The Pardoner is 'among the most self-consciously literary of the pilgrims' (p 257), the clergy having a more complex relation to literature than the other pilgrims. In accepting the Host's tale-telling contest, they accepted a diversion from spiritual goals. The Pardoner, Chaucer's only professional story-teller, points up the tension (lines 319-20; 324-7). For *PardT*, see **867**.

616 Miller, Clarence H., and Roberta Bux Bosse. 'Chaucer's Pardoner and The Mass.' *ChauR* 6(1972), 171-84.

The terms *lessoun, storie,* and *offertorie,* are to be interpreted as 'the epistle, the gospel and the offertory of the mass' (p 174). Within the context of the Mass, even the Pardoner's attack on the tavern vices assumes a coherence. The Pardoner implies a contrast between physical and spiritual food, dicing recalls the soldiers on Calvary and the relation of swearing to the body of Christ is clear. Most of the oaths refer to Christ's body and the cumulative effect is a thematic coherence that keeps central 'the meaning and the means of salvation'(p 180). The 'incoherence' (p 180) of the Pardoner's delivery manifests the depth of lack of comprehension. For *PardT*, see **869**.

617 Ross, Thomas W. *Chaucer's Bawdy*. 1972. See **154**.

See entries for *cokewold* (line 382), *prest* (line 371) and *wench* (line 453). For Pardoner, see **399**; for *Phy-PardL*, see **548**; for *PardT* see **872**.

618 Knight, Stephen. *The Poetry of the Canterbury Tales*. Sydney: Angus and Robertson, 1973.

Knight's work examines the way Chaucer implies meaning in the shape and tone of *PardP* and *PardT* (pp 123-35). The Host, in calling for *PardT*, enunciates the principle of variation. Clear-witted, the Pardoner begins by imitating the Host's *St. Ronyon* and teasing the *gentils*. He moves from teasing with his confession. *PardP* is marked by metrical regularity—which gives the effect 'of a confident, flowing voice, working easily up to an emphatic conclusion'(p 124)—and varying tones—from vivid description, through imitation of persuasive methods and quiet description to his excited insistence on his villainy. Throughout, the confident style becomes stronger as the Pardoner 'speaks with the full power of Chaucer's descriptive poetry' (p 125). *PardP* 'creates with total conviction one of the great confessions in literature' (p 126), thereby setting high expectations for *PardT*. For *PardT*, see **884, 885**.

619 Mehl, Dieter. *Geoffrey Chaucer: Eine Einführung in seine*

erzählenden Dichtungen. 1973; 1986 [cited here]. See **404**.
The Pardoner's 'uninhibited soliloquy' (p 146), a traditional form professionally suited to the Pardoner, adds a genre to *CT*. The confession is at once a form of estates satire and 'a demonstration of brilliant rhetoric used for an evil purpose' (p 146). As such, it elaborates on the portrait in *GP* and provides a frame for *PardT*. Questions about the Pardoner's state of mind are irrelevant, deriving as they do from an anachronistic expectation of psychological realism. For *PardT*, see **886**.

620 Rowland, Beryl. *Animals With Human Faces: A Guide to Animal Symbolism.* 1973. See **406**.
Treats the symbolic meaning of sheep, snake, cow, calf, cock, ox. For *PardT*, see **887**.

621 Andersen, David M. 'The Pardoner's True Profession.' *NM* 75(1974), 630-9.
When Chaucer describes the Pardoner's presentation of two 'pseudo-relics,' the sheep's shoulder bone and the mitten, the Pardoner is 'closest to his real profession, a kind of agrarian witchcraft' (p 638). The formulaic quality for his animal cures conforms to Sir James Frazer's definition of primitive magic; the amalgamation of magic and religion together with the specificity of instructions parallel the Saxon Leechdoms. Understanding that the *lewed peple* are more concerned about their livestock than their souls, the Pardoner turns them away from religion to primitive magic, thereby exposing 'the darker reality of a pagan universe' (p 639) beneath his oratory.

622 Reinecke, George F. 'Speculation, Intention, and the Teaching of Chaucer.' In *The Learned and the Lewed: Studies in Chaucer and Medieval Literature.* Ed. Larry D. Benson. Cambridge: Harvard University Press, 1974. Pp 81-93.
Confronted with uncertainties of text, medievalists necessarily resort to conjecture; for example, the text is inconsistent as to whether the Pardoner is a layman or a mendicant friar. Reinecke speculates Chaucer originally drafted an 'Ur-friar' only later to add the quality of quaestor. Ultimately, two separate characters emerged, Pardoner and Friar, variously connected with the Summoner.

623 Rogers, William Elford. 'Individualization of Language in The Canterbury Frame Story.' *AnM* 15(1974), 74-97.
An exploration of how much individualization of language contributes to *CT* and how that individualization is achieved. The Pardoner, Wife

of Bath and Host become so 'real' their language demands special attention; by contrast, the Pardoner lacks the Wife's enthusiasm and the Host's boisterousness. An assessment of diction, sentence structure and use of imagery shows the Pardoner's language is remarkable chiefly for its range. His shifting of styles (in his sample sermon, for instance) deepens our sense of his deviousness. The Pardoner uses notably little figurative language in *PardP*. His speech lacks the 'homely proverbial wisdom' (p 90) of the Wife and, to a lesser degree, the Host. In describing the bad uses to which preaching can be put, the Pardoner offers a model of exposition (lines 406-19), disposing carefully of the qualifications of the main idea. Judging his speech within the context— semantic, stylistic, dramatic—of the frame, the Pardoner's ordered speech takes on 'the aspect of mechanism' (p 96): the 'unemotional rationality of his rhetorical *dispositio* and his syntax ... become cold-blooded' (p 96); his 'monstrous egotism' (p 96) reveals itself in contempt for the pilgrims. The Pardoner's style is frightening 'because it contends so vigorously with the sense' (p 96).

624 Gallick, Susan. 'A Look at Chaucer and His Preachers.' 1975. See **525**.

In his confession to one audience of how he deceives another, the Pardoner violates a basic tenet of medieval preaching. By revealing his viciousness in *PardP*, the Pardoner misjudges the importance of the preacher's character to the pilgrim audience and creates an atmosphere of 'open hostility' (p 470). For *Phy-PardL*, see **550**; for *PardT*, see **908**.

625 Havely, N[icholas]. R., ed. *The Friar's, Summoner's and Pardoner's Tales from The Canterbury Tales*. 1975. See **102**.

PardP presents the Pardoner's 'quite full assessment of himself, his aims and methods' (p 28). He plays on insecurity and greed; he takes pleasure and pride in his professionalism; he appreciates the irony of the situation. He makes the nature and purpose of his tale clear in advance as if to hint the pilgrims may become his victims. The self-revelation may be understood as the result of pride and drink, or as a pose, or as Chaucer's dramatic device for satire. For Pardoner, see **423**; for *PardP*, see **625**; for *PardT*, see **911**.

626 David, Alfred. *The Strumpet Muse: Art and Morals in Chaucer's Poetry*. Bloomington: Indiana University Press, 1976.

PardP puts us under the spell of his personality. His cynical confession and the blasphemous spirit of his sermon mock the hope of redemption which is the bond uniting the pilgrims. His confession is at once an insult to the company and a plea for acceptance. For *PardT*, see **921**.

627 Ginsberg, Warren. 'Preaching and Avarice in The Pardoner's Tale.' *Mediaevalia* 2(1976), 77-99. Rpt in *Geoffrey Chaucer's 'The Pardoner's Tale.'* [Modern Critical Interpretations]. Ed. Harold Bloom. New York: Chelsea House Publishers, 1988. Pp 63-77.

Critics have neglected the dicta from the *artes praedicandi* on the character of the preacher, thereby missing a possible answer to one of the cruces of the *PardT*. The Pardoner's pause before the tale (lines 327-8) seems a direct parody of Augustine's directive that the preacher give forth what he shall drink from God (*DDC* XXXII, IV, xv p 79). The Pardoner's inspiration is his own, not the Holy Ghost's; he mocks the act of preaching, corny ale replacing the spiritual draught. The reference to cake and ale might well be an ironic reference to the Eucharist (cf **820**) (p 80). For *PardT*, see **923**.

628 Harrington, Norman T. 'Experience, Art, and The Framing of The Canterbury Tales.' See **553**.

PardP conveys the sense of contemporary life beyond the pilgrimage as well as the individual conditions of the Pardoner's life, a life that is still unfolding: 'there is much in his inner life that is as mysterious and inexplicable to him as to his many commentators across the centuries' (p 197). The incoherence of the Pardoner is contrived by Chaucer to demonstrate the incomprehensibility of much of our lives. For *PardT*, see **925**.

629 Howard, Donald R. *The Idea of the Canterbury Tales*. 1976. See **424**.

In *PardP*, the pilgrim's voice has the same ring of direct communication as the narrator's. With the Pardoner, singing and speaking substitute for love-making; his sermon is 'a kind of monstrous verbal rape' (p 347). The Pardoner is an extraordinary performer whose effect is mesmerizing: by turns, he is condescending, intimate, ironical, impudent and invidious. In his performance as preacher, we see the man behind the role. His presentation could be considered 'a study of the obsessional or psychopathic character, of the criminal mind' (pp 353-4). Behind the conventions of *PardP* and *PardT* lies a depiction of self-destroying guilt, the ultimate grotesquerie. For *Phy-PardL*, see **555**; for *PardT*, see **926**.

630 Patterson, Lee W. 'Chaucerian Confession: Penitential Literature and the Pardoner.' *M&H* 7(1976), 153-73.

Though the Pardoner's confession is calculated to win respect from the *gentils*, he reveals conflicting desires for acceptance and release from sin by confession. *PardP*, in its shifts alternately derisory, hesitant, vaunting, candid, reveals a spirit in conflict. *PardP* presents 'inflated self-advertisements and fugitive glimpses of a more genuine self' (p 167). For *PardT*, see **932**.

631 Peterson, Joyce. 'With Feigned Flattery: The Pardoner as Vice.' See **426**.

Criticism reveals a recurring comparison of the Pardoner with Shakespeare's Iago and Richard III: analogies between each of these and Vice in the Morality Drama illumine continuing critical problems with character and intention. Similarities between Vice and the Pardoner in their relations to their respective audiences underline the nature of the Pardoner's performance as drama intended to produce an effect on the audience; analysis of its rhetorical structure discloses the intended effect. The Pardoner, like the Vice, flatters his audience with his confidence, makes them laugh at the sin he embodies, and invites them to feel superior to the Mankind figure he has duped; in so doing, he potentially compromises them as Christians and makes them unwitting victims. For *PardT*, see **933**.

632 Cespedes, Frank V. 'Chaucer's Pardoner and Preaching.' 1977. See **429**.

The Pardoner's text (1 Tim. 6:10) derives from an epistle that warns against the separation between word and deed in the character of a preacher, a phenomenon the Pardoner exemplifies. Paul, Augustine, and later the preaching manuals of Chaucer's time insist that good rhetoric must enlist the appeal of the speaker's life. The Pardoner 'undoubtedly preaches a sermon' (p 6) though his mode is ambivalent as he disregards advice about subdued style. His intent is to channel his listeners' emotions so that 'their "repentance" finds its objective correlative in the purchase of a "pardon"' (p 7). For *Interr*, see **527**; for *PardT*, see **940**.

633 Owen, Charles A., Jr. *Pilgrimage and Storytelling in the Canterbury Tales: The Dialectic of 'Ernest' and 'Game'*. 1977. See **433**.

The Pardoner gives each what he seeks: *japes* to the Host, *som moral thyng* to the gentlefolk. He seeks a validation from the pilgrims, a more sophisticated audience than what he is accustomed to. With the pilgrims, he does as game what he normally does for profit. Simultaneously addressing a fictive peasant audience and the pilgrims, the Pardoner attempts to establish common ground with the pilgrims, thereby making them to some extent accomplices. His repeated acknowledgement of avarice and his denial of any effort to win the pilgrims from sin suggest an ulterior motive of concealment of parts of his life through exaggerated self-exposure. The Pardoner finds joy in the escape that his hypocritical exercise of skill affords. For *Interr*, see **528**; for *Phy-PardL*, see **557**; for *PardT*, see **943**.

634 Pichaske, David R. *The Movement of the 'Canterbury Tales':
    Chaucer's Literary Pilgrimage.* Norwood, Pennsylvania: Norwood
    Editions, 1977. Pp 120-5. Rpt Folcroft, Pennsylvania: Folcroft Library
    Editions, 1978.
    In *PardP*, the Pardoner's self-justification (lines 429-31) becomes 'a
    blanket absolution for his own malice' (p 127). Though the Pardoner
    agreed to present art leading to virtue, he proves himself incapable.
    For *PardT*, see **944**.

635 Fleming, John V. 'Chaucer's Ascetical Images.' *C&L* 28(1979), 19-
    26.
    Chaucer fruitfully employs poetic images and exegetical ideas derived
    from ascetic theology. Chaucer is the rule for vernacular poets of his
    day in employing images from the tradition of exegesis associated with
    ascetical texts. Having dealt in detail with the Summoner elsewhere,
    Fleming concentrates on two images related to the Pardoner: that of
    basket-weaving (in *PardP*), and that of the purse (in *GP*) [see **444**].
    Practically every detail of the Pardoner's literary portrait is controlled
    by a strand of medieval scriptural tradition. Chaucer makes traditional
    exegetical details his own. Parallels have been noted to the Pardoner's
    pronouncement that he will not make baskets (line 445) (**704, 804**); an
    additional parallel, available to Chaucer's audience, is found in St.
    Bonaventure's *Apologia pauperum* (p 22). The Pardoner refuses to
    make baskets because a long tradition of ascetic exegesis, beginning at
    least with Jerome and incorporated into the *Glossa ordinaria*, indicates
    that is how the apostles made their living (p 22).

636 Aers, David. *Chaucer, Langland, and the Creative Imagination.*
    London: Routledge & Kegan Paul, 1980.
    PardP exhibits Chaucer's reflexive imagination by joining 'religious,

social and psychological dimensions, as well as conducting a meditation on reflexivity itself' (pp 89-90). The unusual reflexivity of the Pardoner 'makes religious discourse, devotion and certainty problematic topics' (p 94). With the Pardoner, Chaucer is exposing not only institutional decay in the Church but the very grounds of the institution: 'The Pardoner's knowing acceptance of the material organization and basis of the institution he serves is clear' (p 95). The Pardoner's text 'subverts simple reverence for official authority (**323**) and exposes his reader to a host of disconcerting problems about knowledge, authority and the pursuit of grace in his world' (p 98). Interpretations based on moral treatises (e.g., **323**) neglect the evidence of late medieval dissatisfaction with clergy and hierarchy. For *PardT*, see **958**.

637   Blake, N.F., ed. *The Canterbury Tales*. 1980. See **108**.
Though many of the features of the confession are traditional, *PardP* appears to be 'an original Chaucerian piece' (p 438), drawing inspiration from the confession of Faux Semblant in *RR*. For *Pard-PhyL*, see **558**.

638   McAlpine, Monica E. 'The Pardoner's Homosexuality and How It Matters.' 1980. See **450**.
Synne horrible (line 379) may well refer to homosexuality. For *PardT*, see **967**.

639   Roscow, G[regory] H. *Syntax and Style in Chaucer's Poetry*. Chaucer Studies, 6. Cambridge: D.S. Brewer, 1981.
Characterization of Middle English syntax as colloquial has diverted attention from examination of non-dramatic, mimetic functions. Roscow examines Chaucer's usage within the context of linguistic and literary traditions (particularly Romances) with inconclusive results. The following syntactical elements are examined in the context of *PardP*: word-order (line 308); idiomatic usage (line 386); pleonasm (lines 337-8); ellipsis (lines 429, 459); relative clauses (line 345) and coordination and parataxis (lines 354-7). For *PardT*, see **984**.

640   Noll, Dolores L. 'The Serpent and The Sting in the *Pardoner's Prologue and Tale*.' *ChauR* 17(1982), 159-62.
The Pardoner, in his self description and his selection of relics (one, a sheep bone for the cure of livestock stung by a serpent), participates in an image pattern of serpents who deceive before they sting. The relic is a parodic analogy (cf **874**): while his sheep bone is false, the Lamb of God can heal the sting of death. The Biblical image of death as a viper (1 Cor. 15:54-7) reinforces the Pardoner's vulnerability to spiritual

death. It is instructive to note that at the end of the tale the Pardoner's stinging tongue is still.

641 Taylor, P[aul]. B. 'Chaucer's *Cosyn to the Dede.*' *Speculum* 57(1982), 315-27.

Chaucer holds an ideal view of language wherein intent informs deeds 'through the ministry of words' (p 325). The Pardoner serves as an aberration from the ideals implied by references to Christ and Plato in *GP* and to Christian ritual in *ParsT*. The Pardoner, 'a caricature of a Machiavellian nominalist' (p 326), mocks the idea that words should reflect intent (lines 403-4, 407-8, 427-31, 459-60), promotes the deceptive potential of *tales olde*, and dupes his immediate audience. *[C]osyn to the dede* par excellence, his 'very confessional words disdain the repentance they extol' (p 326). The Parson's 'reconciliation of intent, word, and deed' counters the Pardoner's nominalism; *Ret* 'arbitrates between the performances of the Pardoner and the Parson' (p 327).

642 Cooper, Helen. *The Structure of the Canterbury Tales.* 1983. See **469**.

PardP shows strong similarities with *Dec* VI,10. The 'finer kind of psychological appropriateness' found in *PardP* was introduced late in Chaucer's scheme. The Pardoner's confession, while matched to character, is also rooted in convention and in well known abuses. *PardP*, by casting the diatribe against drunkenness within the fact of stopping at an alestake, alters our understanding of *PardT*, indeed our understanding of what a tale can do. The Pardoner's holy water that will make a husband believe in the faithfulness of his wife comments ironically on the issue of trust and sovereignty raised in several tales. For *PardT*, see **1008**.

643 Glasser, Marc. 'The Pardoner and The Host: Chaucer's Analy(s)is of The Canterbury Game.' *CEA* 46(1983-4), 37-45.

The Pardoner is marked by 'agreeableness'(p 37). Possessed of adaptable art and craftiness in speaking, he casts his lot with the *gentils*, the group in opposition to the Host. He indicates a double purpose in *PardP*: to convince the pilgrims he is greedy and to make them believe he can cause others to repent for their greediness. The Pardoner is a role-player (cf **783**, **629**); his self-description simulates a 'reductio ad absurdum portrayal of Harry Bailly' (p 39). Not only do both govern groups, they are marked by greed. 'As the Pardoner charges admission to see his "relics", so does Harry exact his toll on the way to the shrine of Saint Thomas' (p 39). For *PardT*, see **1011**.

644 Kirkpatrick, Robin. 'The Wake of the *Commedia*: Chaucer's Canterbury Tales and Boccaccio's *Decameron*.' *Chaucer and the Italian Trecento*. Ed. Piero Boitani. Cambridge: Cambridge University Press, 1983. Pp 201-30.

Both influenced by Petrarch, Chaucer and Boccaccio share a fascination with the hypocritical cleric; the Pardoner, a Dantean figure, reveals 'the mysterious force of appetite and the convolutions of the human conscience' (p 203). The Pardoner is a competent, hypocritical and proud narrator; *PardP*, in 'a wholly un-Dantean fashion' (p 221) complicates *PardT*. The background of *PardP* 'is the crushing poverty of the world in which the Pardoner himself operates'(p 223). With the Pardoner, Chaucer writes with greater realism and sympathy than Boccaccio; his moral sensibility may be less sytematic than Dante's but is no less penetrating. For *PardT*, see **1015**.

645 Traversi, Derek. *The Canterbury Tales: A Reading*. See **477**.

The Pardoner initiates a third series of tales whose theme is the disquieting aspects of human nature; they stand apart from the preceding two sections whose theme was pilgrimage. These tales challenge both the moral assumptions of society and the validity of tale-telling to reflect truth beyond human experience. The Pardoner's self-introduction, like that of the Wife of Bath and the Canon Yeoman, present centrally problematic features of human nature. The success of the Pardoner's sermon is such that we doubt the effectiveness of the Parson's preaching and by extension the truth the Parson advances. *PardP*, where Chaucer raises his uneasiness about the motive for tale-telling, finally produces *Ret*; the tension between 'truth' and 'fiction' may be 'the ultimate sense of Chaucer's creative effort' (p 178). For *PardT*, see **1030**.

646 Brewer, Derek. *An Introduction to Chaucer*. London and New York: Longmans, 1984.

The use of *Lordynges* establishes the fictional level of *PardP*. The Pardoner's confession is indebted to *RR*. Such confession may stem from the increasing emphasis on confession after the Lateran Council 1215-6. The literary satire of *PardP* becomes almost fully dramatic, lacking only revealed motive. The voice is authentically the Pardoner's. 'It is a fascinating, self-absorbed explosion of cunning' (p 202). For *PardT*, see **1036**.

647 Yeager, R.F. 'Aspects of Gluttony in Chaucer and Gower.' *SP*

81(1984), 42-55.

John Cassian (writing c 420-5) proposed gluttony as the first sin; this concept of gluttony underlies the Pardoner's description of original sin. In the late Middle Ages a tradition existed which included, as sins of the mouth under gluttony, swearing, blasphemy, sorcery, witchcraft and devil worship. The Pardoner's *develes temple* has its roots in an image of the devil's church or schoolhouse common to penitential tracts.

648   Dane, Joseph A. 'The Pardoner's *Baskettes* (*Canterbury Tales* VI, L. 444-6).' *N&Q* 32(1985), 155-6.

In his renunciation of physical labor, the Pardoner is partially indebted to Faux Semblant. The Pardoner's combination of the motifs of basket-making, labor, and speech-making finds precedent in Virgil's *Eclogue* X. Additionally, the Pardoner rejects begging. This combination of speech-making, labor and begging are features of the begging poem, a genre known to Chaucer.

649   Benson, C. David. 'Chaucer's Pardoner: The Man and His Two Tales as a Defense of Christian Poetry.' *Chaucer's Drama of Style: Poetic Variety and Contrast in the 'Canterbury Tales'*. Chapel Hill and London: University of North Carolina Press, 1986. Pp 44-63.

Dramatic interpretations of the Pardoner are based on inadequate evidence (the Pardoner's self-description), are distracting, and so various as to seem 'idiosyncratic response'(p 46); the current interest in sexual interpretation reveals more about contemporary society than about Chaucer. The Pardoner is an allegorical character, a 'pure example of the corrupt preacher' (p 47). The proximity of poetry and preaching in the Middle Ages establishes the preaching Pardoner as a medium for the examination of the dangers and potential of Christian poetry (p 48). *PardP* presents a serious description of a corrupt preacher whose verbal skill is divorced from truth and prepares for the 'artistic and moral conflicts' of *PardT* (p 49). The Pardoner's lack of substance and reliance on technique make understandable the distrust of art and fiction that runs throughout medieval Christianity. For *PardT*, see **1059**.

650   Ellis, Roger. *Patterns of Religious Narrative in the Canterbury Tales*. 1986. See **486**.

In *PardP*, the emphasis is on process not subject matter. *PardP* 'relativizes' the tale 'implicitly, by creating a context of common practice against which to view it, and explicitly, by offering it as an example of that common practice' (p 254). The division of *PardP* and

PardT creates two 'tales' where one is reinforced by 'the clear signs of disjunction between them' and 'emphasizes the fundamental religious cast of the whole enterprise' (p 258). The Pardoner's self-exposure in *PardP* 'ironically endorses the truths which his practice flouts' and 'criticises the worldliness of his hearers' (p 259). The Pardoner frames his narrative with a challenge to the pilgrims—*And lo, sires, thus I preche*—and thereby denies authority to any single reading of it. The Pardoner uniquely challenges the pilgrim audience to turn their laughter into a prayer. The Pardoner's fiction is a 'truthful expression not primarily of itself but rather of the perversity of the narrator' (p 264). For *PardT,* see **1067**.

651 Hahn, Thomas. 'Money, Sexuality, Wordplay, and Context in the *Shipman's Tale.*' In *Chaucer in the Eighties*. Ed. Julian N. Wasserman and Robert J. Blanch. Syracuse: Syracuse University Press, 1986. Pp 235-49.

In a discussion of *ShT*, Hahn notes that the narratological resonances of *creance* and their relation to the problematics of storytelling in *PardP* invite further attention.

652 Bowden, Betsy. *Chaucer Aloud: The Varieties of Textual Interpretation*. 1987. See **493**.

Bowden reports that *PardP* becomes the first passage of Chaucer to be translated into French. The translator, probably Abbé Prévost, chooses *PardP* to demonstrate that Chaucer 'avoit adopté, si non ses opinions [of his contemporary Wycliffe], du moins sa haine & ses invectives contre les Moines' (p 100). Comments on *PardP* by Elizabeth Cooper, an eighteenth-century reader credited with inventing source-hunting (p 110), are included '[b]ecause no one else has' and because her approach 'has set such precedents for our own' (pp 109-10). Passages recorded on an accompanying tape and analyzed in the text include *PardP* lines 329-34 and 366-71 (cut H1-H3; pp 133-144). For *PardT,* see **1087**.

653 Fritz, Donald W. 'Reflections in a Golden Florin: Chaucer's Narcissistic Pardoner.' 1987. See **495**.

The Pardoner exhibits the personality traits of the *puer* in his exhibitionism, dissembling, fantasies of power of absolution, desire for wealth, avoidance of work and commitments, fear of age and death, and lack of self esteem (p 342). *PardP* is remarkably self-centered in its material and its rhetorical use of *I* (fifty-two times). In his behavior, the Pardoner reveals the characteristics of 'a severe narcissistic personality disorder' (p 345) and leads us to accept his sense of worthlessness. For *PardT*, see **1088**.

654 Ganim, John M. 'Chaucer, Boccaccio, and the Anxiety of Popularity.' *Assays: Critical Approaches to Medieval and Renaissance Tests.* 4(1987), 51-66.

Chaucer is only apparently less concerned than Boccaccio about the appropriation of popular culture; 'the question of literary understanding forms a central motif' in *CT* (p 53). Both the tale of Ciappelletto (*Dec* Day 1, Story 1) and *PardP* treat the nature of belief and *lewed folk*. *PardP* 'is at least partly an essay on the efficacy of fiction and the peculiarities of intention' (p 57). A redemption of sorts is achieved through the reaction of the pilgrims and perhaps through the Pardoner's reaction. By demonstrating that apparently unpromising material 'could be made into something' (p 59), Chaucer provides a defense for poetry. Rejecting the vatic stance of Dante, Chaucer presents his work 'in the manner of a merchant displaying his goods' (p 61). Chaucer is like the Pardoner in his skepticism, pragmatism and irony. He handles his 'anxiety of permanence' (p 63) by making *CT* 'into a fiction of ephemeral performance and presentation, and by including in it structural and formal allusions to provisional, occasional, and temporary forms, particularly those typical of late medieval popular culture' (p 64).

655 Hilary, Christine Ryan.[notes]*The Riverside Chaucer*. 1987. See **117**.

Parallels with Innocent III's *DMC* (cf *MLP*) and Jerome's *Adversus Jovinianum* (cf *WBP*) indicate a mid-decade date for *PardP* and *PardT*. *PardP*, a literary confession, most likely draws on Faux Semblant. Noting that 'the critical bibliography is formidable and the range of disagreement broad' (p 906), Hilary surveys discussion of the Pardoner's performance as a sermon on the tavern sins, the character of the exemplum, the identity of the Old Man, religious symbolism, and the motivation of the Pardoner. For Pardoner, see **498**; for *PardT*, see **1091**.

656 Storm, Melvin. 'Lady Clare's Will and the Pardoner's Hundred Marks.' *NM* 89(1988), 57-62.

Storm cites thematic and biographical connections to support his hypothesis that the Pardoner's *an hundred mark* (lines 389-90), an extraordinary income for a Pardoner, may have been suggested by the 1355 will of Lady Clare where the sum appears in the context of spiritual surrogation ie, to pay for five men-at-arms to travel to the Holy Land should a Crusade take place within seven years of her death.

657 Vance, Eugene. 'Chaucer's Pardoner: Relics, Discourse, and Frames of Propriety.' *NLH* 20(1989), 723-45.

By his transgressions, the Pardoner 'calls attention to both the semiotics and the ethics of truth-making processes in fourteenth-century ecclesiastical discourse' (p 725). *PardP* opens with a cluster of signs, guarantors of the Pardoner's credibility and implicating the ecclesiastical hierarchy from pope to bishop. Chaucer could expect his audience to perceive in the Pardoner's discourse an assertion of contested values. Vance reconstructs the social issues surrounding the diads of Rome/England; lord/vassal; Latin/English; and writing/speech.

658 Fletcher, Alan J. 'The Topical Hypocrisy of Chaucer's Pardoner.' *ChauR* 25(1990), 110-26.

The Pardoner's hypocrisy is qualitatively different from that of other pilgrims. His '[u]nmitigated religious hypocrisy' (p 111) derives its topicality not only from antimendicant satire and traditional criticism of pardoners but the contemporary debate between 'the orthodox establishment and the Lollards' (p 111). Contemporary evidence is cited to support the topicality of such issues as religious hypocrisy, *Thus spitte I out my venym under hewe/ Of hoolynesse, to semen hooly and trewe*(lines 421-2), the eucharistic controversy, *turnen substaunce into accident* (line 539), the validity of spiritual ministrations performed by a corrupt man and the abuse of preaching (lines 407-11). The choice of a pardoner demonstrates Chaucer's 'political and literary tact:' he can introduce into the traditionally corrupt figure 'the resonance of the most urgent and topical theological argument of his day' (p 119). Medieval religious writings did associate pardoners with false relics (contra **314**). The reference to the Pardoner's sexuality may be explicable in terms of the moral equation (religious hypocrite = heretic) as 'aberrant sexual behavior was a standard accusation in heresy charges' (p 120). Examination of contemporary attitudes to religious hypocrisy mitigates against any exoneration that a psychological reading might offer.

659 Ganim, John M. *Chaucerian Theatricality*. Princeton: Princeton University Press, 1990.

In the monologues of the Pardoner and the Wife of Bath, Chaucer creates 'the most fully realized characters in literature before Shakespeare' (p 6). In their theatrically realized performances are found 'precisely the ironic awareness of fiction and interpretation that marks the popular theater' (p 93). The confessional performance of each reveals the doubleness of language or they come close to 'self-redemption through verbal performances that quite often depend upon outright fabrication and wild misstatement' (p 131). *PardP* becomes, in part, an essay on 'the efficacy of fiction and the peculiarities of intention'(p 60). For *PardT*, see **1136**.

660 Kiser, Lisa J. *Truth and Textuality in Chaucer's Poetry*. Hanover, New Hampshire; London: University Press of New England, 1991.

CT is Chaucer's most complex commentary on the nature of human fiction, offering a variety of representational strategies and foregrounding the social and political shaping of discourse. As one of three autobiographers, the Pardoner offers the illusion of immediacy. In *PardP*, he creates an incredible self-fictionalization in an effort to hide from himself the implications of his physical and spiritual state. Chaucer, an 'authority on deauthorization' (p 149) presents the world as a book in which the reader interprets signs through glosses of his own and society's construction.

661 Brown, George. 'Scriptura Rescripta: The (Ab)use of the Bible by Medieval Writers.' In *The Idea of Medieval Literature: New Essays on Chaucer and Medieval Culture in Honor of Donald R. Howard*. Ed. and introd. James Dean and Christian Zacher. Newark: University of Delaware Press, 1992.

Brown examines the tradition of biblical parody in medieval writings to show that Chaucer's penchant is with medieval tradition. The travesty of the Eucharist in *PardT* is the 'least funny but most powerful' inversion of the New Testament in *CT* (p 287). The irreverant comparison between breeches and relics (lines 948-50) employs a biblical motif for hellish contrast.

662 Bitterling, Klaus. 'Goon A Blakeberyed.' 1993. See **566**.

Bitterling draws on two exegetical traditions—the interpretation of the Biblical words for 'blackberry' or 'bramble' as 'vice' or 'sin' and the interpretation of the picking of berries in the wood as a spiritually dangerous activity—to support the interpretation of goon a-blackberyed as 'to go to perdition, to be damned to all eternity.' See also **589**.

663 Spencer, H. Leith. 'English Preaching in the Late Middle Ages.' Oxford: Clarendon Press, 1993.

In this study of sermon material produced in England 1350-1500, *PardP* is discussed in Chapter 3: 'Ancient Customs and New Manners: Medieval Views of Preaching.' *PardP* reveals Chaucer's familiarity with contemporary vernacular preaching styles; though pardoners were not legally empowered to 'preach,' the fact that they could receive permission to read their letters of indulgence following the sermon could lead to the perception they were preaching and associate them with undesirable itinerant preachers. Spencer notes the critical tradition that has understood *PardP* as a sermon (**689, 750, 999, 1018**). Spencer concludes the Pardoner's performance resembles a 'bona fide sermon' in its accordance with the Church's teachings but not in the circumstances of its delivery (p 117).

663a Cooper, Helen. 'Literary and Symbolic Inspiration in the Pardoner's Prologue 1924.' In *Harry Mileham 873-1957: A Catalogue*. Ed Patrick Mileham. Intro Christopher Wood. [Leighton House Museum and Art Gallery, Hove Museum and Art Gallery, Royal Museum and Art Gallery, Canterbury]: University of Paisley, 1995, 45-7.

Illustration reproduced as plate 37 and 38.

Harry Mileham's painting *Pardoner's Prologue* (1924) represents the 'apex of [his] achievement in historical and literary interpretation,' and reveals his concern for characterization, internal dialogue, place, artefacts, and spiritual significance. The painting portrays the moment when the Pardoner announces his theme after insisting the pilgrims stop at an alestake. Mileham's portrayal of the Pardoner is informed by his familiarity with either a fascimile or woodcut version of the Ellesmere miniatures and with a French reliquary (c. 1370) in the Victoria and Albert Museum. True to the spiritual significance of *PardP*, Mileham bases his painting on two models from sacred art: the Marriage at Cana and the *Last Supper*. Cooper reviews the preliminary sketches as evidence of Mileham's developing understanding of the Pardoner, noting finally that the appearance of a boy who provides a segue to the narrative of *PardT*. Both a preliminary sketch and the 1924 painting are reproduced.

663b Furrow, Melissa M. 'Latin and Affect.' In *The Endless Knot: Essays on Old and Middle English in Honor of Marie Borroff*. Eds. M. Teresa Tavormina and R.F. Yeager. D.S. Brewer: Cambridge, 1995. Pp 29-

41.
Latin carried affective power for Chaucer's audience and was not restricted to a literate elite. *PardT* and *PrT* 'turn upon Latin utterances' (p 39) demonstrating their affective power. *PardP* makes explicit reference to the Pardoner's use of Latin to provoke an emotional reaction: *And in Latyn I speke a wordes fewe, To saffron with my predicacioun,/ And for to stire hem to devocioun* (lines 344-6). In a similar fashion, the discrepancy between the stated and intended meaning of *Radix malorum est cupiditas* reveals the efficacy of affect over rational response to literal meaning.

663c   Manzanas Calvo, Ana M. 'The Economics of Salvation in *The Book of Margery Kempe* and *The Pardoner's Prologue*: The Vision of Purgatory.' In *Papers from the VIIth International Conference of SELIM*. Eds. Bernardo Santano Moreno, Adrian R. Birtwistle, and Luis G. Girõn Echevarria. Universidad de Extremadura: Cãceres, 1995. Pp 175-85.

The spirit of vitality emerging in the eleventh century gave rise to a monetized market which, in turn, fashioned images of the other world. By the fourteenth and fifteenth century, with the creation of purgatory, individuals struggled 'to inscribe themselves in the History of Salvation' (p 177). The development of purgatory can be seen as an otherworldly equivalent to the colonization of the New World. Whereas *The Book of Margery Kempe* depicts a well managed other world, *PardP* and *PardT* present a degenerated view arising from the application of human mercenary structures to Christianity.

๛ The Pardoner's Tale 1877-1949

664 Skeat, Walter W. *The Tale of the Man of Lawe, The Pardoneres Tale, The Second Nonnes Tale, The Chanouns Yemannes Tale from the Canterbury Tales.* 1877. See **3**.
Though a considerable part of *PardT* is occupied with digressions, the tale itself is 'told simply, briefly, and well' (p xxvi). The story appears to have been taken from a fabliau now lost but outlined (as Tyrwhitt noted) in *Cento Novelle Antiche* (*Nov* 83). For *PardP*, see **570**.

665 Furnivall, F. J., and W. G. Stone, eds., *The Tale of Beryn with A Prologue of the Merry Adventure of the Pardoner with a Tapster at Canterbury.* London: N. Trübner and Co., 1887; 1909.
Prints the text of the 'continuation,' a contemporary account of how pilgrims like Chaucer's conducted themselves. The Pardoner flirts with a Tapster, revisits her and makes an assignation, finds she is faithless, is beaten by her paramour, hits the paramour with a pan, runs off, hides for a night, then repairs the damage in the morning and escapes detection. Also included are the English abstract of a French original, an Asiatic version of the tale, a plan of Canterbury (c 1588) and a map of the road between London and Canterbury (c 1675). See also **1130**.

666 Lounsbury, Thomas R. *Studies in Chaucer: His Life and Writings,* 1892; rpt 1962. See **265**.
Urry's inclusion of *Pardoner and Tapster at the Inn in Canterbury* and the *Tale of Beryn* as genuine works is 'inexcusable' (1:289); they are later thrown out by Tyrwhitt. The influence of *RR* in *PardT* is a constant quality, no other single source being as influential: a comparison of lines is provided (7099 *RR*/876 *PardT*; 7046/543; 5693/716). The conduct of False-Semblaunt inspires the cynical revelations of the Pardoner. Sources in Cicero (83rd epistle: comparison of drunk man to

madman), Jerome (lines 517-20), John of Salisbury (*Polycraticus*: Chilbon/Stilbon, Demetrius) and Paulus Diaconus (*Historia Miscella*: Atilla) are identified (pp 270, 296, 362, 385). The influence of Innocent III on the wretchedness of mankind, particularly *De Gula*, is noted in ideas and language. Lounsbury suggests it is not unreasonable to suppose that these scattered references 'constitute the translation of which the poet spoke, and that so far as it ever existed at all, it exists now' (2:334). Chaucer shows his lack of familiarity with Avicenna by referring to *fen* as a work independent of the 'Canon of Medicine' (2:394). For *PardP*, see **571**.

667 Ten Brink, Bernhard, *History of English Literature*. 1883-96. See **266**.
When the Host orders a mirthful tale to offset the sadness left by the story of Virginia, the Pardoner pauses at an ale-stake—a long stake decorated with a wreath and typically used as a signboard for beerhouses (p 170)—to think of ideas. The Physician, a doctor of the body, stands as a foil to the Pardoner, a spiritual doctor of miracles. *PardT*, found in outline in *Cento Novelle Antiche*, is a sample sermon and is interrupted by a long digression on the fatal effects of drunkeness, gluttony, gambling, and swearing. In no part of *CT* is the 'connection between individual figure and the general framework so close as in the apotheosis of the Pardoner'(p 172). *PardT* is 'deeply poetic and tinged with mystery'(p 171), the connecting of the treasure with the Wandering Jew 'an extremely happy stroke'(p 171), and the solicitation of relics 'an exquisite touch'(p 172).

668 Kittredge, George Lyman. 'Chaucer's Pardoner.' *Atlantic Monthly*. 72(1893), 829-33. Rpt in *Chaucer: Modern Essays in Criticism*. Ed. Edward Wagenknecht. New York: Oxford University Press, 1959. Pp 117-25.
Critics commonly suppose the harangue of the Pardoner to be a gross violation of dramatic propriety (p 829). Prior attempts to reconcile the Pardoner's behavior with his character have included reference to Faux Semblant and the convention of satire as well as explanations based on drunkenness. The Pardoner is consistent throughout and the 'apparent impropriety of the introductory confession' is 'in conformity to nature' (p 830). The Pardoner is a 'thorough-paced scoundrel' who is 'proud of his dexterity'(p 830). His unsound moral condition known to the pilgrims, and the possibility of him meeting them again being unlikely, he offers a cynical confession rather than be thought a fool. In delivering

his tale or sermon, he is rapt up and in a 'white heat of zeal' (p 831). He offers his relics, just managing to catch himself with the frame, *And lo sires thus I preche* (line 915). In voicing the prayer, the Pardoner recalls his better nature but does not sustain the mood. 'There is no question of repentance or reformation, for the Pardoner is a lost soul'(p 832). The Pardoner seeks to hide his state by jocosely offering his relics; the Pardoner's lack of serious intent is evidenced further by his selection of the Host, 'the last person to yield to seductive suggestions of this sort ...' (p 832). The Host replies with scurrile jest and is surprised by the Pardoner's anger. '[B]y showing us the man in a moment of moral convulsion' (p 833), Chaucer invests the Pardoner with a dignity suited to the tale he tells.

669 Skeat, W[alter] W. 'The Pardoneres Tale.' *The Complete Works of Geoffrey Chaucer.* 1894. Pp 275-90. See **7**.

Skeat cites Novella 82 of the *Libro di Novelle* as a source and notes parallels with Innocent III (III: 444, 445) and *ParsT* which he speculates was written earlier (cf. lines 475, 482, 504, 529, 558, 590, and 631-50 with *ParsT* lines 591, 836, 819, 820, 822, 793, 587-93). He speculates the Flanders setting derives from a lost original and the *pestilence* in line 679 refers to the plague of 1348-9. Skeat accepts Kittredge's identification of lines 727-33 as imitated from the first Elegy of Maximian. In line 734, *cheste* refers to a box for holding clothes and, by implication, his 'worldly goods.' In line 915 ff, the Pardoner, having told his tale, proceeds in 'his usual professional style' (p 290). For Pardoner, see **266**; for *Phy-PardL*, see **530**; for *PardP*, see **572**.

670 Koch, John, ed. *The Pardoner's Prologue and Tale.* A Critical Edition. 1901. See **16**.

The link to *PhyT* is the only certainty in the placement of *PardT*. The date of the pilgrimage 'which cannot have been a merely fictitious one, was the 18th-20th of April, 1385 ...' (p xxii); *PardP* and *PardT* were written after *GP* and the *WBP*, approximately in 1390-1. Analogues for The Robbers and the Treasure Trove are found in *Cento Novelle Antiche* and, as R. Morris first showed (1881), in one of the Buddhist birth stories, *Vedabbha Jataka*. Some of the tale's moral reflections appear to be borrowed from *DMC* and the *Somme de Vices et De Vertues*. It is not known whether Chaucer drew directly from Jerome's *Hieronymus contra Jovinianum* or from the *Polycraticus* of John of Salisbury. For Pardoner, see **269**.

671 Root, Robert K[ilburn]. *The Poetry of Chaucer: A Guide to its Study and Appreciation.* 1906/ rev 1922; rpt 1934/rev 1957. See **270**.

Chaucer drew from the satiric method of Jean de Meun in depicting the hypocritical Pardoner. As the Pardoner begins his tale, the company has reached a tavern 'whose "ale-stake," crowned with its garland, projects far over the muddy road' (p 223). Though the immediate source of *PardT* is lost, Root notes the earliest form is found in the Hindoo *Vedabbha Jataka* and a recent form in Kipling's "The King's Ankus." Root reprints a 1572 analogue from *Cento Novelle Antiche* to demonstrate the distinctive elements of *PardT*: the tavern atmosphere, plague setting and aura of doom. We are tempted to believe the Old Man is Death himself but Chaucer does not say. The tale is 'full of tragic terror,' transacted largely in dialogue, unimpeded with superfluous detail, and 'inevitable as death and night' (p 230). With 'sublime audacity' the Pardoner offers his relics: 'the conscious artist in hypocrisy, who wishes to give a crowning example of his art' (p 231).

672 Hinckley, Henry Barrett. *Notes on Chaucer: A Commentary on the Prolog and Six Canterbury Tales.* 1907; rpt 1964. See **271**.

For *Phy-PardL* (pp 159-62), *PardP* (pp 162-7) and *PardT* (pp 167-83), Hinckley includes notes on *Ronyan* and *Flaundres*. Chaucer originally intended the tale for the Parson but decided it was too brilliant for the 'over-earnest' Parson; 'the drunken confession in *PardP* artistically justifies the telling of a superb moral tale by the conclusion, vv. 895-968.' *PardT* 'is one of the most perfect in all literature' (p 159). In its mystery it approaches the spirit of Greek tragedy.

673 Coulton, G. G. *Chaucer and His England.* London: Methuen, 1908.

The Pardoner begins *PardP* with 'cake in his mouth and the froth of the pot on his lips'(p 161). Carried away by force of habit, he concludes by asking the pilgrims to kiss his relics, make their offerings and 'earn his indulgences' (p 161). The Host replies with words easy to understand 'but not so easy to print here in the broad nakedness of their scorn ...' (p 161). Though Chaucer sympathized with reformers, and must have met Wycliffe, 'all the evidence is against his having belonged in any sense to the Lollard sect' (p 309).

674 Hammond, Eleanor P. *Chaucer: A Bibliographic Manual.* Boston: Macmillan, 1908. Rpt New York: P. Smith, 1933. See **127**.

Hammond notes three positions for Fragment C: after F [Ellesmere and Skeat], after G [Caxton through Urry], and after B² [Chaucer

Society]. She notes the Chaucer Society printing of *PardP* and *PardT* (First Series, Numbers 81, 85, 86, 90, 91 and its supplements 1 and 2), the critical edition by Koch (**16**), modernizations, translations (German, French and Italian), and a dramatization by H. D. Wescott at Yale in 1900. For sources and analogues, she notes *Cento Novelle Antiche*, *Dec* (Day 6, Nov 10) and Kipling's 'King's Ankus' from the Jungle Book. A brief bibliography is included. For *Phy-PardL*, see **532**.

675 Saintsbury, George. 'The End of the Middle Ages.' *The Cambridge History of English Literature*. Vol. 2. Ed. A. W. Ward and A. R. Waller. Cambridge: University Press, 1908. Pp 156-96.

The ancient and grisly *PardT* holds 'a sort of ironic yet avowed impropriety for the pardoner' (p 183). Sainstbury praises *Beryn*, regretting that Skeat excluded it from his edition of *Chaucer and Chaucerians*. Saintsbury notes, however, that those who include *Beryn* as one of Chaucer's works reveal their uncritical attitude in not noting the un-Chaucerian metre (246).

676 Canby, Henry S. *The Short Story in English*. New York: Henry Holt and Company, 1909/ rev 1913.

Though the most perfect telling of one of the oldest Eastern plots, *PardT* is marred by digression. The sermon is too long and overrich in examples illustrating the human nature of the Pardoner, a professional exhorter.

677 Lawrence, William Witherle. 'The Marriage Group in the Canterbury Tales.' *MP* 11(1913), 247-58.

The Wife of Bath's utterances are connected to those of the pilgrims who have already had their say (contra **273**). Critics have acknowledged uncertainty in the relation of Group C. Several (**1, 2, 7**) have insisted Group C is misplaced. The evidence is 'clearly in favor of placing the Physician and the Pardoner elsewhere, and allowing the Wife of Bath to follow the Nun's Priest without delay'(p10).

678 Tupper, Frederick. 'Saint Venus and The Canterbury Pilgrims.' *The Nation* 97(1913), 354-6.

The Chaucer Society placement of *PardT* between *NPT* and *WBT* is opposed not only by manuscript evidence but also by the testimony of the dominant Love motif in *CT*. *PardT* is related to *SNT* through the common motif of the Deadly Sins. See **679, 680**.

679 — 'Chaucer and the Seven Deadly Sins.' *PMLA* 29 (1914), 93-128.

Chaucer uses the familiar motif of the Seven Deadly Sins,

architectonically. A comparison of Chaucer's tales with contemporary treatments (particularly *Confessio Amantis*) demonstrates Chaucer's use of the sins to be deliberate and formalized. The stories are *exempla*, each story is accompanied by a preachment against the particular sin and several storytellers incarnate the sins they preach against. The device of the sins came to Chaucer late; it enters with *WBT*, and culminates in the penitential sermon of the Parson. The Pardoner preaches against two sins—avarice and gluttony—while ironically representing them. Indubitably, Chaucer's artistic purposes incorporated moral ends.

680 —'The Pardoner's Tavern.' *JEGP* 13(1914), 553-65.

Seeking to interpret Chaucer within his horizon, 'his strict confinement within the bounds of fourteenth-century thought' (p 553), Tupper examines *PardT* within medieval tradition. The tavern is the ironic setting of the Pardoner's harangue and the harangue is directed against vices associated with taverns in the medieval tradition. The Pardoner and his fellows remain in the tavern after the drinking of corny ale. The pilgrims are still in the ale-house at the conclusion of the *PardT* when the Pardoner invites them to come forth. At the end of the epilogue, the pilgrims *riden forth hir weye* (line 968), a phrase elsewhere used to indicate resumption of the journey. The Pardoner preaches against 'only the vices of the tavern' (p 558). Chaucer is deriving his application 'directly from the substance of his story' (p 558). The tavern is the abode of gluttony in all its phases. The Pardoner's summary of sins is an orderly exposition of the two deadly sins illustrated in his story: Avarice that leads to homicide and Gluttony accompanied by Luxury, Hasadry and Blasphemy. A comparison of the Pardoner's ban on oaths (lines 651-2) with the Host's blasphemy (lines 288, 314) suggests the Pardoner has convicted the Host of sin long before the summons to his relics. Further evidence that the Pardoner was associated with the tavern sins in the medieval tradition is found in the *Tale of Beryn* where the Pardoner is the gluttonous Pardoner of *PardP* 'lickerish, lecherous, blasphemous ... bibulously preaching sermons against Gluttony from a tavern-bench' (p 564). Close reading suggests the Pardoner is 'a lost soul' (cf **668**) yet the *GP* claims him *a gentil Pardoner*.

681 Kittredge, George Lyman. *Chaucer and His Poetry*. Cambridge, Massachusetts: Harvard University Press, 1915. Rpt many times; Introduction by B. J. Whiting, 1970. Pp 215-8. Rpt in *Twentieth Century*

Interpretations of the Pardoner's Tale: A Collection of Critical Essays. Ed. Dewey R. Faulkner. Englewood Cliffs, New Jersey: Prentice-Hall Inc., 1973. Pp 107-8.

The six lectures delivered at Johns Hopkins University in 1914 have influenced generations of critics, Kittredge's insights still serving as a point of departure for many. 'The Man and His Times' (chapter 1) assesses the Pardoner, at once 'an abandoned wretch' and *a noble ecclesiast*; *PardT* is marked by proportion, skillful construction, and economy. The combination of the 'cynical frankness' of his confession, the 'eloquence' and 'apparent earnestness'(p 21) of the sermon, and the 'impressiveness' of the exemplum produces a 'psychological situation of intolerable stress and strain'(p 22). 'Next to Shakespeare, Chaucer is the greatest delineator of character in our literature'(p 29). Chapters 5 and 6 examine *CT* as a 'Human Comedy.' Kittredge's guideline for interpretation is that 'Chaucer always knew what he was about'(p 151). Pp 215-8, virtually every word of which has been cited by subsequent critics, are reprinted in **882**. Here Kittredge reaches the apex of 'dramatic' interpretation of the Pardoner. The sermon exemplum is one of the best in the world. One passage 'affords a remarkable illustration of effective reticence' (p 107). The Old Man is undoubtedly Death. The momentum of the Pardoner's sermon leads him, inappropriately, to offer the relics, then suddenly his cynicism dissipates as 'he suffers a very paroxysm of agonized sincerity' (p 108) which leads him to pray (lines 913-8). The Pardoner then takes refuge from himself, offering his relics in jest. Harry Bailly, unaware of the Pardoner's 'emotional crisis' (p 108), answers with rough jocularity. The moment is too intense for poise and the Pardoner becomes speechless with fury. The Pardoner is 'the one lost soul among the Canterbury pilgrims' (p 180). Though quite sober, the Pardoner is determined to override the objections of the gentlefolk with a merry tale. *PardP* is in the conventional form of a confession. The pilgrims are well aware of the Pardoner. The cynical frankness of the Pardoner is dramatically inevitable. Though deceiving mankind is his business, this time no deception is possible. The exemplum, one of the best in the world, carries him so far as to append his customary solicitation. The aged wayfarer is undoubtedly Death in person. Realizing too late that his customary summons is inopportune, the Pardoner cynically reminds his fellows that he is merely giving a demonstration. Once the Pardoner was sincere, and now under the spell of his own story, he 'suffers a very paroxysm of agonized sincerity' (p 108). The Host, failing to recognize the Pardoner's emotional crisis, engages in rough jocularity, leaving the Pardoner speechless. With the Knight, a reconciliation amidst laughter is reached; nobody but Chaucer 'divined the tragic face behind the satyr's mask'(p 218; 108). See **882**.

682 Lowes, John L[ivingston]. 'Chaucer and the Seven Deadly Sins.' *PMLA* 30(1915), 237-71.

The presence and prominence of the 'sins motif' delineated by Tupper (**679, 680**) completely collapses under scrutiny. Tupper's claim that each tale represents a sin relies on assumptions and simplification unwarranted by the facts. Though Tupper sees the Pardoner as the representative of two sins, the Pardoner, in fact, mentions five, and states his theme explicitly as Avarice. An examination of the evidence for each of the other sins demonstrates that, while Chaucer makes abundant use of the Seven Deadly Sins, he does not employ a formal schematizing of them. Chaucer is a consummate artist in the use of the exemplum and ironical inconsistency.

683 Moore, Samuel. 'The Position of Group C in the Canterbury Tales.' *PMLA* 30(1915), 116-23.

The most serious defect of the Chaucer Society's arrangement of *CT* is the placing of Group C between the *NPT* and the *WBP*. The arrangement was adopted solely to make the tales of the third day no less than those of the second day. The ms evidence is decisive in indicating the *PardT* is followed by *ShT* and the rest of Group B (CB²): of the accessible mss, thirty-three contain the tales in this sequence; the one that doesn't lacks independent authority. Placing CB² between B¹ and D results in the proper order for place references. The best arrangement for *CT* becomes AB¹, CB², D E F G H I.

684 Tupper, Frederick. 'The Quarrels of the Canterbury Pilgrims.' See **573**.

The 'literary *motif* of clash between precept and practice'(p 257) evident in the Pardoner is found also in False-Seeming of *RR* who preached abstinence and poverty while indulging his appetites and pursuing coin.

685 — 'Chaucer's Sins and Sinners.' *JEGP* 15 (1916), 56-106.

Tupper (**679, 680**) responds to Lowes (**682**) and reiterates a belief in 'architectonic use of the Deadly Sins' (p 56). Lowes, 'heavily impeded by seried masses of minutiae' (p 103) misses the large issues. 'Evidence of each story's purpose lies ... in direct association with the representative

of the respective Vice' (p 57): the motif of Charity and Lechery in
PhyT (pp 59-67); the formal grouping of tavern sins in a tavern setting
in the background and homilies of the Pardoner's exemplum (pp 67-
73); the master theme of Cursing in the *FrT* and the lietmotif of Ire in
the *SumT* (pp 73-7); the function of Cheste or Chiding in the Manciple's
story and homily (pp 77-83); the tenfold emphasis on good works which
relates to the theme of Sloth with the Second Nun (pp 83-7); the thrice
insistent illustration of Detraction (Envy) in the Constance Story (pp
87-95); and the relation of Pride to the inobedience of the Wife of Bath
(pp 96-103). Tupper revises his earlier notion of 'rigid categories' of
sins but stands by his contention that each tale relates to the representative
of a respective Vice (pp 56-7) (cf **679, 680**). That Chaucer used the
Sins as a *motif* can be seen by: the fitness of story; the tag of ironical
assignment to a representative of Vice; insertion of moralizing; the relation
of the sinner's treatment of their sins to the discourse of the Parson
(and, to a lesser degree, discourse in medieval sources; and evidence
of analogues).Chaucer's persistent moral aim is evident in the binding
of *exempla* of Avarice and Lechery in the Doctor-Pardoner link. The
link 'connects with grim humor an unholy union'(p 67). The Pardoner
begins with a sketch of the tavern and a homily on tavern sins. The
medieval mind grouped the tavern sins and associated them with
gluttony. Swearing is related. The association of pardoners with gluttony
and avarice is traditional. The Pardoner is a tavern reveler who knows
his sinfulness, undergoes no 'moral convulsion' (contra **668, 681**), and
denounces, while drinking—'his own tavern sins from the vantage point
of a Tavern bench' (p 72).

686 Curry, Walter Clyde 'The Secret of Chaucer's Pardoner.' 1919. Rpt
1960. [Page numbers from 1919; 1960.]
In his interruption of the Wife of Bath, the Pardoner reveals his
consciousness of physical lack. The pilgrims, perhaps recalling his former
anger in *PardT*, refrain from challenging him. The reason the *gentils*
anticipate an obscene story when the Host calls for a merry tale is
because they 'translate [the Pardoner's] physical peculiarities into terms
of character'(p 602; 65). Contra Kittredge (**668; 681**), the Pardoner's
apparent sincerity (line 915) is 'only a preparation for his proposed
master-stroke of deception'(p 603; 67); the Host's rude speech is more
than jocularity (p 604; 68). The Pardoner's sensitivity about his weakness
is underscored by his incongruous love song and boasts. The Pardoner

admires the Wife of Bath but with her description of husbands as slave and thrall, paying a debt both morning and evening, the Pardoner is provoked, by painful consciousness of his physical misfortune, to interrupt (D line 166 ff). An outcast from human society the Pardoner 'satisfies his depraved desires by preying upon it' (pp 605-6; 70). For Pardoner, see 277.

687   Kuhl, Ernest P. 'Chaucer and The "Fowle Ok".' *MLN* 36(1921), 157-9. Rpt in Ernest P. Kuhl. *Studies in Chaucer and Shakespeare.* Ed. Elizabeth K. Belting. Beloit, Wisconsin: Belting Publications, 1971. Pp 50-3.

Previous critics (**7, 273, 673**) had read the record variously as indicating one, two (**669**), or possibly three robberies. The establishment of three robberies testifies to a considerable amount of travelling in the course of Chaucer's duties at the time of composition of the *CT.*

688   Brussendorff, Aage. *The Chaucer Tradition.* Oxford University Press: London, 1925.

Presents the manuscript tradition of *PardT* (see **16**), noting problems. Suggests provisional textual groups are best established by tracing variants of a few characteristic lines. Treats variants of C 318-28, suggesting that editors should follow Ellesmere but note the London versions of C 297 f, 319 f, and 326-7 as genuine readings rejected by Chaucer himself (p 103). Comments that Ellesmere scribe appears to have been critical of 'Chaucer's tendency to repetition' (p 114), avoiding for example the repetition of *swere* in line 636 f.

689   Chapman, Coolidge O[tis]. 'The Pardoner's Tale : A Medieval Sermon.' *MLN* 41(1926), 506-9.

The structure of *PardT* reveals Chaucer's knowledge of medieval preaching (**668**). Medieval sermon books identify a role for exempla in the sermon. The Pardoner's exemplum comes near the end of his sermon, immediately preceding the recapitulation. Finally, the Pardoner drops the role of 'pious preacher' (p 509) and resumes the role of rascal in offering his pardons.

690   Manly, J[ohn]. M[atthews]. 'Chaucer and the Rhetoricians.' *Proceedings of the British Academy.* [Warton Lecture on English Poetry]. 12(1926), 95-113. Rpt in *Chaucer Criticism 1: The Canterbury Tales.* Ed. Richard J. Schoeck and Jerome Taylor. Notre Dame and London: University of Notre Dame Press, 1960; rpt through 1978. Pp 268-90.

PardT represents Chaucer's growth in artistic power and recognition that observation and imagination were more effective than rhetorical devices as means of amplification. In a listing of tales according to percentages of the larger rhetorical devices they contain, *PardT* has approximately 40 percent (*MkT* 100; *MilT* 1 per cent, p 283). In *PardT*, the long passages of rhetoric between the opening and the narrative itself are justified as part of the Pardoner's sermon. See **778**.

691   —. 'Chaucer as Artist.' *Some New Light on Chaucer*. 1926.   See **286**.

Chaucer, one of the three greatest poets to have ever written in English, 'bids fair to move up from third place to second'(p 265). Many readers still feel that his strength is native wit rather than conscious artistry, but the *PardT*, in its creation of tone and atmosphere, belies such dismissal. Possessing every quality of the ideal short-story centuries before that type of fiction was recognized and defined (p 289), *PardT* displays rapid, vivid narration, verisimilitude in character portrayal, and the creation of a tone so intense as to be matched only once in the next two hundred years (in Henryson's portrayal of Troilus and Criseyde) (p 290). The tragic atmosphere created in the first twenty lines recalls the intensity of the opening of *Macbeth*. The Old Man 'remains perhaps the most tragic and mysterious figure ever created in an equal number of lines in any literature' (p 290). From the appearance of the Old Man, 'the already tremendous theme sweeps to its fulfilment with all the majestic and uncanny terrors of doom'(p 290). See also **515**.

692   Marburg, Clara. 'Notes on the Cardigan Chaucer Manuscript.' *PMLA* 41(1926), 229-51.

Marburg describes the Cardigan manuscript, discusses its relation to other manuscripts of *CT*, and presents a transcription of the Doctor-Pardoner Link, *PardP* and *PardT* (pp 236-51) to enable comparison with the Chaucer Society's *Parallel Text-Specimens* (**1**). Marburg concludes that the Cardigan manuscript belongs to the Dd-subdivision of the A-group, and is most nearly related to Hodson 39 with which it shares a common ancestor influenced by the B-group of manuscripts.

693   Tupper, Frederick. *Types of Society in Medieval Literature*. 1926. See also **288**.

The Pardoner tells one of the world's best short stories and in the telling, 'betters it mightily'(p 94). Then the Pardoner launches his invective at the tavern vices—Gluttony and its accessories, Luxury, Hasardry and

Blasphemy. No digression, this diatribe is warranted by: direct derivation from the setting of the exemplum; the correlation between characters in the exemplum and sins denounced; the tavern setting of the Pardoner's harangue; and the professional reputation of pardoners as gluttons and lovers of gold. The Pardoner knows himself well; rather than undergo any 'moral convulsion' (**668, 681**), the Pardoner hoodwinks his audience with consummate artistry (p 99). The ironical blending of professional and moral elements—class traits and traditional sins is found throughout *CT* (e.g., Friar- Summoner, Cook- Manciple). The bibliographical note lists a history of the convention of the Seven Deadly Sins as well as adaptation in literature, drama, religious songs, and in Romance.

694 Cowling, George H. *Chaucer*. London: Methuen, 1927.
PardT, Chaucer's 'most dramatic story' belongs simultaneously 'to no age and every age' (p 166). Based on an Eastern story, it finds analogues in the tale of the hermit who found treasure (*Cento Novelle Antiche*) and the satire of a begging friar (*Dec*). It is 'a little masterpiece in the grim and gruesome' (p 166).

695 French, Robert Dudley. *A Chaucer Handbook*. New York: Appleton-Century Crofts, 1927/rev 1947.
Noting the capacity for variety in the structure of *CT*, French judges futile attempts to determine intended arrangement or unifying motif. Separate essays on the tale discuss sources and analogues, elements of originality, and indications of date of composition. The Pardoner may have been added late with the Reeve, Miller, Manciple, and Summoner to furnish dramatic incident (**127**). *PardP* is original with Chaucer though contemporary sources document similar abuses. *PardT*, originally of Hindoo origin, worked its way westward, the closest parallel being an Italian verse in *Cento Antiche Novelle*. No known version incorporates the background of the plague or the figure of the Old Man. Some of the moral reflections of the sermon are taken from *DMC*; others, echoed in the *ParsT*, are likely drawn from a common Latin treatise. See **209**.

696 Legouis, Emile. *Geoffrey Chaucer*. Paris: F. Alcan,1928.
Chaucer showed little interest in 'the reverses and internal troubles of his country' (p 32); the plague is simply stated in *PardT* and the setting is Flanders. The Pardoner went into a tavern but came out before telling his tale (cs **680**). Chaucer 'held up the mirror to his age, and presented to it the least distorted image of itself'; no historical document provides as well the people 'in their habit as they lived'(p 157). *PardT* derived

from the East, the counterpart of which is found in *Cento Novelle Antiche.* For Pardoner, see **274**.

697 Manly, John Matthews, ed. *Canterbury Tales.* 1928. See **42**.
Text for *PardT* omits lines 950-5. Notes (pp 616-23) treat the English prejudice against Flanders and the association of Flanders with drunkenness, as well as the appropriateness of a tavern setting. For Pardoner, see **286, 290**; see also **804**.

698 Chapman, Coolidge O[tis]. 'Chaucer on Preachers and Preaching.' *PMLA* 44(1929), 178-85.
A treatment of Chaucer's statements on the methods of sermon making, the times and places of preaching, and the conduct of both preacher and audience reveals Chaucer had a first hand knowledge of the art of preaching. The Pardoner, with his one memorized sermon designed to elicit money, stands in contrast to the learned Parson. The Pardoner uses the amplification of citation and the exemplum of the rioters to entertain rather than instruct his hearers. Further, he violates precautions in preaching manuals by haranguing his audience and letting his glaring eyes rove.

699 Masefield, John. *Chaucer.* Cambridge: Cambridge University Press, 1931.
Next to *KnT*, rank the narrative parts of *PardT*, a tale which comes from France.

700 Montgomery, Franz. 'The Musical Instruments in "The Canterbury Tales".' *Musical Quarterly* 17(1931), 439-48.
Chaucer employs music and instruments in his characterizations. Among the seventeen instruments mentioned in *CT* is the harp which the Pardoner suggests is an instrument of the devil (lines 465-6; 479-80).

701 Dempster, Germaine. *Dramatic Irony in Chaucer.* Stanford University Publications in Language and Literature, 4. Palo Alto: Stanford University Press, 1932. Rpt New York: The Humanities Press, 1959. Pp 77-9 rpt in *Twentieth Century Interpretations of the Pardoner's Tale: A Collection of Critical Essays.* Ed. Dewey R. Faulkner. Englewood Cliffs, New Jersey: Prentice Hall, 1973. Pp 109-11.
Defining dramatic irony as 'the irony resulting from a strong contrast, unperceived by a character in a story, between the surface meaning of his words or deeds and something else happening in the same story' (p 7), Dempster examines *PardT* and four analogues: 1) the fifteenth century Italian miracle, *Rappresentazione di Sant'Antonio*; 2) Hans

Sach's *Der Dot im Stock*; 3) a thirteenth- or fourteenth- century Italian *novella*; and 40 a fifteenth-century *exemplum* printed by J. Klapper (number 98). The first two share two ironical elements: the quest for Death and the frustration of the robbers' hopes. Based on Chaucer's focus on the single tragic irony of the quest for Death in *PardT*, Dempster judges the *exemplum* printed by Klapper, with its economy of ironical detail, to have the best claim 'to a close analogy with Chaucer's source' (p 76). Chaucer introduces the following elements to reinforce irony in the quest for Death: a tavern setting during the pestilence in Flanders which creates an atmosphere of fear and sin; the rioters' challenge of the enigmatic Old Man including an accusation that he is the spy of Death; suspense leading to the discovery of the gold; the rioters' forgetfulness of their purpose upon finding the gold; and the rapid economy that closes the *exemplum*. Despite the fact that *PardT* 'is a sermon, there is room for doubt' (p 79). The Old Man carries the tale beyond the certitude of sermon literature. 'Like Death in the tale, that power is impressive in proportion to its enigmatical character (p 79).

702 Norris, Dorothy M[acbride]. 'Chaucer's "Pardoner's Tale" and Flanders.' *PMLA* 48(1933), 636-41.

Chaucer's decision to set *PardT* in Flanders is deliberate. Despite great prosperity at the beginning of the century, Flanders faced economic and political desolation by the close. In Chaucer's day, Londoners felt considerable antagonism toward the Flemish. Flanders is a pertinent setting for the tale on the evils of drunkeness (**697**) and avarice. The theme of cupidity could also carry a moral for Chaucer's England.

703 Owst, G. R. *Literature and Pulpit in Medieval England: A Neglected Chapter in the History of English Letters and of The English People*. Cambridge: Cambridge University Press, 1933; New York: Macmillan, 1933; 2nd rev ed 1961; rpt 1966.

In a classic study of the influences of preaching upon the general development of literature, Owst presents evidence, published and unpublished, from the sermon tradition to demonstrate the debt in commonplace illustration, allegory, exempla, satire and complaint. The sermon is an 'organ of a virile, picturesque speech and a keen, critical view of society, ... [a] medium for vivid illustration, lively anecdote, homely portraiture, witty and ruthless satire ...' (p 55). Chaucer used classical examples found in Robert Holcot, 'Liber Sapientiae Salomonis' for the *PardT*. Of all the important types of composition in English perhaps none is so little understood as that of Satire and Complaint at its earliest stage (p 213). Chaucer is 'too genial a wit,' 'too little of a preacher and enthusiast,' too much entertained with the world as he sees it, to be very much of a ruthless satirist (p 229). Contrary to his earlier opinion (**577**), Owst notes there were references to pardoners. In view of the poems against Lollards (another lawless group), further sermons dealing with them may be indicated (p 374). Chaucer's hypocritical Pardoner follows the recognized convention when he condemns *the fruyt* that *cometh of the bicched bones two* (line 656). The Pardoner's and the Parson's very words on swearing are found in the homiletic tradition. The *dronke man* like Langland's Glouton and Shakespeare's Falstaff 'have their real prototype as literature in the satires of the pulpit'(p 425). The opening section on gluttony in *PardT* is modelled on current homiletic literature, and specific elements such as the simile *develes temple* (lines 468-70) and the passage on the preparation of food are taken directly from Bromyard. Admonitions on backbiting are also found in the literature. The pulpit was a force to be reckoned with in literature, politics, and religion (p 591). The Christian pulpit kept alive the realism, moral purpose, and dramatic tradition that blossoms in Shakespeare (p 591).

704 Robinson, F. N., ed. *The Works of Geoffrey Chaucer* . 1933/1957. See **51**, **71**.

PardP and *PardT* form a consecutive composition written in the period of *CT*. The Pardoner presents the exemplum, of oriental origin, as a customary sermon. Incidental borrowings include quotations from Innocent III, *ParsT*, and Maximian (for the Old Man, a character largely original with Chaucer). Both *PardP* and *PardT* are delivered while the pilgrims are at a tavern: 'a story which is in large part an attack upon gluttony and revelry is told in a tavern by a man notoriously addicted to the vices he condemns' (p 729). 'And the Old Man, the Messenger of Death, in his mystery and moral sublimity is one of the most impressive apparitions in poetry' (p 11). For Pardoner, see **295**; for *Phy-PardL*, see **535**.

705 Lowes, John Livingston. *Geoffrey Chaucer [and the Development of His Genius]*. 1934; 1958. Pp 229-45 rpt in *Discussions of the 'Canterbury Tales.'* Ed. Charles A. Owen, Jr. Lexington, Massachusetts: D.C. Heath, 1961. Pp 105-10. Republished as *Geoffrey Chaucer*. Bloomington: Indiana University Press, 1958.

The publication of six lectures delivered at Swarthmore College in 1932 is dedicated to Kittredge and appears without reference apparatus. Chaucer's greatest works are 'timeless creations upon a time-honored stage'(p 3). *PardT*, like the other tales whose sources lie in oral tradition, offers 'untrammelled opportunities for development'(p 175). The Pardoner and the Wife of Bath are Chaucer's masterpieces of characterization (p 186): both lay their very selves bare; the Pardoner in a 'cynical disclosure, pitiless in its realism, and daringly outspoken, of the hypocrisy of his preaching'(p 186). The Pardoner is evil to the core with 'perhaps the most haunting of all personifications of Death'(p 186). After a moment of self-recognition, the Pardoner brazenly offers his discredited relics. Together, the prologue, tale, and setting are 'fearless and unsparing satire'(p 187) and more dramatic than any other unit of the pilgrimage. The description of the Pardoner preaching exemplifies Chaucer's 'instinct for the concrete' (p 196). For Pardoner, see **296**.

706 Sedgwick, Henry Dwight. *Dan Chaucer: An Introduction to the Poet, His Poetry and His Times*. 1934. See **297**.

Sedgwick offers a reader's book rather than a scholar's book. Having drunk too many draughts of corny ale, the Pardoner describes his practice as a pardoner. *PardT*, 'a tale of primary human interest' which 'makes the best story in the book'(p 290). Though not among the greatest, Chaucer is 'immensely clever, immensely shrewd, kindly and generous, a consummate master of meter, and a jolly good fellow'(p 357).

707 Brown, Carleton, ed. *Chaucer: The Pardoner's Tale*. 1935. See **55**.

PardT 'is perhaps the finest in the Canterbury collection, whether considered from the point of view of theme or narrative art'(p xi). *PardT* forms the exemplum of a sermon. The apparent disconnection in the homily on the sins of the tavern (lines 135-332) might be explained if it were originally intended for the Parson (cf **672**; cs **590**) with an exemplum on the vices of the tavern to follow. The exemplum of the three rioters was substituted when the tale was assigned to the Pardoner. *[C]heste* refers to a chest for the keeping of clothes and valuables but the word is also used of a coffin—by changing his chest with Mother Earth the Old Man plainly expresses a longing for the grave. To his traditional sources with a hermit fleeing treasure identified as death, Chaucer adds the quest for death calling to mind Maximian as well as the Legend of the Wandering Jew. Brown notes the earliest mention of the legend in England is by Roger of Wendover in his *Flores Historiarum* wherein the wanderer is a Roman soldier, Pilate's doorkeeper whose original name of Cartaphilus was changed upon conversion to Joseph. Following *PardT*, the Pardoner relaxes 'into a mood of pure raillery' (p xxxv) (cs **668**, cs **686**). For Pardoner, see **298**; for *PardP*, see **581**.

708 Tatlock, J. S. P. 'The Canterbury Tales in 1400.' *PMLA* 50(1935), 100-39.

Chaucer left *CT* without any indication of order of groups. He probably had a plan in mind and left internal indicators. The order of the tales has no authority. The order of Furnivall and Skeat is likeliest to match Chaucer's intention.

709 Thurston, Herbert. 'The Conversion of Boccaccio and Chaucer.' *Studies* 25(1936), 215-25.

Chaucer, like Boccaccio, knew that much of what he wrote (e.g., satirizing the clergy) 'was doing the devil's work' (p 220). 'The difference between these writers and the more salacious of the poets and novelists of our day is that [they] had the grace in the end to admit that they had acted in bad faith, and to express their heart-felt sorrow for the scandal which they had given' (p 220). Though Fra Cipolla like the Pardoner is satirized for false relics, Boccaccio's will makes clear he did not despise them. Chaucer's lack of mention of Boccaccio may be a mark of respect due to the fact that he was drawing from a work Boccaccio had repudiated.

710 Hench, Atcheson L. 'On the Subtly Creeping Wine of Chaucer's Pardoner.' *MLN* 52(1937), 27-8.

The reference to the *subtly creeping wine* (line 565) has been interpreted as referring to the illegal mixing of wine by vintners (7), and specifically, the blending of lower priced Spanish wine (**51**). Incidents of mixing bad wine with good are reported in letters and city records.

711 Hamilton, Marie Padgett. 'Death and Old Age in The Pardoner's Tale.' *SP* 36(1939), 571-6.

Scholarly controversy over the significance of the Old Man testifies to Chaucer's success in making him mysterious (p 571). If the character is meant to be more than 'a pathetic Old Man'(p 572), he must stand for Old Age as the Harbinger of Death dressed 'in his master's livery'(p 572). Interpreting the Old Man as Age is consonant with his role as guide to rioters, and suited to the Pardoner's motivational purpose. The Pardoner introduces the Three Messengers of Death—Sickness (plague),

Disaster (death by violence), and Old Age (the Old Man). The motif of the Three Messengers of Death accounts for elements missing in Maximian; e.g., the mysterious nature of the Old Man, his characterization as a servant to Death, and the metaphor of the gate. The futile knocking at the gate is also found in Thomas Sackville, *A Mirror for Magistrates*. Like Sackville, Chaucer conceived of making his Old Man the spy of Death after reading poems in the tradition of the Three Messsengers, then enriched his sketch with details from Maximian, and invested the figure with a glamor that may owe sanctity to the legend of the Wandering Jew (p 576).

712 Patch, Howard Rollin. *On Rereading Chaucer*. 1939; 1967 [Page numbers from 1967.] See **300**.
Chaucer's humor, deemed 'healthy' by James Russell Lowell, the result of seeing life 'steadily' by Kittredge (**681**), and an aspect of 'good sense' by Dryden (p 3) is based on a sense of incongruity between the transitory and the permanent (p 8). As such, it assumes a quality of detachment and a sense of proportion. Chaucer 'spreads the contagious propaganda of a kindly view of human nature'(p 185). 'Chaucer likes everybody in due measure, except perhaps the Pardoner'(p 160); with the Pardoner, Chaucer moves to mordant satire. The Pardoner's recognition that Christ's pardon is best demonstrates that he 'can be honest if need be' (p 164). 'If he really thought that Christ was best, thought it with his whole nature, his life would be different'(p 165). 'And so with deceit in his pleasures, his profession, his idealism and religion, and even in his humor, the Pardoner has that isolation which is Hell'(p 166). Chaucer's work is a drama in the course of action. His characters have another chance: thence his light-hearted quality (p 185). Topical references such as those to the plague are those of a spectator. Dominant in his spirit are geniality and playfulness. For *Interr*, see **517**; *PardP*, see **582**.

713 Bronson, Bertrand H. 'Chaucer's Art in Relation to His Audience.' *Five Studies in Literature*. University of California Publications in English 8: 1. Ed. J. S. P. Tatlock, J. M. Cline, B. P. Kurtz. Berkeley: University of California Press, 1940. Pp 1-53.
The 'final stage of dramatic narrative technique'(p 45) is reached when the personality of the speaker permeates both the tale and the manner of telling. The appropriateness of *PardT* to the Pardoner is beyond doubt and *PardP* ought to be included 'as of equal, if not greater,

importance in the development of dramatic monologue'(p 47). We are indebted to Chaucer's audience because no poet could have gone on producing 'the highly socialized kind of poetry which is Chaucer's characteristic work, without the encouragement of a ready and immediate appreciation'(p 53).

714 Loomis, Roger S. 'Was Chaucer a Laodicean?' Rpt in *Essays and Studies in Honor of Carleton Brown*. 1940. See **301**.

Far from 'invariably good-humored'(p 305) (cs **666**) or detached, Chaucer, in such passages as the Host's response to the Pardoner, expresses contempt and loathing of the Pardoner.

715 Manly, John Matthews, and Edith Rickert. *The Text of the Canterbury Tales*. 1940. See **58**.

Notes provided for lines 488, 532, 544, 552, 598, 644, 659, 700, 705, 760, 769, 771, 796, 826-7, 871, 891, 919f, 928 and 954. Manly-Rickert argue that line 919f is part of the narrative link between tales and might be set off as an epilogue. For Pardoner, see **302**; for *PardP*, see **584**; for *Phy-PardL*, see **536**.

716 Sedgewick, G. G. 'The Progress of Chaucer's Pardoner 1880-1940.' 1940. See **303**.

This article attempts to separate the established judgment from the doubtful in the sixty years following Jusserand (**279**). Critics have variously noted the analogue to the short story (**676**); the debt to the sermon tradition (**933, 698, 703**); the implications of physiognomy (**686**); and a realism suggesting life models (**697, 683**). Criticism has, at various times, overemphasized social commentary (e.g., Flanders), moral intent (e.g., sermon form and digressions from it), and realism in setting (e.g., tavern setting). The Pardoner displays 'demagogic genius' (p 440): the whole 'Pardoner Scheme' is 'a powerfully consistent work of art' (p 443) which must be studied as one block though it is conveyed in five stages: 1) *GP* portrait; 2) interruption of the Wife of Bath; 3) headlink; 4) address (prologue, sermon, benediction); and 5) epilogue or solicitation. In the ending, contrary to Curry who misplaces the transition in tone, and Kittredge (**668**) who argues all on the unsupported assumption that the sermon is too long, the Pardoner realizes he has impressed the pilgrims in spite of themselves and proceeds accordingly. The Host, in responding with 'sheer obscene brutality'(p 457) produces a comic effect. Chaucer presents the Pardoner 'fully rounded and without reservation' in a way that 'enables us to sharpen our senses against the scourge and blight of charlatanism' (p 458). For *PardP*, see **585**.

717 Speirs, John. 'Chaucer: The Canterbury Tales.' *Scrutiny* 11(1942-3), 189-211.

GP and *PardT* are marked by a 'depth of acquired meaning and achieved understanding' (p 189). The Pardoner and Summoner are 'impudently on top of the world, arch-swindlers beneath the Church's capacious cloak, preying on human credulity and superstition' (p 200). *PardP* and *PardT* extend the themes of cupidity and depravity found in the Pardoner portrait.

718 Long, Hudson E. 'Chaucer as a Master of the Short Story.' *Delaware Notes*, 16. Newark, Delaware: University of Delaware, 1943. Pp 11-29.

Long measures several *CT* against the following criteria for the short story: brevity (to allow reading at a single sitting), compression, unity, immediateness, continuous narration, characterization, verisimilitude, style, culmination, and 'soul.' With *PardT*, 'Chaucer has done his job well' (p 26). The Pardoner's digressions are the only potential cause for censure (p 26). If one is willing to allow the digressions as a necessary means of characterization of the narrator, *PardT* needn't be ruled out of the genre. 'Furthermore, ... more than four hundred years before Edgar Allan Poe, Chaucer was writing tales which are such perfect examples of the short story that they have not been withered by age or staled by custom; in fact, they challenge comparisons with the best of O. Henry, Bret Harte, and our contemporary tellers of the short story.'

719 Krishnamurti, S. 'A Note on "The Pardoner's Tale", Lines 237-9.' *MLR* 39(1944), 398.

Lines 237-9 refer to the manner in which vine-shoots of Spanish vineyards become intermixed with those of French vineyards nearby rather than the deliberate adulteration by vintners (contra **710**). This interpretation is evident not only from the use of *growing* and *crepeth*, but from the use of *wyn* and *wynes* wherein Chaucer resorts to a pun (wine/vine).

720 Chute, Marchette. *Geoffrey Chaucer of England*. 1946. See **306**.

PardT, like *WBT*, is the product of Chaucer's 'wisest and most mature technique' (p 292). Around the exemplum Chaucer built a short story 'that Poe could not have bettered for horror or de Maupassant for pace' (p 293). Aware that he is intellectually outmatched, the Host makes a brutal reference to the Pardoner's physical deficiencies. The Knight temporarily takes over the role of master of ceremonies.

721 Bennett, H. S. *Chaucer and the Fifteenth Century.* London: Oxford University Press, 1947; rpt with corrections 1948, 1954, 1988.

The description of the Pardoner indicates that 'the urbane ironic thrusts of Chaucer are more deadly than the blows of Langland' (pp 21-2). The relish with which Chaucer describes the Pardoner convinces us to accept him without judging. The whole conduct of *PardT* is derived from contemporary pulpit practice.

722 Hulbert, J. R. '*The Canterbury Tales* and Their Narrators.' *SP* 45 (1948), 565-77.

Chaucer had hardly any precedent for assigning appropriate tales to tellers. *CT* shows a diversity in kind and degree of appropriateness. Chaucer may not initially have realized the full possibilities of his scheme. *PardT* is dramatically related to the Pardoner; the sermon may have been added to make the connection closer.

723 Long, Richard A. 'John Heywood, Chaucer, and Lydgate,' *MLN* 64 (1949), 55-6.

Long suggests Heywood's displacement of having the quarrel occur between the Pardoner and the Friar (*A mery Play betwene the pardoner and the frere, the curate and neybour Pratte*) rather than the Pardoner and the Host may draw from Lydgate's treatment of tension between a pardoner and friar (*Siege of Thebes*).

724 Lumiansky, R. M. 'A Conjecture Concerning Chaucer's Pardoner.' 1949. See **311**.

Lumiansky builds on suggestions by **716** and **686** to offer a conjecture concerning the Pardoner in eight divisions: the portrait in *GP* (I lines 669-714), the Pardoner's interruption of the Wife of Bath (III lines 163-87), the 'Introduction to the Pardoner's Tale' (lines 318-28), the *PardP* (lines 329-462), the sermon (lines 463-915), the benediction (lines 915-8), the attempted sale (lines 919-45), and the quarrel with the Host (lines 946-68). The tale proper is more completely subordinated to the total performance of the Pardoner than with any other pilgrim. The Pardoner keeps his audience halted and assembled from the introduction of his tale (lines 321-2) to the close of his performance (line 968). *PardT* falls into four divisions (see above). In the sermon, the Pardoner continues flattery and insistence on the value of what he has to offer, 'in an effort to replace in the minds of his listeners the imaginary peasant audience' (p 29; 218) by the pilgrim audience. The benediction completes the substitution of audiences and prepares for the attempted sale. The attempted sale fails because the Pardoner reverts to the crude methods he is accustomed to using with his peasant audiences. He breaks the spell he has created by referring to the mechanics of his speech (line 919), assuming a jocular tone in offering pardon at every mile's end, suggesting the implausible possibility of a fall and approaching the Host in a bantering tone. Though the Pardoner is a master salesman to ignorant peasants, he is a failure among the pilgrims. The closing anger of the Pardoner is triggered both by the Host's reference to his physical lack (cs **686**; cf **716**) and by his awareness of his own error in the attempted sale. For *Interr*, see **519**; for *Phy-PardL*, see **539**; for *PardP*, see **588**.

ᛒᛦ The Pardoner's Tale 1950-1959

725 Everett, Dorothy. 'Some Reflections on Chaucer's "Art Poetical".'
PBA 36(1950), 131-54. [Sir Israel Gollancz Memorial Lecture]. Rpt in
Essays on Middle English Literature. Ed. Patricia Kean. Oxford:
Clarendon Press, 1955. Pp 148-74; with corrected sheets 1959, pp 149-
74; In *Chaucer's Mind and Art*. Ed. A.C. Cawley. London: Oliver
and Boyd, 1969; New York: Barnes and Noble, 1970. Pp 99-124. Rpt in
Middle English Literature: British Academy Gollancz Lectures. Sel.
and introd. John Burrow. Oxford and New York: Oxford University
Press, 1989. Pp 21-44. [Page numbers from 1969.]
To Chaucer, 'art poetical' meant a knowledge of how to write poetry
according to established rules. The method of presentation in *PardT* is
directly related to rhetorical teaching, the whole discourse of the Pardoner
being a 'closely integrated unity' (p 145). If the tale of the three rioters
mentioned in line 661 was not originally connected to the 'homily on the
sins of the tavern' (contra **707**), one can 'only marvel at' (pp 153-4 n
32) the skill of amalgamation. The exemplum and the tirade on the sins
are so closely connected the reader can either regard the story as an
exemplum illustrating the tirade, or the tirade as amplification of the
central point of the story. The Pardoner conveys the illusion of a sermon:
the theme is announced; the final apostrophe acts as peroration (lines
895-903) and is followed by a benediction (lines 916-8); there is a
suggestion of the division of the theme (lines 591-4); Scriptural examples
are employed and the Pardoner directly attacks sins and sinners. The
tale is shaped for the ultimate purpose of completing the portrait of the
Pardoner. The irony of the exemplum cuts deeper than the Pardoner
seems aware; the full extent of the Pardoner's self-deception is revealed
by his own sermon.

726 Lawrence, William Witherle. *Chaucer and the Canterbury Tales.* 1950. See **312**.

Though Tupper's attempt to tie the seven deadly sins to the framework of *CT* is flawed, it does show how vividly the sins were in Chaucer's mind (cs **679, 680**). *PardT* manifests 'fabliau ingenuity of plot, rapid movement, and lively dialogue' (p 68). The dramatic potential of *PardT* suggests that, had he lived in Shakespeare's day, Chaucer might have been a playwright. *PardT*, pointing out as it does to a moral lesson, is compatible with the Retraction. There is no decisive authority for placing *Phy-PardL* between B^1 and B^2; B^2 ought to follow B^1 directly.

727 Thomas, Mary Edith. *Medieval Skepticism and Chaucer.* New York: William-Frederick Press, 1950.

Chaucer's anticlericalism is evident in that four of his five churchmen are false though his indictment of the clergy argues for his devotion to faith. *PardT*, in its conformance to established technique, reveals Chaucer's familiarity with the preaching of his time.

728 Kellogg, Alfred L. 'An Augustinian Interpretation of Chaucer's Pardoner.' 1951. See **590**.

PardP and *PardT* constitute 'an integrated study in Augustinian terms of the secret punishment of evil'(p 465). Kellogg outlines the Augustinian conception of sin and documents its availability to Chaucer. The Gregorian progress of the seven deadly sins and the conception of the sinner carrying hell within himself were available in sources for *ParsT*. *PardT* continues the development of the Augustinian conception of sin found in *PardP*. *PardT* is neatly integrated with the theme of avarice: the Pardoner's method is to begin with offshoots of avarice, embody them as drama and end with an address. The Pardoner's basic sin is pride: *PardT* is a mirror of the struggle in the Pardoner's mind between '"*Goddes wille*" and living "*right at our owene wille*"' (p 473). The protagonists are personifications of the forces; the rioters are characterized by pride; the Old Man, by humility. The Old Man must be 'Death himself' ... (p 479 n 43). Chaucer treats the Pardoner gently because his vice is its own punishment. The Pardoner's final confession (lines 916-8) reveals the good in his being that he has been attempting to conceal. In the benediction '[t]he whole fiction of his joyous life has vanished and the anguish of his soul is laid bare' (p 474). He attempts the solicitation in a desperate effort to have the pilgrims join in his sacrilege. The Pardoner misjudges in selecting Harry Bailly. With the

Knight's resolution, evil 'is absorbed into the pattern of existence' (p 475) and Chaucer's 'profound faith' is revealed. Like Augustine, Chaucer sees the will of God fulfilling itself even in acts of evil. 'The Pardoner has fulfilled virtually every requirement for damnation but like all human beings, to Chaucer he is somehow not quite damnable' (p 475). For Pardoner, see **314**.

729 Malone, Kemp. *Chapters on Chaucer*. 1951; rpt 1979. See **315**.
PardP sacrifices verisimilitude for self-description. *PardT* is the only tale dramatically suited to the teller; the Pardoner makes the tale an integral part of his self-dramatization. In line 915, the scene shifts from church to the frame story, providing a picture of the Pardoner at work.

730 Owen, Charles A. 'The Plan of the Canterbury Pilgrimage.' *PMLA* 66(1951), 820-6.
In proposing that *CT* are played on the 'stage' of a five-day, two-way journey, Owen places Fragment VI on the final day of the return journey when the theme is death. The position for the Fragment is determined, in part, by the Pardoner's interruption of the Wife of Bath which would be 'undramatic and anticlimactic' (p 824) were it to follow *PardP* and *PardT*. The Pardoner's remarks on his being a *suffisant pardoneer* should anyone fall and break his neck indicate a position after the Cook's *fair chyvachee* (Hengwrt line 50), yet with *contree* and possible *aventures* still to ride through (p 824). The positioning of the Pardoner and the Parson on the final day balances the 'equally striking but secular conjunction of the Knight and Miller on the first' (p 826).

731 Owen, W. J. B. 'The Old Man in *The Pardoner's Tale*.' *RES* 2(1951), 49-55. Rpt in *Chaucer: Modern Essays in Criticism*. Ed. Edward Wagenknecht. New York: Oxford University Press, 1959. Pp 159-165.
Working from a supposition that the Old Man is 'merely an old man' (p 160), Owen demonstrates that he is neither symbolic nor mysterious (contra **51, 681, 711**) but 'merely an old man' (p 50). In *PardT*, there is 'an absence of definition' which emphasizes the Old Man's 'seeming triviality' (p 49). In the analogues, the Old Man has seen the gold, has identified it with Death and is fleeing it. By leaving all this out Chaucer adds dramatic irony. Comparison of parallel passages in *PardT* and Maximian's First Elegy suggest it as a possible source for Chaucer's notion of aged humanity. Consistent with Maximian, the Old Man in *PardT* seeks death; in analogues, he flees it.

732 Pratt, R. A. 'The Order of the Canterbury Tales.' *PMLA* 66(1951),

1141-67.

Pratt reviews the editorial tradition for the placement of Fragment VI proposing a modification of both Chaucer Society and Ellesmere orders. The proposed 'Chaucerian' order of IV-V(E-F)-VI(C)-VIII(G) 'offers positive artistic values and interlocking of themes and ideas ... which reveal the actual intention of the poet, and which fully justify this reopening of the whole question of the order in which Chaucer intended to read the *Canterbury Tales*' (p 1167). See **1, 2**.

733 Speirs, John. *Chaucer the Maker*. London: Faber and Faber, 1951; rev 1960; paperback ed. 1964. Pp 97-9, 168-77 rpt in *Discussions of the 'Canterbury Tales.'* Ed. and introd. Charles A. Owen, Jr., Boston: D.C. Heath, 1961. Pp 73-8.

PardP and *PardT*, a single unit, is a self-dramatization in the 'Human Comedy of the Middle Ages'(p 98). The Pardoner's confession is a convention. His digression on the sins integrates his tale with its context; his preaching and entertaining are intertwined for commercial purposes. The Old Man has the force of the allegorical Elde: he knows about Death and is more powerful than the rioters. The final view of the Pardoner—in the Host's retort and the Pardoner's benediction—sets the tale 'in a completed frame' (p 177) which contrasts his pretensions with the widow's sincerity in *NPT*. See **745, 770**.

734 Dunn, Charles. *A Chaucer Reader*. Selections from *The Canterbury Tales*. 1952. See **68**.

In contrast to the Physician, the Pardoner is willing to tell all about his profession. Isolated from the other pilgrims by his abnormal nature, he has only the Summoner as a companion. The Pardoner's hypocrisy contrasts with the Wife of Bath's candor. With the Pardoner the comic elements are submerged in the tragic. The Pardoner is an individualized composite based on False Seeming and the characteristics of a physical degenerate. Dunn sets off *PardT* line 158ff as an 'Epilogue.'

736 Gerould, Gordon Hall. 'The Vicious Pardoner'and 'The Limitations of Chaucer.' *Chaucerian Essays*. 1952. See **316**.

The Pardoner is 'a murky figure and is doubtless best viewed against a murky sky' (p 55). The apparent inconsistency about the Pardoner's voice—small as a goat in line 688 and round as a bell in lines 330-1— may result from an evolving conception on Chaucer's part. The Pardoner's discourse lacks the orderliness of a sermon; his performance can be explained 'only by understanding that he was tipsy' (p 67). Though the Pardoner opens the account of the rioters, the story is never really begun; any attempt to connect the scene in the Flanders tavern with the tale of the rioters is futile. Distracted by his own reference to drunkenness, the Pardoner digresses (lines 485-588). Despite the fact that the Pardoner is a trained preacher, able to display both knowledge of homiletic materials and the tricks of his profession, his performance is not an illustration of medieval sermonizing. When the Pardoner comes to tell his moral tale, Chaucer takes over, sacrificing dramatic propriety for moral force. The voice that continues is that of the Pardoner cleansed; the restraint and precision of the narrative contrasts sharply with the 'scrambled tirade'(p 68) which preceded. The narrative is characterized by compression and understatement, 'tensity of mood' (p 68), irony, and a sense of mystery. At the close of the narrative, the Pardoner exhibits unexpected moral awareness (lines 916-8). His return to 'cynical effrontery' (p 70) with his blasphemous proposal is not surprising. The Pardoner is so amusing that his wickedness fails to shock us. Chaucer is not a reformer; he viewed everything with ironic detachment. In the *PardT*, for example, the closely articulated action is more forceful than the 'confused sermonizing of the scandalous narrator' (p 101). 'The infamous trio who find the death they seek ... are not the rioters of the tavern ...' (p 101). Chaucer preserves the moral force of his fable despite the drama of the Pardoner's performance.

737 Preston, Raymond. *Chaucer*. London: Sheed and Ward, 1952.

PardT, a 'superb sermon from a revolting man' (p 160), stands in ironical contrast to the Pardoner. *PardP* (lines 407-8) explicitly develops the paradox found in *RR* (lines 5763-4). The Pardoner, a doctor of soul, follows the Physician, a doctor of body. *MLT* and the groups of tales begun by the Shipman and Physician may form a sequence demonstrating various ironic relationships between tale and teller; a sequence culminating in the clash between the Pardoner and *PardT*, 'and a perilous cadence, the kiss of Pardoner and Host' (p 227).

738 Schlauch, Margaret. 'Chaucer's Colloquial English: The Structural Traits,' *PMLA* 67(1952), 1103-16.

Schlauch scrutinizes colloquial passages to reveal how Chaucer gained the effect of unstilted ease, fluency, unpretentiousness, and, in dialogue, verisimilitude. In *PardT*, Schlauch notes use of ellipsis (lines 456 ff), subordination and coordination (385-7), and suitability to speaker (859-65).

739 Swart, J. 'Chaucer's Pardoner.' *Neophil* 36(1952), 45-50.

Several slips in *PardP* can be explained only as 'the logic of a man who is slightly drunk'(p 47). In the slight pause before he begins his tale, the Pardoner plots his strategy from confession to the sale of pardons. 'To such a man it would be a singularly attractive proposition to run with the hare and hunt with the hounds' (p 48). The Pardoner's sin, *superbia* is demonstrated in *PardP* and amply documented in *ParsT*. The Pardoner stands revealed 'as a bragging and slightly intoxicated crook' (p 49). *PardT* ironically reveals the Pardoner as 'a Rioter who sets out to seek Death' (p 49). His vanity leads him to miscalculate by offering the pilgrims a chance to realize they are being deceived (lines 915-8). The Knight's call for the kiss appropriately counters the Pardoner: 'Can there be a more humiliating punishment for a professional and superior hypocrite than to be forced to be one' (p 50)? *PardP* and *PardT* are a high point in Chaucer's moral earnestness.

740 Brewer, D. S. *Chaucer.* London: Longmans,Green, 1953. Men and Books Series. 2nd ed. with fuller bibliographical notes and minor revisions, 1960. 3rd ed. 'extensively revised and with additional material,' 1973. Rewritten as *An Introduction to Chaucer.* London: Longman, 1984. Note: The 1973 edition (supplemented) reproduces a chest front carved with scenes from *PardT* about 1400.

In *GP*, the Pardoner is exposed 'for a lying, fraudulent, grasping, conceited eunuch' (p 137). The Pardoner's self-revelation is similar to that of the villain in *RR*; there is no evidence he is drunk. At the close of *PardT*, he 'reverts to his homiletic vein' (p 159) and by a twist of irony solicits the pilgrims. The crudeness of the Host's reply expresses 'something of our feeling'; however, Chaucer consigns none of his pilgrims to 'outer darkness'(p 159). 'Chaucer's satire never seems to spring from personal spleen' (p 160); it is balanced and deepened by irony.

741 Gross, Seymour L. 'Conscious Verbal Repetition in the Pardoner's "Prologue".' 1953. See **591**.

The success of *PardT* lifts the Pardoner into an 'exalted benediction'(p 414). The Pardoner attempts to reestablish his ironic intent with the sale of worthless pardons.

742 Owen, Charles A. Jr., 'The Crucial Passages in Five of *The Canterbury Tales*: A Study in Irony and Symbol.' *JEGP* 52 (1953), 294-311. Rpt in *Chaucer: Modern Essays in Criticism.* Ed. Edward Wagenknecht.

New York: Oxford University Press, 1959. Pp 251-70. Rpt in *Discussions of the 'Canterbury Tales.'* Ed. and introd. Charles A. Owen Jr. Boston: D. C. Heath and Company, 1961. Pp 79-89. [Page numbers from 1959.]

In *CT*, Chaucer adds the complication of a group of observed narrators to a dramatic pose of simplicity. The resulting richness finds concentrated expression in passages that 'at once embody and expose the limited vision of created character and creating narrator' (p 251). The passages foreshadow the outcome of the plot and help to create symbolic values that add a unifying dimension to the narrative. In *PardT*, the crucial passage occurs when the revellers find the gold: *No lenger thanne after Deeth they soughte* (line 772). This line marks a fundamental division in the tale; the revellers no longer seek Death, having found him. Their illusions of brotherhood shattered, they return to the real world. The gold both focuses and limits their vision. The gold is at once effective warning against cupidity, instrument of the Pardoner's greed, and symbol of his victory over physical inadequacy. 'The Pardoner has also found death without recognizing it' (p 263). His life is 'an exemplum of the futility of cynicism' (p 264). At the center of *PardT*, the symbol of gold as unrecognized death reveals the emptiness of the Pardoner's hypocritical attempt to dupe the peasants and vain effort to shock the pilgrims. The simplicity adopted as a mask in *CT* is a 'token' for the deeper simplicity that reflects the 'paradoxes of personality, the contradictions of experience'(p 270).

743 Kökeritz, Helge. 'Rhetorical Word-Play in Chaucer.' 1954. See **543**.
Reexamines the rhetorical background of Chaucer's punning with a view to demonstrating close dependence on his literary models, chiefly Machaut and *RR*. Discusses examples of *traductio*: *ware/avarice/warice* (lines 905-6); and *adnominatio*: *cursed/ cursednesse* (line 895). Contrary to Lounsbury (**666**), Kökeritz argues that, with his ability to transform formalized word play into wit, Chaucer becomes a precursor of the Elizabethans. For *PardP*, see **592**. See also **751**, **756**.

744 Severs, J. Burke. 'Author's Revision in Block C of the *Canterbury Tales*,' *Speculum* 29(1954), 512-30.
Examining Block C to test Manly and Rickert's suggestion (**58**) that some variants might be authentic unrevised editings, Severs concludes that, though Chaucer may have altered one or two words in *PardT*, he conducted no systematic revision. 'Chaucer did not write the Pardoner's

epilogue later than the rest of the tale' (p 530). For *Phy-PardL*, see **544**.

745 Speirs, John. 'The Pardoneres Prologue and Tale.' In *The Age of Chaucer*. Ed. Boris Ford. London: Penguin Books, 1954. Pp 109-17. Slightly revises **733**. *PardP* and *PardT*, which are 'organically one' (p 107) develop and illustrate the themes of *GP* portrait. The Pardoner is a fraudulent preacher, pedlar of pardons and sham relics, and a medicine-man selling false remedies. Inverting normal order, the sermon grows out of the tale, developing themes the suspended tale will illustrate. The recognition that Death is the consequence of Avarice comes as the last in a series of surprises. In lines 916-8, the Pardoner reveals 'a momentary sincerity' (p 115) which sets *PardT* in a frame.

746 Baldwin, Ralph. *The Unity of the Canterbury Tales*. 1955. See **322**. Though edification is the main concern of the pilgrims, they laugh 'at the lewd words with which the Host, unreasonably nettled, it would seem, by the Pardoner's sally (lines 941-2), squelches the bavard (lines 947-55)' (p 77). Each pilgrim and his story combine with the Parson and his homily to make a 'diptych': the Pardoner, 'avaricious and gluttonous ... a blasphemer and a simonist' (p 101) surely would be moved as the Parson takes up his theme. The Pardoner has experienced contrition, the root of penitence, for a brief moment in lines 916-8. For Pardoner *PardP*, see **593**.

- Review by Claes Schaar, *SN* 28(1956), 50-2: Scharr notes Baldwin's claim that vivifying similes attached to churls such as the Pardoner suggest 'a breakdown of the categorical concept of character' and neglects the evidence of the romance (p 52). He concludes that the book is, on the whole, 'ambitious and stimulating, and the points discussed in it are essential' (p 52).

747 Miller, Robert P. 'Chaucer's Pardoner, the Scriptural Eunuch, and the *Pardoner's Tale*.' 1955. See **323**. Like the Pardoner himself, the Old Man in the exemplum is the *vetus homo* representing spiritual death. Through the manipulation of Scriptural images, *PardT* consistently exemplifies the Pardoner's text. At each level of allegorical interpretation, the Pardoner represents the appropriate *radix malorum*. See also **512**.

748 Owen, Charles. 'The Canterbury Tales: Early Manuscripts and Relative Popularity.' *JEGP* 54(1955), 104-10. Challenging Dempster's theory that scribal activity following Chaucer's death was engaged in the production of exemplars, Owen reassesses the circulation of Chaucer's works to conclude 'early readers, probably confined to the court circle in which [Chaucer] moved, were a more discriminating group than the wider audience his tales reached as the fifteenth century advanced' (p 110). He posits early circulation of fragments and individual tales, and deduces '[t]hus a large number of independent textual traditions for a tale points to relative popularity, while the reverse indicates that the tale circulated principally as a part of the collections' (p 109). A review of independent textual traditions, based on Manly and Rickert, suggests immediate popularity for *FranT* (12), *PardT* (8) and *MilT* (8); whereas, in a consideration of 'anthologies,' *PardT* (0) is 'out of the running' (p 110). Among the factors Owen posits for the discrepancy are: a better survival rate for 'respectable material,' hard use for the individually printed tales so as to leave them undesirable for collections, or a change of taste lending to the success of the religious pieces. See **100, 1002**. See also **538**.

749 Schaar, Claes. *The Golden Mirror: Studies in Chaucer's Descriptive Technique and Its Literary Background*. 1955. See **324**.
In the context of his predecessors and contemporaries, Schaar discusses Chaucer's descriptive technique in portraits, landscape and emotions. *PardT* contains no description of isolated individuals. The description of the revellers' habits is unparalleled in the analogues. Behavioristic description such as the rioters' swearing (line 708), menacing the Old Man (line 750), and expressing happiness at finding the gold (line 775) is missing from analogues. In background works, *exempla* typically slight emotive description in favor of plot details. Chaucer's descriptive technique is marked by a degree of independence of immediate sources as well as of general background (p 489). The portraits in stories like the Pardoner's are notable for a greater degree of 'concreteness and fullness' (p 490) than those in originals and analogues. *PardT* contains 'descriptive details of a traditional *fabliau* and *novella* type' (p 365) as well as less common concrete description. *PardT* is similar to Chaucer's models in its lack of scenery description. In the classical doctrine of the three styles, *PardT* belongs to the *genus tenue* classification where behavioristic type and, to a lesser extent, emotive description are used extensively. In contrast to continental conventions of idealizing or drastic description, Chaucer develops to the full '[t]he general inclination for objective description found in Middle English poems' (p 505).

750 Shain, Charles. 'Pulpit Rhetoric in Three Canterbury Tales.' *MLN* 70(1955), 235-45.

Chaucer's familiarity with pulpit rhetoric extends beyond a knowledge of rules or surface consistencies(cs **689, 698**); he selects conventions for dramatic and narrative purposes (cf **707**). Comparison of *MerT* and *PardT* shows Chaucer's ability to 'set his materials to the tune of the man in the pulpit'(p 245); the Pardoner, his 'subtlest preacher,' delivers a sermon that still amazes and confuses us' (p 245).

751 Baum, Paull F. 'Chaucer's Puns.' 1956. See **325**.

In a paper submitted in draft form before Kökeritz's paper (**743**) appeared, Baum challenges the view that puns are uncommon in Chaucer (cs **51, 533, 743**). Baum identifies: *stile* which carries the modern meaning in *PardT* (line 712), the literary meaning in the Clerk's Prologue, and both meanings in *SqT* (line F 105ff); and *crooked* used in the literal and the metaphoric sense (line 761). For *PardP*, see **594**.

752 Coghill, Nevill. *Geoffrey Chaucer.* 1956. See **327**.

The Old Man is one character in Chaucer that comes neither from realistic nor textual sources (save for a few hints in Maximian). This 'ancient, muffled man' comes from 'some unknown half-world'(p 58). The essential creation is all Chaucer's: 'it was his "cyclopean eye" that discerned this eerie figure, tap-tapping his invisible way through the crowds at Queenshithe or by the Custom House, and among the courtiers of Richard II at the palaces of Eltham or of Shene' (p 59).

753 Duino, Russell. 'The Tortured Pardoner.' 1957. See **329**.

In an article intended for high school teachers, Duino reviews the interpretations of Tupper **684** and **685**, Kittredge **681**, Patch **712** and Curry **686** with a preference for Curry. The Pardoner's devout conclusion of his moral tale is only preparation for his '*tour de force* of charlatanry'(p 323).

754 Muscatine, Charles. *Chaucer and the French Tradition: A Study in Style and Meaning.* Berkeley and Los Angeles: University of California Press, 1957, 1964. Rpt (paperback), with brief bibliographical additions, 1965; 6th printing, 1969.

Muscatine examines the contribution of style and convention to Chaucer's 'meaning.' In his mature work, Chaucer exploits the 'nexuses between style and meaning'(p 6) that are characteristic of the courtly and bourgeois traditions of French literature. By 1400, the high Gothic mode had passed into a decadent period typified by the disintegration attributable to 'a loss of purposeful direction in the culture' (p 246). Chaucer's range, mixture of styles, and occasional passages in the fifteenth-century mood qualify him as a late Gothic poet but the main body of his work stands elsewhere. *PardT*, with its cynicism, preoccupation with corruption and death, its flamboyant rhetoric, 'circumstantial realism' and 'vulgarized allegory' explores the limits of the medieval moral order, yet, nevertheless, 'still proclaims the integrity of that order' (p 247). Chaucer is both 'the culminating artist of the French tradition' and the last medieval whose world is 'wide, yet still intelligible, viable, and one' (p 247).

755 Baum, Paull. 'Chaucer and the Scholars: the Pardoner.' *Chaucer: A Critical Appreciation.* Ed. Paull Baum. Durham: Duke University Press, 1958. Pp 44-59.

Noting the general laudatory tendency in Chaucer studies, Baum attempts in Chapter 2 (pp 44-59) to separate Chaucer's Pardoner from the critics' Pardoner. Chaucer's Pardoner tells a story originally meant for the Parson, tells it with great skill, then slips, tries to recover, and boisterously congratulates the pilgrims on having a Pardoner at hand. Hardly an item in the Pardoner's performance has escaped elaboration by the critics, much of it richly imaginative though needlessly imputing to Chaucer 'an elaborate justification for a simple proceeding' (p 52). The Pardoner's address to the pilgrims has tempted the critics beyond their strength. Distinctions in the art of glossing need be observed. The most unfortunate attempt to 'explain' Chaucer rests on the assumption that he can do no wrong. Much of the confusion in interpretation results from the unfinished nature of Chaucer's work. As *CT* are unfinished, so too Chaucer's Pardoner is an unfinished character.

756 — 'Chaucer's Puns: A Supplementary List.' 1958. See **330**.

Baum lists *warice/avarice* (line 905) noted by Pratt. These 'echoic puns' (p 170) are fairly common in Chaucer. See **743, 752**.

757 Cawley, A.C., ed. *Canterbury Tales.* 1958. See **72**.

PardT reveals a depth of character unanticipated in the *GP* portrait. In *PardT*, a 'mock-sermon against avarice' (p x), the Pardoner reveals himself. The Old Man 'is not only Death or the Messenger of Death; he is a symbol of that spiritual death which the three revellers—and the Pardoner himself—have already suffered' (p x).

758 Coghill, Nevill, and Christopher Tolkien, eds. *Chaucer: The Pardoner's*

Tale. 1958; rpt through 1978. See **74**.

The Pardoner's sermon is 'packed with all the virtuosity of Chaucerian rhetoric'(p 30): digressions, comparisons, interpretations and apostrophes. In the condemnation of gambling (lines 589-96), 'Chaucer peeps through the Pardoner more unmistakably' (pp 30-1). Dramatically, the Pardoner shifts to the tale of the rioters whose earliest form is in the *Jatakas.* The personification of Death, a 'peculiarly Chaucerian insight' (p 32), makes a quest possible. Chaucer's habit of suggesting universal implications in small details is evident in the way he depicts the mind of the youngest rioter (lines 837-50); only because the rioter has 'rejected grace in his will', the devil can offer him suggestions (pp 35-6). The 'supreme thing in the story, that ministers most to its irony, is the eeriness' (p 36), chiefly effected by the Old Man. Though one can't speak to Chaucer's intent, 'every sensitive reader will have that pricking of the scalp that comes when we have the intuition of some supernatural presence gliding into our experiences' (p 37). The Pardoner's cynicism and Chaucer's irony meet: at the close of *PardT*, 'before the spell is broken, he plunges in again' and offers a benediction (p 28). For Pardoner, see **332**; for *PardP*, see **596**.

759 Donaldson, E. Talbot. *Chaucer's Poetry: An Anthology for the Modern Reader.* 1958. See **73**.

The Pardoner chooses to preach on drunkenness, gluttony, swearing, and gambling in part because they are credible behavior for the rioters, in part because they 'can be made to sound most exciting,' and in part because they are the sins he practices (p 1093). 'The story itself is one of the most impressive ventures into the supernatural that English literature affords' (p 1093). The naturalism of the dialogue heightens the terror of the supernatural forces. Whatever the reason, the Pardoner makes 'avarice, good-fellowship, humor' (p 1093), the Pardoner makes his first and last intellectual error by insulting the Host's intelligence. 'If it is not the supernatural, it is at least an ironic destiny working through his own nature that impels the Pardoner to provoke his own social destruction among the pilgrims' (p 1094). For Pardoner, see **333**; for *PardP*, see **597**.

760 Murata, Yuzaburo. 'The Swearings in Chaucer.' *Studies in English Grammar and Lingusitics: A Miscellany in Honour of Takanobu Otsuka.* Eds. Kazuo Araki, Taiichiro Egawa, Toshiko Oyama, Minoru Yasui. Tokyo: Kenkyusha Ltd., 1958. Pp 289-99.

Murata surveys Chaucer's structural trait of swearing which 'may rightly be called the backbone of [his] language' (p 289). In his use of swearing, Chaucer adapts style to current speech, and manifests a wide range of usage including colloquial epilogues which serve as springboards to confidential talk (e.g., lines 287-310), and emotional and interjectional phrases (e.g., lines 472-5). The Pardoner speaks about the morals of swearing (e.g., lines 629-60), then violates taste himself by employing several oaths characteristic of vulgar people and an array of strong oaths, milder forms, wishes, and imprecations.

761 Owen, Charles A., Jr. 'The Development of the *Canterbury Tales.*' *JEGP* 57(1958), 449-76.

Owen argues that Chaucer expanded rather than reduced his plan for *CT* and sets forth a hypothesis for the development of *CT*. Among the implications are the following: the *Ret* is 'clearly the conclusion of the treatise on penitence and the seven deadly sins, not of *CT*' (p 458) which had marked influence on, though is antithetic in spirit to, *PardT*; before Chaucer wrote *PardT*, there was a period when he abandoned *CT* (beginning after 1390 and concluding before 1394); the assertion of the Knight's authority at close of *PardT* represents Chaucer's approach to varying the interruptions; *MerT*, a variation on the confession, follows the composition of *PhyT* and *PardT*. For Pardoner, see **334**; for *Interr*, see **521**.

762 Ethel, Garland. 'Chaucer's Worste Shrewe: The Pardoner.' *MLQ* 20 (1959), 211-7.

The character of the Pardoner, the 'wretchedest and vilest' of Chaucer's ecclesiastical sinners, is determined by his 'immortal hate,' trying to revenge himself 'upon God and upon men whose normality he mortally envied' (p 227). His tale and confession fall under the sin of 'double tongue' (p 224): his benediction is the 'crowning impiety' (p 224), aimed not at patronage but mockery of salvation. The Host's compliments to the manliness of other pilgrims indicates the value placed on the quality. Outraged at the Pardoner's sacrilege, the Host struck not where the Pardoner was callously indifferent but 'taunted the worthlessness of his testicles'(p 227).

763 Wagenknecht, Edward [C.], ed. *Chaucer: Modern Essays in Criticism*. London: Oxford University Press, 1959; numerous reprintings.

Essays with reference to the Pardoner include: Arthur W. Hoffman. 'Chaucer's Prologue to Pilgrimage: The Two Voices.' Pp 30-45 (**320**);

J.R. Hulbert. 'Chaucer's Pilgrims.' Pp 23-9 (**722**); George Lyman Kittredge. 'Chaucer's Pardoner.' Pp 117-25 (**668**); Charles A. Owen Jr. 'The Crucial Passages in Five of *The Canterbury Tales*: A Study in Irony and Symbol.' Pp 251-270 (**742**); W.J.B. Owen. 'The Old Man in *The Pardoner's Tale*.' Pp 159-65 (**731**).

❧ The Pardoner's Tale 1960-1969

764 Bronson, Bertrand H. *In Search of Chaucer*. Englewood Cliffs, New Jersey: Prentice-Hall Inc., 1960. Pp 78-87 rpt as 'The Pardoner's Confession,' in *Twentieth Century Interpretations of the Pardoner's Tale*. Ed. Dewey R. Faulkner. Englewood Cliffs, New Jersey: Prentice-Hall Inc., 1973. Pp 15-22.

The self-disclosure of the Pardoner is insidiously provocative. The theories of Kittredge (**668**) and Gerould (**736**), though persuasively argued and dramatically appealing, rest on an assumed intention of psychological realism—a technical achievement probably unknown before the eighteenth century. The answer to the puzzle of the Pardoner may lie in the conditions of composition: the tale may have been written first and rounded off with the prayer (lines 915-8); then, the headlink and conclusion may have been written as a frame, the solicitation being in character. Then the confession may have been added as a prologue. Perhaps to create a pause, to develop the character of the Pardoner more fully, or to lengthen the block of narrative to the customary reading time of one hour to one hour and a quarter, the confession was written as a prologue. The jarring effect on all that follows has been 'explained' by critics 'suckled on psychological realism' (p 87); their efforts reveal the results of 'altering one of the constituents of a cluster that combines conventional with naturalistic effects' (p 87). Though a hypocrite and a rascal, the Pardoner is not an apostate. *PardT* illustrates Chaucer's 'triumphant defiance' (p 101) of the conflict between two-dimensional and three-dimensional representation, between the procedures of allegory and naturalism. Amidst the naturalistic scene of the Flemish tavern, the servant-knave's words move the tale to the realm of personified abstraction. As the rioter's move to kill Death, they enter the world of the miracle play. The Old Man they meet personifies nothing more than the wisdom and gravity of his years. He 'carries an air of uncanny wisdom, and obscure power'(p 103) because he both uses the crude, materialistic personification of Death employed by the rioters, and also understands and applies it in a deeper, figurative sense. The tale acquires the force of allegorical meaning through the manipulation of the figure of Death. Chaucer, here, refuses to be bound by 'naturalistic controls'(p 103); he passes from one plane to another 'with such ease and confident mastery that we are hardly conscious of assenting to a miracle' (p 103). For Pardoner, see **340**; for *PardP*, see **598**. See also **1090**.

765 Schoeck, Richard J., and Jerome Taylor, eds. *Chaucer Criticism 1: The Canterbury Tales*. Notre Dame, Indiana and London: University of Notre Dame Press, 1960; 10th printing 1978.
Includes the following essays relevant to study of *PardT*: Roger S. Loomis, 'Was Chaucer a Laodicean?' (pp 291-310) (**714**); J[ohn] Matthews Manly, 'Chaucer and the Rhetoricians,' (pp 268-90) (**690, 691**); Robert P. Miller, 'Chaucer's Pardoner, the Scriptural Eunuch, and the *Pardoner's Tale*,' (pp 268-90) (**747**); and G. G. Sedgewick, 'The Progress of Chaucer's Pardoner,'(pp 190-220) (**716**).

766 Strang, Barbara M. H. 'Who is the Old Man in "The Pardoner's Tale"?' *N&Q* 7(1960), 207-8.
Chaucer and the Pardoner are such skillful storytellers that any element that does not make sense literally should be interpreted allegorically. Beginning at line 721, the 'Old Man presents himself with the portentous inexplicableness of an allegorical figure' (p 208). In not sustaining the allegory, the Pardoner functions as an oral narrator exploiting the possibilities of the moment.

767 Baker, Donald C. 'Gold Coins in English Medieval Literature.' *Speculum* 36(1961), 282-7.
Editors of Chaucer should not assume *florin* refers to an English coin (cs **7, 71**). The English florin, 'an ill-conceived and short-lived issue' worth 6 shillings, was minted only from January to August 1344. If Chaucer is being technical in *PardT*, given the Flemish setting, he is probably referring to a German or Flemish florin (about 3 shillings); more likely, he is referring to the Italian florin, its imitations, or money in general.

768 Magoun, Francis P., Jr. *A Chaucer Gazeteer*. 1961. See **145**.
See entries for: *Flaundres, Lepe,* the *Rochele, Burdeux, Lacedomye,*

Parthes, Engelond. For Pardoner, see **345**.

769 McNamara, Leo F. 'The Astonishing Performance of Chaucer's Pardoner.' *PMASAL* 46(1961), 597-604.

Avarice is neither the sole nor chief vice of the Pardoner, *a ful vicious man.* The 'drunkeness hypothesis,' though offered to account for both the Pardoner's digression before the exemplum and the Pardoner's psychology, is unnecessary for interpretation of the real consistency of *PardT.* The Pardoner's 'counterfeit humility' (p 599) is sufficient to motivate his confession (cf **742**). The Pardoner adopts a counterfeit humility to meet the suspicion, aversion, and contempt of the pilgrims. With the exception of the Summoner, the pilgrims react to him with disdain: the Wife of Bath at his interruption, the pilgrims at the outset of his tale, and again when the Host retorts using the familiar *thou.* The Pardoner's 'quite clearly satirical offering of relics'(p 603) rules out revenge as a motive. A 'spirit of accommodation'(p 603) accounts not only for his confession and solicitation but quite possibly his blessing, as an effort to prove 'good fellowship'(p 603). This view is implicit in Kittredge (**681**) and suggested to a degree by others such as Patch (**582**). Blake's 'Age's Knave' (p 604) domineering overall seems inaccurate as does the view of Swart (**739**) following Coghill that the performance is a joke. By focusing on the Pardoner's sexual abnormality, the Host blocks the Pardoner's attempt to satisfy his pride and gain acceptance as a 'merry companion'(p 604). The Pardoner is accepted not on his own terms but on those of the Knight.

770 Owen, Charles A. *Discussions of the 'Canterbury Tales.'* Ed. Charles A. Owen Jr. Boston: D. C. Heath and Company, 1961.

This collection, designed for new readers of Chaucer, presents one section of critical essays grouped chronologically and three grouped thematically. Of particular note for study of the Pardoner are: Ralph Baldwin, 'Chronology: Space-Time in the *Prologue*,' (pp 25-7) (**746**); E. Talbot Donaldson, 'Chaucer the Pilgrim,' (pp 18-24) (**759**); Arthur W. Hoffman, 'Chaucer's Prologue to Pilgrimage: The Two Voices,' (pp 9-17) (**320**); John Livingston Lowes, 'The Human Comedy,' (pp 105-10) (**705**); Charles A. Owen, 'The Crucial Passages in Five of the *Canterbury Tales*: A Study in Irony and Symbol,' (pp 79-89)(**742**); and John Speirs, 'from The Canterbury Tales,' (pp 73-8) (**745**).

771 Schaut, Quentin L., O.S.B. 'Chaucer's Pardoner and Indulgences.' 1961. See **348**.

Schaut reviews the historical development of indulgences and their association with pilgrimages, pardoners, hospitals, and accusations of abuse. Improbable as Chaucer's Pardoner may seem, 'after examining the contemporary official documents we feel that nothing has been overdrawn' (p 36). Whereas there may be doubt as to his authorization, the authenticity of his documents, and his status (cleric or lay), there is no doubt as to how he carried out his office or the loathing he inspires. Chaucer's Pardoner is not to be assumed typical; he is 'supreme in his kind' fusing 'all the worst characteristics of the class' (p 39).

772 Stockton, Eric W. 'The Deadliest Sin in *The Pardoner's Tale.*' *TSL* 6(1961), 47-59.

PardT is marked by a plot so serviceable it is still in use (e.g., *Treasure of the Sierra Madre*), and a technique akin to Faulkner's 'cracked lens'; the Pardoner is Chaucer's closest approximation to the Dostoyevskian double man. The psychology of the Pardoner has obstructed interpretation of the tale. Psychoanalytically, the Pardoner is 'a manic depressive with traces of anal eroticism, and a pervert with a tendency toward alcoholism'(p 47). *PardT* is the 'clearest revelation of the man's true character'(p 47). Though the three revellers display a panoply of sins, the deepest meaning of the tale—its focus, pace, and symbolism—shows them guilty of *superbia*; in seeking to kill Death, they presume to supplant Christ. *PardP* and *PardT*, together with the epilogue (lines 919-68), form a unified work, at once self-revelation and demonstration sermon. *PardP* contains: 1) the announcement of the theme (lines 333-4); 2) the protheme (400-34). *PardT* continues with 3) the division of the theme, the 'Homily on the Sins of the Tavern'(lines 463-84;485-659) (p 48); 4) the major exemplum, 'The Robbers and the Treasure Trove' (lines 661-894) interrupted by a digression back to section 3; 5) the peroration (lines 895-915); and 6) the closing formula (lines 915-8). The division of the theme furnishes essential commentary on the exemplum; the Pardoner's strictures on oaths underline the structuralism of oaths in the tale itself. The Pardoner confuses parts 5 and 6; far from sincerity, the closing formula is 'his crowning infamy'(p 56) (cs **668, 681**). The Pardoner errs in selecting the Host, one whose virility he could subconsciously envy (p 56). The Pardoner, more than the Old Man, is 'living death'; he does not understand the symbolic import of what he says; he speaks his epitaph (lines 547-8).

773 Evanoff, Alexander. 'The Pardoner as Huckster: A Dissent from

Kittredge.' *BYUS* 4(1962), 209-17.

The now standard interpretation of the Pardoner is overly subtle (cs **681**). The seeming sincerity of the prologue and the benediction are strategic concessions, the subterfuge of frankness is intended for financial advantage. The Pardoner is 'an insistent, assertive, domineering salesman' (p 212) whose anger at the Host results solely from being thwarted in his sale. Chaucer does not purport to show moral development in his characters; investing the Pardoner with the dignity of moral struggle or regeneration is unwarranted (cs **728**). Contrary to theories of regeneration, the Pardoner's behavior could be variously explained as a consistent desire to dupe the pilgrims; a desire to offer acceptable sentiments; a return to an initial stance after recognizing an incongruous sincerity; or a recognition that the benediction would be recognized as an insincere blunder.

774 Jordan, Robert M. 'Chaucer's Sense of Illusion: Roadside Drama Reconsidered'. *ELH* 29(1962), 19-33.

The conception of 'roadside drama' has encouraged psychological and historical speculation and deterred understanding of Chaucer's sense of illusion. The unity of *CT* 'is less "organic" than "mechanic".' The single focus of dramatic theory has led to 'bizarre interpretations' (p 24). Pilgrims like the Pardoner have 'assumed the infinite and unpredictable variety of "real life," including of course psychological life, and life determined or explained by a past which is assumed to be accessible to the critic' (p 25) (cf **755, 756; 728**). In Chaucerian narrative, the reader's attention is continually shifted from poet to pilgrim-reporter, from illusion to reality, from nature to super-nature. The conflict between poet and Christian is expressed in the 'multiple unity' of *CT* where 'illusion and disillusion stand incongruously together'(p 33). For Pardoner, see **350**.

775 Kantor, Betty. *The Sin of Pride in 'The Pardoner's Tale'*. Stanford Honors Essays in Humanities, 5 and 6. Stanford: Stanford Honors Essays in Humanities, 1962. Pp 1-14.

Reviewing scholarship on *GP* portrait, *PardP*, *PardT* and solicitation, Kantor determines that the fundamental irony of the tale is that, despite announcing the topic of avarice, the Pardoner both preaches against and displays pride. The pride Lumiansky (**588**) and Sedgewick (**716**) discover in *PardP* can be found in *PardT*. The Pardoner is in minor orders (cf **690, 691**); his fraudulence finds a context in historical

238 / Pardoner's Prologue and Tale

evidence. The Pardoner's pride in sinful avariciousness is 'a kind of despair'(p 10), a disbelief in God's saving power. Pride is the climax of the rioters' sin; in seeking to kill Death, the rioters seek to change God's universe. Just as the plot of *PardT* rebounds on the plotters so the pride of the Pardoner enables the Host to bring him down. *PardT* is Chaucer's most extensive venture into indirect characterization (cf. Wife, Franklin, Monk). *PardT* derives inherent unity from its circumstances and the ironic structure of the Pardoner's performance.

776 Robertson, D.W., Jr. *A Preface to Chaucer: Studies in Medieval Perspectives*. 1962. Pp 373-7, 379-82. Rpt in *The Canterbury Tales: Nine Tales and the General Prologue*. Ed. V. A. Kolve and Glending Olson. New York: W. W. Norton, 1989. Pp 530-5.

The framework of *CT* displays a typical Gothic disregard for spatial coherence; the Pardoner's reference to an alehouse is so vague as to invite discounting. Settings such as the grove in *PardT* are iconographic. Characters operate in accordance with their moral natures rather than psychologically. The cupidinous Pardoner fosters cupidity in his audience. Exegetically, he develops his theme vividly, subdividing *cupiditas* into three parts: gluttony, gambling and swearing. *PardT* 'is an excellent illustration of what happens to those who deny the spirit of Christ beneath the letter of the text *radix malorum est cupiditas* and devote themselves to the pursuit of the corporal rather than the intelligible' (p 334). Chaucer's treatment of the Pardoner illustrates 'the abuses of false scriptural interpretation' (p 334); through him, Chaucer implies that those who deny the spirit are 'sterile eunuchs whose life is death' (p 335). The quest for the death of death in *PardT* draws on biblical iconography of the pilgrimage. The Old Man is probably a personification of St. Paul's 'Old Man.' The theme of youth/renewal:age/aridity reaches its climax with the Old Man seeking 'death and that renewal which alone can restore his youth' (p 382). The Pardoner's offer of relics is a logical narrative development that, nevertheless, illustrates the lack of psychological rapport with his audience. For Pardoner, see **352**. See also **634, 945, 1074**.

777 Baugh, Albert C., ed. *Chaucer's Major Poetry*. 1963. See **81**.

PardP and *PardT* are 'admirably integrated,' most likely written at the same time and for *CT*. The exact source of this widespread story has not been found; 'Chaucer has woven much from his own imagination and reading' (p 490).

778 Beck, Richard J. 'Educational Expectation and Rhetorical Result in the *Canterbury Tales.*' *ES* 44(1963), 241-53.

Chaucer employed rhetoric for dramatic realism; consequently, the education, vocation and social standing of a pilgrim should predict the level of rhetoric in the respective tale. The surprisingly low rhetorical content in *PardT* is explained by the largely illiterate nature of the Pardoner's usual audience (p 249). See **690, 691**.

779 Beichner, Paul E., CSC. 'Chaucer's Pardoner as Entertainer.' *MS* 25(1963), 160-172.

The Pardoner is a layman or minor cleric, a fund-raiser by profession, who seeks to entertain the pilgrims. In *PardP*, the Pardoner describes his methods and tricks; in his tale, he offers a sample of his 'money-raising-sermon stuff' (p 172); and in his epilogue he delivers a burlesque demonstration. The Pardoner neither makes a 'false confession (p 171) (cs **747**) nor seeks to raise money from the pilgrims; he entertains by speaking honestly about his 'dishonest practices and his unedifying self' (p 172).

780 Coxe, Louis O. *Chaucer*. New York: Dell, 1963. See **82**.

The Pardoner emerges as a fascinating character; at once clever and evil, he seems to believe the truths he mocks. Drunk, he attempts the sale of relics.

781 Payne, Robert O. *The Key of Remembrance: A Study of Chaucer's Poetics*. New Haven and London: Yale University Press for the University of Cincinnati, 1963, 1970. Rpt Westport: Greenwood Press, 1973.

CT present four times as many serious as humorous tales; *PardT* is a serious tale where the 'starkly schematic action' (p 170) demonstrates one of Chaucer's extreme stylistic developments. *CT* reveal a continuous experiment with the relation of stylistic elaboration to underlying basic narrative.

782 Bowden, Muriel. 'The Influence of Chaucer's Religious and Philosophic World'. *A Reader's Guide to Geoffrey Chaucer*. New York: Farrar, Strauss and Giroux, 1964; rpt 1966. Pp 46-93.

PardT and *ParsT* are both sermons: *PardT* is an 'extraordinary *tour de force*, a sample of one of the Pardoner's own sermons (p 74). Chaucer's references in *PardT* are topical ie, the allusion to cooks who *turnen substaunce into accident* (line 539) is unlikely to refer to Wycliffe's denial of transubstantiation. For *GP*, see **354**.

783 Calderwood, James L. 'Parody in the Pardoner's Tale.' *ES* 45(1964), 302-9.

Whereas the Pardoner's confession has been explained as convention, psychological realism, or theological realism, it is better understood as self-parody. In the headlink, the Pardoner extravagantly exaggerates his evil to demonstrate his relative decency: in the epilogue, he exaggerates his decency by offering a sincere benediction. Yet, in its similarity to the benediction the Old Man gives the rioters, it is also an attack on the *gentils*. In the solicitation, the Pardoner pushes his self-parody to absurdity, his only failure being the selection of the Host, a pilgrim too literal-minded to perceive the parody. The Pardoner's silence results from his indignation as a failed confidence man and his anger at having the Host reveal the one failing he had scrupulously avoided mentioning ... his eunuchry.

784 Corsa, Helen Storm. *Chaucer: Poet of Mirth and Morality*. Notre Dame: University of Notre Dame Press, 1964.

For Chaucer, hypocrisy is the cardinal sin. In the open hypocrisy of his prologue and the spellbinding power of his tale, the Pardoner becomes a threat to the mirthful coexistence of the pilgrims. His hypocrisy is so blatant, however, as to effect 'its own astonished punishment'(p 183) thereby affirming the morality it has threatened. Rascal and rogue, the Pardoner is one of Chaucer's 'most compelling achievements, moral and comic'(p 190). The punishment his own arrogant blasphemy threatens to involve him in cuts deeper than the Host's knife. With the solicitation, his vanity is at its most evident. In singling out the Host, the Pardoner turns his monologue into a scene charged with tension. The vulgarity of the Host's response measures the Host's loss of control, but also the degree of scorn he holds for all the Pardoner represents. The Knight's restoration of order highlights the fact that the Pardoner has become a symbol of disorder; the virtues the Knight practices are the virtues the Pardoner distorts. The Pardoner remains unregenerate: the perversion of values he boasts affirms 'by their rendered inefficiency, the real existence of such values'(p 196).

785 Elliott, Charles, and R. George Thomas. 'Two Points of View: The Pardoner's Prologue and Tale.' *AWR* 14:33(1964), 9-17.

The First View [Charles Elliott] (pp 9-12): Elliott notes the pilgrims succeed in making the Pardoner choose his 'occupational' path of edifying rather than his 'temperamental' addiction to *ribaudye* (p 11).

PardT is authoritative, vivified by an exemplum, fluent, tightly knit and eloquent. *GP* portrait and *PardP* are condemnatory. The Host's response to the solicitation vindicates the details of deception provided in *GP*. Characterization is clear without *PardP*; a conscious insertion, it amounts to 'an assault on a particular corrupting weakness in Church influence' (p 12). Such moral comment by Chaucer calls for reconsideration of Chaucer 'chiefly as a teller of stories wearing his moral conscience lightly' (p 12). The Second View [R. George Thomas] (pp 13-7): Thomas suggests *PardT* challenges our skill in determining whether Chaucer was 'a satirist, an ironist, a moralist, or merely a first-rate, merry story-teller'(p 13). Both *PhyT* and *PardT* are sermons, *PardT* far more skillful. The Pardoner fulfills his commission with astounding self-knowledge and 'impudent self-confidence, matching his superb histrionic skill' (p 15). The Host's outburst at the Pardoner indicates the degree to which *PardT* has affected him. The tolerance of the audience enables the Pardoner's confidence which leads to his self-revelation without impairing the tone of deliberate seriousness of *PardT*. The self-revelation of the Pardoner furnishes 'a double commentary on the central purpose of the pilgrimage' (p 17) and by implication on Chaucer's design. Properly undertaken, the pilgrimage could lead to self-recognition and the quest could be undertaken without sacrificing the 'innocent gaiety of good fellowship' (p 17). As the narrator leads us from *PardT* 'we are conscious of the gulf that separates our "world-picture" from that held by Chaucer; in a minor way this tale ends with the spirit of Canossa in action on the road to Canterbury' (p 17). See **791**.

786 Howard, Edwin. *Geoffrey Chaucer.* New York: St. Martin's Press, 1964.

There is a continual reference to sex in everything said concerning the Pardoner. Additionally, the author of the *Tale of Beryn* assumes the Pardoner is 'capable as need be' (p 160). The Pardoner does not seem to be depicted as a eunuch; he is a hypocritical swindler; his boastfulness is more likely than drink to account for his self-revelation. *PardT*, if a medieval sermon, is 'a poor one' (p 161), lacking as it does power and unity until the introduction of the rioters. The tavern debate indicates how real *CT* has become to critics; to our interpretation of Chaucer, it is inconsequential. The language at the closing suggests a group temporarily dismounted. For Pardoner, see **355**; for *Interr*, see **522**. See also **685**.

787 Maclaine, Allan H. *The Student's Comprehensive Guide To The*

Canterbury Tales. 1964. See **357**.

Maclaine provides a summary of the text, selective glosses, a selective list of commentaries together with data on the text, and a digest of critical interpretations. For Pardoner, pp 38-40; Pardoner's performance, pp 193-209; *Phy-PardL*, pp 196-7; *PardP*, pp 197-201; *PardT*, pp 201-9, is divided into eleven narrative units. For *PardP*, see **600**.

788   Peck, Russell A. 'Number Symbolism and the Idea of Order in the Works of Geoffrey Chaucer.' *DAI* 24(1964), 2894-5. Indiana University Dissertation, 1963. Director: Robert Mitchner.

Number symbolism is one of the methods Chaucer employs in treating the folktale source in Christian terms. Allusions to the Crucifixion run through *PardT* (from the tavern scene to the Pardoner's condemnation of swearing to the Host's reference to the Cross), reminding readers that the rioters' attempt to slay death is a travesty of the Crucifixion. The rioters become an 'anti-trinity' representing Cupidity. They accept the eight bushels of gold at the foot of the oak (Cross) in place of redemption: here, the number 'eight,' which Chaucer traditionally used to signify regeneration, is used ironically as the three find death.

789   Reiss, Edmund. 'The Final Irony of the Pardoner's Tale.' *CE* 25(1964), 260-6.

The dramatic irony of *PardP* and *PardT* is that the Pardoner reveals more than he intends but that his pilgrim audience is unable to grasp the full meaning of what he says. In the Pardoner, evil is tempered with innocence (represented by his sexless condition) and good works (his sermon). With the Pardoner, Chaucer is implicitly questioning the relationship between evil, good and innocence. 'Like Christ, archetype of the incongruously ironic victim, the Pardoner' (p 266) is persecuted because he contains the sins of the world. At the end of *PardT*, the pilgrims indicate through their spokesperson, the Host, that they have misunderstood: 'Nothing has been achieved through the tale, no one understands, and all we are left with is the irony that the Pardoner is the only unpardoned man' (p 266) on the pilgrimage. See also **668**.

790   Steadman, John. 'Old Age and *Contemptus Mundi* in The Pardoner's Tale.' *MÆ* 33(1964), 121-30. Rpt in *Twentieth Century Interpretations of the Pardoner's Tale: A Collection of Critical Essays*. Ed. Dewey R. Faulkner. Englewood Cliffs: Prentice-Hall, 1973. Pp 70-82.

Assessing prior interpretations of the Old Man (**711**, **742**, **766**), Steadman concludes that Chaucer's *senex* is intelligible on the literal level. The Old Man can be understood as an individual as well as a representative of the ideal, portraying the abstract concept of the miseries of senility. In stressing the *greet age* of the Old Man, Chaucer establishes an ethic antithetic to the *yonge folk*: an opposition in years, in attitudes to death, in repentance, in sensuality and treasure. The encounter of the Old Man and the revellers emphasizes antithetical concepts of youth and age, folly and wisdom, avarice and *contemptus mundi*. The Pardoner's regular sermon audience would be reminded by the exemplum that death comes to all; his pilgrim audience would be reminded of the uselessness of worldly possessions, a feature calculated to serve the Pardoner's immediate purposes.

791 Thomas, R. George. 'Two Points of View: The Pardoner's Prologue and Tale.' *AWR* 14(1964), 9-12.
See entry **785**.

792 Battaglia, Salvatore. 'Dall'esempio alla novella.' In *La coscienza letteraria del medioevo*. Naples,1965. Pp 536-47.
The whole *PardT* is a parable which the incident of the Old Man turns into 'myth of the imagination' (p 545). [In Italian.]

793 David, Alfred. 'Criticism and the Old Man in Chaucer's Pardoner's Tale.' *CE* 27(1965), 39-44.
Recent arguments for the overriding symbolic significance of all medieval literature, based upon scriptural allusions and models, dismiss the variety of previous interpretations of the Old Man: **668**, **681**, the Wandering Jew (**212**), Old Age as a messenger of Death (**711**), and a thoroughly realistic old man (**742**). Robert Miller (**747**), for example, interprets the Old Man in the light of the Pauline symbol of the flesh (Col. 3:1-10; Eph. 4:17-24, Rom. 7:1 ff). Though this interpretation enriches our understanding of the Pardoner himself, it is not the only interpretation. The characters of the *PardT*, like those of a work as different as Thomas Mann's *Death in Venice*, arise independently out of a basic archetypal symbolism. The Pardoner shares characteristics with both the revellers and the Old Man. The Pardoner's isolation from natural human love manifests his deeper alienation from divine love.

794 Elliott, Ralph W.V. '*The Nun's Priest's Tale and the Pardoner's Tale (Geoffrey Chaucer)*.' London: Basil Blackwell, 1965, 1982. Pp 52-66. Rpt as 'The Pardoner's Sermon and Its Exemplum.' In *Twentieth Century Interpretations of the Pardoner's Tale: A Collection of Critical Essays*. Ed. Dewey R. Faulkner. Englewood Cliffs, New Jersey:

Prentice-Hall Inc., 1973. Pp 23-32.

Elliott discusses the Pardoner's performance in the following divisions: tale (lines 661-894); sermon (lines 135-575) is 'prologue' to tale, and lines 463-84 and 895-903 are 'epilogue.' The tavern scene of the Pardoner's exemplum leads him to harangue against the tavern sins of gluttony, gambling, and swearing. Following his self-exposure in the prologue and the simple, direct diction of the opening tavern scene, the heightened rhetoric of the sermon becomes an 'appropriate instrument of hypocrisy' (p 23). The intensity and pace of the high oratory is punctuated by colloquial turns of phrase that add 'continuity and a feeling of orderly progression' (p 26). The sermon ends with a summing-up to both moral disquisition and the tale of the three revellers (lines 895-903), and a final ironic touch where the Pardoner simultaneously warns his audience against avarice and invites them to satisfy his greed (lines 427-8). The Pardoner remains hypocritical throughout. The exemplum (lines 661-894) is a moving tale of irony where the Old Man and the revellers serve as poles of good and evil. The hasty and dramatic end of the revellers conveys a strong sense of justice done. Immediately, the Pardoner returns to his lofty eloquence to launch into the epilogue. 'The *exemplum* is finished, the sermon nearly done, the whole performance almost at an end'(p 32).

795 Hussey, Maurice. 'The Church.' *An Introduction to Chaucer*. Ed. Maurice Hussey, A.C. Spearing and James Winny. Cambridge: Cambridge University Press, 1965. Pp 78-80.

The Pardoner's 'hysteria' (p 79) comes through in loud hortatory tones and the lack of a firm moral attitude. His tale shows two classes of men: the riotous and the dead. The Pardoner is full of ambiguity; by contrast, the Pardoner in John Heywood *The Four P's* lacks subtlety.

796 Josipovici, G. D. 'Fiction and Game in *The Canterbury Tales*.' *CritQ* 7(1965), 185-97. Incorporated in Gabriel Josipovici 'Chaucer: The Teller and the Tale,' *The World and The Book: A Study of Modern Fiction*. Stanford: Stanford University Press, 1971, pp 52-99. Pp 193-7 rpt in *Twentieth Century Interpretations of the Pardoner's Tale: A Collection of Critical Essays*. Ed. Dewey R. Faulkner. Englewood Cliffs, New Jersey: Prentice Hall, 1973. Pp 111-4. Rpt in *The Canterbury Tales: Nine Tales and the General Prologue*. Ed. V. A. Kolve and Glending Olson. New York: W. W. Norton, 1989.

The conflict between the moral and the immoral which runs throughout

CT forms the substance of the Pardoner's prologue and epilogue; *Ret* 'appears to reflect Chaucer's final stand' on the issue (p 185). In using this conflict, Chaucer conducts an original strategy aimed at freeing the poem from moral jurisdiction and establishing it as fiction. The ironic 'poise' of *CT* is the culmination of a series of experiments with narratorial persona. In *CT*, the game Chaucer plays with his readers coincides with the game played within the poem by the pilgrims. *PardP* and *PardT* stand at the center of *CT* and reveal 'the final turn of the ironic screw' (p 193). The Host is infuriated not because the Pardoner asks for money but because, through the power of words, he dupes the pilgrims despite having revealed his methods. Modern critics, Miller (**747**) included, have overlooked the crucial fact that the Pardoner is a fictional character. As a paradigm of *CT*, *PardP* and *PardT* demonstrate that it is easier to lay down rules for others than abide by them oneself. 'The Pardoner's ironic self-revelation is a mirror of Chaucer's insistence that his poem is not truth but fiction' (p 196). Chaucer introduces a line of ironical satirists including Rabelais, Cervantes and Sterne whose target is the mind of man. Chaucer is deeply moral not because he is like the Parson but because he is like the Pardoner.

797 Knox, Norman. 'The Satiric Pattern of *The Canterbury Tales*.' In *Six Satirists*. Ed. A. F. Sochatoff et al. Pittsburg: Carnegie Institute of Technology, 1965. Pp 17-34.
If satire is taken, as Frye suggests, as 'militant irony,' *CT* as a whole are satiric. In *PardT*, verbal and philosophic irony work to the same end. The verbal ironies (e.g., statements of the Old Man) focus the dramatic shock of the ironic situation convicting the rioters, for example, of moral obtuseness. Chaucer judges his world through his use of ironies. The Pardoner exemplifies both satiric philosophic irony in preaching against the sin he manifests, and a subtler form in unintentionally revealing his self hatred at the close of his tale. Knox is 'inclined to think' Chaucer 'fully intended the ironic world some readers feel'(p 32).

798 Loomis, Roger Sherman. 'The Pardoner's Headlink and Tale.' *A Mirror of Chaucer's World*. 1965. See **364**.
Figures 168-72 present three miniatures, a mural and a drawing with the following titles and line references: 'The Sins of Swearing and Gambling' (472-74; 651; 654ff); 'A *Tombstere* and Musicians' (477); 'Death with His Spear' (675-7); 'The Black Death' (679); 'The Black Death' (line 679); and 'An Apothecary's Shop' (851 ff). For *Phy-PardL*,

see **547**.

799 Roache, Joel. 'Treasure Trove in the Pardoner's Tale.'*JEGP* 64(1965), 1-6.

Roache cites English Law on treasure troves (Bracton, *De Legibus et Consuetudinibus Angliae*) to clarify the status of the treasure trove in *PardT*; in both instances, the trove is described as a gift of Fortune. Through the careful use of *hoord*, the repeated use of *tresor*, and the emphasis on secrecy, Chaucer indicates the rioters knew enough about the law to subvert it but not enough to do so successfully. In their theft of the treasure trove, the rioters are analogous to the Pardoner who steals from the people, and the Church; in his relation to souls, the Pardoner is analogous to the Lord.

800 Ruggiers, Paul G. 'The Pardoner's Tale.' *The Art of the Canterbury Tales*. Madison and Milwaukee, Wisconsin: University of Wisconsin Press, 1965. Paperback edition, 1967. Pp 121-30.

The Pardoner appears to be physically 'a demonstration of the theory of evil as the absence or deprivation of a natural part' (p 123). *Phy-PardL* is in 'Chaucer's best comic vein' (p 122). The demonstration of evil, resulting in *PhyT* from the gifts of Fortune and Nature, shifts in *PardT* to abuses of the gifts of grace. *PardP* is Chaucer's 'most subtle comment upon evil'(p 123) emanating from a man committed by nature, instinct and intellectual conviction to opposing the good. *PardT*, 'psychologically and structurally one of the great performances' of *CT* (p 122 n 2), represents a conflation of literary types where the didactic elements are subordinated to a larger statement about the 'demonic sublime' (p 122 n 2). The Pardoner is so engrossed in his sermon on the sins as to reveal the cupidity of his own character. In the tale of the rioters, Chaucer, through the 'paradox of art' (p 126), substitutes his own story-telling skill for that of his narrator: 'Our irresistible impression ... is that Chaucer himself has temporarily taken over' (p 127). The Pardoner reveals the full extent of his villainy as he recognizes the validity of Christ's pardon (lines 916-8). *PardT* resembles *FrT* in theme: an unwitting spiritual death resulting from the pursuit of material gain. *PardT* offers the pleasure of 'a punishment gratifyingly commensurate with the wickedness of the agents' (p 129). Because Chaucer's theological vision is comic, the Pardoner's performance closes with a happy ending. The Host, 'barometer of sensibilities'(p 130), responds to the Pardoner's solicitation with 'an appropriately low-comic outburst'(p 130). Recognizing the true identity of the Pardoner is salutary: the kiss reconnects the Pardoner to the community and affirms a Chaucerian vision of social harmony that can admit 'an occasional discordant note' (p 130). For Pardoner, see **365**.

801 Spearing, A. C., ed. *The Pardoner's Prologue and Tale*. 1965. See **86**.

PardT, 'undoubtedly written specifically for ... the Pardoner to tell' (p 2), is a supreme expression of the Pardoner's personality; 'it exposes the nature of a consciousness which has cut all moral bearings and is veering with sick giddiness towards self-destruction'(p 2). The 'sermon-interlude' is closely linked to the exemplum of the revellers for they are 'gluttons, gamblers, time-wasters, deceivers, murderers, and above all blasphemers' (p 32). *PardT* is marked by realistic speech, the resonance of the Old Man and marked brevity as the revellers hurl themselves to death and damnation. Both the Pardoner's life and the core of *PardT* are penetrated by blasphemy: beyond the quest to kill Death lies an allusion to the 'conspiracy-theory of the Crucifixion' that had become a blasphemy in the fourteenth century (p 44). The conclusion of the tale reveals Chaucer's skill in 'the poetry of transitions' (p 49) as we are led through diverse fictional worlds each shift forcing a reassessment. For Pardoner, see **366**; for *PardP*, see **603**.

802 Steadman, John M. 'Chaucer's Pardoner and the *Thesaurus Meritorium*.' *ELN* 3(1965), 4-7.

Chaucer exhibits his concern for decorum in the close relation between narrative and narrator: in *PardT*, the exemplum of *avaryce* both illustrates and serves the Pardoner's vice. *PardT* is both a sermon against vice and an attack on the sale of indulgences: the treasure motif of the *thesaurus meritorium* serves as a concrete symbol for both. Wyclif and his followers attacked the treasury of merits as blasphemous. Chaucer suggests the Pardoner's bulls and indulgences 'entail spiritual destruction' (p 7). Both the Pardoner and the rioters perish in dispersing treasure.

803 Todd, Robert E. 'The Magna Mater Archetype in "The Pardoner's Tale".' *L&P* 15(1965), 32-40.

In knocking upon the earth Mother with his staff ('quite obviously a phallic image' p 35), the Old Man confronts the Jungian *Magna Mater*; with her connections to both womb and tomb, she nourishes and destroys human life. The Old Man and the tavern boy, through their references to their mothers, may symbolize a man's 'early and late' maternal relationships (line 730). The *cheste* (clothes-chest) becomes a dual symbol when the Old Man offers to exchange it for a shroud. The cluster of symbols may well 'have been reborn unmediated in the depths of Chaucer's own unconscious, and originally and incomparably reasserted—hence once again re-liberated—through the magic of his creative instinct' (p 40).

804 Williams, George. *A New View of Chaucer*. Durham, North Carolina: Duke University Press, 1965.

Williams suggests that at least half of Chaucer's poetry reflects his preoccupation with specific personalities or actual events. *PardT* is among his 'genuinely realistic works' (p 127) which date from 1386 or later. The Pardoner is 'so highly individualized that we can hardly help believing that [he was] suggested by real people whom Chaucer knew' (p 9). The 'excessively masculine' Host's violent reaction against the Pardoner's 'eunuchoid nature' is matched only by the Host's reaction to Sir Thopas (p 149) on similar grounds. See **697**.

805 Winny, James. *The General Prologue to the Canterbury Tales*. 1965. See **368**.

PardT provides a deeply ironic commentary on the Pardoner; it would lose much of its force if separated from the teller. In selecting the Host for his solicitation, the Pardoner attacks the life of the company at its center. Typifying 'the optimistic spirit' (p 41) of *CT*, the episode shows Chaucer associates himself with the energy of the natural world yet acknowledges its vitality is threatened by negative forces. The Host's defeat of the Pardoner is as symbolic as the god of summer overcoming the winter spirit.

806 Braddy, Haldeen. 'Chaucer's Bawdy Tongue.' *SFQ* 30(1966), 214-22.

Chaucer's bawdy vocabulary describing ribald situations manifests 'unparalleled artistry with country language and its crude but basic humor'(p 221). The speech always fits the speaker. In *PardT*, Chaucer speaks directly against incest (lines 485-7), whereas in *TC*, Chaucer communicates that incest underlies the relationship of Pandarus and Criseyde by inoffensive verse (III.1574-82). In general, Chaucer shies away from the abnormal; the Pardoner, despite textual suggestions (lines 691 and 453), 'is hardly equivalent to a sex pervert'(p 216). The Host's reply to the Pardoner's offer of relics (lines 946-55) is 'perhaps the most amazing concentration of profanity and rural crudity in the *Canterbury Tales*'(p 219).

807 Brewer, D. S., ed. *Chaucer and Chaucerians*. [Critical Studies in Middle English Literature]. London: Nelson; University, Alabama: University of Alabama Press, 1966. Rpt Norwich: Nelson University Paperbacks, 1970.

See: Charles Muscatine. '*The Canterbury Tales*: Style of the Man and Style of the Work,' pp 88-113 (**812**); Nevill Coghill. 'Chaucer's Narrative Art in *The Canterbury Tales*,' pp 114-39 (**808**).

808 Coghill, Nevill. 'Chaucer's Narrative Art in *The Canterbury Tales*.' In *Chaucer and Chaucerians: Critical Studies in Middle English Literature*. Ed. D. S. Brewer. London: Nelson University; Alabama: University of Alabama Press, 1966. Rpt Norwich: Nelson University Paperbacks, 1970. Pp 114-39.

Chaucer's debt to rhetoric is a matter of neither form nor style but 'know-how in the handling of particular turns and climaxes in his story, to elicit or comment upon some special point' (p 116). Most pilgrims employ the 'natural' style; the Pardoner, beginning with a *sententia*, is the only pilgrim to use the 'artificial' style. *PardT* is typical of *CT* in its swift climax and spring-like close.

809 Elliott, Ralph W. V. 'Our Host's "Triacle": Some Observations on Chaucer's "Pardoner's Tale".' *REL* 7(1966), 61-73.

Close textual analysis of significant repetitions, verbal echoes, hints and allusions, as well as syntactical and lexical devices is a better guide to Chaucer's meaning than fanciful discussion of such topics as the Pardoner's drunkenness (cs **303, 716**) or eunuchry (**277, 736, 739**). The text is inconclusive on the subject of eunuchry. Chaucer's text does not support a reading of drunkenness; the alleged incoherence of the Pardoner's performance overlooks structural elements such as the continuity provided by vices. The connection between Host and oaths which figures prominently in the Pardoner's performance begins in the *Phy-PardL* preceding the Tale and leads to the Pardoner selecting Harry Bailey as his victim. The tale of the revellers acts as a 'double exemplum' (p 66), an exemplum of the tavern vices in the address to the pilgrims and of greed in the sermon to the imaginary village audience. The Pardoner simultaneously addresses two audiences: the actual pilgrims (*lordynges*) and an imaginary audience (*lewed peple*). The solicitation cannot be a serious attempt for it would treat the pilgrims as *lewed*.

The use of *sires* in the benediction (lines 916-8) indicates its address to the pilgrims. The 'comic tone' in lines 927-38 is unmistakable (p 70) (**668, 681, 724, 762**). The joke is directed not at the pilgrims in general but at the Host in particular; beginning in the *Phy-PardL*, swearing has both unified the Pardoner's performance and focused attention on the Host. The Pardoner offers his relics (lines 943-4) as *triacle* for the Host's blaspheming.

810 MacDonald, Donald. 'Proverbs, *Sententiae*, and *Exempla* in Chaucer's Comic Tales: The Function of Comic Misapplication.' *Speculum* 41(1966), 453-65.

The key to Chaucer's use of monitory expressions in characterization is found in context. Characters as disparate as the Pardoner and Prudence in *Mel* (B 2320, 3030) announce *coveitise is roote of alle harmes*.

811 Mitchell, Charles. 'The Moral Superiority of Chaucer's Pardoner.' 1966. See **371**.

The distinction between true and false pardon is a problem of salvation prominent in both *GP* and *CT*. In purchasing 'pseudo-spiritual goods'(p 437), the Pardoner's customers may be morally inferior to him. The Pardoner preaches against his own sin not only to lure the avaricious, but also to remain above his own false pardon. His self-exposure to the pilgrims indicates that his hypocrisy is 'a functional disguise' rather than 'a moral dodge' (p 441). The Pardoner emphasizes his deception of others (rhetorical superiority) and their deception of themselves (moral superiority). The Old Man represents the state of spiritual death as the desire to have it both ways at once; he seeks Death yet flees the rioters. Harry Bailey's gesture points the solution: renounce the Pardoner, 'the unhypocritical emblem of hypocrisy'(p 444). The Pardoner's physical sterility is reflected in his spiritual sterility and that of his customers. The Pardoner commits the unpardonable sin of refusing Christ's pardon. The pilgrims commit the same sin in accepting a false substitute.

812 Muscatine, Charles. '*The Canterbury Tales*: Style of the Man and Style of the Work.' In *Chaucer and Chaucerians: Critical Studies in Middle English Literature*. Ed. D. S. Brewer. London: Nelson; Alabama: University of Alabama Press, 1966, 1970. Pp 88-113.

The mixed style of *CT* is integral to their meaning. Through stylistic juxtaposition, Chaucer demonstrates an abiding interest in comparisons and relationships. Mixed style in *PardT* is an instrument of characterization. The Pardoner is the only pilgrim dramatically given literary powers akin to Chaucer, but the Pardoner ultimately fails in his irony, thereby producing a blend at once grotesque and pathetic.

813 Schmidt, Philip. 'Reexamination of Chaucer's Old Man of the Pardoner's Tale.' *SFQ* 30(1966), 249-55.

Chaucer had 'a great regard, *as a writer*, for the old moral leper' (p 255), the Pardoner. The creation of the Old Man is 'one of the masterworks of all characterization'(p 251); the Old Man, who offers the rioters a choice between his immortality and their mortality is 'extra-human' (p 252) (cs **748**). He is not Odin (cs **226**); Odin is too much of a deity, and Chaucer, being consistent, would not have used a pagan avenger in a 'tale of Christian ethics perverted'(p 250). The rioters play an allegorical role of 'life-misdirected and coming to a reckoning' (p 252). The Pardoner is scared by his own tale, offering a real outburst (lines 895-903), and a moral blessing (lines 916-8) before returning 'to his sales pitch with its vicious hypocrisy' (p 254). Chaucer knew how to 'snatch defeat from the jaws of victory!'(p 254). See **843**.

814 Stewart, Donald C. 'Chaucer's Perplexing Pardoner.' 1966. See **373**.

The Pardoner becomes unduly complex when scholars interpret him in the context of 'single integrated schemes' (p 1). Kittredge opened a Pandora's box (**668**); others, including Lumiansky (**724**), Kellogg and Haselmayer (**728**), and Bronson (**764**) followed. The Pardoner acts predictably with the exception of the benediction. Speculation on the Pardoner's motives for joining the pilgrimage is vain. The Pardoner's confession is the result of his drunkenness and may also be a convention whereby Chaucer satirizes pardoners (cf Brown **707**). The benediction and solicitation were, like the tale itself, originally intended for the Parson (**672**). The tone of the solicitation is jocular; the Pardoner expects the Host to accept his jest.

815 Tuve, Rosemond. *Allegorical Imagery: Some Mediaeval Books and Their Posterity.* 1966. Pp 176-7. Rpt as 'from Allegorical Imagery.' In *Twentieth Century Interpretations of the Pardoner's Tale: A Collection of Critical Essays.* Ed. Dewey R. Faulkner. Englewood Cliffs: Prentice- Hall 1973. Pp 117-8. [Page references from Faulkner.] Pp 139-58 rpt as 'Memory and Form.' In *Geoffrey Chaucer's The General Prologue to the Canterbury Tales.* Ed. Harold Bloom. New York: Chelsea House Publishers, 1988. Pp 37-50. Pp 78-116 rpt as 'The Idea of *The Canterbury Tales*.' [Modern Critical Views]. Ed.

Harold Bloom. New York: Chelsea House Publishers, 1985. Pp 79-104.

Of all Chaucer's tales, *PardT* is the only one 'truly hospitable'(p 118) to allegorical interpretation, an interpretation which does not militate against appreciation of complex characterization. For Pardoner **374**; for *PardP* see **605**.

816 Bishop, Ian. 'The Narrative Art of The Pardoner's Tale.' *MÆ* 36 (1967), 15-24. Rpt in *Chaucer: The Canterbury Tales. A Casebook*. Ed. J. J. Anderson. London: Macmillan Press. 1974. Pp 209-21. Rpt in *The Narrative Art of the 'Canterbury Tales': A Critical Study of the Major Poems*. London and Melbourne: Everyman's University Library, 1987. Pp 90-106. Rpt in *Geoffrey Chaucer's 'The Pardoner's Tale.'* [Modern Critical Interpretations]. Ed. Harold Bloom. New York: Chelsea House Publishers, 1988. Pp 11-21.

The uncanny power of *PardT* results from a threefold economy (of characterization, description and narration), a double perspective (realistic and psychological), and a unifying irony. *PardP* and *PardT* probe the abuse of religion and the possible misuse of talent in creating and performing fiction. The narration exhibits a mastery of timing and pacing, of the use of sound and of silence, as well as the deployment of significant detail, techniques Chaucer may have found in Dante. The digression (denouncing drunkenness, swearing and hasardye) is related to the catastrophe of *PardT*. The tale is told at two removes from the fictional audience; the exemplum fits within the Pardoner's sermon, the sermon within his confession. The tale is marked by a double perspective brought into focus by 'an intertwining irony' (p 23). With all the technical details of the murders established in advance, *PardT* rushes to a dramatic close. Unlike the Parson who offers spiritual remedies for sins, the Pardoner wallows in the sins. Though cynical, he believes in the phenomenon of divine pardon. His mock offer to the pilgrims may be a response to the Host's call for a *myrie tale*. See **1065**.

817 Boyd, Beverly. *Chaucer and the Liturgy*. Philadelphia: Dorrance and Co., 1967.

The liturgy appears in Chaucer's works as part of the way of life. Chaucer's references to saint's legends e.g., John the Baptist (lines 488-91) indicates he was familiar with more hagiography than the *Legenda*. His references to saints' names are most often at the ends of lines requiring rhymes (e.g., Ronyan). Chaucer comments on Penance by implication in the behavior of the Pardoner. He refers to the Canonical Hours in the reference to bells in *PardT* 661-3. His references to the Mass touch on but do not describe liturgical detail (e.g., Offertory in *GP* and *PardP* 400-2).

818 Huppé, Bernard F. 'The Pardoner.' *A Reading of the 'Canterbury Tales.'* Albany: State University of New York, 1967.

In *PardT*, 'a masterpiece of storytelling' (p 215), the tale itself and the Old Man, in particular, reflect the teller. The Pardoner revels in corruption, concluding his 'sermon-tale' with a 'sales-pitch'(p 216) for his false pardons. The Pardoner, like Iago, finds evil its own reward. Motivated by 'his need to express his anguished hate'(p 217), the Pardoner mistakenly tries to include the Host in his mockery. The Host's crude rejection leads the Pardoner to concentrate 'all the venom of his suppressed hate' (p 218) on the Host. The Knight's intervention results in a 'kiss of enforced peace'(p 218), a symmetrical close to the Host's opening call *beel amy* (line 318). It is the 'art of high comedy to have the reader himself ... wake to the fearful truth embodied in the satanic figure of the Pardoner selling the grace of God for the damnation of human souls'(p 219). For Pardoner, see **356**;*PardP*, see **607**.

819 Jordan, Robert M. *Chaucer and the Shape of Creation: The Aesthetic Possibilities of Inorganic Structure.* 1967. See **523**.

Working from the premise that certain structural principles are pervasive in *CT*, Jordan examines the relationship between the world of Chaucer's fiction and the world he knew in cosmology and theology. Chaucer was a maker of tales and, in the case of *CT*, a maker of a framework: his method was 'to adjust the external details of substantially complete artifacts' (p 117). In *PardP* and *PardT* as well as *WBP*, Chaucer moves uncharacteristically 'toward a more fully inner-motivated development of his material' (p 117). For *Interr*, see **523**.

820 Nichols, Robert E. Jr., 'The Pardoner's Ale and Cake.' *PMLA* 82(1967), 498-504.

The Pardoner's demand for ale and cake operates on three levels: as a structural motif unifying Introduction, Prologue, and Tale; as a foreshadowing and component of the gluttony theme; and as an aspect of the Eucharist motif reinforcing irony. The Introduction establishes an 'environment of ale and cake,'(p 500). *PardP* owes its inception and sustenance to the alestake, and the exemplum in *PardT* depends on food and drink for its explication, complication and resolution. Even the interruption of the Wife of Bath is characterized by references to drink.

821 O'Neal, Cothburn M. 'The Syndrome of Masochism in Chaucer's Pardoner.' *CCTEP* 32(1967), 18-23.

Chaucer presents in the Pardoner, 'a clinically accurate case study of advanced masochism' (p 20) including specifically 'castration complex, penis envy, transvestite exhibitionism, and alternate aggressive-submissive tendencies' (pp 21-2). Through his performance, the Pardoner moves from 'an original sexual perversion to an obsessive desire for public humiliation and, ultimately, to the death wish'(p 22). The Pardoner is led by anger at self to set up his rejection by the Host, thereby triumphing over his masochism.

822 Owen, Nancy H. 'The Pardoner's Introduction, Prologue, and Tale: Sermon and Fabliau.' *JEGP* 66(1967), 541-9. Pp 543-7 rpt in *Twentieth Century Interpretations of The Pardoner's Tale: A Collection of Critical Essays*. Ed. Dewey R. Faulkner. Englewood Cliffs, New Jersey: Prentice Hall, 1973. Pp 114-7.

As a majority of the critics have argued (**51, 55, 681, 689, 703, 716, 750**), *PardT* is sermon-like. In fact, *PardP* and *PardT* are structurally a medieval sermon of the 'modern' style (lines 329-918)—theme, protheme, restatement of theme, introduction of theme, process, development, conclusion, and benediction. In place of the 'process', Chaucer fuses narrative technique with homiletic structure as the Pardoner begins the tale of the rioters, his major exemplum. With the interplay between the Host and the Pardoner, the 'sermon' is enclosed within a fabliau framework in which the teller of the tale becomes a victim of scatological jest. In victimizing the Pardoner more than any other pilgrim, Chaucer judges him the most depraved. The Pardoner's self-knowledge saves him from the reader's condemnation.

823 Thompson, Meredith. 'Current and Recurrent Fallacies in Chaucer Criticism.' In *Essays in American and English Literature Presented to Bruce Robert McElderry Jr.* Ed. Max F. Schulz, William D. Templeman, and Charles R. Metzger. Athens, Ohio: Ohio University Press, 1967.

In her critique of ill-founded Chaucer criticism, Thompson lists R.P. Miller's discussion of the Pardoner as a spiritual eunuch (**747**) as an example of the '*rationalistic fallacy (or assumptive fallacy)*' and defined as the unwarranted reliance upon logical "proof" based on insufficient empirical evidence' (p 158). Hoffman's interpretation of the Pardoner (**832**) is identified as an example of 'stylistic fallacy and defined as the unwarranted elaboration of critical style ...' (p 162).

824 Bright, J.C., and P.M. Birch. *Four Essays on Chaucer.* Illustrated by Essell. [Australian High School English]. Sydney and Brisbane: William Brooks & Co., Limited, 1967.

These four essays, focused mainly on the *GP*, introduce first-time readers to Chaucer's poetry. In contrast to the unambiguous ecclesiastical censure of Langland, 'Chaucer's Pardoner ... is not an intensely satirical figure, but an ironical and gently mocking portrait of a suspiciously effeminate and avaricious pardoner' (p 9). 'The Pardoner is, indeed, a most complex and highly individualized character in whose description we notice a certain detachment on Chaucer's part. He is as morally unacceptable as the Friar or the Summoner, and yet he does not quite revolt us. He leaves rather a certain air of ambiguity and contradiction ...' (p 40). A caricature of the Pardoner appears on p 14.

825 Brookhouse, Christopher, 'The Confessions of Three Pilgrims,' *LauR* 8(1968), 49-56.

Chaucer's use of the confession (often operating by implication) to reveal character in *PardT*, *WBT*, and *CYT* suggests his belief that man 'cannot hide the self from someone who will know it' (p 36). The Pardoner does not fully control his confession: although he recognizes what the pilgrims think of him and attempts by interrupting the Wife of Bath to fake physical wholeness, in *PardP* he reveals that his alienation is spiritual as well as sexual. In *PardT*, the rioters and the Old Man comment on the Pardoner's spiritual failure: the digression on the tavern sins demonstrates his personal knowledge and the Old Man's denial of flesh 'is the Pardoner's own condemnation of himself' (p 51).

826 Case, Gilbert. *Geoffrey Chaucer's The Pardoner's Tale.* Adelaide: Rigby, 1968.

A 47-page study guide offering questions on the Pardoner, *PardP*, *PardT*, notes on Chaucer's technique, general topics for discussion and 10-item bibliography [unavailable in U.S.].

827 Curtis, Penelope. 'The Pardoner's "Jape".' 1968. See **609**.

The Pardoner fails to bring the pilgrims under his influence. The tale defeats his attempt by 'detaching itself and all its meanings from the influence of his personality' (p 16). The Pardoner's sermonizing shows a mixture of impulses: towards personality-play (as defined in *PardP*), and towards impersonal truth (in *PardT*). The tale appears to contain the 'sermon' but it is actually a 'new sermonizing habit' (p 23): '[t]he mock-sermon which began the Prologue has never really been discontinued' (p 23). The Pardoner disappears into his tale, reappearing only at the end to maintain its decorum as *som moral thyng*. The Pardoner's performance can be gauged against the standard set by the Parson: the Pardoner, while 'wildly vivacious' (p 28) offers no purposeful movement. When he offers pardons he offers the pilgrimage a mirror image, 'a gloriously impudent parody of Christendom ever journeying towards heaven' (p 29). Appropriately, he selects the Host because he is most enveloped in humanity. In silencing the Pardoner, the narrative holds him up 'to a disdainful view' (p 30), passes judgment on his 'jape', and restores the sense of present time. The 'Pardoner-event' (p 30) casts a new glow on the pilgrim's common existence, 'which can neither realize nor abandon its aspirations in the prologue-scheme of a history' (p 30). The final dimension of time is invoked by the Parson's sermon.

828 Dean, Christopher. 'Salvation, Damnation and The Role of the Old Man in The *Pardoner's Tale.*' *ChauR* 3(1968-9), 44-9.

The Old Man is perhaps 'the most puzzling and enigmatic' of all Chaucer's characters (p 44). The Old Man has been variously interpreted as a symbolic figure (**667, 681, 701, 711, 728, 775, 800**) or as literally an old man (**742, 790**) Some link the Old Man with the Pardoner (**728, 747, 793, 837**). Though some critics have viewed the Old Man as an insignificant figure (**742**), most find him compelling (**695, 728, 811, 820, 869**). The Old Man is the most significant of the three warners who caution the rioters; additionally, he is responsible for a 'crucial twist'(p 47) in the plot. The Old Man is, in several ways, the opposite of the rioters, not the least of which is his manifestation of Christian goodness. Through him are manifested both the mercy of God leading to salvation and the justice of God leading to damnation.

829 Drucker, Trudy. 'Some Medical Allusions in *The Canterbury Tales.*' *NYSJM* 68(1968), 444-7.

Medical symptoms predominate so with the Pardoner and the Summoner that one could suppose the pilgrimage is undertaken in gratitude. Drucker cites a description from an endocrinologist to support her interpretation that the Pardoner is 'beyond question' (p 444) a eunuch.

830 Griffith, Richard R. *A Critical Study Guide to Chaucer's Canterbury Tales.* 1968. See **379**.

The *gentils'* protest is a direct affront to the Pardoner. He finds himself, like several others, in the position of not being able to tell the tale he had planned but his desire to win carries him forward. For *PardP*, see **610**.

831 Harrington, David V. 'Narrative Speed in the Pardoner's Tale.' *ChauR* 3(1968-9), 50-9. Rpt in *Twentieth Century Interpretations of The Pardoner's Tale: A Collection of Critical Essays*. Ed. Dewey R. Faulkner. Englewood Cliffs, New Jersey: Prentice Hall, 1973. Pp 33-42.

As the rhetoric of *PardT* indicates, its value lies in the emotional effect created by the ironic relation of the Pardoner's moralizing to his behavior. As with other dramatic literature, readers should set aside issues of psychological realism and careful analysis to seek the immediate momentary impression, here an 'effect of being startled into a greater awareness by each successive scene' (p 35). The digression on the tavern sins foreshadows the more dramatic expression of the same values. The reader accepts the tension between admiration for the moral excellence of the tale and contempt for the hypocrisy of the teller because of the rapidity and cogency of the Pardoner's style. The narrative speed accelerated by the omissions of transitions (asyndeton) and the variations from the normal order of words and ideas (hyperbaton), together with the extensive use of dialogue in the exemplum, simulates a breathless haste and roughness. The unity of the piece is in the emotion created by the recognition of theoretically irreconcilable values. When the Pardoner provokes the pilgrims at the close of his tale, he provides another example of 'that thrashing, chaotic world of the frame' (p 198) heightened by its juxtaposition with the ordered working of destiny in that tale of the rioters. The scoundrels in the links are not punished as directly as those in the tales.

832 Hoffman, Richard L. 'The Canterbury Tales.' *Critical Approaches to Six Major English Works*. Ed. R. M. Lumiansky and Herschel Baker. Philadelphia: University of Pennsylvania Press; London: Oxford University Press, 1968. Pp 41-80.

The theme of *PardT—Radix malorum est cupiditas*—permeates many *CT* as does its obverse—*Radix bonorum est Caritas* (p 71).

833 Lawlor, John. *Chaucer*. London: Hutchinson University Library, 1968; rpt 1970.

The Pardoner and Wife of Bath present rare congruity between tale and teller perhaps because they are unusually 'fixed' characters (p

113), the Pardoner revealing the depth of contemporary evil. The Pardoner's portrait is unique in opening with irony. His autobiographical confession softens the audience for the trick that follows, a trick that may result as likely from practiced opportunism as planning.

834 Osselton, N. E. 'Chaucer's "clumsy tradition" in the Pardoner's Tale.' *ES* 49(1968), 36-8.

Thise in *Thise riotoures* (line 661) may be 'non-anaphoric, merely forward-looking'; as such, it marks a well-calculated shift from the 'rhetorical tirade' of the sermon to the 'colloquial narrative' of the rioters (p 38).

835 Owen, Charles A. Jr. 'The Design of *The Canterbury Tales*,' in *Companion to Chaucer Studies*. Ed. Beryl Rowland. Toronto, New York, London: Oxford University Press, 1968. Pp 192-207.

Owen reviews and comments on critical approaches to the design of *CT*. Kittredge's discussion of 'gross violations of dramatic propriety'(p 194) (**668**) in the performance of the Pardoner stimulated study of design. Lumiansky's (**724**) interpretation of the Pardoner creates 'a drama that the text hardly supports' though 'his systematic treatment of all the evidence is stimulating' (p 198). Tupper's (**679, 680**) effort to interpret *PardP* and *PardT* as structured on the basis of the seven deadly sins survived the attack of Lowes (**682**) only in the acceptance of the tavern as the setting; that premise was challenged by Gerould (**736**). Mapping a plausible tale order, Owen argues *Ret* belongs with Chaucer's treatise on penitence rather than *CT*.

836 Payne, Robert O. 'Chaucer and The Art of Rhetoric.' In *Companion to Chaucer Studies*. Ed. Beryl Rowland. Toronto, New York, London: Oxford University Press, 1968. Pp 38-57.

Payne discusses the position of medieval rhetoric and reviews critical treatments of Chaucer ranging from Manly (**690, 691**) who saw the 'surface rhetorical cast' of some of his work as a 'historical accident' (p 46) to more recent critics, Baldwin (**746**) and Payne (**781**), who find 'Chaucer closer to the rhetoricians in his primary assumptions about his art than in the surface details of his style' (p 55).

837 Rowland, Beryl, ed. *Companion to Chaucer Studies*. Toronto, New York, and London: Oxford University Press, 1968/ rev with index 1979. Includes: Vance Ramsey. 'Modes of Irony in the Canterbury Tales.' Pp 290-312. See **611**.

838 Toole, William B. 'Chaucer's Christian Irony: The Relationship of

Character and Action in the *Pardoner's Tale.' ChauR* 3(1968), 37-43. The Pardoner's comments on gluttony, gambling and blasphemy set a context for interpreting the relationship between the revellers' blindness to the meaning of events and the judgment that befalls them. Inversion motifs of Christ, Crucifixion, brotherhood and the Trinity intensify the irony. The themes of avarice and the dangers of chance 'pave the way' for the solicitation (p 43).

839   Wagenknecht, Edward. *The Personality of Chaucer*. 1968. See **382**. As well as conventional religious references, Chaucer employs distinctively religious matter in *CT* including the exemplum, *PardT*, three saints' legends, and the pious treatises—*Mel* and *ParsT*. In *PardT*, Chaucer's condemnation of gluttony, drunkenness, gaming and swearing shows he does not take an amoral view.

840   Whittock, Trevor. *A Reading of the Canterbury Tales*. London: Cambridge University Press, 1968.
PardT demonstrates in a way more startling than *PhyT* the rewards of sin; *PardP* and *PardT* are 'a cynical refutation of the Physician's moralizing' (p 185) demonstrating as they do that the wicked may flourish. Together, they provide social satire on the corruption of pardoners, 'a psychological study of an individual scoundrel, and an exploration of the nature of evil' (p 193). The Pardoner proclaims his evil with disconcerting honesty; he seems without conscience yet does not doubt the doctrine of damnation; and manifests a lack of basic consciousness. *PardT* reveals truth is lost on the Pardoner. Death operates as a *privee theef*, as something benevolent, and as retribution. The reconciliation 'affirms the transcendent rightness of gaiety, good spirits and tolerance .... Even the Pardoner is part of the glory of Creation' (p 194).

841   Braddy, Haldeen. 'Chaucer—Realism or Obscenity?.' *AQ* 2 (1969), 121-38.
PardT 'is a corker, but that intolerable business tacked on at the end about the man soiling his breeches just about gags me .... This discreditable sort of filth, Chaucer at his worst, figures small in the total' (p 137).

842   *Chaucer's Mind and Art: Essays Edited by A. C. Cawley*. Edinburgh and London: Oliver & Boyd, 1969.
This collection includes Dorothy Everett, 'Some Reflexions on Chaucer's "Art Poetical,"' pp 99-124 (**725**); and Francis Lee Utley, 'Chaucer and Patristic Exegesis,' pp 69-85 (**352**).

843 Harris, Richard L. 'Odin's Old Age: A Study of The Old Man in *The Pardoner's Tale.*' *SFQ* 33(1969), 24-38.

Adding to Barakat's study of Odin (**229**), Harris counters the objections of Schmidt (**427**) by showing how the decline of Odin's cult might well explain the Old Man of *PardT*. Assuming that the Old Man is the thief, Death, then the spear Death carries may be associated with the staff carried by the Old Man (p 25). Odin's spear became a staff according to Barakat though Harris cannot locate the reference; '... if Odin's spear became a staff for his appearance in the passage which Barakat has found, apparently, somewhere, then there is reason to believe that it could have made the same change' for *PardT* (p 25). The spear is of great significance as a weapon and an implement of sacrifice in the cult of Odin. The cloak and the old age of Odin offer parallels to the Old Man (**226**) though these characteristics are too familiar in medieval literature to be distinctive. Schmidt has noted the voices of the Good Angel and the Bad Angel in the appeal of the Old Man to the rioters: this suggestion is justified but not unique; there are similarities to passages from the Eddic material and *Heimskringla*. Odin's predilection for causing family difficulty finds a parallel in the sworn fraternal relationship of the rioters. Parallels established, the question remains as to how the powerful Odin finds his way to such a degraded position as the Old Man's and how he speaks with a Christian voice. The possibility of Odin 'assuming the figure of the Old Man' (p 38) is enhanced when one considers his degradation in the later Fornaldar Sögur and his mellowing to become a guardian of order in folk-lore rather than a spirit of disorder. The crafty shape-shifter, Odin, might well play the roles of the Old Man. See **93, 94**.

844 Hoy, Michael. 'The Pardoner's Tale' and 'Conclusion.' *Chaucer's Major Tales*. 1969. See **385**.

PardT must be understood against a background of macabre obsession with death: the tale explores the inevitability of death and the fascination surrounding it (p 130). The Pardoner is at once a figure of comedy and sinister evil. Both type and rounded personality, he conveys a sense of delusion and emptiness in his person and his profession. When the Pardoner shifts from reminiscence to direct speech in *PardP* (line 352), the pilgrims become his congregation. Chaucer's style invites us to accept the Pardoner's claims for his relics at face value but throughout there is a 'subtle tone of qualification'(p 111). *PardP* takes the form of a confession. The apparent sincerity of the warning to those in mortal sin (lines 377-84) reveals the Pardoner's obsession with sin, the topic of his tale. The personality of the Pardoner permeates the description in the tale. Blasphemy, the sin the Pardoner judges worst, is a major theme in the tale designed to show the interconnectedness between sins. The 'Sermon Digression,' a 'masterpiece in its technical structure'(p 117), provides unity within the variety of sins and illustrations and links the digression to the story of the revellers. Though the Pardoner's sermon operates as 'a satire of contemporary preaching'(p 121), its primary function is conscious self-dramatization. The Pardoner's sudden return to the tale exemplifies his willingness to use anything for his purposes. The concrete reality of Death, conventionally personified, gives the rioters' quest immediacy. Chaucer intends an association between the Old Man and Death, but 'a specific allegorical reading' confuses (p 123). The Old Man can be associated with Elde (cf *Piers Plowman*) or the Wandering Jew: the ambiguity of the Old Man contributes to his force. Selection of detail creates realism and a simplicity of style which contributes to the inevitability. The final outcome is narrated in 'a deliberately flat style'(p 127). The closing benediction (lines 916-8) is a convention but also 'a grave and sincere expression of emotion' (p 128). The final irony of the tale is found in the Pardoner's invitation to the Host: the Pardoner has deceived himself into believing he is an irresistible preacher. The Pardoner fully recognizes his hypocrisy but ironically fails to understand that the quest of his tale is his own quest. Chaucer's approach to the problem of evil and death contrasts markedly with *Everyman*; Chaucer explores the fascination and horror found in paintings by Bosch or Grünewald. Ultimately, he closes with the Knight's reestablishment of the human comedy. For Pardoner, see **385**.

845 King, Francis, and Bruce Steele. *Selections from Geoffrey Chaucer's The Canterbury Tales.* 1969. See **94**.

PardT is an exercise by Chaucer and the Pardoner 'to arouse strong feelings without any appeal to reason' (p 367); the style and action are full of preacher's tricks e.g., slogans, oaths, calls for attention. More than a parody, *PardT* is genuinely powerful. The Pardoner is 'a professional deceiver,' 'perhaps the most polished professional on the pilgrimage' (p 369). Chaucer has translated allegory (from *RR*) into human character but, apart from his deceptions, the Pardoner does not exist. The setting of *PardP* is sufficient to make his confession believable:

it is not sincere; rather, it is designed to elicit 'reactions gratifying to his self-esteem' (p 370). Avarice is of secondary importance. The opposition between preaching and practice condemns the Pardoner (p 369). Moral perversion is a joke to the Pardoner; the Host coarsely attacks the Pardoner's vulnerability, physical perversion. 'Concerning Pardoners' presents the summary of papal legislation from *Regimen Animarum*, exerpted and translated by A. L. Kellogg and L. Haselmayer in **314** (pp 393-5). Appendix D exerpts the confession by Faux Semblant (*RR*), pp 395-7. For Pardoner, see **386**.

846   Perella, Nicolas James. *The Kiss: Sacred and Profane. An Interpretive History of Kiss Symbolism and Related Religio-Erotic Themes*. Berkeley: University of California Press, 1969.

In tracing religio-erotic themes associated with the central image of the soul kiss, Perella discusses Iseult's kiss of Tristan, followed by the king's kiss of Tristan. Both are kisses on the mouth, and both symbolize reconciliation and peace. The latter marked not only a reconciliation but the establishment of 'something approaching brotherhood' (p 130). Hilary (**1091**) cites this source in commenting on the Knight's call for a kiss of reconciliation.

847   Taitt, P. S. 'Harry Bailly and The Pardoner's Relics.' *SN* 4(1969), 112-4.

The Host misunderstands that the Pardoner's offer of relics is an effort to return the audience to reality and recreate 'a mirthful mood' (p 114). The pilgrims' silence reveals their inability to separate art from reality. Chaucer viewed the Pardoner with compassion.

ᴆᴐ The Pardoner's Tale 1970-1979

848 Currie, Felicity. 'Chaucer's Pardoner Again.' 1970. See **388**.
Fellow pilgrims and critics alike find the Pardoner vile; the Pardoner's
attitude towards the pilgrims has been more elusive. The Pardoner
accepts with a vengeance the challenge of telling a moral tale. He
addresses only one audience, the pilgrims (cs **794**) who have set
themselves up as moral arbiters. As their pride blinds them to the
relevance of the tale, with its theme of death the leveller, any distinction
between *gentils* and *lewed peple* is nullified. The similarity of people
involved—*lewed peple* of *PardP*, rioters in *PardT*, and pilgrims—unifies
prologue and tale. With *feyned flatterye* he shows the pilgrims how he
fools others. Then when he proceeds to tell a moral tale about death,
they are unable to accept its applicability to them. The closing solicitation
(line 919 ff) is simply his final *jape*. The Host's retort reveals his sense
of guilt and proves the Pardoner's point. The Pardoner is like the Clerk
in promising to give the pilgrims what they request and doing so barbed.
Chaucer uses the methods of Faus Semblant to emphasize the
Pardoner's evil doing but the Pardoner is also a scapegoat. Blinded by
the Pardoner's personality and their own moral pride, the Host and
pilgrims reject the moral of *PardT* and turn it into a dirty joke: 'the
Pardoner has had his effect, and who can deny God's use of the
contaminated vessel' (p 21)? For *PardP*, see **612**.

849 Donaldson, E. Talbot. *Speaking of Chaucer*. London: Athlone Press;
New York: W.W. Norton, 1970. 'The Effect of the Merchant's Tale.'
Pp 30-45. Rpt in *Geoffrey Chaucer*. Ed. Harold Bloom. New York:
Chelsea House Publishers, 1985. Pp 37-48. Rpt in *The Canterbury
Tales: Nine Tales and the General Prologue*. Ed. V. A. Kolve and
Glending Olson. New York: W. W. Norton, 1989. Pp 484-92.

The Pardoner, a rascal, elicits grudging admiration for his efficient thievery. Chaucer the pilgrim sees through the Pardoner 'but in Church he remains to the pilgrim "a noble ecclesiaste"' (line 708). The use of *bely* to mean stomach in *PardT* (lines 534-5) is one of three such usages in Chaucer. The Pardoner's sermon is 'a splendid example of what might be called homiletic shock-treatment, or Pauline hortatory vulgarity' (p 39). Unlike the Merchant's 'articulate wrath that keeps wounding our sensibilities', the 'futile, inarticulate wrath' of the Pardoner insulted by the Host evokes laughter (p 42). In a discussion of his opposition to patristic exegesis in its extreme form, Donaldson accepts Miller's (**747**) reading of the patristic significance of the Pardoner's condition but rejects his equation with the Father's scriptural eunuch as 'depreciating the poem' (p 138n).

850 Elliott, R.W.V. 'When Chaucer Swears.' In *Australasian Universities Language and Literature Association: Proceedings and Papers of the Twelfth Congress*. Ed. A. P. Treweek. Sydney: University of Western Australia, 1970. Pp 417-34.

Chaucer employs swearing as an integral part of his technique with character, story, situation, mood and diction. True to the concerns of his time, most oaths are religious. The Pardoner is one of four characters most given to swearing, mocking the Host's expletives, demonstrating his baseness with anatomical oaths referring to Christ's body, preaching against swearing, and telling a tale of rioters given to swearing. The Pardoner's whole performance builds to his confrontation with the Host, Chaucer's most habitual swearer, whose oaths against the Pardoner carry a devastating appropriateness (lines 948-53).

851 Halverson, John. 'Chaucer's Pardoner and the Progress of Criticism.' 1970. See **390**.

Picking up where G. G. Sedgewick left off (**716**), Halverson reviews critical opinion (1940-69) noting both considerable agreement and convergence of interest: the criticism is predominantly interpretive and phenomenological with interest in Freud, the spiritual dimension and ironic modes. Most commentators touch on the 'question of what actually happens while the Pardoner holds the center of attention'(p 185), the character of the Pardoner and the nature of his story. Critical discussions reveal a degree of consensus and a convergence of interest in interpretive and phenomenological topics. The Pardoner, if not drunk, has had his tongue loosened by drink; an unspoken tension exists between the

Pardoner and his audience, and, recognizing his superiority, the Pardoner engages in self-parody. The similarity between modern time and Chaucer's own enables modern critics to see more than their predecessors. 'Of the "real" Pardoner we know next to nothing'(p 196). He is so successful in presenting a sordid image of himself as a revenge against the gentlefolk that the Host (not the Pardoner [**681**]), is carried away by his eloquence. Given the nature of the 'put-on', the benediction remains 'irresolvably ambivalent' (p 198). The nucleus of the tale is death; Chaucer has produced 'an original and profound meditation' (p 202) on the subject. The Pardoner, however, remains unmoved; 'his peroration is the mockery of a necrophiliac'(p 201).

852 Pearsall, D[erek] A. 'Part II. The Canterbury Tales.' *History of Literature in the English Language.* Vol 1. [The Middle Ages]. London: Barrie & Jenkins, 1970. Pp 163-93.

The Pardoner, who is stimulated by Faux Semblant in *RR*, provides 'an extended display of character in verbal action' (p 172). Though density of detail suggests realism in the characterizations, the pilgrims are paradigms of moral evaluation (p 174). Ironically, the Pardoner's 'exhibitionist ill-doing' traps him into doing good. *PardT* seems self-contained, unconcerned with the preceding revelation: 'Chaucer is [probably] not worried by inconsistencies between tale and frame' (p 172). The Old Man seems an embodiment of the Pardoner's outcast state.

853 Woo, Constance, and William Matthews. 'The Spiritual Purpose of the *Canterbury Tales.*' 1970. See **394**.

Chaucer's spiritual purpose is revealed in part by the relation of *ParsT* and the ecclesiatic pilgrims. With its theme 'that the spirit and flesh should join to work toward a single end' (p 93), *ParsT* counters the ecclesiastics in general, and the Pardoner in particular. The Parson is the union, the Pardoner the separation, of appearance and reality. *ParsT* explains as *PardP* reveals the Pardoner's sinfulness—pride, flattery, avarice, gluttony, hearing confession falsely. *PardT* is a sermon with parallels to *ParsT*; with a different purpose, and through the horrible example of himself and the rioters, the Pardoner points the same direction as the Parson, thereby cooperating in the spiritual purpose of *CT*. The Pardoner puts forth a false way, 'a permissive evil that brings about ultimate good if the folk discern and choose the right way' (p 97). The pilgrims protest his tale at the outset and reject him at the close.

854 Belting, Elizabeth K., ed. *Studies in Chaucer and Shakespeare*. Beloit, Wisconsin: Belting Publications, 1971. See **687**.

855 Cartwright, Michael Percy. '"The Alexandria Quartet": A Comedy for the Twentieth Century or Lawrence Durrell, The Pardoner, and His Miraculous Pig's Knuckle.' *DAI* 31(1971), 5391.University of Nebraska (Lincoln) Dissertation. Director: Lee T. Lemon, 1970. [Not seen.]

856 Hussey, S. S. *Chaucer: An Introduction*. London: Methuen; New York: Barnes and Noble, 1971; 2nd ed./rev 1981. Pp 176-88. 1971 edition prints 'Homilies of Morality and Devotion': The *Pardoner's Tale* and *The Nun's Priest's Tale.*' Pp 176-94.

Though exegetical critics led by Robertson (**776**) have suggested that the gluttony, gambling and swearing in the *PardT* are examples of *cupiditas*, Hussey is not persuaded that the exegetical method should be applied to secular literature. *PardT* uses the sermon form but 'keeps up a running commentary by its preacher on his proficiency' (p 181). The Pardoner falsely claims his indulgences can absolve sinners *a culpa*. We accept him because his tale is a performance, a dramatic monologue. The Pardoner's real confession ends at line 642. Serious about the '*theory* of Christ's pardon' (p 188), the Pardoner offers an instant pardon.

857 Josipovici, Gabriel. 'Chaucer: the Teller and The Tale.' *The World and the Book: A Study of Modern Fiction*. Stanford: Stanford University Press, 1971. Pp 52-99.

Chaucer's clarity of vision creates 'a world which mimes our natural propensities for misinterpretation (the result mainly of our belief that the meanings we find in the world are somehow inherently there), and, by miming, relieves us of them' (p 97). That there are right and wrong ways of reading the world is a theme of *PardT*; R. P. Miller's treatment (**747**) results from an overly literal interpretation of text. In the sense of playing the 'game' of *CT*, the Pardoner is the only honest pilgrim: *PardP* and *PardT* are aimed only at those who refuse to recognize them as game.

858 Marks, Jason. 'Tales from Chaucer as Projections of the Tellers' Needs.' *DAI* 32(1971), 1480A. New York University Dissertation, 1971. Director: Charles N. Schirone.

Techniques of thematic apperception supplemented by classical Freudian interpretation are employed to deduce a personality portrait of the

Pardoner, Knight, Man of Law, Pilgrim Chaucer, Clerk and Second Nun. Based on the personality portraits, recreations set in contemporary prose style and milieu are told by present-day storytellers.

859 Robinson, Ian. *Chaucer's Prosody: A Study of the Middle English Verse Tradition.* Cambridge: Cambridge University Press, 1971.

The Pardoner's sermon (lines 549-55) is examined in support of the theory that Chaucer employed the balanced half-line of the alliterative tradition. Comparison of Skeat and Hengwrt (lines 531-43) demonstrate the effectiveness of the balanced pentameter to the 'insane vigour of the Pardoner's sermon' (p 162); Robinson judges Hengwrt's punctuation superior and suggests speaking the lines to discover the unusual foot- and phrase-patterns that produce 'striking rhetorical force' (p 163).

860 Rowland, Beryl. *Blind Beasts: Chaucer's Animal World.* Ohio: Kent State University Press, 1971. See **396**.

Studies the complex significance of Chaucer's animal images. The polecat, not drawn from Chaucer's sources, was found in Flanders; consequently, the rioter's reference to it enabled him to get poison without arousing suspicion. The reference to rats is similarly probable. For *PardP*, see **614**.

861 Taitt, Peter. 'In Defence of Lot.' *N&Q* 18(1971), 284-5.

Peter Comestor (*Historia Scholastica*) appears to be the immediate common source for both Langland's and Chaucer's assertion that Lot's drunkenness led to incest, and the connection of Lot with Noah and Herod. Gen. 19:30-6 shows Lot's daughters conspiring to make him drunk then lie with him in order to insure the continuity of the human race.

862 Conlee, John W. 'The Pardoner's Symbolic Treasure.' *SHum* 3 (1972), 1-3.

Chaucer, generally familiar with number symbolism, uses the number 'eight' in his description of the treasure trove to reflect on the sinful actions and motivations of the rioters, to foreshadow their destruction, and to comment ironically on the folly of pursuing happiness which is merely the prelude to death.

863 Eliason, Norman E. 'The Language of Chaucer's Poetry: An Appraisal of the Verse, Style, and Structure.' *Anglistica* 17. Copenhagen: Rosenkilde and Bagger, 1972.

The ending of *PardT*, though it has provoked more discussion than the endings of all the other tales, remains a puzzle. Inaccurate analysis of the tale as a sermon (cs **716**) confuses what constitutes the ending. *PardT* consists of a story (lines 661-915), introduction (lines 463-660), and a conventional conclusion or benediction (lines 916-8). Chaucer added a prologue (lines 329-462) to suit the tale to the Pardoner and to give it an 'undertone of evil'(p 202). By adding the epilogue (lines 919-68), Chaucer addressed directly the issue of a scoundrel telling a spellbinding tale. The epilogue 'makes peace between the Pardoner and us'(p 206). The Host's malediction, at once offensive and joking, expresses our response, a mixture of contempt at the Pardoner and gratitude for his tale.

864 Fisher, John H. 'Chaucer's Last Revision of the "Canterbury Tales".' *MLR* 67(1972), 241-51.

PardP and *PardT* manifest the interplay between tale, narrator, pilgrim participants and the hearing or reading audience. Dramatic interplay developed as a unifying device through Fragments VI-X and emerged in Fragment VII; at the time of his death, Chaucer was engaged in revising Fragments I-V according to this principle.

865 Kean, P[atricia]. M. *Chaucer and the Making of English Poetry*. Vol. 2. *The Art of Narrative*. London and Boston: Routledge & Kegan Paul, 1972; single volume shortened edition, 1982. [Page numbers from 1972.]

'The *Canterbury Tales*: Chaucerian Comedy' (pp 76-109). The Pardoner offers one of three instances (including the Wife of Bath and the Merchant) where Chaucer shifts the emphasis from the telling of the tale to the presentation of character. Unlike the Wife of Bath and January in *MerT*, the Pardoner's character is not linked to any thematic development. The Pardoner has affinities with self-revealing Vice figures in allegorical writing as well as with Faux Semblant. The Pardoner exemplifies Chaucerian comedy in that he is a typical character who (because of vice and physical abnormality) stands apart from the norm. Overemphasis on the Pardoner's lack of normal masculinity and its social consequences risks anachronistic interpretation; the Pardoner is to be understood in the context of medieval ideas regarding *eunuchus ex nativitate*. The norm is conveyed through characters and reference to the observer whose view the reader is made to share. Chaucer treats his characters with 'an open-eyed consistency in which justice is the ruling principle. In the case of the Pardoner, his eyes are perhaps even too widely open for modern taste'(p 109). The Pardoner has affinities with the self-revealing Vice figure in allegorical writing as well as with Faux Semblant. Chaucer shapes the Pardoner's performance as a totality by adapting the methods of allegorical satire but his approach is fundamentally naturalistic. 'Chaucer has not quite bridged the gap between the kind of presentation in which the confession can be accepted as a necessary and inevitable part of the exposition and that in which it needs a motivation in keeping with the laws of probability' (p 108). The ending is contrived to expose the Pardoner as he really is. The success of his deception depends on 'his own appreciation of the reality for which he offers a shoddy substitute'(p 107).

866 Kellogg, Alfred L. *Chaucer, Langland, Arthur: Essays in Middle English Literature.* New Brunswick, New Jersey: Rutgers University Press, 1972. Rpt as 'An Augustinian Interpretation of Chaucer's Pardoner,' pp 245-68 and slightly revised version of 'Chaucer's Satire of the Pardoner,' pp 212-44. See **314, 590,** and **728.**

867 Khinoy, Stephen A. 'Inside Chaucer's Pardoner?' 1972. See **615.**
A review of interpretation since Sedgewick (**716**) focuses attention on the nature of the Pardoner and the meaning of the Old Man, and establishes that the Pardoner resists consensus (**668, 728, 779, 755, 756, 789, 811**). The diversity of views itself argues that Chaucer intended the Pardoner as a puzzle. If the Pardoner is assessed as a puzzle, our response to the Old Man points to the standard for resolving it. The Pardoner's stance toward fable and moral faces us with 'a paradox that thoroughly subverts medieval doctrine' and invites us to 'accept art for art's sake'(p 258). This reversal that makes the moral disposable operates throughout *PardP*. The relationship between *PardP* and *PardT* is inverted as the immoral prologue imposes its meaning on the moral sermon. The inner truth of the sermon is displaced by a fascination with the Pardoner's performance. Our judgment on him may reinforce his cynical position that things not inner meanings are real. The episode with the Old Man transforms the exemplum into a creation independent of the teller. The Host is almost trapped by the Pardoner. In his refutation, the Host echoes the *RR*. The Host parodies Reason by implying that naming is a matter of convention imposed by human will. Since the Pardoner embodies his argument, the refutation is appropriately *ad hominem*: the Pardoner and all he represents are 'excrement without, impotence within'(p 267). The Pardoner's position, though basic to the modern world, is destructive of the medieval; he

offers the fruit of the tree of language without morality. Only through the Old Man and the Host's word-play, does Chaucer demonstrate that meanings are not arbitrary.

868 Knapp, Daniel. 'The Relyk of a Seint: A Gloss on Chaucer's Pilgrimage.' *ELH* 39(1972), 1-26.

Specific knowledge of Canterbury in Chaucer's time suggests the 'constraints and opportunities inherent in his narrative frame' (p 2). The existence of 'the most astonishing of Becket's relics' (p 13), hair breeches, reveals in miniature the thematic irony in the structure of *CT*. The relic is described by Erasmus in *Peregrinatio Religionis Ergo*. As part of the pilgrim company, Chaucer would likely venerate relics at Canterbury. When Chaucer holds up relics to ridicule in *PardP*, they are clearly spurious. The allusion to the breeches is assigned to the Host with 'great deliberateness and aesthetic propriety'(p 15). Moreover, it reveals Chaucer's attitude toward 'pious fraud'(p 16) and possibly toward the earthly pilgrimage. The frame is 'secular, local, commonplace, earthbound, the tales are profoundly ideal'(p 18). In taunting the Host, the Pardoner has discovered 'a spiritual posture adequate to express his anger, contempt and fear'(p 18). With the juxtaposition of *PardT* and the satiric allusion to the shrine, Chaucer may be expanding the Pardoner's text to include not only the rioters and the Pardoner himself but also the pilgrims and the monks at Canterbury. Chaucer's reasons for closing out the pilgrimage before it got to Canterbury may have been 'more political than aesthetic' (p 23): 'How could the pilgrimage be permitted to end in ... the scene so fatally foreshadowed in the Pardoner's sequence' (p 25)?

869 Miller, Clarence H., and Roberta Bux Bosse. 'Chaucer's Pardoner and The Mass.'1972. See **616**.

Chaucer's Pardoner is 'a negative image of the central image of Christianity, the mass' (p 171). The Pardoner and rioters are anti-Christ figures who find death in life. The contrast between the Pardoner's perversions and the Mass is worked with increasing degrees of intensity in *GP*, the Pardoner's 'sermon-introduction' (p 172) and *PardT*. In *GP*, the Pardoner is uniquely described against the background of the Mass (lines A 707-14). A review of Amalarius shows that the Pardoner (deliberately) and the rioters (unwittingly) pervert the allegory of the Mass. The rioters' sudden deaths ironically pervert the 'fruits' of the Mass, their tavern revelry recalls a condemnation of feasts in church.

The Pardoner is 'a living parody of the good Christian'(p 177). He understands his theme of *cupiditas* to mean worldly pleasure. As Augustine held that evil has no existence in its own right, so the Pardoner's tale of damnation exists only by contrast with the salvation it negates. *PardT* echoes the Mass in preparatory prayer, introit, epistle, homily, creed, consecration, reference to the 'tree' and the eucharistic meal. With their 'Mass of damnation' (p 183), the rioters have perverted the central mystery of the church and portrayed 'a distorted image of the shape of salvation'(p 184).

370 Muscatine, Charles. *Poetry and Crisis in the Age of Chaucer*. Notre Dame, Indiana; London: University of Notre Dame Press, 1972.
In *PardT*, Chaucer treats the implications of dramatic realism. The Pardoner, as rhetorician and storyteller, is akin to Chaucer himself. Muscatine speculates on the connection between the Pardoner's 'almost grotesque perversity' and 'some special baseness Chaucer may feel in the perversion of his talent' (p 116). At the close of his tale, when the Pardoner sets aside cynicism and invokes Christ's pardon, he creates 'a moment of extraordinary psychological complexity' (p 118). Hearing no response from the pilgrims, the Pardoner continues with his tale. *PardT* offers a rare instance of Chaucer approaching 'the blacker stages of the fifteenth century mood'(p 135).

371 Robinson, Ian. *Chaucer and the English Tradition*. Cambridge: Cambridge University Press, 1972.
The Pardoner is 'a sinister madman' (p 88), a eunuch whose association with the Summoner makes clear he is not without sexual gratifications. When the Pardoner interrupts the Wife of Bath, he saves her from the impossible task of connecting the two prongs of her attack (p 101). Where Langland is essentially a preacher, Chaucer is a poet; the Pardoner's treatment of gluttony (line 529 ff) is more accurate than Langland's Glotoun.

372 Ross, Thomas W. *Chaucer's Bawdy*. 1972. See **399**.
Chaucer uses bawdy language to delineate comic characters. Ross lists in alphabetical order more than 300 words that Chaucer may have intended in a bawdy sense. See entries for *breech* (line 948); *coillons* (952); *dong* (530); *fundament* (950); *fyr* (481); *incest* (485); *kiss* (968); *lay* (486); *lecherye* (481); *luxurie* (484); *soun* (536); *styves* (465); and *tappestere* (477). For *Phy-PardL* see **548**; for *PardP* see **617**.

373 Whitmore, Sister Mary Ernestine. *Medieval English Domestic Life* *and Amusements in the Works of Chaucer*. New York: Cooper Square, 1972.

Identifies the following indications of medieval English domestic life: cooking (lines 538-46); gluttony (lines 498-516); clerical costume (lines 681-5); riotous dancing (lines 463-8);gambling (lines 591-602); singing (lines 672-4, 710-3); performers (line 477).

874 Adelman, Janet. 'That We May Leere Som Wit.' In *Twentieth Century Interpretations of the Pardoner's Tale: A Collection of Critical Essays*. Ed. Dewey R. Faulkner. Englewood Cliffs: Prentice Hall Inc., 1973. Pp 96-106.

PardT is a game of wit, at once a self parody and a joke whose aim seems to shift. Two images assume central importance: 'that of the rioters and their poisoned wine, and that of the artist and his audience'(p 99). When the pilgrims realize they have become subject as well as audience, the reader realizes he has been moved one degree closer to the reality of the tale. The Pardoner beguiles himself (missing the point of his own structure), and Chaucer. In the *Ret* when Chaucer breaks with the fiction, the reader is jolted into a fresh awareness that the goal of the pilgrimage is *soothfastness* (p 106). Still, the reader remains nostalgic for the fiction.

875 Barney, Stephen A. 'An Evaluation of the *Pardoner's Tale*.' In *Twentieth Century Interpretations of the Pardoner's Tale: A Collection of Critical Essays*. Ed. Dewey R. Faulkner. Englewood Cliffs: Prentice-Hall Inc., 1973. Pp 83-95.

PardT parodies *PhyT*, capitalizing on two flaws in the Physician's performance and aniticipating several motifs (e.g., the *feend*, notion of bad company, idea of grace, gifts of Fortune and nature, the unknown hour of God's smiting and the moral). Critics since Kittredge have read the Pardoner's performance as a mode of characterization neglecting the qualities of the tale itself. *PardT* is good because it is eloquent (maintaining ethos and style which gather force); intelligent (in its distinguishings and combinings); significantly expressive (with the circumstances of its telling adding to the meaning); unified (in its controlled set of complicated relationships); and instructive (whether the tale is a true analogy to the world or a vain exercise of the imagination). Chaucer asks whether the business of telling tales makes sense from the doomsday perspective or the perspective of natural reason. As a literary artist, the Pardoner uses his craft with his eye cast to the earth. 'If the tale ... in the mouth of the Pardoner ... is true, we may be exercising our imagination to no end, or, like the Pardoner, to mean ends .... The tale is a trial of faith'(p 95).

876   Condren, Edward I. 'The Pardoner's Bid For Existence.' 1973. See **400**.

In *PardP*, the Pardoner affects an inner reality of sinfulness. He proclaims himself an avaricious lecher but reveals himself as neither; rather, he is committed to displaying technical virtuosity as a performer (p 191). The digression consists of homilies designed to stimulate interest and lead into the tale. *PardT* suggests universality, examining the consequences of human action. In *PardT*, the Pardoner seeks to realize a new reality as a thoroughly immoral man capable of persuading others he is a man of God to whom they should give money. He undermines this image, however, by his admission of role-playing and his insistence on moral corruption. The Old Man and the three revellers offer portraits of his unadorned private and his professional life respectively. The Pardoner turns the question of his moral responsibility into the material of art, and in so doing, he has 'sacrificed his moral essence'(p 205). The Pardoner continues a 'figure of utter tragedy, tormented by the self-destructiveness of his game' (p 205).

877   Delasanta, Rodney. 'Sacrament and Sacrifice in The *Pardoner's Tale*.' *AnM* 14(1973), 43-52.

Delasanta considers the implications of recognizing the Pardoner's 'ale and cake' (lines 321-2) as a Eucharist (**820, 838, 869**) by going directly to the language of the medieval Mass. The dual notions of Sacrament and Sacrifice are inseparable: the Eucharist is interpreted 'as a cultic meal which ritualistically represents the Sacrifice of the Cross'(p 45). In a brilliant ironic achievement, Chaucer parodies this teaching through his conjunction of death and meal. The three rioters, sworn in a trinitarian paradigm, extend the parody, becoming Priest and Victim as each offers the other in sacrifice and is slain by his fellows. Thus, Chaucer is 'transubstantiating' the forms of the Mass 'into the eucharist of his own art'(p 52).

878   DeNeef, A. Leigh. 'Chaucer's *Pardoner's Tale* and The Irony of Misinterpretation.' *JNT* 3(1973), 85-96.

The four parts of the Pardoner's performance—the Introduction, Prologue, Tale and Invitation—form a coherent narrative designed to illustrate the inadequate understanding which results from too narrow an angle of vision. Rejected by the pilgrims (the first time the pilgrims have so acted collectively), the Pardoner agrees to a moral tale but complicates the issue by first confessing his depravity. His confession is at the basic level 'a blatant instance of pride ... and *cupiditas*'(p 87). If the Pardoner can still get the pilgrims to respond to his invitation after having revealed his depravity, he will have proved himself *a noble ecclesiaste*. On another level, the invitations can be explained as part of his rote performance. The rioters have ironically found death by taking metaphoric descriptions literally: the remainder of *PardT* is 'an ironic working out in the rioters' own literal terms of what has already happened to them tropologically'(p 90). The meeting with the Old Man extends the literal versus metaphoric duality. The shift from exemplum to invitation actually occurs at line 904. The Host's rejection continues the play on literal and metaphoric. Spokesperson for the pilgrims, the Host sees only the physical eunuchry; symbolically, Bailly rejects the Pardoner's moral words because he fails to see the *sententia* for the *littera*. Not only the rioters and Pardoner but also the Host and pilgrims fail to heed the Augustinian injunction to recognize the symbolic level (p 92). The ultimate ironic twist might be that here the pilgrims reach a collective 'spiritual low-point on the tropological pilgrimage'(p 92). The Knight, in forcing the kiss, forces the Host to enact a 'literal reversal of the latter's metaphoric rejection'(p 92).

879 Elbow, Peter. *Oppositions in Chaucer*. Middletown, Connecticut: Wesleyan University Press, 1973.

Chaucer has an ingrained tendency to see oppositions in such a way as to affirm both sides. The Pardoner, 'the most intriguing and haunting character in Chaucer' (p 135), is endowed with Chaucer's 'own capacity for complex irony, but not with his capacity for relinquishing it'(p 14). The Pardoner and Chaucer have similar vocations (preaching and poetry), give an ironic twist to rhetoric, and enjoy watching themselves. In the solicitation, the Pardoner shows himself 'a compulsive ironist' (p 137) as he reveals the fraudulence of his words and still makes them perform. Unable to relinquish irony, the Pardoner 'seems trapped behind his mask' (p 139). The Pardoner's sin is '*mere sophistication—sophistication never relinquished*' (p 139). In damning himself, the Pardoner plays God; the Host's gross response provides relief: '[t]he body seems to be an antidote both for irony and for paralysis'(p 140).

880 Eliason, Norman E. 'Personal Names in the *Canterbury Tales*.'

1973. See **401**.

Chaucer's consummate control of names is seen in the way he uses them. Not naming pilgrims enabled Chaucer to stress professions thereby setting up dramatic relations and connecting tales to narrators. The anonymity of the revellers in *PardT* converts a possibly inconsequential exposé of folly into 'an ominous revelation of human depravity' (p 150).

881 Elliott, Ralph W.V. 'The Pardoner's Sermon and Its *Exemplum.*' [editor's title] In *Twentieth Century Interpretations of the Pardoner's Tale: A Collection of Critical Essays*. Ed. Dewey R. Faulkner. Englewood Cliffs, New Jersey: Prentice-Hall Inc., 1973. Pp 23-32. See **794**.

882 Faulkner, Dewey R. *Twentieth Century Interpretations of the Pardoner's Tale: A Collection of Critical Essays*. 1973. See **402**.

Contains introductory essay and seven modern interpretive essays: Janet Adelman, 'That We May Leere Som Wit,' pp96-106 (**874**); Stephen A. Barney, 'An Evaluation of the *Pardoner's Tale,*'pp 83-95 (**875**); Bertrand Bronson, 'The Pardoner's Confession,' pp15-22 (**764**); Ralph W.V. Elliott, 'The Pardoner's Sermon and Its *Exemplum,*'pp 52-66 (**794**); David V. Harrington, 'Narrative Speed in the *Pardoner's Tale*,' pp 33-42 (**831**); Robert P. Miller, 'Chaucer's Pardoner, the Scriptural Eunuch, and the *Pardoner's Tale,*'pp 43-69 (**747**); and John M. Steadman, 'Old Age and *Contemptus Mundi* in the *Pardoner's Tale,*'pp 70-82 (**790**). Additionally he excerpts 'view points' by the following: George Lyman Kittredge (**681**), Germaine Dempster (**701**), G.D. Josipovici (**796**), Nancy H. Owen (**822**), Rosemond Tuve (**815**), and D. W. Robertson, Jr. (**776**). Introduction (pp 1-14): After a discussion of the role and status of pardoners in the fourteenth century and an overview of the Pardoner's appearance in *CT*, Faulkner notes that the tales preceding *PardT* prepare the reader for the more serious levels of *PardT* where evil is simultaneously 'far more complex and far simpler'(p 7) than in the two preceding tales. In *PardT*, 'contradictions do not ultimately resolve in paradox; they cancel each other out, leaving only the highly ambiguous kiss at the end' (p 11). The Pardoner begins as a human being and progressively becomes the image of vice.

883 Frost, William. 'What is a Canterbury Tale?' *WHR* 27(1973), 39-59.

Briefly citing critical positions on *PardT* as examples of the move away from allegorization (**796, 827**), Frost offers his criteria for a *CT*, criteria he finds best fulfilled by the performances of the Wife, Nun's Priest and Pardoner (p 56). Frost defines a *CT* as: a narrative of a certain length, composed in a specific literary form, told by a pilgrim on the way to Canterbury in a specific year, told in a manner that illustrates or complicates the teller's individuality, with contents that bear a thematic or other relationship to materials in tales told by other pilgrims, often illuminating one or more medieval forms of narrative, and related to surrounding tales by contrast or some oblique way.

884 Knight, Stephen. *The Poetry of the Canterbury Tales.*1973. See **618**.
In *PardT*, Knight notes the sensational description of the opening 9-line sentence, the direct harangue and the moral analysis as the Pardoner draws devout conclusions from sensational material, skillfully linking the sermon to the exemplum which follows. At the close of the exemplum, the Pardoner speaks with simple honesty (line 918) then moves on with 'comic bravado' (p 134) and self-caricature. The Pardoner's final pain results in silent fury which is manifest in the monosyllabic line 'with alliterating slowness' (line 957, p 134). In the end, the impression of the prologue and tale dominate over the final silence. The Pardoner's performance works at the level of exemplum, revelation of personality, and as masterful poetry.

885 —. *Rymyng Craftily: Meaning in Chaucer's Poetry*. Sydney: Angus and Robertson, 1973.
In a work directed to the detailed working of poetry and the manner in which meaning is 'directly created by the nature and the modulation of the poetry' (p xiii), Knight notes *ManT* resembles *PardT* with slow digressive development followed by a rapid sequence of narration (p 180). The structural similarities between *NPT* and *PardT*—the sequence of long theoretical discussion followed by brisk action and the juxtaposition of closing views—invite analysis (p 206). See **819**.

886 Mehl, Dieter. *Geoffrey Chaucer: Eine Einführung in seine erzählenden Dichtungen*. 1973. Trans/rev as *Geoffrey Chaucer: An Introduction to His Narrative Poetry.*1986 [cited here]. See **404**.
PardT is a demonstration of 'brilliant demagogy' (p 146) which, though appropriate to any pardoner, is tailored as a subordinate part of the Pardoner's total performance. For *PardP*, see **619**.

887 Rowland, Beryl. *Animals With Human Faces: A Guide to Animal Symbolism*. 1973. See **406**.
Treats the symbolic meaning of rat and horse. For *PardP*, see **620**.

888 Wilson, James H. 'The Pardoner and the Second Nun: A Defense of the Bradshaw Order.' *NM* 74(1973), 292-6.

The 'Idleness Prologue' links *SNT* and *PardT* by attempting to reclaim the good the tale might have done without the confusion of the solicitation. Rejecting idleness and bad 'entente,' *SNT* warns against succumbing, like the Pardoner, 'to the bait of his own feigned worldliness in a trap which he thought would catch the pilgrims' (p 295). Both tales present trios unafraid of death. Wilson seeks to establish a definite position for the 'floating' Fragment VI (p 292). He argues in favor of the Bradshaw order offering an examination of the 'Idleness Prologue'(p 296) of the Second Nun (the only lines in the tale for which there is no known literary source) to demonstrate Chaucer's intention of linking the tales of the Pardoner and Second Nun. The Second Nun seeks to reclaim the good that should have resulted from *PardT* had it not become lost in the confusion of the solicitation. In the opening four stanzas, she clarifies what the Pardoner left vague and negative and sets up *SNT* where the legend of St. Cecilia will contrast *ydelnesse* and *leveful bisynesse*. The Pardoner uses *idle* three times: *PardP* (line 446) and *PardT* lines 638 and 642. The rioters in *PardT* live lives of idleness physically and spiritually. Echoing the Pardoner's use of *entente*, the Second Nun moves to replace the Pardoner's emphasis on sinfulness with *leveful bisynesse*: *Wel ogten we to doon al oure entente/ Lest that the feend thurgh ydelnesse us hente* (lines 6-7, p 295). She proceeds to warn that man can be caught unaware as were the rioters and the Pardoner who was so blind that he succumbed 'to the bait of his own feigned worldliness in a trap which he thought would catch the pilgrims' (p 295). Both *PardT* and *SNT* present trios unafraid of Death: the rioters of *PardT* do not expect to find Death whereas the martyrs in *SNT* do. Finally, the Second Nun states that people 'like the Pardoner and his rioters live only *to slepe, and for to ete and drynke,/ And to devouren al that othere swynke*' (lines 20-1, p 295). See **761**.

889 Amoils, E.R. 'Fruitfulness and Sterility in the *Physician's* and *Pardoner's Tales. ESA* 17(1974), 17-37.

PhyT and *PardT* complement one another thematically: the account of Virginia's decision to accept death before the loss of virginity enriches the reader's understanding of the Pardoner and offsets his tale of rioters who pursue and find death. *Fructuousnesse* (p 17), spiritual fecundity, is a major theme of *CT*. The linked themes of spiritual fertility and the defeat of death run through the fragment; yet, the Pardoner, who derives from Faux Semblant, is impotent physically and spiritually. His falseness contrasts directly with Virginia's integrity. The Pardoner is a mockery of the office he claims—guide to the life-giving tree of Penitence. He is the inversion of the Parson. The Pardoner takes words and 'drains them of their reality' (p 36) rendering them *accident* without *substance* (p 36). The Host called for *triacle* after the *PhyT*; the Pardoner delivers venom.

890   Anderson, J[ohn]. J., ed. *Chaucer: The Canterbury Tales: A Casebook.* London: Macmillan, 1974.
Includes: Bishop, Ian. 'The Narrative Art of the Pardoner's Tale.' Pp 209-21. See **816**.

891   Benson, Larry D., ed. *The Learned and The Lewed: Studies in Chaucer and Medieval Literature.* Cambridge: Harvard University Press, 1974.
Includes: Brookhouse, Christopher. 'In Search of Chaucer: The Needed Narrative,' pp 67-80 (**893**); Reinecke, George F. 'Speculation, Intention, and the Teaching of Chaucer,' pp 81-93.

892   Brewer, Derek, ed. *Geoffrey Chaucer.* Cambridge: D.S. Brewer, 1974. Republished as *Writers and Their Background: Geoffrey Chaucer.* London: Bell, 1974; Athens, Ohio: Ohio University Press, 1975; 1990.
Includes: Benson, L.D. 'A Reader's Guide to Writings on Chaucer' pp 321-51 (**155**); Manzalaoui, Mahmoud. 'Chaucer and Science' pp 224-61 (**238**); Shepherd, Geoffrey. 'Religion and Philosophy in Chaucer' pp 262-89 (**901**); Kolve, V. A. 'Chaucer and the Visual Arts' pp 290-320 (**895**).

893   Brookhouse, Christopher. 'In Search of Chaucer: The Needed Narrative.' In *The Learned and the Lewed: Studies in Chaucer and Medieval Literature.* Ed. Larry D. Benson. Cambridge: Harvard University Press, 1974. Pp 67-80.
Though Chaucer portrays the Pardoner's 'need to speak as if he stood by himself,' (p 75) the Pardoner, fearing loss of grace, makes the rioters extensions of himself. Though the Pardoner recognizes victory over death is through Christ, he is unable to act for his own salvation. The Old Man's denial of flesh and insistence on grace is 'the Pardoner's own self-condemnation'(p 77). Chaucer makes *PardT* so appropriate to his inner needs 'the illusion of an autonomous speaker' coexists with

the 'artist's implicit judgment of the speaker'(p 77).

894 Kernan, Anne. 'The Archwife and The Eunuch.' 1974. See **408**.

The Pardoner expresses an outlook in common with the Wife of Bath (C line 403; D line 414). Their prologues and tales possess a formal similarity: the Pardoner presents a sample sermon and exemplum; the Wife presents a 'sort of sermon' (p 4) together with an exemplum of her unorthodox view. Their 'confessions' reveal the irony of speakers exemplifying virtually every charge against their type, be it Wife or Pardoner. Likewise, they each claim false accusation as one of their methods. *WBT* and *PardT* are among the most profoundly reflective of their tellers in *CT*. Each incorporates a mysterious character associated in some way with regeneration: the hag in *WBT* is recognizable as a wish fulfillment fantasy; the Old Man, or *vetus homo*, (**747**) is the Pardoner's comment on himself, a projection of 'unrecognized longings for penitence and renewal'(p 8). The Pardoner's cupidity allies with his eunuchry to ensure both physical and spiritual sterility. For *Interr*, see **524**.

895 Kolve, V. A. 'Chaucer and the Visual Arts.' In *Geoffrey Chaucer*. Ed. Derek Brewer. Cambridge: D.S. Brewer, 1974. Republished as *Writers and Their Background: Geoffrey Chaucer*. London: Bell, 1974; Athens, Ohio: Ohio University Press, 1975; 1990. Pp 290-320.

A chest front carving from 1400 provides the only contemporary 'imagining' of *PardT*. Such material provides 'evidence free from anachronism' and reveals 'what "places" in a literary text exerted the greatest pressure' (p 293) upon the tale's first audience.

896 Manning, Stephen. 'Chaucer's Pardoner: Sex and Non-Sex' *SAB* 39(1974), 17-26.

When the Pardoner is introduced singing a duet with the Summoner (lines 669-74), Chaucer introduces a pattern. When the rioters engage in their fateful meal, the oral motifs of food-drink and swearing are yoked in a parody of a communal meal. The Pardoner's efforts to 'dupe his parishioners' extend the pattern of oral aggression figuratively. The Pardoner's relics, like the sworn brotherhood and, like the Pardoner's absolution, are false appearance which, nevertheless, point 'to an underlying reality'(p 19). The Pardoner presents himself as 'an amusing hypocrite'(p 20), inviting laughter as a 'confirmation of his self-analysis'(p 20). The Pardoner substitutes oral aggression for phallic aggression. In *PardT*, the rioters are diverted from their aggressive intent by greed; so the Pardoner is diverted 'by cupidity, by oral acquisition'(p 23). In his absolution, he functions as a parody of an *alter Christus*. The Old Man is at once the wise old man of folktale and a projection of the Pardoner in his desire for regeneration. The Pardoner speaks sincerely (lines 915-8) before resuming his role as entertainer and embarking on his sales pitch. The Pardoner's tongue is a phallic symbol; Harry Bailly's retort and the pilgrims' laughter serve as oral castration. The pattern of aggression intended by the Pardoner to end with the Host kissing the relics is reversed to become a pattern of reconciliation with the kiss of peace; this reversal suggests a pattern of reconciliation through Christ's pardon. The Pardoner is 'unconsciously in search of pardon'(p 25). He is not the one lost soul: the possibility for repentance remains.

897 Marshall, Carol Ann. 'Love, Salvation and Order in the *Libro de Buen Amor* and *The Canterbury Tales*.' *DAI* 35(1974), 3780A. Saint Louis University, 1973.

CT, like the *Libro de Buen Amor*, is structured around the problem of love; the poet's seeking how to love properly is a search for the relationship between experience and ideal, a search expressed in allegory. The allegorical frame of *PardT* is established by Paul's Epistle to the Ephesians and operates through images and narrative parallels (e.g., old man/ new man). Recognizing the allegory in *PardT* leads to a severe judgment of the behavior of the Pardoner.

898 Millichap, Joseph R. 'Transubstantiation in the Pardoner's Tale.' *RMR* 28(1974), 102-8.

Millichap explores how the imagery of transubstantiation and transformation in *PardP* and *PardT* demonstrate 'the failure to transform God's material gifts into spiritual works' (p 107). By offering blessings as a reward for those who offer gifts (A lines 710-4), the Pardoner sacrilegiously appropriates part of the congregation's offering. The theme of God's gifts misused is carried through the Pardoner's inversion of transubstantiation (lines 538-9), the depiction of bread and wine in the tavern together with the sinful consequences of their abuse (lines 467-70), and the Pardoner's scatological imagery (lines 526-8). The story of the rioters revolves around transformation: the youngest rioter changes wine to poison; the rioters' lives turn material goods into moral poison.

899 Norton-Smith, John. 'The Canterbury Tales.' *Geoffrey Chaucer*. London: Routledge & Kegan Paul, 1974. Pp 79-159.

CT exemplifies a continuous narrative pattern built on contending views. The Pardoner's altercation with the Host extends a pattern initiated with *CkP*. *Phy-PardL* represents 'a basic Chaucerian method of construction: the recurring pairing arrangements indicating that some of the tales have been deliberately written in contrasting "twins" with a single link section between them' (p 97). In terms of a reading version, the seventh section of narrative (2,199 lines) begins with *PhyT*, and takes in the C group and the D group as far as *WBT*, a major sequence in the narrative.

900 Pittock, Malcolm. '*The Pardoner's Tale* and the Quest for Death.' *EIC* 24(1974), 107-23.

PardT is a searching treatment of the difference between notional awareness and substantial knowledge. *PardP* and *PardT* is the most complex of a series of tales told by clerics who lack understanding of their significance. The rioters' quest blasphemously parodies Christ's mission to abolish death and functions as an inversion of any secular undertaking directed to the will of God. Though the literal-minded rioters cannot understand the warnings given, the symbolic overtones of their words and deeds reveal their psychology. Pittock suggests: 'Chaucer saw that the intellectually lucid evil of the Pardoner is made possible when an office which is fundamentally corrupt receives institutional approval ...' (p 123).

901 Shepherd, Geoffrey. 'Religion and Philosophy in Chaucer.' In *Geoffrey Chaucer*. Ed. Derek Brewer. Cambridge: D.S. Brewer, 1974. Republished as *Writers and Their Background: Geoffrey Chaucer*. London: Bell, 1974; Athens, Ohio: Ohio University Press, 1975; 1990. Pp 262-89.

In Chaucer's religious writings, his inventiveness is revealed 'chiefly by his ability to present familiar material with a new confidence and an unexpected verbal enrichment' (p 270). The Pardoner's associations may have been religious but his interest to Chaucer lay in morals and manners. 'A moral indifferentism in principle appears to accompany sympathetic observation and acceptance of the consequences of human action' (p 272).

902 Thorpe, James. *A Noble Heritage: The Ellesmere Manuscript of Chaucer's Canterbury Tales*. 1974; 2nd ed., 1978. See **158**.

Thorpe discusses the Ellesmere portraits and comments that *PardT* is a good story, full of twists and ironies, and a 'slightly horrifying fascination like a Dance of Death' (p 3; 6). The contemporary reader saw in it an allegory on the idea that the love of money is the root of all evil. The action turns on the line *No longer then after Death they sought* (line 772), suggesting on one level that they abandoned their search for death and on another that they had found death. John Huston's *The Treasure of the Sierra Madre* is a simplified version on the same theme; a Somerset Maugham story quoted by John O'Hara in *Appointment in Samarra* provides a parallel about finding Death. The sophistication of *PardT* can serve as an antidote to the poison of modern cultural pride. For *PardP*, see **411**.

903 Black, Robert Ray. 'Sacral and Biblical Parody in Chaucer's *Canterbury Tales.*' *DAI* 35(1975), 6090A. Princeton University Dissertation, 1974.

Parody of sacral sign and symbols in *PardT* produces poetry that can be read allegorically to promote Christian charity. *PardT* parodies the real presence of Christ and the unity of the Church. The Host (*hostia*), as one soaked in wine, is called to offer himself. [Not seen.]

904 Deligiorgis, Stavros. 'Poetics of Anagogy for Chaucer: *the Canterbury Tales.*' In *Geoffrey Chaucer: A Collection of Original Articles*. Ed. George D. Economou. New York: McGraw-Hill, 1975. Pp 129-41.

The reader must be a pilgrim. *PardT* is both cynical and dialectical throughout. The Host's 'explosion' is 'the victory of dialectics suggesting the checking game between statement and life' (p 133). Forgiveness being a dialectic, the Host and Pardoner are reconciled. By acknowledging deceit, the Pardoner earns the grace of the Host. 'The two are one theme; *the* theme, and what makes as much "literature" of readers or listeners as they, in their passivity, make of it' (p 133).

905 Donaldson, E. Talbot. 'Chaucer's Three "P's": Pandarus, Pardoner, and Poet.' 1975. See **413**.

In *PardT*, Chaucer fuses 'the impulse to art' with 'art's frustration' (p 297). In the solicitation, the Pardoner blurs the distinction between fiction and reality thereby destroying himself.

906 Economou, George D. *Geoffrey Chaucer: A Collection of Original Articles*. New York: McGraw-Hill, 1975. [Contemporary Studies in Literature].

A collection of seven pedagogical essays, introduction and selected bibliography intended for undergraduates, teachers and specialists. Items related to the Pardoner include: George D. Economou, 'Introduction:

Chaucer the Innovator,' pp 1-14 (**906**); Stavros Deligiorgis, 'Poetics of Anagogy for Chaucer: the *Canterbury Tales,'* pp 129-41 (**904**); Robert Hanning, 'The Theme of Art and Life in Chaucer's Poetry,'pp 15-36 (**909**); Esther C. Quinn, 'Religion in Chaucer's *Canterbury Tales*: A Study in Language and Structure,'pp 55-73 (**916**); and Winthrop Wetherbee, 'Some Intellectual Themes in Chaucer's Poetry,' pp 75-91 (**920**). Introduction (pp 1-14): Kittredge focused attention on the complexity of interaction among Chaucer's characters; his study of the Host and Pardoner illustrates the 'singularity and subtlety of his insights' (p 5). Chaucer's pairing of pilgrim and tale 'is a completely *new* way of disposing of a variety of stories within a larger narrative frame such as a pilgrimage' (p 10). A full understanding of the pilgrim-tale relationship entails a consideration of the portrait of the Pardoner in the *GP*, his interruption of the Wife of Bath, *PardP*, and *PardT*.

907   Engelhardt, George J. 'The Ecclesiastical Pilgrims of the *Canterbury Tales*: A Study in Ethology.' 1975. See **415**.
'The stereotype of the *illusor* determines the riotous existence of the young prodigals' in *PardT* (p 308). The Pardoner, 'self-proclaimed fellow of the perpetually juvenile' (p 310) resembles the rioters. Since the Pardoner veils his homosexuality, 'Chaucer wishes his audience to infer that the Day of Wrath' (p 310) approaches but is not yet imminent.

908   Gallick, Susan. 'A Look at Chaucer and His Preachers.' 1975. See **525**.
Chaucer employs the sermon to explore character and relationships; he is particularly interested in the central role of the preacher both as teacher and example of morality. Gallick discusses the preaching of the Wife of Bath, Reeve, Friar, Summoner, Nun's Priest and Pardoner. The Pardoner tries unsuccessfully to fulfill the two demands of medieval poetry and sermons—*solaas and sentence*—and, in the process, antagonizes everyone. 'His sermon is a joke on preaching technique which turns on the audience's knowledge of sermon conventions: and it is a moral tale told by an immoral man'(p 467). The Pardoner creates two audiences—the *lewed* and the pilgrim audience—but in confiding to one his methods of deceiving the other, he violates the most basic tenets of medieval preaching. The Pardoner's sermon is so persuasive, even to an audience aware he is a fraud, that his efforts to have the pilgrims laugh with him at his *lewed* audience backfire. At the close of the exemplum, the Pardoner makes a transition from his imaginary

church audience to his pilgrim audience (line 915). The Pardoner misjudges his audience's capacity to separate morality and jest. The Pardoner elicits the pilgrims' fears and the result is 'a farcical performance which collapses in anger and misunderstanding' (p 470). For *Phy-PardL*, see **550**; for *PardP*, see **624**.

909 Hanning, Robert W. 'The Theme of Art and Life in Chaucer's Poetry.' In *Geoffrey Chaucer: A Collection of Original Articles*. Ed. George D. Economou. 1975. Pp 15-36.

Chaucer exploits the scheme of *CT* to address the nature of his art and its relation to *kynde*. The Pardoner, who is insufficient physically, sartorially, and morally, is, nevertheless, effective financially. Thus, Chaucer suggests that art does not need a moral base in experience to succeed. By juxtaposing the 'deceitful virtuosity' (p 32) of the Pardoner with the narrator's claim to be truthful in the *GP*, Chaucer makes an ambiguous statement about the relation of art to truth.

910 Hatcher, Elizabeth R. 'Life Without Death: The Old Man in Chaucer's *Pardoner's Tale*.' *ChauR* 9(1975), 246-52.

Chaucer treated the Old Man as he treated the pilgrims: he made the Old Man define his own meaning by his behavior in a meaningful context (p 246). To understand the Old Man it is better to concentrate on his dramatic function within a context (cf **793, 828**) than to explain him as a static symbol (Death [**681, 728**]; Old Age [**711**]; the *vetus homo* [**747**]); or as a motif with analogues (the Wandering Jew [**228**]; Odin [**226**]). The context for the Old Man's entry (line 713) is the rioters' drunken plan to slay death, an example of a recurrent narrative theme, the 'rash wish' (p 248). The Old Man enters as if in answer to the oath *Deeth shal be deed* (line 710); he is a *reductio ad absurdum* of their wish (p 248). Spiritually blind, the rioters fail to hear the Old Man's instructive answers (lines 721-32) to their questions. The Old Man as a figure warning against folly has literary counterparts (e.g., Elde in *Piers Plowman*, the Struldbruggs in *Gulliver's Travels*) (p 249). Chaucer blends in the Old Man two figures linked with the 'rash wish'(p 247): the traditional figures of the aged person who cannot die and the old man who warns the hero of his folly.

911 Havely, N[icholas]. R., ed. *The Friar's, Summoner's and Pardoner's Tales from The Canterbury Tales*. 1975. See **102**.

Nearly all *PardT* is a sermon (lines 175-627). The Pardoner draws attention to his skill; he creates 'a kind of "mirror-effect" within the

Tale'(p 31) by invoking an imaginary audience. The rioters are broadly representative figures with whom the pilgrim audience is meant to feel guilty identification. Typified by youth and willful ignorance, the rioters are deaf to the Old Man; their quest simulates a 'speeded-up journey through life' (p 34). The Pardoner's presentation of Death as 'a "sly thief" is more subtly menacing' (p 35) than most medieval representations of Death. The Pardoner overreaches when he treats the pilgrims as an extension of his imaginary audience. The Host's rebuff can be seen as necessary to offset the fascination the Pardoner may have. With the kiss, the Pardoner is re-admitted to the ranks of the pilgrims and we are reminded that the pilgrimage represents 'individual souls winding along the road towards judgment' (p 39). For Pardoner, see **423**; for *PardP*, see **625**.

912 Joseph, Gerhard. 'The Gifts of Nature, Fortune, and Grace in The *Physician's*, *Pardoner's* and *Parson's Tale.*' 1975. See **551**.
Chaucer's view of the *goodes* of Nature and Fortune is clear from *ParsT* where the classification is threefold and includes Grace (lines 450-5). Though Ruggiers (**800**) notes the source, he oversimplifies in dividing the non-Christian context of *PhyT* with its evils resulting from Fortune and Nature from the Christian emphasis of *PardT* with its abuse of the gift of Grace. The Pardoner's performance concerns itself with the abuse of Fortune: *richesse, hyghe degrees of lorshipes, [and] preisynges of the peple* (line 453). *PardP* suggests that Nature as much as Fortune has been responsible for his success. The force of Fortune is seen in the exemplum 'which so ironically and, at the same time, broadly recapitulates his own vices and defines his own false gods' (p 243). The unexpected discovery of gold by the *three riotours* is representative of Fortune's dealings. From the Host's words 'concerning the gifts of Fortune and Nature which can often cause death (as they do, respectively, in the two tales)' (p 243), we infer a meaning different from either taken in isolation as well as from the Parson's view which warns that pride sometimes follows these human goods. Group C raises Grace to a higher category than the other two. The 'anti-saint's life' of *PardT* (p 244) argues for the absence of the third and most important gift for those blinded by Fortune and pride.

913 Mandel, Jerome. '"Boy" as Devil in Chaucer.' *PLL* 11(1975), 407-11.
When Chaucer uses the word *boy*, the context consistently evokes

'malicious or demonic overtones'(p 407) extraneous to the Middle English *churl*. Though the meaning of 'boy' in *PardT* (line 670) is servant, his dramatic function suggests more. He informs the rioters of their friend's death, is knowledgeable about death, and advises them (line 683). His speech becomes the impetus for the rioters' action; thus he joins a tradition of 'helpful, knowledgeable, informative, usually smiling guides who lead the unsuspecting gently to hell'(p 410). The appearance of the boy is neither necessary nor derived from source material. Perhaps, he balances the Old Man: both know death and together provide 'a generational frame' (p 410) for the rioters. Perhaps, they are different guises of a shape-shifting fiend. The *boy*, as fiend, ironically works as the agent of God to bring the rioters to their appointed end.

914 Owen, Charles A., Jr. 'The Transformation of a Frame Story: The Dynamics of Fiction.' In *Chaucer at Albany*. Ed. Rossell Hope Robbins. New York: Burt Franklin and Co., 1975. Pp 125-46.

Some contradictions in *CT* are evidence of growth: Owen suggests *CT* develops from a collection of stories to a 'drama of contrasting visions' and, ultimately, to a story-telling contest (p 125). *PardP* and *PardT*, together with the Marriage Group, reveal the drama of conflicting visions. Positing a return journey, Owen places Group C on Day 3, the first day of the return. The Pardoner's performance 'serves as gloss on his own portrait' (p 138): his confession is distinguished by histrionics, admission of villainy and distraction; his sermon is an exemplum spawning further exempla; in the end, he is unable to exempt himself from the judgment of Death or the vulgar censure of the Host.

915 Parsigian, Elise K. 'A Note on the Conclusion of *The Pardoner's Tale.*' *Rackham Literary Studies* 6(1975) 51-4.

More than act of reconciliation or an example of comic irony, the Knight's call for a kiss of reconciliation restores 'the group's faith and its illusions' (p 53). The Host recognizes that, though justified, his outburst is destructive of the community. With the kiss, the Host and Pardoner 'reaffirm faith in the unknown; they reinforce the necessary illusion of protective and holy management in the real world through an hierarchical order which affords compassion and grace to all, even the Pardoner' (p 54).

916 Quinn, Esther C. 'Religion in Chaucer's Canterbury Tales: A Study in Language and Structure.' 1975. See **418**.

Unlike the primarily religious poets, Dante and Langland, Chaucer presents a paradox. To study religion in Chaucer one can examine the religious elements that interested Chaucer considering the relationship between religious language and religious structure and analyzing the way some of the religious elements appear as language and structure in several *CT*. Chaucer uses pilgrimage as both a concept and a structure. The primary identity of about one-third of the pilgrims is established in relation to the Church: the Pardoner, like the Summoner, has taken no vows but operates in the name of the Church. The extent of their effectiveness is a measure of corruption of the fourteenth- century English church. The Host alternately engages in quarrels (as with the Pardoner), and acts as peacemaker. All *CT* contain religious language and are structured so as to support a moral position. *PardT* is 'an imaginative projection of deception, betrayal, and death ...'(p 69). Like the religious tales, *PardT* is serious and aimed at the exposure of vice.

917 Scheps, Walter. '"*Up roos oure Hoost, and was oure aller cok*": Harry Bailly's Tale-Telling Competition.' *ChauR* 10(1975), 113-28.
Harry Bailly's masculinity, one of his salient characteristics, is articulated in his crude response to the Pardoner, the 'least masculine of men'(p 115). *PardT*, though it follows Harry's explicit dictum in telling *Of aventures that whilom han bifalle*, cannot be the winner of the competition since Harry humiliates him at the close of the tale and the Pardoner, in response to the *gentils'* protest, leaves off his plan to tell a merry tale.

918 Taitt, Peter S. *Incubus and Ideal: Ecclesiastical Figures in Chaucer and Langland*. 1975. See **419**.
More significant than the sermon structure of *PardT* is the implicit satire of the avaricious Pardoner preaching against greed. The Pardoner's 'indiscretion' at the end of the tale cannot be explained by drink; only at lines 322 and 328 does the Pardoner have recourse to drink (pp 44-5). The Pardoner seeks to restore a 'mirthful mood' with the sale of relics: 'But it is precisely the failure of the Pardoner's listeners to separate art from reality that accounts for their silence and the Host's outrage' (p 46). With the Host's attack, 'the king of *quaestors* has become the victim of his own quest' (p 47).

919 Taylor, Dennis. 'The Confidence Man From *The Pardoner's Tale* to *The Fall*.' *ArQ* 31(1975), 73-85.
The confidence man entwines the issue of confidence in himself and in a set of beliefs. Chaucer's Pardoner poses a dilemma: if the pilgrims

accept his offer of indulgence, they participate 'in idolatry'; if they refuse, they place themselves 'outside of the church'(p 73). The Pardoner, a 'major confidence man' (p 75) employs three types of dilemma, stressing 'means ends dilemmas'(p 74), consistency of truth, and himself as personal light. He seeks to demoralize his victims by exposing an apparent contradiction in their belief (p 75). In the scale of confidence men, the Pardoner is at the top; his success depends on full awareness in his victims creating a crisis of mind and will. The Pardoner attempts to turn Chaucer's balance of fiction and truth by forcing an interpretation of his sermon either as 'pure fiction or idolatrous truth'(pp 84-5). The prologue to *ParsT* defeats the 'destructive dilemma' of the Pardoner's performance 'as we learn to receive it as a serious fiction, an earnest game' (p 85).

920   Wetherbee, Winthrop. 'Some Intellectual Themes in Chaucer's Poetry.' 1975. See **420**.

The Pardoner's calling for Christ's pardon at the conclusion of *PardT* calls attention to the separation between the spirit and the letter of religious authority. For Pardoner, see **426**; for *PardP*, see **631**.

921   David, Alfred. *The Strumpet Muse: Art and Morals in Chaucer's Poetry*. 1976. See **626**.

Chaucer progressively experienced tension between his obligations as a medieval author and his own artistic vision, his 'strumpet Muse'(p 7). The Pardoner is one of several pilgrims who embody ironic images of the poet. The Pardoner and 'his stock' (p 72) appear at the end of the pilgrims. They express in its 'most outrageous form the discrepancy between ideal and reality'(p 72): the Pardoner symbolizes 'the impotence that infected medieval society' (p 71). *PardT* unfolds with objectivity as the Pardoner 'specifically pronounces judgment upon himself' (p 194). The prologue, tale and following episode serve as a morality play. With his cynical confession and blasphemous spirit, the Pardoner intends to shock. His prologue reveals a longing to be part of the community of pilgrims and a perverse desire to remain isolated in sin (pp 196-7). His sample sermon, 'a superb mixture of the sacred and the profane'(p 197), draws a grotesque picture of sinful human nature. The tale presents an implied analogy between the Pardoner and the Old Man, the Old Man revealing the self-destructiveness of evil (p 199) (**747**). The rioters' quest bears an ironic resemblance to the mission the Pardoner abuses. Though *PardT* is diabolical in its intentional blasphemy, the Old Man conveys the Pardoner's 'subconscious appeal for compassion'(p 201). The language of the attempted sale of relics (lines 918-28) indicates the Pardoner is joking, once again insulting the pilgrims by parodying their quest. The chivalrous peacemaking of the Knight, the *miles Christi* redeems the Pardoner's whole performance and leaves open the possibility of the Pardoner's forgiveness by Christ.

• Review by Howell Chickering Jr., *Speculum* 53(1978), 565-7: 'the most perceptive and convincing interpretations in the book are of the Pardoner, his Tale, and *The Nun's Priest's Tale*' (p 567).

• Review by Charles A. Owen, *SAC* 1(1979), 158-63: '[David's] discussion of the Pardoner's performance ... strikes me as the best yet made' (p 162) ...'Nowhere has the figure of the old man been so judiciously assessed and so well integrated into the Pardoner's histrionics' (p 162). Though David sees the Pardoner as a partial spokesman for Chaucer, the fact that Chaucer exposes and forgives the Pardoner 'provides us with an intensely Christian experience, one of the many instances in which fiction has become the testing ground of morality' (p 162).

• Review by Chauncey Wood, *JEGP* 77 (1978), 423-5: David notes that Chaucer balanced '"judgment of sin with love for the sinner"'... Professor David's own response seems to be to love the sinner and to deny the existence of the sin' (p 425). He supports his claim that Chaucer's sympathy extended to the Summoner and Pardoner by claiming that the Summoner '"needs companionship"' (p 425). 'Those who accept the validity of professor David's approach will be enthusiastic about this volume. Those who do not will find *The Strumpet Muse* to be clear, usually cautious and keeping to the middle of the road in criticism of the individual works, often helpful in detailed insights, but hypersensitive to the affective impact of literary creations' (p 425).

922 Friman, Anne. 'Of Bretherhede: The Friendship Motif in Chaucer.' *Innisfree* 3(1976), 24-36.

Friendship between men, which figures significantly in Chaucer's poetry, is, for the most part, destructive. The simulated friendship between the Summoner and the Pardoner derives from evil attracting evil. Within *PardT*, the brotherhood oath is treacherous: evil has again chosen evil; all are destroyed by it.

923 Ginsberg, Warren. 'Preaching and Avarice in The Pardoner's Tale.'

1976. See **627**.

Ginsberg draws upon medieval treatises on preaching together with homiletic material on avarice and relevant exegetical traditions to address the issue of preacher, sermon and avarice in the Pardoner and his Tale. The dicta for preaching sound doctrine included discerning the hidden meaning of the text, but with the Pardoner, a self-confessed unrepentant sinner: 'spiritual understanding is absent, the tangible reality is all' (p 82). The image of the dove invites allegorical interpretation but with the Pardoner it remains literal. The oak, which seems to have been Chaucer's invention in the *PardT* (p 82), symbolizes '*duritia desperationis*, the obduracy of despair' (p 83) in exegetical tradition. Avarice, as the root of evil, was sometimes depicted as the trunk of the tree of the seven deadly sins. The rioters resemble the Pardoner in seeing the tree literally as a locational marker. The Church fathers reconciled 1 Tim. 6:10 with Eccles. 10:15: sin involved a twofold action, a turning away from God in pride and towards a created thing through avarice (p 85). The Pardoner is 'literal because he is avaricious'(p 87). The Old Man is with the Pardoner 'Chaucer's greatest embodiment of the effects of that sin' (p 87). The Old Man has repented; his wandering is his penance (p 91). It is tempting to think of his chest as a money chest (**882**). The Old Man becomes an archetype, a reminder of the effects of avarice. He is 'another text'(p 93), a 'distinguished player' in an 'expiation myth which seems to require some sort of exchange to effect the protagonist's release' (p 92). We see the Old Man at the moment of exchange and release; unlike the rioters, the reader understands, is instructed and moved. For *PardP*, see **627**.

924 Haines, R. Michael. 'Fortune, Nature, and Grace in Fragment C.' 1976. See **552**.

Though Fragment C is 'not a fully articulated segment' of *CT* (p 232), Chaucer consciously developed the gifts of Fortune, Nature and Grace as a unifying theme: the probable revision in the introduction to *PardT*, the additions to the main source of *PhyT*, and probable additions to *PardT* all support this view. To the Host's explicit mention of the gifts of Fortune and Nature, Chaucer added a second mention of the gifts, and to his folktale source for *PardT*, he added homilies on the abuses of the three gifts and the presumptive quest to slay Death. The three homilies can be read as sermons on the temptations of the flesh (gluttony), the world (gambling), and the Devil (swearing): they can also be read as sermons on the abuses of the gifts of Nature, Fortune, and Grace. Similarly, the three rioters constantly participate in the three sins set out in the three homilies. The Old Man serves as a warning against the pursuit of Fortune. In a note, Haines calls attention to a figure analogous to the Old Man in Passus XI (B-text) of *Piers Plowman*; there Elde warns the dreamer to beware of Fortune (p 235, n 22). Verbal echoes in the revisions suggest Chaucer's attention was focused on *ParsT*. *ParsT* offers the most explicit treatment of the triad but the fullest treatment is found in *PhyT* and *PardT*. *PhyT* deals with the power of Grace to aid in overcoming Fortune and Nature; *PardT* with an abuse of all three kinds of gifts (cf **800**). Other aspects of the theme are found in *ManT*, *PrT*, *SNT* and *MkT*.

925   Harrington, Norman. 'Experience, Art, and The Framing of The *Canterbury Tales*.' 1976. See **553**.

When the Pardoner provokes the pilgrims at the close of his tale, he provides another example of 'that thrashing, chaotic world of the frame' (p 198) heightened by its juxtaposition with the ordered working of destiny in that tale of the rioters. The scoundrels in the links are not punished as directly as those in the tales. For *PardP*, see **628**.

926   Howard, Donald R. *The Idea of the Canterbury Tales*. 1976, 1978. Pp 333-87 rpt as 'The Idea of *The Canterbury Tales*'in *Geoffrey Chaucer*. [Modern Critical Views]. Ed. Harold Bloom. New York: Chelsea House Publishers, 1985. Pp 70-104. Pp 354-71 rpt as 'Modernizing Chaucer' in *Geoffrey Chaucer's The Pardoner's Tale*. [Modern Critical Interpretations]. Ed. Harold Bloom. New York: Chelsea House Publishers, 1988. Pp 49-62.

The organizing principle of *CT* is a concatenated binary system of interlace. *PardT*, a grotesquerie, is appropriately set aside in a 'floating' fragment. *PardT* 'bloats up' an exemplum, subsuming digressions on the other sins while focusing on avarice (p 357). Events happen, episodes are more thematic than narrative. The Pardoner is an ironist who cannot heed his own warning: the Old Man's physical plight reflects the Pardoner's spiritual plight. The hiatus the critics have seen following, *I wol yow nat deceyve* (line 918), is a product of the critics not the scene. The ending of *PardT* is consistent with the Pardoner's motive to draw the pilgrims into his power. The aftermath of the solicitation is remarkably succinct: 'there are scarcely thirteen lines anywhere in Chaucer which accomplish more' (p 367). The Pardoner and the Host exchange 'malevolent wishes to castrate each other' (p 367). The Pardoner's silence reveals a loss of will. The Knight's gesture, which treats the Pardoner as the injured party, is symbolical (uniting courtly civility and Christian charity) though not likely a figure of Christian charity; the brevity of the scene produces an abstract quality. Throughout *PardP* and *PardT* tend toward allegory. *PardT* is the only tale whose ending is not in the pilgrim's voice; the Pardoner is distanced and we may hear the naive objectivity of Chaucer the pilgrim or the ironic detachment of Chaucer the man (p 370). The conclusion concludes nothing but convinces readers of its rightness. For Pardoner, see **424**; for *Phy-PardL*, see **555**; for *PardP*, see **629**.

- Review by D. S. Brewer, *ELN* 15(1977), 122-5: 'after all that has come before, Mr. Howard lays rather surprising emphasis on these [the Pardoner and Parson] and other characters as "real," naturalistic characters, and thus seems to revert the kind of implied novelistic or dramatic criteria which he has seemed to be trying to avoid in his earlier chapters' (p 124).
- Review by Charles Blyth, *EiC* 27(1977), 162-70: 'At many points throughout the book, and especially in the discussion of the Pardoner at the end, Mr. Howard offers valuable particular perceptions' (pp 162-3).
- Review by Florence Ridley, *Speculum* 52(1977), 994-7: [M]any will object to the central role assigned to the Pardoner and 'perhaps to the continuing implication that ideas he presents were shared by Chaucer' (p 995).
- Review by D. W. Robertson, *M&H* 8(1977), 252-5: The final chapter emphasizes *PardT* 'which is treated with passionate expressionism, making it sound a little like a modern horror film with intense psychological realism. In general, the author is stubbornly obtuse to stylistic history and the perspective it affords' (p 253).
- Review by Beryl Rowland, *MLQ* 38(1977), 390-5: 'The range of erudition is dazzling ... the reader is constantly prodded to search for further implications on a variety of topics ...' (p 391).
- Review by Robert Cook, *JEGP* 77(1978), 419-23: 'Few will agree ... with Howard that *GP* portraits are arranged in 'convenient mnemonic groups' ... specially when Howard himself admits that this arrangement' is not really an effective *aide-memoire*' (p 421). Some readers may question the derivation of thematic significance

'from what are probably acccidents of textual transmission' (p 422). The extended psychoanalysis of the Pardoner in Chapter 6 is a strong point. Howard anticipates that some will find his reading too modern. 'But it is not upon modern ears alone that this interpretation will jar, but upon those of any time that have preferred Chaucer's poetry to creative theorizing about it (p 997).

- Review by Robert Edwards, *WHR* 30(1976), 260-63: *CT* is about narrators and orators, two of the finest being the Pardoner and the Parson. The Pardoner and Parson transcend their own discourse. 'Ultimately they point up an artistry committed to experience and not just to description. Howard describes that artistry as skillfully as one could hope' (p 263).

- Review by Lee Patterson, *UTQ* 48(1979), 263-82: Patterson argues against the dominance of a pattern of interlace, noting the concern for narrative coherence that becomes 'virtually epiphanic' (p 271) in *PardT*. 'To call the process of finding "thematic interlace," and then to locate it in the text or, worse, in Chaucer's mind, is not to illuminate the text but to obscure it with a methodological muddle' (p 272).

927 Jungman, Robert E. 'The Pardoner's Quarrel with the Host.' *PQ* 55(1976), 279-81.

The quarrel between the Pardoner and the Host provides 'a perfect illustration of St. Paul's argument in 1 Tim. 6—teaching based on *cupiditas* will lead inevitably to quarreling'(p 281). In *PardP*, the Pardoner convicts himself of *cupiditas*; with the solicitation, he fosters it in the pilgrims. The Host's rejection of the Pardoner's solicitation (lines 946-55) demonstrates *invidiae contentiones, conflictationes, blasphemia* and *suspiciones malae* (p 280).

928 Lanham, Richard. *The Motives of Eloquence.* New Haven and London: Yale University Press, 1976.

Chaucer is even more serious than a poet of 'high seriousness'; he 'saw beyond personality to the way it was formed' (p 81). 'Chaucer's final reality is always a context'(p 66), a game embodying a rhetorically ambivalent attitude. 'The game context weighs more heavily than the pilgrimage context' (p 68). The need for an unbroken context explains the Host's motivation in humiliating the Pardoner; the Host is forced to act when the Pardoner crosses the line between game and life.

929 Luengo, A[nthony E.] 'Audience and Exempla in the *Pardoner's Prologue* and *Tale.*' *ChauR* 11(1976), 1-10.

'"'...The Pardoner fits his rural 'sermon' into an 'address' delivered to the Pilgrims'"' **(716)** with tonal and stylistic consequences for the core 'sermon'(p 1). An examination of terms of address, use of naturalistic images, and control of rhetorical color reveals the Pardoner's shifts between *ensamples* addressed to *lewed peple* (lines 485-572; 629-59; 895-915) and a moral tale or single exemplum directed to the pilgrims (lines 463-84; 573-628; 660-894). The tale differs from the *ensamples* in its non-Biblical origin and its contemporaneity. The Pardoner caters to the taste of the pilgrims with the long dialogue between the Old Man and the rioters serving as a dialogue between courtesy and villainy and deriving dramatic context from the pilgrims listening to the Pardoner. If the Pardoner exacts revenge against the *gentils*, he does so with the brief scatological exempla which he works into the tale.

930 Moore, Bruce. '"I wol no lenger pleye with thee": Chaucer's Rejection of the Pardoner.' 1976. See **425**.

The Pardoner sequence is a theatrical projection; *PardP* is at once self-exposure and a 'compulsive defence from self' (p 56). The obsession with death in *PardT* focuses primarily on the Old Man whose dilemma resembles the Pardoner's. The Pardoner's solicitation must be seen as a joke, a continuation of his performance. In selecting the Host, the Pardoner chooses his natural opposite; the Host reduces him to 'absolute impotence' (p 61). The Host's retort and the Knight's call for reconciliation substitute for a conclusion to the Pardoner sequence: they simply get rid of him.

931 Morgan, Gerald. 'The Self-Revealing Tendencies of Chaucer's Pardoner.' *MLR* 71(1976), 241-55.

Morgan argues the superiority of moral over psychological readings demonstrating his claim with a review of passages from *RR*. Chaucer is fundamentally indebted to the moral scheme of the *RR*. Both the space devoted to *PardP* and the disclosure of the Pardoner's motive (lines 329-462) indicate Chaucer's intention to present the true nature of cupidity and the 'spiritual destitution from which it proceeds' (p 252). In *PardT*, Chaucer brings cupidity and falseness into a coherent relationship. The conclusion of *PardT* fulfills literary expectations if measured by moral principles: the Pardoner's silence (lines 956-7) reveals his 'spiritual and moral destitution'(p 255).

932 Patterson, Lee W. 'Chaucerian Confession: Penitential Literature and the Pardoner.' 1976. See **630**.

Penitential theology and literature, specifically the Middle English penitential lyric and the confession of sins in *Piers Plowman*, afford a context for understanding the Pardoner's spiritual condition and his meaning. Coveting admiration, not money, the Pardoner overreaches and reveals a pattern of self destruction in his offer of relics. He is better understood as *arbor infructuosa* than *eunuchus non Dei* (747). Literally, *PardT* is an exemplum on avarice; spiritually, it is a moral allegory figuring despair. The rioters 'enact the Pardoner's life of self-damnation' (p 166): the emotional center of the tale is the old man; only in the symbolic displacement of the *restelees kaityf* does the Pardoner reveal himself. *PardT* 'displaces into fiction the Pardoner's deepest self-understanding, while hiding its meaning from the man who speaks' (p 167). Inviting at once inclusion and exclusion, the offer of relics fulfills the post-confessional part of penance providing a satisfaction that fits the sin. Penitential theology relates *PardT* and *PardP* 'at the deepest levels of language and doctrine' and provides an epilogue which in addition offers 'emotional release from the problems raised' (p 168).

33 Peterson, Joyce. 'With Feigned Flattery: The Pardoner as Vice.' 1976. See **426**.

Where the Vice typically accuses his audience of being as sinful as he, the Pardoner attempts to make the pilgrims, represented by the Host, demonstrate their sinfulness through actions which, even if performed in jest, would prove them cynical and presumptuous. The Pardoner overreaches himself and, like the Vice, becomes the object rather than the agent of ridicule. The pilgrims' laughter reveals their rejection of complicity in his sin. The Pardoner and the Vice are universalized literary renderings of the force for evil and the recognition that sin, once embraced, becomes a motive force. For *PardP*, see **631**.

34 Ruggiers, Paul G. 'A Vocabulary for Chaucerian Comedy: *A Preliminary Sketch*.' In *Medieval Studies in Honor of Lillian Herlands Hornstein*. Eds. Jess B. Bessinger, Jr., and Robert R. Raymo. New York: New York University Press, 1976. Pp 193-225. Rpt in *Chaucer's Humor: Critical Essays*. Ed. Jean E. Jost. New York: Garland Publishing, Inc., 1994. Pp 41-77.

Focusing on plot and character, Ruggiers draws from Aristotle to set forth a vocabulary for discussion of Chaucerian comedy. *PardT*, an ironic comedy, figures among the half of comic tales that are nonsexual, lack lighthearted humor and raise ethical considerations. *PardT* demonstrates the tendency to move from the old law or bondage toward freedom in its unmasking of illusion and hypocrisy. The emphasis of the tale falls on describing the ethos of society as the group of hypocrites is unmasked. *PardT* is discussed under the headings of deception (pp 51-2), compacts and conspiracies (p 55), and laws (p 56). The reader is called upon to recognize a double world, that above which recognizes virtue and the temporal state where characters are interesting for their vices.

935 Thomas, Richard George. 'Conscience and Eloquence: Chaucer's Pardoner.' An Inaugural Lecture. Cardiff: University College, 1976. [Not seen.]

936 Tristram, Philippa. *Figures of Life and Death in Medieval English Literature*. New York: New York University Press, 1976.
Elde appears as a prototype of death in the Old Man of *PardT*. The three rioters are Pride of Life figures impervious to the warnings of corpse, pestilence and the Old Man. In *PardT*, death has no personified being. 'By centering on the figure of Age, and denying the existence of the abstract figure of Death—Chaucer never portrays one—the Pardoner makes death the more terrifying in its omnipresent invisibility' (p 71). The Pardoner makes his point that warnings go unnoticed by arousing and frustrating dramatic expectations. Even the Pardoner has redeeming qualities although his religious and psychological insight intensify the darkness of his character. When the Pardoner makes his solicitation, he too becomes a Pride of Life figure impervious to the warning his tale has offered. With their references to relics, *PardP* and *PardT* reveal the corrupt nature of the materialist tendency of medieval spirituality. The difference between anticipated and sudden death is demonstrated in *PardT*; for the unprepared rioters, death signifies mortality of body and souls.

937 Wenzel, Siegfried. 'Chaucer and the Language of Contemporary Preaching.' 1976. See **526**.
Sermons and the art of preaching contribute to Chaucer's poetic world and enter his idiom: sermon influence is found in story plots, images and the use of technical terms. The 'entire performance of the Pardoner' (p 138) reflects the professional activity of preachers. Despite critical efforts (**689, 697, 704, 750, 772, 827**), however, the *PardT* has not been demonstrated to be patterned on actual sermons. In the case of the Pardoner, as Pratt (**89**) has shown, sermon material may have

been drawn from collections of commonplaces in order to characterize him as a hypocrite.

938 Zacher, Christian K. *Curiosity and Pilgrimage: The Literature of Discovery in Fourteenth-Century England.* 1976. See **428**.

PardT presents refractions of the Pardoner's 'own hateful loves' (p 120)—disorder and curiosity. The rioters seek the curious man's most forbidden goal finding 'the death that comes for those whose inquiry takes them too near the tree of hidden knowledge' (p 120). *PardT* does in microcosm what most *CT* do—shatters the piety of the pilgrimage with the lure of curiosity. The Pardoner would have avoided his fatal error at the end of his tale had he understood the verses on false teachers that precede his text (1 Tim:6). 'Hold your tongue' is a theme variously expressed by *WBT*, *PardT*, *FranT*, and more explicitly by *ManT*.

939 Burlin, Robert B. 'The Pardoner and the Canon's Yeoman: "Gylour Bigyled".' In *Chaucerian Fiction*. Princeton: Princeton University Press, 1977. Pp 169-80.

CT are psychological fictions whose logical coherence lies in the dramatic use of narrators. Often the genre appropriated by a pilgrim carries assumptions that are at odds with the character of the speaker. The Pardoner's genre, though professionally suitable, is perverted: the Pardoner is a 'self-confessed hypocrite'(p 159). The sexually deficient Pardoner senses his true antagonist in the Host. In *PardP*, the Pardoner flaunts his hypocrisy; at the end of the tale, either as a further taunt or because he thinks he can carry his audience along, he equates them with his usual rustic congregation. *PardT* 'absorbs the generic allusion usually found in the pilgrim's prefatory maneuvers'(p 171). The Pardoner consciously explodes the 'secondary pose'(p 171), the authoritative role of the preacher. In *PardP*, the Pardoner inverts his usual procedure, inviting pilgrims backstage 'guiding them into the dressing-rooms of motive and intention' where they must acknowledge a kinship in such performing (171). *PardT* shows the Pardoner's competence as a preacher, while the subject matter reinforces his 'primary pose' as a *riotour* himself (p 171). Though the Pardoner feels himself in control of his tale and his audience, other motifs such as the fellowship of the rioters, the ambiguity of the Old Man, and the rioters' oaths prove otherwise. As the Pardoner culminates his performance with overweening bravado, the Host becomes his 'Old Man,' his secret is revealed, and his world is reduced to 'pitiful physicality' (p 175). Like the Pardoner, the Canon's Yeoman begins by conceding the ill use he has made of verbal ability, then tells a moral tale both self-serving and self-defeating. The Canon's Yeoman, however, is not bright enough for the sustained aggressive hypocrisy of the Pardoner (p 180).

- Review by Robert M. Jordan. 'Romantic Unity, High Seriousness and Chaucerian Fiction.' *Review* (1980), 49-69: ' ... Burlin marshalls his considerable resources of resonant and persuasive language and intricate and subtle argumentation to demonstrate how much tales tell about their tellers. Contradictions, digressions, or inconsistencies in the narrative are dismissed with the reiterated emphasis upon character, particularly the character of the (fictional) teller' (p 61).

940 Cespedes, Frank V. 'Chaucer's Pardoner and Preaching.' 1977. See **429**.

The Pardoner's eloquence is an essential aspect of his character at odds with his evil nature. The Pardoner's text, drawn from Paul's epistle to Timothy, has relevance to the Pardoner's cupidinous nature as well as the plight of the rioters. Though critics have argued that the Pardoner is essentially good (**681, 728, 783, 876**), the fact that his villainy is unmitigated by actions deriving from a better nature justifies his interpretation as 'an archetypal study in some sort of evil' (p 11). From the standpoint of the Pardoner's epistle to Timothy, the danger of the Pardoner's salesmanship is not the sale of relics but the fact that the tale has occupied the pilgrim's attention with 'the profane novelties of words' (1 Tim. 6:11) causing them to forget a more important set of values. *But, sires, o word forgat I in my tale* (line 919) ironically reinforces the division between eloquence and villainous character (lines 459-61). The Pardoner makes the pilgrims aware of the equivocal nature of their choice of storytelling. As the Host calls attention to the moral and physical nature of the Pardoner, he comically reasserts the superiority of deeds over words. The pilgrim's laughter is ambiguous: the object may be the Pardoner, the Host or both. The Knight's request that the Host and Pardoner kiss is 'further acknowledgment that he and the other pilgrims must come to terms with the dilemma' (p 13) that as storytellers they are prey to the evil that Paul warns against and the Pardoner epitomizes. If Chaucer, in the Pardoner, is denying admiration for art apart from the artist's morality, *CT* as a whole with its counterpoise of the Parson, ideal in nature but limited in his capacity to communicate to a fallen world, is an open-ended investigation. For *Interr*, see **527**;

for *PardP*, see **632**. See also **729**.

941 Gardner, John. 'Fragment VI and VII: The Theme of Pride and The Uses of Unreliable Art.' 1977. See **431**.

Fragment VI is a pivotal point in *CT* the tales, looking back to illustrate the principle that justice in the world comes only from God (Frag II-V), and looking forward to the tales on human pride (Frag VII) and the closing tales. From this point on, Grace will be increasingly important. Although both Physician and Pardoner are 'proud, self-loving dissemblers' (pp 298-9), only the Pardoner knows what he is. As storytellers, their human limitations suggests limitations in art. 'The idea, grounded in nominalism, that art is futile ... will become increasingly important' (p 299). In *PardP*, the Pardoner confesses he is a fraud motivated by avarice and guilty of all seven deadly sins. The Pardoner silences the pilgrims 'with a sermon not to be matched elsewhere in English literature'(p 300). Specifying the identity of the Old Man is wrongheaded; he is 'a dark, mysterious figure, suited to the Pardoner's dark legend'(p 386). At the close of his sermon, the Pardoner covers his self-consciousness by 'nasty jokes' about fraudulent relics and pardons and a 'mock homosexual proposition'(*Unbokele anon thy purs* (line 945) (p 302). The resolution of conflict between the Host and the Pardoner comes through the Knight, the upholder of social order and the order of nature; 'the Pardoner is not so much vicious as he is a foolish, ill-behaved child'(p 303). Where *PhyT* makes bad art despite good intentions, *PardT* 'makes good art for mostly base reasons'(p 303). For *Phy-PardL*, see **556**.

- Review by Lee Patterson, *UTQ* 48(1979), 263-82: '... [T]hose of us who are caught between the Scylla of the text and the Charybdis of uninformed undergraduates will rue the day this book first appeared' (p 268). Gardner's reading of the Pardoner surprisingly rejects 'his usual allegorizing on the one occasion when it has enjoyed general acceptance.' The Pardoner figures for him 'simply the anxiety of the repressed homosexual' (p 267).

942 Johnson, Judith A. '*Ye* and *Thou* among the Canterbury Pilgrims.' *MichA* 10(1977), 71-6.

Though entitled by rank to use intimate pronouns, the Knight's use of *thee* in addressing the Pardoner (line 966) is an exception. Perhaps he seeks to soothe the Pardoner by appealing to him as a comrade; more likely, he is establishing social superiority in order to effect a reconciliation.

The Pardoner addresses the Host with the intimate pronoun and the Wife of Bath more formally.

943 Owen, Charles A., Jr. *Pilgrimage and Storytelling in the Canterbury Tales: The Dialectic of "Ernest" and "Game."* 1977. See **433**. *PardT* is, in part, a repercussion of the Wife's monologue (p 168). Fragment C is the only part of *CT* lacking indication of time or place. A position near Fragment D is suggested by the Pardoner's interruption of the Wife and the fact that the drunken Cook's fall (C line 936) may inspire the Pardoner's claim that his presence is the pilgrims good fortune (line 935) gives 'a very slight confirmation' to assigning the Wife and Pardoner 'on the first day of the homeward journey'(p 169). 'The Pardoner's performance best illustrates the set of complex relationships between ernest and game that the pilgrimage generates'(p 216). In *PardT*, the Pardoner seeks validation from an audience more sophisticated than the one he usually bilks. In so doing, he gains satisfaction from doing as game what he normally does for profit. His effort to 'prolong the association' with the pilgrims, mocking with them the relics and pardons, has an unintended and 'shattering result'(p 171). In the sermon on the tavern sins, the Pardoner addresses both audiences simultaneously using morality immorally. Interestingly, the Pardoner does not address lechery. 'The exemplum has swallowed the sermon of which it is ordinarily a part, and then the sermon proceeds to spawn new exempla' in tavern scenes (p 175). When he turns from sermon to story, the Pardoner controls the proportions and detail. The Old Man's quest for death is a comment on the revelers' quest. That the Old Man's impenetrability 'certifies the instinctive grasp of artfulness which Chaucer grants to the Pardoner' (p 180). The exemplum is followed by 'a comedy of misunderstanding and inadvertent insult that unexpectedly exposes the Pardoner's eunuchhood' (p 180-1). With the blessing, he 'mocks for the pilgrims his own venal histrionics ... He has won for himself a temporary release from the avarice that grips his life' (p 181). The episode of the Pardoner's anger concludes a series of incidents that began in *GP* and are directed at concealing the Pardoner's lack. The Pardoner's blindness to his own teaching 'reflects the intensity of his efforts to find some compensating fulfillment for what nature has denied him'(p 182). For *Interr*, see **528**; for *Pard-PhyL*, see **557**; for *PardP*, see **633**.

944 Pichaske, David R. *The Movement of the 'Canterbury Tales':*

Chaucer's Literary Pilgrimage.1977. See **634**.

PardT 'is one of the most artistically dense performances' (p 120) in *CT*, its naturalism more akin to the first half of the pilgrimage. The Pardoner is motivated, in each aspect of his performance, by a desire to overcome his estrangement from the pilgrims. His art proves 'insufficient to its intended ends' (p 130). The failure of the revelers to kill death is frustrated by their corruption. The exhortation against sins is ineffective. The admonitions against drunkenness and gluttony are undermined by the tavern (or alestake) setting of *PardT* (p 130). With his solicitation, the Pardoner oversteps the acceptance he has won with his tale: he wins neither money nor respect. Finally, the kiss represents acceptance of the Pardoner into the pilgrimage.

945 Scheps, Walter. 'Chaucer's Numismatic Pardoner and the Personification of Avarice.' *Acta. The Fourteenth Century*, 4. Ed Paul Szarmach and Bernard S. Levy. Binghamton: Center for Medieval and Early Renaissance Studies, 1977. Pp 107-23.

The verbal, iconographic and symbolic connections between avarice and sterility are represented by the medium of money. Scheps explores the literal and symbolic resonances of fourteenth-century numismatics. The Old Man is the personification of goodness; the Pardoner of Avarice (**739**). The Pardoner is guilty of usury (the unnatural breeding of money) and witchcraft (e.g., ' the worshipping of ymages or of other werkes of "mannes hande",'*Speculum Christiani*, cited p 116) both associated with physical and spiritual barreness. The association of Avarice with the horse and the representation of Avarice alternately as man and woman explain the *geldying* or a *mare* reference (p 120).

946 Bolton, W. F. 'Structural Meaning in The Pardoner's Tale and The Nun's Priest's Tale.' *Lang&S* 11(1978), 201-11.

In the midst of critical disagreement about *CT*, interpretations that begin with types of discourse and discourse signals are on firm ground. With *PardT*, the greatest critical disagreement centers on the final 'benediction' and what follows. If, guided by the mirrored, symmetrical structure of *PardT*, the epilogue is understood as something that occurs in the same fictive plane as *PardP*, the epilogue is seen to extend the game the Pardoner is playing. The Pardoner's invitation betrays, at most, a weakness in his awareness of his sway over the pilgrims. Attributing the symmetry of prologue and epilogue to the Pardoner gives a reading where structure substantiates content.

947 Brewer, Derek. *Chaucer and His World*. New York: Dodd, Mead & Co., 1978. 2nd ed. 1992.

In this work where Brewer intends a vivid impression of Chaucer's life and historical circumstances, he includes illustrations of tavern scenes as well as of a carved chest front held by the Museum of London and portraying three scenes described in *PardT* (p 172; not included in 2nd ed.).

948 Payne, Robert O. 'Chaucer's Realization of Himself as Rhetor.' *Medieval Eloquence: Studies in the Theory and Practice of Medieval Rhetoric*. Ed. James J. Murphy. Berkeley: University of California Press, 1978. Pp 270-87.

Chaucer's self-consciousness as a poet and his study of the rhetorical treatises produced in him an unusual mode of awareness (p 273). With him, the 'idea/language model which *rhetorica*-turned-*poetria* had generated became again something much more like the speaker/language/audience one of earlier rhetoric' (p 273). The Pardoner goes directly to the point of the Sophistic question: can a corrupt preacher produce good (lines 427-31; 457-61). By his command of the skills of the *artes praedicandi* and *artes poetriae*, the Pardoner produces the results they recommend. The fragmentation of *CT* notwithstanding, the Pardoner and Parson can be placed at opposite ends of a continuum which 'defines Chaucer's sense of the problem of rhetoric—and ... part of his sense of the problem of poetry' (pp 275-6). The Chaucerian narrator compresses the three issues of persuader, audience and language. Chaucer's realization of himself as rhetor provides him the device of 'impersonating' himself in order to participate in a continual re-creation of his poetry.

949 Patterson, Lee W. '"The Parson's Tale" and the Quitting of the "Canterbury Tales".' *Traditio* 34(1978), 331-80.

In the course of addressing the question of relation to other tales and date for *ParsT*, Patterson notes passages in *PardT* which are among the thirty-five *ParsT* passages echoing preceding tales (*PardT* lines 633-7; 472-5; 591-4; 504; 529-33; 558-9; 481-4). The lines of influence run from the tales to *ParsT*; consequently *ParsT* was composed after them. *ParsT* includes an echo of conventional phrasing in *Phy-PardL* lines 294-6. The Pardoner, in his set-piece of vernacular preaching, is one of five tale-tellers for whom substantial echoes are found in *ParsT*. Like the Wife of Bath, he creates himself 'not merely in language but *as* language, giving to a generalized mode of speaking a unique voice that implies a coextensive character' (pp 360-1). The echo of the Pardoner's distinction between blasphemy and perjury (lines 631-2) found in *ParsT* is added by Chaucer to his source works.

950 Rudat, Wolgang E. H. 'The *Canterbury Tales*: Anxiety Release and Wish Fulfillment.' *AI* 35(1978), 407-18.

Deeply rooted in his Christian beliefs, Chaucer employs bawdy for religious purposes; the Pardoner releases fears and anxieties through the springtime ritual of the pilgrimage. The Pardoner mirrors his own state in his presentation: *PardT* reflects his avarice; his interpretation of original sin as gluttony is 'an attempt to sublimate his sexual handicap'(p 415). *PardT* can be read as an unconscious confession; as such, it is 'an adroit psychoanalysis' by the poet (p 415). A conscious confession, the offering of relics leads to a 'perceptive psychoanalysis' of the Pardoner by the Host (p 416). Expatiating on the sexual connotations of *purs* (872), the Host analogizes the spurious relics to the Pardoner's non-existent testicles. The Knight understands the full meaning of the Host-Pardoner dialogue though the other pilgrims do not. Whereas the Host leaves the Pardoner in isolation, the Knight seeks to 'reintegrate the Pardoner into humanity' (p 417). The firmness of Chaucer's religious convictions allows even 'the most obscene situation' to be 'easily absorbed into the spiritual significance of the pilgrimage'(p 418).

951 Trower, Katherine B. 'Spiritual Sickness in the Physician's and Pardoner's Tales: Thematic Unity in Fragment VI of the Canterbury Tales.' *ABR* 29(1978), 67-86.

The Physician and Pardoner play upon 'the theme of disease and death, physical and spiritual, a theme countered by the full scriptural implications sounded by the Pardoner' (p 86). The *PhyT* is 'merely a prelude' to the Pardoner's performance (p 85). *PhyT* and the Pardoner's performance are linked by the use of *boughte* and *triacle*, (*PardT* provides no remedy to the untranscendent *PhyT*). The Pardoner, an antitype of the Physician, is associated with healing (Rouncivale, role as preacher/*medicus*, claims of healing with relics) yet poisons the spirit with his temptations and deceit. A type of Antichrist, the Pardoner's insistence on the physical and of death seems an attempt to undermine the Church. He may resemble the Old Adam but he undergoes no regeneration. The only spiritually redeeming qualities in Fragment VI are found in the pattern of the Pardoner's biblical allusions which stress transcendence and in Chaucer's use of the *topos* of the Atonement (the reconciliation may be a parody of the aftermath of the Harrowing of Hell).

952 Coletti, Theresa. 'The Pardoner's Vernicle and the Image of Man in the Pardoner's Tale.' 1979. See **443**.

PardT weaves the themes implied by the vernicle—the juxtaposition of the Old Man and the New Man, the image of man, man's relationship to God, and the nature of flesh and spirit—while undermining the positive associations implicit in the vernicle. By punctuating his treatment of the tavern sins with references to Christ's sacrificial death, the Pardoner at once 'defiles and dismembers the body of Christ just as he corrupts his own' (p 11) and also holds out hope for man. The vernicle, like the Knight's call for reconciliation, suggests that the Pardoner 'still has a place in the Christian community' (p 12).

953 Jungman, Robert E. 'The Pardoner's "Confession" and St. Augustine's *De Doctrina Christiana*.' 1979. See **245**.

The discrepancy between the highly moral and effectively presented *PardT* and the Pardoner's character replete with moral flaws is a striking incongruity. The hypocritical preacher is a late medieval commonplace. In addition to the parallel to Faux Semblant, there is a discussion of an immoral man preaching morality in Augustine's *De Doctrina Christiana* (Book IV, xxvii, 59) which provides a significant *glose* if not an outright source.

954 Manning, Stephen. 'Rhetoric, Game, Morality, and Geoffrey Chaucer.' *SAC* 1(1979), 105-18.

The study of rhetoric as game establishes Chaucer's 'creative vision'(p 118). Departing from Richard Lanham's notion that the struggle between play and purpose is the base of Chaucer's art (**928**), Manning notes that the Host converts the pilgrimage into a contest where each pilgrim is both pilgrim and contestant then develops an analysis of the Pardoner's performance and *FranT* (pp 111-8). The tension between rhetoric and seriousness sheds light on Chaucer's most enigmatic pilgrim, the Pardoner. The Pardoner creates a 'social self'(p 108) in the headlink (lines 318-28). He continues in *PardP* to build on the *gentils'* conception of him. He 'traps himself between his public selves and his central self'(p 108). After the tale, when he turns to salesmanship, he overstates, 'combining his roles as vicious man and as entertainer' (p 109). The Pardoner 'pretends to be *homo seriosus* before the pilgrims, with a central cupidinous self to which he is true while he plays *homo rhetoricus* in his preaching'(p 110). The seriousness he portrays in his self-portrait is part of his performance. Manning modifies his earlier position to suggest the Pardoner's stance is more complex than simple sincerity: the tension between play and seriousness is underscored in lines 915-8, a moment which is 'unconsciously both'(p 110) truth and playful hypocrisy. The Host acknowledges the game and plays to win, turning the exchange into what Huizinga has called a 'slanging match'(p 110). The Pardoner, unwilling to acknowledge the psychological and social consequences of his central self (A line 691), 'seeks a series of public selves which must be constantly re-established'(p 111). The Pardoner's search for a social self leads to the spiritual death of his central self but healing images are present. In the 'paradoxical acrobatics' of '[d]eath and healing ... public self and central self—play and purpose' (p 111), Chaucer presents the Pardoner.

955 Miskimin, Alice. 'The Illustrated Eighteenth-Century Chaucer.' 1979. See **445**.

A widening range of attitudes towards *CT* appeared at the end of the century. In a set of nine drawings which stress the fabliaux and the supernatural (published in a quartro edition of Tyrwhitt 1987; rpt 1798), J.B. Mortimer included the Pardoner's 'Three Gamblers and Time.' Miskimin reports that Blake's *Descriptive Catalogue* characterizes the Wife of Bath as 'a scourge and blight' (p 54).

956 Rowland, Beryl. 'Chaucer's Idea of the Pardoner.' *ChauR* 14(1979-80), 140-54.

Rowland takes up the question: 'why should a diabolically clever, self-confessed charlatan try to persuade his listeners to behave in the same way as his customary dupes?'(p 140). Chaucer presents 'a disastrous physical ambivalence as both counterpart and cause' (p 150) of the Pardoner's behavior. Curry **(686)** and Howard **(1092)** related the Pardoner's moral condition to his biology. Previously, Rowland **(601)** suggested the Pardoner was 'a testicular pseudo-hermaphrodite of the feminine type'(p 143). This paper adduces evidence from ancient and medieval authors to demonstrate 'the values attached to the hermaphrodite were ambivalent. The hermaphrodite could be the image of perfection; it could also be an image of frustration or incontinence. Philosophically it meant an ideal unity; physically it was an evil and a misfortune'(p 148). Chaucer draws upon the medieval understanding that 'the hermaphrodite's dual nature represented a duplicity, a doubleness of character' (p 149).

957 Satow, Tsutomu. 'More Serious and Sinful Development of Human Life: *Pardoner's Tale.*' *Sentence and Solaas: Thematic Development and Narrative Technique in 'The Canterbury Tales.*' Tokyo: Kobundo Publishing Company, 1979. Pp 228-54.

In this undifferentiated overview the Pardoner is presented as the 'greatest moralist' and most complicated pilgrim; his tale has a 'strong moralistic and antisexual bias' (p 228). Though he proclaims himself a figure of avarice, his aim is 'verbal and practical blasphemy, the desecration of religion and of the sacrament of penance' (p 232). *PardT* is part of a seven part structure: interchange of Pardoner and Host; Pardoner's speech to pilgrims; tale; principals of three deadly sins; tale continued; another speech to pilgrims; interchange between Pardoner and Host. *PardT*, like *PhyT*, is a tale of death, evil and grace. *PardT* is 'a cynical and ironical refutation of the Physician's moralizing' (p 232). *PardT* resembles *MerT* in persistent irony and 'the seriousness which informs even the farcical climax' (p 239). The basic concern of *PardT* is death; the Old Man, a self-dramatization of the Pardoner, 'is a splendid example of hypocrisy' (p 241). The value of *PardP* and *PardT* lies 'in the inexpressible emotion created partly by the self-revealed character of the narrator' (p 245).

• Review by Thomas Ross, *SAC* 3(1981), 176-7: The insights are ... for the most part familiar ... There is a more sophisticated critical perception in Satow's treatment of *The Physician's* and *Pardoner's Tale*, both of which deal with the 'gift' of death ... More important are some undeniable—and some probable—errors of fact (e.g., *PardT* has 'a strong ... antisexual bias' [p 228]).

∾ The Pardoner's Tale 1980-1989

958 Aers, David. *Chaucer, Langland, and the Creative Imagination.* 1980. See **636**.

In the Pardoner, a figure central to *CT*, Chaucer created 'an endlessly fascinating self-reflexive vision of one possible fate of reflexive imagination in his own world' (p 102). The Pardoner concludes his performance by referring to *PardP*. After framing his calling within the bounds of a moral tale (lines 904-15), the Pardoner steps into his official vocation targeting the Church, his Christian audience and himself (lines 920-40). Chaucer has taken us beyond conventional moral condemnation 'disclosing the complicated and fluid interrelationships between social practices, contemporary ideologies and individual consciousness' (p 102). The Pardoner negates the institution the pilgrims rely on: the Host's reaction to the Pardoner represents his rejection of any critical analysis of self, society or Church (lines 941-57).

- Review by Elton D. Higgs, *SAC* 3(1981), 121-4: Aers sees Chaucer explaining the Pardoner 'primarily by reference to the interaction of social forces.' In rejecting the 'elitism' of those in political and religious power, Aers establishes 'just as indefensible a kind of elitism by assuming the superiority of his modern moral sensitivity and his behavioristic convictions [over the common ideologies and assumptions of the Middle Ages]' (p 122).

959 Hilary, Christine Ryan. 'The "Confessio" Tradition From Augustine to Chaucer.' *DAI* 41(1980). University of California, Berkeley Dissertation,1979.

The *confessio fidei*, one of three modes of religious confession, provides the dominant mode for the secular literary confession tradition. All literary confessions include 'a self-witnessing speaker' who witnesses a philosophy of life or communal attitude. The confessions of Faus Semblant, the Wife of Bath and the Pardoner are treated in the final chapter.

960 Holley, Linda Tarte. 'The Function of Language in Three Canterbury Churchmen.' *Parergon* 28(1980), 36-44.

Chaucer dramatizes the irony of disjuncture between word as intended, spoken, and heard in the presentations of the Pardoner, Friar and Summoner. In all three, language fails to function as 'an index to the reasonable nature of man'(p 43). The Pardoner, in *PardP*, warns the pilgrims that what he is and what he says are at odds. With the pilgrims, the Pardoner substitutes one illusion for another, dropping his regular role in favor of a self-dramatization as Avarice. When he moves back to his customary role, the Host reacts with indignation. The vacuity of the Pardoner's rhetoric contrasts with the eloquence of the *PhyT*. 'Avarice is only the accident of the Pardoner's nature; the nexus for his thought, word, and deed is pride' (p 37). The Pardoner beguiles himself. His sin is the abuse of reason, the sign of which is speech (p 38). Though an ironist, the Pardoner is unaware that, through his words, he lives physically but dies spiritually. The illusion-making power of language is evident in the variety of the Pardoner's verbal stances. For all their effectiveness, the Pardoner fails to appreciate the distance between accident (his hypocrisy) and substance (his pride in the misuse of his gift)(p 43). Standing between the external sign and the substance is man's limited understanding.

961 Kane, George. *The Liberating Truth: The Concept of Integrity in Chaucer's Writings.* London: Athlone Press, 1980.

The current consensus that Chaucer ought to be understood as a man of his own time rather than a precursor of later times is an improvement capable of further refinement. Chaucer's work reflects a general moral concern and a specific concern with the character of uncorrupted virtue: integrity, in our time; *trouthe* in his. Chaucer's work is typified by accuracy in representing the 'condition of conflict between the absolute excellence of the ideal and the power of the urge away from it'(p 17). Consequently, the concerns for grace and liberation expressed in the Retraction are consistent with overriding thematic concerns.

962 Lawler, Traugott. *The One and the Many in the Canterbury Tales.* Hamden, Connecticut: Archon, 1980.

The complementary relationship between unity and diversity, oneness and multiplicity, is the most pervasive issue and the major unifying force of *CT*. Though Chaucer grants value to diversity, he places higher value on unity. *CT* can be considered a *metafabliau* where professions are stereotyped and in conflict. The Pardoner is *all* professional: 'the best way to understand him is to take him absolutely literally when he says *myn entente is nat but for to wynne*' (line 403). When the Knight demands the Pardoner kiss the Host, he is demanding a genuine act of pardon. Though distinctive in the brilliance of his skill, the Pardoner fits himself to the stereotype of the manipulative exposed professional. Marriage, authority and experience are one-and-many themes. The general structure of *CT* moves between continuation and closure, ultimately resolving itself in the unity of *ParsT*.

963   Lehr, John Robert. 'The Old Man in Fourteenth and Fifteenth-Century English Literature.' *DAI* 40(1980), 50645A. University of Toronto, 1979. Director: D. Fox.

Within a study of background to the representation of old age in medieval literature, Lehr examines the confrontation of youth and age in *PardT*, in Gowers' 'The Trump of Death,' and Henryson's 'The Ressoning Betuix Aige and Yowth.'

964   Leicester, H. Marshall, Jr. 'The Art of Impersonation: A General Prologue to the *Canterbury Tales*.' *PMLA* 95(1980), 213-24. Rpt in *Geoffrey Chaucer's The General Prologue to the Canterbury Tales*. Ed. Harold Bloom. New York: Chelsea House Publishers, 1988. Pp 85-100. Rpt in *The Canterbury Tales: Nine Tales and the General Prologue*. Ed. V. A. Kolve and Glending Olson, New York: W. W. Norton, 1989. Pp 503-18.

In *CT*, Chaucer practices impersonation creating himself as a fiction: 'there is nobody there, ... only the text' (p 217). Howard's 'unimpersonated artistry'(p 215) requires the reader to decide which part of a narrative ought to be assigned to a pilgrim teller, which to the author. Though the tales are individually voiced, the overriding impersonation leads the reader to see the entire narration as the work of a single speaker. Donaldson's work on Chaucer the pilgrim, valuable as it is, encourages the reader to treat the speaker as if he can be known apart from his utterances. In the tales, the narrator directs our attention to the variety and complexity of the roles he plays; he seems to suggest we can know him only through the pilgrims eg, through the Pardoner. The speaker of *CT* is 'a self-constructing voice'(p 222). See also **926, 1142.**

965 Luengo, Anthony E. 'Synthesis and Orthodoxy in Chaucer's *Parson's Tale*: An Analysis of the Concordance of Different Authoritative *Sententiae* According to the Principles of the Medieval *artes praedicandi.*' *RUO* 50(1980), 223-32.

The Parson adopts several methods outlined in Thomas Walley's *De modo componendi sermones* in part to counter the Pardoner's careless and misleading use of *sententiae*. Comparison of the Parson and the Pardoner's treatment of swearing shows the Pardoner uses fewer authorities, handles them in a misleading fashion and includes distracting fables. The Pardoner is a specific target of the Parson's comment on Ire (line 623 ff).

966 Justman, Stewart. 'Literal and Symbolic in *the Canterbury Tales.*' *ChauR* 14(1980), 199-214. Rpt in *Geoffrey Chaucer*. [Modern Critical Views]. Ed. Harold Bloom. New York: Chelsea House Publishers, 1985. Pp 123-35.

CT breaks with the symbolic view of the world that insists on the reality of analogical thought. Though the Pardoner's rhyme of *swere* and *totere* (lines 473-4) attests to the idea that words are contracts with reality (p 200; 124), the Pardoner is himself 'a false exemplification, a counterfeit' (p 206; 130). A false sign with false relics, the Pardoner ironically 'confirms the connection of symbols and controls' (p 206) as the literalist rioters fail to understand the symbolism of the Old Man. The Pardoner's digression (approximately half the tale) recalls that words themselves are a 'digression' from reality. '[T]he Pardoner may ironically remind us of the purely symbolic, un-real character of words' (p 207; 130).

967 McAlpine, Monica E. 'The Pardoner's Homosexuality and How It Matters.' 1980/ rpt 1988. See **450.**

With the Pardoner, Chaucer explores the inner reality of an outcast despised by his society and misunderstood by his Church. Through his manipulation of the sacrament of Penance, the Pardoner covertly seeks forgiveness (p 17). The pardons and relics provide the Pardoner a link with his Church. Unable to confess his sin, the Pardoner seeks forgiveness vicariously through the sale of pardons. Compulsion for validation leads him to offer relics to the pilgrims. In addressing the Host, the Pardoner at once uses his homosexuality as a weapon and asks for love (p 17). The latent aggression and sexual implication in the

Pardoner's statements to the Host turn the scene into 'one of implied seduction or even rape'(p 17). But the Pardoner simultaneously asks for love: '[t]he goal of the final scene, as of all the Pardoner's maneuvers, is a kiss'(p 17). The Knight engineers a reconciliation that at once restores mutual tolerance and avoids all the issues. Although Chaucer views homosexual acts as sinful, he appears not to view them as uniquely detestable; the suggestion of homosexuality contributes not to the portrait of a damned soul but to a representation of the *sondriness* of humanity. For *PardP*, see **638**.

68 Allen, Judson Boyce, and Theresa Anne Moritz. *A Distinction of Stories: The Medieval Unity of Chaucer's Fair Chain of Narratives for Canterbury*. Columbus: Ohio State University Press, 1981.
In *CT*, Chaucer proposes a normative definition of human society based on the paradigm of human marriage. The principle of unity in *CT* is best understood by reference to medieval commentaries on Ovid's *Metamorphoses*. Medieval commentaries regard poetry as valid description of the real world, a world organized on principles of analogy; Chaucer's stories define ethical norms for the good society. The Pardoner, who intends to deceive, presents a powerful lesson on the effects of avarice. *CT* is a *distinctio*, a collection of transformations arranged in four major parts: tales of natural changes, of magic, of moral struggle, and spiritual interpretation. The tales of magic begin and end with a tale of death; *PardT* closes the group (*SNT,CYT, SqT, FranT, WBT, FrT, SumT, PhyT, PardT*). The exemplum of *PardT* presents earthly riot and deserved punishment but, viewed in the context of *SNT*, *PardT* seems, ironically, the part of a saint's life visible to mortal vision. Death, then, is not only just punishment but the last anagogical peace.

69 Beidler, Peter G. 'Noah and The Old Man in the *Pardoner's Tale*.' *ChauR* 15(1981), 250-4.
Interpretations of the identity of the Old Man misread his character: the Old Man's longing for death does not imply immortality; nor does his role in the revellers' deaths mean he is evil (rather he is contrasted with evil). Medieval explanations of the plague as a scourge for sin connect the Old Man with Noah, a survivor of the earlier holocaust brought about by man's depravity. A reading of the exemplum and the Wakefield 'Noah' suggests specific parallels.

70 Benson, Larry D. 'The Order of *The Canterbury Tales*.' *SAC* 3(1981),

77-120.

Benson takes issue with the conclusions of Manly and Rickert (**42**) to argue that two tale orders—A B¹ D E F C B² G H I and A B¹ D E F G C B² H—can be assigned to Chaucer and that the former (El-a) is Chaucer's final arrangement.

971 Chamberlain, David. 'Musical Signs and Symbols in Chaucer: Convention and Originality.' *Signs and Symbols in Chaucer's Poetry.* Ed. John P. Hermann and John J. Burke. Alabama: University of Alabama Press, 1981. Pp 43-80.

The Pardoner sings in Church for greed and on the pilgrimage for lechery. In *PardT*, music is a sign of riot or debauchery. This use of song, the 'Old Song' or 'Song of Man,' Chaucer would have found in the treatise he translated from Innocent III '*Wreched Engendrynge of Mankynde*' (p 59).

972 Coleman, Janet. *Medieval Readers and Writers, 1350-1400.* New York: Columbia University Press, 1981.

Coleman examines the growth in lay literacy and social mobility as expressed in fourteenth-century literature, a time when most works were intended to instruct, exhort and eventually inspire reform. Chaucer worked in a tradition favoring *ordinatio* of a *compilatio* of *exempla*; *PardT* is not only patterned on actual sermons but reveals influence of sermon language (p 201). See **89**.

973 Dello Buono, Carmen J. *Rare Early Essays on Geoffrey Chaucer.* [Rare Early English Essays Series]. Pennsylvania: Norwood Editions, 1981. See **268**.

974 Diekstra, Frans. 'The Language of Equivocation: Some Chaucerian Techniques.' *DQR* 11(1981), 267-77.

There is a peculiar aesthetic fascination in the way the Pardoner practices his deceit. Chaucer's poetic idiom habitually recreates the effects of equivocation (e.g., the young reveller's mutually exclusive lies to the apothecary, a slip of the tongue) in his characters and narrators.

975 Gill, Richard. 'Jung's Archetypes of the Wise Old Man in Poems by Chaucer, Wordsworth and Browning.' *JEP* 2(1981), 18-32.

The resemblances among the Old Man in Chaucer's *PardT*, the Leech-Gatherer in Wordsworth's 'Resolution and Independence,' and the hoary cripple encountered in Browning's 'Childe Roland to the Dark Tower Came' are better explained by their relationship to Jung's archetype of the wise Old Man than by literary influence. Discussions of literary archetypes (notably Frye's) have remained purely descriptive. The archetype of the 'wise old man' typically appears suddenly, combines wisdom and good will, and creates an irresistible fascination.

976 Kawasaki, Massatoshi. 'Chaucer no Menzaijouri no Seikaku to Imi ni Tsuite.' In *Bungaku to Ningen: Nakajima Kanji Kyoju Tsuito Ronbunshu*. Tokyo: Kinseido, 1981. Pp 21-40. Fisher gives English translation of title as: 'The Character and Meaning of Chaucer's Pardoner.' In *Literature and Man—the Papers for the late Professor Kanji Nakajima*.

Reportedly discusses the character and meaning of the Pardoner in relation to a submerged irony. [In Japanese; not seen.]

977 Kuntz, Richard Alden. *The Pardoning of the Pardoner: Critical Approaches to the Morality of Chaucer's Pardoner*. University of California Irvine Dissertation,1981. See also *DAI* 42(1981), 1141.

In presenting the Pardoner as both a lost soul and a human being of dignity, capable of being affected by the eloquence of his tale, Kittredge lays the basis for two distinctive trends in twentieth century criticism **668**. Following a period when the weight of critical response rested on the Pardoner's sinfulness (1893-1948), interest in the Pardoner's moral character grew (1949-61), with opinion balanced between condemnation and a mitigation based on the Pardoner's capacity for revealing truth or his psychological torment. Efforts to pardon the Pardoner are most evident between 1962-71, with the Pardoner's apologists shifting or sharing guilt, variously implicating the Host, other pilgrims, or the reader. In the ten years following, the trend veers again toward a judgment of depravity.

978 Lanoue, David G. 'Musical Imagery in the Poetry of Juan Ruiz, Guillaume de Machaut, and Chaucer: A Comparative Study.' University of Nebraska Dissertation, 1981. Director: Paul A. Olson. See also *DAI* 42(1981), 1141-2A.

In this study which examines iconographic conventions regarding music, and argues that those conventions provide a key to unity in fourteenth-century poetry, Lanoue demonstrates that a 'consistent perversion of sacred music'(p 1142-A) underscores the Pardoner's perversion of ecclesiastical 'degree' and illustrates his collusion with the Summoner, his 'fellow corrupter[s] of divine harmony' (p 1142).

979 Lawton, D[avid] A. 'The Pardoner's Tale: Morality and Its Context.' 1981. See **457**.

The juxtaposition of villainous Pardoner and impressive tale is examined as a structural dichotomy of tale (lines 463-903) and frame (all remaining lines). The denunciation of sins is relevant to the concerns of the tale, orthodox in its theology, and within the range of convention in tone. The rioters, scarcely individualized, function as a 'pattern of action which we see laid over all the sins'(p 47). It is essential to recognize the Pardoner's fictionality; few moments in the tale focus on his personality. The tale is full of bones: the Old Man is whatever we think of old age and death. Following the 'splendidly understated and unemotive apotheosis' of the tale in line 888 (p 50), Chaucer returns to moral purpose with mankind replacing the rioters three. The true climax of the tale (lines 903-5) has been undervalued by the 'psychology heresy' which draws attention to the less effective benediction (lines 916-8) (p 51). *PardP* is an analysis of the Pardoner's challenge to ourselves and our world. The Pardoner, indeed the C-Group of *CT*, has been shaped by Chaucer's reading of the *RR*. Textual scrutiny implies Chaucer intended us to recognize the Pardoner as a type of Faux-Semblant. The Pardoner puts forward 'a grotesque, reductive view of the pilgrims and their *pley*' (p 58). The frame turns back to the 'moral absolutism' of the tale (p 60), highlighting its potency. In shrinking from 'the absolute standards and intractable logic of the Tale'(p 60), are 'victims of Chaucer's game' unwilling to consider the judgment of the tale (p 60)?

980 Leffingwell, Wm C., Jr. 'Some Versions of Chaucerian Irony.' *DAI* 41(1981), 3592A. University of Maryland Dissertation, 1980.

A central irony ties together the Pardoner's relations with the other pilgrims, the lesson of the Pardoner's performance and the theme of the exemplum.

981 Nitecki, Alicia K. 'The Convention of The Old Man's Lament in *The Pardoner's Tale.*' *ChauR* 16(1981), 76-84.

Chaucer mines the medieval convention of the old man's lament for structural elements: the questioning of existence, the elegiac complaint,and the expressed fear. The Old Man in *PardT* shows affinity with the portrayal of age in the meditative lyrics. Chaucer varies the tradition slighting the physical and stressing the sense of desolation. The Old Man is alive because the world clings to youth and refuses age. Chaucer uses the convention to depict the horror of a world with no death, the world the rioters seek. By presenting the Old Man mimetically, Chaucer establishes an identification with him, thereby showing the necessity for death. The deathless world becomes a trope for the human longing of transcendence.

82　Payne, F. Anne. *Chaucer and Menippean Satire*. Madison: University of Wisconsin Press, 1981.

Payne identifies the Old Man as a *Deus* figure in Menippean dialogue, a dominant structural feature of Chaucer's work. The Old Man is characterized by his desire to give the rioters what they ask for when they query him as to the location of Death.

83　Peck, Russell A. 'St. Paul and the *Canterbury Tales*.' *Mediaevalia* 7(1981), 91-131. Rpt with revisions as 'Biblical Interpretation: St. Paul and *The Canterbury Tales*.' In *Chaucer and Scriptural Tradition*. Ed. David Lyle Jeffrey. Ottawa: University of Ottawa Press, 1984. Pp 143-70.

The idea of pilgrimage is maintained in *CT* through configurations of Pauline imagery; *PardT* employs such *topoi* as old men and new men, doctrine hidden amongst enigma, full and empty psyches with attendant iconography, concepts of redeeming time and the search for grace. The Pardoner, an exhibitionist like the Wife of Bath, compensates for his deficiencies by tyrannizing others. The Pardoner seems dedicated to death: he 'projects the most depraved view of human nature' in *CT* (p 167). He ignores the fullness of Paul's commentary, selecting only the depraved parts. His attitude comes to the inevitable, self-destructive conclusion in his solicitation of the Host: the Host's reaction is appropriate 'for it is in the dung of an unclean animal that the Pardoner has already set his talents' (p 169). See **1041**.

84　Roscow, G. H. *Syntax and Style in Chaucer's Poetry*. 1981. See **639**.

The following syntactic elements are examined as they appear in *PardT*: word-order (lines 713, 871); idiomatic usage (lines 538, 796, 811, 859-60); pleonasm (lines 621-3, 776); ellipsis (lines 885-6); relative clauses (lines 649-50, 664-5, 675, 766); and co-ordination and parataxis (lines 851, 865).

85　Sato, Noriko. 'The Old Man in the Pardoner's Tale.' *TCEL* 54 (1981), 11-36. [Not seen.]

86　Standop, Ewald. 'Chaucers Pardoner: Das Charakterproblem und die Kritiker.' In *Geschichtlichkeit und Neuanfang im Sprachlichen Kunstwerk: Studien zur Englischen Philologie zu Ehren Von Fritz W. Schulze*. Ed. Peter Erlebach et al. Tübingen: Gunter Narr Verlag,

1981. Pp 59-69.

Attempting to separate the *chaf* and the *fruyt* in the numerous character studies of the Pardoner, Standop concludes that the proportions are akin to those of iceberg and tip. The Pardoner's sexual deviancy is only one example of critical absurdity. Most critics fall into one of two traps: either the fallacy of psychological realism which claims to know more about the 'real' Pardoner than the text itself, or the intentional fallacy which denies the obvious inconsistencies among prologue, self-revelation, tale, ending and the artlessness of Chaucer's lame attempt at a humorous afterthought. Most Chaucer criticism is more decorative than informative and is better judged by aesthetic than scientific standards.

987 Allen, Judson Boyce. *The Ethical Poetic of the Later Middle Ages: A Decorum of Convenient Distinction*. Toronto: University of Toronto, 1982.

PardT, in its presentation of the rioters' encounter with the Old Man, affords an instance of *consideratio*, 'a specification of that quality of descriptions of customs and beliefs which renders those customs and beliefs important, normative, definitional, connected with the eternal fitness of things' (p 30). In this event which 'argues itself' (p 31), Chaucer exploits the power of folk tale atmosphere.

988 Barney, Stephen A. 'Chaucer's Lists.' In *The Wisdom of Poetry: Essays in Early English Literature in Honor of Morton W. Bloomfield*. Eds. Larry D. Benson and Siegfried Wenzel. Kalamazoo, Michigan: Western Michigan University, 1982. Pp 189-223.

'To list is to attempt to comprehend, and Chaucer revels in and distrusts lists' (p 223). Barney analyzes the characteristics (smaller than stories, adjectival and principled, and symmetrical and intransitive) and sources (oral mnemonic sources, OF *voie*, art of rhetoric) of Chaucer's lists; comments on *PardP* 394 where the Pardoner threatens a list, and *PardT* 821; and examines *PardT* 538 to show Chaucer's closest approximation to satire.

989 Bauschatz, Paul C. 'Chaucer's Pardoner's Beneficent Lie.' *Assays* 2 (1982), 19-43.

Bauschatz examines the Pardoner's speech in the context of the predicational options inherent in Anselm's logical model of truth. 'The Pardoner is Chaucer's fiction, and his discourse is Chaucer's artifact. The questions which it raises work back against the whole fiction in which Chaucer has plunged us' (p 33). With *PardP* and *PardT*, the tests of human understanding raised in *CT* reach 'their fullest extreme' (p 33). With the Pardoner, the rational model of scholastic discourse has become 'a weapon for the destruction of that very understanding' (p 31). For the Pardoner, Anselm's 'supreme truth' has become consentient with the 'beneficent lie' (p 32). Whereas God speaks only truth, the Pardoner has a greater linguistic range. He replicates 'the weakness of all fictionalizing' (p 34). *CT* ends by asking the reader to participate in the consideration of the value of its fictions. See **1162**.

990 Beidler, Peter G. 'The Plague and Chaucer's Pardoner.' *ChauR* 16(1982), 257-69.

By neglecting the implications of the plague setting, scholars have failed to acknowledge the full richness and artistic unity of *PardT*. A knowledge of medieval attitudes towards the bubonic plague elucidates the exemplum (providing a rationale for the rioters' carousing, the existence of unattended gold, and even the identity of the Old Man); underscores the Pardoner's skill at extortion (if, as was commonly thought, the plague was a scourge for sin, then a pardon was of timely value), and suggests a motivation behind the Host's reaction; he may well have seen the sinful Pardoner as bringing plague upon himself and all those in contact with him.

991 Boitani, Piero. *English Medieval Narrative in the 13th and 14th Centuries.* Cambridge: Cambridge University Press, 1982.

Chaucer depicts reality through the use of genre, narrative style and the interior workings of the pilgrims. Chaucer recreated both the official and the unofficial culture of his age; *PardT* both overturns the official ecclesiastical culture and reaffirms the Christian model. The three rioters are the only characters in *CT* who do not share the official culture. Referring to the structure of *PardT* as one of two 'Chaucerian' structures (the other being *NPT*), Boitani offers a reading to demonstrate its polyphonic character, its multiplicity of styles (pp 260-5). The episode of the Old Man is 'a parable within a parable' (p 264). Here the poetry is a 'poetry of pathos' proceeding through '*impossibilia*' and '*aenigmata*' (p 264). 'For the first time in English literature he [Chaucer] creates a figure such as we find in the three witches of *Macbeth*, in the "fool" of *King Lear*, in the Phlebas of the *Waste Land*' (pp 264-5). See **1114**.

992 Leicester, H. Marshall, Jr. '"Synne Horrible": The Pardoner's Exegesis of His Tale and Chaucer's.' In *Acts of Interpretation: The Text in its*

Contexts, 700-1600: Essays on Medieval and Renaissance Literature in Honor of E. Talbot Donaldson. Ed. Mary J. Carruthers and Elizabeth D. Kirk. Norman, Oklahoma: Pilgrim Press, 1982. Pp 25-50. Rpt in *Geoffrey Chaucer's Pardoner's Tale.* [Modern Critical Interpretations]. Ed. Harold Bloom. New York: Chelsea House Publishers, 1985. Pp 79-102.

PardT is both the tale that best responds to patristic or Augustinian analysis (**747, 818, 949**) and also one of the most fully dramatized (**681**). Acknowledging a bias in favor of dramatically inclined criticism, Leicester examines the typological elements of the tale as indicators of Chaucer's attitude toward exegetical methods, methods he unquestionably employed. *PardT* reveals a 'deliberate forcing of mundane and particular matters into a general and spiritual framework while at the same time refusing to let go of the literal level' (p 28). The Pardoner is the first exegetical critic of his own tale. Through his tale, he indicates that he himself knows and wishes others to know: 'that he is the *eunuchus non dei*, the embodiment of the *vetus homo*, the Old Man whose body is the body of this death, and guilty of the sin against the Holy Ghost'(p 29). Through parodic representation in his sermon, the Pardoner satirizes the corruption of the Church. By presenting himself as an exemplar of the sins he describes, he presents himself as a figure of those aspects of the Church that fail to come to terms with the reality of sin in the world. The Pardoner elevates words above experience as he fails to distinguish literal from spiritual. The Pardoner modifies the exemplum, a form whose 'institutionalized literalism' (p 35) is ill-suited to his ends, by making it increasingly typological as he proceeds. The Pardoner rejects his tale at the literal level but is propelled by a frustrating consciousness of self to force the issues of sin and spirit into the pilgrimage. The Pardoner's typological imagination makes him the main example of spiritual corruption implicit in the Old Man, his alter ego. The real moral (lines 915-8) is a continuation of what the Pardoner has been saying. The other half of the Pardoner's message is found in the solicitation (lines 919-45). The tale, as a whole, represents the poet's critique, though not rejection, of typology as a way of thinking about the world. But it is important to Chaucer that the Pardoner's voice is heard, for the Pardoner is 'a considerable part of the poet'(p 49). Both exercise the power of language over reality. Chaucer, however, sees more than the Pardoner, for Chaucer subordinated his own vision to the portrayal of other consciousnesses. In *PardT*, Chaucer both embodies and chastens his impulse to play God.

993   Leitch, L. M. 'Sentence and Solaas: The Function of the Hosts in the *Canterbury Tales*.' *ChauR* 17(1982), 5-20.

Harry Bailly's criterion of *best sentence and moost solaas* (line 798) introduces a thematic tension between pleasure and edification, festivity and repentance, himself and the Parson. The Host shares the role of editor and timekeeper with several of the pilgrims; his position is ultimately usurped by the Parson. By the time of his quarrel with the Pardoner, the Host is fast losing control. The *gentils* resist the Host's call for *som myrthe* (line 319) because the pilgrimage is drawing to a close and their concern is shifting to edification.

994   Item cancelled.

995   Rex, Richard. '"Spiced Conscience" in the Canterbury Tales.' *MP* 80(1982), 53-4.

In homiletic contexts *spiced* was the equivalent of 'delicate', delicacy being an aspect of gluttony. Both the Parson (I line 827) and the Pardoner (lines 517-20) refer to the *tendre, deyntee*, and *delicaat mete* of gluttons to mean spiced food. The spiced food of gluttons is, in moral terms, like exaggerated sensibility affected by hypocritical religious. The Parson does not pretend to have *a spiced conscience* (A line 526).

996   Rhodes, James F. 'Motivation in Chaucer's *Pardoner's Tale*: Winner Take Nothing.' *ChauR* 17(1982), 40-61.

Few characters have generated as much hostility as the Pardoner. To understand the tolerance with which the medieval audience greeted him, the modern reader must translate him into the modern idiom: the Pardoner has affinities with the 'homeless and desolate'(p 60) confessional hero. The Pardoner, like the Wife of Bath, is obsessed with regeneration. Sex and avarice only partially explain his compulsive behavior; his deeper secret is that, for him, the 'inner man' does not exist. Like the Old Man, the Pardoner's true intent is to lead people (his sermon audience being like the rioters) to spiritual death. The attempt to sell relics to the pilgrims is an intellectual experiment to see what the pilgrims think of him. Though unmasked, he remains on the pilgrimage as the Knight restores order. Having received the Pardoner's performance in the spirit of game, the pilgrims refuse either to judge him or to enter his cycle of despair; consequently, they 'open the road to Canterbury anew to him'(p 59). See **1162**.

997 Rowland, Beryl. 'Seven Kinds of Irony.' *Earle Birney: Essays on Chaucerian Irony*. Ed. Beryl Rowland. Toronto: University of Toronto, 1982. Pp xv-xxx.

Irony is Chaucer's 'most consistent position' (p xxvii) and is expressed variously as verbal irony, irony of manner, dramatic irony, irony of values, irony of theme, and structural irony. *PardT* is an example of thematic irony in that the Pardoner's theme ... *radix malorum est cupiditas* ... unifies all the lesser ironies, creating a perspective beyond that of the central character (p xxv).

998 Rudat, Wolfgang E. H. 'Sexuality and Self-Recognition in *The Pardoner's Tale*.' *JEP* 3(1982), 124-9.

PardP functions as a 'pseudo-confession by a sinner-displaying-his-sinfulness' that 'leads to a genuine confession which may actually achieve the salvation of the sinner' (p 127). The Host interprets the Pardoner's attempts to sell relics as homosexual aggression; in so doing, he makes a causal connection between the Pardoner's sexual anomaly and his selling of false relics. Startled that the Host has found him out, the Pardoner is left speechless. Though the other pilgrims miss the full depth of the Host's analysis, the Knight does not. He ironically assumes the role of spiritual counselor, thereby giving a religious meaning to an otherwise bawdy episode.

999 Stevens, Martin, and Kathleen Falvey. 'Substance, Accident, and Transformations: A Reading of The *Pardoner's Tale*.' *ChauR* 17(1982), 142-58.

PardT is Chaucer's first poetic statement that art and morality are inextricably linked. In the Pardoner, Chaucer invents an 'unethical spellbinder' (p 146) who attempts to 'woo an audience with a highly moral tale'(p 146). The failure of the Pardoner's attempt is Chaucer's rejection of sophistry. The Pardoner, unbeknownst to himself, becomes the central character of his own fiction. In the tale, the Pardoner replaces the rioters, then Chaucer replaces the Pardoner as the teller of the tale. The imagery of transformation (dove to serpent, Death to rioters, food to dung), all underscoring moral decay, reveals the poet's own voice. By showing the Pardoner as an anti-poet, Chaucer rejects the Host's theory that limits the role of literature to delight or profit (i.e., the dinner).

1000 Storm, Melvin. 'A Culpa et a Poena: Christ's Pardon and the Pardoner's.' *NM* 83(1982), 439-42.

The Pardoner's benediction is neither out of character nor contradictory to his solicitation. He offers his pardons only after invoking divine forgiveness (lines 904-6; 916-8) and acknowledges a difference between Christ's pardon (*a culpa*, from guilt) and his own (*a poena*, from penalty).

001 ———. 'The Pardoner's Invitation: Quaestor's Bag or Becket's Shrine?' *PMLA* 97(1982), 810-8.

Storm initiates a discussion of the Pardoner that provokes response from Lawrence Besserman (**1005**), William J. Hyde (**1013**), Charles Owen (**1023**), and Claude Summers (**1029**) as well as replies from Storm (**1027, 1028**). Storm suggests that in *PardT*, Chaucer employs the abuse of relics and pardons as a portent for the abuse of pilgrimage. In a series of parallels between the Canterbury pilgrimage and the rioters' quest, Storm notes that, were the pilgrims to accept the Pardoner's invitation at the alestake, they could become, like the rioters, distracted by the physical. Despite his efforts with false relics and possibly ineffectual indulgences, the Pardoner fails to detour the pilgrims. *PardT* is unique among *CT* in reestablishing the *status quo* at its conclusion. The Pardoner's implicit threat to the pilgrims becomes explicit with his solicitation. His choice of the Host, the pilgrimage's guide, is appropriate to his effort in diverting the pilgrimage. The confrontation of Host and Pardoner marks the turning point of the pilgrimage as the Host averts the failure of the pilgrimage. In referring to Becket's shrine (lines 946-50), the Host juxtaposes images of true and false relics. See **1005, 1013, 1023, 1027, 1028, 1029**.

002 Strohm, Paul. 'Chaucer's Fifteenth Century Audience and the Narrowing of the "Chaucer Tradition".' *SAC* 4(1982), 3-32.

Strohm delineates the reduced capacity of fifteenth-century audiences to appreciate the full range of Chaucer's poetic tradition as the primary close-knit audience of the fourteenth century was replaced with 'a far-flung and disparate secondary audience' (p 32). *PardT* is cited together with *FranT*, *PrT*, *ShT*, *CYT* and *MillT* as one of the most popular tales among Chaucer's contemporaries (cf **748**); whereas, analysis of anthologized tales in the fifteenth century indicates *PardT* was not included. Typical of tales popular in the fourteenth century, *PardT* frustrates generic expectations (i.e., the frame renders it deliberately equivocal) and offers an alternative to social hierarchy, sworn oaths, and established bonds. By contrast, the tales most popular in the fifteenth century reaffirmed *obeisance* and subordination to authority.

1003 Taylor, P[aul]. B[eekman]. 'Chaucer's *Cosyn to the Dede*.' *Speculum* 57(1982), 315-27.

Chaucer's use of *Will, intent, word*, and *work* more often suggests breach than harmony. Chaucer holds an ideal view of language wherein 'intent informs deeds through the ministry of words' (p 325). The Pardoner serves as an aberration from the ideals implied by reference to Christ and Plato in *GP* and to Christian ritual in *ParsT*. The Pardoner, 'a caricature of a Machiavellian nominalist' (p 326) mocks the idea that words should reflect intent, promotes the deceptive potential of *tales olde*, and dupes his immediate audience. The Pardoner 'is ... a *cosyn to the dede* par excellence, whose very confessional words disdain the repentance they extol' (p 326). The Parson's 'reconciliation of intent, word, and deed ... [counters] ... the Pardoner's nominalism' (p 327). See **1162**.

1004 ——. '*Peynted Confessiouns*: Boccaccio and Chaucer.' *CL* 34(1982a), 116-29.

Chaucer repeatedly explores disjunction in human communication and sensibilities. According to Augustine, the moral consequences of a breach of identity between thought, word and deed rest with the writer. The Pardoner sets himself apart by suggesting that evil intent, through the power of words, can serve a good end. The tale of Ser Ciapelletto in the *Dec* offers an analogue to the confusion of intent. Ser Ciapelletto dupes his audience into believing a lie; the Pardoner dupes his audience into disbelieving a truth. Like the Pardoner, Ser Ciappelletto is a trader in lies but the effect of his lies on various audiences can be delineated; with the Pardoner, meaning is obscured in 'its plenitude of suggestion' (p 128). The tale of the rioters is a grotesque reflection of the pilgrimage. Chaucer, like Boccaccio, refers to audience reception rather than inherent moral substance as the working criterion for assigning value. In the *Ret*, Chaucer turns away from the nominalistic implications of his work.

1005 Besserman, Lawrence. 'Chaucer's Pardoner.' Forum Response to Storm. *PMLA* 98(1983), 405-6.

Besserman notes that the opposition Storm sets up between the Pardoner's false relics and the relics at Canterbury is challenged by Lollard criticism of the practices both of carrying false relics and corrupted pilgrimage, specifically the pilgrimage to Canterbury and the veneration of the relics of St. Thomas. Noting that Storm allowed a Lollard perspective in his explication of the Pardoner-Summoner relationship, Besserman suggests Chaucer shared the same perspective on the question of pilgrimage and false relics. See **1000, 1001**.

006 Braswell, Mary Flowers. *The Medieval Sinner: Characterization and Confession in the Literature of the English Middle Ages.* London and Toronto: Associated University Presses, 1983.
By the late Middle Ages, theologians had worked out an elaborate theology of sin. The sinner, unlike the antagonist, articulates an awareness of sin and motive. Previous critics who have assessed Chaucer's treatment of sin and sinners have largely ignored the pilgrims themselves. The presumptuous Pardoner, the most hardened sinner (p 113), plays the role of confessor and in *PardP* conducts his own investigation. The Pardoner understands the confessional nature of his remarks but also revels in the sin he reveals. Starring in a self-staged confessional drama, the Pardoner refuses to seek grace, and is, thus, unpardonable (p 116). The epilogue keeps with the penitential format, insofar as one is made to feel humiliated in the most vulnerable area. The Pardoner, like the Wife of Bath, luxuriates in sinfulness: their egos remain intact; they remain commanding presences for the duration of *CT* (p 127). The *pax* commanded by the Knight fulfills the post-confessional part of Penance. Chaucer's sinners are at once the 'best' sinners and the 'best' characters (p 127).

007 Burnley, David. *A Guide to Chaucer's Language.* Norman, Oklahoma: University of Oklahoma Press; London: Macmillan, 1983.
Treats interpretive implications of grammar and syntax. Relevant items which can be traced through index include: *Interr* D 175 (reflexive pronoun), D 186-7 (*'eth'* forms); from *Phy-PardL* C 304-7 (unusual use of *'cors'* as live body); and from *PardT* C 492-7 (*difference* suggests ironic similarity), C 642 (use of *or* possibly to suggest conceptual affinity), C 702-10 (variation between preterite and perfect tenses), C 713 (adjective lacking *e* when used after an indefinite article), C 764 (use of *nothyng* for emphasis), C 823 (periphrastic with *wol* to refer to future).

008 Cooper, Helen. *The Structure of The Canterbury Tales.* 1983. See **469**.
Frag VI (C) always occurs immediately before VII B²; only in Ellesmere and its group does it follow *FranT*, a placement that is probably best. *PhysT* and *PardT* are 'antitypes' giving exemplary portrayals of virtue and sin, close in plot and pairing gifts of Nature and Fortune (p 154). *PardT* demands 'two mutually exclusive moral readings' (p 74). *PardT*

gains morality-like quality from its lack of proper names: only Death is named; the rioters are '*other* people ... potentially, the audience' (p 157). The central theme is the nature of death. Though *PardT* derives richness from resonances with other tales, the immediate context is the Pardoner himself. *PardT* fulfills traditional literary purposes of delighting and teaching as well as the practical purpose of enriching the Pardoner. Aesthetically, *PardT* ranks high; ethically, the Pardoner resembles the Friar though *PardT* lacks even the momentary glimpse of virtue found in *FrT*. For *PardP*, see **642**.

- Review by Charles A. Owen. *SAC* 7(1985), 178-80: '... in the case of the Pardoner, the *Prologue* and the quarrel with the Host are largely ignored. Instead we get the effort to connect the Physician's digression on governesses, not with the historical events in John of Gaunt's family, but with the Pardoner...This connection depends on Cooper's not Chaucer's description of the Pardoner in the wolf-and-shepherd imagery that brings the Physician's digression to an end. Cooper's final point about *The Pardoner's Tale*, that it differs from the other "moral" tales by concerning itself exclusively with vice and evil, needs qualification: there is, after all, the encounter with the old man' (p 179). Owen concludes that the book 'breaks new ground' but fails to follow its own plan of seeing the fragments of *CT* as stages of a developing but unfinished plan with 'sufficient rigor' (p 180).

1009   Erickson, Jon. 'Chaucer's *Pardoner's Tale* as Anti-Märchen.' *Folklore* 94(1983), 235-9.

Including the notion of 'marking' in the definition of *märchen* can account for the atypical character of stories like *PardT*. Röhrich argued that tales with unhappy endings be excluded from the *märchen* classification (Aarne-Thompson 763, cited in **71**), and suggested that stories centering on the activities of a negative hero be seen as *anti-märchen*. Structurally, the exemplum corresponds to the *märchen*: an initial situation, a villain (in this case unusual both as an abstraction and the goal of the quest), and a hero who decides on appropriate counteraction, meets a test and acquires a helper. More important than the negative character of the hero is the systematic relationship of hero to ending: the negative character of the hero demands he come to a negative end. The negative characteristics can be seen as a variety of 'markings': the anti *märchen* a systematic transformation within the *märchen* genre.

Not all stories under Aarne-Thompson 763 are *anti-märchen*; 'The King's Ankus', though an analogue to *PardT*, is not a *märchen* because it lacks a quest and Death is neither villain nor goal.

1010   Ginsberg, Warren. 'The Cast of Character: Chaucer and the Conventions of Originality.' *The Cast of Character: The Representation of Personality in Ancient and Medieval Literature.* Toronto: University of Toronto Press, 1983. Pp 134-65.

Chaucer's characters manifest a 'submerged conventionality' (p 141): irony often results from the juxtaposition of conventional expectations and behavior in *CT*. The Pardoner derives power from 'his conscious denial of the processes of literary typology' (p 142). By introducing images with spiritual connotations (e.g., the dove, the Old Man) yet allowing only literal meaning, the Pardoner reveals his lack of faith.

1011   Glasser, Marc. 'The Pardoner and The Host: Chaucer's Analysis of The Canterbury Game.' 1983/84. See **643**.

When the Pardoner narrows his general theme of *cupiditas* to the sins of gluttony, gambling and swearing, he moves to the Host's 'turf'(p 40). His manner of denouncing the sins virtually specifies the Host. Gluttony is 'the raison d'être of the Canterbury tales' (p 40) which the Host has arranged to end with a supper; *hasard* is seen in the Host's conversion of a pilgrimage into a tale-telling competition; and swearing is evidenced by the Host in the introduction (p 40). *PardT*, with its rioters journeying in search of Death, is a 'savage, mocking parody of the Host's conception of and plan for the Canterbury pilgrimage' (p 41). The Pardoner's parody reveals the 'darker implications'(p 42) of secularizing the pilgrimage. *PardT* concludes with as dense a series of dialogue interchanges as any part of *CT*. In offering his relics, the Pardoner invites the pilgrims to share in his sacrilege. The Pardoner reverses the roles of himself and the Host, mocking the Host's early control of the pilgrimage. When the Knight reasserts the sense of community, the sacramental pilgrimage continues.

1012   Hallissy, Margaret. 'Poison Lore and Chaucer's Pardoner.' *MSE* 9(1983), 54-63.

Asking why Chaucer alludes to Avicenna (an author with whom he demonstrates familiarity) rather than describe the poisoned wretches' suffering leads to a consideration of poison lore, a subject which in turn develops the paradox of the evil Pardoner as a channel of grace. Both medieval medical writers and early exegetes offer precedent for linking poison with the notion of evil. When the Pardoner describes himself as a serpent, he perverts the usual signification of the image: a would-be confessor, he spews forth venom. Paradoxically, and according to the principle of homeopathic medicine where like cures like, the tale becomes a *moral thyng* serving a *treacle* whose medical sense is that of a universal antidote and whose spiritual sense is one of healing. Despite the Pardoner's attempts to make Christ's truth an instrument of his greed, the tale becomes an occasion of repentance for the hearers. Ironically, the Pardoner becomes a concrete example of the possibility of mercy and forgiveness.

1013 Hyde, William J. 'Chaucer's Pardoner.' Forum Response to Storm. *PMLA* 98(1983), 253.

The Pardoner is not a threat to the continuance of the pilgrimage (though such is the assumption of the pardoner in *Four P's*) because he openly asserts his covetous aims and fraudulent relics. Rather than as substitute benefit to Canterbury, the Pardoner offers himself as travelers' insurance. The Pardoner's challenge to the Host may be an effort, engendered by sexual embarrassment, to test his manhood. The Host's reply is carefully chosen for its offensiveness. See **1000**.

1014 Kanno, Mashiko. '"Purs" and "Relikes" in *The Pardoner's Tale*.' *Bulletin of Aichi University of Education* 32(1983), 31-8.

Through a consideration of diction, particularly the use of pairs of associative words (bag/relics; belly/excrement; purse/testicles), Kanno examines Chaucer's treatment of the Pardoner [in Japanese]. For the English translation of this article, see **1140**.

1015 Kirkpatrick, Robin. 'The Wake of the *Commedia*: Chaucer's Canterbury Tales and Boccaccio's *Decameron*. *Chaucer and the Italian Trecento*.' 1983. See **644**.

PardT is considered in an examination of the dissimilarities between the *Dec* and *CT*. Chaucer's Pardoner and Boccaccio's 'guileful priests' (p 203) reveal a fascination with the force of appetite and call into question the schemes of pardon manipulated by false clerics. *PardT* provides 'a comprehensive history of man's unhappiness' and a dramatic investigation of 'the consequences of sin' (p 221). In scope, intensity and moral subject, the work is Dantean. Despite their similarity as hypocritical orators, the Pardoner differs consistently from Cepperello and Cipolla (*Dec*) in that his lies reveal his true self.

1016 Knapp, Robert S. 'Penance, Irony, and Chaucer's Retraction.' *Assays*

2(1983), 45-67.

In a discussion of authorial self-elimination in irony, *Ret* and penance, Knapp comments that the Pardoner is one of several pilgrims who succeed at the literal task of entertaining but less clearly in terms of the spirit of pilgrimage. The Pardoner correctly reads the meaning of his tale but misses its significance both as a mirror of his condition and in terms of its impact on his audience.

17 Knight, Stephen. 'Chaucer's Pardoner in Performance.' 1983-4. See **472**.

In an examination of some implications of accepting performance as the mode basic to *CT*, Knight moves beyond his argument for the 'orally persuasive' character of *CT* (**884, 885**). Performance alters the text, the performer necessarily resolving some ambiguities and creating others 'by making two kinds of syntactic and semantic analyses possible' through the onward movement of the language (p 24). *PardT* is rich in the verbal play and visual delights common to oral material; primary among the visual, sensual delights are the gold coins. The Pardoner is a type arising from the tradition of a speaker simultaneously confessing and performing villainy (cf Faux Semblant). Such contradiction is particularly disruptive in the medieval context where the individual is seen as a fragment of a social whole, and fulfilling a role is understood as a social duty rather than falseness to individuality. The Pardoner, 'a deeply shocking figure' is 'a truly dialectical figure in that the contemporary vigour of one system—external values—is the cause of its overthrow' (p 32). The Pardoner is 'a self-conscious, anti-communal, individualist revolutionary'(p 32). His performance is an acute realization of a theme running through *CT*, the tension between 'society as a community and its constituent members' (p 33). The late fourteenth century shows an increasing awareness that the public 'semblance' may be 'false'(p 34). Chaucer's imagination derives power from the rapidly developing social and cultural individualism. The Pardoner's obsession with cash receives context from the transition from the 'use value' system of the manorial economy to a cash economy. With the Pardoner, Chaucer realizes the 'socio-economic history of his period' (p 35).

18 Merrix, Robert P. 'Sermon Structure in the *Pardoner's Tale.*' *ChauR* 17(1983), 235-49.

The debate over the relation of *PardP* and *PardT* to the medieval sermon

328 / Pardoner's Prologue and Tale

continues to range widely. The major problem in defining the relationship derives from an unfounded assumption that the medieval sermon was strictly defined as a form with 'clearly delineated parts within a unique structure'(p 235). The *artes praedicandi* identified elements and called for systematic development as each element arose out of the previous one. Examination of sermons during the later Middle Ages reveals a definable genre known as the modern medieval sermon. The *PardT* exhibits an analogous structure to the '"modern" medieval sermon' based on the *artes praedicandi* (p 235): theme (lines 333-4), protheme (lines 335-462), introduction to theme (lines 463-482), division and subdivision (lines 483-660), major exemplum (lines 661-894), and recapitulation (lines 895-915). Consequently, the *PardT* is a representative example of a medieval sermon.

1019 Moisan, Thomas. 'Shakespeare's Chaucerian Allegory: The Quest for Death in *Romeo and Juliet* and the Pardoner's Tale.' In *Chaucerian Shakespeare: Adaptation and Transformation.* Ed. E. Talbot Donaldson and Judith J. Kollmann. Medieval and Renaissance Monograph Series, 2. Michigan Consortium for Medieval and Early Modern Studies, Ann Arbor: 1983. Pp 131-49.

Central to PardT and *Romeo and Juliet* is the resistance, in the form of 'a rhetorically heightened quest' (p 131) of youth to the demands of death and its attendant concepts (e.g., time, providence). In both cases the quests turn on irony (though successful, they produce unexpected results), and the paradox that the rhetoric of the quest is the means of evading death. The Pardoner's 'harangue' like the cries of Juliet's 'presumptive mourners,' both specimens of 'rhetorical insincerity,' distance their audiences (p 136). The figurative action of the Pardoner's exemplum and the final act of *Romeo and Juliet* is governed by the tragic necessity determined not only by providence but the human will.

1020 Nakagawa, Tokio. 'Chaucer no menzaifu Uri no Seikaku Byosha to Kare no Hanashi no Geifutsu sei.' In *Eibungaku to no Deai.* Ed. Naomi Matsuura. Kyoto: Showado, 1983. Pp 251-9. [Not seen.]

1021 Olhoeft, Janet Ellen. 'Division and Connection: Mediation in Chaucer (England).' State University of New York at Buffalo Dissertation, 1983. See also *DAI* 44(1983), 2143.

Chaucer's interest in mediation is reflected in his creation of mediator figures, mediated worlds and use of language as connection. The Pardoner, like the Host, Clerk and Narrator, functions as a connector.

In his mediated worlds, Chaucer presents situations in which two characters are influenced by the presence of a third. Language is defined as the mediation between the artist, audience and truth. Ultimately, the reader is placed in a position of mediating ambiguity.

022 Olsen, Alexandra Hennessey. '*They Shul Desiren to Dye, and Deeth Shal Flee Fro Hem*: A Reconsideration of the Pardoner's Old Man.' *NM* 84(1983), 367-71.

The Old Man in *PardT* should be interpreted in the context not only of the tale (**910**) but also of the entire *CT*. Many of the modern learned explanations would probably not have occurred to the pilgrims. If one assumes that each of *CT* gains resonance from comparison with those that precede it, one can compare *PardT* to *FrT*. The memory of the Green Yeoman, a devil wandering the earth in search of prey, makes the appearance of the Old Man more ominous, as does the Parson's reference to the medieval doctrine that the damned seek death which flees them (*ParsT* lines 213-6). Both the Green Yeoman and the Old Man seem courteous, mysterious and prescient; in each tale a character is betrayed by sworn brothers and the damnation of the characters is underscored by futile pious wishes. Reminding the pilgrims of the damnation awaiting sinners who refuse to repent and the way sinners can be tricked by the devil, *PardT* prepares us for the Parson's closing sermon on the seven deadly sins.

023 Owen, Charles A. 'Chaucer's Pardoner.' Forum Response to Storm. *PMLA* 98(1983), 254.

The Pardoner does not seek to divert the pilgrims from their journey. The Pardoner calls the pilgrims 'however seriously or jocularly, to repentance and to recognition of their journey in spiritual terms'(p 254). The quaestor's bag and Becket's shrine enhance each other; seeking pardon at every milestone would underscore the spiritual nature of the pilgrimage. The Pardoner distinguishes between his ordinary audience and the pilgrims at the outset and again at the close of his tale. His shift in tone and the context of his boasting 'makes it difficult to see the invitation as anything but parody' (p 254). The Host serves as guide in storytelling. In his confrontation with the Pardoner, the fellowship of the pilgrimage rather than the journey itself is threatened. The Host's verbal assault on the Pardoner does not contribute to the pilgrims' well being. See **1000, 1013, 1029**.

024 Pearsall, Derek. 'Chaucer's Pardoner: The Death of a Salesman.'

ChauR 17(1983), 358-65.

PardT is the most fully articulated tale within its dramatic context. Chaucer, while clearly interested in the inner workings of character, deliberately creates zero-psychology in the Pardoner: the Pardoner represents the 'horror of vacuity'(p 361), existing only in the act of performance. Theologically dead himself, his profession appropriately reduces a system of spiritual solace to mercantile exchange. The tale of the rioters presents a trick depending on a double meaning of death which we understand but they do not; the trickery of the narrative is reinforced by *PardP*, homily and profession. The chill of the *PardT* is mitigated by an 'ambiguous movement of inner life'(p 364) prompted by his imaginative act of telling a story. See **1162**.

1025 Schauber, Ellen, and Ellen Spolsky. 'Conversational Noncooperation: The Case of Chaucer's Pardoner.' *Lang&S* 16(1983), 249-61.

A study of the speech acts of the Pardoner reveals that he violates discourse conventions of the commentary; by his refusal to fill the expectations of his audience, he sets himself outside the communication circle. The Pardoner's hearers are angered by the collocation of his speech acts in *PardP* (e.g., boasting, confiding, arguing weakly, and relying on assertion in place of argument). In the exemplum, his speech acts identify him with the rioters. Most grievous, his sermon is insincere. The Host's reference to castration reflects an awareness of the Pardoner's inability to connect with his community. See **1039**.

1026 Shoaf, R[ichard]. A. 'The Pardoner and the Word of Death.' In *Dante, Chaucer and the Currency of the Word: Money, Images, and Reference in Late Medieval Poetry*. 1983. See **475**.

Deriving a Chaucerian poetics of reference from Canto 30 of *DC*, Shoaf proposes an extended equation: poetry = language = sign = image = coin. *CT* is a collection of possible positions on poets and poetry. The Pardoner is obsessed with language and money, using 'the one as a magnet for the other' (p 211): he takes avarice as his theme; announces the breach between vicious *entente* and his moral tale; insists upon 'buying' Redemption; and expects his audience to 'buy' his tale. With his multiplicity of selves, the Pardoner offers the 'extreme of "irreference"' (p 224). He transforms content into intent, turning himself 'inside out' through torrents of speech (p 225). Radically asserting the priority of the private, he exploits the community's need for a medium of exchange by converting the substance of language into the accident of coin. The anxiety of his isolation simultaneously motivates and frustrates his confession. His exemplum is 'about the old man he meets every day in his own body' (p 227). Forgetting that words *refer*, he invites thee pilgrims to accept his pose; he receives a violent reaction precisely because words *do refer and refer, moreover, to the truth* (p 227).

027 Storm, Melvin. 'Chaucer's Pardoner.' Forum Reply to Besserman. *PMLA* 98(1983), 406.

Storm differs with Besserman **(1005)** on two counts: he cites support from Kellogg and Hasselmayer, Arnold Williams, Jusserand and Herbert Thurston to maintain that the association of pardoners with false relics was rare in the documents of the day; and he opposes Besserman's suggestion 'that because the Lollards denounced pilgrimage to Canterbury and veneration of Becket's relics, so too must Chaucer' (p 406). On the latter point, Storm discounts the implication that Chaucer repudiates the Canterbury pilgrimage framework. See **1000, 1001, 1005**.

028 —. 'Chaucer's Pardoner.' Forum Reply to Hyde, Owen, and Summers. *PMLA* 98(1983), 255-6.

Storm suggests an inconsistency in Hyde's criticism **(1013)**: if the Pardoner's disclosure precludes his deception of the pilgrims then it would also preclude his function as 'traveler's insurance'(p 255). Actually, the Pardoner's self-revelation does not preclude his deception of the pilgrims: it is a deliberate effort to heighten the challenge (if the Pardoner is motivated by sexual embarrassment, so much the more so). Storm rejects Owen's reading **(1023)** of an altered pitch for the Pardoner's invitation: by invoking Christ's pardon, the Pardoner distinguishes between indulgence *a culpa* and indulgence *a poena* **(1001)**. The Host is spiritual guide not in his own view but in Chaucer's. Storm rejects the concern raised by Summers **(1029)** as being irrelevant to historical criticism.

029 Summers, Claude J. 'Chaucer's Pardoner.' Forum Response to Storm. *PMLA* 98(1983), 254-5.

Summers charges that Storm's article presents 'insensitive and offensive characterization of homosexuals' (p 254) **(1000)**. Summers alleges that by failing to separate his own views from those of Chaucer, Storm endorses 'noxious and antiquated attitudes' (p 255). See **1000**.

030 Traversi, Derek. *The Canterbury Tales: A Reading.* 1983. See **477**.

PardT consists of a denunciation of the sins of Gluttony and Avarice and an exemplum. Beyond the comic effect of the Pardoner's sermon, he strives simultaneously to stimulate and undercut a sense of sin. The tree with gold at its base is a parody of the Cross, the rioters' meal a parody of the Eucharist. The rioters have found *cupiditas*: the root of all evil and the occasion of the Pardoner's exclusion from grace. By invoking the superiority of Christ's pardon, the Pardoner draws the pilgrims' attention to the efficacy of his sermon and the poet's audience to a recognition that pardon and penitence are the substance of pilgrimage. With the Pardoner's performance, Chaucer poses the question of whether the 'reality' by which we live is not a creation of our 'faith' (p 194). In *CT*, the question of the validity of fiction and the efficacy of 'truth' remains. For *PardP*, see **645**.

1031 Tristram, Philippa. '"Olde stories longe tyme agoon": Death and the Audience of Chaucer's Pardoner.' In *Death in The Middle Ages*. Mediaevalia Lovaniensia. Series 1. Studia 9. Ed. Herman Braet and Werner Verbeke. Leuven: Leuven University Press, 1983. Pp 179-90. When *PardT* is seen as a comment on the theme of death, the tales that are not told are significant. Both the opening tavern scene and the meeting with the Old Man arouse expectations which are not met: the result is a tale memorable to the *lewed* and instructive to the *gentils*. Chaucer's refusal to create a figure of animate death in a setting as inviting as *PardT* 'can only be construed as his own challenge' to the figure (p 188). *PardT* attempts to redirect the conception of Death common in England at the close of the fourteenth century. The Pardoner's 'mediating consciousness' (p 180), with his relics and oaths, both exhibits and denounces the materialistic apprehension of mortality. *The Pride of Life* and the motif of the three Living and three Dead would have led Chaucer's audience to 'expect some salutary encounter with an animate corpse' (p 184) and speculate whether the rioters would live to repent or die damned. Initially, the rioters would have found the Old Man more traditional than mysterious. He is nontraditional in the lack of both the detail of decrepitude and nostalgic life view, as well as in the manifestation of avarice: these nontraditional characteristics suit his posture as one who longs for rather than fears death. The address to earth as *leeve mooder*, though paralleled in Maximian, is rare in English before the Renaissance. Chaucer's Egeus (*KnT*) and Troilus suggest the grave as a place of peace. With the rioters' discovery of gold 'even

the *lewed* must have bartered their expectation of an animate corpse
for a wittier donouement'(p 188): Death is assimilated into the rioters'
moral being as their sin becomes the instrument of self-destruction.
Anticipating the Renaissance, Chaucer resisted the obsession with
mortality which impeded a true perception of temporal life indicated an
'intrinsic denial' of the hope of resurrection (p 190).

32 —. 'Strange Images of Death.' *LeedsSE*, 14(1983),
196-211.

Like Shakespeare in *Pericles*, Chaucer seems to allude in *PardT* to the
familiar legend of the three living and the three dead. The tale frustrates
audience anticipation of the legend's denouement: there is no figure of
death. The tale traces 'the genesis of such horrible imaginings'(p 200)
from metaphor (line 683) through personification to actual figure (line
700). The Old Man is not charnel; he is exceptional in his longing for
death; 'for the first time in English literature—and the last until the
Renaissance—he addresses earth as a mother in death as in birth'(p
201). When the rioters are destroyed by their avarice, death is
'assimilated to man's moral being'(p 201). Surprisingly, Shakespeare's
allusion to the legend in *Pericles* is more medieval than Chaucer's since
it restores the original significance of the legend by disposing of the
animation of the three princes.

33 Ames, Ruth M. *God's Plenty: Chaucer's Christian Humanism.*
1984. See **478**.

Ames reviews *CT* to show Chaucer was an educated medieval Christian
whose Catholicism was an operative force in his thinking. Chaucer's
references to the Jews (e.g., the Pardoner's references to *Lamuel,
Samuel, Sampsoun*, the holy Jew) reflect popular knowledge rather
than Old Testament theology. It is 'chilling' (p 193) that, with one exception
in *CT*, Jews are characterized as violently anti-Christ and anti-Christian.
The Pardoner compares blasphemers to Jews who rent Christ's body.
The response to the problem of evil in *CT* is more devotional than logical.
In *PardT*, the devil is subordinated to Providence. The Pardoner uses
the concept of the devil metaphorically. The kiss at the close of *PardT*
dramatizes the theme of reconciliation, integral to Chaucer's Christianity.
The Knight's act suggests Chaucer did not damn the Pardoner despite
condemning his sins. Humor and a sense of community moderate
Chaucer's satire; the Pardoner can be pardoned 'because finally all
share with Chaucer in God's plenty' (p 259). For Pardoner, see **478**.

1034 Andreas, James R. 'The Rhetoric of Chaucerian Comedy: The Aristotelian Legacy.' *Comparatist* 8(1984), 56-66.

The literary tradition that Chaucer worked within—sanctioning topicality, festive release and erotic candor—ultimately derived from Aristotle. Within the '"unstable," processional' structure of *CT*, the unruly pilgrims 'are ready to assist the Host in the threatened castration of the Pardoner'(p 60). 'The reconciliation of the Host and the Pardoner ... represents a high comic moment in the poem'(p 61). The Pardoner's sexual ambiguity, an aspect of the comic grotesque, is not an emblem of moral failure; moral judgment 'is suspended during the liminal moment of festive release'(p 62).

1035 Besserman, Lawrence. 'Chaucer and the Bible: Parody and Authority in the Pardoner's Tale.' In *Biblical Patterns in Modern Literature*. Brown Judaic Studies, 77. Ed. David H. Hirsch and Nehama Aschkenasy. Chico: Scholars Press, 1984. Pp 43-50.

Late fourteenth-century controversy about Biblical interpretation finds a parallel in Chaucer's satire of the abuse of glossing. In *PardP* and *PardT*, rich biblical allusion produces the 'darkest' parody in Chaucer (p 47). In particular, by investing the judicial prescription for a wife suspected of adultery (Num. 5:11-31), 'the adulterous woman's ordeal has become the cuckolded husband's surefire cure' (p 50).

1036 Brewer, Derek. *An Introduction to Chaucer*. 1984. See **646**.

PardT is read in the light of the Pardoner's self-revelation. His sermon within the tale has elements of caricature. Chaucer enters the Pardoner's spirit so they speak as one. The astonishing tale, marked by a touch of horror found nowhere else in Chaucer, closes with 'the wonderfully calm fullness of Chaucer's plain style' (p 203). The Old Man 'is the weariness of old age incarnate' (p 204). 'A sense of the ineluctable mystery of life lies beneath the simple plot' (p 204).

1037 Collette, Carolyn P. '"Ubi Peccaverant, Ibi Punirentur": The Oak Tree and The *Pardoner's Tale*.' *ChauR* 19(1984), 39-45.

When the Old Man directs our attention to the exact location of death, the sudden slowing of narration and concentration of detail signal thematic importance. Chaucer builds on the connections among death, idolatry, and the oak which is familiar from the Old Testament. Through the detail of the oak, the exemplum becomes 'anagogically an allegory of grace offered and refused'(p 43), a theme suited both to the rioters and the Pardoner.

38   Dean, James. 'Spiritual Allegory and Chaucer's Narrative Style: Three Test Cases.' *ChauR* 18(1984), 273-87.

Chaucer employs spiritual allegory as a narrative technique to deepen the mystery of characters and situations (p 283). Using three test cases of the summoner in *FrT*, the rioters in *PardT*, and the false canon in *CYT*, Dean shows the way each moves 'toward identification with their baser natures and their sin' (p 275). The rioters' ignorance of Death and desire to kill it mark them as allegorical figures. The oak tree can be interpreted within two related contexts: the classical (Roman) phase suggesting a golden age and the medieval phase adding the moral significance of the 'hard but fortunate existence of virtuous simplicity' (p 279). Chaucer obfuscates the Old Man's significance by linking him both with the ideal symbol of the oak and symbols of carnality (e.g., gold, crooked way). The thrust of *PardT* is away from the narrative and the personality of the teller to the sin of avarice.

39   Dürmüller, Urs. 'Sociolinguistics and the Study of Medieval English.' In *Linguistic and Stylistic Studies in Medieval English*. Ed. André Crepin. Publications de l'Association des Médievistes de l'Einseignement Supérieur, 10. Paris, 1984. Pp 5-22.

Following Schauber and Spolsky (**1025**), Dürmüller examines the characterization of the Pardoner in terms of speech act theory, considering the intentions of the Pardoner, and the presumptions of his audience. The Pardoner is 'stylistically off the track, in his appearance, his behavior and his speech' (p 17). The Pardoner's audience condemns him only after he violates 'conventionalized appropriateness conditions' (p 21).

40   Fleming, John V. 'Gospel Asceticism: Some Chaucerian Images of Perfection.' In *Chaucer and Scriptural Tradition*. Ed. David Lyle Jeffrey. Ottawa: University of Ottawa Press, 1984. Pp 183-95.

Chaucer's primary appeal in presenting the worldliness of the Pardoner is to ascetic texts. Using the central image of the spiritual eunuch (cf **747**), Chaucer employs image patterns of sterility (sexual) and increase (silver, crops, cattle) to underscore the victory of flesh over spirit in the Pardoner. In lieu of sexual organs, the Pardoner has a purse, a detail available to Chaucer 'in the exegetical vocabulary of Christian perfection' (p 189).

41   Jeffrey, David Lyle, ed. *Chaucer and Scriptural Tradition*. Ottawa: University of Ottawa Press, 1984.

A collection of eleven essays on Chaucer's relationship to scriptural tradition, four of which treat *PardT*: John V. Fleming, 'Gospel Asceticism: Some Chaucerian Images of Perfection,' pp 183-95 (**1040**); Russell Peck,'Biblical Interpretation: St. Paul and *The Canterbury Tales*,' pp 143-170 (**983**); and Edmund Reiss, 'Biblical Parody: Chaucer's "Distortions" of Scripture,' pp 47-61 (**1042**).

1042 Reiss, Edmund. 'Biblical Parody: Chaucer's "Distortions" of Scripture.' In *Chaucer and Scriptural Tradition*. Ed. David Lyle Jeffrey. Ottawa: Ottawa University Press, 1984. Pp 47-61.

A consideration of the Pardoner's purposeful 'distortions' of Scripture indicates that Biblical parody plays a distinctive role in Chaucer's art (p 61). Although the Pardoner more than anyone else in Chaucer urges his audience to read the Bible, his Biblical allusions, whether Old Testament (Lot, Herod, Adam and Eve) or New Testament (1 Cor. 6:13; Phil. 3:18; Matt. 5:34), are suspect.

1043 Sklute, Larry. *Virtue of Necessity: Inconclusiveness and Narrative Form in Chaucer's Poetry*. Columbus: Ohio State University Press, 1984.

Inconclusiveness functions in *CT* as a principle of structure and a tactic to control meaning. As such, it underlies the fictional voices and motivates composition in fragments. Chaucer imbued his fictions of the inner form with the voices of the characters developed in the outer form. In *PardT*, where self-revelation is explicit, the distinctions between inner and outer form disappear. During the Pardoner's recitation, the boundary between tale and performance merges within the Pardoner's consciousness; he enters his own fiction and turns to the pilgrim audience as if they were *lewed* folk, thereby producing an intensely dramatic moment. Chaucer 'fragmentized' his material, dialectically presenting in each fragment one valence and at least one alternate valence (p 123). Fragment VI is 'unified by a common assumption about how language means' (p 123). Both *PhyT* and *PardT* take accident for substance; the Pardoner transposes the spiritual matter of salvation with the material matter of profit.

1044 Birney, Earle. 'Is Chaucer's Irony a Modern Discovery?' In *Earl Birney: Essays on Chaucerian Irony*. Ed Beryl Rowland. Toronto: University of Toronto Press, 1985. Pp 36-53.

Birney notes that the seventeeth-century Oxford antiquarian, Bryan Twyne wrote on the irony of *PardT*.

045 Bloom, Harold, ed. *Geoffrey Chaucer*. [Modern Critical Views]. New York: Cheslea House Publishers, 1985.

Includes: E. Talbot Donaldson, 'The Effect of the "Merchant's Tale",' pp 37-48 **(849)**; Donald Howard, 'The Idea of *The Canterbury Tales*,' pp 79-104 **(926)**; and Stewart Justman, 'Literal and Symbolic in *The Canterbury Tales*,' pp 123-35 **(966)**.

046 Cowgill, Bruce Kent. '"*By corpus dominus*": Harry Bailly as False Spiritual Guide.' *JMRS* 15(1985), 157-81.

The interaction of Host and Pardoner is one of four scenes which evoke the allegorical import of the Host as 'a burlesque Christ/mass-priest' (p 170). The comic identification of the Host as Christ the Redeemer is indicated through the anti-sacramental blasphemy of *Phy-PardL*. In *PardT*, the unholy trinity end their 'dark anti-mass'(p 174) with the sacrificial slaying of the younger and the subsequent death of the other two. The concluding kiss of peace works on the ironic level as a comic inversion of the ritual sequence in the Mass of the kiss of peace followed by communion. In *PardT*, a burlesque communion takes place as the Pardoner pauses at the alestake.

047 Ferster, Judith. *Chaucer on Interpretation*. Cambridge: Cambridge University Press, 1985.

In addition to the hierarchical model, Chaucer shows his awareness of dialectical models of power in *ad hoc* leaders like Harry Bailly, Nicholas, and the Pardoner who attempt to control situations over which they have no authority. The Pardoner, as narrator, acknowledges the audience's power in the selection of his tale. 'Chaucer's emphasis on the reader's rewriting of texts may have been motivated by an anxiety about his influence on his audience's spiritual health' (p 11). The Pardoner and Manciple give differing evaluations of 'the word's escape from the author' (pp 11-2). The Pardoner contemplates the possibility his words will have a different effect on his listeners than that which motivates him to speak.

048 Lawton, David [A]. *Chaucer's Narrators*. Cambridge: D. S. Brewer, 1985; Cambridge and Wolfeboro, New Hampshire: Boydell and Brewer, 1986.

This book sets the earlier discussion of narratorial voice in *PardT* within a fully developed theory of narratorial voice informed by structuralist and post-structuralist criticism **(979)**. Chaucer's narratorial voice moves increasingly from ostensibly oral to self-consciously written medium.

In the process, it loses authority and presence: the Chaucerian 'I' is 'more self-effacement than self-projection'(p xiv). The 'I' loses 'meaning' and gains 'supplementarity'; the transferred 'I' given to fictional narrators of *CT* is doubly 'supplementary,' the introduction of a new character (p xiv). The '*persona*-oriented criticism ... diverts attention from language and styles into a reckoning that is dramatic and psychological' (p 7). In place of the blanket term, *persona*, five functions are delineated: 'narrator,' 'open *persona*,' 'closed *persona*,' 'narratorial voice,' and 'character'(p 7). To read *PardT* as an extension of the Pardoner is to apply a critical model better suited to the novel. The persona of *PardT* is open (i.e., a clearly marked narrator who remains a neutral voice): that of the 'frame' is closed. During Chaucer's period, the narratorial voice moves from 'a kind of moral anonymity to poetic individuality' (p 14). Chapter II 'The Pardoner: Morality in its Context'(pp 17-35) reprints (**979**). In *PardP* and *PardT*, 'persona and theme are dramatically at odds'(p 36). The dramatic monologue of *PardP* sets up a fictional persona that is suspended until the end of the tale. Unlike Gower and Langland who employed a persona to create a confidence in the writer, Chaucer often uses a persona to fictionalize the writer. In *PardT*, where penance is at the thematic core of the poem, Chaucer employs a narratorial voice that is close to 'the standard voice of "public poetry" in the last decades of the fourteenth century' (p 37). The Pardoner-frame, with its appropriation of False-Seeming, 'alienates the public voice from its authority and immediately produces a new and unstable literary context'(p 37). It is unstable by design; it is 'unauthorized,' challenging precedent as it does (p 37).

- Review by Joerg O. Fichte, *SAC*, 10(1988), 165-8: With the exception of Bakhtin's concept of 'heteroglossia,' studies of narratology do not shape the argument. Chapter 2 on *PardT* illustrates Lawton's interpretation. Though Lawton is right to reject the 'highly psychological reading of the narrator-persona,' the 'supposed neutrality of the narratorial voice' is difficult to accept (p 167). Lawton's analysis is thought-provoking and his conclusions challenging to one's own assumptions about Chaucerian narrators though one may 'hesitate to follow all the leads he gives to their ultimate conclusions'(p 168).
- Review by David Benson, *Speculum* 64(1989), 182-3: 'Although not every reader will read the sermon on the three sins as

straightforwardly as Lawton, he is certainly right to note the modern tendency to "shrink from the absolute standards and intractable logic, of the Tale" and instead "base most of our criticism on nine lines of quizzical anatomy in the General Prologue" (p34).'

49 Lindahl, Carl. 'The Festive Form of the *Canterbury Tales*.' *ELH* 52(1985), 531-74. Rpt (partial) In Chap 4. *Earnest Games: Folkloric Patterns in the Canterbury Tales*. Bloomington: Indiana University Press, 1987. Pp 44-61.

Chaucer shaped *CT* to simulate the structure of the medieval festival, fitting the action of the frame to the model of oral group performance. In festival art, any powerful objection can end the performance; in this manner, the *gentils* prevent the Pardoner from telling a bawdy tale. Medieval performances engaged two distinct classes. Though the Host chose a *gentil* form of competition, the churls react with quarrels evoking the dynamics of the Corpus Christi plays. For Pardoner, see **500, 1094**.

50 Pearsall, Derek. *The Canterbury Tales*. 1985. See **483**.

Pearsall reviews criticism of the Pardoner in an extended original essay. *PardP* extends the *GP* portrait and gives rise directly to *PardT*, a specimen of the Pardoner's preaching. The interruption of the Wife of Bath 'is a nice dramatic touch in itself' and sets her off on autobiographical reminiscences (p 83). The Pardoner 'performance' is 'a uniquely consistent exploitation of the dramatic potentialities of the pilgrimage framework' (p 92) but the Pardoner resists the frame of either drama or moral allegory. He uncovers 'his consiousness of his outcast state' (p 104) in the imaginative act of telling a story in which the portrait of the Old Man mirrors the stirring of his spiritual life.

51 Phelan, Walter S. 'Vocabulary in *The Canterbury Tales*.' *ALLCJ* 6(1985), 39-54.

Includes 'A Thesaurus Proprius for the Pardoner's Tale' pp 41-54. *CT*, in its more than 182,000 word-occurrences presents a mirror of Chaucer's world. In part 1, Phelan deals with deductive procedures testing 'cultural paradigms in the text'(p 39). Phelan uses structuralist theory (Todorov, van Dijk, Chatman, Fillmore). He posits that Chaucer had a macrostructure, and examines the possibilities of the Seven Deadly Sins (**679, 680**), character, and 'array of narrative forces' represented in the Tarot deck (p 41) to establish that Chaucer's was an 'age of allegory' (p 41). In part II, which deals 'with inductive techniques for generating a macrostructure from the text itself' (p 39) Phelan presents a prototype of a *thesaurus proprius* for *PardT* in order to test some inductive procedures for thesaurus construction. Phelan assumes that 'thesaurus and macrostructure have a worthy equivalence, that we retain a structure of motifs which is sequential and a structure of themes which is organizational' (p 43). The *thesaurus proprius* is a 'fresh construction of familiar IDEAS in THINGS which can have considerable heuristic value' (p 45). Potential uses of a *thesaurus proprius* include: a semantic concordance can be printed; the pattern of semes can be studied; differences in the influence on scenes in Chaucer and the source documents can be identified; bridging semes can be examined to clarify structure; and since the semantic structure of a word changes with each tale, the *thesaurus proprius* can 'provide a shorthand for describing the best scene-contexts for a given lexical entry' (p 46). Supporting data includes a frequency chart for *CT* of the word *Sle*, a distribution list of lexical morphemes in scenes or subsections of the *PardT* (pp 50-4).

1052   Rowland, Beryl, ed. 'Seven Kinds of Irony.' In *Earle Birney: Essays in Chaucerian Irony*. Toronto: University of Toronto Press, 1985. Pp xv-xxx.

In an introductory essay, Rowland cites the theme of *PardT* which unifies all the tale's lesser ironies and 'creates a perspective beyond that allowed to the central character' (p xxv) as the sixth kind of irony; other forms include verbal irony, irony arising from the discrepancy between narrator and poet, dramatic irony, philosophic irony, irony of value, and structural irony.

1053   Smallwood, T. M. 'Chaucer's Distinctive Digressions.' *SP* 82(1985), 437-49.

PardT is one of six *CT* (*WBT, MerT, FranT, PhysT, ManT*) in which Chaucer inserts a substantial digression early in his narrative. The digressions show Chaucer's 'unparalleled confidence and flexibility' (p 444) as well as his originality (as demonstrated by comparisons with the *artes poeticae*). After twenty lines in *PardT*, the narrative is interrupted with 178 lines of sermonizing (lines 483-660) only incidentally related to the theme of the tale. The digression in *PardT*, as long as the tale itself, characterizes the Pardoner, accommodates the inclusion of popular preaching materials (attractive for their pace and vitality), and allows the presentation of sentence. To consider *PardT* in its entirety as a sermon 'would be a case of the *exemplum's* swallowing the homily' (p 445). The display of the Pardoner's 'professional self' (p 445) provokes a more complex response than could have arisen from the actual telling of a tale.

1054 Weiss, Alexander. *Chaucer's Native Heritage.* American University Studies, 4. New York: Peter Lang, 1985.

Chaucer's decision to write in English was a risk calculated on his recognition of the literary potential of the English language. Didacticism is a pervasive element of Chaucer's work; on the one occasion when the pilgrims voice their literary taste (C 324-6), they call for a moral tale. Earlier they have shown themselves willing to tolerate bawdy but they reject ribaldry for ribaldry's sake.

1055 Aers, David. *Chaucer.* [Harvester New Readings]. Atlantic Highlands, New Jersey: Humanities Press International Inc., 1986.

Chaucer's art characteristically invites reflection on the contexts of holy writing and speaking as well as exploration of its 'role as a discursive and economic *practice* within a web of social relationships'(p 47). *PardP* and *PardT* together are a 'supreme and characteristic moment' (p 51) in which Chaucer works over problems of religious authority. Pardoners were important official agents of the Church in Chaucer's time: with the exception of his sale of confessedly false relics, Chaucer's Pardoner is 'typical' in his practices and theological assumptions (p 46). The Pardoner, his 'clients,' the 'holy corporation' employing him, and the laity were bound in a unity marked by severe tensions and contradictions, later to emerge in the Reformation (p 48). The Host, responding as a 'conventional bourgeois Christian' (p 50), misses the institutional issues and scapegoats the Pardoner for 'the massive problems and anxieties in the late medieval Church' (p 50). Chaucer continues to expose 'uncritical acceptance of authority and its self-images, the conventional separation of the "spiritual" or "ideal" from the social, economic and material dimensions of human being'(p 51).

- Review by Edward Donald Kennedy, *SAC* 10(1988),114-6: Aers presents his work as a concise critical introduction to Chaucer's poetry focussing on Chaucer's representations of society, religion, and marriage and sexual relations. In view of the book's several provocative views it may be more suited to the experienced reader.

056 Ando, Shinsuke. 'The English Tradition in Chaucer's Diction.' In *Chaucer in the Eighties.* Ed. Julian N. Wasserman and Robert J.

Blanch. Syracuse: Syracuse University Press, 1986. Pp 163-74.

Fetys (line 478) in *PardT* is used ironically. As one of two instances of the term in *CT*, its ironic use indicates an abandonment of stock phrases borrowed earlier.

1057 Arrathoon, Leigh, ed. *Chaucer and the Craft of Fiction*. Rochester, Michigan: Solaris, 1986.

Includes: J. D. Burnley, 'Chaucer's Host and Harry Bailly,' pp 195-218 (**1063**); and Janette Richardson, 'Intention and the Pardoner,' pp 85-95 (**1079**).

1058 Benson, C. David, 'The *Canterbury Tales*: Personal Drama or Experiments in Poetic Variety?' In *The Cambridge Chaucer Companion*. Ed. Piero Boitani and Jill Mann. Cambridge: Cambridge University Press, 1986. Pp 93-108.

Dramatic interpretation of *CT* has obscured recognition of the literary comparisons between tales that reveal Chaucer's 'drama of style' (p 107). *PardT* demonstrates that Chaucer creates poetic variety even within a single tale: the corrupt but skillful sermon on the tavern sins differing markedly from the symbolically charged narrative of the exemplum. Together, these approaches suggest 'both the dangers and the opportunities of moral fiction' (p 106).

1059 —. 'Chaucer's Pardoner. The Man and His Two Tales as a Defense of Christian Poetry.' 1986. Pp 44-63.

Chaucer's Pardoner, long interpreted dramatically, actually provides an example of the limitations of the dramatic theory (**681, 926**). As a verbal performer, the Pardoner is 'a tool to explore the dangers and potential of literature in the service of morality'(p 44): the contrast of *PardT* with *Mel* and *Thop* poses the question of the right mix of doctrine and art. Artistic contrast between tales is a central principle of *CT*. *PardT* contains such internal contrast it appears two different poems: the first an energetic denunciation of sins (lines 463-660) along with an address to the pilgrims (lines 895-918); the second, the exemplum of the three revellers (lines 661-894). These two parts, the sermon and the exemplum, are demonstrations of the use of eloquence; the one commendable, the other reprehensible. The sermon, while technically accomplished, illustrates a misuse of language condemned by Aquinas as self-regarding and 'presumably despised' (p 52) by Chaucer (cs **809, 932**). The effect of the sermon is 'manipulative, demagogic, and often vulgar' (p 52); it offers no spiritual remedies and is not at all prohibitive (cf **801**). The exemplum which contrasts morally and aesthetically to the 'sermon' is spare, energetic and elegant. At the close of the tale, the mood is shattered by a return to 'cheap rhetoric' (p 62). The attempted sale of relics should be seen as 'tomfoolery' and 'a comic modulation down from the serious issues of the tale itself' (p 62). The Pardoner's prologue and two tales both illustrate the dangers of misusing the power of fiction and justify 'the ways of Christian poetry to medieval (and modern) man' (p 63). *CT*, in its drama of style, is Chaucer's attempt to reconcile the demands of Christianity and poetry. In *PardT*, Chaucer set out to prove that some truths can best be conveyed 'through the shadows of poetic fiction'(p 163, n51). Paradoxically, Chaucer is able to indulge in daring literary experiments like the Pardoner's two tales 'precisely because of his faith'(p 149). For *PardP*, see **649**.

• Review by Eugene Vance, *SAC* 9(1987), pp 176-8: Though this 'well-written book challenges the tendency of generations of Chaucerian critics to construe [*CT*] as disclosures of the personalities of their tellers' (pp 176-7), it fails to establish the incompatibility of dramatic interpretation with the author's 'loosely conceived' drama of style (p 178). Oddly, Benson omits mention of Augustine's *DDC* and 'shuns medieval rhetorical theory as bases for his concepts of the mixed style' (p 177). Devoid of any new perspectives of non-Chaucerian, modern criticism, this work could for the most part 'have been written twenty years ago' (p 178).

060 Bixler, Frances. 'Links Between Chaucer's "Pardoner's Tale" and "Second Nun's Tale".' *PAPA* 12(1986), 1-12.

The parallels between central characters, symbols, lifestyles and consequences in *PardT* and *SNT* suggest that they form an antithetical pair of stories. Recognition of the link supports a placement of Fragment VI after IV-V and before VIII.

061 Blanch, Robert J., and Julian N. Wasserman. 'White and Red in the *Knight's Tale*: Chaucer's Manipulation of a Convention.' In *Chaucer in the Eighties*. Ed. Julian N. Wasserman and Robert J. Blanch. Syracuse: Syracuse University Press, 1986. Pp 175-92.

'White and red,' an expression of complementarity and thereby totality, is used in reference to wine in *PardT* (lines 526, 562) where it marks a secondary folk application of theory and observable fact.

062 Boitani, Piero, and Jill Mann, eds. *The Cambridge Chaucer*

Companion. Cambridge: Cambridge University Press, 1986.
Includes: C. David Benson, 'The *Canterbury Tales*: Personal Drama or Experiments in Poetic Variety?,' pp 93-108 (**1058**); A.C. Spearing, 'The *Canterbury Tales* IV: Exemplum and Fable,' pp 159-77 (**1083**); and Barry Windeatt, 'Literary Structures in Chaucer,' pp 195-212 (**1085**).

1063 Burnley, J. D. 'Chaucer's Host and Harry Bailly.' In *Chaucer and the Craft of Fiction*. Ed. Leigh Arrathoon. Rochester, Michigan: Solaris, 1986. Pp 195-218.

In an examination of the characterization of the Host, Burnley reviews the diversity of methods Chaucer employs with other pilgrims. Many critical difficulties with respect to the Pardoner derive from an assumption of dramatic technique. *PardP*, however, proceeds on an exemplary or representative basis; the Pardoner's admission of pulpit misuse, his comparisons to toads and snakes as well as his self confession as a *ful vicious man* all are evidence of a second viewpoint, that of a critical observer. The discontinuity between his sermon and his challenge to the pilgrims is explained by a switch from representational to dominantly dramatic mode of characterization. The interaction between the Host and the Pardoner is to be understood within the context supplied by the discussion in *RR* between the courtly dreamer and personified Reason regarding words and referents. Here, Chaucer goes beyond credible fiction and employs an allusion intended not for the Host but some members of the audience. The voice of Chaucer is also found in lines 958-9 which are drawn from Prov. 22:24-5 and echoed in *SumT* D 2086-8 and *RR* 3265-8. The Host's condemnation of the Pardoner as an angry man is consistent with a theme running through *CT* (cf headlink to *MLT*); consequently it can be understood as a mouthpiece for the poet. See **1057**.

1064 Cook, Jon. 'Carnival and *The Canterbury Tales*: "Only equals may laugh" (Herzen).' *Medieval Literature: Criticism, Ideology and History*. Ed. David Aers. New York: St. Martin's Press. 1986. Pp 169-91.

Bahktin's treatment of carnival is invoked to explain the convergence of the pilgrims, their description and resistance against the pressures of feudal hierarchy. In the Pardoner, the corruption of the official Church is confronted by a 'comic corruption, the representation of sacred symbols in terms of base matter and the body' (p 183). The Host's speech is informed by three carnival motifs: arse-kissing, the threat to castrate the Pardoner and debasement (p 183). The Pardoner's silence may be seen as a triumph of the carnivalesque idiom and a refutation of the Pardoner's way of life. The Knight's intervention frames the quarrel as a comic spectacle.

65 Edden, Valerie. 'Reading the *Pardoner's Tale.*' In *Talking About Text.* Ed. Malcolm Coulthard. Birmingham: English Language Research, 1986. Pp 61-74.

Edden borrows techniques from transformational grammar to apply the notion of 'narrative competence' (p 62) to *PardT*. Narrative competence assumes norms for storytelling as well as an ability to recognize genre, complete unfinished stories and evaluate various endings. In the complex act of reading (or hearing) *PardT*, the reader perceives deep structure—the two linked contractual stories of the rioters' quest for death and the mutual treachery of the rioters—assumptions based on genre (sermon exempla and quest), the association of gold with avarice as well as clues from the surface structure (e.g., reference to drink and drunkenness). See **816**.

66 Elliott, Ralph W. V. 'Chaucer's Clerical Voices.' *Medieval English Religious and Ethical Literature: Essays in Honour of G. H. Russell.* Ed. Gregory Kratzmann and James Simpson. Cambridge: D. S. Brewer, 1986. Pp 146-55.

Elliott adds to G. H. Russell's identification of a distinctive clerical style—'statuesque, formal stanzas'(p 146)—a second style typified by narration in heroic couplets and employed by clerical rogues. 'Clerical voice' denotes a composite of speech mannerisms, linguistic and stylistic range, thematic issues and stance of teller. *PardT* and *PrT* are antipodes. The Pardoner, with his small voice, is 'sonorous one moment and wheedling the next'(p 153); his entire performance reflects the 'professional training and activity of preachers'(p 153) (cf **937**). Typical of the tales of the clerical rogues, *PardT* lacks both the even homiletic tone and the 'statuesque solemnity' (p 154) of the stanzaic tales. The stanzaic clerical tales are probably among Chaucer's earlier tales; generally lacking in irony, they reveal a controlled use of language and rhetorical colors. The later clerical tales (e.g., *PardT*) offer the couplet's 'inexhaustible scope for narrative and stylistic variety' (p 155) and a moral tone embracing 'wit and humour, irony and satire' (p 155).

67 Ellis, Roger. *Patterns of Religious Narrative in the Canterbury Tales.*

1986. See **486**.

PardT can be seen as one of Chaucer's *omelies*. *PardT*, like the *NPT*, focuses on the problem of producing a simple religious narrative defined primarily in terms of content (p 13). In *CT* each tale continues the forward movement and also marks a new beginning; consequently, individual tales are both 'subordinated to the total pattern' and a 'symbolic realisation' of it (p 7). The 'real importance' (p 229) of the *PhyT* is in its paired tale—*PardT*. Like *PhyT*, *PardT* is interrupted by a digression. The Pardoner's narrative realizes 'its own literal dimension' vividly (p 242). The deliberate dislocation of the opening statement of the tale emphasizes its symbolic nature. The solicitation (lines 904 ff) directs the audience to read the tale in its entirety as the moral offering requested by the *gentils*. The tension between subject matter and process, characteristic of a religious narrative, is a crucial element of the Pardoner's performance. Replete with ambiguity, *PardT* expresses 'a single and coherent religious position' (p 265). By contrast, the specific detail of the closing kiss permits but does not compel a religious reading. This reticence reflects an awareness that 'religion is both more and less than the particular forms it chooses for its own expression'(p 265). For *PardP*, see **650**.

- Review by Helen Cooper, *RES* 39(1988), 102-3: It is good to have so much material on Chaucer's use of Biblical sources, an area increasingly noted in criticism. 'There are moments none the less when doubts set in: are biblical groves, oaks, and terebinths, whether *in bono* or *in malo*, necessarily behind the tree of the Pardoner's Tale?' (p 102).

1068 Friedman, John B. '"He hath a thousand slayn this pestilence:" The Iconography of the Plague in the Late Middle Ages.' In *Social Unrest in the Late Middle Ages*. Ed. Francis X. Newman. Binghamton, New York: Medieval and Renaissance Texts and Studies, 1986. Pp 75-112. Whereas the conservative traditions of medieval manuscript illustration copied and adapted old pictures to represent the plague, writers were more influenced by contemporary reality. The outdoor funeral procession with clinking bell in *PardT* draws on Chaucer's familiarity with real life as well as art. 'Chaucer's personified Death pierces his victim's heart with a spear' (p 78). The spear, rather than a scythe, results from a development in the iconography of death that began with the onset of the plague.

069 Jost, Jean E. 'Foreswearing in Chaucer's *Pardoner's* and *Franklin's Tales*: A Recurring Motif of Tale and Teller.' *MedPers* 1(1986), 75-88.

Within *CT*, unified by the theme of vow-breaking, *FranT* and *PardT* revolve around a triple bond; *PardT* adds a pact of brotherhood. Chaucer's evaluation of vow-breaking depends on: 1) the legitimacy of the vow; 2) his respect for the victim; and 3) his attitude toward the vow-breakers. The vow-centered narrative reveals the rioters' self-interest and the Pardoner's 'obsessions, concerns, fears, and desires' (p 87). His evaluation of the rioters as 'evil, greedy and unwise' (p 87) leads him to kill them off in unmourned tragedy.

1070 Knight, Stephen. 'Chaucer's Religious Canterbury Tales.' In *Medieval English Religious and Ethical Literature. Essays in Honour of G. H. Russell*. Ed. Gregory Kratzmann and James Simpson. Cambridge: D. S. Brewer, 1986. Pp 156-66.

Manuscript evidence suggests that, in the fifteenth century, not only were individual tales viewed as religious, but *CT* as a whole was seen as having religious impact (p 156). Through the religious tales, Chaucer transmuted the conflicts of his period into art. *CT* can be viewed as four sequences (*GP-MLT*, *WBT-PardT*, *ShT-NPT* and the last four tales) which begin by posing the conflict between traditional structure, and opposing forces and ultimately move to the assertion of the voice of the orthodox Church and the rejection both of secular conflict and art as its mediator (p 158). The second sequence (*WBT-PardT*) presents narratives which 'project the inherent sociopolitical positions of particular pilgrims ... [and] produce[s] most of the tales thought to be inherently great' (p 158). With the *PhyT*, the Pardoner continues the 'realisation of an increasingly feeble secular conservatism and an increasingly powerful disruption' (p 161). *PardT*, the 'most powerful and thoroughly imagined projection of disruptive forces' (p 162), is 'individualistic,' 'cash-obsessed,' 'anti-conservative,' and 'revolutionary in clerical, economic and ontological terms' (p 162). The only containment offered, other than moral disgust and promise of damnation is the Pardoner's sexual peculiarity. With that detail, Chaucer has transformed a commonplace on the sterility of cash economy (lacking progeny in the form of profit on capital) into imaginative characterization.

1071 Knight, Stephen. *Geoffrey Chaucer*. 1986. See **487**.

PardT centers on a figure that symbolizes the 'threat of cash-based acquisitive individualism'(p 126). The false exterior of the Pardoner defies the medieval idea of the person (ontology) which considered people to be primarily social and only in aberrance or in transition, individual (p 126). The Pardoner's whole significance comes down to 'private, sensual interest' (p 127). The Pardoner combines the two elements necessary for 'capitalist take-off': mobility and capital formation (p 128). The backdrop of the plague which provoked rapid development of a cash economy and new social relations is noteworthy. The closing of *PardT* recapitulates the positioning of the Pardoner: lines 915-8 present the ideal situation which is followed by the Pardoner's role-reversal in offering his relics and concluded by the rejection of the Host, 'the voice of normative judgements' (p 131). The required kiss of the Host and Pardoner is 'the embrace of urban business and radical individualism' (p 131). In its ambivalent ending, *PardT* sums up the sequence beginning with the *WBT*. For Pardoner, see **487**.

1072 Kraztman, Gregory, and James Simpson. *Medieval English Religious and Ethical Literature. Essays in Honour of G. H. Russell.* Ed. Gregory Kratzmann and James Simpson. Cambridge: D. S. Brewer, 1986.

Includes: Elliott, Ralph W. V. 'Chaucer's Clerical Voices,' pp 146-55 (**1066**); and Knight, Stephen. 'Chaucer's Religious Canterbury Tales,' pp 156-66 (**1070, 1071**).

1073 Mehl, Dieter. *Geoffrey Chaucer: An Introduction to His Narrative Poetry.* Cambridge: Cambridge University Press, 1986. See **886**.

1074 Minnis, Alastair. 'Chaucer's Pardoner and The "Office of Preacher".' In *Intellectuals and Writers in Fourteenth-Century Europe.* Ed. Piero Boitani and Anna Torti. Tubigen: Gunter Narr Verlag; Cambridge: D. S. Brewer. Cambridge, 1986. Pp 88-119.

[Given in the J.A.W. Bennett Memorial Lectures, Perugia, 1984.] Chaucer was aware of the 'theological dimensions of the literary problem' (p 118) posed in *PardT*; namely, can an immoral man tell a moral tale? A review of thirteenth-century quodlibets establishes the issue as a topic of scholastic debate; evidence drawn from the *ars praedicandi* focuses attention on the authority, knowledge and personal character of the preacher. Chaucer presents the issue clearly, using as a model for the Pardoner, the type of bad preacher found in the scholastic debate. The Pardoner lacks neither knowledge nor skill; he lacks in intention. Even the traditional understanding that a bad preacher can do good if his sin is secret fails to save the Pardoner who revels in his sinfulness. 'The Pardoner sins in his very act of preaching' (p 111). His tale, itself a masterpiece, is rendered void of moral effect in his telling. 'By these means, all the paradoxes, contradictions, anomalies and shortcomings of the traditional approach—which Chaucer, as far as one can judge, accepts—are revealed in a way which is as exciting as it is uncompromising' (p 118).

1075 Mohan, Devinder. 'Chaucer's Poetic Ideal and the Contexts of "Cupidity" and "Marriage" in "The Pardoner's Tale" and in "The Merchant's Tale".' *PURBA* 17(1986), 3-17.

Chaucer exposed the degeneration from the medieval idea of marriage as aesthetic ideal to the practice of cupidity through the idea of pilgrimage. 'Through the structural combination of religio-cultural individualities, the ethical ideals, and the metaphysical vision of love and marriage, Chaucer reveals the corruption of the Church hierarchy in the degenerating use of free will' (p 10). The Pardoner is 'most illustrative of corruption streaming out of church in the cultural life-style' (p 10). The theme of cupidity, with the medieval idea of marriage represented in the motif of pilgrimage, is illustrated more vividly in *MerT*.

1076 Newman, Francis X. *Social Unrest in the Late Middle Ages.* Binghamton, New York: Medieval and Renaissance Texts and Studies, 1986.

Contains: John B. Friedman. '"He hath a thousand slayn this pestilence": Iconography of the Plague in the Late Middle Ages,' pp 75-112 **(1068)**; Russell A. Peck. 'Social Conscience and the Poets,' pp 113-48 **(1078)**; D. W. Robertson, Jr. 'Chaucer and the Economic and Social Consequences of the Plague,' pp 49-74 **(1080)**.

1077 Olson, Paul A. *The 'Canterbury Tales' and the Good Society.* 1986. See **490**.

The Pardoner treats both the partial forgiveness of Roncesvalles and the plenary indulgence of 1383 by preaching two sermons. He hawks the Roncesvalles pardon to the pilgrims in a new sermon beginning line 928; the plenary indulgence he offers in an old sermon to an imaginary crusade-related audience (lines 911-5). The latter adapts rhetoric of the kind associated with the indulgence preaching that supported the Despenser 1383 Low Countries crusade. In contrast to Wycliffe's predestinarian attack on indulgences, Chaucer's 'black humor' indicates that indulgences externalize the penitential act. Appearing to preach against sin, the Pardoner preaches against avarice, a wrong that can be undone by a few offerings (lines 904-9). 'We are back in an Epicurean world. Purse is the Pardoner's heaven' (p 209). Chaucer's satires of the Summoner and Pardoner 'constitute his most indignant "Juvenalian" work' (p 213).

1078 Peck, Russell A. 'Social Conscience and the Poets.' In *Social Unrest in the Late Middle Ages*. Ed. Francis X Newman. Binghamton, New York: Medieval and Renaissance Texts and Studies, 1986. Pp 113-48. Chaucer shared a common audience with the Langland alliterative tradition; the Plowman's Tale (lines 669-74) echoes *PardT*. Chaucer probably wrote the Marriage group as well as *Interr* about the same time as the Wycliffite *Piers Plowman's Crede* and the *Plowman's Tale*. The satire of the Friar and Summoner together with *PardT* 'remain the most brilliant satires on ecclesiastical corruption ... [and] win Chaucer the reputation of reformer which he carried with him into the Renaissance' (p 140). See **1076**.

1079 Richardson, Janette. 'Intention and the Pardoner.' In *Chaucer and the Craft of Fiction*. 1986. See **491**.
Though Chaucer seems to denigrate rhetoric, his work reveals rhetorical expertise, *PardT* being the most 'quintessentially rhetorical'(p 85). *PardT* raises three rhetorical situations: the Pardoner's persuasive stance with the uneducated folk; his role as entertainer to the pilgrims (though he shifts when he seeks to sell pardons to them); and Chaucer's rhetorical stance to his audience. With relation to the naive audience, the Pardoner excels using, as Cicero recommends, the indirect approach suited to discreditable causes (p 86). The latter portion of *PardT* conforms to sermon structure recommended by the *artes praedicandi*, but compared to *ParsT* has very little of doctrinal significance. Though the Pardoner claims incidental good comes from evil intentions, such is not the case with his fellow pilgrims because he motivates them with worldly rather than spiritual intentions. The exemplum is open to anagogical interpretation. Chaucer apparently agreed with the sermon manuals of his day that an effective preacher must teach by deeds as well as words. Good does not proceed from evil intentions. 'The real sermon here is Chaucer's own for his own audience'(p 94). See also **1057**.

1080 Robertson, D.W., Jr. 'Chaucer and the Economic and Social Consequences of the Plague.' In *Social Unrest in the Late Middle*

Ages. Ed. Francis X. Newman. Binghamton, New York: Medieval and Renaissance Texts and Studies, 1986. Pp 49-74.

What Chaucer called *cupiditas* seemed 'the true queen of the commonwealth' (p 55). *GP* is 'a humorously exaggerated attack on the lack of "steadfastness" in the hierarchy of the realm' (p 63). The effect of pestilence on the realm might be represented by the abandonment of brotherly obligation in *PardT*, the only tale where pestilence is featured.

1081 Rogers, William E. *Upon the Ways: The Structure of 'The Canterbury Tales.'* English Literary Studies Monographs, 36. Victoria, B. C.: University of Victoria, 1986.

Despite the futility of seeking Chaucer's final intention for *CT*, the attempt to see *CT* as a whole is justified: placing the fragments into relation with each other enables fuller understanding of each fragment. The Ellesmere order places *PardT* and *NPT* in suitably crucial positions. The atmosphere of Frag VI is one of 'irremediable evil'(p 79) where both tales are reactions against the superficiality of the happy endings in the tales of Frag V. The Pardoner claims his tale is not fictive with respect to the frame; as a recital of recent events and self-quotation, the tale presents the world as it is and will continue to be. Evil in the real world, unlike the world of story, often triumphs. The non-fictionality of the Pardoner's sermon underscores the reality of the world in the tale (pp 82-3). The world of *PardT* is preeminently a 'world of waste' (p 83). Beside the waste of the tavern sins, the first part of the Pardoner's sermon is wasted both on the rioters and the preacher himself. Ironically, the impact of the tale is not wasted on us: the terror derives from a balance, in large part linguistic, between 'the supernaturally horrible and the everyday'(p 84). In his mystery, the Old Man suggests 'the hostile unintelligibility of the world of the tale'(p 85). In *PardT*, '[*CT*] as a whole finally comes directly to grips with the darkest side of human experience ... The Pardoner casts his shadow on the rest of the work'(p 85). Frag VII attempts to respond to the Pardoner's vision of evil in a literary way. *ShT* inverts *PardT* parodically. *NPT* calls into question the attempt to deal with the problem of evil linguistically, and by extension the whole literary enterprise.

1082 Scott, William O. 'Chaucer, Shakespeare, and the Paradoxes of Dream and Fable.' *CEA* 49(1986-87), 25-32.

Scott explores the relations between dreams, lying and art in Shakespeare and Chaucer. Chaucer's mature work, in its use of irony, is related to his explorations of the ambiguity of fiction in the earlier dream poems. The Pardoner exemplifies the liar paradox as he at once discloses his nature and attempts to hoodwink his audience. 'A slippery kind of self-reference' (p 30) figures in his offering of Christ's pardon (lines 915-8). Though not deceptive on the surface, this move prepares for his attempt to sell pardons and have the pilgrims kiss his false relics.

1083 Spearing, A.C. 'The *Canterbury Tales* IV: Exemplum and Fable.' In *The Cambridge Chaucer Companion*. Ed. Piero Boitani and Jill Mann. Cambridge: Cambridge University Press, 1986. Pp 159-77.

Before denouncing *fables and swich wrecchednesse* in *ParsT*, Chaucer employs exemplum and fable to explore the relation of narrative to moral doctrine. Spearing analyzes a series of those relations in *FrT*, *PardT*, *NPT*, and *ManT*. With *PardT*, the exemplum subsumes the sermon, leaving moral exhortation as an interlude in the narrative. The exemplary function is enriched with imaginative power (e.g., the enigmatic Old Man, the 'metamorphic energy' (p 167) of the mingled sins, the sinful materialism of oaths and relics, and the blasphemous parody of the Crucifixion heresy that two persons conspired against the third). Despite the Pardoner's persistent self-exposure, his narrative is effective. With fiction separated from moral *entente*, even exemplary narrative is exposed as false.

1084 Wasserman, Julian N., and Robert J. Blanch, eds. *Chaucer in the Eighties*. Syracuse, New York: Syracuse University Press, 1986.

Contains: Shinsuke Ando, 'The English Tradition in Chaucer's Diction,' pp 163-74 (**1056**); Blanch, Robert J. and Julian Wasserman. 'White and Red in the *Knight's Tale*: *Chaucer's Manipulation of a Convention*,' pp 175-91(**1061**); and Thomas Hahn, 'Money, Sexuality, Wordplay, and Context in the *Shipman's Tale*,' pp 235-49 (**651**).

1085 Windeatt, Barry. 'Literary Structures in Chaucer.' In *The Cambridge Chaucer Companion*. Ed. Piero Boitani and Jill Mann. Cambridge: Cambridge University Press, 1986. Pp 195-212.

Chaucer's inventiveness often consists in the '"art of context"' (p 198). The Pardoner provides two prefaces—his confession in *PardP* and his exposition of sins—which provide moral momentum. Three 'experiences of ending, frames within frames, boxes within boxes' are created by the Pardoner's close to his exemplum, his effort to apply the effects of the exemplum to the pilgrims and the reconciliation (p

198). This frame releases the fullest force for the tale. See **1062**.

1086 Blamires, Alcuin. *The Canterbury Tales*. [The Critics Debate]. Atlantic Highlands, New Jersey: Humanities Press International, 1987.

As a work directed to students beginning advanced work in English for the first time, this text presents a critical survey, an appraisal from a standpoint that acknowledges the multifaceted quality of Chaucer's writing, and a 7-page bibliography. The Pardoner's performance at the close of *PardT* is discussed in the context of psychological readings (pp 37-9); *PardP* is used to illustrate issues of intent and resonance.

1087 Bowden, Betsy, *Chaucer Aloud: The Varieties of Textual Interpretation*. 1987. See **493**.

PardT is treated in Chapter 5, 'The Pardoner on Tape' pp 114-31; Chapter 6, 'The Old Man in the *Pardoner's Tale*' pp 132-53; and the accompanying tape. Illustrations including *The Pardoner's Tale* (lines 760-2) by S. Williams are taken from an 1835 school edition, *The Riches of Chaucer* and *Three Gamblers and Time* drawn by J. H. Mortimer and bound into a copy of Urry's edition appear (pp 142,144). Bowden uses examination of modernization, illustrations and performance as a basis for understanding interpretations of *PardT*. William Lipscomb's modernization of *PardT* (1792, lines 882-969 reprinted here for the first time) is cited as reader response: Lipscomb's Pardoner, a 'hapless comic figure ... shares more traits with his fifteenth-century counterpart than with either of his contemporaries' (p 109). Passages recorded on an accompanying tape and examined in the text include: lines 895-906 and 913-36 (cut F1-7, pp 117-23); lines 960-5 (cut G1-26, pp 124-7); lines 711-75 (cut H1-3, pp 133- 44); lines 713-24 and 737-67 (cut I1-4, pp 145-53). For *PardP* see **652**.

1088 Fritz, Donald W. 'Reflections in a Golden Florin: Chaucer's Narcissistic Pardoner.' 1987. See **495**.

Kittredge intuited the compulsive psychology of the Pardoner. The etiology of the Pardoner's behavior lies in a narcissistic character disorder; the Pardoner's behavior is consistent with the image of the *puer aeternus*. The positive side of the archetype includes youthfulness (seen in the Pardoner's appearance, interruption of the Wife, and tale of three youths); the office of Pardoner heralded rebirth and restitution. The darker side of the archetype prevails, however. The Pardoner is dedicated in his profession to corruption and vice: 'this malefic side of the *puer* ... ultimately ... provides a clue to the violent and demonic nature of his behavior as well as the dark vision of his tale' (p 341). *PardT*, which is shaped by his *puer* personality, leads us to the conflict with the negative *senex*, the puer's fear of aging and death, his eternal wandering and longing for the mother, his wish for wealth, fantasy of omnipotence and 'murderous rage' (p 345). Of psychological interest is the fact that the news of death is reported by a child taught by his mother. The Old Man represents the realm of the father and forms of reality: age, boundaries, and time. The Pardoner's solicitation, whether in jest or earnest (and Fritz believes it earnest), expresses a grandiose fantasy of the Self as Messiah (p 350). The Host declines to participate in either the Pardoner's spiritual or sexual fantasy. The collision of Host and Pardoner has been anticipated since their juxtaposed portraits in *GP*. Both Host and Pardoner are mother-bound. The aggressive threat of the Host may reawaken the threat of a psychologically castrating parental figure. The Pardoner's speechlessness reveals the close psychological connection between genital exhibitionism of the *puer* and his verbal social skills. The Knight, a positive *senex* figure, succeeds in reconciling the *puer* and the *senex*. For *PardP*, see **653**.

1089 Grennen, Joseph E. 'The Pardoner, The Host, and The Depth of Chaucerian Insult.' 1987. See **497**.

The hostile encounter between the Pardoner and the Host, which reaches 'blasphemous intensity'(p 18), indicates the potential depth of Chaucerian invective. The Pardoner sets the stage 'for a kind of flyting which centers upon witty lexical innuendo' (p 19) with his use of *enveloped* (line 942). In context of the medieval fondness for false etymologies, *enveloped* carries insinuations of sensuality (L. *volup*, pleasurably) and deceit (L. *volupes*, falsely derived by Isidore from *vulpes*, fox). The Host's retort (lines 946-50) which imagines an imprint of the Pardoner's *fundement* (buttocks, anus) on his breeches 'is quite clearly a sacrilegious version of the image of Christ's face imprinted in blood on Veronica's veil' (p 21). The Pardoner himself wears a *vernycle*. Aside from its original meaning as *foundation, fundement* was regularly understood by ecclesiastical commentators (e.g., Augustine, Wyclif, Grosseteste) as *faith*, the *foundation* of the Christian religion. The Host intuitively grasps that the Pardoner with his vain promises (e.g., sheepbone, lines 350-60; mitten, 372-6) as Chaucer's parody of the Divine Physician.

1090 Higuchi, Masayuki. 'On The Integration of the *Pardoner's Tale*.'

ChauR 22(1987), 161-9.

Linguistic analysis leads to insight on the unity of *PardT*. An 'integrator' is the 'lexical item ... which links major chains of lexical cohesion'(p 161). The 'integrator' associates itself with other expressive units until, theoretically, at least, it is interrelated with all the other expressions in a literary work. Chains of lexical cohesion in *PardT* are associated with *sin, deeth, pardoner*. The word *deeth* is the integrating factor of *PardT*: *deeth* recurs in *PardT* with various meanings; sin-related words are scripturally associated with *deeth*; the Pardoner is suggestive of *deeth* in his sterility and his sinfulness; and the recurrent rime *Deeth:sleeth* reinforces the meanings of *deeth*. The conclusions of this textlinguistic view align with those of Bronson (**764**) who employs a quite different methodology. Melding the findings of this textlinguistic analysis with Bronson's proposal regarding sequence of composition suggests: first, when Chaucer wrote *PardT* he had *deeth* as the core of his composition; next, when he added the 'headlink' and 'conclusion' the theme was developed to the 'cause of death' and the Pardoner's sterility; lastly, in the 'confession,' the association proceeded from 'physical sterility' to 'spiritual sterility'(p 168).

091 Hilary, Christine Ryan. [Notes to *PardP* and *PardT*.] *The Riverside Chaucer*. 1987. Pp 904-10. See **117**.

Hilary treats *PardP* and *PardT* together 'since they are so closely linked by Chaucer' (p 904). Reviewing the range of analogues with their recurrent motifs—quest-for-death, scorn for the Old Man, mention of rats when the poison is purchased—she concludes that Chaucer knew a related version. Unique to Chaucer are the setting in Flanders, the theme of the plague and some details of the Old Man's character. Critical views are reviewed regarding the nature of the Old Man, religious symbolism, the Pardoner's motives and the intent of the solicitation. Hilary concludes by noting 'the critical bibliography is formidable and the range of disagreement broad indeed' (p 906). For Pardoner, see **498**; for *PardP*, see **655**.

092 Howard, Donald. *Chaucer: His Life, His Works, His World*. 1987 [page references from this edition]. See **499**.

With the exception of *PardT*, Chaucer had the order of *CT* 'for the most part clear in his mind' (p 488) at the time of his death. Relating to 'the overarching idea' (p 488) of *CT*, *PardT* 'is a commentary on the pilgrimage itself' (p 488). The Pardoner reveals the corruption of the central complex of medieval institutions—saints, relics, indulgences, pilgrimages—and deals with fundamental Christian lessons of charity, forgiveness, death and eternity. That *PardT* is linked to *PhyT* shows only that Chaucer was trying to fit it in. The Pardoner allows his tale to swallow his customary sermon and does his sermonizing through digressions. The archetypal image of Death, 'an image Chaucer retained from his childhood' (p 490), provides the occasion for the tale. The Pardoner seeks in the Host someone who will go along with him but finds himself insulted 'on the one matter he would have kept secret' (p 491). After the ritual act of charity and forgiveness, the Pardoner 'is absorbed into the pattern of existence and the universe goes on undisturbed' (p 491). *PardT* is contrived to make us laugh at the sin but hate the sinner; the closing emblematic kiss reverses those feelings. 'In postmedieval literature, this would make an effective ending' for *CT* (p 492).

1093 Jordan, Robert M. *Chaucer's Poetics and the Modern Reader*. Berkeley: University of California Press, 1987.

Chaucer's poetry expresses an uncertainty about the truth of poetry and the role and status of the poet. As the pilgrims narrate, they shed their nominal dramatic identities and merge to a single Chaucerian voice. Dramatic interpretation notwithstanding, the Pardoner is a fiction subject to textual constraints. *PardT*, which begins with relatively subdued description, proceeds with moral energy to explode in the digression (line 485); the illusion of a narrating persona is replaced by a 'story-oriented text' (p 132). The principle of verisimilitude competes with the 'principle of aggregative composition' more powerfully with the Pardoner than other pilgrims; yet, it is the text not the Pardoner that is alive (pp 134-6). In the closing of the tale, Chaucer's methods are similar to the Pardoner's in crafting a melange of genres and styles.

1094 Lindahl, Carl. *Earnest Games: Folkloric Patterns in the Canterbury Tales*. 1987. See **500**.

The Pardoner, the one professional oral artist in *CT* '"plays himself" in his fiction' (p 67); in making his profession part of his performance, the Pardoner follows oral tradition dating from the Cycle plays. Lindahl undertakes a reading based on '"traditional play realism"' (p 68). The Pardoner engages in 'a *performance of a performance*' (p 68), at once a description and enactment of his typical role. In so doing, he reveals his own capacity for deceit and the audience's capacity for

self-deceit. The audience is stunned at the close of his tale. Extending
the play to demonstrate the audience's self-deceit (they are at once
simple pilgrims and 'tavern' pilgrims capable of error), the Pardoner
jokingly invites the Host to kiss the false relics; however, the contrast
between the piety of the tale and the Pardoner's impiety explodes the
fiction and the pilgrims recognize they have participated in a
performance at their own expense. The Pardoner is the only character
who subjects the group to scorn; ultimately, the audience judges. See
also **481**.

1095 Lloyd, Joanna Eve. 'Chaucer's Acts of Interpretation and Interpreting
Chaucer.' *DAI* 47(1987), 4081-2A. Rutgers University State University
of New Jersey, New Brunswick Dissertation, 1986. Director: Andrew
Welsh.

Chaucerian characters demonstrate both human fallibility and problems
of interpretation. *Thop* and *Mel* show the errors of 'writing at a distance
from the Biblical text'; the Pardoner's portrait and tale show us
'additional error, including our own' (p 4081).

1096 Steimatsky, Noa. 'The Name of The Corpse: A Reading of *The
Pardoner's Tale*.' *HUSL* 15(1987), 36-43.

A deconstructive reading of *PardT* presents the Pardoner as 'a breeder
of paradoxes and thus, [as] a kind of deconstructive reader and story-
teller of his own literary self' (p 36). The Pardoner employs paradox to
conceal his truth, his eunuchry: his is 'a despairing quest for health' (p
41). As a story of paradox, open to innumerable possibilities, *PardT*
remains enigmatic. *PardT* manifests an 'uncanny anonymity' (p 39) as
the boy refuses to disclose the name of the corpse, the rioters interpret
the allegorical Death literally, and the Old Man's anonymous identity
mirrors 'the Pardoner's ambiguous identity, his Liars' Paradox and his
living deathliness'(p 40). The 'moral' of *PardT* is that the quest must
be unfulfilled, despair must continue to operate, story-telling must go
on without closure. When the Host silences the Pardoner, the end of
play and story-telling become a threat. In restoring order, the Knight
produces a shift back to the open road and the open page.

1097 Stone, Brian. *Chaucer*. 1987; rpt 1989. See **501**.

In *PardP* the Pardoner reveals his nature shamelessly; he is kin to
False-Seeming (*RR*), Vice in the medieval morality plays and the rogues
of Shakespeare. *PardT* offers an exemplum based on an oriental
folktale, a homily on three vices and a closing formula promising

heavenly bliss. The Old Man appears to be Chaucer's addition. In the closing soliciation, the Pardoner is carried away and errs badly; the Host responds with the worst abuse in *CT*.

1098 Taylor, Paul B[eekman]. 'Wife of Bath, Pardoner and *Sir Thopas*: Pre-Texts and Para-Texts.' In *The Structure of Texts*. Swiss Papers in English Language and Literature, 3. Ed. Udo Fries. Tübingen: Gunter Narr Verlag, 1987. Pp 123-32.

The performance of the Wife of Bath comprises a pre-text for the Pardoner's performance; the Pardoner's performance of reading and refiguring the Wife's is Chaucer's pre-text, *Thop* being a refraction, para-text, of both texts and invites a reading through them (p 124). In all three, the quest is diverted by a screening force which doubles as an instructor to the questor (the Old Man in *PardT*; Olifaunt in *Thop* figures the Pardoner's cupidity). The Pardoner imitates the Wife's display of self in his revelation, and his quest-tale reads hers so as to raise possibilities of interpretation in another critical context. The Pardoner's interruption of the Wife 'trivializes her narrative sense by a calculated misreading that both masks and marks his reading of her' (p 126 n). The Pardoner abstracts himself as a figure of cupidity (answering the Wife's self-portrait as concupiscence) and screens the implications of his tale with 'self-avowed viciousness of character'(p 126). He sets up a misreading of his tale which itself turns on a number of misreadings. *PardP* reshapes the 'progress to grace into viciousness of intent, hypocrisy of word and selfishness of deed' (p 127). The Host's attack only confirms the Pardoner's implication that the pilgrims cannot read the truth of his person, his tale or the pilgrimage (p 127). 'Even the subversive narrative of the Pardoner cannot prevent continued renewal of the journey of the human soul toward grace' (p 131).

1099 Williams, David. *The Canterbury Tales: A Literary Pilgrimage*. Boston: Twayne Publishers, 1987.

Chaucer makes the function of language and poetry the very subject of his poetry. The debate between nominalism and realism underlies *PardT*. The Pardoner constructs his tale on the basis of nominalist theories; his challenge to a theory of universals and language threatens the pilgrim authors and the pilgrimage itself. As a moral sermon, *PardT* promotes repentance; as an intellectual proposition, it confuses the nature of signs. The Old Man is a disconnected sign who 'can lead others to what they seek, but is forever separate from it' (p 82). In offering his relics, the Pardoner attempts to extend the terms of the tale into the world of the pilgrimage. The Pardoner not only voids words of their signifying power and relics of their incarnating power, he assaults the Eucharist, at once sign and symbol. In projecting his spiritual decay through his tale, and attempting to extend the terms of the tale into the pilgrimage through his offer of relics, he threatens the basis of fiction. The artistic achievement of *PardT* renders ironic Chaucer's rejection of the hypotheses on which it is built.

- Review by Christian K. Zacher, *SAC*(10), 208-10. Chaucer is unsympathetic toward the nominalist view that language is heuristic. 'Particularly in the tales of those entertaining but deconstructively misleading pilgrims the Miller, the Wife of Bath, and the Pardoner (a "radical" nominalist), Williams sees various attempts at disconnecting fiction from reality' (p 208). The Host's reply to the Pardoner reflects a belief that the basis of fiction is reality. Williams suggests some new ways of understanding semiotic creations like the Pardoner's Old Man who, like the Pardoner, 'seems to be a sign disconnected from anything signified,' (p 210).

1100   Bloom, Harold, ed. *Geoffrey Chaucer's 'The Pardoner's Tale.'* [Modern Critical Interpretations]. New York: Chelsea, 1988.
Bloom brings together a representative selection of 'the best modern critical interpretations' (p vii) in chronological sequence: 'The Narrative Art of the Pardoner's Tale,' pp 11-21 (**816**); 'The Pardoner's "Jape",' pp 23-42 (**827**); 'The "Floating" Fragment,' pp 43-7 (**926**); '"Modernizing" Chaucer,' pp 49-62 (**926**); 'Preaching and Avarice in the Pardoner's Tale,' pp 63-77 (**923**); '"Synne Horrible": The Pardoner's Exegesis of His Tale, and Chaucer's,' pp 79 -102 (**992**); 'The Pardoner's Homosexuality and How It Matters,' pp 103-24 (**967**); 'Sermon Structure in the Pardoner's Tale,' pp 125 -38 (**1018**); and 'The Pardoner and the Word of Death' pp 139- 58 (**1026**). A selective bibilography (1958-84) is included pp 165-7 and an index pp 171 - 7. In an introductory essay (pp 1-10), Bloom meditates on Chaucer as 'Shakespeare's truest precursor in the representation of moral and emotional change brought about by and in a figure such as the Pardoner, who reacts to what he himself has said'(p vii). Citing Donaldson as '[t]he most Chaucerian and best of all Chaucer critics'(p 1), Bloom rejects contemporary modes of interpretation, ('mad on method,' p 5), that deny any value in the 'illusion of vitality' (p 2), and argues that

Chaucer's vision, 'a supermimesis ... of human possibility' (p 4), demands an 'experiential' (p 5) criticism of humane observation leading to testing 'in every context that indisputably is relevant'(p 5). With Chaucer, the critic is thrown back 'to become a vitalizing interpreter' (p 7) charged with carrying 'more life forward into a time without boundaries'(p 7). The Pardoner is at once 'obscenely formidable and a laughable charlatan'(p 8). The 'very type of the eunuch,' the Pardoner accompanies the Summoner 'so as to pick up some sexual coloring' (p 8). The Pardoner is like the Old Man in approximating an emblem of death: the association of castration, blindness and death, so crucial in Freud, is a given here. The Pardoner is 'the most powerful representation of depravity'(p 8) in English before Shakespeare's Edmund and Iago. In the telling of his tale, the Pardoner 'achieves a kind of vertigo' (p 9) mixing pride and 'something dangerously authentic out of the supernatural order of grace' (p 9); he is driven to the social suicide, (or 'moral masochism' in Freudian terms (p 10), in insulting the Host. Unconsciously, but shrewdly, the Pardoner has sought the Host's violent response; consciously, he is stricken as silent as Iago.

1101 Chance, Jane. '"Disfigured is thy Face": Chaucer's Pardoner and the Protean Shape-Shifter *Fals-Semblant* (A Response to Britton Harwood).' *PQ* 67(1988), 423-37.

The dialectic of inner and outer in *PardT* (**1105**) originates in Fals-Semblant where 'false-seeming' depends less on boxes, chests or doors than on religious clothing as signs of identities. In *PardP* and *PardT*, Chaucer transforms the symbol of clothing into an emblem of the body as cover for the soul and the shape-shifting Fals-Semblant into the protean faces of the Pardoner. The Pardoner's sincere offer of relics at the close of his tale tests the pilgrim's spirituality: if the spirit not the body is important, it matters not that they are false; if real, purchase would be blasphemy. Another explanation of the Pardoner's offer occurs through the image of Proteus: Fals-Semblant employs the image implying that one shape is insufficient if deceit is the goal; and Protean shape-shifting characterizes the Pardoner's abrupt and hypocritical changes in behavior. The Pardoner's abrupt changes free him to manipulate others: he can shift *personae* to profit; on another level, he is fettered by his vices; and, on 'a more providential (and authorial) point of view' (p 431), he works *for* God. See **1105, 1106**.

1102 Davenport, W.A. *Chaucer: Complaint and Narrative.* Chaucer

Studies, 14. Cambridge: D.S. Brewer, 1988.

Besides the use of the complaint of soul against body and the regrets of old age in the words of the Old Man, in *PardP* and *PardT*, Chaucer employs the complaint as a rhetorical device to explore the morality of art, the relationship between appearance and intention and the death of the spirit. *PardP* turns *PardT* 'into a self-consciously rhetorical performance' (p 58). The Pardoner's boasts function as 'a perverse version of the "modesty" prologue'(p 58). The duality of narrative and complaint evident in *PardP* and *PardT* related for Chaucer to the complexity of the role of the poet. Like *CYP*, *CYT* and *WBP*, *WBT*, *PardP*, and *PardT* move from an 'interest in oral effects to conclusions which include explicit didacticism and a degree of literary purpose beyond the range of merely imitative, naturalistic devices' (p 205). The reader understands *PardP* and *PardT* as a dual form ironically relating the Pardoner's corrupt purpose to the efficacy of his tale. The tale works as a complaint 'against the times'(p 205). The quarrel places the dual form of complaint and narrative in context.

03 Dinshaw, Carolyn. 'Eunuch Hermeneutics.'1988/ rpt1989. See **503**.

Chaucer engages a sexual poetics; the control of signification is associated with the masculine in patriarchal society. The Pardoner's 'eunuch hermeneutics' suggests a poetics beyond gender and fallen language. The Pardoner's eunuchry permeates the thematic and narrative strategy of his tale as well as his behavior: he enunciates a eunuch hermeneutics, a hermeneutics of the partial. Wanting to believe in his own wholeness, the Pardoner 'plays on his audience's desire to believe in theirs; he exposes everyone's radical longing for completeness' (p 29). There is extraordinary focus on the body (more properly, parts of the body) in *GP*, *PardP*, and *PardT*. The association of relics, testicles and writing at the close of the *PardT* is found also in the *RR*: *coilles*, *reliques*, and *paroles* are fragments (p 37). The Pardoner with his *hauteyn speche* (p 330), missing *coillons*, and false relics is 'the focus of anxiety about language' in *CT* (p 37). Language, at best a fragment, can be cut off from the Significator: the Pardoner is Faux-Semblant's descendent. *PardT* is 'a narrative representation of the fetishist's conflicted psyche' (p 40). The rioters are representations of the Pardoner's belief in the impossibility of atonement with the father. The Old Man articulates the Pardoner's 'incompatible assertions' (p 41). The Pardoner obsessively desires wholeness, claims his pardons will deliver wholeness and knows that is the desire of the pilgrims. The exemplum is not only a lie that tells the truth, 'it formally demonstrates the psychological stagnation of the fetishist, caught between incompatible affirmations' (p 42). The Pardoner is caught between knowledge of his fragmentation and belief that he can be made whole (p 43). The solicitation is 'the final gesture of the fetishist among his peers' (p 43). The Host's retort is at once an apt reply and, like all language, itself a fragment. For *Interr*, see **565**; for *Phy-PardL*, see **565**. See also **1117**.

1104   Emmerson, Richard Kenneth, and Ronald B. Herzman. '*The Canterbury Tales* in Eschatological Perspective.' 1988. See **504**.

PardT reflects the mixture 'of the universal and the personal elements of eschatology'(p 420): the rioters are representative of moral decline often associated by chroniclers with the plague, and, in personal terms, are blinded by sin and headed for death and destruction. The Pardoner typifies the archetypal simoniac and eschatological deceiver. A showman, he encourages idolatry (urging worship of his bulls, lines 907-9), and inverts sacrament and ritual (in the false confession of *PardP* and the attempted solicitation at the close of *PardT*).

1105   Harwood, Britton. 'Chaucer's Pardoner: The Dialectics of Inside and Outside.' *PQ* 67(1988), 409-22.

The Pardoner begins with the Summoner. Chaucer, 'having composed the summoner's [sic] derision on the question of what could be inside a purse' (p 411), creates the Pardoner as he works through the consequences of opening a purse and closing it. Containers, which have played little part earlier in *GP*, flourish with the Pardoner: the *jurdones*, *galouns*, and boxes of the Physician presage the Pardoner; the Pardoner carries *walet* in a *lappe* which contains his *hood*, a *male* with a pillowcase and a glass case; the Pardoner mentions containers rare in the Chaucer canon—poison in a *box*, *boyste*, *botelles*, *stones*, *cod*, and *latoun* (perhaps a box of latten); when the Pardoner describes the Host as *envoluped*, the term is both original in *Middle English Dictionary* and unique in Chaucer. The Pardoner arises from the dialectical relationship between inside and outside: he opens up his secrets and makes money by exploiting closed chests. The Old Man, 'a cylinder of rags' (p 412), provides a model for imagining what closed containers contain. Other closed containers include the mitten, the unseen depths of the well, belly, womb, *stynkyng cod* and *paire of dees*. Giving his sermon uncharacteristically free from his material intent, the Pardoner is moved/ left open. The Pardoner's sermon is performative. The sermon 'bristles with warnings inside a constative context, a context that both frees the pardoner (sic) to listen and recedes from consciousness' (p 416). Because *PardT* has become constative for him, it is as if he has been situated in his own interior space. The Pardoner's sermon ironically moves him to contrition; his blessing (lines 915-8) is his response to his own warning. Aware of the tawdriness of his relics, the Pardoner extrudes a new mask; metaphorically, he shuts a box. The Pardoner is like a door simultaneously open and shut, bracketed by the Host and Summoner.

1106 ——. 'A Response to Jane Chance.' *PQ* 67(1988), 435-7.
Harwood replies that, in calling for attention to context and conventions, Chance misunderstands phenomenological criticism which grants conventions as precisely the problem. Rather than offer an alternative account, Harwood continues, Chance has taken the Pardoner's performance as a set of significations unchanged from Servius to Jean de Meun to Chaucer; Harwood's focus has been 'Chaucer's attempt to understand the ways in which he makes the world' (436). Taking Chance's essay within its own terms, Harwood notes that he questions the Pardoner's frankness, and thus Chance's reading of candor, as one more Protean shape. See **1101**.

1107 Kendrick, Laura. *Chaucerian Play: Comedy and Control in the Canterbury Tales.* Berkeley: University of California Press, 1988.
In a study of the mechanisms, meanings and purposes of Chaucer's literary play (p 2), Kendrick examines *CT* as a 'model for the equilibration by means of fictions and laughter of the badly disrupted late-fourteenth-century English social body' (p 43). The Host, with his aggressive obscenity (lines 947-55), tries to dethrone the Pardoner. The Host subversively mimes the Pardoner (*beel amy* line 318) and calls for a merry tale. In his 'anxiety-enhancing fictional sermon'(p 39), the Pardoner demonstrates his ability to control Death fictionally; to the extent that his audience identifies with his (and the church's) power to control what they fear, they respond to his solicitation. *PardT* is akin to the 'abreactive play' (p 39) discovered by Millard Meiss in post-plague painting in Florence and Siena and by Huizinga in late medieval art.

1108 Koff, Leonard Michael. *Chaucer and The Art of Storytelling.* Berkeley and Los Angeles: University of California Press, 1988.
Challenging the critical view that Chaucer's opinions emerge only

obliquely, Koff argues that Chaucer's art encourages us to observe a 'conceptual distinction' between 'allegorical reading and parabolic listening'(p 3). Chapter 5 pairs *PardT* with *KnT* to demonstrate that Chaucer's text has voice everywhere, any distinction between 'pure voice' and 'pure bookness' being misleading (p 4). Because the Pardoner seems a fully dramatized character, *PardP* and *PardT* taken together (a unit Koff refers to as the 'Pardoner's Prologue') as performance is the 'best example in Chaucer of how the performative idea of dramatic irony' renders it as much a storyteller's performance as any pilgrim narrative in *CT* (p 158). Critical attention should focus on what a medieval audience would make of the Pardoner's self-revelation rather than the 'lifelikeness' of the Pardoner. *PardP* and *PardT* keep a distinction between language and speaker, a distinction essential to understanding the benediction. 'Because the Pardoner is a feigned preacher through whom Chaucer ... is examining the nature of performance, religious and artistic, the Pardoner can equivocate without our imagining any psychological trauma on his part'(p 164). The ending of *PardT* shifts first from the Pardoner's sermon to Chaucer the Pilgrim's recollection of the interchange between Pardoner and Host, and then from Chaucer's recollection to Chaucer's performance now (p 170). The distancing at the end of *PardT* is instructive. The Pardoner is 'perhaps Chaucer's *only* storytelling counterpart in his work'(p 172). Our response to the Pardoner's *techne* can tell us about our faith and our theory of knowledge (p 173).

1109 Lerer, Seth. 'Rewriting Chaucer: Two Fifteenth-Century Readings of the Canterbury Tales.' *Viator* 19(1988), 311-26.

Describing 'scribes' as 'those who read, wrote and rewrote Chaucerian manuscripts for their own purposes' (p 311), Lerer reviews the individual reader response of the Helmingham ms (Princeton University Library ms 100) of *PardP* and *PardT* for implications of fifteenth-century expectations. Similes and asides are pared down in *PardP*, examples are eliminated in *PardT* and the closing exchange between the Pardoner and the Host is removed (lines 895-968). The result is 'a more coarsely tuned version of the poem' (p 320), one marked by narrative speed but lacking nuance. This minimizing of ambiguity alters the verbal texture and dramatic meaning of the text and evidences a critical attitude different both from the 'disambiguating' Patterson has found in fifteenth-century audiences and the critical interests of modern readers. Prints

Helmingham ms corresponding to *PardP* lines 412-42 and *PardT* lines 551-90. See **1186**.

110   Mahoney, John. *The Pardoner's Tale: Geoffrey Chaucer*. London: Charles & Letts Co., 1988.
This study guide for A-level examinations includes line-referenced commentary directing students back to the text, study questions, and a brief bibliography.

111   Sleeth, Charles R. "'My Dames Loore" in *The Canterbury Tales.' NM* 89(1988), 174-84.
PardT employs the motif of a mother's teaching as authoritative. The rioters are instructed about death by three persons arranged in order of increasing gravity: a boy (lines 670-84), a taverner (lines 685-91), and an Old Man (lines 713-67). The boy counsels readiness for death. *Thus taughte me my dame* (line 684) may serve as the boy's entitlement to advise his elders; it may also suggest the rioters lack even rudimentary knowledge. The taverner, an adult, vouches for the importance of the boy's warning. The Old Man speaks with irony from 'his own heartfelt religion and his painful personal experience' (p 179).

112   Smith, J.J. 'Spelling and Tradition in Fifteenth-Century Copies of Gower's *Confessio Amantis*.' In J.J. Smith, ed. *The English of Chaucer and His Contemporaries: Essays by M.L. Samuels and J.J. Smith*. 1988. Pp 96-113.
In an effort to explore the continuity and dissolution of Gowerian forms in fifteenth-and sixteenth-century copies of the *Confessio Amantis*, Smith examines a set of items in *PardP* and *PardT*. Smith concludes that Gower mss were produced within a strong orthographic tradition.

113   Baumlin, Tita French. 'Theology and Discourse in the *Pardoner's Tale*, the *Parson's Tale* and the *Retraction.'Renascence* 41(1989), 127-42.
The problem of fruitfulness, introduced in *GP*, comes to a head in *PardT* and *ParsT* but is not resolved until *Ret*. The Pardoner can distinguish between wholesome and deadly speech and, though spiritually sterile himself (cf **747**), he deceptively insists his language is fertile. 'The Pardoner is caught in the vicious circle of sin and self-delusion' (p 131). The only fruit of his solicitation is the 'bitter brokenness of fellowship' (p 132) which remains until the Parson insists on the union of intent and word. In *Ret*, Chaucer ensures fecundity by transforming art.

114   Boitani, Piero. 'The Old Man and the Earth: Alterity and Otherness

of a Medieval Story.' In *The Tragic and the Sublime in Medieval Literature*. Cambridge: Cambridge University Press, 1989. Pp 1-19.

In an examination of the mental and representational differences between modern and medieval attitudes towards death, Boitani contrasts the Old Man in *PardT* with Santiago in Hemingway's *The Old Man and The Sea*. The episode of the Old Man is a parable within a parable. The Old Man is 'culturally stratified,' (p 10) half Biblical and half Christian. '[A]n image powerfully created through concretions,' the Old Man 'represents the borderland, the *limen* or threshold where division is oneness, and his uncanniness is therefore supremely, "sublimely" tragic'(p 19). See **747, 748, 801, 991, 1024**.

- Review by Ronald B. Herzman *SAC* 13(1991), 165-8: The more rigorous analyses of medieval poems are generally more illuminating than the discussions of modern examples. 'I found his discussion of Apoc 9:6 as a source for the Old Man to be genuinely illuminating; the extended reference to Hemingway's Old Man from *The Old Man and the Sea* I did not' (p 167).

1115 Canfield, J. Douglas. *Word as Bond in English Literature from the Middle Ages to the Restoration*. Philadelphia: University of Philadelphia Press, 1989.

The Pardoner, Volpone, and Dorimant (*The Man of the Mode*) are comic protagonists who overreach; societal bonds ultimately restrain their greed. The Pardoner perverts word (e.g., his fiction of forgiving sin, abuse of the Offertory and manipulations of his audience) and Word (e.g., his perversion of Scripture). Ironically, the motif of swearing carries the ultimate answer to the problem of death. The Knight's call for the kiss, an exchange of charity, reinforces the meaning of Word, thereby enforcing word as bond. Thus, the Pardoner is reinscribed into the discourse that enforces feudal power relations.

1116 Cooper, Helen. *The Canterbury Tales*. The Oxford Guides to Chaucer. New York: Oxford University Press, 1989. Rpt (paperback with corrections), 1991.

Cooper provides a handbook to *PardP* and *PardT* covering such topics as date, text, sources and analogues, genre, structure, themes and style. *GP* Pardoner portrait, *Phy-PardL*, *PardP* and *PardT* are interpreted within the context that *CT* most resembles an anthology of genres whose stories are thematically linked. Though *PardP* and *PardT* work together 'brilliantly,' there is no proof the tale was composed with the prologue in mind and the tale possesses a power independent of its speaker (p 260). Rather than tortured agonizing, the tone of *PardP* is 'self-congratulatory complacency' (p 263). *PardT* shows more similarity to the structure of *CT* (e.g., *MerT* and *ManT*) than to the sermon form. Unlike any of the other tales, *PardT* presents characters that are not particularized. The tale embodies contradictory meanings at once a moral tale against avarice and, in the mouth of the Pardoner, an immoral ploy to further his avaricious aims. The Old Man is the one figure who can see beyond materialism. The Host's final outburst is the last reduction of the spiritual to the earthly. 'Chaucer's Pardoner is a forerunner of the Reformation, not only as an instance of corruption within the Church and as a peddler of false pardons, but because he opens the way to questioning the connections between outward forms and spiritual meaning' (p 271).

117 Dinshaw, Carolyn. 'Eunuch Hermeneutics.' In *Chaucer's Sexual Poetics*. 1989. See **506**.

Dinshaw significantly expands and revises **1103**. The Pardoner and the Wife of Bath produce a perspective outside of patriarchal discourse, a perspective that is carried forward in *PardP* and *PardT*. In his critique of patriarchal discourse, the Pardoner reveals the inadeqaucy of categories such as masculine/feminine, letter/spirit, or literal/figurative. In so doing, the Pardoner calls into question the possibility of making morally redeeming tales. By inversion, the Pardoner leads the pilgrims to think about the language of the divine, 'about radical Being in which there is no lack and in which all difference and division are obviated' (pp 183-4).

- Review by Sheila Delany, *WS* 20(1992), 354-61: 'One might also claim that other pilgrims [than the Pardoner] ... also tell tales conducive to contemplation of the absolute, that as human and fallen beings they too can only offer a "hermeneutics of the partial"' (p 179).... 'In what strikes me as a particularly clumsy reading, Dinshaw sees the old man's desire for death as a yearning for a "lost ideal realm of unity and plenitude"' (p 179). 'But the old man's expressed wish is for burial ...' (p 360).
- Review by Catherine La Farge, *YES* 23(1993), 314-6: The chapter on *PardT* is 'by far the most stimulating and original' with its implications for 'the gendered hermeneutic of the veiled feminine body as text and meaning'(p 315). 'Reading the Pardoner as a study

in fetishism, and noting a medieval nostalgia for wholeness and unslipperiness in language, Dinshaw argues that the Pardoner suggests an alternative hermeneutic': one based not on gender but 'something unmediated' (p 316).

- Review by Derek Pearsall, *Speculum* 67(1992), 134-8: 'The Pardoner, in a chapter unfortunately entitled "Eunuch Hermeneutics," suggests the confusing possibilities of ungendered reading .... [The] technique of interpretation is based on a trope: since patriarchal society has historically governed the forms and interpretations of discourse, all forms of that discourse are gendered male, and thus by implication antifeminist'(p 136). Pearsall questions the over-intricate argument and asks whether 'allegory' would be 'a better figure of masculine textual control than translation' (p 136).
- Review by Monica McAlpine, *CE* 54(1992), 595-602: Dinshaw draws on neo-Freudian theory on fetishism to interpret the Pardoner as figurative eunuch, language being for the Pardoner 'as much a fetish as his relics .... Still, the Pardoner does not validate traditional hermeneutics, Dinshaw argues (rather too briefly), but points to the need for an inclusive hermeneutics grounded on the Incarnate Word' (p 602).
- Review by Sarah Stanbury, *Envoi* 3(1991), 86-92: ' While acknowledging feminist challenges to the phallocentric models of both Freud and Lacan, she asserts that their accounts of castrated existence seem fully descriptive "of the gendering of culture in Western patriarchal society" (167) with the fourteenth century, apparently, in unbroken continuity with our own time. Where this leaves the Pardoner, however, is as a twentieth-century castrato, defined by lack ...' (p 91). 'The chapter on the Pardoner ... would thus profit from a fuller historical consciousness of the play of gender in the fourteenth century and a greater willingness to look at the differences between the patriarchal consciousness of Chaucer's world and our own' (p 91).

1118 DuBruck, Edelgard E. 'Inviting Tacit Agreement: *"The Pardoner's Tale"* and Its Modern Reception.' In *The Living Middle Ages: Studies in Mediaeval English Literature and Its Tradition*. A Festschrift for Karl Heinz Göller. Ed. Uwe Böker, Manfred Markus and Rainer Schöwerling. Stuttgart: Belser Wissenschaftlicher Dienst., 1989. Pp 103-13.

Modern criticism of *PardT* has focused on the psychology of the Pardoner and the Old Man to the neglect of the exemplum and Chaucer's narrative skills. The exemplum is marked by dramatic narrative speed and establishes that covetousness is a metaphor for spiritual death. The Pardoner presents two prologues: the first (*PardP*) bridges the gap between his rustic audience and the pilgrims to encourage them to take his exemplum seriously; the second (the digression) is a serious sermon whose implication is that if one avoids sin, he needs neither pardons nor Pardoner. The exemplum follows immediately reinforcing the message that the time of death is uncertain. The Pardoner may be carried away at the end of his tale but the audience 'is barely listening, for they still ponder the violent ending of the story' (p 112). Restoring *PardT* to its author highlights Chaucer's narrative skills: characterization, psychological insight, mastery of rhetorical and linguistic devices, flexibility of idiom, and 'the calculated distribution of climactic and anticlimactic points by variations in speed' (p 112).

19   Fletcher, Alan J. 'The Preaching of the Pardoner.' *SAC* 11(1989), 15-35.

PardP and *PardT* are not organized according to the norm of *modernus modus predicandi*, found in the *artes predicandi* (**737, 1018**). Arguments championing the modern sermon form, require combining *PardP* and *PardT* and blurring the separation of the two audiences in *PardP* to comprise the sermon. *PardP* and *PardT* follow a homiletic genre found in Mirk's *Festial* (now known to have been composed between 1382-92), *Jacob's Well*, *Speculum sacerdotale*, Bodleian Hatton 96 folios 193-97 and three texts arguably intended for sermon use (Ashmole 750 42v and 48); this form typically lacks a formally announced theme, is structured associatively rather than systematically and is illustrated with exempla. *PardP* and *PardT* could have been perceived as polemical, appealing to *lewed peple*; Chaucer's audience would have found it suspect.

20   Gillmeister, Heiner. 'Chaucer's *Pardoner's Tale* as a Poetic Sermon.' *Poetica* 29-30(1989), 58-79.

PardT is compared with two previously unpublished sermons on the *radix*-theme by Honorius de Augutoduno and Giles of Rome. Sophisticated literary structures distinctive to Chaucer are analyzed by applying the rules of transformational grammar to reveal deep structures underlying selected passages (lines 883-4, 664f, 668, 784-6, 768-72 and 900-5). In the peroration (lines 900-5), Chaucer uses chiasmus to contrast the ideal conduct of God and the sinfulness of man thereby underscoring the identity of the rioters as 'perverted imitators of Christ' (p 77). An English translation of Honorius' sermon is included; the Latin text appended.

1121 Rooney, Anne. *Geoffrey Chaucer: A Guide Through The Critical Maze*. State of the Art. Bristol: The Bristol Press, 1989.

Surveys critical approaches beginning with the Edwardians through a trend of increasing diversification. Includes fourteen-page bibliography. Critical treatments of *PardT* are briefly noted as examples of patristic criticism (**747**) and studies of voice which show Chaucer's interest in the gap between knowing and showing (**1093**). Current criticism evidences a movement away from realist treatments towards issues of literariness, intertextuality, poetics, voice and tone, and away from the search for unity towards an acknowledgement of contingency, plurality, uncertainty and tension.

1122 Schaber, Bennet Jay. 'The Lettered Body: Chaucer in the Place of Analysis.' *DAI* 49(1989), 3359A. Brown University Dissertation, 1988.

Using Lacanian analysis to explore the relation of body and signifier, Schaber maps the lost thing on which representation depends (the *objet petit a* or lost object of fantasy) in the representational economy of *PardT*. The body, itself a manifestation of the *objet a*, is understood as fantasy both erotic and political, framed by social psychical and somatic contexts.

1123 Strohm, Paul. *Social Chaucer*. Cambridge: Harvard University Press, 1989.

Strohm examines the 'shifting structure of social relations in Chaucer's lifetime'(p ix) as an interpretive context for *CT*. The mention of *floryns* is one of few details that connects *PardT* to fourteenth- century realities. In examining the inscribed audience of pilgrims, Strohm notes Chaucer's bold stroke of dividing his pilgrims into different literary camps based on social position notably, *gentils* and *cherls* (lines 319, 323-5). Chaucer critiques the casual relations replacing vassalage; *PardT* links false swearing with the falsification of human ties. The Pardoner, with his marginality and animosity, threatens the presuppositions on which the community is founded: he offers a discourse artful and false within a community founded for the purpose of exchanging edifying discourse. Following a moment of candor (lines 916-8), he moves to 'conciliatory buffoonery' (lines 919-45, p 156); the pilgrim's laughter indicates they share the Host's response. *PardP* and *PardT* threaten the discursive community of *CT* in questioning 'the reliability of fabulation as a means of embodying the truth' (p 174).

1124 Vance, Eugene. 'Chaucer's Pardoner: Relics, Discourse, and Frames of Propriety.' 1989. See **507**.

In an examination of some dramatic links between the Pardoner's discourse and the frame of *CT*, Vance notes that the Pardoner's words challenge the *CT* pilgrimage and also 'the power of fiction itself to frame human evil' (p 740). The Pardoner conspires to set himself at the center 'as a moveable shrine' (p 741); in so doing, he challenges the necessity of pilgimage itself. For *PardP*, see **1146**.

1125 Volk-Birke, Sabine. 'Literacy and Orality in Late 14th Century Vernacular Sermons and in Chaucer.' In *Anglistentag 1988 Göttingen: Vorträge*. Ed. Heinz-Joachim Müllenbrock and Renate Noll-Wiemann. Tübingen: Max Niemeyer Verlag, 1989. pp 209-19.

Volk-Birke analyzes *PardP* and *PardT* against a framework of characteristics drawn from the oral-aural sermon tradition in the last quarter of the fourteenth century and the first quarter of the fifteenth. *PardP* and *PardT* juxtapose contrasting levels of moral injunction and deceit. Of six characteristics identified, *PardP* and *PardT* manifest four: strong interaction between the Pardoner and his audience; syntactic patterns such as parallel constructions, comparisons, if-clauses and particular causal relations; structural organization of a five-part sermon (in *PardP*, the Pardoner comments on preaching; in *PardT*, he preaches a sermon); and a sophisticated narrative style arising from a complex cultural and literary tradition. See **698**.

1126 Wetherbee, Winthrop. *Geoffrey Chaucer: The Canterbury Tales*. 1989. See **509**.

The Pardoner, 'a professed materialist,' is also 'the most spiritually alive' and his worldly and religious selves are in conflict (p 75). His sermon reveals his intense self-absorption; the tale presents a futile quest paralleling the Pardoner's state. In lines 916-8, the Pardoner's call for Christ's pardon highlights the separation between the spirit and the letter of religious authority. More than any other literary character the Pardoner conveys 'a sense of fallenness' and Chaucer suggests no comfort (p 79).

The Pardoner's Tale 1990-1995

127 Alton, Angus. 'The True Morality of *The Pardoner's Tale.' Critical Essays on the Pardoner's Prologue and Tale*. [Longman Literature Guides]. Ed. Linda Cookson and Bryan Loughrey. Burnt Mill, Harlow, Essex: Longman House, 1990. Pp 75-85.

PardT evokes complex responses including recognition of the morality of the tale and laughter at the irony of the Pardoner who seems self-aware yet undone by the greed he preaches against. See **1131**.

128 Benson, C. David and Elizabeth Robertson, eds. *Chaucer's Religious Tales*. Chaucer Studies 15. Cambridge: D. S. Brewer, 1990.

Includes: Jane Cowgill, 'Patterns of Feminine and Masculine Persuasion in the *Melibee* and the *Parson's Tale*,' pp 171-83. See **1132**.

129 Boenig, Robert. 'Musical Irony in the *Pardoner's Tale.' ChauR* 24(1990), 253-8.

The tavern music in *PardT* (line 466) 'sounds a note of irony' (p 253) as well as provides verisimilitude. Chaucer ironically depicts the tavern musicians as playing the wrong instruments for fashionable music. Chaucer preferred the complexities of the French style, *Ars Nova*, popularized by Machaut over the more conservative English style. The music of Machaut is typified by interweaving parts individuated by timbre or the specific sounds of instruments rather than pitch. Woodwinds outnumbered stringed instruments in the fourteenth century according to music historian, Willi Appel; a point underscored by the evidence of manuscript illuminations (e.g., ms Ashmole 1523, fol 99r and *Visconti Hours*, fol BR 76v, 120v). The *harpes, lutes, and gyternes* of *PardT* are unsuited to the fashionable music of Chaucer's time. The 'musical paradox' of the tavern music is analogous to the life of the rioters:

'attempted cooperation with inherent competition undermining the artistic success' (p 257).

1130 Bowers, John M. '"Dronkenesse is Ful of Stryvyng": Alcoholism and Ritual Violence in Chaucer's *Pardoner's Tale.' ELH* 57(1990),757-84.

A re-examination of the Pardoner's drunkenness in light of the symptomatology of the alcoholic provides a reading of *PardT*, the Pardoner's rhetorical strategies and his sexual deviance. The Pardoner's theme is drunkenness in that his 'acting-out in the frame narrative and the moral metaphorics of his tale' are explicable in terms of alcoholism (p 759). Through a series of expanded readings of specific lines (*WBT* III 170-1; VI 327-8; 359-60; 693; 549-50; 558; I.689; 58; 468-9; 867; 886; 952; 957; 963), Bowers indicates parallels. Both the restless Old Man and the drunken rioters serve as correlatives for the Pardoner who engages in a religious charade; the Pardoner may suffer 'alcoholic testicular atrophy' (p 768); the Summoner's leprosy may suggest an external projection of the Pardoner's gluttony; the Physician who treats the plague yet suffers the corruption of greed 'anticipates the Pardoner's own metaphoric substitution'(p 770); the two taverns in *PardT* suggest the two faces of alcoholism; and the Host's assault transforms the Pardoner into a scapegoat. The interpretation 'of alcoholism as a subversion of the ritual and aesthetic of pilgrimage as a spiritual quest' (p 779) extends through *CT*.

1131 Cookson, Linda, and Bryan Loughrey, eds. *Critical Essays on the Pardoner's Prologue and Tale.* [Longman Literature Guides]. Burnt Mill, Harlow, Essex: Longman House, 1990.

Directed to a student audience, this volume includes ten original critical essays, study questions, a guide to student writing and a brief bibliography. Essays include: Angus Alton, 'The True Morality of *The Pardoner's Tale*,' pp 75-85 (**1127**); John E. Cunningham, '*The Pardoner's Tale*: An Unholy Mess?' pp 104-12 (**1133**); Mark Spencer Ellis, 'States of Mind—Action—Moral Judgment,' pp 29-45 (**1134**); Alan Gardiner, 'The Pardoner as Preacher,' pp 86-95 (**1137**) ; Charles Moseley, 'The Cosmic Banana Skin: The Pardoner v. his Tale,' pp 46-54 (**1144**); Paul Oliver, 'Confusion and Concealment in *The Pardoner's Tale*,' pp 65-74 (**1148**); Pat Pinsent, 'Narrative Techniques in Chaucer's *Pardoner's Tale*,' pp 96-103 (**1149**); Michael Read, 'The Tale Outside the Tale: The Pardoner and the Host,' pp 55-64 (**1150**); Richard Smith, '*The*

Pardoner's Prologue and Tale: Poetry For Performance,' pp 18-28 (**1151**); and Cedric Watts, 'Problem-Areas of *The Pardoner's Tale*,' pp 9-17 (**1152**).

1132 Cowgill, Jane. 'Patterns of Feminine and Masculine Persuasion in the *Melibee* and the *Parson's Tale*.' In *Chaucer's Religious Tales*. Chaucer Studies, 15. Ed. C. David Benson and Elizabeth Robertson. Cambridge: D. S. Brewer, 1990. Pp 171-83.

The Pardoner's abuses are rooted in his masculine form of discourse which mirrors the male-dominated medieval world of hierarchical power by assuming a distance between authoritative speaker and unlearned listener; this distance enables the Pardoner to see his audience as manipulable. The Pardoner reflects the potential for corruption in the masculine mode of discourse: he makes explicit the irrelevance of personal virtue; appeals to authority (e.g., seals and bulls); flavors his speech with Latin; and employs *hauteyn speche*.

1133 Cunningham, John E. '*The Pardoner's Tale*: An Unholy Mess?' *Critical Essays on the Pardoner's Prologue and Tale*. Ed. Linda Cookson and Bryan Loughrey. [Longman Literature Guides]. Burnt Hill, Harlow, Essex: Longman House, 1990. Pp 104-12.

Cunningham charts the relationship of *PardT* to the character revealed in *GP* and *PardP* to show that the seeming 'mess' of three divisions and three styles is actually a 'careful package of tale and teller' (p 111). See **1131**.

1134 Ellis, Mark Spencer. 'States of Mind—Action—Moral Judgement.' *Critical Essays on the Pardoner's Prologue and Tale*. Ed. Linda Cookson and Bryan Loughry. [Longman Literature Guides]. Burnt Mill, Harlow, Essex: Longman House, 1990. Pp 29-45.

PardT challenges our assumptions about the relation between character and event. The ethical structure of *PardP* and *PardT* is based on the assumption that '[E]verything, even life itself, is property' (p 41). In place of morality, *PardT* sets up an alternate scale. See **1131**.

1135 Fletcher, Alan J. 'The Topical Hypocrisy of Chaucer's Pardoner.' *ChauR* 25(1990), 110-26.

The Pardoner's hypocrisy is qualitatively different from that of other pilgrims. His '[u]nmitigated religious hypocrisy' (p 111) derives its topicality not only from antimendicant satire and traditional criticism of pardoners but the contemporary debate between 'the orthodox establishment and the Lollards' (p 111). Contemporary evidence is cited to support the topicality of such issues as religious hypocrisy—*Thus spitte I out my venym under hewe/ Of hoolynesse, to semen hooly and trewe* (lines 421-2); the eucharistic controversy—*turnen substaunce into accident* (line 539); the validity of spiritual ministrations performed by a corrupt man and the abuse of preaching (lines 407-11). The choice of a pardoner demonstrates Chaucer's 'political and literary tact:' he can introduce into the traditionally corrupt figure 'the resonance of the most urgent and topical theological argument of his day' (p 119). Medieval religious writings did associate pardoners with false relics (contra **721**). The reference to the Pardoner's sexuality may be explicable in terms of the moral equation (religious hypocrite = heretic) as 'aberrant sexual behavior was a standard accusation in heresy charges' (p 120). Examination of contemporary attitudes to religious hypocrisy mitigates against any exoneration that a psychological reading might offer.

1136 Ganim, John M. *Chaucerian Theatricality.* 1990. See **659**.
Seeking to reorient criticism from dramatic interpretation to a paradigm based on 'theatricality,' in turn based on materials from urban and court spectacle as well as forms of late medieval performance, Ganim considers 'theatricality' as 'a governing sense of performance, an interplay among the author's voice, his fictional characters, and his immediate audience' (p 5). As such, theatricality becomes 'a paradigm for the Chaucerian poetic, and seeks to define Chaucer's 'own manipulations of the forms of popular culture and the varying discourses of inherited high literary forms'(p 5). With *PardT*, Ganim suggests the influence of Chaucer's Italian masters. By examining parallels between *PardP* and *PardT* with Boccaccio's tale of Ciappelletto in Day 1, Story 1 of *Dec* as well as comparisons with Cipolla (Day 6, Story 10), Ganim demonstrates that Chaucer has put the pilgrims in the place of his *lewed* audience and forced them to react.

1137 Gardiner, Alan. 'The Pardoner as Preacher.' *Critical Essays on The Pardoner's Prologue and Tale.* Ed. Linda Cookson and Bryan Loughry. [Longman Literature Guides]. Burnt Mill, Harlow, Essex: Longman House, 1990. Pp 86-95.
The Pardoner's abuses—forged documents, exploitation for personal profit, and 'peddling of false relics' (p 86)—were common. Similarily, the structure of *PardP* and *PardT* adheres to medieval convention. Throughout, the Pardoner's aim is to induce fear of sin to motivate his

audience to seek absolution and part with their money. See **1131**.

1138 Georgianna, Linda. 'Love So Dearly Bought: The Terms of Redemption in *The Canterbury Tales.*' *SAC* 12(1990), 85-116.

Challenging the view that Chaucer satirizes religious practices, Georgianna argues that religious understanding underlies Chaucer's treatment of pilgrimage and the theology of penance, the twin frames of *CT*. In offering absolution from the guilt of sin and ignoring the prerequisites of contrition and confession, the Pardoner reduces redemption to mundane exchange. Though the Pardoner uses orthodox language in reminding his audience that Christ bought back the world (lines 500-1, 766-7, 900-3), he falsely implies an analogy between Christ's buying and his selling. Chaucer exposes the Pardoner's fraudulent terms without rejecting the idea of the pardon.

1139 Holley, Linda Tarte. *Chaucer's Measuring Eye.* Houston: Rice University Press, 1990.

Through the Host, Chaucer links *PhyT*, the exemplum, and the Pardoner's telling to instruct in the proper use of gifts of Fortune, Nature or Grace. *Phy-PardL* fascicle forms a diptych in which narrative patterns mirror each other. Virginia's text is the gloss for the Pardoner; the Pardoner's sermon is the gloss for *PhyT* and the rioters. This narrative structure 'adjusts to the reader's increasing clarity of vision, requiring one to read to and fro ... to perceive connections' between the texts (p 66).

1140 Kanno, Masahiko. 'Word and Deed in The Pardoner's Tale.' *SMELL* 5(1990), 45-55.

This article translates **1014**. Through a consideration of diction, particularly the use of pairs of associative words (bag/relics; belly/excrement; purse/testicles), Kanno examines Chaucer's treatment of the Pardoner. See **1014**.

1141 Knapp, Peggy. 'Three "Noble Prechours": Pardoner, Nun's Priest, and Parson.' In *Chaucer and The Social Contest.* New York and London: Routledge, 1990. Pp 77-94.

Arguing that *CT* includes a pervasive adaptation of subversive Wycliffite discourse, Knapp considers the ways in which *PardT*, *NPT*, and *ParsT* comment on each other and serve as candidates for *knyttin up* the feast. *PardT* and *ParsT* present opposite readings of the relation between tellers' intent and the moral effectiveness of telling; *PardT* and *NPT* address the role of fiction in the teaching of morality. Following

Aers (**958**) and Leicester (**964**) in recognizing the psychological complexity of the Pardoner, Knapp proceeds to examine the psychological problem his role creates as an analysis of the institutional church. The Pardoner's performance results in 'ugly self-revelations, gestures which demystify some disturbing ecclesiastical practices, and pulpit brilliance' (p 84). The balancing of the demystification of the Pardoner's techniques and those of the institutional church in *PardP* with the skill of *PardT* results in 'a riddling equivocation concerning both preacherly intent and the value of fiction in teaching Christian virtue ...'(p 84).

1142 Leicester, H. Marshall, Jr. *The Disenchanted Self: Representing the Subject in the 'Canterbury Tales.'* Berkeley: University of California Press, 1990.

Leicester builds on his treatment of the art of impersonation (**964**) to establish a method of reading which: 1) treats the tales as *texts*, and 2) reads them with a view to analyzing the individual subject, the voice of the text. Thus read, the pilgrims are products, rather than producers, of their tales. *CT* is comprised of texts about the subjectivity of their speakers; 'Chaucer's subject is the subject, not, or only incidentally, the self' (p 15). Leicester applies his method to *PardT*, *WBT* and *KnT*. Part I 'Chaucer's Subject' analyzes the Pardoner's 'disenchanted' perspective and draws from 'Kierkegaard's description of the phenomenology of theological despair' (p 29) to assess his despairing consciousness. Part II 'The Subject Engendered' examines the connections between sexuality and authority by comparing the Pardoner and Wife of Bath. Here, consideration of the Pardoner's style of subjectivity and representation of sexual difference suggests application to other gendered subjects; brief comparison of the role of *jouissance* in *SNT*, the Prioress, and the Nun's Priest demonstrates the potential. Recognizing the appeal of the dramatic interpretive tradition, Leicester directs attention to 'the institution of exegetical interpretation' in *CT* (p 35). At the center of *PardT*, lies a fundamental failure to distinguish literal from spiritual levels; the most important determinant of meaning is found in the allegorical relation of spirit and letter. The Pardoner is the most 'self-conscious' of the pilgrims; he is 'the first exegetical critic of his own tale' (p 39). Through his own over-literalness, he satirizes the way in which the transcendence of religious institutions has been reduced to solely human practices. The Pardoner's motives does not reveal his motives; the text affords the representation of an activity rather than an entity. See **964, 1143**.

- Review by Monica McAlpine, *CE* 54(1992), 595-602: The Pardoner provides one of Leicester's two 'easy' cases ... 'Whatever the eventual consensus on Leicester's argument, his teller-centered criticism can immediately be cleared of any suspicion of distracting attention from the tales; his theory motivates an intense focus on the letter of the text, and every teacher of Chaucer will want to be acquainted with his brilliantly detailed readings' (p 600).
- Review by Ruth Cameron, *C&L* 40(1991), 307-9: 'His revisionary treatment of *PardT* concludes that the Pardoner is "disenchanted," a person who is in Kierkegaardian despair because he embodies the corruption of the Church and knows that he does so but is unable to attain the true spiritual state espoused by a pure Church' (p 308). Leicester's deconstructive and humanistic view denies the category of transcendence and affirms that there are only human constructs and institutions' (p 309).
- Review by Mary B. Campbell, *Envoi* 3(1991),150-5: 'The readings (auditions?) provided here of the Pardoner, the Wife of Bath, the Knight, and the *General Prologue's* "Chaucer" are nearly clairvoyant commentaries on these characters "impersonated" utterances ...' (p 150).

143 Leicester, H. Marshall, Jr. 'Structure as Deconstruction: "Chaucer and Estates Satire" in the *General Prologue*, or Reading Chaucer as a Prologue to the History of Disenchantment.' *Exemplaria* 2(1990), 241-61.

GP encourages a 'disenchanted perspective' on society (e.g., pardoning), on the pilgrims, and on discourse by deconstructing estates satire (cs **403**). Leicester defines 'disenchantment' as what had been thought to be other-originated but in fact is the product of human creation. In the 'failed performance'(p 255) of *GP*, the Narrator adopts and discards the hierarchical and 'apocalyptic'(p 254) classification procedures. As one of the final seven pilgrims, the Pardoner's portrait is marked by an apocalyptic drive to strip surface complexity from underlying truth and the emergence of the Narrator as the source of the drive. The Pardoner is 'the darkest example and the most trenchant spokesman of an attitude the speaker [Narrator] here comes close to sharing' (p 253). See **1142**.

144 Moseley, Charles. 'The Cosmic Banana-Skin: The Pardoner v His

Tale.' *Critical Essays on The Pardoner's Prologue and Tale. Geoffrey Chaucer.* [Longman Literature Guides]. Ed. Linda Cookson and Bryan Loughrey. Burnt Mill, Harlow, Essex: Longman House, 1990. Pp 46-54.

The major ironies of *PardT* revolve around the sermon and its context. Though the Pardoner is subverted by his tale, the tale is 'told to an audience that deserved it, and genuinely needed a pardon he does not believe in' (p 53). See **1131**.

1145   Neuss, Paula. '*The Pardoner's Tale*: An Early Moral Play?' In *Religion in the Poetry and Drama of the Late Middle Ages in England.* The J. A. W. Bennet Memorial Lectures, 1988. Cambridge: D. S. Brewer, 1990. Pp 119-32.

Within the larger 'play' of *CT*, *PardT* is an early moral play with the Pardoner the personification of covetousness. '[T]he response of Chaucer's audience ... is very close to that of the audience of an early play' (p 122). Narrative images function similar to dramatic devices: the rioters in the tavern are related to the device of Riot in the moral plays. When the Pardoner turns on his audience, he almost succeeds in bringing them and us into his moral drama; if successful that collective subject would be akin to the Mankind figure in drama. The Host rejects the role of sinful mankind and the moral play on covetousness concludes.

1146   Nichols, Stephen G. 'Empowering New Discouse: Response to Eugene Vance and Hope Weissman.' *Exemplaria* 2:1(1990), 127-47.

Nichols responds specifically to the issues of 'power semantics' and the 'thematic of castration'(p 129) in **507**, **657**, and **1124**. Vance's concept of 'power semantics' delineates how Chaucer uses transgressive exempla to critique the discourse of medieval history in *PardT* and predicates a literal critique of medieval institutions. The Pardoner's confession (lines 423-34) is 'structured around a circular pattern of repetition that stresses contradiction and hypocrisy by way of signifying the Pardoner's intention to flaunt institutional norms'(p 131). As a 'symbol of the hegemonic discourse of identity,' the Pardoner becomes 'a didactic metaphor' (p 133). Nichols questions that *PardP* and *PardT* can bear 'the freight of the critical discourse' (p 135) Vance suggests, but notes that the closing solicitation indicates unmistakeable subtlety. The parody becomes a political metaphor which equates *exemplum-as-narrative* with *exemplum-as-sign* (p 136). The Host's threat of castration parallels the Pardoner's exhibitionism in *PardP*.

147 Nolan, Edward Peter. 'Knocking the Mary Out of the Bones: Chaucer's Ethical Mirrors of Dante.' In *Now Through a Glass Darkly: Specular Images of Being and Knowing From Virgil to Chaucer*. Ann Arbor: University of Michigan Press, 1990. Pp 193-217.

Part of the clarity of the *Commedia* is the result of depicting the world dead: part of the ambiguity of *CT* is the result of depicting the world of the living, 'reality seen in a glass darkly' (p 194). In his ethical configuration, the Pardoner reflects Francesca da Riminni (*Inferno*). The Pardoner's missing sexual identity is substituted for by his appetite for eating, drinking and talking. Like Francesca's, his is 'an energetically evil will ... such souls can only image themselves forth as parody of the truly Other' (p 197). The words of both are the inverse of the saving Word; both are figured perversely as doves. The imagery of *PardT* 'is an externalised [sic] imaginary landscape of the Pardoner's soul' (p 199). The Pardoner 'plays all the parts' in 'his personal psychomachia' (p 200); he speaks of himself in speaking of the cooks knocking the *mary* out of bones, turning substance into accidence. 'In parodic inversions of Bread, Wine, and the mediating Word, he eats the world; he is the *imitatio Antichristi* ...' (p 201).

148 Oliver, Paul. 'Confusion and Concealment in *The Pardoner's Tale*.' *Critical Essays on the Pardoner's Prologue and Tale*. Ed. Linda Cookson and Bryan Loughrey. [Longman Literature Guides]. Burnt Mill, Harlow, Essex: Longman House, 1990. Pp 65-74.

PardT, with its irrelevancies and unsolved problems, is as much an oral performance and piece of self-exposure as *PardP*; whereas in *PardP* the Pardoner is proud of his self-exposure, in *PardT* he is unaware of it. See **1131**.

149 Pinsent, Pat. 'Narrative Techniques in Chaucer's *Pardoner's Tale*.' *Critical Essays on the Pardoner's Prologue and Tale*. In *Critical Essays on the Pardoner's Prologue and Tale*. Ed. Linda Cookson and Brian Loughrey. [Longman Literature Guides]. Burnt Mill, Harlow, Essex: Longman House, 1990. Pp 96-103.

PardT, with its characteristic pace, economy, characterization and style, creates an unexpectedness suggesting on one level that Chaucer is in control and on another that Fate or Fortune is directing the outcome. Consequently Chaucer's technique reminds that God is in control and justice will be done. See **1131**.

150 Read, Michael. 'The Tale Outside the Tale: The Pardoner and the

Host.' *Critical Essays on the Pardoner's Prologue and Tale*. Ed. Linda Cookson and Bryan Loughrey. [Longman Literature Guides]. Burnt Mill, Harlow, Essex: Longman House, 1990. Pp 55-64.

Chaucer intends his pilgrims to be understood realistically as well as symbolically. The Pardoner stands for the artist, the Host for the audience: in the Pardoner, Chaucer 'confronts the moral ambiguities of his own profession'; in the Host, he vents 'his frustrations at his unresponsive or inappropriately responsive audience' (p 62). Chaucer's irony encloses Pardoner, Host and reader: the Pardoner, master of words, is silenced; the Host, who by silencing the Pardoner, 'proves the power of the words he rejects' and the reader 'because, once we have registered the ironies, the questioning of fiction and of language itself,' we recall Chaucer's images (p 63). See **1131**.

1151   Smith, Richard. '*The Pardoner's Prologue and Tale*: Poetry for Performance.' *Critical Essays on the Pardoner's Prologue and Tale*. Ed. Linda Cookson and Brian Loughrey. [Longman Literature Guides]. Burnt Mill, Harlow, Essex: Longman House, 1990. Pp 18-28.

Understanding *PardT* in spoken terms redirects questions of psychological consistency to issues of performance. See **1131**.

1152   Watts, Cedric. 'Problem Areas of *The Pardoner's Tale*.' *Critical Essays on the Pardoner's Prologue and Tale*. Ed. Linda Cookson and Bryan Loughrey. [Longman Literature Guides]. Burnt Mill, Harlow, Essex: Longman House, 1990. Pp 9-17.

Sexually the Pardoner is 'impossibly inconsistent'(p 10); apparently Chaucer, in developing his character, made him steadily more potent and formidable. The power of the Old Man 'derives from the combination of question-begging particulars and an answer-frustrating inner opacity' (p 14). Amidst the ironies of *PardT*, the ultimate irony may be that the Pardoner wins over audiences as well as pilgrims. See **1131**.

1153   Wurtele, Douglas J. 'The Concept of Healing in Chaucer's Pardoner's Tale.' *ABR* 41(1990), 59-79.

The Pardoner displays the Augustinian principle of concupiscence as self-inflicted punishment of the sinner and refers to the related principle of Christ as healer of sinners. Additional sources for Christ as spiritual healer include Burchard of Worms, William of Auvergne, Alan of Lille, Aquinas, the *Lay Folks Mass Book* and *ParsT*. Under normal conditions the Pardoner, like the Physician, capitalizes on ailments while claiming to heal them. The conditions of *PardT* differ and, in the benediction,

Chaucer seems to be depicting the beginning of his conversion. With the solicitation, the Pardoner reverts '[I]n a burst of grotesque japery' (p 78) to his old self expecting the Host and audience to join in his joke. The Pardoner's silence reveals the humiliation of 'the partly changed man' (p 79). 'In his benediction and even in the "afterthought" is glimpsed the outward sign of the inward moment of prevenient grace' (p 79).

1154 Allen, Mark. 'Moral and Aesthetic Falls on the Canterbury Way.' *SCRev* 8(1991), 36-49.

The imagery of falling on the Canterbury road reinforces the topos of falling-into-sin which suggests interruptions in the progress of the pilgrimage. The reference to falling at end of *PardT* (lines 927-40) links the themes of sin, penance and progress toward God. Because of the questionable nature of the Pardoner's credentials, his offer of *seuretee* becomes an example of the falling topos and signals the danger of false confession. The Pardoner's pun that he has *yfalle* among the pilgrims reinforces the imagery. The Pardoner, like the Old Man, serves as a distraction whereby others are distracted; his story represents the lure of false confession. The contrast between immoral intent and superior craft in *PardT* manifests a concern for the moral dimension of art. *Phy-PardL* brings the issue of literary response to the foreground by invoking a rhetorical triangle of concern for a merry vs moral tale, audience and manipulative narrator. *PardT* presents itself as an aesthetic death offering the satisfaction of a well-told tale though its intent is vicious.

155 Brown, Peter, and Andrew Butcher. *The Age of Saturn: Literature and History in the 'Canterbury Tales.'* Oxford: Basil Blackwell, 1991. Chaucer uses the metaphor of the malign influence of Saturn to typify the social disintegration of the fourteenth century. In *PardP* and *PardT*, Chaucer examines the politics of religion (specifically policy on papal taxation) to demonstrate the result of defaulting on Christian doctrine. 'The voice of Lollardy is heard, unexpectedly, through the rhetoric of the Pardoner, which also identifies him as a God-denying fool' (p 13). The Pardoner undertakes a satirical critique of the late medieval Church but also of conditions in England in the 1370's. *PardP* and *PardT* 'seem intended to embody the attitudes of both the papacy and the late fourteenth-century church' (p 245). The following topics are discussed in the context of contemporary historical analysis: drunkenness, covetousness, blood and wine, flesh and bone, and the Pardoner as 'fool.' The symbolism of the eucharist extends to the description of social and political harmony and the contemporary debate over the nature of the eucharist epitomizes the challenge to the authority of the Church. Most likely, Chaucer approached the composition of *PardP* and *PardT* incrementally, beginning in the late 1370's and extending through the 1390's. The Old Man anchors the tale and offers a foil to the rioters. The Pardoner aims to reveal rhetorical sensationalism for what it is: 'In the process of anatomizing his practices the Pardoner allows the distanced audience to anatomize him' (p 155). *PardT* recoils upon itself and the Pardoner becomes his own exemplum thereby creating moral impact. The Pardoner's rhetoric together with his narrator serve as 'reflexive masks' (p 156).

1156 Cigman, Gloria. 'Chaucer and the Goats of Creation.' *L&T* 5(1991), 162-80.

Cigman argues that, in the popular view reflected in medieval vernacular literature, the underlying polarity is between sin and evil rather than good and evil. Unlike Langland who targeted both sinner and evil-doer, Chaucer directed his attack specifically against those who are evil. The Pardoner, Friar and Summoner, irredemably evil pilgrim-narrators, tell fabliaux representing 'the phenomenon of evil and its impact' (p 177). The Pardoner, '[t]he most striking example of evil' (p 177) demonstrates that evil, unlike sin, is a medium without primary existence. Untroubled by his own *cupiditas*, the Pardoner, in *PardP*, manipulates the guilt of his audience of ordinary sinners. The Pardoner is an instrument of God both as a preacher and a personification of hypocrisy. Unlike the Friar and the Summoner who defeat each other through their tales, the Pardoner brings himself down. His fate, like that of the characters in *PardT*, demonstrates the failure of evil. Like the Friar and the Summoner, the Pardoner is a 'goat' of creation but through the imaginative dimension of literature, they assist the 'sheep' (ordinary sinners) to salvation.

1157 Dillon, Janette. 'Chaucer's Game in the *Pardoner's Tale*.' *EIC* 41(1991), 208-21.

'Chaucer uses the Pardoner to underline to his audience the extent of its own contribution to the meaning of the text' (p 219). The intervention of the audience in choosing the Pardoner's text satirizes the urge to categorize the tale before it is told; the playfulness in vocabulary and structure of *CT* encourages the audience to consider the text as 'open questions' (p 210); the impossibility of authenticating the Pardoner's credentials and relics preclude judgment. The Pardoner, scornful of his gullible audiences, delights in the gap between his falseness 'as Pardoner—author and the authority of his text' (p 212). The Pardoner's interest lies more in manipulating his audience than in telling his tale *per se*. *PardT* 'mimics the undermining of over-simplified boundaries between "truth" and fiction' (p 215). The Pardoner, like the rioters, is characterized by exaggerated playfulness; his explicit boundaries (lines 915, 919) are not real. His offer of pardons (lines 928-30) is a joke but doesn't preclude earnest response. Through layers of artifice, leading in and out of *PardP* and *PardT*, the Pardoner directs 'the audience towards continual revision and postponement of their judgements' (p 219).

1158 Frese, Dolores Warwick. *An 'Ars Legendi' for Chaucer's Canterbury Tales': Reconstructive Reading*. 1991. See **510**.
In this study of Chaucer's intertextuality, Frese examines Chaucer's memorial practice of anticipation and retrospective correction designed to encourage re-readings which ultimately reveal Chaucer's authorial intention. Fragment VI operates as a fulcrum for the pilgrimage; in its demand for retrospective reading, it affords the first 'fully articulated model' for Chaucer's intertextual practice, a form of reading which distinguishes between *implication* and *ramification* (p 4). Frese proceeds through a close reading of the Pardoner portrait which she claims prejudices the Pardoner's performance more than any other portrait does a tale, *PardP* and *PardT*. Chapter 1 offers a reconstructive reading detailing the coupling of money and male sexuality in the Pardoner's performance. Chaucer's method is instructive: 'By repeatedly reworking his own prior text into subsequent portions of the ongoing poem, where the transported phrase or line carries an entirely new burden of signification, and by having narrators and narratives regularly confirming and challenging one another's utterances even when such explicit verbal quotation is withheld, the very "Tales," as well as their tellers, are put into a state of perpetual discourse' (pp 49-50). Chaucer realized the serial experience of listening to stories, then reading, then writing. The experience of both readers and Chaucer-the-poet replicates the culture's shift from orality to literacy. The pilgrim-poet invites the connections between the acts of listening, reading and writing and those of the Augustinian faculties of Memory, Intellect and Will. Chapter 2 extends theoretical notions specific to the Pardoner to medieval literary

theory. The figural practices of *involucrum* (veiling of meaning) and *integumentum* (extension of inventive fictions) are examined in terms of 'relics' and 'testicles.' The Pardoner 'both conceals and records Chaucer's penetrations of Jean de Meun's ingenious *involucrum* in the matter of *reliques* and *coillons*' (p 5).

1159 Homan, Delmar C. 'Chaucer's Pardoner and the Grotesque.' *Proceedings of the Medieval Association of the Midwest*, 1. (1991), 82-96.

In the English Middle Ages, the grotesque is embodied in the English Decorated Style. With the Pardoner, the grotesque moves beyond a contextual style to become an integral part of *CT*. The Pardoner's portrait is placed emphatically at the end of the pilgrims and in mirror relationship to the portrait of this fellow grotesque, the Summoner. Both *PardT* and *SumT* (which are not grotesques) develop psychological revelation through their main characters' intent in preaching and both are integrated into the central action of *CT*. The Pardoner's inclusion is central to the 'tolerant vision of humanity' in *CT* (89); it is also consistent with elements of the English Decorated Style—fantastic and ill-assorted subjects marked by vitality and action (89). See **926**.

1160 Jonassen, Frederick B. 'Cathedral, Inn and Pardoner in the Prologue to the Tale of Beryn.' *FCS* 18(1991), 109-32. Rpt as 'The Inn, the Cathedral, and the Pilgrimage of *The Canterbury Tales*.' In *Rebels and Rivals: The Contestive Spirit in The Canterbury Tales*. Ed. Susanna Greer Fein, David Raybin, Peter Braeger. Kalamazoo, Michigan: Medieval Institute Publications, 1991. Pp 1-35.

Using the socio-historicism of Mikhail Bakhtin and the social anthropology of Victor Turner, Jonassen explores Chaucer's evocation of the opposing value systems of the carnivalesque and the lenten. The Pardoner manifests a 'dual relationship with the Inn and the Cathedral'(p 113); he threatens to supplant both the Parson and the Host, the respective representatives of Inn and Cathedral. The Pardoner 'structurally engages the symbolic poles of the *Canterbury Tales* as the one pilgrim most alienated from both'(p 121). In a range of figures of alienation extending from the medieval pilgrim to the Renaissance fool (as in Bruegel's painting, *Battle Between Carnival and Lent*), the Pardoner is closer to the fool.

1161 Kamowski, William. '"Coillons," Relics, Skepticism and Faith on Chaucer's Road to Canterbury: An Observation on the Pardoner's and the Host's Confrontation.' *ELN* 28(1991), 1-8.

Kamowski reviews conditions that evoked valid skepticism about relics and concludes that the Pardoner's relics were 'as good as many, if not most, in England, and less absurd than some'(p 7). The Pardoner's solicitation raises the issue of faith and skepticism: he may expect a donation but he doesn't expect the pilgrims to assert faith in the relics. By inviting the pilgrims to 'play along'(p 5), the Pardoner 'hopes to capitalize on their pretense of wholesale faith in the apparatus of pilgrimage'(p 6) which included the veneration of relics. Despite the Knight's peacemaking, the 'discomforting confrontation'(p 6) remains unresolved.

62 Montelaro, Janet J. 'The Pardoner's Self-Reflexive Peyne: Textual Abuse of *The First Epistle to Timothy.*' *SCRev* 8(1991), 6-16.

Building on earlier analyses of the Pardoner's discourse, Montelaro examines the Pardoner's textual manipulation of 1 *Tim* as evidence of his anxiety over his spiritual and sexual deficiencies. The Pardoner flaunts his 'ministerial perversity' (p 6); through his *peyne*, he draws attention to his speech and actions creating 'a semiotics of compulsion and verbal violation' (p 7). Contrary to 1 *Tim*, the Pardoner indulges in fabulous narration and uses his 'tales' to generate personal wealth. Unlike Paul, who distinguishes himself as 'instrument' from Christ as 'mediator,' the Pardoner represents himself to the pilgrims as spiritual mediator. The Pardoner's textual distortions thematize the rioters' *going astray* and reveal his perverted spirituality: examination of these textual manipulations and silences (e.g., the latter half of 1 *Tim* 6:10 which spells out the Pardoner's spiritual inadequacy is omitted) reveals Chaucer as 'a witty as well as a scrupulous reader of Biblical texts' (p 9). See also **989, 996, 1003, 1024,** and **1088** .

63 Owley, Steven. 'Chaucer's *The Pardoner's Tale.*' *Expl* 49(1991), 204.

In his call for a show of solidarity, a rioter unknowingly foreshadows the doom of the three with a blasphemous pun on bones/dice (line 695). In *we thre been al ones* (line 696), *al ones* may be understood as 'all together' or as 'all ones' i.e., snake-eyes, always a loser in games of hazard.

64 Patterson, Lee. *Chaucer and the Subject of History.* 1991. See **512**.

In this influential work, Patterson argues that the social meaning of Chaucer's poetry is to be found in 'the institutional context from which it derived, the audience to which it was addressed, above all the class values it expresses' (47). In chapter 8: 'The Subject of Confession: The Pardoner and the Rhetoric of Penance' and 'Afterword,' Patterson elaborates his earlier work (**932**) locating *PardP* and *PardT* in relation to the discourse of penitential literature. Considering *PardP* and *PardT* a 'confession,' Patterson examines the institution of penance, medieval precedents for the 'confession,' Chaucer's revision of inherited materials and the exchange between the Host and the Pardoner. As the first post-medieval poet, Chaucer approaches history as a subject and humans as individualized subjects within history. In *PardP* and *PardT*, Chaucer employs the rhetoric of penance for an act of self-constitution. '[T]he subjectivity constructed ... is shaped according to the medieval understanding of the privation of sin and its antidote in the sacrament of penance ...'(p 371). In the treatment of the Old Man's expression of desire, the Pardoner offers a mode of discourse that 'stands as an alternative to the inauthentic language of confession' (p 373). *PardP* and *PardT* paradoxically present the impenitent man performing a penitent act. The exemplum about Avarice becomes a psychological allegory revealing despair. At the 'imaginative center' (p 372) of *PardT*, the Old Man gives voice to 'the very desire that the paternal justice of penance has proscribed' (p 372). Sufficiency is imagined 'not as atonement with the judgmental Father but as reengorgement by Mother Earth' (p 373). Here the Pardoner articulation privileges 'an illicit language of the subject [representing] perhaps Chaucer's most radical imagining' (p 374). The central gap between intention and language is dramatized in the exchange between Host and Pardoner. Ultimately the Pardoner's confession challenges the institution of penance: it is an anti-confession, 'a mockery of the Church's penitential procedures' and 'an oppositional political statement' (p 420). See also **747**.

- Review by Helen Cooper, *N&Q* 238(1993), 85-6: In an attempt to 'think socially' about Chaucer, Patterson traces three motifs: class conflict, relationship to social upheavals of the 1380's; and 'Thebanness,' ... 'which in the chapter on the Pardoner emerges as a full-scale Oedipal reading of the Old Man' (p 85). Noting Patterson's resistance to 'defining his concepts' Cooper suggests that as a book '"that will shape the way that Chaucer is read for years to come," it has its dangers' (pp 85-6).
- Review by Seth Lerer, *MLQ* 54(1993), 422-7: Patterson offers

'an extended meditation on the nature of society both medieval and modern, and on the place of poetry and criticism in the construction of the writing self and the reading community' (p 423). The essay on the Pardoner provides an 'encyclopedic' treatment of the nature of penance. In an examination of the institution of the Church, Patterson 'adjudicates between traditionally exegetical approaches to the Pardoner and more modern, psychologically or sexually oriented readings of his "rhetoric of penance"' (p 423).

- Review by N.F. Blake, *ES* 74(1993), 387-9: Chaucer develops the relation of self to society through the process of creating characters. The Pardoner 'illustrates the importance of confession and reveals a spirit in conflict' (p 389). 'The book assumes that the Ellesmere order of *The Canterbury Tales* is Chaucer's, even though we all know it is not .... However, it does represent an important achievement and anyone interested in Chaucer studies will have to take account of this book in the future'(p 389).

1165 Volk-Birke, Sabine. *Chaucer and Medieval Preaching: Rhetoric for Listeners in Sermons and Poetry.* Script Oralia, 34. Tübingen: Gunter Narr Verlag, 1991.

Part I develops criteria for textual analysis of medieval sermons; Part II applies the criteria to *PardP* and *PardT*, *Mel*, *NPT*, and *ParsT*. In the chapter, 'Preaching Perverted,' Volk-Birke explores features of *PardT* that indicate it was written for oral delivery and aural reception. The features include: interaction between speaker and audience (e.g., forms of address, exhortations, recurrent formulae); structural elements (established by scholastic sermon or homily); narrative (e.g., elaborations and exemplary elements); syntactic patterns (e.g., repetition, parallelism); and rhetorical figures and images. Volk-Birke concludes that, in *PardP* and *PardT*, the Pardoner applies features recognizable from the preaching tradition (e.g., conditional clauses) for evil ends and that *PardT* does not conform with contemporary preaching patterns in its arrangement of parts (cs **1018, 1119**).

- Review by Siegfried Wenzel, *Speculum* 68(1993), 903-5: Volk-Birke's contribution lies more in demonstrating stylistic similarities between sermons and Chaucer's poetry than in offering major new views. Additionally, 'the study raises several larger questions that are left wide open. Thus, her analysis and comparison rest on the assumption that "it is highly likely that the resemblance between the wording of the oral performance and the wording of the sermon in the manuscript was close"' (p 62 cited p 904).

- Review by D.S. Brewer, *Rev* 14(1992): 'The interaction between the Pardoner and his pilgrim-audience, the formulas he employs, his structural organization, his narrative and his patterns of development are analyzed in terms of the practices of sermons. These are not matters simply of surface structures but of deeper meanings and Volk-Birke moves easily between the larger structures of rhetoric and detailed analysis of individual phrases' (p 97).

1166 Astell, Ann W. 'The *Translatio* of Chaucer's Pardoner.' *Exemplaria* 4(1992), 411-28.

The rhetorical trope *translatio*, which subsumes metaphor, allegory and irony, patterns the Pardoner's way of speaking and acting and informs the structure of *PardP* and *PardT*. The Augustinian distinction between one who speaks his own word and one who speaks another's glosses the relationship between prologue and tale: in *PardP*, a homodiegetic narrative, the Pardoner presents his own word; in *PardT*, a heterodiegetic narrative, he presents a sermon, words not his own and alien to his life. In *PardT*, the Pardoner translates himself into the rioters and the Old Man whose Otherness he deflects into the abstraction *cupiditas*. Purposefully, the Old Man's benevolence disfigures him as a sign and creates a void seeking replacement in the youths and rendering his meaning indeterminate. The meeting with the Old Man, as displaced sign, results in a series of translations which reflect the 'mental universe of the Pardoner as a trafficker in words' (p 426). The Pardoner's *translatio* of sermons into silver reveals his lack of words of his own, his alienation from self.

1167 Bowers, John M., ed. *The Canterbury Tales: Fifteenth-Century Continuations and Additions*. Kalamazoo, Michigan: Medieval Institute Publications, 1992.

Bowers presents the text of 'The Canterbury Interlude and Merchant's Tale of Beryn' (pp 55-164) as well as a variant of the Pardoner-Shipman Link (pp 49-50) as spurious supplements to *CT*. Noting that the unfinished state of *CT* was as much an aesthetic embarrassment as a commercial drawback, Bowers speculates that following Chaucer's death, his son Thomas together with remnants of Chaucer's literary circle, and various professional scribes sorted and arranged the fragments of *CT*. The Canterbury Interlude and Merchant's Tale of Beryn (Northumberland ms 455 c. 1450-70) recount the pilgrims' arrival in Canterbury, the overnight escapade of the Pardoner and the Tapster and first tale of the return journey. In this sequence the Pardoner is sexually potent, heterosexual, and temperate; he offers no indication of his profession. Unsuccessful in romance, he ends the night beaten and shivering in a dog kennel. The Pardoner-Shipman Link, or spurious Shipman's Prologue, is drawn from BL Royal 18.C.ii (c. 1425-40); this prologue occurs in thirteen manuscripts between the tales of the Pardoner and Shipman, connecting *Gamelyn* with *ShT* in four, and linking the Clerk and the Shipman in one. Bowers indicates that the number of the links and the frequency of their appearance in manuscripts indicates that fifteenth-century scribes were 'intent upon tying together and unifying ... fragments that had been left maddeningly disconnected by the poet himself ...' (p 42).

168 Brown, George H. '*Scriptura Rescripta*: The (Ab)use of the Bible by Medieval Writers.' In *The Idea of Medieval Literature: New Essays on Chaucer and Medieval Culture in Honor of Donald R. Howard*. Ed. James M. Dean and Christian K. Zacher. Newark, Delaware: University of Delaware Press, 1992. Pp 285-300.

Though Chaucer could draw textual evidence from the Bible to support an argument, his distinctive artistry is found in his use of 'clipped, well-chosen biblical reference and allusion' (p 286). In the Pardoner's exemplum, Chaucer employs a biblical motif to provide a 'hellish contrast': the travesty of the Eucharist in *PardT* is '[p]erhaps the least funny but most powerful inversion of the New Testament' in *CT* (p 287).

169 Burger, Glenn. 'Kissing the Pardoner.' *PMLA* 107(1992), 1143-56.

Burger argues that neither masculinist hermeneutic, (found from Alain de Lille to contempories such as Vance (**1124**), nor feminist models (e.g., Dinshaw **1117** and Leicester **1142, 1143**), allow for understanding the Pardoner as 'a nexus of intermingling discourses about the subject and its meaning that cannot settle into a reassuring ordered hierarchy but must work in conjunction, even in competition, with one another' (p 1145). The kiss of Host and Pardoner aligns the Pardoner with the audience; the Host does what he earlier rejected, i.e., kiss a worthless relic. The kiss may move the pilgrimage forward but 'it also perpetuates the play of storytelling and postpones the "final" word of the Parson's Tale and Retraction' (p 1147). The kiss indicates a commerce between subordinate and dominant cultures. 'Kissing the Pardoner, ... means embracing the discoherence of masculinity (and power and authority) that is taking place in the tale' (p 1152). See **1180, 1182**.

1170 Calabrese, Michael Anthony. 'Meretricious Mixtures: Chaucer's Ovid and the Poetry of Love and Exile.' *DAI* 53(1992), 804A. University of Virginia Dissertation, 1991.

The overall shape of Ovid's career is analogous to Chaucer's contrasts between *game* and *ernest*. The Pardoner who is 'steeped in Ovidian rhetoricity' creates a reality to win false profit; ultimately, he subverts natural and divine law. Chaucer's *Ret* recognizes that, depite his fiction-making, his poetic career is accountable to God.

1171 Emmerson, Richard K., and Ronald B. Herzman, ed. '*The Canterbury Tales*: Apocalypticism and Chaucer's Pilgrimage.' *The Apocalyptic Imagination in Medieval Literature*. Philadelphia: University of Pennsylvania Press, 1992. Pp 145-81.

The structure and allusions in *PardT* are consistent with reading *CT* within an eschatological perspective. The pilgrimage can be seen as a microcosm of salvation history. *PardP* and *PardT* reflect personal eschatology in the portrayal of moral blindness leading to damnation, and a more universal eschatology in their parodies of the penitential system (*PardP*) and the Eucharist (*PardT*). The portrayal of the Pardoner, himself, associates him with false spiritual leaders such as Simon Magus and the Antichrist. 'The presence of the Pardoner ... is Chaucer's most extended commentary on the Church *in novissimis diebus* and on the sharp division between its ideals and its practices' (p181).

1172 Finnegan, Robert Emmett. 'Bovine (E)sc(h)atology: Papal *Bulles Assoilling* in The *Pardoner's Prologue and Tale*.' *NM* 93(3-4) (1992), 303-12.

The terms *assoillen* and *bulle* cluster in *PardP* and the epilogue to *PardT* thereby offering insight into the self the Pardoner reveals to pilgrims. An examination of *bulles* and the homophone *boles* suggests a scatalogical pun relating the Pardoner's relics and *bulles* to animal excrement. In the epilogue, the Pardoner exposes his 'soiled spiritual condition' as he moves to usurp the Host as leader of the pilgrimage and God as source of absolution (p 310).

1173 Gerke, Robert S. 'Avarice and Mercy in The Pardoner's Tale.' *BWVACET* 14(1992), 23-33.

PardT draws from the vice/virtue tradition in medieval homiletic and theological tracts in its use of avarice and mercy. The Pardoner, motivated by avarice and lacking mercy, may choose to distance himself as a hardened sinner from the Host's compassionate response to *PhysT*. The Old Man portrays, 'the subtle relationship of mercy and the Gift of the Holy Spirit—counsel' (p 28). He follows the way of poverty preparatory to death but directs the avaricious rioters who reject his counsel on the path that leads most directly to death. In its treatment of avarice, lack of mercy and deficient counsel, *PardT* reflects a Chaucerian theme also found in *Lak of Stedfastnesse* (lines 15-21).

1174 Mandel, Jerome. *Geoffrey Chaucer: Building the Fragments of the 'Canterbury Tales'*. Rutherford, Madison, and Teaneck, New Jersey: Fairleigh Dickinson University Press; London and Toronto: Associated University Presses, 1992.

Mandel notes that while *CT* is unfinished, most Fragments are finished and reveal Chaucer's principles of order, coherence and propriety. Though modern readers note parallels between the Pardoner and the Wife of Bath or Canon's Yeoman, the medieval audience would have understood him in the context of medieval pardoners and 'the *Weltanschauung* generated by the characters and action' of *PhyT* (p 53). Fragment VI has a distinctive structure wherein *PhyT* and *PardT* reveal a parallel structural pattern. Nature and the Pardoner open the respective tales with a self-description and a description of their characteristic action. The following parallels are noted: Nature/Pardoner; Virginia/Rioters; interruption to governesses/digression of sermon; as well as parallels in the impulse for action, conspiracy, confrontation scene, discussion and death. The Pardoner's reference to Christ's pardon contributes to the unity of the Fragment as the Physician also shows the pardoning of error out of love. The Host closes this Fragment, as he does others, by turning earnest into game. The Old Man and Virginia are the only two characters in the Fragment to take God's will seriously. A bibliographic note reviews comparisons of *PardT* with other tales (pp 200-1).

1175 Matsuda, Takami. 'Death, Prudence, and Chaucer's *Pardoner's Tale*.' *JEGP* 91(1992), 313-24.

PardT is contextualized by the growth of a pragmatic attitude toward life and death and a consequent usurpation of a Christian virtue by worldly prudence. The Pardoner exploits the established system of salvation by offering 'an answer born out of worldly prudence' (p 314) in place of a spiritual solution as he forces a literal interpretation on spiritual texts. In its treatment of individual salvation, *PardT* manifests 'the danger of literalism inherent in the reception of a spiritual text' (p 324).

1176 Purdon, L.O. 'The Pardoner's Old Man and the Second Death.' *SP* 89(1992), 334-49.

The doctrine of the second or eternal death would appeal to the Pardoner's desire to control, motivate contrition and produce dramatic effects. A summary of the theological tradition (including Augustine, Innocent and Aquinas) provides a context for interpretation of the Old Man. The *proudeste* rioter calls attention to the Old Man's 'paradoxical death-like state lacking death' (p 343); the Old Man describes his *sory grace*, knocking at his *moodres gate* and referring to his *cheste* (coffin); and the rioters ironically become what the Old Man personifies. Finally, the Pardoner in his approach to the Host reveals his own perversion of will, a condition predisposing him to 'the death of the whole man and its dire consequence, the second death'(p 349).

1177 Ridley, Florence. 'The Friar and the Critics.' In *The Idea of Medieval Literature: New Essays on Chaucer and Medieval Culture in Honor of Donald R. Howard*. Ed. James M. Dean and Christian K. Zacher. Newark: University of Delaware Press, 1992. Pp 160-72.

Ridley identifies the affinity between the Friar and the Pardoner, both corrupt clergy and powerful story-tellers who tell narratives similar in action, effect and significance. Since *PardT* is superior in consistency, conciseness, completeness and revelation of the teller, Ridley speculates *FrT* is a 'work-in-progress' for *PardT* (p 168). As the Friar is undone by the Summoner so the Pardoner by the Host. Howard's image of 'interlace' suggests a method for understanding the full effect of the tales See **926**.

1178 Aspinall, Dana E. 'I Wol Thee Telle Al Plat': Poetic Influence and Chaucer's Pardoner.' *University of Mississippi Studies in English* 11-12(1993-5), 230-42.

Aspinall offers a psychoanalytic reading in which he argues that 'the Pardoner's psyche rebels from the "Father" figure of God, relinquishes the role of priest, and adopts instead the role of poet' (p 231). The Pardoner's behavior 'mirrors the traditional practice of Freudian analysand/therapist relations' (p 231). Throughout his performance, the

Pardoner reveals 'the complex struggle between id and ego and their relation to his profession' (p 240). Like the Old Man, the Pardoner seeks death though the death he seeks is that of his creative impulses; the final silence relieves the Pardoner of guilt and 'allows him to remove the laurels of the poet' (p 240).

1179 Brandt, Paul R. 'An Answer to the Problem of *The Pardoner's Tale.*' *UDR* 22(1993-4), 113-21.

The Pardoner is not self-deceived; rather, he accepts his own death and sinful nature. He is able to prey upon the pilgrims because they do not accept their *cupiditas*. He mirrors the pilgrims' attempts to absolve themselves and deny death. 'It is ironic that the character who appears to be the most effeminate and the most sinful is the character who is strongest and perhaps most worthy of forgiveness' (p 118).

1180 Burger, Glenn. 'Forum: The Medieval Kiss: Reply.' *PMLA* 108(1993), 334-5.

Burger replies to Gardiner's reply (1182) to his earlier article (1169) that both Chaucer's text and the historical evidence are ambiguous as to whether the Pardoner's kiss was on the mouth or on the cheek. He cites evidence of mouth-to-mouth kisses that are both public and intimate, and redirects attention to his central point: '[t]hat which has been constructed as "naturally" and absolutely other is now reconstituted as a sign of sameness and contiguity because of the traditional signification of the kiss as a mark of equality or near equality' (pp 334-5).

1181 David, Alfred. 'The Presidential Address. *Old, New,* and *Yong* in Chaucer.' *SAC* 15(1993), 5-21.

The deep structure of nostalgia in *PardP* and *PardT* reflects Chaucer's positive response to 'the brave new world of the 1380's' (p 14). The Pardoner values the *newe* in style (A 680-2) and rejects age in *PardT*. The reference to the rioters as *yonge folk* is a rare use of *yonge* with a negative valence. 'By feigning a frame in which young and old, lerned and lewed indulge themselves ... in the fascination and pleasure of feigning ... [Chaucer imagines] recovery of loss in the power to manipulate and control imagined worlds' (pp 20-1).

1182 Gardiner, Anne Barbeau. 'Forum: The Medieval Kiss.' *PMLA* 108(1993), 333-4.

Interpreting Burger's claim regarding the Pardoner's kiss (1180) to be that the kiss had to be a mouth-to-mouth kiss, Barbeau calls for evidence that 'men unrelated by blood ordinarily gave each other mouth-to-mouth kisses as public, ceremonial signs' (p 333). See **846, 1180**.

1183   Green, Richard Firth. 'The Pardoner's Pants (and Why They Matter).'
SAC 15(1993), 131-45.

Interpretations of the Pardoner as eunuch, hermaphrodite or homosexual
are based on slender and ambiguous evidence. The term *olde breech*
may contain an allusion to the general folktale type 'Adultress Outwits
Husband' which circulated widely in the Middle Ages as the tale 'the
Friar's Pants'(p 132). Recognition of this allusion would support the
view of the Pardoner as a philanderer, a view consistent with the
Pardoner of *Beryn* and suggested previously by Benson (**1058**) and
Green.

1184   Hamilton, Christopher. 'Poet versus Priest: Narrative and Balanced
Portrait in English Literature.' *CSR* 23(1993), 145-58.

Hamilton outlines his theory that, until the mid-eighteenth century, in
efforts to reform society, most authors viewed themselves as adjuncts
to the clergy, and generally balanced negative portrayals of clergy with
positive ones. In times of crisis, however, authors tended to suggest the
poet as more effective reformer than the clergy. Medieval literature
draws from the biblical topos of contrastive portraits and expands the
social vision to set religious satire of such figures as the Pardoner within
a larger frame that indicts professional corruption in general. Satirical
portraits of religious figures were also generally balanced with an ideal
portrait such as the Parson.

1185   Kelly, H. Ansgar. 'Sacraments, Sacramentals, and Lay Piety in
Chaucer's England.' *ChauR* 28(1993), 5-22.

Noting that the Pardoner does not sell relics (cf **508**), Kelly examines
the use of relics in *PardP* and *PardT* within the contexts of canon 62 of
the Fourth Lateran Council of 1215 and contemporary complaints.
Chaucer treats the charlatan Pardoner critically, indicating that his
sympathies lie with the Parson.

1186   Lerer, Seth. *Chaucer and His Readers: Imagining the Author in
Late-Medieval England.* Princeton: Princeton University Press, 1993.

Lerer reads the marginalia, additions and physical appearance of the
Helmingham manuscript (Princeton University Library MS 100) as
evidence of personal response impatient with prolixity and directed to
narrative. The manuscript 'transforms essays in authorship into fables
of decorum for a gentry readership' (p 100). *PardT* is 'de-authorized,'
becoming an exemplum of moral action whose subject is no longer

Chaucer or the Pardoner but 'the childish reader' (p 100). The post-Chaucerian literary system is explored as a 'phenomenon of subjection' (p 5) wherein Chaucer's authority subjects his readers. The literature of the fifteenth century, based on the fictional persona of the subjected reader, operates within a larger universe dubbed the '"cult of childhood"' (p 6). In *PardP*, Helmingham reduces similes, asides, and the Pardoner's ironic self-revelation (omitting 361-4, 391-4, 415-22 and 427-40). In *PardT*, the omissions (547-50, 555-62, 565-6, 571-88, 599-602, 617-20, 622, 627-8, and 643-8) and editorial actions '... effectively realign the narrative force and conception of character that modern critics have grasped as governing the shape of Chaucer's poem' (p 99). Notably, and consistent with the possible objective of a child audience, the Helmingham omits the closing exchange between the Pardoner and the Host, ending the tale with the death of the rioters. The resulting poem, shorn of 'rhetorical sleights, confidential asides, and revealing admissions' (p 99), differs radically from the one reflected in twentieth-century psychological interpretations. The text of portions of *PardP* and *PardT* revised in the Helmingham manuscript are reprinted (Appendix p 221). See **1109**.

187 Rudat, Wolgang E.H. 'Revealing the Church's *Pryvetee*: The Pardoner and Various Otherworldly Loins.' *Earnest Exuberance in Chaucer's Poetics: Textual Games in the "Canterbury Tales."* Lewiston, New York: E. Mellen Press, 1993. Pp 121-158.

Situating his work in relationship to Kendrick (**1107**), Dinshaw (**1117**), McAlpine (**967**), and contra Lindahl (**1094**) and Jordan (**1093**), Rudat attempts to 'read-and-explicate the portrait of the Pardoner palimpsestically in the light of the Prioress' portrait' (p 144). With *PardT*, Chaucer satirizes 'the Church's practice of selling pardons to multiply its economic power, power which it could then use to force vulnerable women into a life of celibacy' (p 158). In so doing, Chaucer exposes both the Pardoner's and the Pope's *privitee*. Rudat offers distinctive sexual readings of the Pope filling the eunuch Pardoner's *lappe* with pardons and the Pardoner becoming 'an anal-erotic version of Mary' (p 145). By presenting a redemption scene for the Pardoner but not the Prioress, Chaucer satirizes 'the sexo-economic policies of the Church' (p 155). See also **567**.

188 Wilson, Grace G. '"Amonges Othere Wordes Wyse": The Medieval Seneca and the *Canterbury Tales*.' *ChauR* 28(1993), 135-45.

Though in *CT* Chaucer refers to Seneca thirty-three times (more than any author except Solomon), the Pardoner cites Seneca only once—a passage from *De Ira* indicating no difference between a madman and a drunkard. This reference reinforces the sense of the Pardoner's glibness and his command of 'the sermon literature on anger and drunkenness' (p 139). By having a wide range of characters cite Seneca, Chaucer offers his audience as much wisdom as they might variously want while safeguarding his ambiguity.

1189 Brown, Peter. *Chaucer at Work: The Making of the 'Canterbury Tales.'* London and New York: Longman, 1994.

A study guide for teachers and students that approaches *CT* through sources and contexts. Based on the *GP* portrait and the solicitation, Brown provides a reading of the Pardoner, drawn in sharp contrast to the Parson. He raises questions about the abuses of the institution of pilgrimage, the implications of the Pardoner's sexuality, his materialism, the principle of organization in the portrait and the narrator's stance. The solicitation focuses on the pilgrims' motives and raises questions about the nature of comedy. Wycliffite commentary on Psalm 13 establishes a discourse sharply critical of the clerical hypocrisy displayed in *PardP*. The role of dicing in the iconography of the Crucifixion elucidates the sin of the rioters and the use of bones or relics by the Pardoner.

1190 Burger, Glenn. 'Queer Chaucer.' *English Studies in Canada* 20(1994), 153-70.

Queer theory destabilizes hegemonic heterosexual assumptions, problematizes the past, and challenges the essentialist position that the Pardoner's body and language alert the pilgrims to his otherness. Proximity to *PhyT*, where the Physician and Host attempt to make masculinity 'cohere,' gives a 'deconstructive edge and subversive menace' to the Pardoner's performance of masculinity (p 162). The Pardoner's body, 'ceaselessly performing gender and sexuality but never getting it "right"' may illuminate 'the complexities of a medieval politics of representation that the characters and tales of Fragment VI ... enact' (p 163).

1191 Calin, William. *The French Tradition and the Literature of Medieval England.* Toronto: University of Toronto Press, 1994.

In a study of Chaucer's Frenchness, Calin undertakes a reading of *PardP* and *PardT*. 'The Pardoner is a textual, psychological, and archetypal reworking of Faux Semblant' (p 337). Chaucer transforms the 'personification of hypocrisy' into a novelistic trickster-villian (p 338). The Pardoner, an egocentric rhetor, is guilty of sin himself and instills it in those who buy his pardons. The Pardoner is an alienated outcast; by having him fail, Chaucer establishes 'that art cannot be separated from moral and civic concerns' (p 345). Chaucer's imitation of Jean de Meun's achievement with Faux Semblant serves as a 'satire on hypocrisy, on the Church and on sodomy' (p 346). The kiss at the close of *PardT* indicates that despite the corrupting action of the Pardoner, a higher Justice offers love to all.

192 Copeland, Rita. 'The Pardoner's Body and the Disciplining of Rhetoric.' In *Framing Medieval Bodies*. Ed. Sarah Kay and Miri Rubin. Manchester, England: Manchester University Press; New York: St. Martin's Press, 1994. Pp 138-59.

In an exploration of the linkage between sexuality, 'disciplining of the body' (p 138), and the discipline of rhetoric, Copeland examines the ways in which gender and sexuality 'are part of the political text of rhetoric's institutional history' (p 138). Through the sexual ambiguity of his bodily presence, the Pardoner figures rhetoric as 'an emasculated or effeminate male body' (p 149). In his body, the Pardoner joins '[t]he social politics of sexuality and the institutional politics of rhetoric'(p 149). In *Phy-PardL*, the Host moves the group from the power of arbitrary law demanding obedience in *PhyT* 'to the affective power of rhetoric' (p 150) in *PardT*. Manifesting rhetoric's compulsion 'to perform its disciplinary instabilities by performing the exposure of its own vices,' *PardP* 'is a consummate performance of rhetoric's self-exposure of its transgression and counterfeit' (p 151). 'The corruption or moral vacuity of character that the Pardoner manifests ... is metonymic for the deficiency or permeability of his sexual body and the incontinence of his rhetoric' (p 153). The public display of the interaction between the Host and Pardoner ultimately contains rhetoric thereby inducting it into disciplinary order. 'The legitimisation and "disciplining" of rhetoric is inevitably its repression, a process in which rhetoric participates by naming its own bodiliness' (pp 155-6).

193 Frantzen, Allen J. '*The Pardoner's Tale,* the Pervert, and the Price of Order in Chaucer's World.' In *Class and Gender in Early English Literature: Intersections*. Ed. Britton J. Harwood and Gillian R. Overing. Bloomington: Indiana University Press, 1994. Pp 131-47.

Applying Marxist and gender criticism, Frantzen examines how Chaucer negates the interdependent model of the world of the three estates in the imagery of the three rioters and of the tavern sins and demonstrates the price of destruction paid by those who resist its order. Frantzen argues that 'understanding the Pardoner's perversity is part of understanding the Christian values his prologue and tale so bitterly expose' (p 145). A 'double threat' with his gender ambiguity and his exposure of the social hierarchy, the Pardoner lays bare 'the death-threatening, life-denying, spirit-crushing construction of lack' (p 145).

1194 Hoerner, Fred. 'Church Office, Routine, and Self-Exile in Chaucer's Pardoner.' *SAC* 16(1994), 69-98.

A psychoanalytic reading of *PardP* and *PardT*. The Pardoner inverts the Host's request that he participate in the healing of community, thereby signalling 'analogous institutional and psychological inversions that occur when, in Max Weber's phrasing, charisma turns to routine' (p 69). The Pardoner's pervasive gluttony implies 'corporation,' which violates the Eucharistic origins of the Church by confusing institutional with fleshly bodies (p 70). Hoerner reads *PardT* as a manifestation of the Pardoner's 'own corrupt state, displaced into doctrinal formula (gluttony) and allegory (of the rioters and the Old Man)' (p 86). In his routinization, the Pardoner perverts himself and implicates the pilgrims and the Host who becomes a figure of corportion and institutionalization.

1195 Ireland, Richard W. 'Chaucer's Toxicology.' *ChauR* 29(1994), 74-92.

Chaucer's knowledge of poison lore reveals a 'latent element of diabolical presence' (p 74) in *PardT* and underpins the discussion contraception and abortifacients in *ParsT*. The association of poison, sin, the serpent and Envy is found in medieval literary texts and operates in *PardP* (353-7, 366-8). The theme of physical and supernatural poisoning in *PardT* contrasts with the theme of medicine in found both in *PhyT* and in the reference to Christ as *oure soules leche* (line 916).

1196 Kruger, Steven, 'Claiming the Pardoner: Toward A Gay Reading of Chaucer's Pardoner's Tale.' *Exemplaria* 6(1994), 115-39.

Through a historically structured investigation into the Pardoner's possible homosexuality as reflected in *PardP* and *PardT*, Kruger explores 'a historical understanding of the late-medieval construction of male homosexuality and of homophobia' (p 120). If the Pardoner is constructed as the medieval equivalent of a gay man, he is 'a character written out of homophobia' (p 121). Reviewing the literature on the Pardoner as homosexual, Kruger concludes: ...'I am convinced that Chaucer wants us to see, as part of the Pardoner's sexual "queerness," the possiblity of homosexuality' (p 125). The exemplum of *PardT* presents a 'constellation' of ideas about male homosexuality including 'an exclusion of the female, with heterosexual behavior replaced by a homosocial parody of procreative sexuality; a failure of reading; an involvement in and debasement of the body' (p 131). In the Pardoner's encounter with the Host, the fear of the loss of signification (associated in the Middle Ages with heterosexual fecundity) is set aside in favor of 'a heterosexual hegemony' (p 135). Claiming the Pardoner's text requires modern readers to resist 'what might have been the homophobic intentions of its author, celebrating ... the Pardoner and his disruption of the heterosexual constructions of dominant medieval culture' (p 137).

1197 Myles, Robert. *Chaucerian Realism*. Cambridge: D.S. Brewer, 1994.
In an examination of Chaucer's realism—foundational, epistemological, ethical, semiotic and linguistic—Chaucer's intentionality is desribed as 'an understanding of the *directed* relationship between word and thing, and the effects of that on the consciousness, and on the 'condicioun', the human *being*, of each individual (p 134). Though Myles' focus lies with other pilgrims, he comments on the Pardoner, 'master of improper couplings, verbal and otherwise' (p 125) in conjuction with the Summoner, and traces relationships between *wynnyng*, *purchas* and *rente* in *PardT* and *RR*.

1198 Pelen, Marc M. 'Murder and Immortality in Fragment VI(C) of The *Canterbury Tales*: Chaucer's Transformation of Theme and Image from the *Roman De La Rose.*' *ChauR* 29(1994), 1-25.
Raison's images and ideas of sexual violence and natural generation in *RR* are opposed in *PardT* and *PhyT*, thereby providing thematic unity. The conflicting stances taken by Raison, Genius and Nature seed Chaucer's opposition of murder to immortality. The influence of *RR* goes beyond the Pardoner's debt to Faux Semblant, his apparent eunuchry, and his reference to relics 'to a larger theme contrasting natural generation to divine providence' (p 9). The Pardoner's 'gross materialism' stands in opposition to the Physician's yoking of physical purity and penance; the Pardoner's hypocritical condemnation of the rioter's quest for immortality in gold reveals an interest in the naturalism of *PhyT* (p 9). Within Fragment VI(C), murder and immortality are

opposed to their sacramental analogues of contrition and Redemption.

1199 Scanlon, Larry. *Narrative, Authority, and Power: The Medieval Exemplum and the Chaucerian Tradition*. Cambridge: Cambridge University Press, 1994.

As a means of moving beyond the tension in Chaucerian criticism between narrative complexity and authority, Scanlon examines the exemplum arguing that it is a dynamic form that reproduces moral authority. 'The congruence between narrative discourse and moral authority' embedded in the exemplum enables it to transmit social and rhetorical authority, thereby serving 'as a process of empowerment and appropriation'(p 5). In *PardP* and *PardT*, Chaucer takes up the relation of the doctrinal to the lay. Returning with the mendicant Pardoner to the theme of anticlericalism, Chaucer employs it as 'the platform for a more general adumbration of the moral authority of narrative' (p 192). Scanlon focuses on what the production of the Pardoner's subjectivity in *PardP* and *PardT* reveals 'about the nature of the cultural authority that produces him' (p 195). Despite the instabilities exposed by the Pardoner's quarrel with the Host, the anticlericalism of *PardP*, and the sexual ambiguity of the Pardoner, *PardT* ends by reaffirming the authority of narrative and anticipating Chaucer's treatment of lay authority in *Mel*, *MkT*, and *NPT*.

1200 Shynne, Gwanghyun. 'Chaucerian Textuality: The Politics of Allegory in "The Canterbury Tales".' *DAI* 54(1994), 3046A. University of Wisconsin, Madison Dissertation, 1993. Director: Larry Scanlon.

In a dissertation that examines exegetical allegory in *CT*, Shynne reads *WBT*, *CYT*, and *PardT* as full-blown examples of Chaucer's metatextual awareness. Shynne argues that though Chaucer provides a critique of allegory and makes a deallegorizing move, he ends by staying within the problematic of allegory, both appropriating and reaccentuating it.

1201 Smith, J.J. 'Spelling and Tradition in Fifteenth-Century Copies of Gower's *Confessio Amantis*.' In *The English of Chaucer and His Contemporaries: Essays by M.L. Samuels and J.J. Smith*. Ed. J.J. Smith. Pp 96-113.

In an effort to explore the continuity and dissolution of Gowerian forms in fifteenth- and sixteenth-century copies of the *Confessio Amantis*, Smith examines a set of items in *PardP* and *PardT*. Smith concludes that Gower mss were produced within a stong orthographic tradition.

1202 Braswell, Mary Flowers. 'Chaucer's Palimpsest: Judas Iscariot and

the *Pardoner's Tale.' ChauR* 29(1995), 303-10.
The elements of avarice, inability to die, oak, and treasure in *PardT* create a '"palimpsest" of Judas Iscariot' (p 303) which both broadens and darkens the tale. Judas lore, popular from Biblical times, reached a high point in the fourteenth century. The Pardoner's theme (1 Timothy 6:10) was often associated with Judas; both the Pardoner and Judas were outsiders and hypocrites steeped in despair.

203 Chance, Jane. *The Mythographic Chaucer: The Fabulation of Sexual Politics*. University of Minnesota Press, Minneapolis and London, 1995.
Chapter 10 'Conclusion: The Artist Pygmalion, the Subject Chaucer, and Self-Seduction' (pp 263-82) discusses *PardP* and *PardT*. Chaucer is motivated by '[t]he concealment of embarrassing secrets, often sexual in nature, and the burden of political alliances and strategies' (p xix). To analyze Chaucer's sexual politics, Chance uncovers implicit truths in his mythological references. The Ovidian-based tales of Physician, Pardoner and Maniple explore the nature of poetic as counterfeit. The Pardoner's counterfeiting undermines his self-knowledge as his duplicity is ironically turned to good. An additional dimension, elucidating the Pardoner's '"poetics of absence,"' (**1117**) is provided by mythographic commentary on Proteus, a figure found in *RR* though not explicitly mentioned by Chaucer (p 272). The metaphor of outside vs inside, embodied in clothing imagery and characterizing the relation of body to soul, dominates the portrayal of the Pardoner. With the Pardoner, meaning is determined by 'what is not said,' the silence serving as a 'noetic symbol for the idea of *fabula*, and an appropriate determinant for Chaucer's purposes in the fabulous Retraction' (p 280).

204 Crafton, John Micheal. 'Emptying the Vessel: Chaucer's Humanistic Critique of Nominalism.' In *Literary Nominalism and the Theory of Reading Late Medieval Texts: A New Research Paradigm*. Ed. Richard J. Utz. Medieval Studies 5. Edwin Mellon: Lewiston, N.Y.; Queenston, Ont.; Lamperer, Wales, 1995. Pp 117-34.
Examining what appears to be contradictory evidence regarding Chaucer's views on nominalism and language, Crafton concludes that Chaucer's method of presenting then undermining essentialist and nominalist positions reveals his acceptance of 'the new rhetorical attitudes' that construe the poet's words as dictated 'by the civil needs of society and the desire to create beauty and glorify God' (pp 133-4).

The Pardoner operates as a 'Machiavellian Nominalist' who disregards any ontological relation between words and universals (p 129). He creates disjunction between his prologue and his opening sermon, his sermon serves as a 'verbal false relic,' and he literalizes the metaphor in *radix malorum* by placing the scene of greed at the root of the oak tree (p 129). In a patterrn similar to *PhyT*, the Pardoner has the major characters in his tale act out his theory in the perversion of the Eucharist. Ultimately, the sanction of the Knight critiques 'this free-wheeling, free-wording nominalist' (p 130).

1205 Dinshaw, Carolyn. 'Chaucer's Queer Touches/ A Queer Touches Chaucer.' *Exemplaria* 7(1995), 75-92.
The 'queer' problematizes heterosexuality, rendering control structures visible. When the Pardoner 'starts up' to interrupt the Wife, he disrupts the 'robust heterosexuality' of her presence and denaturalizes 'the field of sexuality' (p 77). The Pardoner not only operates as queer but 'as some kind of hermeneutic or ideological key to the *Tales*' (p 79) (cf. **926; 1103, 1117**). The Pardoner's first audience recognized his departure from the norm of heterosexuality (established in the opening imagery of *GP* and the thematic relevance of marriage throughout *CT*); the Pardoner makes that departure explicit in his mimicry of the Host in *Phy-PardL*. Gendered attitudes characterize reactions to the Pardoner: Kittredge's critique of the closing frame of *PardT* is remarkably gendered (**668**); the Host's retort may constitute '[t]he first threatened queer bashing in English literature' (p 89). Ultimately, through his presence, the Pardoner marks 'heterosexual incompletenes' (p 92).

1206 Gross, Gregory Walter. 'Secrecy and Confession in Late Medieval Narrative: Gender, Sexuality and the Rhetorical Subject.' Brown University Dissertation, 1994. Director:Elizabeth D. Kirk. See also *DAI* 55, 1945.
The emergence of the concept of the 'secret' can be historicized in a late medieval rhetorical trope that complicates the relations among truthfulness, sexuality and gender. This trope is used in twentieth-century criticism of *PardP* and *PardT* 'for locating the "authentic" Pardoner within an essentialist view of homosexuality' (p 1945).

1207 Irwin, Bonnie D. 'What's in a Frame? The Medieval Textualiztion of Traditional Storytelling.' *Oral Tradition* 10(1995) 27-53.
As a frame tale, *CT* evidences the 'constantly fluctuating relationships between traditional and literary narrative in the Middle Ages' (p 51). A

narrative designed primarily for the presentation of other narratives, the frame tale provides a continuity between the acts of listening and reading. As one of the more literary frame tales, *CT* provides distinct identities for characters and narrators such as the Pardoner.

208 Hallissy, Margaret. *A Companion to Chaucer's Canterbury Tales.* Greenwood Press: Westport, CT, 1995. Pp 49-53, 213-23.

In a work designed to accompany a first reading of Chaucer, Hallissy cautions that, in the context of medieval Christianity, the Pardoner is 'a mortal sinner,' fully aware of the gravity of his act and choosing it nonetheless (p 49). Talented preacher and *vicious man*, the Pardoner presents a typical medieval sermon, building a digression through example, then returning to his tale of the revelers. Chaucer does not intend readers to sympathize with the Pardoner; the Host's insults portend the Pardoner's eternal punishment. Paradoxically, the Pardoner is at once an 'agent of pardon' and possibly the single damned soul on the pilgrimage (p 223).

209 Johnson, Bruce A. 'The Moral Landscape of The Pardoner's Tale.' In *Subjects on the World's Stage: Essays on British Literature of the Middle Ages and Renaissance.* Eds. David G. Allen and Robert A. White. Newark: University of Delaware Press; London: Associated University Presses, 1995. Pp 54-61.

The twenty-eight geographical references in *PardT*, depict a moral landscape in which the *stile* figures centrally. The *stile* of *PardT* (one of three uses in *CT*), figures as 'an ethical crossroads' (p 58) where the rioters meet the Old Man. Their humanity debased, the rioters do not cross the stile. 'The three rioters, already spiritually dead, journey through the very landscape of death to be met at a stile by a mysterious, priestly figure who directs them to their own common grave in unconsecrated ground' (p 60).

210 Masri, Heather. 'Carnival Laughter in the *Pardoner's Tale.' MedPers* 10(1995-6), pp 148-56.

The Pardoner's performance can be understood in the light of Bakhtin's treatment of 'carnival' and its relations to the tradition of medieval drama [cf 933]. In *Phy-PardL*, the Host's language (e.g., his reference to *Seint Ronyan*, traces 'the boundaries between prayer and cursing' (p 152). In the solicitation, the Pardoner invites complicity as much as actual payment; the pilgrim laughter is a form of 'carnival laughter' directed simultaneously at the object and the laughing subject (p 154).

Since the Pardoner's virtuous sermon is presented by a wicked man, the pilgrims cannot accept it on the authority of the speaker; rather, they must contemplate the paradox and, in so doing, discover their own moral insight.

1211 Snell, William. 'Chaucer's *Pardoner's Tale* and Pestilence in Late Medieval Literature.' *SMELL* [Studies in Medieval Language and Literature]. [Tokyo, Japan] 10(1995), pp 1-6. [Not seen.]

1212 Strohm, Paul. 'Chaucer's Lollard Joke: History and the Textual Unconscious.' The Biennial Chaucer Lecture. Ninth International Congress of the New Chaucer Society. *SAC* 17(1995), pp 23-42.

Strohm solicits the Freudian psychology of jokes together with New Historicist readings of Lollard views and views of Lollards to explicate the silences or unconscious text of the Pardoner's reference to cooks turning *substaunce into accident* (*PardT* 538-40). The joke 'enters a period of social unrest that complements its own restless center' (p 37). Strohm proceeds to examine: unacknowledged sources (eg, the context of Eucharistic debate surrounding the source in *DMC*); the context of political power; textual meaning as a contract between author and audience; the task of uncovering meaning by deflecting distraction; the revelation of aggressivity through the examination of the linguistic, of comparison and temporality; and the reversible relationship between outer and inner (hull and kernel), the 'constant instability' which suggests a more generalized theological and social anxiety, and figures the relations between history and theory (p 42).

1213 Taavitsainen, Irma. 'Narrative Patterns of Affect in Four Genres of the *Canterbury Tales*'. *ChauR* 30(1995), 191-210.

Analysis of interjections and short exclamations reveals their role in the creation of narrative suspense, interpersonal effects and genre-specific patterns of audience involvement. As sermons, *PardT* and *ParsT* differ stylistically. *PardT* is a folktale transformed into a sermon; the two layers are stylistically distinct. The interjection (e.g., *o, allas*) is an indicator of stance.

❧ Index

References are to item numbers. Boldface identifies the author or editor of an item, regular typeface indicates that the person or topic is discussed in that item, and a bold lowercase **r** following an item number indicates that the person named is the author of a review of that item. Thus 'Blake, N.F. **45**, 49**r**, 179' indicates that Blake is the editor of item 45, reviewed item 49, and is mentioned in item 179. Chaucer's works are entered under their full names, not their abbreviated titles. Biblical references are grouped together under 'Bible' and manuscripts under 'manuscripts'; saints are entered individually under 'St'.